To: Dr Michael Newhouse

In appreciation for
your help and support

Yours sincerely,

[signature]

The Royal College of Physicians and Surgeons of Canada 1960-1980

The Pursuit of Unity

To
Pilar

And for
Fiona and Tandy

The Royal College
of Physicians
and Surgeons
of Canada

Le Collège Royal
des Médecins
et Chirurgiens
du Canada

The Royal College of Physicians and Surgeons of Canada 1960-1980

The Pursuit of Unity

David A.E. Shephard, FRCPC

Ottawa 1985

Shephard, David A.E.
   The Royal College of Physicians and Surgeons
of Canada, 1960-1980

Includes index.
Bibliography: p.
ISBN 0-9692155-0-9

1. Royal College of Physicians and Surgeons of
Canada — History. 2. Medicine — Specialties and
specialists — Canada. I. Royal College of
Physicians and Surgeons of Canada. II. Title.

R15.R74S54 1985   610.69'52'06071   C85-090193-6

Contents

Acknowledgements ix

Citation of Source Material and Usage of Abbreviations xii

Introduction
  The Pursuit of Unity 1

PART 1   THE COLLEGE TRANSFORMED

Chapter 1
  Legacy of the First Three Decades: The Fellowship, The
  Certification Program and The "Dual Standard" 11

Chapter 2
  Nature, Objectives and Membership. 31

Chapter 3
  Constitutional and Bylaw Changes 77

Chapter 4
  Changes in Committee and Administrative Structure 95

Chapter 5
  Relations With Other Medical Organizations 125

Chapter 6
  The College and National Issues 159

PART 2   THE DEVELOPMENT OF THE SPECIALIST

Chapter 7
  Legacy of the 1950s: The College and Postgraduate Medical
  Education. 183

Chapter 8
  The Evolution of Training Requirements 191

Chapter 9
  Evaluation and Examination for Specialist Competence. 231

Chapter 10
  The College and Research: The Work of the McLaughlin Centre
  and Other Aspects of Scientific Investigation 269

PART 3   THE MAINTENANCE OF COMPETENCE

Chapter 11
The College and Continuing Medical Education 307

PART 4   RELATIONS WITH THE SPECIALTIES

Chapter 12
The College and the Development and Recognition of the
Specialties 335

PART 5   THE DELICATE FABRIC

Chapter 13
The Quintessence of Fellowship: Biographical Sketches of
the Presidents, 1960-1980. 373

Chapter 14
The College and Medicine in Canada: A Conclusion 395

Appendices 411

About the Author 491

ILLUSTRATIONS

PAGE

Past Presidents at The Convocation, Montreal,
    January 22, 1970   20

Charter Fellows at the Fiftieth Anniversary
    Meeting, Montreal, February 7, 1979   20

Dignitaries at the Annual Dinner,
    Quebec City, January 18, 1964   35

Council 1968-70   35

Pauline Crocker   111

Françoise Lemieux-Moreau   111

James H. Graham   111

T.J. Giles   111

Kenneth T. MacFarlane   112

Frederick J. Tweedie   112

Robert A.H. Kinch   112

James H. Darragh   112

W. Gordon Beattie   115

Jacques Robichon   115

Fraser N. Gurd   115

John B. Firstbrook   115

Council 1960-62   135

Dedication of the Roddick Memorial Room,
    College Building, September 10, 1962   135

Presentation of the Mace — Convocation,
    January 16, 1964   153

Conference of Presidents, Annual Meeting,
Quebec, January 17, 1964   153

Joint Conference of Surgical Colleges,
Ottawa, March 29 & 30, 1973   154

Representatives of other Colleges, Annual
Meeting, Vancouver, January 27, 1978   154

Donald R. Wilson   278

The First Duncan Graham Award, Edmonton,
June 25, 1969   278

Honorary Fellows Admitted at Convocation
January 21, 1966   314

Honorary Fellows Admitted at Convocation,
January 22, 1976   314

Herbert Knudsen Detweiler   315

Donald A. Thompson   372

G. Malcolm Brown   374

Walter C. MacKenzie   376

Robert B. Kerr   378

Jacques Turcot   380

Robert C. Dickson   382

Charles G. Drake   384

K.J.R. Wightman   386

Robert B. Salter   388

Douglas G. Cameron   390

Bernard J. Perey   392

Acknowledgements

The publication of this book is the result of cooperation on the part of many individuals. To all who contributed, in ways both large and small, I express my profound gratitude.

The primary source of research was the College's collection of archival material. The organization and management of the College's files and committee minutes by Dr. J.H. Graham and Mrs. Rita McClymont made my task a straightforward one and I am much in their debt. I also thank Mme Louise Papineau, of the Examinations Section, for assistance in interpreting examination results; Mrs. Wilma Tinnish, of Computing Services, for her assistance in collating statistics relating to membership; Mr. Glen McStravick, Financial Manager, for his guidance in interpreting the presentations of the College's annual budget in the minutes of the annual business meetings; and Claudia Pittenger, Director, Medical Photography, South Saskatchewan Hospital Centre, Regina, for preparing Figures 4.1 and 4.2.

Many Fellows were kind enough to write to me, sometimes in great detail, about the College's activities from 1960 to 1980. Their letters enabled me to develop a much needed perception of the College during my research. Others granted me interviews and these Fellows, including six Past-Presidents, likewise oriented me. Many other individuals were of great assistance in various ways and it is a pleasure to thank the following (while apologizing for any inadvertent omissions): D.A. Baird; M. Bérard; E.H. Botterell; F.S. Brien, Mrs. Helen Brown; D.G. Cameron; R.V. Christie; A.L. Chute; J.G. Couture; C.H. Crosby; J.H. Darragh; R.A. Davis; the late R.C. Dickson; C.G. Drake, J.H. Duff; F.W. DuVal; A.E. Eistetter; J.R. Evans; C.C. Ferguson; J.B. Firstbrook; T. Gelfand; J. Genest; T.J. Giles; W.M. Goldberg; R. Gourdeau; J.H. Graham; R.W. Gunton; F.N. Gurd; L. Horlick; B. Hudson; R.C.A. Hunter; G. Hurteau; R.B. Kerr; R.A.H. Kinch; S. Kling; G.R. Langley; D.G. Langsley; J.-M. Loiselle; F.H. Lowy; R.A. Macbeth; W.B. MacDonald; J.T. MacDougall; K.T. MacFarlane; J.W. MacLeod; D.F. McAlpine; J.L. McCallum; J.D. McHattie; H.W. McIntosh; L.E. McLeod; C.B. Mueller; A. Naimark; V. Neufeld; B.J. Perey; D.I. Rice; J. Robichon; H.R. Robertson; E.C. Rosenow; R.E. Rossall; I.E. Rusted; R.B. Salter; R.W. Samson; C.F. Scott; E.N. Skakun; V.H. Skinner; W.B. Spaulding; L.C. Steeves; J.F. Stokes; J. Strong; G.W. Thomas; F.J. Tweedie; R. Watts; S. Waugh; D.R. Webster; C.H. Weder; D.R. Wilson; and E.R. Yendt. Some of these individuals aided me while I was planning the book and some, while I was writing it. In the latter respect, general comments made by Dr. F. Fenton were instructive. Of great value were two meetings with the College's Archives Committee (Drs. H.R. Robertson, J.H. Graham, R.A.H. Kinch, T. Gelfand and R. Jackson) in the early phase. Invaluable later were the comments on the early drafts by an informal review committee comprising Drs. D.G. Cameron, J.H. Darragh, J.H. Graham, R. Gourdeau, R.W. Gunton, F.N. Gurd, G. Hurteau, R. Jackson, B.J. Perey and H.R. Robertson; to them I am most grateful for the time and trouble they took in critiquing the early drafts. Among them, Drs. J.H. Darragh and J.H. Graham read the later drafts, and Drs. H.R. Robertson and J.H. Graham assisted me in selecting the illustrations for the book.

In the production phase I was similarly fortunate, for Mr. R.A. Davis and Dr. J.H. Darragh oversaw the scheduling and adherence to deadlines. A special word of thanks is due to Dr. R. Gourdeau for his interest and concern regarding translation, which was skillfully executed by Dr. G. Nadeau. Thanks are also due to Mrs. Lois Nelson for advice concerning indexing of the book and to Ms. Kate Schissler, who laboured for long hours in proofreading the galleys, pageproofs and blues.

For generous support in the research and production phases it is a pleasure, on behalf of the College, to thank the Hannah Institute for the History of Medicine and the Institute's Executive Director, Dr. G.R. Paterson. It is not inappropriate here to acknowledge, too, the enormous contribution the Hannah Institute has made to the advancement of Canadian medical history in supporting projects such as the present one sponsored by the College.

The very multiplicity of acknowledgements suggests, I hope, that publication of this book was a cooperative endeavor. This I sensed, and appreciated, particularly on my numerous visits to the College, where all the members of the College secretariat and the headquarters staff made my hours there comfortable as well as productive. Particularly supportive were Mrs. Rita McClymont, a diligent and courteous research assistant; Dr. J.H. Darragh, Executive Director, to whom I express my appreciation of the College's giving me the opportunity to research the College's history; and Dr. J.H. Graham, former Secretary of the College. To Dr. Darragh and Dr. Graham I further acknowledge their acting as sounding boards against which I was able to assess my progress in becoming familiar with the College and its history.

The practice of medicine is demanding of time, and much of the writing of this book was necessarily done in the pre-dawn hours and at weekends. My wife was patient, understanding, tolerant and forbearing, and to her I am thankful beyond words. I am grateful also to Dr. G.H. Hodgson, Acting Head, Department of Anaesthesia, Plains Health Centre, Regina, both for his encouragement during the completion of the writing and for permitting the Department secretary, Marlene Bast, to type some of the manuscript; to Marlene Bast I offer my thanks for splendid secretarial assistance. Thanks are due also to Dr. M.A. Spooner, Associate Dean, College of Medicine, University of Saskatchewan at Regina, for permitting Marion Butler to type another portion of the manuscript, and to Marion Butler in turn I offer my thanks too for typing so competently under the pressure of deadlines.

Finally, to Dr. Graham it is not possible for me to express my gratitude adequately. This physician and gentleman gave continuity to the evolution of the College in his years as Secretary from 1953 to 1979, and he was therefore of invaluable assistance to me as consultant. The book could not have been written without his assistance, and his collaboration with me in the preparation of the Appendices will, I hope, signify my deepest gratitude to him. The Appendices will, I also hope, become identified with Jim Graham and serve to remind those who know him better than I do, and to indicate to those who do not know him, that his contribution to the College was unique. It has therefore been a special privilege to work with a Fellow who is, in many respects, representative of the dedication to specialist health care that The Royal College of Physicians and Surgeons of Canada endeavored to achieve in its pursuit of unity from 1960 to 1980.

David A.E. Shephard, FRCPC
Regina, Saskatchewan

Citation of Source Material and Use of Abbreviations

The primary source of material for this history comprises the minutes of the College's committee and annual business meetings. Virtually every event and issue of note is covered in the minutes of either Council or the Executive Committee (or both), and the minutes of other committees supplement these sources. The minutes of the annual business meetings document somewhat different aspects of the College's evolution: the Presidents' annual state-of-the-College reports, the contributions made by the Fellows to debates on important issues and the introduction of new bylaws or amendments. Other primary source material includes briefs, reports and memoranda prepared by the College officers, Fellows and staff, correspondence between the College and the Fellows, files relating to the Fellows and files concerning the College's relations with other organizations.

Because complete (and compulsive) citation of statements made in this book would prove distracting in the text, specific references to the primary sources have not been cited unless it seemed essential or clarifying; references to Council or committee sources are usually clear in the context of a particular discussion. Readers who wish to pursue a specific line of inquiry might, however, note three points. The first draft of the manuscript, which is available for inspection at College headquarters, contains a relatively complete series of citations; Appendix 1 provides a chronological summary of those events and resolutions that were central to the College's evolution from 1960 to 1980; and the primary sources themselves are readily available for study at the College headquarters.

Usage of abbreviations also requires explanation. Certain abbreviations refer to the names of organizations with which the College has enjoyed close relations and which are mentioned frequently — the Canadian Medical Association (CMA) and the Association of Canadian Medical Colleges (ACMC) are two examples. After the name of the organization has been mentioned for the first time, the appropriate abbreviation is used thereafter. For convenience, the abbreviations of names of organizations that have been used are listed here: the Association of Canadian Medical Colleges (ACMC); the Canadian Association of Internes and Residents (CAIR); the Canadian Medical Association (CMA); the Canadian Psychiatric Association (CPA); the Canadian Society for Clinical Investigation (CSCI); the College of Family Physicians of Canada (CFPC); the College of Physicians and Surgeons of Ontario (CPSO); la Corporation professionnelle des médecins du Québec (CPMQ); the Medical Council of Canada (MCC); and the Society of Obstetricians and Gynaecologists of Canada (SOGC). In general, apart from abbreviations for these organizations, abbreviations have been avoided, although the abbreviations for continuing medical education (CME) and Regional Advisory Committees (RACs) are exceptions.

Abbreviations are, of course, necessary in references to cited books and journals. Two sources of information that have frequently been consulted are D. Sclater Lewis's invaluable *The Royal College of Physicians and Surgeons of Canada: 1920-1960* (published in 1962 by the McGill University Press) and the informal account of the main events in the College's first-half century, which was published by the College in 1979 and was edited by A.W. Andison and J. Robichon. These two volumes are referred to in chapter notes as 'Lewis' and 'Andison and Robichon', respectively. References to books in the chapter notes are cited in the customary manner and references to journals have been abbreviated in accordance with the so-called Vancouver style. Two exceptions to use of the latter style concern the abbreviation *'Ann RCPSC'* for the *Annals of The Royal College of Physicians and Surgeons of Canada*, and 'ABM' for the minutes of the College's annual business meetings.

Asking why others thought as they did
challenges us to ask why we think as we do.

— Owsei Temkin

Introduction

The Pursuit of Unity

Between 1960 and 1980 The Royal College of Physicians and Surgeons of Canada underwent a remarkable transformation. The high point occurred in 1972, when, within a few months, the size of the membership doubled and the nature of the membership was transformed from a minority elite among Canadian specialists into a large cadre that was truly representative of medical and surgical specialists across the country. This transformation was the most notable aspect of change and growth in the College from 1960 to 1980, but this two-decade period was one of change and growth in many other respects also, and a steady course was necessary in a time of flux. Serving to steady the College was its pursuit of unity. This pursuit facilitated and gave a sense of purpose to the College's principal activities between 1960 and 1980 — those concerning membership, specialist training and evaluation, maintenance of competence and specialty recognition.

The essential reason for the transformation of the College was simple: the College could no longer accept the long-standing situation whereby there were two standards of clinical competence and two classes of specialists in Canada. The issues surrounding this situation, however, were complex. The need for change was recognized in committee in 1955 and the key decision that led to implementation of change was made by Council in 1958. But between 1958 and 1972, when this decision was acted on, a great deal of discussion and debate was necessary and a great many interrelated steps were required before the Fellows at large could approve Council's decision that there should be only one standard of clinical competence and only one class of specialist in Canada — and in the College. Nor was approval given unanimously, for the issue was an emotional and controversial one. Because the change meant that pre-1972 Certificants could, by means of a grandfather clause, now be admitted to Fellowship, the meaning of the Fellowship changed; indeed, the very "culture" of the College changed. In essence, a new College was created.

The majority of Fellows accepted the decision that Certificants should be permitted to apply for admission to Fellowship and so become members in the College alongside them. This says much for the tolerance and understanding of the Fellows and for the flexibility and democracy of the College. The Fellows

1

constituted an elite whose distinguishing designation was the hard-won and widely respected Fellowship diploma; the Certificants formed a much larger body of specialists whose designation was the less demanding journeyman Certificate. For some Fellows, the Certification program was neither a central nor a proper concern of the College; some Certificants were regarded as second-class specialists and others, who had attempted but not passed the Fellowship examination, were thought of as "failed Fellows". This view may seem extreme but a small revolt against the admission of pre-1972 Certificants without examination at the Fellowship level among Fellows in 1972 demonstrated its reality. The revolt failed to gain support at the 1973 annual business meeting, and the evolution of the new College continued unimpeded. In Canada thereafter the terms 'specialist' and 'Fellow' were, for practical purposes, synonymous.

The year 1972 was historic, too, for a second reason: henceforth, a specialist candidate would be required to take one examination instead of having the option of taking the Fellowship examination or the Certification examination (or both). Somewhat confusingly, the new single examination — now the sole test of specialist competence in Canada — was named Certification and the Fellowship examination (as opposed to Fellowship as membership in the College) was discontinued. But the greater understanding of medical education and evaluation that had developed in the 1960s made the new Certification examination perhaps superior to any former College examination; and, paradoxically, passing the Certification examination became the principal prerequisite for Fellowship-as-membership in the College. The nature of "Fellowship" therefore changed quite fundamentally in 1972, but it was a change that was consonant with the changes in this era in medical education, specialty development, specialty health care and, indeed, Canadian society also.

The pursuit of unity in this period of change, was, however, no easy task; the forces for disunity were often attractive and always powerful. It was not easy to keep a growing number of specialists in an increasing number of specialties unified. It is therefore useful to consider how the College succeeded. Two factors in particular explain the College's success — the process of professionalization and the Canadian condition.

The traditional sociological view holds that a profession tends quite naturally to be cohesive and homogeneous, and in Canada this is, in general, true of the development of the specialist segment of the medical profession. But a tendency towards separation is just as natural, for, as Bucher and Strauss have observed, professions are "loose amalgamations of segments pursuing different objectives in different manners and more or less delicately held together under one common name"; moreover, as specialties develop they define themselves and identify for themselves "unique missions".[1] Indeed, in many countries specialties are organized separately within their own individual colleges, and specialty certifying boards are separate and autonomous. Canada

2

has therefore been fortunate. The College has opposed and contained the tendency to fragmentation, and it has served successfully as a unifying force. In doing so, the College has turned to its good the positive features of professionalization — the process whereby the production of knowledge and skills shapes and becomes integrated into the precepts and practices of a profession.[2]

A profession is characterized by five bonding elements: community sanction, a body of systematic theory, authority, an ethical code and a "culture".[3] All of these elements are recognizable in the Canadian specialist profession, as reflected in the College. Thus, while community sanction of the activities of specialists has always been granted in a general sense, society's sanction in a particular sense has been given, first, in the granting of Royal Assent, in 1929, to the parliamentary bill that led to the Act of Incorporation and, second, in ministerial approval of the Letters Patent of Continuance in 1971; it was implicit, too, in the report of Justice Emmett Hall's two reports on health services in Canada of 1964 and 1980. Similarly, over the years, a body of systematic theory developed under College aegis; two examples are the corpus of work relating to theoretical aspects of evaluation as understood and applied by the R.S. McLaughlin Examination and Research Centre, and the criteria for specialty recognition that were formulated by Dr. R.W. Gunton and his colleagues in 1974. Regarding the College's authority, the College's successful efforts to convince universities of their responsibility for specialty training form just one example of such authority. The College's ethical code has been quite evident also, for the Ethics Committee has always been a prominent element in the College's committee structure (as has the Biomedical Ethics Committee more recently) and the Code of Ethics occupies a place in the College's documents alongside the Act of Incorporation and the bylaws.

A profession's "culture" is a central characteristic. Greenwood has claimed that "if one were to single out the attribute that most effectively differentiates the professions from other occupations, this is it".[4] The culture of a profession is reflected in its values, its mores of behavior and its symbols — all of which join the profession's members together and facilitate the pursuit of unity. In Canada, the College has provided the forum in which, over the years, the values, mores and symbols that specialist physicians recognize have evolved and have been preserved. Hence the worth of the Act of Incorporation (and of its continuation in 1971 in the Letters Patent, which contain a reference statement on objectives), of the pattern of behavior as exemplified in Council and committees and of the coat of arms. All these cultural characteristics have linked Canadian specialists together and have tended to unify the profession — and so aid in the pursuit of unity. As, of course, has the existence of the College itself — "a body of persons having a common purpose or common duties".

A cultural duty that is common to all Fellows is to ensure that they and their colleagues are appropriately trained and educated, whether this concerns basic specialty training or the continuing education of established specialists. In this manner, the quality of specialty practice is steadily refined and the profession's culture is tempered to serve society. In the period from 1960 to 1980, the College took enormous strides in applying educational methodology to the evaluation of specialist candidates, and it was the intense efforts of a handful of Fellows, particularly in the second half of the 1960s, that enabled the College to introduce the revolutionary single examination process in 1972 — and so to demonstrate that a single, rather than double, specialty standard was a practical as well as a desirable attainment.

None of this, however, specifically explains the College's unique success in preserving unity among its specialists, for fragmentation rather than unity has been the rule in most other countries having a similar approach to specialist health care. The College is virtually unique in combining under one roof the representatives and interests of numerous specialties and, besides, the functions and responsibilities of a traditional physicians' college. Not surprisingly, the College has been much envied for its success, and the reasons for this success may be summarized here.

The Canadian quest, par excellence, is unity; this is the holy grail that has inspired the nation since Confederation. In a country as large and diverse as Canada, the presence of a unifying force is necessary to counteract tendencies of the geographic regions or the provinces to either separatism and autonomy within Canada or even to union with the United States. The College is a microcosm of the country, and the tendency of specialties to separation and autonomy is analogous to that dreamed of sometimes by some of the provinces. The concerns that the College has had in this respect have existed from the founding of the College, but it is precisely because of this that the College has been conscious of the need to pursue unity actively rather than to pay it lip-service only.

The need for unity was in fact recognized at the very first Council meeting in 1929. Two surgeons attempted to reject the original plan for an integrated college of physicians and surgeons; they wanted physicians and surgeons to form two separate colleges. Their opposition was soon quashed and the joining together of the Division of Medicine and the Division of Surgery under the common roof of the College set a pattern for the College's later pursuit of unity.

Not long after this first crisis had been resolved, another arose. This concerned the need to certify and thus recognize specialists. In the early 1930s Canadian radiologists expressed concern that no organization in Canada served their needs for a body that would lay down training requirements for, and examine and certify in, radiology. (At this time the College emphasized a broad education in medicine or surgery as the basis for specialist practice rather than a narrower training in a specific specialty such as radiology.) The College had, in fact, been engaged in discussions with the Canadian Medical Association (CMA) concerning a certification program, but progress was slow. The radiologists, impatient at an apparent impasse, threatened to establish their own college, and other specialties considered seeking specialty recognition by way of joining American specialty boards. The danger of separation was real and the College, as a result, accelerated progress in the planning of the Certification program. This satisfied the specialties, which entrusted their future to association with the College, and the Certification program, which was quite separate from the College's own well-established Fellowship program, was introduced in 1942.

It was, therefore, the active pursuit of unity to satisfy a peculiarly Canadian need that led to the introduction of the Certification program and, thereby, to recognition by the College of an increasing number of specialties. Yet the introduction of the Certification program achieved, for the moment, only a limited degree of unity. On the one hand, the program did serve to unify a number of specialists in Canada and indirectly to associate them, through the College's granting them Certificates, with the College; moreover, if the College had not introduced the program, separate specialist colleges and boards almost certainly would have been established, after the manner of the United Kingdom and the United States, so that the unified and representative Canadian College as we know it today would never have developed. On the other hand, the Certification program was peripheral to the College proper because, constitutionally, only Fellows could be members of the College, and the Certificants remained, for the time being, outside the College in this respect. A more forceful pursuit was then required before total unity could be gained.

The lessons of those early years were learned well. The need to actively pursue unity was at least recognized. As obstetricians and gynecologists, psychiatrists and pathologists sought autonomy and independence, the College, motivated by the pursuit of unity, managed to keep these specialties within the fold. Much the same is true as new specialties developed in the 1960s and 1970s; the College's careful attention to appropriate means of recognizing specialties and subspecialties kept the specialist profession in Canada unified. As a result, the College grew even stronger.

The same is true of the College's relationships with other organizations. The desire for unity, difficult though its achievement might sometimes have seemed, has lain behind the College's relationships with various medical organizations. These organizations are numerous and could not be ignored if the College was to remain in the mainstream of health care: the Canadian Association of Internes and Residents (CAIR); the CMA; provincial medical colleges such as la Corporation professionnelle des médecins du Québec (CPMQ) and the College of Physicians and Surgeons of Ontario (CPSO); the Medical Council of Canada (MCC); the Association of Canadian Medical Colleges (ACMC); specialty groups such as the Canadian Psychiatric Association (CPA) and the Society of Obstetricians and Gynaecologists of Canada (SOGC); the Canadian Society for Clinical Investigation (CSCI); and the College of Family Physicians of Canada (CFPC). The College has been largely successful in building and maintaining a harmonious and fruitful relationship with each of these organizations and so in achieving a measure of unity in specialty health care — in part, no doubt, because College Fellows often have been members of these organizations and of their executives.

The need for the active pursuit of unity was, however, never more important than in relation to the College's relationship with the Certificants. That the College eventually succeeded in accomplishing the enormous task of unifying virtually all Canadian specialists under its broad roof is the most eloquent tribute to its pursuit of unity. That the College, in 1972, was able to take the revolutionary step of opening its membership to all specialists in Canada rather than a minority and thereby to change the very nature of the College is a testament to the value it placed on unity (and negates, perhaps, the cynical view that unity is but a synonym for Canadian compromise). In brief, the College sought a democratic and all-inclusive approach to Fellowship in the College, rather than an elitist and exclusive one.

The College's pursuit of unity is the principal theme of this book. Although it is exemplified in many events and issues throughout the period from 1960 to 1980, the pursuit of unity has clearly woven a pattern in the College from the start. It explains much that has occurred as the College has evolved. But the evolution of the College from 1960 to 1980 was shaped by forces that had not previously existed, and the pursuit of unity consequently served different needs in this period. Four such forces provide the greater part of the framework of this book. Part 1 of the book discusses the way the College itself changed from 1960 to 1980, especially in relation to its nature, objectives, membership, constitution, organization and administration. The changes in this respect were closely related to changes in society, for Canada and the medical profession were not untouched by the universal sociocultural upheaval of the 1960s. The 1960s also brought to fruition advances in the understanding of new educational methods that had been developing since the Second World War, and Parts 2 and 3 of the book deal, respectively, with the development of the specialist and the maintenance of competence among established specialists. Finally, the period from 1960 to 1980 witnessed the rapid development of specialties, which both changed the face of medicine and caused the College, which has always been intimately concerned with specialty health care, to consider how it should adapt to this particular force — the concern of Part 4 of the book.

The period from 1960 to 1980 was a most eventful one for the College and, while the College's unitarian nature and purpose is envied by other specialists' colleges around the world, Canadians for their part should be proud of their College, for the pursuit of unity has resulted in evolution rather than revolution. The nation, as well as the College, has benefitted, and will continue to benefit, from the unifying process to which this history bears witness.

NOTES TO INTRODUCTION

1. R. Bucher, A. Strauss, "Professions in Process." *Amer J Sociol* 1961; 66:325-334.
2. M.S. Larson, *The Rise of Professionalism: A Sociological Analysis*, Berkeley, University of California Press, 1977, p. 50. The concept of professionalization is a complex one, and its application to medical historiography is problematic. While it is useful to remain aware of trends within a profession that enable its practitioners to share various commonalities and to facilitate the performance of tasks that need to be achieved, it is also necessary to remember that different professions (and even different segments within a single profession) differ in their approaches to key dualities such as altruism versus self-interest regarding service, and inclusiveness versus exclusiveness regarding membership. To make matters more complex, the viewpoints of the many authors who have interested themselves in professionalism are widely divergent. Larson, for example, relates knowledge and skills to social and economic rewards, and Eliot Freidson (e.g. *Profession of Medicine*, New York, Dodd and Mead, 1970) stresses the implications and dangers (for the profession and for the public) that are inherent in professional autonomy. A useful and pleasingly short introduction to the subject is Terence J. Johnson's *Professions and Power* (London, Macmillan, 1972).
3. E. Greenwood, "Attributes of a Profession." *Social Work* 1957; 2(3):44-55.
4. Greenwood, 1957.

PART 1

THE COLLEGE TRANSFORMED

Chapter 1

Legacy of the First Three Decades: The Fellowship, The Certification Program and the "Dual Standard"

To understand the evolution of the College between 1960 and 1980, one must understand its early history. The history of the period from 1929 to 1960 has been described by Lewis,[1] and here only the origins of those events and issues that were the College's chief concerns in the later years are emphasized. Among these later concerns, the abolition of the "dual standard" of specialist competence was paramount. This chapter summarizes the development of the College in relation to the original nature of the Fellowship, the introduction of the Certification program and then the rise of the dual standard of competence that resulted from the College's decision to approve two standards of clinical competence.

The Fellowship

The College was formally founded when a Bill petitioning the Governor General of Canada received Royal Assent on June 14, 1929. The College's Act of Incorporation was set out in this Bill, and an early task of the College's founding Fellows was to draw up a set of bylaws. Dr. A.T. Bazin presented the bylaws for approval at the annual meeting in November 1930. These bylaws contained but one Object, but the wording of this object was sufficiently clear for it to serve as a guideline for the following three decades. The object was stated simply in Article 1, Section 2, as follows:

Because of the growth and development of the science and art of medicine and its division into various specialties, it is considered necessary and advisable that a practising physician essaying to do 'special work' should have the opportunity of obtaining a distinguishing designation from The Royal College of Physicians and Surgeons of Canada whereby it may be known that he is properly qualified.

The simplicity of this statement, however, belied its significance. The College was conceived in a period when there was little formal distinction between the general practitioner, the consulting physician and the consulting and operating surgical specialist. The profession was concerned about patients' lives being "endangered or lost" as a result of the performance of major surgical operations by practitioners who, though legally qualified under current licensing laws, nevertheless for lack of special training and of surgical experience were "absolutely and fundamentally incompetent in matters of surgical diagnosis and treatment".[2] The need to identify — for both the medical profession and the public — those physicians who were qualified to practise as specialists was urgent, and the bylaw stood the test of time well.

In the early years, the College was concerned also with more general goals that seemed so obvious that they were not even defined in the original bylaws. Such goals, however, were often articulated in other statements. Thus, an early statement emphasized "the furtherance of scholastic and scientific attainment among medical men in order that the highest ideals and standards of medical education may be preserved";[3] another suggested that a goal of the College was "to provide means through which the highest standards of specialized practice may be maintained throughout the country".[4] Even so, the original bylaw's object still serves as a valuable text in any attempt to understand the nature of the College in its early years.

Terms of note in the original object are 'special work', 'a distinguishing designation' and 'properly qualified'. Considering the implications of these phrases enables one to understand the College's activities in its early years.

Although some physicians have, through the ages, always engaged in special work, specialization did not become an accepted part of medical practice until the late 19th century. In Canada, the view that specialism should be discountenanced, which was held as recently as 1881, was not entirely unfounded, for some self-styled specialists, it was claimed, had a "superficial professional education and a want of success as practitioners of medicine and surgery".[5] For these practitioners, the rewards of specialist practice overrode any ethical integrity. The First World War aggravated the situation, for men who had, as medical officers, practised military medicine now had a taste for surgical specialization, but many, of course, lacked formal surgical training. By the 1920s, therefore, a standard for the qualification of specialists was much needed, and this need constituted one of the proposed aims for the Canadian college of specialists that was then being considered.

The need for well-conducted 'special work' — and for a Canadian college of specialists — thus became clear. What kind of distinguishing designation should mark *bona fide* specialists?

Although the motivating force underlying the creation of the College was provided by three stalwarts from the plains of Saskatchewan — dubbed, according to Lewis, "the Regina Bronchos"[6] — the College from the first was an academic organization. The Act of Incorporation prescribed that the Charter Fellows be university professors, and the College was intended to serve as "an incentive to medical men, both physicians and surgeons, to aspire to higher qualifications and therefore higher standards of service to the public".[7] The distinguishing designation was, therefore, to be academically oriented. The Fellowship diploma would indicate that a Fellow had passed a rigorous test, for the College's founders preferred that the College become known through its worthy diploma, high standards and a slower rate of growth than by rapid growth, low standards — and a meaningless diploma.

Both the content and the pass rate of the College's Fellowship examination reflected these early concerns. The written part of the primary examination comprised papers in anatomy (including histology and embryology) and physiology (including biochemistry); the final examination consisted of searching questions on pathology (including bacteriology) and the principles and practice of either medicine (including therapeutics and preventive and forensic medicine) or surgery (including surgical anatomy and operative surgery). Early Fellows wanted the examination to be nothing less than a "severe test of the knowledge, ability and judgement of the candidate".[8] The pass rate was never high: in the very first final examination, held in 1932, not one of the three candidates passed, and from 1932 to 1944 the pass rate for the final averaged 50 per cent.

The distinguishing designation offered by the College, then, identified those specialists with an academic orientation and constituted a distinguished diploma in itself. "Fellowship", said Dr. J.W. MacLeod, "is the hallmark of an academic man."[9] Fellows were proud of their diploma. They had worked long and hard for it, and the Fellowship meant colleagueship as much as a diploma; and medical and surgical specialists in other countries respected it. The Canadian Fellowship soon came to represent the best in medical and surgical practice.

But how did the College ensure that specialists to be awarded its distinguishing designation were properly qualified? This was not easy in the early years; indeed, it never became easy and remained a perennial problem. What was the College's approach in its early years?

The College examination, reflecting the College's parent divisions, emphasized general medicine and general surgery. Even the major specialties were virtually excluded, despite a provision in Article 3, Section 2, Subsection B of the original bylaws that allowed for a candidate to be examined in one or more of the recognized special branches of medicine or surgery. For the Charter Fellows and early examiners, a Fellow was properly qualified only if he had passed an examination in either general medicine or general surgery. The examinations were hardly tailored to the needs of the candidates, some of whom might already be specialists in major hospitals. This so irritated one well-known professor of pediatrics that he tendered his resignation from the College. Another physician, Dr. E.H. Botterell — then a budding neurosurgeon and, later, dean of medicine at Queen's University — summarized the situation by describing his own experience:

My first event was the taking of the FRCS(C) examination in general surgery — the only surgical examination that existed at that time. The primary examinations in anatomy and in physiology were conducted by professors of anatomy and physiology and bore little or no relationship to applied anatomy or physiology as a surgeon saw it. They were searching exams in anatomy and physiology. A plastic surgeon on the staff of a Toronto teaching hospital took the oral examination in the Royal Victoria Hospital [in Montreal] the same time that I did — at that point in time we were members of the attending staff of the T[oronto] G[eneral] H[ospital], U[niversity] of T[oronto]. We were both examined by general surgeons; he got the neuro patient and I was examined at length on plastic surgical problems, the first attempt at examination in a specialty gone wrong. Happily we both passed. The experience pointed out the need for proper exams in major specialties to me.[10]

The restrictive nature of the examinations kept at bay many younger specialists, who were not prepared to subject themselves to a test of this kind — and who knew that the pass rate in the 1930s was about 50 per cent. One result of the approach that the College took was that the College was perceived as breeding an elite. It was a perception that was not unrealistic, as the following pronouncement on a Fellow's standing suggests: "It may be accepted as one of the primary responsibilities of the Royal Colleges when they elect a candidate to Fellowship that they are satisfied that his preparation and knowledge of medicine are of such an order as to place him above his fellows in his chosen profession."[11]

The examination problem was corrected to some extent in 1944, largely through the work of the Committee on Educational Standards. The charge of this committee, which had been formed in 1938, was to review the much criticized examination system. The mandate was timely, for the regulations for the examinations were considered obsolete and the period of required training was thought to be too short. The committee also recommended, and Council agreed, that the Fellowship examination be modified to permit Fellowship candidates to be examined in the specialties of dermatology/syphilology, neurology and/or psychiatry, pediatrics, neurosurgery, obstetrics and gynecology, orthopedic surgery and urology. Now, therefore, the concept of being 'properly qualified' to do 'special work' was extended so that the 'distinguishing designation' of the Fellowship would, in literal and realistic terms, reflect the original object of the College: the recognition of specialty practice.

At the same time, an amendment of the Act of Incorporation, assented to on June 3, 1939, had empowered the College to conduct examinations that would enable it to award specialist certificates to physicians who sought an alternative distinguishing designation that was less academic than the Fellowship — in other words, Certification. But the fact that the College introduced Certification as a second distinguishing designation confused the answer to the question as to which specialists were "properly" qualified. Why, therefore, was the College willing to create this second qualification? After all, the College's original object — a deceptively simple statement — had guided the College well in its early years, and a cadre of well-trained specialists was created. Canadian specialists received a broad education in general medicine or general surgery, and then comprehensive training in one of the few medical or surgical specialties. An ideal solution to the question of a 'proper' qualification for a Canadian specialist appeared to have been found. Yet, at the same time, for perfectly practical reasons, there did seem to be a need for Certification — this alternative, less academic, qualification.[12]

The Certification Program

While the College had been concerned with the qualification of specialists since its founding, its concern with the Certification of specialists (as opposed to the Fellowship program) did not develop until 1934. In the spring of that year, the College of Physicians and Surgeons of Saskatchewan asked the Royal College for its opinion on the use of the title 'specialist' and whether any restrictions and conditions might govern its use. The College had never discussed this issue before, but the matter was considered important enough to warrant formation of a committee to study the issue. Drs. W.E. Gallie and A. Primrose were appointed to a committee chaired by Dr. J.G. Fitzgerald.

Drs. Fitzgerald, Gallie and Primrose were familiar with the broad outlines of the issue. They would have read, the previous summer, an editorial on "The Qualification of Specialists" in the *Canadian Medical Association Journal* by Dr. E.S. Ryerson;[13] and, with Dr. D. Graham, the College President, they were members of the CMA's Committee on Specialists, which was chaired by Dr. Ryerson and appointed in June 1934. Dr. Ryerson, the moving spirit behind the initial efforts to introduce a Certification program, had noted that as many as one-third of the country's physicians were specializing, though it was impossible to know who had received adequate special training and who had not. To protect the public, he advocated "a particular identification" for those who professed to be specialists; it would be granted only on the successful completion of training that was adequate to prepare the individual for practice in the limited field of a specialty. Because recognition of specialists was of interest to the provinces, it was possible that the provinces, "with vested rights and other conditions", might wish, in their separate ways, for control. That, said Dr. Ryerson, would be a mistake; unity, not disunity, was needed. So he asked: "Is not now the time to avoid different standards and different methods in the regularization of specialists in Canada by devising some common minimum standard of qualification for the practice of the specialties?" He recommended a standard that would be midway between that of the MD degree and that of the Fellowship diploma.

15

This argument proved compelling enough for the College to work with the CMA in determining which body should certify Canadian specialists. The MCC initially seemed the appropriate one, for it had been conducting qualifying examinations for 20 years and its membership comprised representatives of the medical profession at large, the provinces and the universities. But the Canada Medical Act did not empower the MCC to undertake the certification of specialists.[14] That left the CMA and the Royal College as possible certifying bodies. It was now June 1936, two years since the original question on specialists had been asked of the College, three years since Dr. Ryerson's editorial had been published — and five years since the CMA's Section of Radiology had initiated a movement to establish a Canadian college of radiology. The radiologists were impatient: in Britain, standards of training for radiology were controlled by radiologists and, in the United States, the independent Board of Radiology exerted similar control; but in Canada the CMA's discussions on specialization were stalled in an "impasse" and the Royal College offered "no standard of training nor examination [to] guide the candidate educationally or designate him as a radiologist".[15] The Canadian radiologists, who felt the need at that time to protect their interests and those of the public should a health insurance scheme be introduced into Canada, therefore resolved to press ahead with their plan to establish their own college. Dr. W.A. Jones, president of the Canadian Association of Radiologists, however, left room for negotiation. He reassured Dr. A.T. Bazin, President of the College, that, if the College's Committee on Specialists or the College itself could offer an alternative scheme that would meet the situation, the members of the Section of Radiology would be agreeable to work within that scheme.[16]

The radiologists' action produced the desired effect. Neither for the first nor for the last time in its history, the College now hurriedly pursued the cause of unity. Dr. D. Graham, chairman of the College's Committee on Specialists, urged "prompt action" and recommended that the College take on the responsibility for certifying specialists. He thought that the best interests of the medical profession of Canada would be served by having a single responsible body conduct examinations and grant certificates or diplomas for those qualified to practise a specialty.[17] In England, The Royal College of Physicians of London and The Royal College of Surgeons of England, rather than the British Medical Association, examined candidates and granted diplomas in different specialties. In Canada, the College was, after all, conducting its own examinations and granting diplomas for a higher qualification in medicine and surgery; moreover, its Charter Fellows represented the different specialties to whom Council might appeal for advice and suggestions concerning the drafting of regulations governing qualifications, training and examinations. And it was not only the radiologists who were impatient: the anesthetists, ophthalmologists and otolaryngologists were taking the same viewpoint. The need for action was indeed urgent. Moreover, there was a particular demand across the country for physicians who, though not academically oriented, could deliver the specialist services that were required in the maturing nation of Canada.

Dr. D. Graham's argument prevailed. He learned from the CMA that its executive committee would eventually urge the College to take on the responsibility for Certification. Meanwhile, the College's Committee on Specialists drew up tentative plans for Certification. Subcommittees were established to define training requirements for the different specialties identified for eventual Certification; these subcommittees were the forerunners of the College's valuable specialty committees. Federal, provincial and university bodies were consulted and their support solicited. Their support was essential, for a prerequisite to the College's Certification program was amendment of the Act of Incorporation; the Act did not permit the imposing of standards and the granting of a diploma unless it was related in some way to Fellowship in the College. Amendments were therefore drafted; a key amendment was the clause stating that "the Council shall have power to grant special diplomas to persons who shall have shown such degree of proficiency in such examinations as the Council may consider entitles them to such special diploma, provided that the granting of such diploma shall in no way qualify such persons to be Fellows of the College".[18] Most of the bodies consulted were favorable to these several steps and the amended Act received Royal Assent on June 3, 1939.

The College's Certification program was now constitutionally valid and could be formally introduced.

The College's plan had the general support of the medical profession, but support was not unanimous. Although Council, in November 1935, had apparently "unanimously" favored some recognized standard being established for specialists in Canada, some councillors were not entirely supportive and others were sceptical and negative. Thus, in regard to the developing Certification program, Dr. R.E. Valin, the College's first Honorary Treasurer, asked, in June 1937, "What effect will this have on the College?" He added, "I'm afraid that we are going to kill the College". Dr. E.G. Bourgeois, of the University of Montreal, wondered whether the College was the right organization to certify specialists and whether the universities should recognize specialist competence by offering mastership degrees.[19] Another fear in those early days — indeed, a fear that was felt also, from 1970 to 1973, when the merits of the *new* Certification qualification, were being debated — was that the prestige of the Fellowship would suffer. The opinion of the Canadian Association of Clinical Surgeons was an example. In relation to urology, Dr. Gallie told Council in October 1937 that the Canadian clinical surgeons were unanimous in thinking that Certification in specialties requiring a thorough knowledge of surgery would diminish the prestige of the Fellowship in surgery, and that it would be "exceedingly unwise" for the College to grant a diploma or certificate in urology. Many Fellows thought that the Certification should be developed "quite outside" the mainstream of the College's activities and agreed with Dr. G.S. Young, who said of the 1939 amendment to the Act of Incorporation the following: "The College was set up for a definite purpose. I question whether we can mix two departments in its activities, the one we started with and the one that we have added with this amendment".[20]

Prominent among Canadian urologists was Dr. F.S. Patch. If Dr. D. Graham, the first chairman of the College's Committee on Specialists, laid the foundation of the Certification program from 1934 to 1937, Dr. Patch built its main structure from 1937 to 1947. With Dr. Graham, Dr. Patch proposed arguments in favor of Certification that overrode those of the opponents of the Certification program. While Drs. Graham and Patch valued the Fellowship as a fine diploma and entirely appropriate as a distinguishing designation for specialists in teaching hospitals, they realized that some competent specialists would, for one reason or another, never qualify for Fellowship, even though, from a technical and practical viewpoint, they were entirely qualified to practise. Rather than reflect the narrower concerns of an elite, Drs. Graham and Patch preferred to take the broader view that Certification would serve a particular need, especially in the smaller cities and towns where there were no teaching hospitals. Canadian patients there needed specialist care as much as those in the larger cities; if there were specialists who were interested in working there, without having taken the Fellowship, it was better to at least encourage them to take formal training and then an examination appropriate to their needs. What the proponents of the Certification program, like Drs. Graham, Patch and Ryerson sought, then, was what Dr. Ryerson had recommended in 1933 — a standard of qualification between the high one of the College's Fellowship diploma and the standard one of the MD degree.

This view ultimately won the day and the Certification program was introduced in 1942. The first Certificants were seasoned specialists whose credentials indicated that a formal examination need not be a prerequisite for the specialist certificate. By the end of 1942, 152 such specialist certificates had been awarded in anesthesia, dermatology and syphilology, pediatrics and urology. By the fall of 1947, when the last "grandfather" certificates were granted, the total had risen to 3,468, but the specialties recognized by Certification then included internal medicine, general surgery, neurology and psychiatry, neurosurgery, pathology, radiology, orthopedic surgery and physical medicine and rehabilitation. Now, Certificants were having to earn their specialist certificates by examination, for the first Certification examinations were held in September and October 1946.

Such are the origins of the College's initial Certification program. This first phase had occupied the College for no less than 12 years, and the College's role in this period was moulded by a program that some had thought should not be part of the College's activities.[21] The impact of the Certification program, both on the College and the medical profession, was considerable. Dr. Patch indicated this in 1947 in these words:

> *The* success of Certification by the College would seem assured and it is therefore quite proper to review the advantages which have thereby accrued to the College.
> 1. The prestige and authority of the College have been greatly enhanced. The diploma of Fellowship and the specialist Certificate are now universally recognized as denoting the highest standards of graduate qualifications.
> 2. Certification has awakened an active and increased interest by medical schools and hospitals in the matter of advanced graduate training.
> 3. It has created a demand for the formulation of standards of approval of hospitals in the field of advanced graduate training.
> 4. It has raised the standards of medical education in Canada.
> 5. It has played an important role in inducing the College to broaden the scope of its Fellowship examination.
> 6. More than anything else, Certification has acted as a quickening ferment to the College. ...on the Council an originally pessimistic outlook has been changed to one of enthusiastic optimism. ...[one can] note the livelier interest of medical graduates, who in increasing numbers are planning their training with a view to obtaining one of the qualifications of the College.[22]

Dr. Patch suggested that "there may be developments in the future, which none of us can foresee at the present moment". He noted that, already, there was evidence of an effort to alter the policy of the College with regard to Certification. Dr. Patch saw clearly. An effort to alter the policy of the College was indeed underway, even as the Certification program itself was getting underway. This effort stemmed from dissatisfaction with the dual standard that was created when the College approved the Certification, in addition to the Fellowship, as a designation of specialist competence.

The Dual Standard — and Early Moves Towards Its Resolution

While there were understandable reasons in the 1940s and 1950s for having a practically oriented as well as an academically oriented standard of specialist competence, the dual standard was not, in the long run, an ideal solution to Canada's problems of specialized health care. The ideal would be to develop a cadre of specialists, all highly trained and taught by university physicians whose standards of practice were based on sound theoretical principles. The College's Fellowship examination reflected this ideal, but the Certification examination of the 1940s and 1950s did not. The dual standard was, therefore, an acknowl-

Past Presidents at The Convocation, Montreal, January 22, 1970

(L. to R.) W.C. MacKenzie, W.G. Penfield, R.B. Kerr, D. Graham,
President J. Turcot, D.S. Lewis, D.A. Thompson, G.M. Brown

Charter Fellows at the Fiftieth Anniversary Meeting, Montreal, February 7, 1979

(L. to R.) W.R. Waddell, W.J. McNally, E.J. Maltby, J.B. Scriver,
President D.G. Cameron, G.S. Fahrni, A.C. Abbott, D.M. Baltzan,
M.R. MacCharles

edgement that the College condoned less than the best; in the long run, the dual standard was not an acceptable solution as the standards of health care, the standards of specialist training and the numbers of available trainees in Canada rose.

The dual standard, then, was an only partially desirable expedient that reflected the need to fulfil Canada's requirement for adequately, rather than ideally, trained specialists in the 1930s, 1940s and 1950s. The defects of the dual standard were soon apparent, and some of them were the subject of vigorous criticism. Thus Dr. R.I. Harris, in 1953, while admitting that the Certification program had brought uniformity of standards to the country, stressed its negative consequences, especially the isolation of Certificants from the College:

> *In* certain fields of medicine the program of Certification is useless, futile, and detrimental. It sets up dual standards. It isolates from this College a certain group who choose to take the Certification examination rather than the Fellowship and this group takes no part and makes no contribution of fees, knowledge or initiative to the College's activities. They have been certificated and that is the end of their association with the College. They have no active participation in our work and we have no control over them.[23]

Thus the problem of a dual standard of *competence* was compounded by a second problem of a dual standard of specialist *status*: those who were Fellows and so were members of the College and those who were Certificants and so were not members of the College — even though these Certificants had once been certified as being competent by the College. The consequences of the complexity of this dual standard for the evolution of the College vis-a-vis specialists' standards and the College's pursuit of unity as a whole were considerable; and the polarization of views about the College's Certification program and the position of the College in relation to its Certificants obscured or distorted the dimensions of the problem. The consequences became clear only much later, as Dr. R.C. Dickson suggested in 1979. Dr. Dickson's perspective developed from his having been a councillor during the 1960s and President from 1970 to 1972. Of the situation in the late 1940s and of the consequences for the College of views held then by the Fellows, Dr. Dickson wrote as follows:

> *From* a perusal of the minutes of Council of this era it is possible to discern clearly the opinions that were held on the subject. Most of the members of Council felt there would be relatively little interest in the Certification program and that it would continue for only a short time. In this they were proved wrong indeed. One group of Council members thought that the new Certificants should be brought in as Fellows of the College at once, others thought that Certification must be at a lower level than the Fellowship and that those qualifying for the former

should not have any relationship whatever with the College. In retrospect both groups were partly right and partly wrong. Had either been powerful enough to prevail, the College would have been very different from what it is today. Fortunately that was not the case and although it was to take 25 years to reconcile these two positions, the College is immeasurably stronger than it would otherwise have been. Holding examinations as it does in 36 specialties and subspecialties, and maintaining comparable high standards in all, it is the envy of the medical world. Had the group favoring admission of all specialists to Fellowship carried the day, a definite lowering of the standards of the College would have been the result and it is doubtful whether they could ever have been satisfactorily raised later. Had the view been adopted of those who believed Certificants should have a lower status and never be brought into the College, it is likely that the College would have constituted a small elite group and that the Certificants would have formed their own organization, much larger than the College and probably far more influential. For the people of Canada no other solution could have provided the uniformly high standards of specialist training and identification that have now been achieved.[24]

The move to reconcile the two positions and thereby to resolve the dual standard was initiated during the Council meeting of October 1953, only seven years after the Certification examinations had been inaugurated. Dr. Harris asked Council to appoint a special committee to study the Certification program. Dr. C.W. Burns, who believed that the usefulness of Certification had passed and that 75 to 90 per cent of Fellows would favor the abolition of Certification, seconded Dr. Harris's motion. The motion, however, lacked sufficient support to pass at the time. Dr. N.W. Philpott suggested that most of those who wanted Certification to be discontinued were from university centres; and it is true that those who favored the abolition of Certification were specialists who were, for the most part, university-based and drawn from specialties such as neurosurgery, neurology, thoracic surgery and plastic surgery, in addition to Dr. Harris's own specialty of orthopedic surgery. Dr. E. Dubé also pointed out that British Columbia, Alberta and Ontario relied on the College's Certification for recognition of specialists. The issue did not disappear, however, and during the November 1953 Executive Committee meeting Dr. H.R. Robertson, seconded by Dr. Philpott, proposed that the matter be referred back to Council and that a committee be appointed to study the question.

By June, 1954, the Certification program loomed large as "a real problem", and it was reported that many people did not realize the difference between Certification and Fellowship and that Certification was beginning to undermine the influence of the Fellowship. Action was clearly necessary. (Not for the first time did the need for "urgent" action appear to become evident quite suddenly.) As a result, the Robertson committee was appointed forthwith "to study the wisdom and necessity of modifying our present program of Certification". It was to be the first of four committees that would study the issue in the 1950s — and thus provide the College with issues to debate in the 1960s. The others consisted of two that were appointed in December 1955 to study the Robertson committee's report following its discussion by Council (an Ontario group, or subcommittee, and a Quebec subcommittee) and one that was appointed in October 1957 to study the relationship of the certificated specialists with the College and the implications should Certificants be included in the College (the Botterell committee).

These four committees identified the principal issues, and the Botterell committee, in particular, led Council in October 1958 to pass three crucial resolutions. The most far-reaching was the resolution that placed Council on record as favoring the abolition of the Certification examination. The second was highly significant also: Council supported the principle that the certificated specialists be allowed a closer relationship or association with the College. The third resolution directed that the Credentials Committee and the Examinations Committee study the matter. Because the work of these four committees and the resolutions of Council in October 1958 paved the way for the College in the 1960s to take the steps that finally enabled it to resolve the dual standard, the complex discussions in committee and in Council should be summarized here.

The Robertson committee presented its report to Council in October 1955. The committee, chaired by Dr. H.R. Robertson, comprised Drs. C.W. Burns, R.B. Kerr, J.W. MacLeod, F.P. Patterson and J. Saucier as nucleus members and E.H. Botterell, C.W. Holland, W.A. Jones, W.J. McNally and J. Turcot as corresponding members. The committee noted that, while the activities of the College had improved the standard of specialist practice in Canada, the Certification program had prevented the College from fully achieving its aims since many physicians were preferring to take the easier Certification examination; the College, therefore, was losing potentially valuable members. At the same time, the proportion of Canadian physicians who would become specialists appeared to be rising: specialists represented approximately 40 per cent of all physicians compared with 35 per cent some 20 years earlier. Hence the College should do all it could to ensure that those who obtained Certification were thoroughly trained and fully deserving of the status of specialist.

As the Robertson committee observed, the current program of training and examination leading to Certification was, however, deficient in several respects. Thus there was no formal system of assessing candidates before they were selected for training; many hospitals approved for training did not in fact provide adequate training; the College's requirements dealt only with the time that was to be spent in training, whereas, particularly in the surgical specialties, an essential consideration was not so much time as adequacy of practical experience; and the standard of the Certification, which comprised two relatively easy papers and a single short oral examination before only two examiners, was not particularly high. (The last point was confirmed by Dr. G.M. Brown when Council discussed the Robertson report. It was becoming increasingly difficult to pass the Fellowship examination but not more difficult to pass the Certification examination: in 1947, the pass rate for the Fellowship had been 62.0 per cent and for the Certification, 81.3 per cent; by 1955, while the Fellowship pass rate had fallen to 46.0 per cent the Certification pass rate of 73.9 per cent was little different than it had been earlier.)

The committee made three recommendations. First, the committee thought that, since Certification seemed to be advantageous in certain specialties with respect to supply of physicians, the dual standard should be retained in internal medicine, anesthesia, pediatrics and radiology. Second, the committee suggested that a long-term benefit would result if the double standard of *training* were abolished and a single standard based on minimum training requirements were established for each specialty, much along the lines of the Fellowship examination requirements. And third, the committee proposed that all candidates in each specialty take the same initial set of examinations marked by the same board of examiners, who would then segregate the candidates who were evidently potential Fellows, potential Certificants and failures. This plan would stream the candidates into five categories: outright failures; those judged to be of Certification quality who would proceed only to the Certification orals; those acceptable for further evaluation by a second written examination — the Fellowship; those who then failed this second examination but who could proceed to the Certification oral examination; and those who passed the second examination and who could proceed to the Fellowship oral examination.

Council approved the Robertson committee's recommendations in principle and asked the Executive Committee to work out the details or to appoint a committee for this purpose. The Executive Committee appointed two committees, one in Ontario and a second in Quebec.

The Ontario committee, chaired by Dr. A.L. Chute and consisting of Drs. E.H. Botterell, R.F. Farquharson, R.A. Mustard, D.L. Wilson and G.E. Wodehouse as members, made six points. They first noted that the current system failed to assure full training and competence of Certificants and that any system of screening of candidates for specialist training would be impractical. They recommended that approval for specialist training should be granted only to those hospitals that provided proper training. The committee then stated that the College's policy regarding the type and periods of training for the different specialties was too rigid. The dual system of training and examinations, however, should be retained, since it was quite reasonable to want to take the Certification examination without having to be branded as a "failed Fellow"; however, the Certification examination should be of the same type as the Fellowship examination, and there was a case for abolishing the Certification examination in specialties like neurosurgery and internal medi-

LEGACY OF THE FIRST THREE DECADES

cine. Finally, admitting Certificants to the College in some capacity would strengthen the College and give it a more representative voice in the country's medical affairs.

The Quebec committee was chaired by Dr. W. de M. Scriver and included Drs. G.A. Bergeron, R.L. Denton, F.N. Gurd, W.J. McNally, L.P. Roy and J. Saucier as members. They likewise recommended that the dual system should be continued for the present but suggested that some other body eventually take over the responsibility for conducting the Certification examination. The committee thought that in certain parts of the country and in certain specialties the time was not right to insist that everyone take the lengthy period of training for the Certification examination that would be required if the standard of training for the Certification and the Fellowship examinations was made the same — even though this would obviate the need for Certificants to take more training before sitting the Fellowship examination later. Certificants should be encouraged to write the Fellowship examination later, for many had developed into first-class doctors and it was undesirable that so many certified specialists should take no part in College affairs.

The Ontario and Quebec committees both recommended that a way should be found to bring the Certificants into a closer relationship with the College. With the Robertson committee, the Ontario and Quebec committees also held that the dual standard still served a useful purpose.

The Ontario and Quebec committees' reports were not formally adopted by Council, but momentum was beginning to accelerate. One indication of this was Council's directing the Executive Committee, in October 1956, to consider the abolition of the Certification examination, within a five-year period, in neurology, neurosurgery, orthopedic surgery and thoracic surgery. In June 1957 Council decided that the Certification examination should be abolished in neurology and neurosurgery as from 1962. Yet the College was still unsure how far to go. Councillors of 1957 had thoughts in common with those of councillors of two decades earlier, for the latter had seen that the issues were problematic and complex. Thus in October 1939, when the Act of Incorporation was amended to empower Council to grant Certificates to specialists, Dr. G.S. Young expressed concerns that perhaps were still evident in 1957:

> We are entering on a new field. We know nothing about what we are undertaking as yet. We can scarcely be guided by precedents of other Royal Colleges, or by their bylaws. We must find our own way. It will be necessary that we proceed very slowly. We shall have to be careful to avoid mistakes.[25]

So, in 1957, yet another committee was asked to study the issues. This fourth committee was chaired by Dr. E.H. Botterell, who had been a corresponding member of the Robertson Committee and a member of the Ontario committee. He was firm in the view that there should be only one standard of examination, and the fact that his own training program in neurosurgery had yielded Fellowship candidates who, over a nine-year period, achieved a 100 per cent pass rate in the Fellowship examination supported his view. His committee was made up of Drs. W.B. Barton, A.L. Chute (secretary), P.E. Ireland, S.V. Railton and G.E. Wodehouse, all of Ontario, together with Drs. J.D.B. Baird, F.N. Gurd, F.C. Heal, J.M. Kilgour, R. Lemieux, R.R. Mutrie, H.R. Robertson, L.C. Steeves, D.A. Thompson and D.R. Wilson as corresponding members. Despite being encumbered with the longest name for a committee in College history ("The Nucleus Committee Concerning the Relationship of the Certificated Specialists to The Royal College of Physicians and Surgeons of Canada and the Future of the Certification Program in Canada"), the committee studied the problems with dispatch and reported to Council in time for the letter's meeting of October 31 and November 1, 1958.

The Botterell committee constructed its report around three questions:

- What is the future of the Certification program?
- Is there a place for certificated specialists within the College, and what are the relevant implications?
- What would be the status of Certificants if admitted to the College?

The committee then made six telling points:

1. The Certification program was initiated before the Fellowship program had provided the numbers of the specialists that Canada required, but that situation no longer existed in 1958.

2. It was incongruous that specialists with similar training and practising beside each other within a community should neither have a common meeting ground nor be able to speak authoritatively about a specialty's position or needs in relation to the medical profession or the community.

3. Because the existence of a dual standard was an admission that a standard of specialist care "less than the best" was countenanced, Certification should, through a planned process of evolution, give way to the Fellowship.

4. As most specialists did not practise in teaching centres, two goals became logical: the Certification examination, while extant, should become more comprehensive and progressively more nearly equal to that of the Fellowship and, as the Certification examination became obsolete in a specialty, the Fellowship would reflect first-class clinical competence more and academic issues less.

5. The majority position of the Certificants, who outnumbered Fellows by five to one, made two things likely: the College would be unable to continue influencing the quality of specialist care unless all specialists participated in the College; and Certificants would otherwise form their own group ("a most undesirable, divisive effect").

6. Admission of Certificants, however, might lower the academic standard of the College and it might annoy those who had worked hard

to obtain the higher degree. (This was a discerning observation, the validity of which was proved by the reactions that Fellows showed in the 1960s and 1970s.)

The committee was unanimous in recommending to Council that the current Certification program should be discontinued; that the Certification examination should be terminated in all specialties within three years of the adoption of this report by Council; that current Certificants should be admitted to the College; and that the admitted Certificants, who would be known as "Associates" or some such designation, should be entitled to participate in all of the College's meetings and to elect 12 councillors to represent their interests — but that, with the eventual abolition of Certification, the number of Certificant councillors would be systematically reduced over a 30-year period.

The Botterell committee clearly defined the College's responsibility for the 1960s. The committee stated its belief that the measures it proposed should raise the standards of medical practice and facilitate the provision of the best medical care to the public. The committee stressed that, although it had envisaged rather radical changes, power to maintain its high standard remained with the College. This was not, the committee observed, the first time that changes in the examination procedures had been undertaken, nor was it likely to be the last. Indeed, the committee concluded, it was only by the constant reappraisal of its role in relation to the profession and the community that the College could continue to give the leadership that was expected of it.

In the second half of the 1950s, four committees had studied the issues surrounding the dual standard, and the chairman of the fourth of these committees, Dr. Botterell, now placed the onus squarely on Council's shoulders. Reminding Council at the meeting of October 31 and November 1, 1958, that the several committees had presented their reports as requested, Dr. Botterell stated that matters had reached the stage of decision-making by responsible committees; in short, he told Council, "the College must decide what it wants to do".

Council was, in fact, responsive, and its positive response showed how far the College had come, in 1958, towards resolving the dual standard. Councillors were open-minded regarding change, and some admitted that their opinions had changed since they had read the various committees' reports, particularly the Botterell report. The discussion in Council late in 1958 also provided an example of decision-making that was based on councillors' being able to consider a complex problem over a lengthy period. Dr. P.E. Ireland, for example, who had been a member of the Botterell committee, admitted that at first he did not agree with much in the report but, as the matter was discussed, his view changed and he was able to endorse the report. Dr. Ireland also communicated to those who would study the problem afresh in the 1960s a sense of the feelings that had developed in those Fellows who had studied the problem in the 1950s; he and his colleagues felt strongly that Certification should be discontinued and that those already certificated should be admitted "in some manner" to the College.

Dr. R.M. Janes shared Dr. Ireland's response to the Botterell committee's report; he admitted that he was "startled" when he first read the report, but he added that each time he reread it he was more impressed by it. Dr. Janes's remarks are also of interest because they summarized the position that many Fellows were now beginning to take regarding the Certification program:

> I think we have to admit that Certification has done a tremendous amount of good for Canada. It has raised the standards of practice. However, we have to appreciate the fact that perhaps we have gone through that period in our evolution when Certification was imperative and perhaps there is no longer the great need for the production of specialists. It is interesting to look back over the years. At the outbreak of the First World War there was only one man in Toronto confining himself to the practice of a specialty.
>
> The position of the certificated specialists must be clarified. We cannot go on as we have been doing to date. The certificated specialists now outnumber the Fellows four to one. It is wrong for this College to believe that if we go on as we are going that the Fellowship group will be able to control Certification.

Dr. Janes added that Council should be asked two questions: first, whether they favored the abolition of Certification and, second, whether they favored the admission of certificated specialists to the College without for the moment considering how this could be done.

That Dr. Janes should take this view says much both for him and for the College's decision-making process. Here was a distinguished Fellow and Past-President, a member of the elite, who had once told Council that Certification would destroy the Fellowship. Now this senior Fellow not only praised the virtues of the Certification program but also accepted the logic of the Botterell report, which its author had even labelled "radical", that the time for change had come. But Dr. Janes did urge caution. He advised that this radical step was likely to arouse criticism and urged that the issue be placed before the Fellowship at large before any final step be taken. But it was also he who had moved, seconded by Dr. Chute, that the Credentials Committee and the Examinations Committee study the matter and that they bring in reports by the next meeting of Council.

Council's meeting in the fall of 1958 was a key one: in making the decisions that were reflected in the three crucial resolutions that were passed at that meeting, it passed on to councillors of later years a legacy of policy-making that would give the College a sense of direction in resolving the thorny issues of the dual standard — even though the way it was finally resolved differed somewhat from the manner of its resolution as foreseen by the councillors of 1958. Dr. D.A. Thompson was perceptive in assuring Council in October 1958 that "this College has the initiative and ability to bring this most undesirable situation to a successful solution". The nature of the principal challenge for the College in the 1960s was clear.

NOTES TO CHAPTER 1

1. D.S. Lewis, *The Royal College of Physicians and Surgeons of Canada, 1929-1960*. Montreal, McGill University Press, 1962. (Hereinafter referred to as Lewis.)
2. CMA Committee on Education, *Can Med Assoc J* 1926; 16(Suppl): xvi.
3. Lewis, p. 12.
4. Council, October 1954, p. 35.
5. Lewis, p. 143.
6. Lewis, p. 17. The medical flavor of this alternative form of the word 'bronco' is worth noting. The three were D. Low, D.S. Johnstone and S.E. Moore.
7. Lewis, p. 25.
8. Lewis, p. 102.
9. Council, October 1954, p. 36.
10. E.H. Botterell, letter to D.A.E. Shephard, May 6, 1983.
11. Council, October 1940, p. 36.
12. In this respect, a direct and illuminating question was asked in 1934: "Why should not all specialists become Fellows of the Royal Colleges?" A meeting of the CMA's Committee on Specialists gave a ready and lengthy answer to this question on Oct. 23, 1934. There were several reasons. Time and money were two, as the answer indicated:
    - The primary examination in the basic sciences was so comprehensive that the average would-be specialist could not spare the time to study for it, and for the final examination time was often insufficient to permit a physician to study the broad range of subjects encompassed by medicine (or surgery) in addition to those of his own specialty.
    - The graduate who wanted to specialize in a limited field was more interested in spending his time studying the basic sciences as applied to his intended specialty than in studying the broad range of anatomy, physiology and pathology that the Fellowship examination covered.
    - Money, too, was a factor, for the expense of obtaining a Fellowship was greater than if he had to pass just one examination in his own specialty conducted by specialists.

    But another reason was in a different category:
    - "If all graduates entering specialties became Fellows of the Royal Colleges, the value of the FRCP or S as a distinguishing designation indicative of a very high standard of knowledge, would be materially decreased".

    It seems, therefore, that there was both recognition of the practical value of a Certification program and also a desire to preserve especially high standards among Canadian specialists who, in contrast, had the Fellowship. But while the Certification program seemed attractive, the blunt and perhaps elitist question contains the germ of the idea of the dual standard — the issue that was to occupy the College's attention for so much of the period from 1960 to 1980.

13. E.S. Ryerson, "The Qualification of Specialists in Canada". *Can Med Assoc J* 1933; 29:72-73.
14. MCC's solicitor informed its Registrar of this opinion in October 1935, but it was not until September 1936 that MCC finally decided that because of difficulties with its Charter, the Council could do nothing about Certification (Lewis, p. 149). More often than not, the wheels of the decision-making process within the medical profession appear to move slowly. The CMA also required a lengthy period to permit itself to decide that the College should in fact be the body to certify specialists; that was in the fall of 1937. Lewis's comment on the key resolution indicates that "it had taken twelve months to go through the regular channels" (Lewis, p. 151). By then it was, therefore, no less than three years after the matter had been first studied by the CMA and the College.
15. Council, October 1936, p. 13.
16. Council, October 1936, pp. 13-14.
17. Council, October 1936, p. 14.
18. Council, October 1936, p. 13.
19. Lewis, p. 151.
20. Council, October 1939, p. 44. The work of Dr. Patch's Committee on Specialists, nevertheless, influenced the College's ideas about educational standards. Dr. Patch said that "in as much as Council has not approved of the standards of qualification [for Certification], it is an excellent opportunity to re-study them in the light of the discussion...with regard to Fellowship qualifications". In fact, some specialties had proposed standards for Certification that were higher than those for the Fellowship.
21. See, for example: Council, June 1937, p. 116; October 1937, p. 27; and October 1939, p. 46.
22. Council, November 1947, p. 25.
23. Council, October 1953, p. 44.
24. A.W. Andison and J.G. Robichon (editors), *The Royal College of Physicians and Surgeons of Canada/Le Collège Royal des médecins et chirurgiens du Canada: Fiftieth Anniversary, 1979*. Ste. Anne de Bellevue, Québec, Harpell's Co-operative Press, pp. 80-81 (hereinafter referred to as Andison and Robichon).
25. Council, October 1939, p. 45.

Chapter 2

Nature, Objectives and Membership

Of paramount concern to the College in the 1960s — and the principal factor that led to the transformation of the College between 1960 and 1980 — was the need to find an acceptable solution to the problems caused by the existence of the dual standard. The eventual solution, which was implemented in 1972, was a twofold one. One part of this solution was entirely acceptable: all specialist trainees henceforth had to pass a new, single qualifying examination before they could be recognized as specialists and before they could apply for Fellowship in the College. The second part of the solution was controversial. All those specialists who had the Royal College Certification (but not the Fellowship diploma, so were not Fellows of the College) were now permitted to apply for Fellowship in the College without being required to take the Fellowship examination. Previously, because the College had limited its membership to specialists who became Fellows by passing the rigorous Fellowship examination, membership in the College was small and somewhat exclusive. All this changed in 1972. The College was transformed in an instant. A 'new' College emerged.

The historic year of 1972, therefore, marked a change in the nature of the College, principally because the nature of its membership changed. Fellowship in the College now embraced not only those specialists who had passed the respected (and difficult) Fellowship examination but also those whose recognition as specialists had been granted by passing the less academic Certification examination. This change in the nature and the membership of the College created new needs and activities in the College, for the membership suddenly doubled in 1972 as a majority of the 6,734 pre-1972 Certificants applied for admission to Fellowship. As a 'new' College emerged, it became appropriate — and necessary — to formulate new objectives. Both quantitatively and qualitatively, therefore, the College in 1972 and thereafter was different from the College it had been before 1972.

Sudden though this transformation was, finding the successful solution was a lengthy and complex process that was pursued throughout the 1960s. Many steps had to be taken. The training requirements for the Fellowship and the Certification examinations were made uniform; a system was developed to enable residents to train in programs that were organized to provide postgraduate (and coordinated) educational opportunities as well as service responsibilities; new requirements were formulated for approving hospitals participating in training so that they became integrated with university training programs; a single examination process was designed to evaluate, as a primary objective, *competence* in would-be specialists; and previously certificated specialists were enabled to become affiliated with the College. Once these steps (fully described elsewhere in this book) had been taken, a vision of a 'new' College appeared. In this chapter, the nature of the College that underwent this transformation is discussed in relation to the formulation of new objectives and the evolution of new categories of membership.

Formulation of New Objectives, 1969-1970

Until 1969, the College's objectives had been formulated only once, when — four decades earlier — the College's single Object had been written into the bylaws to indicate what the College was then attempting to accomplish. The 1950s and 1960s spawned an interest in behavioral objectives and, accordingly, a group of Fellows in 1969 (the Expanded Executive Committee) developed a set of new objectives that would be appropriate for the College in a time of great social change. As Dr. E.D. Gagnon, a member of the Expanded Executive Committee, suggested to his fellow committee members in October 1969, "we are asking ourselves to redefine, to put...in the bylaws... or put in the Act [of Incorporation] somewhere, what we are actually doing in 1969... ." The nature of the objectives that the Expanded Executive Committee developed for Council to refine and introduce as College policy indicates how senior Fellows in 1969 envisioned the College's role in society 40 years after its founding.

The Expanded Executive Committee provided a group of wise men[1] with a forum in which to debate issues concerning "the heart of the College's reason for existing".[2] The committee, led by President J. Turcot, met four times in 1969, and out of these four meetings evolved the philosophical basis for a 'new' Royal College. Although the committee was formed as the result of Council's concern, expressed in January 1969, over the need to grapple anew with the perennial but now acute problem of the College's examinations (especially the Certification examination, for which intelligent planning was seemingly negated by Council's decision of 1958 to phase out the examination), the committee's mandate was in fact much broader. As President Turcot pointed out during the first meeting, held on April 26, 1969, the problem of the examinations was related to many other problems, and the committee's task was to debate "the whole aspect of the future role of the College". The implications of the committee's work were far-reaching and, as Dr. C.G. Drake had suggested a month earlier to the members of the Executive Committee, it seemed that the

College might well have to relinquish some long-held views regarding the Fellowship and Certification qualifications.

When, therefore, President Turcot asked, during the committee's second meeting, held on June 4, 1969, "What is the College and what should it be in future and how?", it was natural that the members of the Expanded Executive Committee should begin to ask themselves what objectives should be formulated. At their first meeting the members had agreed that the College should do more in Canadian medicine than simply identify clinically competent specialists, and now Dr. I.E. Rusted observed that "this is one of the criticisms of the College, that apart from this very short paragraph in the regulations the College has really not spent very much time or spelled out its objectives.... ." Discussion of the College's "objects" was therefore placed on the agenda of the committee's third meeting, scheduled for October 24, 1969.

At the beginning of this third meeting, Dr. Gagnon claimed that the College's single Object was inadequate as a definition of the College's current functions. Dr. W.C. MacKenzie stressed the need to emphasize patient care as well as specialist training; Dr. K.J.R. Wightman, the need to include in any set of objectives monitoring of the profession's performance and disciplining of its members; and Dr. Drake, the need to stress the postgraduate education of physicians, the examinations and certification of specialists and the promotion of excellence in the practice of medicine. Laudable though these proposed objectives were, they were general rather than specific, but discussion of them led Dr. R.B. Salter to identify a more specific set of objectives. Agreeing with Dr. MacKenzie that the aim of the College was to improve the standard of patient care, Dr. Salter suggested that the College might achieve this aim by fulfilling seven functions or responsibilities at a national level. The seven functions or responsibilities were as follows: achieving a high standard of postgraduate education of specialists; assessing the clinical competence of specialist trainees; providing continuing education for specialists; stimulating clinical and experimental research; maintaining a high standard of ethics among specialists; delivering specialized care to the whole population; and ensuring effective liaison with provincial and national medical organizations, universities and governments.

Dr. Salter's objectives reflected what was now more clearly recognized as the College's responsibility — its role on a national level in ensuring that the public receive adequate specialty care. Dr. Salter's statement was refined by a sub-committee consisting of Drs. Salter, Gagnon, J.H. Graham and Wightman and Mr. C.F. Scott, QC, the College solicitor. The revision was then considered by Council, and by March 1970 the following definitive statement enshrined objects that would serve for the 1970s and beyond:

> *The* objective of The Royal College of Physicians and Surgeons of Canada is to further the excellence of professional training and the

standards of practice in the various medical and surgical specialties in Canada.

The College contributes to the improvement of health care of Canadians through the provision of designations for specially trained physicians and surgeons whereby it may be known that they are properly qualified. This involves communication and liaison within the College and with various specialty groups, with universities and teaching hospitals, with governments and with provincial, national and international medical organizations. With this cooperation, the College in providing specialty designations:

a) establishes requirements of graduate training relating to its examinations
b) establishes standards required of hospitals and institutions that provide such graduate training
c) assesses and approves hospitals and institutions providing graduate training
d) assesses the credentials of candidates for the examinations of the College
e) conducts examination processes for the obtaining of the College's specialty qualifications.

The Royal College has further responsibilities beyond those immediately related to the function of providing specialty qualifications. They include:

1. The maintenance of a high standard of professional ethics, conduct and practice among medical and surgical specialists.
2. Continuing medical education.
3. The encouragement of research in medicine and medical education.
4. The study of quantitative and qualitative aspects of specialized health care in Canada.
5. Continuing concern with health matters which the College considers to lie within its competence.

The College, in 1970, was now 40 years old. While it was still concerned with enabling each specialist to obtain a "distinguishing designation...whereby it may be known that he is properly qualified", the College in 1970 was prepared to go beyond this single concern and emphasize the importance of the "further responsibilities" that would make the College a truly national professional organization dedicated to improving the health care of Canadians. Less than a half-century old, the College had gradually built for itself a position of respect and strength in the health care field, and the responsibilities that the College made its policy in 1970 attested to its maturity as well as its adaptability to the needs of changing times.

Dignitaries at the Annual Dinner, Quebec City, January 18, 1964

(L. to R.) President G.M. Brown, Mrs. Brown, Mme Lesage,
Mme Turcot, Premier Jean Lesage, Dr. J. Turcot

Council 1968-70

(L. to R.) F.E. Bryans, K.T. MacFarlane, W.D. Miller, C.G. Drake, J.H.B. Hilton,
R.C. Dickson, W.M. Goldberg, C.H. Crosby, J.P. Gemmell, R.C. Laird,
G.M. Brown, President J. Turcot, F.N. Gurd, W.C. MacKenzie,
F.G. Kergin, R.V. Christie, I.E. Rusted, D.R. Wilson, R.B. Kerr,
E.D. Gagnon, D.F. Moore, J. Grandbois, C.C. Ferguson

Membership: Evolution of Criteria for Admission to Fellowship

Important as the definition of the new objectives was, the Expanded Executive Committee spent most of its time wrestling with more radical issues. Three such issues occupied the committee's attention for much of the time: the nature and purpose of the Fellowship and Certification examinations; the question as to whether the College should in fact continue to hold both examinations and, if not, whether to retain either the Fellowship or the Certification examination as the College's test of clinical competence; and the nature of criteria for admission of candidates to the new type of Fellowship, which was a controversial and contentious issue. In addressing these most complex issues, the committee did indeed do what Dr. Drake had earlier suggested it might very well do — abandon traditional views on the Fellowship and Certification qualifications in favor of an examination that was more appropriate to the 1960s. The way in which the College was transformed in 1972 can be understood only by understanding how these issues were resolved. Their resolution was a complex and lengthy process, an exposition of which requires a detailed summary of events from 1969 to 1973.

The essence of the committee's approach, shaped by discussions in four meetings over a period of eight months, is found in a statement made by Dr. MacKenzie on December 13, 1969:

> *Some* of us are trying to see that the College better represents the qualified specialists of Canada...we honestly feel that you can't have two standards of Fellows or two standards of membership in this College...we feel that in the future we are going to have to have a Fellowship in which more people can belong.

Before the Expanded Executive Committee met, it was generally considered acceptable that the College was a medical elite and that the Canadian community of medical and surgical specialists was made up of two classes of physicians who were differentiated by a dual standard of competence. The validity and logic of this view had been questioned from time to time but it governed the day-to-day policy of the College and formed the basis of specialist practice in Canada. The meetings of the Expanded Executive Committee changed all this. The outcome of these deliberations was the simple yet complex conclusion that, once and for all, The Royal College of Physicians and Surgeons of Canada must embrace all, and not just the minority of, Canadian specialists. The committee's meetings constituted a four-act play wherein was caught the conscience of the College regarding membership.

Expanded Executive Committee, April 26, 1969

When the Expanded Executive Committee first met, on April 26, 1969, the concept that clinical competence could be assessed by relatively new techniques such as the objective, multiple-choice question examination and in-training assessment was generally accepted, and the innovative concept of a single examination process for this purpose was developing. The Expanded Executive Committee, however, found that it could not validly define so vexing and central a matter as the essential difference between the Fellowship examination and the Certification examination in determining clinical competence. Worse still, no one could even define the essence of the term, 'Fellowship'. Thus, 40 years after the founding of the College, Dr. MacKenzie, in speaking of the Fellowship and "the kind of a person" who might become a Fellow in an organization like the College, was forced to admit, "now I don't believe that we can define this very readily"; and Dr. F.N. Gurd admitted that he and his colleagues did not really know "what this Fellowship was all about". One of the great accomplishments of the Expanded Executive Committee was to reach agreement not only on the College's objectives but also on the nature of Fellowship in the College.

How did the Expanded Executive Committee view the nature of Fellowship in the College, such that the College would better represent Canadian specialists? How did the committee's thinking develop? To answer this question, it is necessary to follow the discussions of the committee.

Early in the committee's first meeting, Dr. Gurd pointed out the College was perpetuating an anomaly that made the College a laughing stock. Candidates were taking the same training but then taking two different examinations — sometimes the Fellowship examination or the Certification examination but sometimes both. An examiner might well find it difficult to tell the difference between a "Fellow" and a "Certificant", particularly when, as happened occasionally in the mid-1960s, the same candidate might pass the supposedly more difficult Fellowship examination but fail the Certification examination — which was supposed to be the easier examination, and which, according to Council's resolution of 1958, was supposed to be obsolescent.

Yet in 1969 there were good reasons to retain some type of certificate of competence. Three such reasons were advanced at this time. One reason was the introduction, the year before, of Medicare; a standard of specialist competence was required in all the provinces as a basis for recognition and remuneration apart from anything else. Here was a threat to unity, for the need to provide a comprehensive plan of medical care made each province acutely conscious of the need to compete for and attract specialists. The College's decision, in the mid-1960s, to abolish Certification in neurology, neurosurgery, orthopedic surgery and thoracic surgery now presented a problem. British Columbia, for example, had already felt the effects of this decision to make the Fellowship the only qualification in orthopedic surgery, for specialists who had not obtained the Fellowship left to practise in the United States.

The situation in Quebec constituted a second, and particular, reason why some Fellows now thought that the College should not discontinue Certification — even though its stated policy since 1958 had been to ultimately discontinue Certification. The Quebec Certification, which had been introduced in 1955, was the legal and obligatory specialist qualification in Quebec; it was a separate provincial Certificate and was not equated with either the Royal College Certification or Fellowship. If the Fellowship were the sole Royal College qualification, few physicians in Quebec would be interested in acquiring it as well as the Quebec Certification. The Quebec constraint operated as a key decision-making factor throughout the Expanded Executive's discussions, and the threat to national unity that abolition of Certification posed vis-a-vis possible reactions in Quebec served, as much as any other factor, to lead the committee to recommend that the College's single qualification for competence should be named Certification rather than Fellowship. This was stated several times by President Turcot and most emphatically by Dr. Gagnon. The statement that Dr. Gagnon made during the Expanded Executive Committee Meeting on December 13, 1969, explained the nature of this consideration in unequivocal terms:

> I would be tremendously concerned, and I have stated this and will repeat it again, that you would be encouraging discontinuance of interest from Quebec. There are people who practise entirely in Quebec and more particularly, French-Canadians. The Quebec College and the Liaison Committee, on which I sit on behalf of this College with Dr. Gurd, has reiterated at every meeting that there is a distinction in the Quebec College between the Certificate that they issue, which is legal tender in the province, and the Fellowship, which is something else and is highly respected. Certainly if we equate by one single examination Fellowship to the Certificate of this College, the Quebec College and more particularly the French-Canadians who have separatist tendencies will separate all the more, and ten years from now you will have very few French-Canadians in this College. I am convinced of that.

A third reason related to the College's obligations to the affiliated Certificants. Dr. MacKenzie, who had led the movement to offer Certificants affiliation with the College five years earlier, was just as emphatic in this respect as Dr. Gagnon was regarding the Quebec consideration. "The College has a much wider responsibility than just to the deans...[and] academic people...", Dr. MacKenzie said. "It is all very well", he continued, "to say that you are going to have one standard — the Fellowship — and do away with the Certification. But as an organization which just a few years ago took the Certificants in, we have an obligation to these people rather than washing them down the drain right away". And, indeed, the Certificants themselves, as Dr. N.K. MacLennan had emphasized in the Council meeting of January 1969, wanted the College to retain Certification.

That the College had instituted Certification, with its various consequences, was, as Dr. MacKenzie suggested, one of the "constraints of history" that limited the College's space in which to maneuver in an era of "a great deal of turmoil" and anti-establishment feeling that exerted pressure on the College to change. Two other facts tightened the constraints of history. One was the Council's stated policy that Certification would eventually be abolished — the constraint that constituted an obstacle against which, as Dr. Wightman observed, Fellows who wanted progress "stubbed their toes". The other was the question as to what the difference was, "if any", between Certificants and Fellows — the difference that Dr. R.B. Kerr admitted was "very vague" and constituted " 'the snag' on which we fall down, i.e., whether there is a difference or whether there should be a difference".

So, as Dr. Gurd emphasized, there was indeed a strong argument for the retention of Certification as the essential qualification of specialist competence, and this argument would remain compelling throughout the Expanded Executive Committee's debate.

On the other hand, an argument in favor of the Fellowship as the single standard of specialist competence could be put forward just as readily. One good point was made by Dr. Gurd: "Orthopedic surgery, neurosurgery and neurology have had the Fellowship alone for about five years now and the opinions of each of the Specialty Committees in Orthopedic Surgery and Neurosurgery appear...to indicate that...their specialty has been benefitted by the sincere effort to work under this one high standard". The newest specialties such as cardiovascular and thoracic surgery clearly favored the Fellowship; and the other specialties, if the pattern was at all consistent, would ask for Fellowship as the one standard. Moreover, to take just one specialty as an example, in orthopedic surgery there was no evidence of either a fall in the standard of the examination or an unduly high failure rate. Dr. Gurd also referred to the training program in plastic surgery at The Montreal General Hospital: 21 of the last 22 trainees had succeeded in passing the Fellowship at their first attempt. All this showed what could be done and it raised the question of why the College should perpetuate the "Certification mentality" when such levels of quality were now within the College's grasp.

A second reason for favoring the Fellowship as the single qualification of specialist competence was the desirability of leaving the Act of Incorporation undisturbed. The Act required that only Fellows could be members of the College and that Fellowship not be granted before five years had elapsed since graduation. To open the Act, moreover, would be an uncertain and lengthy procedure. If the College was to accept a single qualification, the simpler course would be to make this qualification the Fellowship, regardless of any pressure (as from the universities) to provide a specialist qualification four years after graduation.

But deeper than these reasons, both of which were entirely logical to those who wished to preserve the status quo, were others that were more emotional than logical. Many Fellows feared any change that appeared to threaten the cherished concept of the Fellowship both as an examination, which was not easily passed, and as membership in the College, which was limited to relatively few well-qualified specialists. Preference for the Certification as the single qualification of specialist competence was one such threatening change. It was sufficiently apparent a threat to lead Dr. Graham to state it in these terms: "You couldn't conceive, under the present Act of Incorporation, of going to one standard and calling it Certification because the College would then slowly die over the years. If you go to one standard you have to go to Fellowship or change the Act". Dr. G.M. Brown readily discerned this feeling when he expressed his personal response to the discussion early on April 26, 1969, as follows:

> I think that there is a lot of sentiment around this table that hasn't yet been expressed. I think there is a great disinclination to use this precious word Fellowship for an examination which is going to be completed successfully by the same proportion of candidates who now complete the Certification examination successfully. I think this is one reason why people are holding off.

But times had been changing during the 1960s and members of the Expanded Executive Committee began to realize that the primary function of the College now was quite different from breeding a medical elite. Dr. Drake was among those who realized early that this was no longer possible; as he said, "we are trying to do something with the Fellowship that we can't do and that is, pick out...a medical elite". While Dr. Drake favored the Fellowship as the preferable qualification, his openness of mind led him to look carefully at Article 1, Section 2 of the College's bylaws and to relate the Object of the College contained therein to current circumstances. The wording of that section had remained relevant since the founding of the College and it was by no means an anachronism: "Because of the growth and development of the Science and Art of Medicine and its division into various specialties, it is considered necessary and advisable that the practising physician, essaying to do 'special work', should have the opportunity of obtaining a distinguishing designation whereby it may be known that he is properly qualified". Dr. Drake was wise enough to understand the need to review, in the light of the work of the R.S. McLaughlin Examination and Research Centre, the basis for any decision that a specialist in 1969 rather than in 1929 was "properly qualified". Even though for years he had staunchly defended the Fellowship and the way in which competence was assessed in the essay examination, Dr. Drake now realized that the examination could not be "the final measure of a man". One should regard the process more as a hurdle, as Dr. Gurd had said, that everyone must pass before, as a qualified specialist, a physician could finally practise. He concluded that this would mean retaining the Certification function.

Dr. Brown's thinking was similarly flexible and adaptable to changing circumstances. He endeavored to formulate an approach that would provide a compromise between Certification (as a recognition of competence) and Fellowship (as a recognition of professional and collegial "higher values"). Dr. Brown preferred a simpler course than was suggested by, for example, Dr. Gagnon. Dr. Gagnon, visualizing the Certification as the basic competence qualification and the Fellowship as "something else", proposed that the Credentials Committee participate in the evaluation of candidates for Fellowship (that is, for membership in the College the committee would be examining not only the credentials of the individual but the quality of the individual over the first three or four years). Dr. Brown preferred this simpler approach:

> I do think the future system of classification of the Royal College should be something quite simple. It should be as simple as possible, and it should be something that permits a good deal of flexibility as the College deals with men who want to have an association with the College. Let us translate that right away to mean "as the College deals with men who want to do specialty practice in Canada".

Dr. Brown went on to say that the College's main function was to identify those physicians who are competent to practise a specialty and that it should act accordingly. He continued by emphasizing his democratic and unitarian vision of the College in these times but he also identified a most significant paradox:

> ...as we decide about different categories of persons and decide about different methods of examination of them...we should keep in mind, not that the College is, as many of us used to think of the College, a group of men with common interests, but...[performing] this national job of identifying people for specialty practice. This is the prime goal of the College now...not to maintain a "club" of specially trained men who have met on a specially high level; that seems to be secondary. I am, of course, talking about the Certificate and not the Fellowship, and...this is...[the] paradox...that the principle of Certification now is more important than the Fellowship. Do what you want with the names but I think that is the case. Now...the College must be just as strong as possible and that strength must be built up, maintained and nurtured by various means so that it can do this primary function, which is to identify to the country those who are competent in a specialty, because its position in this field is really a moral position if not a legal position... .

Dr. Brown defined four principles that were emerging. In this way he contributed greatly to this first meeting of the Expanded Executive Committee

— and, indeed, prepared the ground for the three later meetings. First, he advocated simplicity in any approach to a system of qualification of specialists. Second, he recommended flexibility in any method of assessment of specialist candidates. Third, Dr. Brown formulated the concept of the purpose and nature of the College for modern times. He saw the College as being no longer an elite "club" but a national organization having the task of identifying physicians for specialty practice. This national role had not been fully achieved, but it was a desirable one; as he said later in the meeting, "to be nationally understood is an ideal goal and not one that has been achieved by the College at any point". Unity within a national context remained the ideal. Dr. Brown's fourth principle was in some ways the most interesting: the paradox that Certification had become more important than the Fellowship. But since there were good reasons for retaining Certification and strong emotional ties to the Fellowship, the eventual solution would have to be based on compromise — so often a synonym for, and a path to, unity. And this compromise must take account of the real issue before the Expanded Executive Committee — the question that President Turcot asked: "should the two qualifications remain?".

Several possible solutions to this issue were put forward during this meeting. Dr. Brown offered one. This would consist of a college degree in association with a basic qualification. He and others offered another: Fellowship in the College based on criteria other than clinical competence, as the American College of Physicians and the American College of Surgeons, for example, did. This solution, however, had disadvantages, especially if admission to Fellowship were based on some form of selection or election that was inevitably associated with a dual standard of membership. This was distasteful to many Canadians, who agreed with President Turcot that "this election system is all wrong".

An interesting perspective was offered by Mr. C.F. Scott, QC, who, as the College solicitor and legal advisor, had no vested interest in either Certification or Fellowship. In observing (as did Dr. Gagnon) that the Expanded Executive Committee was taking the same course as the Robertson committee had in 1955, Mr. Scott clarified the issues before the committee in the following terms:

> ...*the* basic question is: "Are you going to have two qualifications?". It has been said earlier that the basic responsibility of this College is to determine clinical competence. Now if that is the sole responsibility of this College, I think you move to a one-tier system. To get to the two-tier system you have to determine that you are going to have certain people who are more clinically competent or else that they have a broader vision than is simply clinical competence. I take clinical competence as the first level for a person who has claim to be a specialist, more than a simple degree of Doctor of Medicine. Now you have to determine that broader interest... . There can be that in the practical field, there can be that in the academic field, there can be that in the research field, but that gives that second level, as well as the greater

competence. I think the College now is coming back to determine whether they will endow with a special name those who are "an elite". You can call them part of the "club". You can give them any name you want. But looking at this Act, and looking at it without reference to the Certificants, it seems to me that is was originally intended to provide for the picking out of "the elite". Later on came the requirement where the College took on the duty of judging a basic clinical competence.

The committee had by now agreed that the single standard of clinical competence was desirable, and that admission to Fellowship should be based on an initial evaluation of competence followed by definition of criteria regarding suitability for Fellowship that were yet to be determined. While most members of the Expanded Executive Committee felt that it would be desirable to develop specific criteria for admission to Fellowship, two members were open-minded enough to make statements that demonstrated considerable prescience. Thus Dr. MacKenzie:

What would happen if we gave all the present Certificants Fellowships? We gave a great many Fellowships under the grandfather clause right from the very beginning to people with very little in the way of qualifications. All the Certificants have been trained and examined. The reaction would be, I suppose, from our young Fellows who have taken the Fellowship by examination. But is it not one thing that we should perhaps take a look at? If we are going to establish one basic examination of competence and call it the Fellowship, then we should re-name all our Certificants Fellows of the College.

This view was shared by Dr. Drake:

I was thinking more of the one standard, one qualifying examination, common to all, which might be called Fellowship, or give them the alternatives, and...that there would be a melding of the Certificants and the Fellows of the past. Then this would end up, five years from now, as being nothing but the Fellowship.

During this first meeting of the Expanded Executive Committee, the important issues had been raised and discussed. But Dr. MacKenzie reminded the committee that one of the purposes of the meeting was to answer for the Examinations Committee the question as to whether clinical competence should be assessed by one examination rather than two. The discussion so far had indicated that everybody would favor that, but Dr. MacKenzie added that "what we do beyond that is something else again".

A little earlier, Dr. D.R. Wilson had remarked that it was quite feasible to suggest that there should be one standard and one set of examinations for clinical competence. President Turcot asked what the group thought, and Drs. Drake and Kerr suggested that a "straw vote" would help to answer this question, but their colleagues were reluctant to vote on a motion unless it dealt specifically with the desirability of a single basic qualification of competence for all candidates. It was partly a matter of wording. Dr. Brown stressed the need to be certain what one standard meant, and what was meant by two standards. With his customary precision and clarity, Dr. Brown submitted a motion to test the opinions of his colleagues. The motion both crystallized the thinking that had been formulated during the day and advanced immeasurably the decision-making process. The motion read as follows:

> *That* be it resolved by this committee that all candidates, for membership of any type in the College, write the same examination, and that the examination be at a level which the passing...of...means that the man is clinically competent in his clinical specialty, [and] that admission to Fellowship be by several routes: by an additional examination in clinical specialties taken after completion of the earlier specialty qualification; by submission of published work any time ten years after the MD; and by "election" from among Certificants, the candidates being people who have held their Certification for a mini-

Dr. Brown's crucial motion was well received. President Turcot responded by suggesting that "slowly we might agree that Certification is really the basic examination". The motion also answered the urging of the medical schools that specialist candidates should take the qualifying examination after four years; and the College was not bound at the Certification level by the five years as required by the Act of Incorporation. It also left flexible the development of criteria for admission to the Fellowship.

The motion, though not formally seconded and though amended slightly, succeeded, as Dr. Brown had hoped, in testing the feelings of the committee members. When the motion was put to the vote — though it was not a binding vote — five votes were counted in favor and none were recorded against it. The day's meeting had been long but productive. A step forward had been taken. Informally stated by Dr. Wightman, the Committee's view was this: "All we are saying is that we tell people that they can try a Certification examination in four years, must try it in those specialties that now have a Certification examination and that Fellowship will be attained a year or more later on the basis of various criteria".

The Expanded Executive Committee's first meeting thus went far in clarifying the nature of the basic issues that confronted the College in 1969. In summary, the committee had agreed that the objectives of the Fellowship and Certification qualifications had not been clearly defined in the past; the national standard of a basic specialty qualification, now desired, must be realistic, supplying sufficient qualified specialists for delivery of health care; the basic qualifying examination should be available after four years of postgraduate training; all specialists should take the same basic certifying examination in their field, whatever the qualification might be called; the Certification program leading to a basic specialty qualification had become of national importance and, in some practical respects, even more important than the current Fellowship program; any new plans introduced should be simple and flexible; there was sufficient evidence of the need for change in the Act of Incorporation, which should be amended at the appropriate time by the best method; and, finally, the College should have more of a role in Canadian medicine than simply identifying clinically competent people.

Expanded Executive Committee, June 4, 1969

The committee's second meeting took the members, and the College, closer to approving policy whereby clinical competence would be assessed by a single qualifying examination. Dr. Wilson urged his colleagues to formulate "very clearly defined" aims and objectives of the Certification qualification and he stressed the need to be "absolutely sure" that there would be just a single standard of competence, regardless of its name. Dr. I.E. Rusted agreed that there should be a single standard of competence but recommended that the College consider determining "at least a minimal standard of competence" below which the College would not go.

While the committee was in general agreement that the single standard of competence was desirable, agreement was still lacking as to its name. Drs. Drake and Salter favored naming it Fellowship on the basis that it was not fair to tell a fully trained specialist, "You have a diploma now and later on if you are good you will have the Fellowship". On the other hand, Drs. Wightman and Gurd felt that the College would play roles in addition to that of a certifying body. Dr. Wightman, seeking to indentify potential Fellows by their broad interests and sense of responsibility, suggested that academic value, outside of clinical competence, was a quality by which Fellows might be identified and that a proportion of specialists might be encouraged to pursue further efforts beyond Certification if Fellowship served as something else to be achieved; and Dr. Gurd thought that the College's involvement in continuing medical education would retain interest among those specialists who wished to proceed to Fellowship. A "single-shot" Fellowship, with no further objective, would leave this continuing function of the College to other bodies like specialty groups and universities. Dr. Gurd's concept would complement and unify the activities of specialty bodies and universities in a national way; unity, as always, was an important consideration. After leaving the previous meeting, Dr. Gurd had asked himself, "Is there anything for the College to do after it has given a man a Certificate of competence?" and he had come to conclude that there was.

Of further concern was the thought among some Fellows that, with the introduction of the single qualifying examination that all candidates must take, the standard of Fellowship would fall. Dr. Gagnon, for example, expressed the fear of many when he said that he was not sure whether the new examination would be a "glorified Certificate" or a "bastardized Fellowship". Yet the enlightenment in medical education of the 1950s and 1960s and the more recent studies that had been conducted by the R.S. McLaughlin Examination and Research Centre suggested that the new examination process would in fact be a more exacting type of examination and more accurately reflective of the steady improvement in training programs.

At this stage in the evolution of the College and in the Expanded Executive Committee's deliberations, many Fellows were uncertain of the way the College, and its Fellowship and Certification, should develop. Drs. Brown, Drake, Gurd and Salter envisioned a relatively simple and modern approach, as did Dr. MacKenzie, who now articulated the concept of simplicity in the following statement:

> *We* have...read something into the Fellowship which Dr. Wilson and colleagues now tell us we should not have read into the Fellowship, because we didn't have any real basis for doing this. So, instead of creating a new Fellowship, if we do this I would submit that we confine ourselves to measuring in the new Fellowship or Certification, or whatever you want to call it, what we are capable of measuring with it, that is basic clinical competence, and that we are not reading into it as we have been ever since we established [it] something that we really can't measure.

Even so, this would not be easy, even for the experienced Fellows who were now wrestling with the issues that faced the Expanded Executive Committee; as Dr. MacKenzie said, "we are perhaps the hardest people to educate around here because we have hung onto something in this Fellowship that wasn't really there".

With this statement, the initial phase of the Expanded Executive Committee's second meeting was concluded. Dr. MacKenzie had earlier said that the College should move forward, and he now took a step forward by moving that the first half of the motion that had developed out of the previous meeting be adopted. His motion would read:

> *That* it be resolved by this committee that all candidates for membership of any type in this College write the same examination (in their field), and that examination be at a level the passing of which means that the man is clinically competent in his specialty.

The motion was not formally voted on in this form, but it stimulated discussion that yielded unanimous agreement that the College should indeed introduce a single basic examination to determine clinical competence. Although this first motion remained before the committee — it was taken for granted that it would pass — Dr. Gagnon, concluding from the earlier discussion that it was becoming evident that there was no need to continue a double standard in specialist recognition, then moved that it be recommended to Council that there was no further need to continue a double standard of specialist recognition in the Royal College.

This motion took account of changes that were taking place in medical education. The medical schools' trend to provide medical students with clinical experience in the clinical clerkship year (equivalent to that of the rotating internship) and to make the first year of postgraduate training a year of straight internship was an imperative. It demanded an answer to the question as to whether specialty training programs would be planned around a four-year curriculum rather than a five-year one, as stipulated in the College's training requirements. A four-year program was possible and there was no problem in devising a single examination leading to Certification at the end of it. The problem remained that of the five-year limitation in Article 8, Section 2 of the Act of Incorporation: it would not be possible for an examination taken at the end of four years to lead directly to Fellowship. To obtain the necessary changes in the Act would take time, while the medical schools wanted an indication of the College's intention soon.

Now two motions were interrelated. They were therefore combined into the following single motion, since the second provided the rationale for the first. Moved by Dr. MacKenzie and seconded by Dr. Salter, the motion read as follows:

> *Whereas* this committee believes that there is not further need to continue the double standard of clinical competence determined by the current Fellowship and Certification examinations, therefore be it resolved that all candidates wishing to obtain a Royal College specialty qualification be submitted to a single examination procedure, the passing of which indicates that the candidate is competent in the specialty involved.

Discussion of the motion was brief, part of the discussion being directed to minor changes in wording. The most interesting modification concerned the substitution of the word 'process' for 'procedure', for this was the first occasion on which the term 'single examination process' came to be used. The intent of the motion was straightforward: the committee wanted one examination to test clinical competence. The name of the examination, however, still remained uncertain, because the group was still unclear as to the course that the College should take. Dr. MacKenzie explained the implications of the motion by saying that to name it Certification would mean establishing the Fellowship on any other basis except by examination. If, however, it was decided that the examination was to determine Fellowship, there would be no further attainment. There might be recognition, but the College would not be involved in any further recognition of the individual.

The motion was carried unanimously. It formed the basis of the first of a series of resolutions that were later presented to Council.

Development of the other resolutions that were formulated during this meeting followed the lines earlier advocated by Dr. Wightman. He suggested that graduates of Canadian schools should be permitted to sit the basic examination after four years of specialist training and, for graduates of other schools, the possibility should be determined later; that successful candidates would be granted Certification in their specialty; and that Fellowship would be granted "by whatever means" at the end of five years, or later. The committee was now able to clarify its conceptions regarding the terms Certification and Fellowship, and to agree that the basic specialty qualification should be termed Certification and that specialists who passed this examination might be encouraged to apply for admission to Fellowship later. The committee was also enabled to approve three resolutions for presentation to Council. The first resolution proposed that the specialty qualification indeed be termed Certification, that it constitute a prerequisite for admission to Fellowship and, further, that Fellowship be obtained on application at a later date by criteria to be determined. The second resolution proposed that candidates who had had an acceptable undergraduate clinical clerkship be exempted from the year of internship prescribed in the training requirements for the various specialties. And the third resolution proposed that, if Council agreed to the foregoing proposals, a committee be empowered to recommend regarding the objectives of Fellowship, when it would be granted and the criteria for granting it. The proposed admission criteria included evidence of professional growth such as an additional year of full-time training, involvement in educational activities, research or the advancement of knowledge, activities in professional medical societies and outstanding competence.

Of all the Expanded Executive Committee's recommendations, admission to Fellowship through such criteria, which were yet to be determined, was the least specific; indeed, this would remain the weak point in the proposals that Council developed in the following two years. Dr. Wightman, who had always favored the institution of such criteria, recognized the problem when he remarked, "I hope it doesn't seem that I am trying to produce some elite group of people, but it seems to be that such a group does stratify, that it really is interested in the College as a whole". To this, Dr. Gurd responded by saying that membership in the College should not be exclusive and that he would like to see 80 or 90 per cent of qualified specialists in the College rather than 10 or 15 per cent.

This exchange led Dr. W.O. Rothwell, the Certificant representative on the Committee, to refer to "the whole kettle of fish" of admission of *current* Certificants. Dr. Wightman stated that they could become Fellows if they wanted to; and Dr. Turcot added that this would follow when all the "qualities necessary" had been studied by the Credentials Committee and accepted by Council. Dr. Rothwell pressed the point. Echoing what Drs. MacKenzie and Drake had said earlier, he stated that it was "a very good idea to give something to the great body of Certificants who are now [affiliated] in the College". Furthermore, he asked for reassurance that this did not refer to Certificants who had just passed the examination but included, Dr. Rothwell hoped, "the ones in the past". Dr. Kerr answered Dr. Rothwell by saying, "anyone who passes the basic qualification" — that is, the Certification examination.

The door to admission of all current Certificants for Fellowship had been opened.

The committee became aware that other aspects of what they had proposed were problematic. Dr. Wilson referred to the problem of "automatic" admission to Fellowship, a problem that, like the admission of current Certificants, would remain controversial. Dr. Wilson suggested that Fellowship might become automatic provided the applicant had a "clean copybook". He saw nothing wrong with it being automatic as long as this was recognized; otherwise, it would become a problem.

The committee had achieved much this day, and recognition of potentially contentious issues was one achievement. The committee was now ready to adjourn. Before a motion for adjournment was entertained, however, Dr. Graham took the initiative of guiding the committee in a necessary final step. This related to the need to consult Fellows on the drafting of any plan for the future of the College. "It would not be the kind of thing", Dr. Graham advised, "that you could announce as a fait accompli without some sort of consultation with Fellows". Dr. Graham recalled that certain actions in the past had aroused considerable discussion and commentary at the College's annual meetings. Continued Dr. Graham: "It involves the concept of Fellowship for many people and it is a rather radical change in that concept which quite a few people may not agree with. It seems to me that it would be a course of wisdom to figure out somehow or other how the Fellowship is to be consulted at some point". Dr. Graham's concern led the committee to recommend to Council that, if the resolutions were approved, the Fellows and affiliated Certificants should be consulted at the appropriate time to assess their opinions regarding the resolutions.

The committee, now halfway through its deliberations, had drawn a blueprint for the future development of the College. The remaining two meetings would refine thinking on the Fellowship, Certification and the interrelationships of Fellows and Certificants and would formulate objectives for the nascent new College. But these first two meetings had taken the Expanded Executive Committee far on the College's path into the future. Before a further meeting could be held, however, Council must scrutinize and debate the proposals that had been developed by the committee.

Council, June 6-7, 1969

Council considered the Expanded Executive Committee's resolutions on June 6 and 7, 1969. Council modified the resolutions somewhat, but, in general, Council's response was favorable. As Dr. D.G. Cameron observed at the October 1969 meeting of the Expanded Executive Committee, "it was clear that there was a great sense of relief that things were beginning to move".

The chief change that Council entertained lay in the motion that proposed that the specialty qualification be termed Certification and that this qualification be a prerequisite for admission to Fellowship. Dr. F.G. Kergin opposed this motion on the basis that it would only perpetuate one of the College's main problems by continuing the two types of membership. If Fellowship was to be attained later, either the Fellowship would become automatic, and therefore pointless, or the multiplicity of criteria to be considered in admission to Fellowship would create a "monster" that would be too difficult to handle. Dr. Kergin wanted one set of examinations leading directly to Fellowship; to attempt any partial solutions to current problems out of consideration for past traditions would breed other problems in the future. Dr. L.C. Steeves was opposed to the motion because elevation to Fellowship necessitating judgement of a candidate's performance in fact constituted a second examination; the qualification obtained as the result of the single examination process should be named the Fellowship. If there was need for a further qualification, it might be termed Mastership, for example. Dr. D.F. Moore then suggested that the motion consisted of three parts and that the part following the word 'Certification' be deleted. This amendment was approved. Thereafter the remainder of the motion was approved separately.

Council approved the other resolutions with relatively little discussion. The most important concept was discussed by Dr. Wightman: in his view, the Fellowship represented not so much the passing of an examination as membership in a national organization that was attempting to "set things right" in relation to standards of specialty training and practice throughout the country. The deliberations of the Expanded Executive Committee concerned many aspects of the College's future. But underlying all these aspects was the concept of nothing less than a new College. Council recognized this. The way to the future would now become clear.

Expanded Executive Committee, October 24, 1969

When the committee met for the third time, the members had gone far in reaching a consensus as to where the College was going. Yet an understanding of the essential nature of Fellowship in the College still eluded them. To accurately and completely define a Fellow and his role was difficult, even for the logical and sagacious Dr. Brown. As late as October 1969 Dr. Brown could only admit, "I'm a little uncertain as to the purpose of Fellowship".

The committee attempted to clarify the purpose of the Fellowship by defining criteria for admission to Fellowship. Points touched on included eligibility of candidates; the kind of qualities to be expected of candidates; the difficulties to be expected if assessment of candidates was delegated to a local level; the desirable interval between Certification and Fellowship; and the status and activities of the new Certificant before being eligible for admission to Fellowship. The discussion clarified the issue sufficiently for a motion to be passed concerning the criteria for admission to Fellowship of candidates who were successful in passing the new, single qualifying examination. It read as follows:

> *After* three or more years, a person who has obtained his Certificate in his specialty by examination and wishes to participate in furthering the objectives of the College, may apply for Fellowship, which may be granted by the College after appropriate assessment of his/her ethical standards and evidence of his/her continued professional competence in the specialty.

The Expanded Executive Committee's deliberations were now nearly complete. The committee had continued to make progress, and the members were particularly fortunate in one respect: time was on their side, for they had been granted the luxury of being able to ponder and discuss the problems over a period of months. Dr. Cameron recognized the value of time when he said that he was "deeply concerned that we might try to rush too fast into this thing and find that we haven't achieved very much at all". The patient approach was beneficial, and Dr. Cameron, who first joined the Expanded Executive Committee at this third meeting, stressed the need, in identifying "the thing that we are looking for", to be "pretty broad in our thinking".

Simplicity, like patience, was a virtue. As Dr. Brown had praised the virtues of simplicity earlier, now Dr. Cameron echoed Dr. Brown's approach in his own iconoclastic but democratic approach:

> ...We have made a big step forward in this clinical competence. It is a clear crisp thing. How you decide it, I am not sure yet. But if we can decide that, here we have a group of people who graduated from university. They now spend four or five years of training under rather rigorous conditions and now pass this business whatever it is, and are now responsible clinically to practise the specialties represented in this College. Now what would such a man lack that he couldn't do anything in the College? His I.Q. is quite adequate, academic performance isn't too bad. We all know that there are some people who apparently have the Fellowship, but who don't turn into very brilliant characters, and there are some Certified people who are undoubtedly leaders in their own community. So I am really asking why do we have to have the Fellowship at all? Why don't we make them all Fellows the first time around? Then we have a real solid College which goes across the country and people will then carry on as officers of the College.

His question was how establishing new criteria for Fellows would identify specialists for the public and how this would assist in their competency as specialists, once their competence had already been established.

But the basic and underlying problem remained: no one could give a clear and specific definition of the purpose of the Fellowship. For his part, Dr. Brown responded by putting a question in which much of the previous meetings' discussions was implicit and in which the direction of future discussions would lie: "When we talk about...Certification and Fellowship, are we thinking of the College being operated in the immediate future as it has in the past, that is, with the Certificants playing a regrettably small part, or are we thinking of working into the entire operation of the College all of those who pass this initial Certification examination?" It was now quite clear that the vision of a new College was developing.

Expanded Executive Committee, December 13, 1969

At its final meeting, the committee further considered criteria for admission to Fellowship, though the concept of an all-embracing representation in the College of all specialists currently in practice took firmer hold in the minds of the committee members. Most significantly, the committee concluded its deliberations by passing a motion that *all* Certificants — past, present and future — should be given the opportunity to apply for Fellowship in the College.

In the discussion of criteria for admission to Fellowship, the emphasis on simplicity of criteria and on liberality of an admission policy grew stronger. Dr. Brown facilitated this; for example, he asked "the terrible question...why don't we just have one examination and give the Fellowship then?" He added that it had been suggested that, three years after the examination has been passed, Fellowship could be awarded to 99 per cent of successful candidates and asked, "so what is all this ado about?" Dr. R.C. Dickson's response to Dr. Brown's questions illustrated the point of view of those who advocated specific criteria rather than the simple approach. He argued that it was not possible to examine for clinical competence at the Fellowship level at the end of the shortened interval since graduation (based on inclusion of a straight internship) without opening the Act of Incorporation; that it did seem possible to identify, among those who were certified as clinically competent individuals, those who would contribute or want to contribute to the College; and that awarding Fellowship on the basis of the single examination process would be interpreted as an indication of the need to lower the standard to provide the needs of the country. To these reasons Dr. Gagnon added two others: the need to avoid alienating Quebec and the desirability of demonstrating that the College was not only a certifying board (like the American specialty boards) but also a *bona fide* college.

Dr. Drake, like Dr. Brown, advocated simplicity and liberality of admission; with respect to the degree of representation of specialists that was desirable in the College, he wanted this to be "total or as near totality as possible". And Dr. Salter suggested that it was desirable to look at the question from the point of view of what the Certificants merited. After all, the College had set the standard for their training and had set the examination that they had been required to take. Dr. Salter concluded that they deserved some type of affiliation with membership in the College. It was not right to make the College "a very elite club". The College's responsibility towards the Certificants was a higher priority than the Fellows' feelings as to what they wanted in the College.

President Turcot, too, took the liberal view, stating that the main desire was to have all specialists in Canada "of the same qualification of competence and that is all". He recognized the need, in formulating a workable plan for the future, to "get away from the idea of the old Fellowship...to look at the future not trying to adjust the old pattern". Dr. Turcot was suggesting a simple approach to admission. Of the potential applicants, the only thing that was hoped was that they would join the College voluntarily. Improvements in training programs, in evaluation resulting from the introduction of in-training assessment and in examination techniques following the widening use of multiple-choice question papers meant that the residents were better trained and assessed; when they reached the level of true assessment of competence they were immediately qualified.

The desire among many of the committee members for a complex system of criteria for admission to Fellowship, therefore, was fading; the practical advantages of a relatively simple system became evident. Dr. Brown sensed this and moved that one of the criteria for admission to Fellowship be approval by a Fellowship credentials committee that would examine evidence concerning the applicant's continued professional competence in a specialty. The motion was almost immediately carried. Dr. Wightman then presented a motion that would delineate guidelines for a Fellowship credentials committee; this, too, was soon carried. The wording of the motion indicates the point that the Expanded Executive Committee had reached:

> *Fellowship* may be awarded to a Certificant in recognition of his interest and willingness to become involved in the objectives of the College, his contributions to the standards of medical care in the community, his contribution to the growth of his specialty, his contributions to the educational life of his university, his contributions to medical knowledge and evidence of satisfactory discharge of his responsibility to his patients.

This motion, while offering guidelines on criteria that were broad enough to allow a wide embracement of applicants, did, however, have one disadvantage. The question remained as to the status for Certificants in relation to the College while waiting for the time to elapse before they could apply for admission. This, in effect, meant another type of dual membership — which Dr. Turcot rejected, saying, "we should have only one class of members in the College".

The committee was now on the point of taking the quantum leap of stating quite clearly that current Certificants should definitely be admitted to Fellowship. Dr. Drake took the initiative in taking this giant step. Admitting that the College had made mistakes in the past and that provision should be made somehow for those existing Certificants to become Fellows, he wanted to see some means whereby they could elect to become Fellows; then, within a period of five years, the number of Fellows would have tripled. His statement met with the approval of President Turcot, who said that "this is what we are aiming at". It also found favor with Dr. Rothwell, representing the Certificants; "Now that you can become a Fellow", he said, "if this goes through, it is a new ball game".

The essence of the committee's thinking at this stage was expressed by the President. The questions that he had placed before the Expanded Executive Committee at the beginning of its work — "what is the College and what should it be in future and how?" — had been answered. He himself gave part of the answer: "Everybody", he enthused, "would have the same opportunity to become a Fellow if they had qualified". In short, the College would embrace a membership that would be truly representative of all specialists across Canada; "the ideal goal" of national recognition and representation would thus be realized.

It was therefore fitting that the Expanded Executive Committee's meeting should close with a motion that indicated how far the committee had come and how far the College would go as a truly representative, national organization. Dr. Drake simply asked:

> Would it be in order, Mr. President, to make a motion that implicit in the discussion of this Expanded [Executive] Committee today is the idea of all of the Certificants of this College, by that I mean past as well as present and future, shall have the opportunity to apply for Fellowship in the College.

The motion was carried at once. Dr. Rothwell and the Certificants would indeed see a new ball game.

By the end of 1969, the Expanded Executive Committee had taken the College far on a course that would radically alter the nature of membership in the College. Before the committee's proposals could become policy, however, much work remained for Council to complete. Besides developing appropriate resolutions regarding new policies, Council would have to take any proposals before the College membership and then to amend the College's constitution accordingly.

The Development of Council's Proposals, 1970

One of the first items of business on the agenda of Council's meeting in January 1970 was the response of Fellows and affiliated Certificants to a letter that had been mailed to them from College headquarters on December 8, 1969. This letter apprised its nearly 9,000 recipients of the changes that the Expanded Executive Committee had proposed and, by the time Council met, 318 replies had been received. Most of the correspondents supported the proposed plan, largely because they condemned the dual standard of competence and of examinations or found it unnecessary, but some were concerned that changes would debase the Fellowship, and several thought that the standard of the Fellowship examination would fall after the single examination process had been instituted. Many referred to the difficulties that would result from the descision to award Fellowship on the basis of as yet undetermined criteria, and the lack of well-defined criteria for admission to Fellowship was an apparent weakness in the plan. One Fellow wrote that "the establishment of the criteria on which attainment of Fellowship would be judged could certainly be a major stumbling block", and he asked that the College inform Fellows of suggested methods before any criteria were approved.[3] Another summarized the difficulties that Council should consider in the following clear and direct terms, writing to Dr. Graham as follows:

> In your letter you state that the conditions under which Fellowship would be awarded would have to be determined. I should suggest respectfully that this is the primary consideration before the proposed changes can be proceeded with. Before I personally can take an intelligent stand in this, I should like to know who would screen selection of Fellows, how they would be proposed and what the criteria would be for attaining this distinction. Is it to be on the basis of academic achievement, clinical service, economic prowess or a combination of all of these? Fellowship in the Royal College and its meaning would be greatly influenced by the emphasis any of these factors might be given. Who is going to propose names of prospective Fellows to the Council of the Royal College? Is this to be done by local Fellows whose judgement may be colored by their relative isolation or by fierce parochial loyalties, or is it to be made by university faculties, who while being able to judge academic excellence may not be fully familiar with local conditions in all remote places or is it to be made by individual Fellows on the "you scratch my back, I scratch yours" basis. These are weighty and important questions which I believe must be solved before the matter of the Fellowship by election can receive consideration.[4]

It was imperative, therefore, that Council carefully consider the criteria of admission to Fellowship. While President Turcot had stated at the beginning of the January 1970 Council meeting that "it is obvious that the studies in depth of the College structure and future does interest many of its members", he might equally have said that many were concerned rather than interested. They *were* concerned about the way in which Council would introduce the proposed changes, and Council now had to develop a course of action that would take account of the opinions of the Fellows regarding the criteria for admission to Fellowship.

In developing criteria for admission to the Fellowship, Council suggested criteria that ranged from assessment based on means other than the evaluation of clinical competence and academic excellence to those that invoked a liberal and all-inclusive policy of admission to Fellowship. Continuing to favor the introduction of criteria to be satisfied before a candidate could be admitted to Fellowship was Dr. Wightman, who explained why three years should elapse before admission. It would, he suggested, take at least three years in practice following Certification for a person to function as a member of the community and it would take at least those three years for anyone to identify the qualities to be looked for in a potential Fellow. Others were concerned that the award of Fellowship might become automatic.

A liberal and progressive spirit was apparent in Council, however, and, as Dr. Cameron observed, no one was saying that they had to fight "tooth and nail" for the old order. Nor was it the younger Fellows who were necessarily the progressive councillors. Dr. F.G. Kergin, for example, was one of those favoring a liberal and all-inclusive policy of admission:

> I don't see much point in delaying or setting up such criteria, which are not measurable things and which we can't [use to] demonstrate that a certain person is worthy of this added level of acknowledged competence. ...it should be simplified. If a person has successfully passed the Certification examination test, has his Certification and is in good standing with his colleagues (and we perhaps have obtained three references), then we should let him voluntarily become an active part of the College as soon as he has reached the five-year graduation. Then we do have people who are actively and willingly participating in the membership of the College.

Dr. W.M. Goldberg shared Dr. Kergin's view; apart from a demonstration of competence and of interest in the College's concerns, "anything else", he said, "is a fault".

Council then approved three resolutions concerning admission to Fellowship of physicians after passing the new Certification examination. The first resolution proposed that the person who had obtained the Certificate in a specialty by examination and wished to further the objectives of the College might, after a minimum waiting period of three years, apply for admission to Fellowship and be granted Fellowship after the College had assessed the candidate's ethical standards and continued professional competence. The three-year waiting period was thought not to be excessive since the Act of Incorporation required

56

that Fellowship could not be attained in less than five years after graduation; the point of the motion was the acceptance that the Fellowship is something that was to be gained by a Certificant in the shortest possible time. The second resolution proposed that an individual's continuing professional competence be assessed by a Fellowship credentials committee. Additional guidelines for judging appropriateness of advancement from Certification to Fellowship were provided by the third of these resolutions. These guidelines suggested that Fellowship might be awarded to a Certificant who showed interest and willingness in discharging the functions of the College as reflected in the physician's contributions to the standard of medical care in a community, to the educational life of a community or university, to the growth of a specialty and to medical knowledge.

Two other resolutions concerned the admission of *current* Certificants to Fellowship. Under amendments to the bylaws approved in 1967, any Certificant who wished to do so was enabled to affiliate with the College and benefit in ways that demonstrated the growing concern of the College that many Canadian specialists practised outside the College's sphere of influence. (These amendments permitted Certificants the following privileges: the right to be known and designated as a Certificant of The Royal College of Physicians and Surgeons of Canada (CRCP[C] or CRCS[C]), full participation in the College's scientific meetings and representation (albeit non-voting) on Council.) One resolution approved the Expanded Executive Committee's recommendation that all current Certificants should indeed have the right to apply for Fellowship under the proposed regulations. The other resolution approved the need to rescind the 1967 resolution that specialists certified after January 1970 must affiliate with the College; because, under the new plan, it was proposed that, in order to demonstrate willingness on an applicant's part, application for admission to Fellowship should be voluntary, any date could not be specified.

By January 1970, therefore, Council had approved virtually all that the Expanded Executive Committee had proposed. Even so, before Council was ready to take its proposals to the Fellows for their approval, some issues still required clarification. One such issue was the question as to whether the proposed single examination really should be termed Certification rather than Fellowship, which latter name some members of the Executive Committee still favored. But the arguments in favor of 'Certification' remained considerable. At this point, the arguments were the following: first, terming the examination for competence Certification would bring the qualifying examination into line with what was done by American specialty boards; second, in Quebec, where a provincial Certification examination had been in existence since 1955, it would be easy for the College and CPMQ to conduct conjoint (simultaneous) Certification examinations, and the Fellowship would remain as a respected higher diploma to which Quebecers could continue to aspire; and, third, terming the examination Certification would be consistent with the universities' wish to shorten the interval between graduating from medical school and qualifying as a specialist to four years, whereas terming it Fellowship at the end of four years would be inconsistent with the Act of Incorporation. Moreover, the term Certification was more in tune with the modern concept that the College should embrace all Canadian specialists; the view that the College was a relatively small exclusive group of "Fellows", as President Turcot himself came to admit, was outmoded.

It was a crucial period. Long-standing ideas about the Fellowship were indeed being relinquished — although, as Dr. Cameron observed, it was hard to stop worshiping sacred cows. The meaning of Fellowship in the College had perhaps been clarified by formulating new objectives, but established Fellows, such as Dr. F.J. Tweedie, could say only that the meaning of Fellowship in the College of the future would be the meaning of the College itself. If the College itself were not to remain sound, the Fellowship would not retain significant meaning. But the meaning of the new College was becoming clear, as is apparent from remarks made by Dr. L. Horlick during Council's meeting of June 1970 on the function of the College of the future:

> ...if we mean the College to be an important national organization, concerned with the new objectives drawn up before us, it has to be a much more democratic institution, much more inclusive. It has to cease to be a club of the elite and it has to bring into it the working specialists in this country and give them a voice in its management and in its hopes. Once we do that, of course, we remove the element of elitism. Now there may be some people who still feel that there should be a special elite organization for physicians in this country and undoubtedly they will find some way or other of creating such an organization... . ...if we can get the working specialists into this body, if we can reach out toward the new objectives which this College has set for itself, then this College will grow tremendously in strength and interest in the country and community and everyone will feel that the proposals are...important and worthy of support.

The second basic issue concerned the "screen" of criteria through which specialists whose competence had already been established by examination would be admitted to Fellowship. This issue was clarified during the Council meeting of June 1970, when Dr. Cameron tentatively proposed that the interval between attainment of Certification and admission to Fellowship should be as short as possible and that admission to Fellowship should be dependent not on fulfilment of a series of criteria but simply on an indication from each individual Certificant of a desire to further the objectives of and work with the College. Council then focused on what Dr. Salter identified as a critical question, "Are we going to be inclusive or exclusive?" Put in this form, the issue was simply a question as to whether membership in the College was either, by simplifying criteria, to include a large number of specialists or, by making the criteria more complex, to exclude a large number. For technical reasons, Dr. Cameron withdrew his motion, but it was now clear that a majority of councillors favored inclusiveness rather than exclusiveness.

Dr. R.C. Dickson, now President, sensed this consensus. It would now be timely to take the Executive Committee's proposals as approved by Council to the Fellowship. An initial step was to publish an article in the *Annals* of July 1970 about the proposals. Prepared by Mr. Giles and also by Dr. Dickson, the article (entitled "Council Proposes Single Qualification and New Approach to Fellowship") served to give Fellows further information on Council's plans. The article also provided Fellows with background material in preparation for two other important steps — a cross-country tour that President Dickson was planning for the fall of 1970 and a plebiscite on the proposals, which would be conducted towards the end of the year. There were six such proposals.

The six proposals were stated as follows:

> *Whereas* it is believed that there is no further need to continue the double standard of clinical competence represented in the current Fellowship and Certification examinations, it is proposed:
>
> 1. That all candidates wishing to attain a Royal College specialty qualification be submitted to a single examination process, the passing of which indicates that the candidate is considered competent in the specialty involved.
> 2. That the specialty qualification obtained by examination as described in Proposal No. 1 should be termed Certification...
> 3. That attainment of Certification will constitute a prerequisite for admission to Fellowship under Section 8 of the Act of Incorporation with Fellowship being attained on application at a later date under criteria deemed suitable for the purpose.
> 4. That each person who has obtained Certification by examination is encouraged to participate in furthering the objectives of the College and to apply for Fellowship which may be granted by the College three (3) years after Certification and following appropriate assessment of his/her achievements such as contributions to the standards of medical care in his community, the growth of his specialty, the educational life of his community and university, medical knowledge, the benefit of his community generally, together with evidence that he has satisfactorily discharged his responsibilities to his patients.
> 5. That as potential Fellows of the College all new Certificants are encouraged to participate in the College's scientific meetings.
> 6. That all Certificants have the right to apply for Fellowship under the proposed new regulations.

To this statement of the proposals was added the statement of the College's objectives and functions that had been developed earlier in the year.

President Dickson, besides listing the proposals (and their rationale) as well as the objectives, defined earlier, explained Council's two principal aims in developing its blueprint for change. One was to construct a more simple and rational basis on which to discharge its responsibility as an examining and certifying body; the second was to define the means by which the majority of specialists could become full members of the College — a college with important roles in addition to that of the examining and certifying ones. Council believed that the proposals indicated the kind of dynamic "new look" that it envisaged for the College of the future and Dr. Dickson said that he hoped that the membership would support them.

President Dickson's cross-country tour, which took him across the country in visits to 21 cities, from St. John's to Victoria, was conducted between September 14 and November 6, 1970. It was indeed a *tour de force*, made more remarkable by the manner in which the President stomped the country even though crippled by osteoarthritis of the hips. On this tour, the College's business was Dr. Dickson's sole concern, and facilitating a consensus among Fellows (and affiliated Certificants) regarding Council's proposals his chief goal.

President Dickson's address in each city was low-key and free of rhetorical and persuasive devices; the only trace of emotion came at the end of his speech, when he told the Fellows, with strong conviction, that the changes envisaged by Council, together with acceptable further suggestions from the Fellows, would produce a college "unequalled anywhere in the world".

President Dickson made five points. First, as a health-care organization, the College must broaden its objectives beyond formulating distinguishing designations for specialists. Second, the dual standard was inherently divisive and weaknesses in the examination system had developed because of it; the dual standard was now no longer required. Third, the new single examination for assessment of clinical competence would be a more searching and more objective examination than even the present Fellowship examination. Fourth, the name 'Certification' for the new single qualifying examination was, on practical grounds, preferable to the name 'Fellowship'. And fifth, since Fellowship was the only category of membership in the College permissible under the Act of Incorporation, a way was needed to enable those who passed the Certification examination to advance to Fellowship.

The cross-country meetings were informative to the President. There was almost unanimous support for the proposed single examination, though only 129 of 452 Fellows and Certificants favored Certification as a name for the examination. Of more concern to Dr. Dickson was the adverse reaction to Proposal No. 4 — the proposal that Certificants could advance to Fellowship after a waiting period of three years, based on an assessment of their performance. Fellows had several misgivings about this proposal, based on several possibilities: regional variations in standards; influence of personal feelings in selection (or rejection) of candidates; a preference for candidates with academic appointments; and even a perpetuation of a form of dual standard. In fact, Proposal No. 4 was rejected at 18 of the 21 meetings.

The next step was to conduct a plebiscite. Council in June 1970 had recommended that this be sent to Fellows and affiliated Certificants, but by a vote of three to two the Executive Committee in November 1970 decided that the plebiscite would be conducted among Fellows only. The plebiscite was mailed, in November 1970, to the College's 4,828 Fellows. The plebiscite asked four questions:

1. Do you believe that it would be preferable to discontinue the present double system of examinations (Fellowship and Certification) and instead conduct a single examination process for specialist competence?
   (The next questions were to be answered only if Question 1 was answered in the affirmative.)
2. Do you believe that the qualification of specialist competence obtained by the proposed single examination should be called Certification?/Fellowship? (If your reply to the question is "Certification" please answer questions 3 and 4. If your reply is "Fellowship" please omit question 3 and answer question 4.)
3. Having completed the training and examination process to demonstrate clinical competence do you believe that successful candidates should be admitted to Fellowship
   i)   automatically?
   ii) on completion of an application accepting the responsibilities inherent in membership in the College?
   iii) after a period of 3 years and having satisfied the additional criteria suggested by Council?
   iv) after a longer period of time?
4. As part of the revision of the Fellowship and Certification programs and in the interest of unity of specialists qualified by the College, do you believe that a method should be devised to admit presently certificated specialists to Fellowship in the College without additional formal examination?

Analysis of the plebiscite returns was based primarily on the 3,320 questionnaires that were completed, in order and received by December 4, 1970. Four conclusions were warranted. First, naming the qualifying examination 'Certification' was now acceptable to 74 per cent of Fellows. Second, almost 20 per cent of Fellows had voted against discontinuing the dual standard, which implied support of Fellowship determined by examination; and, on the cross-country tour, more than 75 per cent of the Fellows had favored an examination-determined Fellowship. Third, although the plebiscite appeared to show majority support for the proposal whereby Certificants would be admitted after waiting three years and satisfying admission criteria (the replies to Question 3 showed that the third option was preferred by 77.6 per cent), a further look at the mathematics showed that the denominator in arriving at the proportion of 77.6 per cent should have been 2,976 (the total number of qualified ballots) rather than 1,772 (the number of qualified ballots with respect to Question 3 only). In other words, this proposal was in fact supported by only 46.2 per cent of the plebiscite respondents — and President Dickson therefore recommended to Council in January 1971 that Proposal No. 4 be revised. And fourth, admission of currently certificated specialists to Fellowship was favored by some 60 per cent of the respondents.

The results of the cross-country meetings and the plebiscite made President Dickson aware of Fellows' views, and he and other councillors were prepared to change their own views accordingly. The President had not stated his own opinion publicly, though he had up to now accepted the dual standard because of the nationwide shortage of Fellowship specialists; Dr. Dickson thought that the Certification qualification had served practical ends. But now, with great sincerity, honesty and statesmanship, the President told his colleagues, "I freely admit that my opinion changed as I listened to the excellent and objective discussions at the meetings". He now favored Fellowship being earned by examination because it preserved the tradition of the College; yet, at the same time, it was unrealistic to expect a specialist first to earn a certificate of competence by passing a hard, objective examination, and then to be submitted to a process of subjective evaluation before being able to attain Fellowship. This respected conservative had become an admitted liberal; his change of mind reflected not only the power of reasoning over many months but also the victory of the spirit of inclusiveness over exclusiveness.

In keeping with the spirit of inclusiveness, and with an eye to gaining the greatest amount of support possible for the proposals, Council resolved to provide alternatives to two of the proposals. Here the alternatives to Proposals 4 and 6 are set beside the originals:

Proposal	Alternative Proposal	Original Proposal
No. 4	That each person who has obtained Certification by examination is encouraged to participate in furthering the objectives of the College and to apply for Fellowship which may be granted by the College on his/her completion of an application accepting the responsibilities inherent in	That each person who has obtained Certification by examination is encouraged to participate in furthering the objectives of the College and to apply for Fellowship which may be granted by the College three (3) years after Certification and following appropriate assessment of his/her achievements such as contributions to the standards of medical care in his community, the growth of

	membership in the College and having satisfied the terms of the Act of Incorporation.	his specialty, the educational life of his community and university, medical knowledge, the benefit of his community generally, together with evidence that he has satisfactorily discharged his responsibilities to his patients.
No. 6	That all current Certificants shall have the right to apply for Fellowship under new regulations to be determined by Council and to be agreed upon by the membership.	That all Certificants should have the right to apply for Fellowship under the proposed new regulations.

Affirmation of the 'New' College, 1971 to 1973

The next step was to take the proposals — there were eight now, all told — before the 1971 annual business meeting. Held on January 22, 1971, in Ottawa, this meeting attracted some 400 Fellows, who now heard President Dickson explain that the meeting was the final stage in the planned program of communication and discussion with the Fellows concerning Council's proposals.[5] President Dickson first summarized the results of the plebiscite and then introduced the Council's proposals by explaining Council's two basic aims: to discontinue the production of specialists at two standards in favor of a single standard, and to end the divisiveness that had resulted from the two-standard system over the past 25 years. Proposals Nos. 1 to 4 were designed to achieve the first objective and Proposal No. 6, the second. (Proposal No. 5 was not controversial.) Regarding the College's relationship to current Certificants, Dr. Dickson suggested two possible courses. First, the College could leave them "in limbo" until time eliminated the problem. Second, the College could take the broader and more generous view and admit them into the College by means yet to be devised, in the knowledge that if they participated in College activities the College could help them maintain and improve their competence. Council recommended the latter course; it would achieve greater unity among specialists.

Proposals Nos. 1 and 2, concerning the requirement for a single examination process to be termed Certification, were approved quickly. Proposal No. 3 — that Certification would be a prerequisite for admission to Fellowship, with other criteria yet to be determined — was not so readily accepted, in part because some Fellows had not grasped that this proposal concerned the future Certificants and not current Certificants. This understood, Proposal No. 3 was approved.

The June 1970 version of Proposal No. 4 and its derivative of January 1971 were then discussed. Dr. Dickson explained the existence of these two similar proposals as follows: "The old Proposal No. 4 suggested re-evaluation of the man's performance over three years; the new Proposal No. 4 means that he gets his Fellowship by examination provided he applies for it". Council recommended the newer version, Dr. Dickson said.

Dr. P. Chevalier, of Sherbrooke, regretted what he saw as the removal of the Fellowship as a diploma of excellence and thus of "a good motivation for our doctors in the Province of Quebec who might remain at the level of the Certificant of the [Quebec] College of Physicians". There was no need for two Certificates in Quebec; for Quebec, it was the Fellowship that was important. He also stressed the importance of unity: "In view of national unity", Dr. Chevalier said, "in view of our sense of professional necessity, I think that this body should consider very seriously to keep somehow a motivation for our doctors of Quebec to try to obtain an affidavit of excellence other than the certificate which will be issued by the Royal College [and] which will be called a Certification".

Some Fellows were concerned at the use of the word 'may' instead of 'shall' in the proposals. "That", said Dr. J.A. Tallon, of Cornwall, "puts a very broad application to the motion". Dr. Dickson explained that the object of the new proposal was to ensure that the examination was the determining factor, together with the expression by the successful candidate that he wanted to be a Fellow, and he said that the College reserved no discretion to itself by using the word 'may', and Dr. Kergin recommended use of the word 'may' "just in case some unfortunate incident should happen".

These concerns to some extent appeased, voting was called on the newer Proposal No. 4. The motion relating to it was carried.

Proposal No. 5 was "just a 'motherhood' cause", Dr. Dickson claimed — it encouraged new Certificants to attend the College's scientific meetings — and so he went on to the newer version of Proposal No. 6. The newer version was recommended to the meeting because the older version had been designed "to go along with old Proposal No. 4" — and this had just been rejected in favor of the newer Proposal No. 4. This stated that "All current Certificants now have the right to apply for Fellowship under new regulations to be determined by Council after further consultation with the membership". Voting on it would indicate whether Fellows would wish Council to proceed to develop ways and means to bring the present body of Certificants into the College. Reactions to this proposal were predictably mixed, but the discussion was not long and the motion was carried.

The conduct and outcome of the 1971 annual business meeting was not unsatisfactory to Council and it was now necessary to determine how current Certificants might be admitted to membership in the College. At the cross-country business meetings and in the plebiscite of 1970, some Fellows had favored their admission but others were opposed to this. The problem was discussed in detail by the Executive Committee in March 1971. Dr. Dickson reminded his colleagues that there were different categories of Certificants, and that some had preferred to take the Certification rather than the Fellowship examination for entirely valid reasons. A few established specialists had been granted Certification without examination before the Certification examination had been introduced in 1946. Another group of Certificants comprised those who were certificated by examination when no Fellowship was available in their specialty; pathologists were an example. Another group consisted of specialists who had deliberately preferred the Certification examination, either because they were not planning to practise in academic centres or because they considered the Certification a better specialty qualification than the Fellowship; the psychiatrists were an example. Still others included specialists who had been awarded Certification on the basis of near-success at the Fellowship examination and specialists who had taken the Certification as an alternative, having failed the Fellowship examination on a number of occasions. Thus "Certificants" were a varied group of specialists — and not always too different from Fellows.

By the spring of 1971, the mood of Council provided less support for specific admission criteria than previously. Dr. Salter, for example, advocated the College's requiring either a shorter waiting period before admission, such as one year, or perhaps no time limit at all. Dr. Turcot, too, was becoming convinced of the desirability of a liberal and inclusive policy of admission, as free of criteria as possible. He spoke eloquently and passionately on this issue and set the tone for the remainder of the discussion:

> I think this is a real occasion to decide once and for all what is the College of the future, and we should decide right now to set the new pattern. I think the membership-at-large in a great majority is waiting for us to move ahead. If we don't, they will ask questions, "What are you doing?", "What is the delay?" I feel all Certificants are waiting for that also. Waiting is not really the result of a rationalized approach. It is sentimental and I think we should get rid of it and ask all Certificants into the College right now, and remove from the bylaws all those items that suggest we are keeping two standards, two levels, two classes and so on. This is not Canada. I think all Certificants have been trained in our programs. The heads have been agreeable to keep them. They are specialists. They are performing operations on Canadian citizens and, really, don't you believe they are first-class citizens and ought to be members of this College? We are not being realistic and I think we should think hard and make a decision...to include them all.

The meeting was moving towards a consensus that was based on a desire to see current Certificants become members of the College and, even more fundamentally, on the desire for a unified College. Dr. Cameron, discerning a "remarkable" expression of a need for speed and for the greatest simplicity in this matter, moved that current Certificants should be admitted to Fellowship on submission of an application and on condition that it was accepted. To him that was one end of the spectrum of opinion; the other comprised screening meshes of different gauges. Dr. Cameron was right; Council was coming to favor a simple approach. Time, and Council meetings, served as clarifying elements in the decision-making process. Councillors were not proposing to judge the competence of Certificants but to ask them if they wanted to take part in the future expanded activities of the College. Insisting on a waiting period, Dr. J. Beaudoin thought, was being discriminatory, and he asked for a simple screening mechanism such as two letters of approval. Dr. C. Gaudreau admitted to having become "more liberal" in the past year because of his opposition to the waiting period. Not surprisingly, therefore, Dr. Cameron's motion was carried.

A subcommittee then drew up a statement incorporating the two ends of the spectrum of opinion that Dr. Cameron had referred to. Drs. Wightman, Horlick, T.W. Fyles and Salter then worked on a proposal entitled "Mechanism for Admission of Present Certificants into the College". Following a preamble relating to the College's objectives, three guidelines would govern application for admission to the Fellowship: (i) all current Certificants who obtained Certification prior to the new examination would be permitted, and encouraged, to apply for admission to Fellowship; (ii) the application form would contain a statement indicating that the candidate would support the College's objectives and would ask for the names of three referees; and (iii) in the event of controversy, the final recommendation would be referred to Council by the Fellowship credentials committee. Slightly modified, the statement proved acceptable to Council. Council had now arrived at the basis for consultation with the membership on the admission of current Certificants to Fellowship, and the next step was to consult the Fellowship by means of a referendum.

The referendum form was mailed to the College's 5,426 Fellows on November 8, 1971. A letter signed by President Dickson, Vice-Presidents D.G. Cameron and R.B. Salter and Immediate Past-President J. Turcot reminded Fellows that the annual business meeting of 1971 had directed that Council would consult the membership on regulations that would govern the admission to Fellowship and provide them with a statement describing Council's most recent decisions. The key paragraph of the letter was the following:

> The Executive Committee and Council have given much thought to the matter of regulations which could be developed for the admission of present Certificants into Fellowship in the College. There had been earlier consideration of this by the Executive Committee and Council

in 1969 and 1970 when certain quite general criteria were developed. In its recent deliberations the Council members were impressed with the opportunity which they believed to be at hand to attain a maximum degree of unity amongst specialists in Canada and to develop the strongest possible College if the provisions for admission of present Certificants into the College could be liberally conceived and administratively simple. The Council, therefore, rejected complicated formulae in favor of the following proposal...:

> The Council shall admit to Fellowship all persons to whom the College shall have granted prior to July 1, 1972, a certificate of qualification, who are in good standing with the College and who shall:
>
>> i) submit a written application for admission to Fellowship in prescribed form, which application shall include an agreement by the applicant, if admitted to Fellowship, to support and further the interests of the College and its objectives, and which application shall be endorsed by signature thereto of three Fellows who are resident in the applicant's geographic area and who shall by such signatures attest to the good standing of the applicant in his profession in his community, provided that where an applicant resides outside Canada, the application may be endorsed by three persons other than Fellows acceptable to the Council;
>> ii) subscribe to the declaration as prescribed by Section 5 of this Article 4...; and
>> iii) pay the prescribed fees.

The letter concluded by saying that, "after the intensive work of the past three years in planning improvements for the College, the Council hopes that all Fellows will cast a vote in this referendum and that the proposal will be acceptable to the majority of Fellows".

The referendum asked a single question that demanded the answer Yes or No. The question was the following: "Are you in favor of the method of admitting presently certificated specialists to Fellowship in the College as described in the letter from the officers of the College dated November 8, 1971?" All ballots received up to December 8, 1971, were accepted. The College received 3,529 completed referendum forms (a return rate of 65.3 per cent). Of the Fellows responding to the College's question, 2,118 (60.0 per cent) answered 'Yes' and 1,411 (40.0 per cent) answered 'No'. (The balance of the total 5,426 ballots consisted of 20 that were not delivered and 1,877 [34.6 per cent] that were not completed.)

The return rate of 65.3 per cent was considered good. Council concluded that the majority favoring its proposal, while not great, was substantial and took comfort in the probability that the 1,877 Fellows who refrained from voting had not opposed Council's proposals.

The referendum provided more than a tabulation of answers in the affirmative or negative. Some Fellows added comments to their completed ballots. Of 52 such Fellows, 39 had voted 'No'. Their reasons for voting as they did varied, but their reasons included the following: the lack of guarantee of knowledge and ability of a candidate, formerly indicated by the Fellowship, in the elevation of Certificants to Fellowship; the likely devaluation of the Fellowship and the denigration of the College's good name; the pointlessness now of having worked hard to gain the Fellowship; the distastefulness of acquiring three signatures from Fellows; "the process of beheading the level of excellence in dressing up the level of competence of the Certificant with a title of Fellow"; the simplicity or inadequacy of requirements; and the needlessness of giving Certificants the Fellowship when other means of considering them active members of the College could be devised. One Fellow, who said that "time marches on", saw both sides of the picture; he had voted 'No' but he had concluded that the suggested solution seemed the best for the College and the older Certificants. It was, he added, "a grand chance to make one complete unit".[6]

A clear view of the situation as of December 1971 was expressed by Dr. F.J. Tweedie, who commented on the results and implications of the referendum in a letter to President Dickson.[7] Dr. Tweedie's comments reflected the thinking of the Expanded Executive Committee in 1969 and of Council since then, his own awareness of the way in which decisions had been reached and the need now to decide on the next step. He had participated in much of the decision-making process over the past three years, and his letter offers a succinct explanation of both the way Council works in order to take a lead on a controversial issue and the problems that face the Fellowship-at-large in reaching a decision on a complex issue.[8] The major part of Dr. Tweedie's letter is therefore quoted verbatim:

> The results of the referendum are not as decisive as on previous occasions and certainly not as clear cut as you would wish, even though the weight of opinion does favor the Council proposal. The overall 40 per cent opposed (including 47 per cent of French-speaking Fellows) is, of course the disturbing fact, and one has to be concerned as to their reasons for opposing the resolution and how they might react if it is pushed through.

> When one takes a retrospective glance at our discussions of the past three years, this attitude is perhaps not too surprising. At the outset of our deliberations, many of us started out with it — then, as the debate developed, I think we all underwent a process of re-thinking and re-education, the trend being progressively away from the traditional concept of the College as a special or elite group who qualified through the ability to clear a difficult hurdle, to a more liberalized, more representative view of a College which had defined objectives

and a larger job to do in Canadian medicine. For some of us the educational process was gradual and took many hours of discussion around these points to bring about a change in viewpoint. It is therefore not surprising to me that a substantial proportion of the Fellowship, not having had the benefit of such exposure, even though informed in other ways to the extent reasonably possible, still hold a traditional view of the Fellowship standard, mainly in terms of the effort which they undertook to achieve it. It is also not surprising that they indicate resistance, by their vote, to any action which would tend to lower their standard by giving it to some who, in their view, are less deserving.

In relation to the problem which is posed by the referendum result, I believe that we have to proceed more or less according to a schedule and plan. I think that the resolution re[garding] admission of Certificants should be presented to the annual business meeting as it exists, or with minor modifications. If it passes, I think there should be further educational efforts to pave the way for its smooth acceptance before implementation. If it is defeated, reconsideration of the whole matter will be necessary in light of the discussion preceding the vote. My present inclination is not to offer a watered-down alternative at the same time, as the present resolution is the product of evolutionary thinking and discussion over a period of time, and other resolutions defining criteria and complicated mechanisms just have not stood up to critical appraisal.

In conclusion, I think we have long since set our sights on a widely representative 'new' College with a well-defined course for the future. I think the entry of the existing pool of Certificants is an essential element to this philosophy and the mechanics of admission have been reduced to the simplest denominators to accomplish this. This may be the hardest package to sell, but we now have a certain momentum in our design for change, and we should take advantage of it to complete the job.

The final step in the evolution of Council's proposals could now be taken; the College's sacred cows could be sacrificed at long last in the name of the 'new' College. Council would now go to the Fellows at the 1972 annual business meeting on January 28, in Toronto. There President Dickson would do two things: ask for firm approval of the proposal to give current Certificants the right to apply for admission to Fellowship and move the adoption of the remainder of the new Bylaw No. 1. (Bylaw No. 1 is discussed in chapter 3.)

Some 400 Fellows attended the 1972 business meeting. President Dickson reminded them that, because the principle of admission of current Certificants to Fellowship had been established at the 1971 annual business meeting, this particular issue was not under debate in 1972. What had to be discussed was the means by which the principle would be implemented. This would be the first order of business, after which — while the votes on just this subsection of the new bylaw were being tallied — Dr. Dickson would preside over the discussion relating to the remainder of the bylaw.

President Dickson could always simplify issues. In introducing the proposed Subsection B of Section 2 of Article 4 (on which Fellows had answered the referendum), he gave the following guidance to the Fellows:

> *If* you believe that admission of those Certificants who wish to further the objectives of the College will strengthen it and at the same time improve the standards of health care for Canadians by encouraging participation in the expanding program of the College in continuing medical education, then you should support the motion of Council.

The discussion of the controversial proposal was surprisingly brief. Of the 400 or so Fellows attending the meeting, only 10 who were not councillors spoke. Most Fellows, and certainly the majority of councillors, were "talked out". Some concerns were expressed, however, particularly relating to the requirement that three Fellows "attest to the good standing of the applicant in his profession in his community". Dr. Dickson clarified the reasons for this requirement. He explained that because Fellows had expressed their reluctance to serve on the proposed regional credentials committee, and because a central credentials committee could not effectively screen applicants from all over Canada, Council had looked for a simpler alternative.

A vote was soon called. Fellows in favor of this subsection of the bylaw were asked to stand, whereupon Dr. Dickson stated that it seemed clear that the motion had been carried. But, in order to cast out doubt, ballot forms were passed out so that the voting could be documented. The votes having been counted, Dr. Cameron reported that the motion was carried by 191 to 130. This majority of 59.5 per cent was almost the same as the majority given Council at the plebiscite and the referendum.

While the votes were being counted, Dr. Fyles, Chairman of the Bylaws Committee, moved the adoption of the new bylaw's 20 articles, several at a time. The discussion again was brief, clarification being required only on the inclusion in the bylaw of the requirement of a two-thirds majority in approval of bylaws. Mr. Scott explained this as follows:

> ...*If* the Royal College were going to proceed without a general requirement of a two-thirds majority there would be certain types of bylaws which would require a two-thirds majority.... . The Council, in proposing this to the Fellowship, had deemed it wise to recommend a two-thirds majority in respect of all bylaws. Under the Canada Corporations Act, certain bylaws would have to have a two-thirds majority, but the Council felt that it would be desirable to have all bylaws approved by the same majority.

The various articles were approved, and Dr. Fyles was then able to ask both for adoption of his report in its entirety and then for agreement that all previous bylaws be revoked and repealed. Both of the motions were carried. The College now had become legally and constitutionally transformed.

The final words in the annual business meeting of 1972, were, appropriately, those of Dr. C.G. Drake, who had now been elected President. Dr. Drake would lead the College under a new banner, as he told the meeting:

> *Today* you have taken a giant step forward: the unification into a common Fellowship of the specially trained physicians and surgeons of this country, long desired and sought. As a part of Canada it is fitting that our strength is based on two languages and two cultures and that the future lies in the strength of these bonds.

The College indeed had taken a giant step forward. It would now be a new College, ready to face the remainder of the 1970s and whatever challenges they would bring.

*   *   *

To this account of some of the pivotal events in this momentous period in the College's history, a postscript must be added. The College's decision to admit pre-1972 Certificants to Fellowship upon presentation of an application form signed by three Fellows, subscription to the declaration as prescribed in Section 5 of Article 4 and payment of $150.00 as the admission fee was opposed by perhaps one-third of the Fellows. Among some of them, this opposition lingered on. It was led by a group of Fellows in Victoria, B.C.; led by Dr. D.A. Baird, this group named itself The Concerned Fellows of Victoria. These Fellows thought it unjust and illogical to award Fellowship without examination to physicians who had previously rejected or failed the difficult and respected higher diploma of Fellowship. They had (as all Fellows had) worked hard for their Fellowship and they objected to the way it had become, as Dr. C.A. Simpson told the 1973 business meeting, a "mail-order" qualification. The view of Dr. Baird was typical: "My Fellowship" he wrote 10 years later, "was one of the highlights of my life. I worked hard for it, as all of us did, and because of this tremendous effort, I felt very proud of it".[9] The fact that Dr. Baird felt bitter about the College's decision 10 years later indicates how strongly these Fellows felt about a perceived devaluation of the Fellowship. These Fellows were concerned about a fall in standards and did all they could to have the College's decision rescinded.

The Concerned Fellows of Victoria failed to have the 1972 decision reversed, but much of the first half of President Drake's term, and much of his time and energy, was consumed in a hectic pursuit of unity that was necessary in order to heal this breach that threatened the integrity of the Fellowship in 1972. President Drake and Council had reason to be concerned, as an unofficial referendum conducted by the Concerned Fellows of Victoria among the College's

5,926 pre-1972 Fellows in the early summer of 1972 appeared to show. [10] Two questions in this referendum were significant: (1) "Are you in favor of existing Certificants becoming Fellows without examination or thesis?" and (2) "Do you approve of existing Certificants obtaining Fellowship for $150.00 and the solicitated [sic] signatures of any three Fellows?" 'Yes' or 'No' answers were required. Thus directed, 76.2 per cent replied 'No' to Question 1 and 81.2 per cent replied 'No' to Question 2. In the opinion of The Concerned Fellows of Victoria, approximately 80 per cent of the 3,362 Fellows who responded disapproved of the admission of pre-1972 Certificants to Fellowship. The results of this referendum spurred both sides on to defend their positions, and the strong feeling that was generated led to the largest attendance ever at a College business meeting — some 835 Fellows attended the College's next business meeting, which was held in Edmonton on January 26, 1973. They attended this meeting in order to express their own opinions if need be and certainly to vote on an issue that appeared to be increasingly divisive as 1972 passed by.

Somewhat surprisingly, The Concerned Fellows of Victoria's attempt failed by a large margin — the key motion, labeled 'B', which proposed that pre-1972 Certificants must pass the current qualifying examination (or submit an acceptable thesis) or else have their recently granted Fellowship cancelled and rescinded was defeated by 675 votes to 86, with 74 abstentions. This result appeared to many Fellows to be an anticlimax, but it may be interpreted as a remarkable demonstration of the desire of the majority of Fellows for unity. The Edmonton meeting was a memorable one in that so many Fellows seemed to be aware of the need to pay close heed to what was happening. Tension and excitement filled the Alberta Room of the Chateau Lacombe, where the 1973 business meeting was held; the meeting had elements of drama in it and the drama that was played out on that unusually warm January day befitted the significance of the decision that had to be made once and for all: whether the College was indeed to be a 'new' College embracing all those specialists who agreed with President Drake that unification of the specialty components of the medical profession could release "tremendous positive forces" [11] or whether it was to return to its former nature as the elite, minority "academic club" that Dr. Baird believed to be the role of the College. [12] The fact that the 1973 meeting was so much of an anticlimax indicated that the position taken by President Drake and Council represented the beliefs and wishes of the majority of the College's Fellows.

The crisis of 1972, however, was not without benefits, for it permitted President Drake to articulate concisely, clearly and convincingly the nature and the role of the 'new' College — and the hopes and aspirations of those, like President Drake and his predecessors, who had worked so hard in the pursuit of unity and a better College. President Drake wrote three letters to the Fellows in the last quarter of 1972, and the effects these letters produced explain why the voting at the 1973 annual business meetings was so unexpectedly one-sided. It is therefore appropriate to conclude this chapter on the transformation of the College by discussing the content of these letters,[13] which made many Fellows reflect further on the complexities of the issue and which made many withdraw their support for The Concerned Fellows of Victoria.[14]

President Drake's first letter was straightforward and made three simple points about the admission of both those specialists who had been certificated before 1972 and those who were certificated after July 1972. Dr. Drake told the Fellows that Council was not empowered to withdraw Fellowship except as a disciplinary measure; that to postpone the admission to Fellowship of specialists certificated after July 1, 1972, for five years would be to break faith with them; and that now, for the first time, the objectives cited in the Letters Patent of Continuance could be pursued with every expectation of support across Canada. "Now", concluded the President, "is the time for this great new Fellowship to apply itself to the fulfilment of these expanded objectives".

President Drake's second letter was directed to those Fellows who, at the urging of the Concerned Fellows of Victoria, had asked the College to stop admitting Certificants to Fellowship and even to cancel the admission of those who had been admitted. But, Dr. Drake argued, Council was simply implementing the will of the Fellowship that had been expressed when the new bylaw was approved at the 1972 annual business meeting. Furthermore, since thousands of Certificants had responded in good faith to the invitation to apply for admission to Fellowship (by the end of 1972, the College's offer of admission to Fellowship had been accepted by no fewer than 5,283 pre-1972 Certificants, so that the Fellowship doubled in 1972[15]), the College had both a moral and a legal duty to honor the invitation and to comply with the requirements of the bylaw.

In his third letter the President addressed all the Fellows. He referred to points of misunderstanding that should be clarified, some differences of opinion that should be discussed and some assertions that were "simply not true". The changes in the College, Dr. Drake explained, had involved the creation of a newer concept of the meaning of Fellowship: the College was seeking to identify specialists who were willing to participate in the affairs of the College and further its aims. These changes would neither diminish the professional status of a given Fellow nor enhance the professional status of a given Certificant; Dr. Drake stressed that such status in the long run was determined by a physician's own professional record of performance in contribution to health care rather than by the fact that an individual was either a Certificant or a Fellow. When Fellows were asked to sign a Certificant's application form for Fellowship, they were not testifying to professional competence of the Certificant so much as good professional standing in the community.

The President also answered the criticisms that an admission-to-Fellowship fee was required either because the College was greedy or because it was losing money. To these criticisms Dr. Drake responded by making the following points:

- The College was financially sound before the plan was introduced, as the 1971 audited statement, which was sent to all Fellows in March 1972, proved.

- The College's financial assets had been built up over 40 years, largely from registration fees from Certificants and admission-to-Fellowship fees from Fellows. Continuation of the fee for admission to Fellowship was approved at the 1972 business meeting. The fees derived from the admission of Certificants to Fellowship were being placed in a fund designated for educational purposes only (the Educational Development Fund).

- "Positively and unequivocally", the motives for the change were the adoption of a single examination process and the promotion of unity of specialists in the College. The motives were neither financial nor "political".

President Drake also referred to the oft-stated criticism that Certificants were either failed Fellows or persons who did not have the fortitude to pursue the higher qualification. Many Certificants had taken the Certification examination because it seemed, at the time, more appropriate to the setting in which they would practise; others had been advised that the Certification examination, which concentrated on the content of a particular specialty rather than on the broader dimensions of medicine or surgery, was a better test of specialty competence than the Fellowship; and still others had taken the Certification because the Fellowship was not then available in the specialty. The President also suggested that some Certificants had failed Fellowship by just a very small margin and that Certificants, as well as Fellows, had achieved distinguished places in medicine. Such Certificants included physicians who were well known nationally and internationally and persons who had already served the College well in various capacities such as committee members and examiners. The gain, Dr. Drake added, had been for the College.

This third letter, which the Fellows received a few weeks before the 1973 business meeting, concluded with a simple and concise statement that summed up the position Dr. Drake had held over the past three years. His statement is also an adequate summary of the end-result of the transformation of the College that had been finally and successfully executed:

> *Preoccupation* with the distinctions of the past fails to recognize the primary and essential point that we are creating a new College, a new Fellowship, which can embrace the entire specialist corps of physicians and surgeons in Canada. We cannot, in all fairness, leave behind our current Certificants, specialists created by this College, as we move forward. Fellows have been asked to relinquish [a] separate designation in order to promote this goal.

NOTES TO CHAPTER 2

1. The members of the Expanded Executive Committee included the following individuals: G.M. Brown, D.G. Cameron, R.C. Dickson, C.G. Drake, E.D. Gagnon, T.J. Giles, J.H. Graham, F.N. Gurd, R.B. Kerr, W.C. MacKenzie, J. Robichon, W.O. Rothwell, I.E. Rusted, R.B. Salter, C.F. Scott, J. Turcot, F.J. Tweedie, K.J.R. Wightman and D.R. Wilson. Not all of them attended all four of the committee's meetings, but the combined experience and knowledge of these individuals, which was directed over a period of eight months towards solution of the College's most problematic issues, served as a most potent decision-making force.
2. T.J. Giles, Executive Committee, March 1969, p. 7.
3. J. Balfour, Letter to J.H. Graham, Jan. 19, 1970.
4. G.M. Wyant, Letter to J.H. Graham, Dec. 30, 1969.
5. The previous six stages in the College's program of communication were the following: (i) the July 1969 article in the *Annals* by Mr. T.J. Giles, entitled "Certification? Fellowship? or Both?"; (ii) the letter to Fellows and affiliated Certificants of December 8, 1969; (iii) Dr. Turcot's presidential address given at the previous year's annual business meeting and published in the *Annals* of April 1970; (iv) the article Dr. Dickson had written in the *Annals* of July 1970, a reprint of which had been mailed to all Fellows and affiliated Certificants; (v) the 21 business meetings held in the fall of 1970; and (vi) the plebiscite of November 1970.
6. J.H. Graham, summary of correspondence, November 1971.
7. F.J. Tweedie, Letter to R.C. Dickson, Dec. 10, 1971.
8. This problem, of course, is not unique to the Canadian College. A.M. Cooke, in studying the history of The Royal College of Physicians of London, observes that "if the College's affairs have sometimes seemed to be largely in the hands of the President and officers, it is because these men have spent much more time and trouble on College business than the generality of the Fellows...." (*A History of The Royal College of Physicians of London*, Oxford University Press, 1972, p. 1126). See also page 395 of the present history.
9. D.A. Baird, Letter to D.A.E. Shephard, April 15, 1983.
10. See Executive Committee, September 1972, Attachment 1, for details of this referendum.
11. C.G. Drake, Letter to Fellows, Oct. 20, 1972.
12. ABM 1973, p. 12.
13. President Drake's three letters are included with the minutes of the meetings of the Executive Committee for Dec. 2, 1972 (letters of Oct. 20 and Nov. 3, 1972) and Dec. 28, 1972 (letter of Dec. 13, 1972).
14. The President's three letters produced many responses; as of the beginning of December 1972, 148 Fellows had written since the middle of September 1972. Their responses fell into three categories. Strong approval and equally strong disapproval made up two categories. The arguments in these letters were familiar by this time. Letters written in support of Council's plans stressed the adverse effects of divisiveness and of the dual standard and praised the pursuit of unity. Letters opposing Council's plans emphasized the devaluation of the hard-won Fellowship or the means by which Certificants were enabled to apply for Fellowship. But the third category of letters was different: some Fellows, having become convinced of

the correctness of Council's position, changed their minds since they had replied to the referendum that was conducted by The Concerned Fellows of Victoria and now supported Council. This was especially true of those Fellows who had supported the request of The Concerned Fellows of Victoria for a special meeting to discuss their demands. One Fellow, for example, explained that he had misunderstood the Victoria group's position and that President Drake's letter of Nov. 3, 1972 led him to wish to withdraw his support for a special meeting (C.J. Chacko, Letter to C.G. Drake, Nov. 15, 1972). Another Fellow responded to this letter from the President by reviewing an earlier letter from the President that had been written on March 27, 1972 (which described the plan for admission of Certificants to Fellowship) and by stating that he was open-minded enough to accept the President's viewpoint and to support it wholeheartedly (W.G. Frances, Letter to C.G. Drake, Nov. 24, 1972). A third Fellow said that he had responded to The Concerned Fellows of Victoria in haste and without sufficient knowledge of the facts; he regretted this and wished to make amends (I. VanPraagh, Letter to C.G. Drake, Nov. 3, 1972).

15. Council, January 1973, p. 6.

Chapter 3

Constitutional and Bylaw Changes

C onstitutionally, the essence of the changes in the College that were engineered from 1969 to 1972 lies in two documents — the Letters Patent of Continuance, granted on November 4, 1971, and Bylaw No. 1*, approved at the College's annual business meeting on January 28, 1972. These two documents reflect the most obvious changes in the College between 1960 and 1980, but throughout this period other bylaw changes reflect other changes in the College. For example, a bylaw amendment in 1967 brought Certificants of the pre-1972 era into a closer relationship with the College — an amendment that was a step towards the admission of Certificants in 1972; a 1970 amendment introduced electoral reform, a Fellow's ballot for election of candidates for Council now no longer becoming void if the Fellow did not vote for a *full* quota of vacancies — an amendment that was in tune with the desire for electoral reform on a greater scale in these years; and another amendment, approved in 1980, changed the title of the College's chief executive officer from Secretary to Executive Director — an amendment that reflected one aspect of administrative reform of the College in the 1970s.

The constitutional and bylaw changes that are summarized in this chapter are discussed in relation to the more important developments in the College between 1960 and 1980.

Constitutional Changes

The Letters Patent of Continuance and Bylaw No. 1

Council's proposals of 1970 and 1971 had profound constitutional implications. The College's Act of Incorporation (see Appendix 3) states that, except for Honorary Fellows and Fellows *ad eundem gradum*, "no person shall become or be admitted as a Fellow of the College...unless he shall have passed

---

*Bylaw No. 1 was so termed because it was the first bylaw that was introduced after the College adopted its new constitution in the form of the Letters Patent of Continuance. The numbering of the College's bylaws was started afresh with Bylaw No. 1; later amendments were signified by the terms Bylaw No. 2 (1976), Bylaw No. 3 (1978) and Bylaw No. 4 (1980).

such special examinations...as the Council shall...prescribe and direct for candidates for Fellowship...."; furthermore, the candidate had to be a graduate of not less than five years' standing. The new proposal to admit Certificants, both old and new, was incompatible with Section 8, which did not permit holders of Certificates to become Fellows. This would apply to both the pre-1972 Certificants (who had not passed the Fellowship examination) and to post-1971 Certificants, who, under new regulations, would not necessarily have been graduated for five years at the time of Certification. An appropriate course of action was therefore required.

One course that Council considered was to open the Act of Incorporation in order to amend it, as had been done in 1939, when the Certification program was being organized. But opening the Act would be a lengthy and complicated procedure, the outcome of which was by no means certain; moreover, Parliament was so busy that it was unlikely that high priority would be accorded College business.

Fortunately, the provisions of the Canada Corporations Act, Part II, permitted an alternative course: the College-as-corporation could be transformed into a non-profit company and its activities could simply be regulated by Letters Patent of Continuance. The CFPC had taken this course in 1969, when it changed its name from the College of General Practice of Canada to its new name and it seemed appropriate for the Royal College to take this course now.

To effect the changes that Council saw as being necessary, Mr. C.F. Scott, QC (the College solicitor) therefore advised Council to apply to the Department of Consumer and Corporate Affairs for the Letters Patent and not to attempt to have the Act of Incorporation opened in Parliament. The procedure was relatively simple. Information would be required regarding the reason for the change in status, which would entail drafting the proposed bylaws under the Letters Patent; the purposes of incorporation would have to be stated in terms much broader than those of Article 1, Section 2; as much material as possible should be included in the bylaws (hence the reason for the new Bylaw No. 1) rather than the Letters Patent; and as much administrative detail should be set down in regulations rather than in the bylaws. All this would facilitate potential changes in the future. The possible loss of status in the College's giving up its "special" Act would be more than compensated by flexibility with respect to future changes in the College's constitution; thus, amendments to the constitution would merely require scrutiny by the Minister of Consumer and Corporate Affairs to ensure that these amendments were within the power of the corporation under the Letters Patent.

No change in the College's day-to-day functions was likely.

The Letters Patent of Continuance (see Appendix 3) constitutes a short document, but it permitted the College's "carrying on without pecuniary gain to its members, objects, to which the legislative authority of the Parliament extends, of a national...[and] scientific...character...." The Letters state that the Minister of Consumer and Corporate Affairs would continue the College as if it had been incorporated under Part II of the Canada Corporations Act, but two provisions had to be observed. The first required that the College's seven objectives be listed, that these objectives were "to continue to be carried out in more than one province of Canada" and that "any profits or other accretions to the Corporation" were to be used in promoting its objectives. The second provision was that the College extend its powers, earlier detailed in the Act of Incorporation, by the insertion of six clauses, Clause (a) of which stated that "the Corporation may prescribe the qualifications for Fellowship notwithstanding any provision, restriction or qualification in the Act incorporating the Corporation, as amended. ...[and] may provide for the admission to Fellowship of holders of any certificate heretofore or hereafter granted."

Mr. Scott's draft of the Letters Patent was accompanied by a "second and little thicker piece." This was the draft of a new bylaw for the constitutionally refashioned College. This was Bylaw No. 1. It differed from the College's existing bylaws in several significant respects. Most important of these was Article 4, Section 2, concerning admission to Fellowship after Certification. Section 2 was divided into Subsection A, dealing with specialists who would receive a certificate after approval of the bylaw, and Subsection B, relating to current Certificants. A further difference resided in Article 21, which stated that for repeal or amendment of bylaws and for enactment of new bylaws an affirmative vote of at least two-thirds of the Fellows present at the meeting was required.

The application for the Letters Patent of Continuance and the new bylaw were considered by Council on May 31, 1971. Said President R.C. Dickson, "this is a most important matter and one that we want to do with complete understanding." He invited Mr. Scott to go through the draft with the councillors. This first draft was discussed and approved, which permitted Mr. Scott to work on the final draft of the application during the summer. The final draft of this application and of the new bylaw was considered at a special Council meeting on October 23, 1971. After the final touches had been put to the application, the College then submitted it to the Minister of Consumer and Corporate Affairs and remaining action was a formality. The Letters Patent of Continuance were finally granted to the College on November 4, 1971.

Constitutionally, the College now was reborn. The approval given to Bylaw No. 1 by a majority of Fellows at the 1972 business meeting testified to the viability of the new College.

Other Notable Bylaw Changes

While the College bylaws do not make exciting reading in themselves, they are not devoid of interest. Interest is heightened when they are seen in light of the various changes that made the period from 1960 to 1980 so remarkable.

The bylaws become more interesting if they are considered in the context of Owsei Temkin's dictum: "Asking why others thought as they did challenges us to ask why we think as we do."[1] Here, comments are made only on the more important of the bylaw changes from 1960 to 1980' and on related issues.

1964

In 1964, two bylaw amendments gave greater protection against possible manipulation and unauthorized use of ballot papers. Until then, it was ruled that "each Fellow must sign the ballot paper and include his address", and that "within three days after the closing date for receipt of ballots, the Secretary in the presence and under the direction of the official auditors of the College, or their nominees, shall open and count the ballots." Dr. R.B. Kerr, Chairman of the Bylaws Committee, explained to the annual business meeting that year that some Fellows had been critical of the previous requirement that a Fellow's ballot paper must be signed or else invalidated. The bylaw amendments of 1964 changed the procedure. In future, a Fellow would return the ballot paper inside two envelopes, only the outer one bearing his signature and address. Within three days after the closing date for the receipt of ballots, the College Secretary, "in the presence and under the direction of the official auditors of the College", was now required to open and destroy the outer envelopes and then to open the inner envelopes and count the ballots.

These amendments were straightforward and provoked no discussion among the Fellows, who readily approved them during the annual business meeting in 1964.

1966

By 1966, however, a "widening restlessness" — to use Arthur Schlesinger's apt observation regarding the temper of the 1960s[2] — was apparent among some of the Fellows, and this restlessness infected and animated the sterile arena of bylaw amendments. Election to Council was again the focus of concern, along with admission to Fellowship. Led by Dr. E.C. Cockings, 23 Fellows from Saskatoon sought to change the bylaws so that the College might become more representative of the Fellows at large. During the 1966 annual business meeting, Dr. Cockings formally gave notice that he and his colleagues wished to propose no fewer than seven bylaw amendments at the 1967 meeting. They wanted the following changes: admission to Fellowship by means other than examination to be restricted; admission to Fellowship by any such other means to be accepted only on a two-thirds' majority by secret ballot of the Fellows at large; Fellows admitted to Fellowship without examination to be encouraged to use the appellation 'Honorary' after the designation FRCP(C) or FRCS(C); only Fellows admitted by examination to be allowed to hold office; nominations to Council to be drawn only from the Fellows in respective geographic areas; Fellows to vote only for councillor candidates in their own particular geographic area; and areas 1, 2 and 5 to be divided into provincial areas.

Although the Saskatchewan Fellows' seven motions did not find favor with Council and were not in fact approved by the Fellows attending the 1967 annual business meeting, they were by no means insignificant. In considering them, Council was made aware of the need to listen to what was being said by Fellows and was provided with an opportunity to consider the nature and mission of the College in changing times. The restlessness among some of the Fellows from Saskatchewan — a province that, not for the first time, loomed large in the history of the College — also presaged a profounder restlessness that would be felt in 1970.

With respect to the Saskatchewan Fellows' notice of motions, Council's views were based on past practice and on the power vested in Council. Of particular concern to Council were representation of Fellows on Council and admission to Fellowship without examination. Concerning representation of Fellows on Council, the main point that Council made related to the question of whether the College should be a national rather than a regional organization. Council's view was twofold: first, the College was essentially a national body and, second, while a preponderance of councillors would be drawn from the universities, the need for representation on Council of non-university Fellows would always be recognized by Council and the Nominating Committee. Representation on Council was a complex matter and Council explained its position in a letter to the Fellows dated October 14, 1966. It made three points. First, in selecting nominees for the Council, the Nominating Committee and the Council must not only keep in mind the geographic areas and the matter of French and English representation, but also attempt to achieve an equitable representation of the 21 specialties for which the College was then an examining body. This was a formidable task in a Council of 24 members. Council had tried to achieve a fair representation of the medical and surgical specialties with rotation of representation of these specialties. Second, Council held that most Fellows would agree that Council should retain the right to make nominations for vacancies as they developed so that there could be the necessary coordination of planning on a national basis to provide for attention to important issues, which could hardly be done on a regional and *ad hoc* basis. Fellows should retain, of course, the right to also nominate for any vacancies occurring. And third, arguments could be, and frequently had been, advanced both for regional and national voting. However, in view of Council's concept of the College as a national organization and not a federation of specialists with regional interests, Council believed it preferable to maintain the current system of national rather than regional voting in Council elections. Council added that, of the 3,407 Fellows as of April 1966, 63 per cent were based in Ontario and Quebec, yet these provinces were in fact represented by just 50 per cent of the councillors.

Council had accurately discerned the feelings of the majority of Fellows across the country. Two statements made at the 1967 annual business meeting appeared to support Council. Dr. D.A. Thompson, from New Brunswick, stated that he was opposed to the principle that left nominations to the regional level. He expressed his belief that the College was "a great national body with a great national duty." From Saskatchewan itself, Dr. (now Senator) E.W. Barootes supported Dr. Thompson in the following terms:

> This organization has grown rapidly in influence and in the good of medicine on a national scale. If we are to become a federation of provincial organizations in matters of representation, we can't scream democracy on one side and then ask for disproportionate representation on the other. ...the work that is being done by the Council and has been done as it has grown and progressed in Canada on a national scale, should be commended at this time. I would feel, particularly in the centennial year, that we keep this organization national rather than regional.

The other issue of special interest concerned admission to Fellowship without examination. Council made three points. The first was that admission to Fellowship without examination was a privilege that had been granted sparingly. It had been, and remained, the policy of Council that the Fellows should preferably qualify by examination. During the decade from 1956 to 1965, of the 2,061 Fellows who had been admitted to membership in the College, 1,982 (96 per cent) had been admitted by examination: 74 (3.6 per cent) under Article 3, Section 3 (without examination) and five (0.24 per cent), *ad eundem gradum*. Second, it would be "impractical, undesirable and probably undignified" to subject the question of admission to Fellowship without examination to a national referendum. The third point was that in Council was vested a discretionary power that, legally, must be exercised only by the authority to whom it was committed; moreover, that discretionary power had been vested in Council by Parliament.

In view of Council's argument, the basis for the Saskatchewan Fellows' proposals was not strong. Council argued that the proposed changes in Article 3, Sections 3 and 4 of the bylaws were contrary to the Act of Incorporation and, therefore, out of order or unacceptable.

Even though the motions dealt with matters that were, strictly speaking, out of order, the Executive Committee considered them important with "far-reaching effects" and recommended that they be allowed to stand. The question concerned unity as much as anything else. Drs. E.D. Gagnon and J. Turcot, from Quebec, expressed their concern in this respect: Dr. Gagnon feared that the College would then become simply "a federation of its provincial subdivisions with all the attendant political and other disadvantages of such an organization, rather than being a truly national body"; and Dr. Turcot, that it would be opening a dangerous door to provide a geographic division based on the same political divisions of the country.

For his part, Dr. Cockings remained convinced that he was right in saying that the College should be more representative of the Fellows at large; he was, however, unable to prove this, though he made the good point that since Council initiated the nominating process it was always at an advantage, particularly because, as he noted, "little or no information" was given regarding its choice of candidates." He also exposed for discussion the regulation that all Fellows must vote for candidates in all geographic areas, and that if they failed to do so the ballot would be ruled invalid. Dr. J.J. Marian, of the Saskatchewan group, supported Dr. Cockings, saying that the fact that Fellows had to vote for candidates unknown to them would hardly be consistent with the College as a national representative body.

Although the Saskatchewan Fellows' motions were soundly defeated, points emerged that did influence the thinking of Council. Dr. D.F. Moore, for example, identified important implications for Council to ponder. Dr. Moore, professor and head of the Department of Pathology at the University of Saskatchewan and member of the Council, submitted comments and recommendations that he hoped would be of some help in the resolution of "a considerable area of unrest." His observations were astute: "It seems to me that the annual business meeting wisely avoided traumatic conflict, but that it would be unwise to assume that the basic unrest had been dispelled. Also it was my impression that there was a much broader basis for complaint than was indicated by the notice of motion localized to a small group of Fellows in Saskatoon." Dr. Moore made five constructive suggestions, a common aim of which was to make for fairer voting procedures.

The Saskatchewan Fellows' initiative, therefore, was not wasted. In the long term, it was not uninfluential and one specific outcome soon emerged: the policy of circulating a curriculum vitae for each nominee to Council, which was approved in June 1967. Democracy had served the College's pursuit of unity.

1966 was, however, notable for one bylaw amendment regarding elections that would give the College greater flexibility in choosing its Presidents. Until then, the President and the Vice-Presidents had customarily been elected by the Council from among the members of Council. Since, in addition, a President must be elected alternately from among Fellows in the Division of Medicine and from among Fellows in the Division of Surgery, many well-qualified nominees were excluded from consideration. The solution lay in the 1966 amendment whereby it was stipulated that the President could be elected also from among Fellows who were not necessarily currently on Council but who had served at least two full terms (the maximum permitted) on Council and, further, that if the President were to be elected from among past Councillors, he would become a member of Council ex officio. The first Fellow to be elected under this new custom was Dr. R.C. Dickson, who became President in 1970.

1967

Five bylaw amendments that were introduced in 1967 by Dr. I.E. Rusted, chairman of the Bylaws Committee, are historically interesting because they brought the Certificants into a closer relationship with the College. One amendment granted each Certificant who so desired them three privileges: to be known and designated as a Certificant of the College, in either the Division of Medicine or the Division of Surgery (and to be permitted to use the abbreviation CRCP(C) or CRCS(C) after the Certificant's name); to be permitted full participation in the College's scientific meetings; and to be represented on Council, and on Council's committees, by three Certificants — though, because of the restrictions imposed by the Act of Incorporation, these representatives would not be permitted to vote at Council meetings. A further privilege was the holding of a special business meeting of the Certificants during the College's annual business meeting. These privileges would be granted provided Certificants gave notice to the College before 1970. An additional amendment made it a duty of the Secretary to keep a register of all Certificants who were not Fellows.

These significant amendments were approved by the Fellowship at the 1967 meeting, apparently without discussion.

1969

A bylaw amendment in 1969 extended the representation of Certificants on Council. The number of representative Certificants was increased from three to five. Each would be representative of Certificants in one of the College's five geographic areas (British Columbia and Alberta; Saskatchewan and Manitoba; Ontario; Quebec; New Brunswick, Nova Scotia, Prince Edward Island and Newfoundland). A further amendment provided for a method of nominating and electing these representative Certificants to Council, so that they would be elected rather than appointed.

Introduction of these amendments by Dr. F.E. Bryans, the chairman of the Bylaws Committee, provoked considerable discussion that echoed objections that had been raised at the 1966 business meeting. Dr. E.C. Cockings recalled that he and his colleagues from Saskatoon had suggested that Council should not put forward the names of nominees until the Fellows at large had had time to put forward their own nominees; he said that "there are some very deep-rooted objections to the type of balloting in elections that we have for Fellows, and...these are just as valid for Certificants." Dr. A. Aronoff also referred to the bylaw whereby "each person voting must vote for the full quota of vacancies or the ballot paper is void", and he suggested that it would be better if members from each province were to vote for candidates in that province, who would be more likely to be known than nominees further afield.

The discussion at the 1969 business meeting revealed fundamental differences between two groups of Fellows. One group was represented by Dr. Cockings, who was concerned that election to Council was not sufficiently democratic and that electoral reform in the College was not moving fast enough. The other group was represented by councillors who spoke at this meeting. Dr. E.D. Gagnon, for example, agreed with Dr. R.B. Kerr, in saying that it would be unfortunate if the election of Certificant representatives to Council with the College were delayed in any way, since more than 4,000 Certificants had opted for affiliation. Dr. W.C. MacKenzie, who had worked hard during his presidential term of 1964-1966 to encourage the affiliation of Certificants, stressed that Fellows had an obligation to the Certificants and that the manner of voting reflected Council's conviction that the College was primarily a national organization and not one that was made up of "various local bodies." A further comment was made by Dr. E.H. Botterell, who had chaired the committee that had reported on the role and relationship of the Certificants in 1958; his opinion was that Council had made a "steady and progressive advance" in establishing a closer association between Canada's Certificants and Fellows and that the proposed amendment was a further milestone in the process of integration.

The amendments were approved at the 1969 business meeting, but it was quite clear that the College was now being affected not only by the "widening restlessness" of the 1960s but also by other characteristics of that year noted by Arthur Schlesinger: "freshening attitudes in politics;...a new acerbity in criticism;...stirrings, often tinged with desperation among the youth; [and]...a spreading contempt everywhere for reigning cliches...."[3] These characteristics would become even more apparent at the 1970 business meeting.

Meanwhile, one other amendment introduced in 1969 deserves comment. This amendment recommended the deletion of the original but heraldically unrecognized shield as used in the College Seal and its replacement by the formal and official coat of arms. How the coat of arms came to be granted by the College of Arms in 1963 and how the coat of arms was designed has been well described elsewhere by Dr. R.B. Salter,[4] but two points may be made here. The first is that, though the College had, at its founding, been granted the use of the term 'Royal' in its title, the College had never obtained a formal grant of arms from the College of Arms in London. True, the College had used a shield in certain of its documents, yet the shield had neither specific reference to Canada nor good heraldic form.

The second point is that the coat of arms, as designed by Mr. Alan Beddoe in 1961, provided the College with a symbol that became entirely appropriate both to the nature of the College and to the College's pursuit of unity. Thus, the simple shield is divided into a right half that is purple (purpure) and symbolic of the physician, and into a left half that is red (gules) and symbolic of the surgeon.

(The side of the shield refers to that of the bearer rather than that of the viewer.) Overlying the centre of the shield, the rod and the serpent, taken from the original College seal, are surmounted by a coronet incorporating maple leaves, which connotes both royalty in the College's title and charter and the national emblem of Canada. Above the shield stands a helmet, and, above that, an eagle clutching a mace. The crest was intentionally designed to resemble that of The Royal College of Surgeons of England so that the close ties between the two Colleges, and the Canadian College's gratitude to the English College, might be indicated. (The Canadian College's crest is "differenced" from that of her sister College in that the body of the Canadian eagle is gold rather than brown and its beak and talons red rather than grey; and a maple leaf rather than a crown is used on the top of the mace.) The shield is wreathed with leaves and its pointed base rests on a scroll bearing the College motto, *Mente Perspicua Manuque Apta* ("With a Keen Mind and Skillful Hand").

The proper heraldic description, or blazon, of the armorial bearings is derived from Old English and Norman French. It reads as follows:

> *Per* pale Purpure and Gules Rod of Aesculapius ensigned by a Coronet composed of four Maple leaves set upon a rim Or. And for the Crest on a Wreath of the Colors An Eagle regardant Or armed Gules Crowned with an Imperial Crown and supporting with a dexter talon a Mace erect Or tipped with a Maple leaf Gules veined Or.

The College Coat of Arms has heraldic significance but, in the context of this history, it has a particular significance in relation to the College's pursuit of unity. Both the purple and the red of the shield and the Old English and the Norman French in the wording of the blazon symbolize an intimate relationship between, on the one hand, the Division of Medicine and the Division of Surgery and, on the other, Canada's two founding linguistic and cultural groups. The coat of arms is, therefore, the very essence of the College. That the armorial bearings decorate the facade of the College's headquarters in Ottawa and that they are represented on the College tie that is worn by Fellows across Canada is a daily reminder of the College, of its objectives and what it continues to strive for.

1970

The bylaw amendments that were introduced in 1970 were, in themselves, not controversial, but the discussion stemming from their introduction provoked intense feeling on the floor of the annual business meeting of that year. In particular, the implications of the motion proposed by Drs. B.J. Perey and A. Trias, both of Sherbrooke, were so far-reaching that the essence of the debate at the 1970 meeting should be discussed here, for its implications remained in the forefront of Council's meetings in 1970 and 1971, when the great proposals for change that were implemented in 1972 were being formulated.

Three amendments were quite straightforward and devoid of controversy. The first related to the lack of a heraldic description of the coat of arms. The first amendment ratified the new wording: "Per pale Purpure and Gules a Rod of Aesculapius ensigned by a Coronet composed of four Maple leaves set upon a Rim."

The second amendment corrected another deficiency: the Fellowship diplomate was referred to as a "learned *man*" [italics added]. This was clearly unsatisfactory, and the amendment then declared that "such alterations as are requisite should be made in the case of *women*" [italics added]. The appropriate Article was further amended so that the wording on the diploma would read not "a man or a woman skilled in medicine" but "a man or a woman skilled in [the name of the specialty]." This last amendment was an attempt to bring into the bylaws a more accurate description of the now numerous specialties in which Fellowships were being granted.

A further amendment reflected another recent change in College activities. Previously, the bylaws had stated that the President was the chairman of the Arrangements Committee for the annual meeting. Now the bylaw was amended so that mention of the President as chairman of this Committee was deleted. The reason for this amendment was simple: the College's annual meeting had, by 1970, become so complex that the President could no longer take primary responsibility for its programs.

One other amendment lacked a controversial nature. This rescinded the requirement whereby Certificants had to give notice of their wish to affiliate with the College by 1970. This amendment was introduced because Council was developing a single examination and it was thought wise to delete mention of a deadline pending a definite decision about the College's future.

The amendment that opened a veritable Pandora's box was worded as follows: "Each Fellow has the privilege of voting for candidates [for Council] in all geographic areas." Voting along these lines was not a new idea, for the Saskatchewan group had advocated this at the 1966 business meeting, but the proposed amendment gave Dr. Cockings a further opportunity to express his well-known views — though he did admit that the proposal on the floor represented a "halting step" on the part of Council towards much-needed electoral change. The amendment also provoked Dr. R.N. Richards into decrying the College's resistance to democratization and identifying four reasons for this resistance: the College lacked a sense of urgency and therefore temporized when confronted with calls for change; the College was characterized by inertia and "blind observance of tradition"; the bylaws prevented those most affected by the College from having any say in its affairs; and new Fellows were too exhausted from their recent training, and residents too scared, to challenge the College. The amendment, however, was approved.

What *was* revolutionary at the 1970 meeting was the critique of the College that was so articulately and so vigorously expressed towards the end of the meeting by Dr. B.J. Perey, of Sherbrooke. Because his ideas, and indeed his charismatic personality, greatly influenced the evolution of the College in the 1970s, it is necessary to discuss Dr. Perey's argument in some detail.

Dr. Perey was but one of several Fellows who were concerned over the College's crustacean rigidity in a time of change. Thus, Dr. E.H. Botterell, dean of medicine at Queen's University and well versed in College affairs, wrote to President J. Turcot on March 25, 1968, to comment on the varying degrees of flexibility or inflexibility, that marked the College's guidelines on training.[5] He said that, because the College not only set the examinations but also defined training programs and approved residencies, the College was "overwhelmingly powerful" in university-sponsored postgraduate medical education and that the College should take pains to avoid becoming blind to the vital role of universities — which, after all, had in part shaped the education of Fellows. Dr. Botterell urged the College not to monopolize, but to share, power.

A year later, another surgeon, Dr. J.R. Gutelius, of Montreal, wrote to Dr. Turcot to express his views on the current role of the College and the need for reorientation of senior Fellows in light of the changes in Canadian society in the 1960s. He complained, of the College, that its interest in renewal was "not obvious" and continued in more specific vein as follows:

> The failure to recognize that all specialists in Canada must become members [of the College] in the near future, the failure to recognize that a double standard of examination is inappropriate when we all know that examinations are inadequate and inappropriate methods of identifying superior achievement and its inability to move quickly into a functioning partnership with the universities, are examples of situations which are becoming increasingly unacceptable to younger members of the College, be they at university hospitals or not.[6]

Dr. Gutelius recognized that this period was a critical one if the College was to continue as a unified body for the recognition of specialists. He suggested that the time had come for Council to appoint a committee properly balanced between members and non-members of Council, university specialists and community hospital specialists to reexamine the objectives and future of the College so as to provide a broad base for the years ahead.

For his part, Dr. Turcot agreed with Dr. Gutelius and Dr. Botterell that the current time was a challenging one — he observed that "a real educational revolution, at all levels, is taking place"[7] — but he believed that Council's approach through discussion with other bodies such as ACMC and special studies such as those of the Expanded Executive Committee would make it possible to reach agreement for the greater benefit of postgraduate medical education in Canada. For Dr. Turcot, the pursuit of unity was by no means unimportant and the pace at which the College had moved in the 1960s was by no means disturbing.

But for Dr. Gutelius the pace of the College's advance was indeed too slow, as he pointed out to Dr. Turcot in a further letter, dated May 1, 1969:

The fact that many of us are not aware of rapid changes in the College indicates a problem of communication between Council and the Fellows of the College. Change has often seemed slow and patchy and has usually resulted from external pressure rather than any clear leadership of the part of the Royal College.

I am, of course, aware that there are many plans for the institution of new regulations. These proposed changes would continue the double standard. This will simply not do! There is no proof that this system improves the quality of surgery. To believe this will be to state that the standard in Canada is higher than in the United States. It is clearly necessary that a single qualification be established; this should be termed the Fellowship to avoid conflict with the provinces or the Act [of Incorporation]. Additional recognition or titles may be given to teachers, superior clinicians or scientists after a period of performance after the training period. It is essential that specialists enter practice with a single qualification.[8]

Dr. Gutelius assured Dr. Turcot that he hoped Canadian specialists would continue to be grouped "in one house", fearing that "it is likely to dissolve in the next few years unless radical change occurs."

"Unless radical change occurs... ." Dr. Gutelius' view was shared by another Quebec surgeon — Dr. Perey. Claiming in a letter of April 1, 1969, to Dr. C.C. Ferguson, that he was "not impatient by nature" he linked his own demands for change to the dynamic nature of the milieu in which he lived:

...*many* of the troubles that afflict Canada are due to the unpredictably rapid social and cultural evolution taking place in Quebec. Quebecers are on the move. They have lost their passive approach to life. They are thrown into a fascinating adventure and they resent anything that slows down their progress as a people. ...I am not a French-Canadian myself [Dr. Perey was born in France] and I am not a separatist. However, I find life around here exciting and what I say reflects the feelings of my colleagues.[9]

To Dr. Perey the need for change was urgent: "It is the rapidity and ingenuity with which the College will adapt to new situations and grasp new opportunities that will decide whether it stands or falls."

Dr. Perey expressed clearly and forcefully the view of a young man who was reaching maturity in the 1960s and whose sensibility permitted him to draw from this era of vitality and energy a spirit that liberated so many in Canada and elsewhere. A sense of this spirit of the 1960s has been conveyed by Marshall Berman:

...*as* the decade developed and we began, tentatively at first, to let it all hang out, and act it all out and bring long-suppressed feelings into the open, and free our bodies and expand and implode our minds, we found — for a time at least — that our new self-expression, far from threatening our survival, was bringing us new sources of life and energy, and helping us cope, not only more happily but even more effectively than we ever had before.[10]

It was Dr. Perey's role, both in the late 1960s and the early 1970s, as well as during his presidency from 1980 to 1982, to bring "new sources of life and energy" to the College.

In another letter, dated March 27, 1969, and written to Dr. F.N. Gurd, Dr. Perey amplified his argument. The points he made in his detailed letters to Drs. C.C. Ferguson and Gurd[11] may be summarized as follows:

- Of major concern were the "appalling" failure rates in the Fellowship examinations. In the Fellowship examination in general surgery in 1968, only 18 per cent of the candidates had passed. Many of those who failed were respected and admired by their colleagues and teachers and it seemed that there was no correlation between the examination results and the value of the failed candidate as a competent or even a scholarly surgeon. The Fellowship examination was like a game of roulette. The results seemed to depend as much on the name of the examiner or the weather, Dr. Perey claimed, as the value of the candidate.
- As a factor explaining the examination failure rates, defective examinations were just as likely as inadequate trainee calibre or poor training. Much superior as a form of assessment was the day-to-day evaluation by teachers watching trainees operate, treat patients, teach, conduct research and relate to their colleagues. This form of assessment, in use at the University of Sherbrooke, had not yet been introduced by the College. (In-training evaluation was introduced by the College in 1972.)
- The College lagged behind centres that were interested in modern ideas on evaluation. The College relied on outdated examination methods, which were not related to modern objectives or, added Dr. Perey, "any other known objective for that matter."
- The Royal College was far behind the CPMQ in understanding the current revolution in medical education, and for this reason the Quebec milieu was an unusually stimulating one. His own ideas being progressive, Dr. Perey was frustrated because the Royal College did not realize what could be achieved on a national level. "The most frustrating aspect", Dr. Perey wrote, "is the slow motion of the College."
- The College was rapidly becoming isolated. An increasing number of specialists across the country were becoming critical of the College because it was not communicating with them. The College must give up its sentimental attachment to "clubbishness" and accept, as full partners, all certificated specialists across the country. Since the College's examinations were flawed — as the work of the College's own R.S. McLaughlin Examination and Research Centre was beginning to show — there was no reason to perpetuate "two

bad standards instead of one." The College could no longer be the privileged instrument of a selected minority. "Its future", Dr. Perey emphasized, "resides mainly in providing a national standard of competence."

Thus, when Dr. Perey rose to speak at the 1970 annual business meeting, his speech was the outcome, not of the "acerbic criticism" that other speakers had displayed but of profound thought both on medical education and on the College's character and objectives. He was as concerned as much as other speakers about the lack of democratization in the College, but he was more concerned than they had been about the lack of flexibility of the basic structure of the College in an era of change. Because Dr. Perey's speech led to a major change in the bylaw governing the membership of the Nominating Committee — and indeed in the thinking of many senior Fellows about the College's role at this time — Dr. Perey's remarks are reproduced verbatim. The significance of Dr. Perey's remarks went beyond reform just of the membership of the Nominating Committee, for the approval of the amended bylaw reflected a stated commitment to the need for and value of democratic evolution in the College that might readily have found it easier to look inward. By looking outward instead, to its Fellows, unity was preserved.

Mr. President, ladies and gentlemen, it is slightly disappointing that after the few hours...[since] we...met we really haven't got down to the fundamental issues. I don't think the amendments to the by-laws presented today are of a nature and magnitude to satisfy the expectations of a sizeable number of the profession that is not really in accord with the way the Royal College is conducting its affairs and the way it is preparing itself to face the problems in the few years to come. I think it is clear from a meeting such as this one that there is a sizeable group of responsible people, people who do not agree with fundamental issues as they are being tackled by the Royal College. There are more than enough in this room who have taken a more negative attitude, I would even say sometimes a destructive attitude, and I am amazed at the number of departmental chairmen that I meet and are so incensed by what they feel is wrong that they are willing to resort to anything constructive. We mustn't misunderstand the enthusiasm of youth and the lack of experience of some of us and we must accept there is an underlying discontent. An increasing number of people are being aggravated; they feel no part of the Royal College, they feel that they don't have adequate opportunity to participate in the affairs and the planning and the decision-making process of the Royal College. The young people, particularly, who will actually make up the majority of the membership before long, are more progressive and a substantial sector of the elite of the profession are having serious doubts about whether the Royal College is taking sufficient steps to meet the difficult years ahead. The Royal College as we know was created with certain objectives which are definitely not the ones we are pursuing at the moment. It was started by a group of elite individuals who meant to start a sort of an association of [the] elite, a sort of clubbish affair and which had attained its objectives of raising the standards of medicine throughout the country and it has succeeded. However, it has now entered other fields such as certification of competence and matters of medical education which overlap the responsibilities of the universities, and the question that I would like to raise is whether the present structuring of the Royal College, which represents the same structure that it had in the beginning, is sufficient to meet the challenge of a few years ahead. I, personally, along with many others, am concerned that unless radical steps are taken to seek the advice of the members of the profession or the universities or medical societies about a basic change in structure for the Royal College, unless this is done, the next few years may see the relative or complete destruction of a body which has the unique opportunity of being the unifying factor in the medical profession across the country. If we see what is going on south of the border we must realize that we are privileged in having at least a body such as the Royal College, a unique body, which if it is fast enough and smart enough can gather all the energy and all the hopes of the profession. Mr. President, these few remarks are just to introduce a motion which is of a general nature. My motion reads that the Committee on Amendments of the Bylaws of the College be asked to give special attention to the structure of the Nominating Committee of the Royal College, the election of Council and the structure of Council itself. This motion states further, that the committee consult with the members-at-large, with universities and other important medical bodies on amendments to the by-laws, and further that proposals of amendments be circulated to members of the College in time for discussion at the general annual meeting in 1971. Thank you, Mr. President.

1971

Although the motion that Dr. Perey proposed, and Dr. A. Trias seconded, was readily approved immediately it was put to the vote, it was not implemented until 1972, when the concepts underlying the motion were incorporated into the College's new Bylaw No. 1.

During the 1971 business meeting, President R.C. Dickson explained that the "extensive changes" envisaged in the Fellowship and Certification examinations made it necessary to postpone implementation of "any appropriate changes with respect to the Nominating Committee, the Council elections and the structure of Council" for another year. Drs. Perey and Trias agreed to Dr. Dickson's request for deferral of consideration of the complex motion, but, in agreeing, Dr. Perey made further contributions to the facilitation of change. In the past year, Dr. Perey said, he had changed his opinion and was less sceptical about the ability of the College to induce change. He explained his new stance by becoming aware of President Dickson's "vitality and open mind." He had, perhaps, gained a greater understanding of the problem, as his exposition of it, offered during the 1971 business meeting, revealed:

> The problem as many of us see it is as follows: the College in its structure appears to many of us as a self-perpetuating body by its very own bylaws which indicate that the Nominating Committee of Council will be made up of the President and the past three Presidents. This means that if the Presidents remain for two years each, individuals that were at the head of the College for the past eight years will have a tendency normally to nominate individuals that they know best and therefore they may not have as easy access to newer members. The trend of the time being youth, many of us feel that that is not the mechanism that encourages the entrance of youth into Council. I am not implying that youth and vitality naturally go together and that age and lack of it also go together. Regarding the methods of election of Council members, many of us also feel that some members of Council have been elected who did not represent the views and didn't have the respect and support of their regional colleagues. The reasons being that all Fellows across Canada can vote for the slate proposed by Council and these individuals sometimes may have been elected by people who did not know them and were elected against the wish of their regional colleagues. So many of us hope that Council will, this coming year, give us consideration to improve on the democratic process and also improve on the representativeness of Council members on a regional basis. I will now present my motion, Mr. President; it reads: "That the mandate given last year to Council to study and propose changes in its structure and in its method of election be extended for one year."

Council did indeed fulfil its mandate and its action led to the drafting and approval of Bylaw No. 1 in 1972.

1976

After 1972, approval of one or more bylaw amendments was marked by the numbering of a new bylaw. Amendment of Article 6, Section 2 and Article 9 of Bylaw No. 1 in 1976 gave greater flexibility in committee appointments and making a certificated specialist who had been censured or suspended by a province or another country liable to censure and suspension by Council also, respectively. With this amendment, Bylaw No. 2 was brought into effect.

1978

Bylaw No. 3 came into effect in 1978 when two amendments were approved. One amendment regularized by bylaw rather than Council regulation the use of the abbreviations FRCP(C) and FRCS(C). The other introduced the term 'Chief Executive Officer' as a synonym for the term 'Secretary'.

1980

Finally, Bylaw No. 4 came into effect in 1980, after the Bylaws Committee, chaired by Dr. G.W. Thomas, revised Articles 2, 4, 6, 8 and 9 through 21. These revisions included the following:

- The office of President-Elect was created. The President-Elect would be elected approximately one year before becoming President. If the President-Elect was chosen from outside Council, that individual would become a member of Council and the Executive Committee, which would familiarize the President-Elect with current College affairs before taking office as President.
- The designation of the College's chief executive officer was changed from Secretary to Executive Director.
- The following provisions were clarified: a President or Vice-President was not eligible for re-election to the same office; a Council member could not serve more than two full terms on Council; and the Executive Committee member chosen at large was to be elected at the first meeting of an incoming Council.

NOTES TO CHAPTER 3

1. O. Temkin, "The Historiography of Ideas in Medicine." In E. Clarke (ed), *Modern Methods in the History of Medicine*, London, Athlone Press, 1971, p. 15.
2. A. Schlesinger, "The New Mood in Politics", in G. Howard (ed), *The Sixties: The Art, Attitudes, Politics and Media of Our Most Explosive Decade*. New York, Washington Square Press, 1982, p. 44.
3. Schlesinger, p. 44.
4. R.B. Salter, "The Armorial Bearings." In Andison and Robichon, pp. 35-46.
5. E.H. Botterell, Letter to J. Turcot, March 25, 1968.
6. J.R. Gutelius, Letter to J. Turcot, April 8, 1969.
7. J. Turcot, "The Essence of Surgical Training: The Role of the Universities, the Faculties of Medicine and the College." Paper presented at the annual meeting of the Canadian Association of Clinical Surgeons, Saskatoon, March 1969.
8. J.R. Gutelius, Letter to J. Turcot, May 1, 1969.
9. B.J. Perey, Letter to C.C. Ferguson, April 1, 1969.
10. M. Berman, "Faust in the '60's", In G. Howard (ed), *The Sixties: The Art, Attitudes, Politics and Media of Our Most Explosive Decade*. New York, Washington Square Press, 1982, p. 497.
11. B.J. Perey, Letter to F.N. Gurd, March 27, 1969.

Chapter 4

Changes in Committee and Administrative Structure

While revision of the Act of Incorporation and the bylaws reflected changes in the College's constitutional powers in the 1960s and 1970s, changes in the College's regular activities were reflected in revisions of the College's committee and administrative structure. These revisions reveal further change and growth in the College from 1960 to 1980.

Changes in Committee Structure

Under the basic constitution, the only committee that is obligatory is the Council; "the business and affairs of the College", it is stipulated, "shall be administered by a committee of the Fellows to be known as 'The Council' of the College." One of Council's duties is to appoint committees, which are of two types — standing committees and such "other committees as become necessary."

Certain standing committees have been of primary importance, but of the currently identified standing committees only the Credentials Committee and the Examinations Committee have existed since the College's founding. These committees testify to the basic activities of the College. The other standing committees currently identified in Bylaw No. 1, as amended in 1980, were created at different times since 1929, and even these standing committees differ from the standing committees identified in the 1962 version of the bylaws.

Even more reflective of change is the third category of committee — "such additional committees (not otherwise provided for) as Council may from time to time deem expedient for the better effecting of the purposes of the College." Examples of such committees are the Fragmentation Committee (1964), the Committee on Policy (1964), the Committee on Certificant Relationships (1968) and the Expanded Executive Committee (1969). These committees were created to deal with specific problems that loomed large at a particular time. On other occasions, ad hoc committees were formed to deal with specific charges — as, for example, the ad hoc committee that preceded the formation of the Education Committee in 1970 and the Task Force on the Single Examination Process that developed the single examination process in 1970 and 1971.

The most important of the committees that were struck between 1960 and 1980 are the following:

Arrangements for the McLaughlin-Gallie Visiting Professorship Committee (1960)

By agreement with the trustees of the R.S. McLaughlin Foundation, representatives of the College have worked with a representative of ACMC to select the McLaughlin-Gallie Visiting Professor to Canada for each year. This responsibility is now that of the Awards Committee, which reports to the Fellowship Affairs Committee.

Archives and Library Committee (1961)

Numerous archival documents have been collected, catalogued and analyzed since 1961. The results of the committee's work are evident primarily in the handsome Roddick Memorial Room. Officially opened on September 10, 1962, this room at College headquarters honors Sir Thomas Roddick, founder and first president of the MCC. The Medical Council of Canada graciously donated $15,000 to the College to furnish the Roddick Room. The committee's chairmen have included Drs. D.S. Lewis, E. Desjardins and H.R. Robertson.

Specialty Development and Manpower Committee (1962)

An ad hoc committee on specialist manpower, formed in June 1961, assisted in the preparation of the brief that the College submitted to the first Hall commission on March 21, 1962. The value of a committee on manpower was recognized in the formation in 1962 of the Committee on Specialist Manpower in Canada (later, the Committee on Supply and Distribution of Specialists). This committee, though a standing committee, was not particularly active. Meanwhile, specialty development became increasingly important to the College, and a committee to deal with this complex issue was formed in June 1964. Dubbed at first the Fragmentation Committee, this committee became known formally as the Committee on Specialty Development. These two committees — the one on specialist manpower and the other on specialty development — increasingly studied matters of common concern, and in 1970 the Committee on Supply and Distribution of Specialists was integrated with the Committee on Specialty Development, to form the Specialty Development and Manpower Committee.

Publications Committee (1963)

An ad hoc committee was formed in 1963 in order to review the College's position regarding an official publication. Chaired by Dr. G.M. Brown, this committee developed the College's *Annals* and participated in developing the College's co-sponsorship, with the CMA, of the *Canadian Journal of Surgery*. The committee was renamed the Communications Committee in 1976.

Committee on Policy (1964)

Council's 1958 decision that the original Certification examination should eventually be abolished led President W.C. MacKenzie, in 1964, to consider the form of a relationship that the College should develop with the Certificants. The committee, chaired by the President, met on December 1, 1964, and May 16, 1965, to make recommendations on "the whole future development of the College." The work of the committee, which was in part based on a referendum mailed to the Fellows on September 1, 1965, led to formulation of the 1967 bylaw amendments that enabled Certificants to affiliate with the College.

Films Committee (1964)

This committee was established to advise commercial firms, universities and others concerning medical educational films to be produced in Canada and later to develop a film library in the College. The project had limited success. Although more than 100 films were available, relatively few were used. The films are now housed in the Canadian Film Institute. The committee was discontinued in 1974.

Committee on Certificant Relationships (1968)

To determine the nature of the Certificants' relationship with Council, a committee, chaired by Dr. R.B. Kerr, was formed that included the three Certificant representatives to Council (Drs. G. Drouin, N.K. MacLennan and W.O. Rothwell). The committee met on October 25, 1968, and made five recommendations that were approved by Council. One resolution recommended that the Certificant representatives be permitted to vote at Council meetings. This recommendation, however, was incompatible with the wording of the Act of Incorporation. However, Mr. C.F. Scott, QC, the College solicitor, advised Council that a recently enacted section of the Canada Corporations Act, Part II, would enable the College to be "converted" to a corporation by means of Letters Patent of Continuance and so avoid having to amend the Act of Incorporation in Parliament. But the committee's work was overtaken by faster moving events, as the Expanded Executive Committee in 1969 and then Council in 1970 developed proposals that led to the admission of the Certificants to Fellowship in 1972.

Expanded Executive Committee (1969)

A further, highly significant step in considering the "whole future development of the College" was taken when President J. Turcot established this committee in the spring of 1969 (see Chapter 2). It met on four occasions in 1969 and, in effect, laid the basis for the 'new' College that emerged in 1972. Its work was of the utmost importance. The minutes of the committee's meetings reveal an unfolding of a liberal and all-inclusive philosophy that enabled Council to develop its proposals both for the admission of Certificants to Fellowship and for the single examination process — the twin highlights of 1972.

Education Committee (1970)

When this committee was formed in June 1970, the goal was to coordinate a variety of educational activities, ranging from granting awards to arranging visiting professorships. The terms of reference were both self-defined and lengthy, in part because, initially, a clear policy on continuing medical education for the College was lacking. In 1974, the Executive Committee assigned to the committee a clearer objective of continuing medical education and agreed that the committee should be reorganized. Named members of the new Continuing Education Committee were the chairmen of the existing regional committees in continuing education (which had been formed in 1971) and the chairmen of the committees on publications, scientific meetings and the Educational Endowment Fund. Additional members included liaison representatives from ACMC and CMA. The first chairman of the Committee on Education was Dr. D.G. Cameron; the first chairman of the Committee on Continuing Education was Dr. R.B. Salter.

Conference of Specialties (1971)

During the development of the single examination process, the College sought the reactions of specialty groups to this important innovation. A conference of the chairmen of the College's specialty committees and the presidents of the national specialty societies with senior College officers was accordingly convened in April 1971. The value of holding periodic meetings on topics of mutual interest to the College and the specialties soon became apparent. From 1971 to 1980, five such conferences were held (see Chapter 12), and the groups that met on this basis came to be known as the Conference of Specialties.

Emergency Medical Care Committee (1972)

A Committee on Trauma had been formed in 1958, but this committee remained relatively inactive. As a result of the growing interest in the multidisciplinary field of emergency medicine, a special interest committee was struck that comprised Fellows of different specialties who were concerned with the care of patients with emergency conditions. The committee's potential for stimulating the development of training in emergency medicine was considerable, and, after an abortive conjoint endeavor planned with the CFPC, the College recognized emergency medicine as a specialty in 1980.

Training and Evaluation Committee (1972)

The formation of the Training and Evaluation Committee reflected the increasing complexity of the work of the College's three primary standing committees on accreditation of specialty training programs, credentials and examinations. Each of these committees was engaged in several different activities. The Accreditation Committee* had to survey and accredit a growing number of programs in an increasing number of specialties. The Credentials Committee was faced, in addition to assessing the training credentials of more and more candidates, with the need to develop criteria for assessment of candidates educated and often trained outside Canada. The Examinations Committee was required to appoint examiners, develop and organize both written multiple-choice and essay examinations and oral and clinical examinations (all in English and French) while simultaneously developing the new single examination process and participating in some of the activities of the R.S. McLaughlin Examination and Research Centre, particularly the arduous work of the multiple-choice question test committees. At the same time, because Fellows with an interest in education began, in the 1960s, to realize that the College's examinations should not dictate but rather reflect training requirements, a need for coordination of the work of the three major committees emerged. The result was the formation of the Training and Evaluation Committee.

Initially, the committee assessed and made recommendations on problematic evaluations of In-training Evaluation Reports. In 1974, a shortage of headquarters personnel who had to deal with the steadily increasing amount of work in the Division of Training and Evaluation became critical, and the Training and Evaluation Committee showed its mettle by examining the functions and roles not only of the division but also of headquarters staff. The committee's work led to the Horlick report of 1975 and prevented a crisis from worsening by making constructive recommendations on the problems of 1975 (see Chapter 8). Later, the committee played a valuable role in drawing up guidelines for acceptable training by non-Canadian specialist candidates.

---

*This committee, later more completely known as the Committee on Accreditation of Specialty Training Programs, was previously termed the Committee on Approval of Hospitals (until 1964), the Committee on the Approval of Hospitals for Advanced Graduate Training (until 1971) and the Committee on the Evaluation of Specialty Training Programs (until 1976).

Advisory Board for the R.S. McLaughlin Examination and Research Centre (1973)

The R.S. McLaughlin Examination and Research Centre, established in 1968, was entirely a College operation, but the MCC, while recognizing the Centre's expertise, wished both to use its resources and to participate in its management and financing. The mechanism that was devised was an advisory board, comprising five members representing the College and two, the MCC. The MCC's membership in the advisory board made it easy to arrange that test committees developing examination questions should have a common core of members and the development of examination techniques and the study of evaluation in general were facilitated. It became easier, too, to develop examinations on a national, Canadian basis.

Committee on Horizons (1973)

This committee was created as a result of President C.G. Drake's request in the summer of 1973 that a committee scan the horizons of the College's future "from every aspect." Dr. Drake wished to examine how the College might best play a responsible and influential role with respect to the standards of medical education, the practice of medicine and the delivery of health care in Canada. This tall order was carried out by a nucleus committee comprising Drs. R.A. Macbeth (Edmonton, chairman), L. Deschenes (Quebec City), R.W. Gunton (London), L.K. McNeill (Halifax) and B.J. Perey (Sherbrooke), assisted by members of the College's specialty committees and of the national specialty societies.

The committee, after studying many aspects of the College's future, presented no fewer than 76 recommendations to Council in December 1977. Some idea of the nature of these recommendations can be gleaned from Table 4.1. Excerpts from the report give some idea of the committee's approach:

- *Our* committee...interpreted our charge to be one of producing a document that would form the basis and the focus for discussion, and ultimately for decision by the Council of the College.
- We are not presenting a blueprint or even a strategic plan. The report is rather a conceptual plan which presents possible approaches which the College might find appropriate in developing a structure and function designed to effectively deal with some of the challenges which are taking form on the horizons of medical specialty practice...to which our College must, without question, address itself.
- We would hope that the report may cast a little light in some of the dark corners that have, as yet, only been perceived dimly, and perhaps shed further light, and even provide a new perspective, in relation to those areas that have been independently identified as horizons... .

- In general...the College has been a body that reacted, often very effectively, to its external environment, rather than an organization which assumed positions, based on conviction, and attempted to modify that external environment. As such, it often found itself in the direct path of change, harassed by previously unrecognized influences that had undergone subtle change and now appeared as full-blown threats, or endangered by the possibility of domination by newly emerging pressures. There is every reason to believe that, unless steps are taken to anticipate the future, this type of confrontation will occur with increasing frequency and with disastrous consequences.
- ...as the College approaches the 50th anniversary of its foundation, there are those who would believe it would be appropriate and desirable for the College to assume a bold new image and undertake a greater leadership role in determining the future of specialty practice, in all its manifold aspects, in Canada. Such a role would require increased sensitivity to developing public and professional aspirations, discriminating observation of social trends, a more representative structure and...a continued scanning of the horizon for evidence of subtle mutations which will foretell major future requirements.

The report of the Horizons Committee, then, was intended to provide a basis for continuing discussions. That it succeeded in this respect is evident from the fact that the Executive Committee took the report as a subject of special study in their retreat of August 1980.

TABLE 4.1 The Committee on Horizons Report, 1977: Classification of Recommendations.

Interest Area	Total No. of Recommendations	Comments	Recommendation Nos. in Report
Continuing medical education	11	Leadership role of College; RACs to play significant role; needs of specialty groups to be met; self-assessment and evaluation stressed.	6, 12, 13, 20, 32, 33, 40, 41, 42, 49, 51
International relationships	8	Liberal attitude regarding international role.	9, 62, 63, 67, 68, 74, 75, 76
Training	7	Excellence the primary criterion for approval; interest in undergraduate education.	24, 25, 26, 27, 48, 70, 72

Interest Area	Total No. of Recommendations	Comments	Recommendation Nos. in Report
The specialties	7	Reassessment of specialties in primary and secondary categories; relations with specialty societies important.	2, 16, 28, 29, 39, 45, 61
College organization and structure	6	Unicameral and bicameral structures compared; increased grass roots involvement in Committees; Committee charges to be better defined; value of RACs stressed; redefine roles of President, Vice-Presidents.	17, 18, 19, 21, 34, 60
Research	6	Report cotemporaneous with decrease in federal funding and formation of Committee on Research and reflective of close relationship with CSCI.	30, 31, 43, 54, 64, 65
College's relationships	4	Reporting mechanisms to be more formal; extend to voluntary health agencies; increased relations with France, fewer with U.K.	55, 56, 66, 69
Social issues	4	Liberal view on College's responsibility in becoming more active as a Canadian organization.	3, 5, 23, 59
Fellows	3	Need for merit recognition; consideration of emotional health of Fellows.	22, 71, 73

Interest Area	Total No. of Recom- mendations	Comments	Recom- mendation Nos. in Report
Multi- disciplinary nature of College	2		47, 49
College honorees	2		46, 57
Recertification	2	Much interest in this issue at time of report.	14, 15
Quebec and separation	2		7, 36
Patient care	2	Stress on compassionate care; reference to intern and resident strikes.	8, 50
Immigration	2		11, 38
Annual meeting	2	Right mix of scientific and CME content in meeting now achieved.	4, 49
Manpower	1		10
McLaughlin Centre	1		52
Archives	1		58
Automation	1		53
Foreign medical graduates	1	Need for assessment of undergraduate medical edu- cation in non-Canadian schools.	25

Interest Area	Total No. of Recom-mendations	Comments	Recom-mendation Nos. in Report
Professionalism	1		35
Surgical 'mother' discipline	1	Question of whether interests in surgery-in-general should be maintained.	37
Role of internist	1	Need to define role and enhance image of internist.	1
Regional meetings	1	"Mothball"	44

Regional Advisory Committees (1975)

In 1974, President K.J.R. Wightman told the Executive Committee that "the College would function more satisfactorily if there was a constant feedback of critical and constructive material from each region." The College's regional scientific meetings (which were inaugurated in 1959) and the regional committees on continuing education (which were created in 1971) were useful in decentralizing College activities, but President Wightman thought that an additional need was to take account of the attitude of the Fellows in the different regions. Besides, the two regional mechanisms were defective in several respects. Regional meetings were not always successful because it was difficult to attract enough registrants to justify the effort and expense of these meetings, and because it was difficult to make their educational value great enough to warrant physicians' travelling often great distances to a regional meeting; and the associated business meetings failed to elicit many comments from Fellows about College policies and activities. Nor did the regional committees on continuing education encourage the desired grassroot support, for their members included the elected members of Council for each region, the university heads of divisions or departments of continuing medical education within the region and an elected representative from each of the College's divisions of Medicine and Surgery.

The Continuing Education Committee therefore suggested the development of a stronger regional structure, and Council considered this suggestion at its meeting of June 1974. During this meeting, Dr. W.C. MacKenzie advocated the formation of an advisory committee for each region, and Council resolved to establish five regional advisory committees (RACs).

The benefits of the RACs, as discussed by Council in January 1975, were seen to be several. In particular, communication between Council and Fellows would be facilitated, allowing discussion of various matters, especially those on which regional considerations, such as to continuing medical education and manpower planning, were important. Councillors could become more active in their constituencies, instead of tending to deal with College affairs solely at Council meetings in Ottawa and the opinions of the Fellows at large in relation to the College's broadened objectives would be readily understood. And with members appointed rather than elected, it would become evident that the committees served a particular function, and so activities such as nominating Fellows for Council seats could be encouraged. With the approval of the formation of the RACs, a new type of committee structure was created. Up to 15 members were appointed by the regional councillors, one of whom would be the chairman of the RAC. Thus, each RAC consisted of a large group of Fellows who were immediately enabled to communicate with the College through Council, which, in turn, was better enabled to communicate with the Fellows.

Fellowship Affairs Committee (1976)

While the Training and Evaluation Committee coordinated the reports of the Accreditation, Credentials and Examinations Committees, all of which were concerned with pre-Fellowship affairs, no one committee coordinated all post-Fellowship affairs. The creation of a Fellowship Affairs Committee, which was approved by Council in January 1976, was intended to fill this gap. It replaced the Continuing Education Committee because it included educational affairs in addition to its other terms of reference.

The Fellowship Affairs Committee was intended to report to Council on matters of concern to Fellows on topics that had so far not fallen within the realm of College activities. Its charge was as follows: to formulate policy concerning communication with the Fellows; to develop and carry out programs for specialists in the general area of maintenance of professional competence; and to recommend the establishment of subcommittees to oversee and execute College functions concerning continuing education, publications, awards and fellowships. In addition, the committee would consider policy on such aspects of College interests as self-assessment, peer review, medical audit and continuing Certification.

These latter concerns were later taken up by the Maintenance of Competence Committee, a subcommittee of the Fellowship Affairs Committee. Of particular interest to the committee were self-assessment programs and medical audit and peer review. The committee noted the absence of hard data on continuing medical education and the maintenance of competence and therefore focused on a technique to facilitate the maintenance of competence among Fellows that could be developed in association with the advisory specialty committees and the national specialty groups. The work of the committee became increasingly important, as maintenance of competence came to concern both the medical profession and the public.

Bioethics Committee (1977)

The suggestion that the College establish a Bioethics Committee came from Dr. J. Genest, who delivered the Royal College lecture during the annual meeting in 1977 on "Bioethics and the Leadership of the Medical Profession." President R.B. Salter announced the formation of the committee during the annual meeting the same year, with Dr. Genest as chairman. The growing importance of bioethics in medicine soon attested to the value of this committee. The committee's present name is the Biomedical Ethics Committee.

Research Committee (1977)

Concern regarding the need for financial support of medical research grew in the early 1970s, and reached a head in 1976, when the federal government decided to freeze financial support for medical research in Canada. President Salter wrote Prime Minister Trudeau expressing the College's concern over the implications of the government's decision on graduate research, and other organizations, including CSCI, also made representations to the federal government. The government then made possible a modest increase in the current support for the Medical Research Council through allocation of other funds.

Research was one of President Salter's major interests — his research in pediatric orthopedics was world-renowned — and Dr. Salter was instrumental in creating this committee. The committee was given terms of reference that covered the following areas of interest: the role of research in the postgraduate education of specialists; the importance of research in faculties of medicine; monitoring of quality research posts allied to training programs in medical schools; ways in which the College might beneficially influence the federal and provincial governments regarding allocation of research funds; and means by which the College might enhance the quality of medical research through recognition of its importance, teaching and adequate remuneration.

Changes in the Administrative Structure

In 1960, when the College moved into its new home at 74 Stanley Avenue, Ottawa, the headquarters staff comprised just five individuals and the College's membership numbered just over 2,000 Fellows. The secretariat was headed by Dr. J.H. Graham, an Ottawa internist, who had joined the staff in 1953 as Honorary Secretary, at first working part-time and then, from 1966, full-time. Before Dr. Graham joined the College, Miss Pauline Crocker had served as Executive Secretary, and she remained with Dr. Graham as his capable assistant when the College moved from the cramped rented quarters at 150 Metcalfe Street, Ottawa, to the new and spacious building. Mr. T.J. Giles joined the headquarters staff in 1958 as Executive Secretary, and his long career (he retired in 1984), like that of Dr. Graham, extended over the entire period from 1960 to 1980. In 1960, the basic functions of the College were relatively few, consisting of prescribing the requirements for specialty training programs, assessing the credentials of candidates in training, approving training hospitals and examining trainees. Also members of the secretariat were Mlle Françoise Lemieux (later, Mme Françoise Moreau) whose responsibility it was to organize examination matters, and Mrs. Isabel Mitchell, who assisted in the execution of financial affairs.

In 1980, the headquarters staff constituted a large secretariat comprising almost 30 people. The College was now a large organization: its membership exceeded 18,000 Fellows (Fig. 4.1), its budget topped $3 million (Fig. 4.2) and its administrative structure was a complex one that was built around the three divisions of Training and Evaluation, Fellowship Affairs and Administration and Finance. The College's day-to-day affairs now were the responsibility of an Executive Director, Dr. J.H. Darragh, rather than a Secretary — Dr. Graham

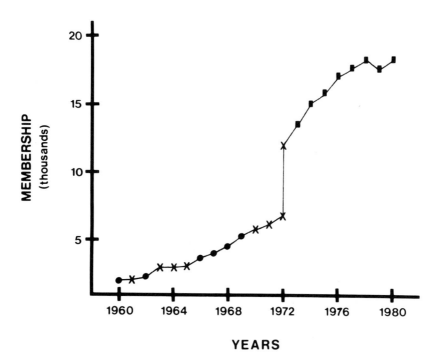

Fig. 4.1 Growth in College membership, 1960-1980. The data are taken from three sources: the College's computer services (●), the minutes of the College's annual business meetings (×) and the records of members in good standing (■). The sharp increase in membership in 1972 resulted from the admission of Certificants, of whom there were, at the beginning of that year, 6,734.

retired after more than a quarter of a century's remarkable service to the College at the end of 1979. The College thus was transformed not only in its membership and objectives, but also in the nature of its administrative support structure.

Changes in the administrative structure of the College between 1960 and 1980 were, therefore, extensive. The greater part of this change occurred in the

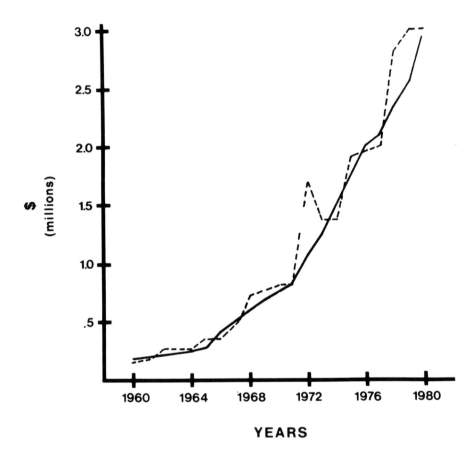

Fig. 4.2 Growth in College income and expenditure, 1960-1980. Income is represented by the solid-line curve; expenditure, by the dashed-line curve. The break in the latter curve indicates a change in accounting policy. From 1972 onwards, donations, grants and endowment receipts and expenditures were included in operating funds; earlier, these were reported elsewhere. the sharp rise in income after 1971 is attributable partly to admission-to-Fellowship fees paid by pre-1972 Certificants; monies thus accruing were appropriated in the specially created Educational Development Fund.

1970s. How some of the problems attendant on this change were solved are summarized in the remainder of this chapter.

A great stimulus to thought about the structure and organization of the College was provided by the remarks made at the 1970 annual business meeting by Dr. B.J. Perey and by the motion that he and Dr. A. Trias then proposed (see Chapter 3). Mr. T.J. Giles, for example, prepared two memoranda on the subject. The first concerned the constitutional and governing structure of the College.[1] His premise was that, if the College was to play a useful role apart from its examining and certifying functions, fundamental deficiencies of the current structure must be corrected and a new structure introduced. There appeared to be three deficiencies: the lack of a mechanism by which three-quarters of clinical specialists might be able to participate in administration of the College; the absence of a forum permitting a dialogue between the College and the medical schools on basic philosophies, principles and policies relating to postgraduate training programs; and the lack of an interface between academicians and community clinicians that might facilitate definition of realistic training program objectives. The suggested cure for these ills was the creation of two boards that would be interposed between the Council and the standing committees. A board on specialty training and qualification would include representatives from medical schools and would be related to the Approval of Hospitals, Credentials and Examinations Committees. The second board, on membership affairs, would comprise representatives of the practising profession from each of the five electoral areas and would encourage the development of a grassroots organization. It would relate to the committees dealing with ethics, film, grants and awards, scientific meetings, specialist supply and trauma. Its membership might be more representative than Council of the Fellows at large; thus, there might be eight representatives each from Ontario and Quebec, two each from British Columbia, Alberta, Saskatchewan and Manitoba and four from the Atlantic provinces.

Mr. Giles's second memorandum dealt with the organization and staffing of the College secretariat.[2] He analyzed the organizational structure and staffing required to manage the proposed changes in the examining function, the admission of Certificants to Fellowship and the achievement of the new objectives. There were several weaknesses in the current system: understaffing of the secretariat, especially in view of the publication of the *Annals*, the automation of records and accounting and the always increasing workload related to the examining and qualifying functions; lack of contingency mechanisms in the staffing structure that would ensure continuity of vital functions if any senior staff members were to be absent; less than desirable capability of functional bilingualism among the senior staff; lack of definition of areas of interest or activity in which it was proposed that the College become involved; and uncertainty regarding sources of financial support for College activities — for example, the R.S. McLaughlin Examination and Research Centre and the accreditation of specialty training programs. The message was clear: more personnel and funds were required.

President R.C. Dickson also drew up a statement on organization.[3] He had his own vision of the College of the future: "a new vital College, widely representative of the specialties, accepting equally widely increased responsibility for delivery of the best possible health care to the Canadian people within the scope of the new objectives." For this vision to be realized, two goals were evident: improved examinations and improved administrative organization of the College and its secretariat to handle the increased activity.

As far as reorganization of the College was concerned, Dr. Dickson identified four objectives. He wished to give Council more time to consider policy developments; to improve communication between Council and College members and to increase the potential for participation by them in College activities; to make more effective the relationship between the College and the universities; and to draw the specialist societies into a more effective relationship with the College. These objectives might be accomplished in various ways. One way was to create some kind of grassroots organization, based perhaps on an annual regional business meeting in designated sites in each area, arranged by Councillors in the region and attended by officers of the College. Another was through the committee structure: the Education Committee would be responsible for all matters pertaining to the welfare of College members (especially regarding continuing education); a committee on training and evaluation would be responsible to Council for all matters pertaining to the selection, training and evaluation of new specialists and would receive reports from subcommittees on credentials, approval of hospitals and programs and examinations and the Nominating Committee would be enlarged by the addition of a representative of each region not represented by the President and three immediate Past-Presidents. A third way was to involve the specialties — national specialty societies would be permitted to take over the responsibility of the College's specialty committees, and two pools of representatives of all the specialties would be created, the members of one pool being nominated by universities and the second by Fellows, both of which would aid the Nominating Committee so that nominees would be satisfactory to the Fellows. No change was recommended in the structure of Council or the Executive Committee.

While neither Mr. Giles's nor President Dickson's plans were put into effect in their original form, they did crystallize the ideas of the time. The two plans stimulated discussion on solutions to problems brought into the open by the Perey-Trias motion. They also generated ideas on other aspects of the College's interests. Thus, the idea of a meeting with representatives of the specialty societies was raised at the meetings of the Executive Committee and Council in June 1970, and the first of what would become a periodic series of such

Pauline Crocker

Françoise Lemieux-Moreau

James H. Graham

T.J. Giles

Kenneth T. MacFarlane

Frederick J. Tweedie

Robert A.H. Kinch

James H. Darragh

meetings of the specialty societies was the meeting of April 29, 1971. Some of the ideas were implemented later. An example of this was the idea of a grassroots structure, which was realized in 1975, when the RACs were created.

By 1972, to these many concerns was added the College's new concern with the needs of a suddenly increased membership, for within the space of a few months, the number of College Fellows rose sharply from 6,000 at the beginning of the year to almost 11,000 in October 1972. These many concerns necessitated an expansion of the secretariat. Thought had to be given, therefore, to new staffing arrangements and new committee structures. At the beginning of 1972, the post of Associate Secretary was created and, as of January 1, 1972, Dr. F.N. Gurd joined the secretariat in that position. He continued to oversee the work that he had started, as chairman of the Examinations Committee, on the development and implementation of the single examination process and he gave increasing attention to the College's activities related to training and evaluation. At the same time, thought was given to hiring a third physician (to develop membership affairs and continuing medical education activities) and to finding an administrative assistant for Mr. Giles, a search that had begun in 1971. The increase in complexity of the College's administrative work was reflected, too, in a new committee organization, and the formation of the Training and Evaluation Committee in January 1972 is an example of the new approach to committee organization. A further example was the formation, somewhat later, of the Fellowship Affairs Committee.

Greater concern over the consequences of the change and growth that attended the emergence of the 'new' College in 1972 was reflected in the attention given to the College's administrative structure between 1974 and 1977.

In 1974, as Dr. K.J.R. Wightman began his presidency, three divisions employing 27 individuals carried out duties related to training and evaluation, administration and finance and membership affairs (including continuing education). The Division of Training and Evaluation, directed by Dr. F.N. Gurd since January 1972, and with Mr. T.J. Giles as Assistant Director, comprised three sections — Accreditation of Training Programs (headed by Mr. V.H. Skinner), Credentials (Mrs. J. Burrow) and Examinations (Mlle F. Lemieux). The Division of Administration and Finance was directed by Mr. P.L. Muir. The Division of Membership Affairs was the responsibility of the Acting Director, Mr. R.A. Davis. (As of December 7, 1974, the posts of Director of the Division of Membership Affairs and of Associate Director of the Division of Training and Evaluation were vacant.)

At this time, the growing membership and the steadily increasing number of trainees whose credentials had to be assessed before they could be accepted for the qualifying specialty examinations created heavy administrative demands on the secretariat, and in 1974 the situation became critical. Three reasons were apparent. First, illness forced Mr. Skinner's absence for a period;

second, the efforts to find a second physician to support Dr. Gurd in his back-breaking duties were unsuccessful; and third, Mlle Lemieux's impending marriage might mean her removal from Ottawa. Mr. Giles, in 1970, had observed that the back-up for staff was inadequate then;[4] now, the situation might become desperate at any moment.

Some urgency, therefore, underlay the discussion of these problems by the Executive Committee in December 1974. Dr. Gurd held that the Division of Training and Evaluation was strained to the limit. He suggested that the post of Director of the Division of Training and Evaluation should be occupied by a young and vigorous person and that he himself should be free to undertake special projects. (One such project was his useful study, conducted in 1975, of the criteria for and methods of specialty training in Great Britain, which was of great value to the College during the revision of the College's document entitled "Requirements and Guidelines for Accreditation of Specialty Training Programs" [see Chapter 8].)

To some extent, the problem was aggravated by the College's own considerate manner of operating. The approach taken to credentialling, for example, required that extraordinary trouble be taken to individualize attention to each candidate. (The approach was very different in the United States of America, where the requirements are rigorous and computerized rather than personalized.) All in all, the College was reaping the fruits of the seeds that had been planted in the 1960s — the uniformity of training requirements and standards in the first half of the decade; the affiliation of Certificants in 1967; the publication of the *Annals* beginning in 1968; the establishment and rapid growth of the R.S. McLaughlin Centre from 1968 onwards; the introduction of a new examination process in 1972; and, of course, the transformation and rapid growth of the College in 1972. The College had grown from a small operation to a large one, and the administrative structure was inadequate to cope with the stresses imposed on it. Even the much envied College's unitarian operation that permitted all the specialty board functions to be combined under one roof, relationships with faculties of medicine to be developed and the College to evolve as a professional college in the traditional sense made current problems more complex rather than simpler.

In view of these problems, the decision was taken to re-examine the functions such as assessing credentials and examining. Dr. L. Horlick proposed that a task force, comprising senior Fellows, review the College's current administrative structure. It was decided that the Training and Evaluation Committee should be enlarged and given the mandate to examine the functions of the Division of Training and Evaluation with a view to making recommendations as to its future structure, organization and staffing. Chaired by Dr. Horlick, the members included Dr. G. Hurteau (chairman, Evaluation of Specialty Training

W. Gordon Beattie

Jacques Robichon

Fraser N. Gurd

John B. Firstbrook

Programs Committee), Dr. L.E. McLeod (chairman, Credentials Committee) and Dr. B.J. Perey (chairman, Examinations Committee). Dr. J.B. Firstbrook, soon to join the secretariat as Director of the Division of Training and Evaluation to take over from Dr. Gurd, attended as an observer. The committee met on February 27 and 28, 1975. It interviewed all members of the secretariat.

Almost immediately, the committee found that it was necessary to examine the interrelationships of the Division of Training and Evaluation with the other divisions and with the Executive Committee and Council. It was also necessary to assess the roles of the senior officers of the secretariat. The committee therefore expanded its mandate.

The committee's study, and the Horlick report that summarized the findings and recommendations, was a remarkably candid self-appraisal on the part of the College. The study occasioned close examination and probing of the College's vital senses and functions. It revealed serious, but not irreversible, effects of stress and fatigue.

The problems that the committee identified and the recommendations that it made were numerous. The principal ones are summarized in Table 4.2.

Each section was plagued with its own problems. The examinations section was functioning adequately but there was "an overriding need" for a senior physician to perform roles that required both strength and sensitivity of character. The examinations were not validated and a closer relationship with the R.S. McLaughlin Centre was considered desirable. The committee suggested that "at some time in the future" a feasibility study should be set up to determine whether the interest of the McLaughlin Centre and its major users would be better served by combining the English and the French units in Ottawa.

In the section on evaluation of training programs, the main need was for an experienced deputy for Mr. Skinner. Of the other problems, the principal ones were the general lack of standardization of operations and the delay of up to a year in Council's recommendations regarding training programs reaching a medical school.

Particularly hard-pressed was the credentials section. Because of new examination regulations, the section was now dealing with some 3,000 fresh applications each year, as well as reopening and reviewing numerous old files; moreover, in this period it was necessary to provide a more or less individual eligibility assessment for each ruling. One perennial problem and one recent problem imposed a particular burden on Dr. Gurd. The perennial problem was that of assessing the credentials of foreign medical graduates; a lack of clear policy regarding foreign medical graduates and the great flexibility of College regulations meant that the staff under Dr. Gurd could, on their own, deal only with the simplest problems. The recent problem was the incorporation of program directors into the new single examination process, by way of the In-Training Evaluation Report; this required a major educational effort on the part of the section (in practical terms, this meant Dr. Gurd) and much time, patience and correspondence. These problems were compounded by the personalized, rather than the systematized, approach that the section had always used.

With respect to the senior secretariat staff, the committee recommended a more prominent role for both Dr. Graham and Mr. Giles. They should be granted greater authority in terms of bringing issues, position papers and planning (including alternative plans of action) before Council and the Executive Committee. Mr. Giles's administrative capabilities could be used more fully, and Dr. Graham, who had always seen himself as the servant to Council, should be freed from routine administrative work in order to spend most of his time on policy matters and forward planning. The committee sought to redefine the role of these two "loyal servants": instead of giving advice only when asked or giving it "very quietly and discreetly", the two veterans might assume a more active and forward role in proposing new policy.

In this respect, the members of the committee were perceptive. They concluded their report by saying that "as in most things 'Canadian' we are seeking a middle way between the traditional role of the Secretary and that of his American counterpart, the Executive Director."

Both the Executive Committee, in April 1975, and Council, in June 1975, gave the Horlick report close attention. Few suggestions were made and serious reservations were expressed on four recommendations only. The suggestion that survey reports should go to Council "for information only", which was intended to reduce Council's work, was amended by including a statement to the effect that a summary of important items should be appended to the agenda for discussion before the Council meeting. The recommendation that medical schools assume responsibility for assessing candidates' credentials was thought impractical and potentially divisive, for 16 different standards might well result. The tentative proposal that the College conduct a study of the feasibility of moving the R.S. McLaughlin Centre to Ottawa was countered by the Executive Committee's opinion that the examination systems being conducted at three widely separated centres required continued thought. And concerning the recommendation that the public should be represented on the Evaluation of Specialty Training Programs Committee, the Horlick report had recommended this on the basis that the College should be proud of the system of approving training programs, that a better image of the medical profession would result if this work of the College was better known and that selection of a knowledgeable individual to represent the public would protect the public, the College and the profession. But Drs. C.G. Drake and G. Bethune were concerned about those survey reports in which certain programs might be heavily criticized; and Dr. Firstbrook warned that having the public represented would not be the same as informing the public. In Council, the point was made that, if the objective was to demonstrate public accountability in relation to the College and its functions, a better place for public representation would be

TABLE 4.2 The Horlick Report, 1975: Summary of Principal Problems in Division of Training and Evaluation and of Recommendations.

Section	Problems	Recommendations
	• Lack of MD member and thus of continuing check on work of examining boards and of MD-authored letters to failed candidates.	MD to work with section head, to liaise with examining boards and to monitor examination process.
Examinations	• Lack of validation of short-answer and essay-type examinations by MD with expertise.	Validate all examination questions and close liaison with McLaughlin Centre.
	• Lack of precision in examination process if training program objectives not clearly defined; increasing involvement of program directors in test committees and examining boards.	Preparation of training objectives by specialty committees and questioning of propriety of program directors on test committees and examining boards.
	• Lack of trained back-up for section head.	Strengthening of staff, possibly with MD.
	• Lack of systematic coding or recording of training program status.	Systematic coding or recording system.
Evaluation of Training Programs	• In survey program, lack of: standardization overall; surveyor information and education; standardized surveyors' guidelines and report forms; report deadlines; encouragement of innovation and flexibility.	Standardize all aspects of survey system; shorten period between survey and report to Council; more authority for committee chairman and secretariat to liaise with deans.
	• Inadequate lines of communication between College and medical schools.	Encourage residency committees in medical schools for continuing self-review.

TABLE 4.2 **The Horlick Report, 1975: Summary of Principal Problems in Division of Training and Evaluation and of Recommendations.**

Section	Problems	Recommendations
	• Narrow base to committee.	Broaden committee base with representation from public, CMA, provincial licensing body in addition to residents.
	• Enormous workload from personalized service to candidates at all levels, both in Canada and abroad, and to program directors; no development of "streams" dealing with particular types of candidates.	Find middle way between personalized service and streamlined planning: delegate processing of Canadian medical school graduates to universities; recognize only certain foreign medical schools and implement recommendations of Task Force on Acceptable Non-Canadian Training Programs*; cease dealing with ineligible foreign medical graduates.
Credentials	• Delegation of tasks to only the most senior staff due to Council and Committee's failure to provide clear guidelines on accreditation of candidates.	Release staff from other sections (e.g., examinations) to assist.
	• Even simplest task requires exchange of correspondence and little procedural change over the years and lack of automation.	Use programmed or systematized approach.

*The Training and Evaluation Committee drafted guidelines for acceptable non-Canadian training in 1975. See Chapter 8, pp. 214 to 217.

Council, where "the total endeavors" of the College could be seen rather than just one aspect of them.

Although not all of the recommendations made by the Horlick report were immediately feasible, the report did bring into a wider forum a number of important points for discussion. The report identified problems and made recommendations (some of which the secretariat had already pushed for) and it showed that the College cared about its secretariat. It was one of a number of factors that contributed to the College's assuming a more businesslike posture in the latter 1970s.

The College's administrative structure continued to be the object of concern in 1976 and 1977. At the request of the Finance Committee, Mr. Giles, for example, in a memorandum entitled "The Administrative Organization of the College Secretariat", made no fewer than 18 recommendations relating to administration of the College.[5] The Executive Committee, as well as the Finance Committee, received the memorandum favorably. The committees agreed with the suggestions that the Secretary be designated as Chief Executive Officer; that the post of Associate Secretary, as defined in the bylaws, be abolished, while that of Honorary Assistant Secretary be retained; that the three-divisional structure of Training and Evaluation, Administration and Finance and Membership Affairs be formalized; and that the Finance Committee develop a policy on personnel that would address the remuneration of senior staff.

The College's administrative structure was further considered towards the end of 1977, after a team, again led by Dr. Horlick, studied the position of the R.S. McLaughlin Examination and Research Centre vis-a-vis the College, and vice versa.[6] Most of the issues identified and the recommendations made by the study team concerned the roles and activities of the Centre (see Chapter 10), but it was noted that relations between the Centre and the College were poorly defined and ambiguous. It was recommended that the Centre should remain separate from the regular line organization of the College and even retain the potential for autonomy. Members of the secretariat, however, believed that the Centre should, rather, be an integral part of the College's administrative structure and that the Centre's director should report to the College's chief executive officer in the same way that the three divisional directors reported to him. In part, the secretariat's minority opinion resulted from the belief that rising costs in the College could best be controlled if the Centre were treated as an integral part of the College's administrative structure; but in part also the secretariat's objections stemmed from a lack of communication and clear-cut responsibility, as Dr. J.B. Firstbrook put it, and the lack of, as Dr. B.J. Perey saw it, "a little bit of understanding." The need was to ensure that the various individuals in the College and in the Centre understood each other's roles and responsibilities. This need was recognized when the Executive Committee and Council approved the Horlick recommendations in June 1978.

A month after the Horlick report was received by the College, Dr. Graham submitted his resignation in a letter to President R.B. Salter. Noting the recommendation by the managerial consultant member of the Horlick study team, Dr. E.B. Shils, of Philadelphia, for a well-organized hierarchical system with a clear-cut definition of authority and of lines of reporting and operating with a chief executive officer, Dr. Graham wrote as follows in explaining his wish to resign:

> I have discussed with you privately on more than one occasion my concerns that after close to 25 years as Secretary of the College (under varying titles and conditions), consideration should be given as to whether I should step aside from that role to make way for a new incumbent. This is a long time for the imprint and style of one person. The retirement of Dr. Wilson, the recent intensive studies we have had, the enormous changes and growth of the College in the past ten years with further expansion to come and to a certain extent also some personal factors of mine would all seem to make this a very appropriate time to have the subject of the chief executive officer discussed fully by the officers, Executive and Council. The subject is one on which you will be aware I have given a good deal of thought for some time, not out of any self-sacrificing tendencies but I hope on the basis of realistic appraisal of what may be best for the College at this stage in its history and at this time in my own career and life.[7]

With wisdom and insight, Dr. Graham indicated that one of the reasons he was writing was to bring these matters into the open and to urge that Dr. Horlick's and Dr. Shils's proposals be examined with an open mind without attempting to fit the total administrative pattern and, in particular, the role of the chief executive officer to the overall qualifications of the current incumbent.

Dr. Graham remained firm in his intention, despite the Executive Committee's pledge of support for his services, and his notice of resignation, to become effective on December 31, 1979, was accepted by Council in January 1978. President Salter pointed to the reactions of his predecessors as well as his own when he said, "I think it is fair to say that for each President of the College over the past 25 years, happiness is having had Jim Graham as the Secretary." The value of his services was acknowledged formally in June 1979 in a motion that the Executive Committee record its recognition of "the outstanding contribution" that Dr. J.H. Graham had made as Secretary of the College for more than 25 years and by the decision to hang a commissioned portrait of Dr. Graham in College headquarters during his lifetime (the portrait then to become the property of his estate). The value that Canada recognized in Dr. Graham was acknowledged when the Order of Canada was bestowed upon him in 1980.

By the date of his retirement as Secretary — he preferred this title to that of Chief Executive Officer — Dr. Graham had served the College faithfully and diligently for just over one-half of the College's existence. For a quarter of a century, James Graham personified the objectives and the style of the College. He joined the College in 1953 as Honorary Secretary, combining his practice as an internist with his College duties, which often meant that the lights in the Honorary Secretary's office burned late into the evening. His increasingly responsible duties later necessitated his working half-time rather than part-time — whatever that euphemism meant — until, in 1966, he was appointed full-time Secretary.

It was often said of Dr. Graham that he was "Mr. Royal College", though he himself might well graciously say that he was, rather, "Dr. Royal College" so that his long-time colleague as from 1958, Mr. T.J. Giles, might wear the hat of "Mr. Royal College." Be that as it may, it was Dr. Graham's sterling personal and intellectual qualities that so immeasurably benefitted the College. A courteous and modest man, Dr. Graham advised a dozen presidents, hundreds of councillors and thousands of committee members during his secretaryship. His knowledge of the College was encyclopedic and his memory of its affairs was computerlike. He became, and remained after his retirement from the post of Secretary, the *eminence grise* that unsure presidents, officers — and historians — felt bound to consult.

It was, perhaps, the Secretary's style that won him lasting respect, and the imprint he thereby made on the College over so long a period, that constituted Dr. Graham's primary contributions to the College. His style was that of both servant and guide, giving advice with consideration and deference and drawing on his knowledge of College affairs in order to suggest rather than dictate action. The College's successes during Dr. Graham's 25 years of stewardship were, to a considerable degree, attributable to his awareness of his advisory role. This in turn was based on the wisdom and knowledge attendant upon the lessons learned in a long and distinguished career in administrative medicine.

Dr. Graham was suceeded by Dr. J.H. Darragh on January 1, 1980. Interested in management — he studied health systems management at Harvard University before taking up his position with the College and he preferred the title of Executive Director to that of Secretary — Dr. Darragh had joined the College as Director of the Division of Fellowship Affairs in 1977. He therefore knew the College, and its workings, from an inside viewpoint.

Before taking office, Dr. Darragh considered the subject of communications and the possible changes related to organization of the secretariat in particular. Communications constituted a priority because, following a recommendation by the Committee on Horizons, Council in June 1978 had recommended the establishment of a communications office in the College, and the communications office was established in 1980, with Mr. T.J. Giles as Director. One of Dr. Darragh's proposals was that, commencing on January 1, 1980, Dr. Graham would be invited to accept a new post in the College — that of Director of Specialties. Creation of this new post would satisfy two objectives: to enable Dr. Graham to remain within the College orbit and to maintain an improved level of communication between the College and the specialties. Dr. Graham accepted this invitation and so brought his knowledge of the College to bear on the coordination of the activities of the 40 specialty committees and to advise in the work of the Specialty Development and Manpower Committee. A second priority of Dr. Darragh's was to streamline the organization of the activities of the secretariat. The secretariat now was both adequate in comparison with the situation in the early 1970s and enormously sophisticated in comparison with the situation in January 1960, when only five staff members had moved into the College's new home.

NOTES TO CHAPTER 4

1. T.J. Giles, Memorandum on The Constitutional and Governing Structure of the College, February 1970. Executive Committee, April 1970, Attachment 5.
2. T.J. Giles, Memorandum on Organization and Staffing of College Secretariat, February 1970. Executive Committee, April 1970, Attachment 6.
3. R.C. Dickson, Memorandum on College Organization and Staffing, n.d. (1970). Executive Committee, June 1970, Attachment 3.
4. T.J. Giles, see note 2 above.
5. T.J. Giles, Memorandum on the Administrative Organization of the College Secretariat, Jan. 15, 1976. Executive Committee, January 1976, Attachment 12.
6. L. Horlick (chairman), Report of the Survey Team on the R.S. McLaughlin Examination and Research Centre, Nov. 17, 1977. The survey of the McLaughlin Centre is discussed in detail in Chapter 10.
7. J.H. Graham, Letter to R.B. Salter, Dec. 7, 1977. The letter is reproduced in full as Attachment 9 to Executive Committee, Dec. 19, 1977.

Chapter 5

Relations With Other Medical Organizations

The pattern of complex relations that contribute to an effective system of specialist health care in Canada has been likened to a delicate fabric. In formulating this image, Dr. L. Horlick was thinking particularly of the complex relations between the College, the provinces, the Departments of Health, the medical schools and the federal government, "consisting largely of a gentlemanly or otherwise give and take between these bodies for the establishment of a state of creative tension."[1] One of the College's tasks has been to preserve this delicate fabric of relationships, and the College's pursuit of unity has been linked to its efforts to preserve it.

Many of the College's relations with other medical organizations make up this delicate fabric. Some, like those with the CMA and the CFPC, have been concerned with the interaction of general and specialty health care. Some, such as those with the MCC and the provincial medical colleges, have been based on licensing — a provincial responsibility — and the basic requirements that specialists with a Royal College qualification must observe in order to practise in the provinces. Also valuable have been the College's relations with the Canadian Council on Hospital Accreditation, which facilitated the College's early efforts to approve hospitals and to survey training programs.

Particularly important have been the College's relations with the universities and medical schools. Over the years, a continuum was created in which medical schools, hospitals and specialty departments of university faculties have each played a role in determining the specialist's basic educational requirements. Especially through its relations with ACMC, the College has both responded to the needs of this continuum and impressed its own educational standards and requirements of training on it.

Still other relations have been fruitful in different ways. The College's relations with CSCI, for example, have been valuable because useful and harmonious discussions have enabled both parties to reach agreement on topics of narrower but common interest — the timing and nature of the annual meeting and the funding of medical research are two examples. At the same time, each organization benefitted immeasurably: CSCI, by sharing a forum such as the annual meeting, and the College, by keeping the nation's foremost clinical researchers close to its orbit.

In a different category are those relations that have reflected the need to acquire information from special interest groups. With the Canadian Association of Professors of Medicine, discussion of the value of In-Training Evaluation Report (ITER) and of the Certificate of Special Competence stimulated the College to broaden its approach to decisions and to proceed with its implementation of change. With the Association of Canadian University Departments of Anaesthesia, exploration of new avenues of educational liaison contributed to the College's work in training and examination. And the College's relations with the Canadian Association of Internes and Residents (CAIR), which originated in the liberalization and democratization that shaped the College in the 1970s, was useful in requiring the College to react to the views of the vigorous group, some of whose members would, in fact, eventually become Fellows.

Still other relations have been fruitful in a more formal manner, as befits the College's relations with sister colleges and organizations such as the American Board of Medical Specialties. These relations have enabled the College both to compare its own role and objectives with those of other organizations and to make known its individual nature and activities to them, especially in other countries.

The Canadian Medical Association

The College's relationship with the CMA is unique in that the Act of Incorporation was originally presented to the Governor General of Canada by means of a petition from the CMA. The CMA was also instrumental in initiating the College's Certification program in the 1930s. The College's relations with the CMA have been almost filial, and it was therefore appropriate that the College be regularly represented, as an affiliate, at some of the CMA's meetings, particularly those of General Council and those between the CMA and its affiliates. The College's President is always a member of the platform party at the CMA's annual ceremonial formalities and the CMA's president fulfils a similar role during the Royal College Convocation. This formal filial relation has also included the giving of gifts to the CMA: the College presented a sterling silver cigar box on the occasion of the CMA's centenary in 1967 and donated $5,000 to the CMA in 1969 towards furnishing and decorating the new headquarters building.

The College's relations with the CMA have benefitted the College in several distinct ways. First, the CMA's system of identifying and approving internships facilitated the College's ensuring that specialist candidates take an approved internship before starting a residency. This long-standing model of identifying and approving internships was the stimulus to the College in identifying and approving residencies for its own system of developing requirements for training. An early statement from the CMA's Committee on Approval of Hospitals for Internships provided a stimulus to the College in this respect. The report of this committee for June 1946 suggested that "serious consideration should now be given to the listing of those residencies and specialties which could be recognized for the Royal College Certification." The CMA's Executive Committee, noting that there were no approved centres for postgraduate training, then directed the CMA's Secretary-General, Dr. A.D. Kelly, to ask the College "as to its future plans in this connection." One year later, the College inaugurated its hospital approval program.[2]

A second benefit of the College's relations with the CMA was the co-sponsoring of the *Canadian Journal of Surgery* with the CMA. Publication of the journal was started in 1957 by the CMA, and in 1973 the CMA and the editors of the journal invited the College to share in its publication. The College agreed, and a three-year trial of co-sponsorship turned into a successful permanent partnership that has benefitted the continuing education needs of both organizations.

The third way in which the College has benefitted from its relations with the CMA is a less tangible yet perhaps more significant one than the other two. This stems from the College's collaboration with the CMA in developing a code of ethics. The CMA's Code of Ethics was adopted by the College on its founding, though later the College developed its own code. In 1953 a joint CMA-Royal College committee was struck to formulate a code that would be appropriate for both organizations, and since 1956 the two organizations' codes have been similar. The CMA revised the code in 1970, when it published its "Code of Ethics and Guide to the Ethical Behavior of Physicians of the Canadian Medical Association." This code was adopted by the College, which recognizes that the CMA should delineate the standard of ethical behavior expected of all Canadian physicians.

The College's relations with the CMA have been fruitful and constructive, not just for the two organizations themselves, but also for the medical profession as a whole. The desire of the CMA, as stated in 1957, to counter "the forces of disunity" by establishing liaison with the College "in the interests of the profession as a whole"[3] was welcomed by the College, which had, through its own policies and activities, long been concerned with the pursuit of unity itself.

The College of Family Physicians of Canada

Like its relations with the CMA, the College's relations with the CFPC have provided an avenue through which organizations such as these two might seek greater unity in the medical profession, better public relations and ultimately, better medical care. A need for unity was felt, particularly by the CFPC (then the College of General Practice of Canada), which was concerned in 1960 that "areas of differences between specialists and general practitioners... may be working for disunity in the medical profession."[4]

The relationship between the Royal College and the CFPC might have taken any of a number of forms. That it took the form of a correct and formal relationship may perhaps be attributed to various factors, in terms both of the personalities and of the values and norms of each group, but it is clear that each college wished primarily to follow its own path — rather than to join together from the start of the relationship. Unity was thought to be desirable for the profession as a whole rather than a desirable goal in terms of the two colleges' combining together to form one college.

A professional relationship between the two groups of physicians appears to have originated in 1952, two years before the CFPC, as an autonomous organization, was founded. Dr. M.R. Stalker, chairman of the section of general practice of the CMA, wrote to Dr. J.E. Plunkett, then Honorary Secretary of the Royal College, to request the Royal College's advice and assistance. Dr. Stalker explained that the chief objective of the CMA's section of general practice was to raise the standards of general medical practice and that the section sought to accredit competent practitioners who voluntarily might wish to work towards that goal. Dr. Stalker added that the Royal College's success as a certifying body led his colleagues to ask for the help and advice of the Royal College as to how best to proceed.[5] The Royal College formed a committee of Drs. G.G. Miller, E. Dubé and E.S. Mills for this purpose, and these Fellows met with Drs. C.L. Gass, J.R. Lemieux, E.C. McCoy and M.R. Stalker of the CFPC, on January 20, 1953. Neither group evidently looked for a particularly close relationship. With respect to the general practitioners, it was reported that "although they are prepared to proceed with their objectives at once, and *alone if necessary*, they would prefer to have *a loose affiliation* with either the CMA, The Royal College of Physicians and Surgeons, or both." [italics added][6] The Royal College's view was reflected in a letter Dr. Plunkett wrote to Dr. Miller at the end of 1952. Dr. Plunkett emphasized that while "the views of the CMA committee should be accorded a sympathetic reception and the experience of the College put at their disposal... the feeling [in Council] was that this College does not plan to Certificate general practitioners *either now or in the future* [italics added]."[7] That is history. One is left to speculate on the possibility of a different outcome had the Royal College and the section of general practice been closer to each other's views. If, instead, unity had been pursued more vigorously in this instance, the general practitioners might have been able to form a third division of the College, as happened for a time in South Africa.

A meeting to discuss matters of mutual interest, held on November 12, 1960,[8] marked the beginning of a more formal relationship between the two organizations. In addition to representatives of the Royal College (Drs. D.A. Thompson, J.W. Scott and G.M. Brown) and of the CFPC (Drs. F.M. Fraser, I.W. Bean, E.C. McCoy and W.V. Johnston), representatives of the CMA (Drs. E.K. Lyon and A.D. Kelly) were present. Dr. Fraser stressed the importance of unity in the profession but mentioned that some differences did exist, and expressed the hope that some form of permanent liaison might be set up at some time in the future.

The two colleges did continue to work together on the further development of plans for Certification of family practitioners. By the mid-1960s, the CFPC had established two pilot projects in advanced postgraduate training in family practice, one in Calgary and one in London; Queen's University also had been working for several years towards the development of a postgraduate residency training program for family practitioners. It was, therefore, appropriate for the Royal College, universities interested in developing this field of medical education at the postgraduate or residency level and the CFPC to study postgraduate education for family practitioners. The CFPC therefore called a meeting to discuss programs for training in family practice leading to Certification. This meeting was held on November 10, 1966, and it furthered liaison between the CFPC and the Royal College. Following this meeting, Dr. D.I. Rice, Executive Director of the CFPC, set down five specific points for consideration by the current Council of the Royal College and, preferably, by a liaison committee of the two colleges. These five points related to the following objectives:

- Acknowledgement by the Royal College of the continuing need for the general practitioner-family physician in the provision of quality medical care, and, to ensure the position of the family physician of the future, of the need to develop specific training programs of family practice at the postgraduate level of medical education.
- Endorsation by the Royal College of the principle that the CFPC had the major responsibility in the development of advanced training for family practice.
- Since programs of training in family practice would include training in some special disciplines such as medicine and pediatrics, establishment of a mechanism whereby an appropriate curriculum might be developed conjointly by the CFPC and the Royal College.
- Development of a program assessment and certification procedure for programs of advanced training in family practice with the assistance of representatives from the Royal College and representatives of university medical faculties.
- Acknowledgement by the Royal College that the CFPC be the recognized authority for the setting of standards and the granting of Certification in advanced training for family practice.

The Executive Committee, at its meeting in January 1967, considered this matter "worthy of exploration." Council subsequently appointed representatives to a liaison committee to act with the representatives of the CFPC to consider further the five points, and in due course the CFPC introduced its Certification in 1969.

A second educational project on which the Royal College worked with the CFPC concerned the recognition of emergency medicine as a specialty and the appropriate qualifications for emergency room physicians. The efforts of the two organizations are more remarkable for the development of a conjoint and innovative approach to Certification in a specialty than for the fact that, eventually, the project failed as each college went its own way. In this instance, the Royal College's grip on unity was insufficiently strong for its pursuit of unity to be completely successful.

Discussions on these topics were given impetus by a joint meeting, on January 16, 1976, of the Royal College's Emergency Medical Care Committee and the CFPC's Committee on the Emergency Care Physician. The joint meeting agreed to recommend to both colleges that a joint training committee on the emergency care physician be established. This recommendation was made in light of agreement on other points: (i) there was a need for doctors to be fully trained in emergency medicine and to work full-time in the emergency departments of some hospitals; (ii) the physicians who received adequate training in emergency room medicine would remain in this career in the same way that other physicians and surgeons continue to practise their specialties; (iii) in the CFPC's view, most of the work of emergency care consists of primary care and is therefore the responsibility of the family physician, even though in some areas hospitals would require, and physicians would prefer, to have the emergency department staffed by full-time and formally trained emergency room physicians and therefore such physicians should be trained forthwith; and (iv) the training proposed by the CFPC would include 18 months of residency training in family medicine followed by 18 months training in emergency medicine. The joint training committee would need to establish educational requirements and standards, approve training programs, assess the performance of emergency care physicians and grant appropriate recognition of qualified physicians.

The question of recognition of emergency medical care as a specialty had been discussed by the Royal College's Specialty Development and Manpower Committee on and off since 1972. A problem for the Royal College was how to grant recognition on the basis of the CFPC's training program, which was shorter than the College's specialist training programs. One possibility was to grant recognition by a diploma rather than the usual Certification leading to Fellowship in the College.

The joint training committee met on January 17, 1977, and presented a preliminary report to Council the following week. The proposed educational requirements meant that those entering the field from family practice would require a total of only three years of training while those proceeding from one of the specialties would need a minimum of four or even five years of training. For Dr. R.W. Gunton, chairman of the Specialty Development Committee, this requirement might imply the existence of a double standard. Council, however, approved the report of the Emergency Medical Care Committee, which presented these requirements, as further discussions were anticipated.

The joint training committee developed its definitive report in the form of a proposal dated April 15, 1977.[9] The comprehensive proposal comprised four parts — the educational requirements and standards, the approval of training programs, the examination procedure and a jointly issued Certificate of Special Competence.

Given the delicacy and the complexity of the objection that had been raised concerning the length of training, the proposal was a skilled display of compromise in the interest of unity. The section dealing with eligibility to sit the examination reflected this. Eligibility would be determined according to two categories of candidate — the "resident-eligible" and the "practice-eligible." The resident-eligible candidate would be required to have obtained an appropriate Certificate of the Royal College or the CFPC, spent a minimum of three years in postgraduate training, completed two years of identifiable training in emergency medicine within the total period of the candidate's postgraduate training and spent six months of the third year or subsequent years of training as an identified chief or senior resident in an emergency medicine residency program. The practice-eligible candidate would be required to have obtained the Certificate of the Royal College or the CFPC, spent the majority of time in the delivery of emergency medicine (in service, teaching or administration) with a minimum of three years immediately prior to the evaluation, obtained the basic medical degree at least five years previously and shown evidence of continuing medical education appropriate to emergency medicine.

The innovative aspect of this proposal was the conjoint nature of the qualification: the Certificate of Special Competence in Emergency Medicine would be granted conjointly by both colleges. (The Certificate, however, "would not bestow the privileges of either college beyond those inherent in the primary Certification.") In this respect, a precedent in specialty recognition seemed forthcoming. It was one that, as Dr. Rice said, might well form a model for similar collaboration in other areas, including perhaps geriatric medicine. This possibility, however, was of some concern to the Royal College in view of the possibility of the awarding of multiple Certificates of Special Competence in the same fields and the confusion that would result therefrom. The proposal, however, was accepted by Council in June 1977 and it appeared that a new chapter in specialty recognition had been completed.

The outcome of these protracted discussions — they had been conducted since 1973 in one form or another — was, however, not what might have been expected following Council's approval of a conjoint Certificate of Special Competence. For a while, all seemed well, and the joint specialty committee that was struck subsequently to fulfil the recommendations of the conjoint proposals met several times from 1977 onwards. On October 2, 1979, the joint specialty committee actually recommended the formation of a Conjoint Board on Emergency Medicine, to be sponsored by the two colleges. But, shortly after this, pressure grew for a primary qualification, as opposed to a conjoint

Certificate of Special Competence in Emergency Medicine. Pressure was exerted partly as a result of a telegram that nine concerned Fellows had sent to members of Council. These Fellows urged the Royal College to take a leadership role in the development of emergency medicine and encourage some form of primary qualification.

This view came to be held also by the Royal College's Emergency Medical Care Committee, which in January 1980 recommended a primary specialist qualification in this field. The committee made five recommendations: (i) that the College recognize emergency medicine as a primary specialty; (ii) that the primary specialty of emergency medicine be established within the Division of Medicine; (iii) that the Specialty Committee in Emergency Medicine be representative of the specialties concerned in the training of emergency physicians; (iv) that the specialty of emergency medicine consider for its training curriculum not less than three or more than four years of training following graduation from medical school; (v) that an observer from the CFPC be invited to participate in the Specialty Committee in Emergency Medicine.

The CFPC also concluded that the conjoint approach would not in fact serve its membership. Because so many family physicians worked in emergency departments, and because up to 85 per cent of the work done in emergency departments was "episodic first-contact care," the family physicians wished to develop a combined qualification in family medicine and emergency medicine. They proposed that departments of family medicine offer residency training in emergency medicine consisting of one- to two-year training programs added to or integrated with the existing two-year program in family medicine.

These developments constituted a reversal of the position that had been held jointly by the two colleges in 1977. The question now was whether some kind of dual standard was acceptable. On this, Council, which discussed the question in June 1980, was divided. There were two issues. The first was whether there was room for both types of emergency physicians; there was some basis for the view that the family physician worked mostly in small hospitals while the Royal College-qualified specialists would work mostly in major hospitals with a trauma unit. The second issue related to the justification of a new free-standing specialty: if there were good reasons for establishing a specialty and a Royal College Certification, one should vote for specialty recognition; otherwise, one should vote against it. Ultimately, the vote on the motion to accept the five recommendations was carried, and in 1980 the College created its own specialty of emergency medicine.

Although the College's relations with the CFPC were not always mutually productive in terms of specific projects, the two colleges recognized the importance of continued collaboration. Liaison was maintained through periodic meetings and by representation, at Council and Board level and, since 1976, each college has been reciprocally represented at the other's policy-making level. Similarly, the CFPC has been represented as an observer on the advisory board of the R.S. McLaughlin Examination and Research Centre, at the College's annual meetings, at various conferences and on several College committees, notably those concerned with training and evaluation. The basis for such mutual representation was laid in December 1977, when the two colleges' chief executive officers, Drs. J.H. Graham and D.I. Rice, drew up a memorandum on liaison between the two organizations. The principal proposals that were agreed on at that time and that were accepted by the Royal College's Executive Committee were the following:

- Senior officers of each college should attend at least one of the semi-annual Council or Board meetings of the sister college, the appropriate meeting being determined by the agenda items.
- Joint meetings of the officers of the two colleges might be desirable on occasion.
- When thought to be mutually profitable, representation at the committee level would involve the three chief committees of the Royal College (Accreditation, Credentials and Examinations) and the Assessment and Evaluation and the Examinations Committees of the CFPC. The concept of regular exchange of representatives at committee meetings was not supported.
- From time to time, representation on other committees might be desirable — for example, the Royal College's Training and Evaluation Committee, the Specialty Development and Manpower Committee and one or more of the educational committees, and the CFPC's Educational Process Committee. Representation at special or ad hoc committees might also be desirable; the joint training committee on Emergency Care Physicians was an example of such a committee.
- Representation from the CFPC at meetings of the Board of Governors* of the R.S. McLaughlin Centre, which was initiated in 1973, should be continued.
- A potential source of consultative assistance to the CFPC might be one of the Royal College's specialty committees, particularly those in internal medicine, general surgery, pediatrics, psychiatry and obstetrics and gynecology.
- The two colleges might wish to act jointly, perhaps with other organizations as well, in making representation on important issues to a third party such as government.
- Liaison mechanisms would be regularly evaluated in order to develop the most productive systems.[10]

---

*At this time, the Advisory Board was known as the Board of Governors (see Chapter 10).

While the Royal College and the CFPC differ in their own objectives, the proposals that they agreed on in December 1977 did testify to a continuing desire for unity within the medical profession.

The Medical Council of Canada

Like the College, the MCC is an examining body that grants a qualification that is accepted by all licensing authorities in Canada. The MCC's licentiateship is the basic form of medical licence in Canada, just as the College's Certification is the basic form of specialty qualification. The College's relationship with the MCC is evident within the College in three different ways.

One way in which the College's relationship with the MCC is daily made manifest takes the form of the College's Sir Thomas Roddick Memorial Room. An attractive room that houses the College's archives and library, the Roddick Room was decorated and furnished by means of a grant of $15,000 that the MCC graciously donated to the College to serve as a memorial to the MCC's founder. Apart from honoring Sir Thomas, the purpose of the Roddick Room, as far as the MCC is concerned, is to be able to deposit archives there and, if desired, to permit it to hold its meetings in the College building.

The College's relationship with the MCC is also apparent in the latter's occupying three seats on the advisory board of the R.S. McLaughlin Examination and Research Centre. As the McLaughlin Centre's expertise in examination methods developed in the 1970s, the MCC, as the College's client, began to use the McLaughlin Centre for the production of its examinations. But the MCC wished to be more than a client, and its financial and participatory interests in the McLaughlin Centre were recognized by the College's granting the MCC representation on the McLaughlin Centre's advisory board.

The College's relationship with the MCC has also grown close since the MCC regularly invited the College to its annual meetings — the third way in which the relationship is evident.

Provincial Medical Colleges and Licensing Authorities

Since health care in Canada comes under provincial jurisdiction, the responsibility for recognizing physicians as specialists and permitting them to practise as specialists in particular provinces is that of the provincial medical authorities. The College's relations with the provincial medical colleges and licensing authorities are therefore based on a respect of provincial autonomy and, at the same time, on a desire to integrate with provincial jurisdictions the College's concerns about specialist qualifications. In part, the College's relations with the provinces have been developed through its membership in the Federation of Provincial Medical Licensing Authorities of Canada, which was founded in 1968. In part, however, the College's relations with the provinces have been shaped through the need to explore and to collaborate with them on specific

Council 1960-62

Front (R. to L.) W.K. Welsh, J.H. Graham, K.T. MacFarlane, C.E. Hébert,
President D.A. Thompson, J.W. Scott, L.G. Bell, W.G. Beattie
Mid (R. to L.) D.G. Cameron, R.B. Kerr, L.C. Steeves, G.A. Bergeron,
G.M. Brown, P.E. Ireland, G. Hooper, J.G. Dewan,
W.C. MacKenzie
Rear (R. to L.) A.L. Chute, C.E. Corrigan, E.F. Ross, D.R. Wilson, R.V. Christie,
D.R. Webster, R.C. Dickson, C.H. Crosby, J.W. MacLeod

Dedication of the Roddick Memorial Room, College Building, September 10, 1962

Front (L. to R.) G.M. Brown, President RCPSC, and G.A. Bergeron, President MCC
Rear (L. to R.) C. Macpherson, D.S. Lewis, G. Hooper, C.J. Houston, R.G. Lea,
J.H. Graham, W.G. Beattie

issues affecting specialist practice. Particularly noteworthy issues have been the need for temporary Certification (with CPSO) and the simultaneous Certification of specialists in Quebec (with CPMQ). The College's relations with CPSO and CPMQ are therefore emphasized here. They provide further examples of the pursuit of unity.

The Ontario Stimulus: The Temporary Certification Program

An entirely new twist to College responsibilities in specialist qualifications developed in the summer of 1966. The minutes of the Executive Committee for June 1966 refer to possible problems following the hiring of faculty members by new and expanding medical schools in Canada. Many of these specialists came from outside Canada, and there was no reciprocal basis for the granting of Certification without examination. The problem was most acute in Ontario. It was compounded by the introduction of the Ontario Medical Services Insurance Plan (later, the Ontario Health Insurance Plan), which stimulated additional applications for Certification without examination from those working in special fields but who did not have Royal College qualifications.

These concerns, which were considered by the Executive Committee in June and September 1966, led to the creation of the College's program of temporary Certification. It was a solution to a problem that was uniquely Canadian. Dr. W.C. MacKenzie explained the need for the program in the following terms: "Because of the rapid expansion in medical educational facilities in Canada, the country is at a crossroads; there are not enough highly qualified Canadians to fill the academic posts and a considerable number of 'imports' would be required." Dr. MacKenzie referred to an 'acting while holding' type of certification in Alberta and Dr. E.D. Gagnon stated that the CPMQ provided a temporary certificate while a physician was holding an academic post.

It was then agreed to recommend to Council that the Council consider "a mechanism for granting Certification without examination on a temporary basis to highly qualified individuals heading academic departments in Canada." Each case of this type would be considered by the Executive Committee on an individual basis, the final decision authorizing such temporary Certification resting with the Council. The certificate would be valid only during the individual's tenure of office as a departmental head.

Although the discussion had arisen because of the need to consider the problem of a single individual in Toronto, the Executive Committee thought it wise to frame the resolution in general terms. The committee advised that any recommendation for a temporary form of Certification should be limited, initially at least, to heads of departments.

At the September 1966 meeting the Executive Committee considered a letter on this problem from CPSO.[11] Dr. J.C.C. Dawson, the CPSO Registrar, wrote to Dr. J.H. Graham on August 24, 1966, to report that the Ontario deans were disturbed that the current regulations of the CPSO, which recognized only those specialists certificated by the Royal College, would impede the recruiting of staff for new or expanding faculties of medicine. The deans had requested the CPSO to recognize the foreign specialty qualifications of individuals receiving faculty appointments. The CPSO's Education and Registration Committee did not favor this suggestion because of the CPSO's policy of recognizing only the Royal College's qualifications, but it supported the deans' second request, that the Royal College reconsider its policy on the recognition of foreign specialty qualifications. The Ontario committee concluded that "it would be a proper function of the Royal College to make provision to grant its Certification without examination to holders of specialty qualifications from abroad which the Royal College considered to be equivalent in all respects to its own Certification." The committee drew up recommendations for the Council of the CPSO to consider in November 1966, but requested that the Royal College be advised of this immediately. The committee would request the Royal College to offer *ad eundem gradum* specialty Certification or Fellowship to graduates from abroad with training and qualifications equivalent to Canadian standards.

The College was faced with a new imperative. The Executive Committee, before taking its recommendation to Council, wished to be sure of its ground for, as Dr. Graham reminded Council in January 1967, the granting of Certification (or Fellowship) without examination was one of the "touchiest problems" the College faced. One of the first questions to be answered was the legality of granting temporary Certification. Mr. C.F. Scott, QC, (the College solicitor) reviewed the minutes of Council meetings as far back as 1935 with respect to the granting of Certification without examination, but could find no legal obstacle to the College's proposed solution, as long as the applicant possessed a specialist qualification obtained by examination from another acceptable qualifying body. The matter could now be discussed by Council.

Dr. W.C. MacKenzie explained why the program should be developed. One reason related to the consequences that would result should individual provincial colleges begin to recognize the various specialty qualifications of other countries. Acceptable, though, for example, the American Board Diploma or the English Fellowship or Membership might be, recognition by Canadian provincial colleges of qualifications other than those of the Royal College would eventually have a marked effect on the Certification of the Royal College. The pursuit of unity — or the prevention of disunity — again influenced the College's decision-making process. Dr. Graham stressed the Executive Committee's wish to proceed cautiously and to grant temporary Certification to heads of academic departments in the first instance, even though eventually Certification might be granted to members of departments. Dr. Graham added that, because there could be no assurance that the individuals thus certificated would remain in their posts, the granting of permanent Certification might create a situation that would be considered unfair and lead to abuse.

Two other principal reasons lay behind the introduction of the temporary Certification program. One was the requirement of many hospitals that applicants for staff positions should be certificated. The other reason was the need for a specialist to be certificated in order to receive remuneration consistent with specialists' services.

The temporary Certification program was indeed a touchy problem, and discussions on it engendered strong feelings. The motion that the Executive Committee submitted to Council was therefore conservative as well as being all-embracing. The motion was worded in careful terms as follows:

> *That* the Council consider a mechanism for granting Certification without examination on a temporary basis to highly qualified individuals heading academic departments in Canada, each case of this type to be considered by the Executive Committee on an individual basis with the final decision authorizing any such temporary Certification resting with the Council, and the certificate to be valid only during the individual's tenure of office as a department head.

The Executive Committee's arguments were convincing and the motion was duly carried. The program could now be implemented.

By the summer of 1967, however, it became apparent that the resolution that had been approved in January was too restrictive a definition of eligibility to permit the objectives of the program to be achieved. It was therefore agreed that temporary Certification without examination could be extended to heads of divisions of university departments and to heads of services in major university teaching hospitals. It was also agreed that each applicant should obtain a supporting letter from the dean of the faculty and that the temporary Certification program would not be extended to Canadian physicians.

At this June 1967 meeting, Council also approved the granting of the first temporary Certificates to six department heads. These physicians were the following: Drs. C.B. Mueller and W.P. Cockshott, of McMaster University; Drs. W.R. Drucker and L.E. Morris, of the University of Toronto; Dr. J. Parkhouse, of the University of Manitoba; and Dr. J.W.R. Redford, of the University of Alberta. They were the first six of 303 physicians and surgeons who, by June 1982, were granted temporary Certification. Their contributions to Canadian medicine were invaluable. Dr. J.H. Darragh assessed the value of their contributions in these words:

> *In* the medical schools, there are many professors and chairmen of departments [who hold temporary Certification]. In the College, temporary Certificants have been chairmen and members of examining boards, chairmen and members of specialty committees and surveyors. In addition, temporary Certificants have made enormous contributions to educational programs sponsored by the College and other aspects of the work of the College. [12]

The temporary Certification program, which was administered on behalf of Council by the Executive Committee, did meet a particular need and was judged successful, particularly in its first five years, but modifications of the program became necessary from time to time. Three such modifications were introducing a time limit and extending the program to more junior full-time faculty members in 1969 and, in 1972, permitting temporary Certificants without time limit to apply for Fellowship.

Aside from the benefit that the temporary Certification program gave to the College's relationship with CPSO, this relationship was constructive in another way. It demonstrated the importance of the College's maintaining relations with other organizations and understanding other points of view, for only in that way could the College test the validity of its own position and policies. An example of this aspect of the College's relationship with a provincial college is afforded by a meeting between the College and CPSO on March 31, 1965, which was discussed by the Executive Committee in May 1965. The issue was professional incompetence among Royal College specialists.

This meeting with Ontario representatives (Drs. E.R.S. Wyatt, D.L. Wilson, R.I. MacDonald, J.W.R. Webster, A.R. Turnbull, J.C.C. Dawson and J.W. Kucherepa and Mr. W.H. Noble, QC) was held primarily to discuss action that might be taken by both colleges in relation to professional incompetence in those possessing Royal College specialist qualifications. (The College was represented by Drs. W.C. MacKenzie, K.J.R. Wightman and J.H. Graham and Mr. C.F. Scott, QC.) To maintain a register of specialists in Ontario, the CPSO used the Royal College's specialist certificate as the basic criterion. In the previous two years, the CPSO had been faced with the need to consider whether six specialists had demonstrated professional incompetence. But, under the current regulations of the CPSO, if the specialist certificate from the Royal College remained in good standing the CPSO could not remove the holder from the list of registered specialists of the province, even though professional incompetence seemingly had been demonstrated. Therefore the CPSO had been drafting amendments to their regulations that would provide for revocation of specialty standing in Ontario if this appeared indicated.

Dr. MacKenzie indicated how the College stood with respect to professional incompetence. Originally, the British position had been followed: the College was considered analogous to a university and the "degree" simply attested to the fact that the holder of the degree had satisfied the requirements of training and had passed an examination. In general, this had proved acceptable for, until 1964, some 11,500 physicians had been granted specialist status by the Royal College and, remarkably, the secretariat could recall only one disciplinary problem that had been handled by Council. But since early 1964, Dr. MacKenzie added, Council had changed its attitude regarding responsibility relating to professional misconduct, and during that time Council had imposed disciplinary measures on seven individuals. Close relationships with the provinces were important because, in most instances, the College was dependent on facts supplied by a provincial licensing body as a basis for action (and, in turn, the College kept the provincial organizations informed of its actions).

The problem of incompetence was not easy to deal with, either for the Royal College or for a provincial college. It was doubtful from a legal standpoint that the Royal College had the right to reexamine a Fellow or Certificant to determine his or her present degree of competence and, as a voluntary body incorporated by a federal Act, the College did not have judicial powers allowing it to conduct true judicial inquiries for which it could subpoena individuals for testimony. The College needed to rely on voluntary testimony and on information provided by institutions, such as the Ontario College, that were empowered to conduct judicial inquiries. Partly for this reason, the bylaws were amended in January 1965 so that any certificated specialist who had been censured or was suspended by a local provincial licensing body because of "professional incompetence, negligence or malpractice" would then "be liable to censure or suspension or removal from the register of certificated specialists. . . ."

This discussion between the Royal College and the CPSO further demonstrated the importance and value of the College's fostering and strengthening its relationship with other medical organizations. Only in this way could the College preserve its credibility in matters that did not lie strictly within its area of responsibility. Legally, the College was empowered through its Act of Incorporation only "to provide for and hold special examinations for physicians and surgeons in Canada" and to "grant special Certificates to persons who shall have shown such degree of proficiency in such examinations as the Council may consider entitles them to special Certificates." Much of the College's influence has always been exerted through the respect that accrues to it through expertise in the field of postgraduate medical education and through the power of moral suasion that it can call on when appropriate. Only through its relationships with other organizations could the College create, to quote Dr. G.A. Bergeron, "an exceptional forum."[13]

The Quebec Stimulus: The Simultaneous Certification Program

For a long time, the College's relations with the CPMQ, though special in the College's pursuit of unity, were based largely on formal exchanges of courtesies and ideas. During the meeting of the Executive Committee in February 1964, Dr. J. Turcot, of Quebec City, said that he had often been asked why the Royal College and the CPMQ should not meet occasionally to discuss matters of mutual interest, such as listings of approved hospitals and residency programs in these hospitals. To emphasize the importance of fostering the College's relationship with the CPMQ, Dr. Turcot suggested that attendance of Quebec physicians at the Kingston conference on residency education in the clinical specialties, scheduled to be held in October 1965, would benefit both the Royal College and Quebec physicians. This was a valuable suggestion, and thereafter the College's relations with the CPMQ became increasingly important and mutually beneficial.

One of the most useful results of collaboration between the two organizations was the development of Certification examinations planned and conducted simultaneously. This collaboration was joined towards the end of 1965. President W.C. MacKenzie received two letters that initiated both this project and a continuing liaison with the CPMQ. The first letter, written on November 15, 1965, was from Dr. N.J. Belliveau, president of the Quebec Medical Association. He reminded Dr. MacKenzie that he had recently brought up the question of Certification for physicians from the province of Quebec and the duplication of effort on the parts of the candidates, who thus had to write two separate sets of examinations.[14] Dr. Belliveau informed Dr. MacKenzie that the Quebec Medical Association's Education Committee had recently initiated studies on this. The committee had concluded that duplication should be abolished and that one set of examinations for Certification should be acceptable to both Colleges. The idea was accepted in principle, and Dr. Belliveau added that the road was now open and that the details and methods of implementation would be a matter for further discussion. Because Dr. D.G. Cameron was chairman of the Quebec committee and because Dr. J. Turcot was a member of the committee, the Royal College, through these senior Fellows, was well aware of Quebec views from the beginning of the discussions on simultaneous Certification examinations.

The second letter, dated December 22, 1965, was from Dr. R. Dufresne, director of professional relations for the CPMQ. Dr. Dufresne recalled for Dr. MacKenzie that they had met together during the previous September concerning a future discussion of common problems with representatives of the Royal College and that this information had been well received by Dr. Dufresne's colleagues.[15] Dr. Dufresne now wrote to arrange a meeting that would enable them to exchange views in an informal way.

Representatives of the College and the CPMQ met on June 7, 1966.[16] The Royal College was represented by President R.B. Kerr and Drs. R.V. Christie, E.D. Gagnon and J.H. Graham; the CPMQ, by Drs. G.A. Lachaine, R. Dufresne, H. Gagnon, V. Goldbloom and A. Roy. It was agreed that there had been little contact in the past between the two bodies and that the two should try to work together in the best interests of the medical profession. Talks of this nature would lead to closer cooperation between the two organizations. The meeting also clarified activities in common and those that differed.

Training requirements were of interest to both organizations. The CPMQ currently approved 29 specialties and the Royal College, 21 — though with recognition by the latter of additional specialties in principle, the difference was not as great as it seemed; moreover, the training requirements were the same in

11 specialties and differed little in another eight. Even so, differences in outlook and organization appeared to give a sense of liberalism to the CPMQ and of conservatism to the College. Dr. Christie attributed the conservatism of the College partly to its wish to ensure that specialists in a medical specialty, for example, would have a grounding in internal medicine, while Dr. E.D. Gagnon feared stereotyping with that type of training and urged more variety. The Royal College's manner of operation tended to be "ponderous" since the Credentials Committee, the Examinations Committee, one or more of the specialty committees, the Executive Committee and Council all might have to advise before a decision could be made on a difficult problem. The CPMQ's operation was leaner: its Credentials Committee comprised the executive and three deans and it contained no specialty committees. But a problem for the CPMQ lay in the fact that the specialty groups in Quebec were separately constituted bodies looking after the interests of their individual specialties, which tended to support the opposition of some specialties to the CPMQ's training requirements; the psychiatrists, for example, had "worn down" the CPMQ regarding the requirement for an obligatory period of training in internal medicine. And the CPMQ had to bear in mind its responsibility to the public regarding licensure as set down in the Quebec Medical Act.

Apart from these differences, the two organizations shared the same concerns regarding residents who took irregular and uncoordinated training, especially those who satisfied training requirements by taking four uncoordinated years of residency training posts that were each approved only for one year. The CPMQ, like the College, was trying to encourage the development of organized plans of training.

Differences in the two systems for approval of hospitals were then considered. For each organization, the quality of training in the hospitals was important, the basic concern being the need to avoid subjecting the public to professional work from inadequately trained physicians. Because the two lists of approved hospitals were not identical, it was important to know why certain fields of training might not be approved by the College or the CPMQ and to learn the positive reasons for approval of those accepted fields. The differences might be attributed in part to more recent knowledge on the part of one of the organizations on a particular area of training. In fact, it was agreed that their standards did not really differ, which was as it should be for, as Dr. Goldbloom put it, "there should really be no difference at all since there should only be one quality."

The third topic that was discussed at this meeting in June 1966 concerned examinations. Again, it was recognized that certain differences might be more apparent than real. Many of the examiners were members of each other organization's examining boards; many of the candidates in Quebec tried both organizations' examinations. The total of such candidates in 1966 amounted to 365; a supplemental oral examination in the spring was available for candidates taking the examinations of both organizations; and, while the essay type of examination was the standard one in each body, there had been much questioning of the value of essay-type papers. The College had introduced a multiple-choice type of paper in internal medicine in 1965; and the CPMQ examiners were aware that the multi-choice technique was being used in examinations of five of the undergraduate subjects at McGill University and that the technique was making great strides in medical schools in France.

With respect to the possibility of the two organizations' holding simultaneous Certification examinations, which was the underlying reason for this initial meeting and which would be the basis for further meetings in the 1960s and 1970s, both the rationale and the prospects therefore looked good. As the June 1966 meeting adjourned, it was agreed that further meetings of the two colleges should be held and that the CPMQ might send observers to meetings of the Royal College's Credentials Committee, Hospitals Approval Committee and Examinations Committee.

Efforts to lay a basis of agreement were extended at a further meeting of high-level representatives on December 4, 1967. CPMQ was represented by Drs. G. Gingras, J. Mathieu, F. Hould, R. Gingras, G. LaSalle, P. Latour, A. Roy; the Royal College, by Drs. R.B. Kerr, E.D. Gagnon, D.R. Wilson, F.G. Kergin, F.J. Tweedie and J.H. Graham. This meeting revealed ways in which the CPMQ's thinking had advanced ahead of the Royal College's, raised the problem of attaining equivalent status for the two Certificates and reached agreement that a liaison committee should be formally established.

Two aspects of a change in policy in Quebec were of particular interest to the Royal College. One concerned the imminent implementation of the proposal that the medical schools take charge of the postgraduate training of physicians and of standards that would be presented by the CPMQ. This proposal reflected the wishes of Quebec governmental authorities, the influence of whom facilitated the rapid implementation of various policies in Quebec. The second aspect of a policy change was the proposal that the junior internship year, as previously conducted, would be dropped in the case of postgraduate training in specialties since the current final-year clinical clerkship appeared to provide the same experience as currently conducted in the junior internship. The significance of this change was clear: this plan would raise the question of whether the total training period could be reduced by one year to four years or whether it should be retained at five years. On this matter, consultation with the specialty groups in Quebec was "very active" at the time of the meeting.

Although both these proposals were of great interest to the College, its somewhat ponderous decision-making machinery and its national composition and wider responsibilities meant that it was not able to introduce changes as quickly as the CPMQ could. The College's position, which was influenced by these two factors, was expressed well by the President. Dr. Kerr pointed out that the College had urged the development of the university-directed programs for postgraduate training for many years — in fact, since 1950 — but it was still not compulsory that postgraduate training programs be under university direction. And with respect to the length of postgraduate training programs, in view of the changes of the internship year, the Royal College had not given much consideration so far to any change in duration of training.

The philosophical, pedagogic and political distance between the two organizations had practical meaning. Dr. Gagnon, of Montreal, an astute and acute observer of these matters, feared that if one of them should move too fast the difference between the examinations of the two organizations might be extended. Dr. Hould felt that the Royal College might lose a great deal in the province of Quebec if there were not a real effort to attain equivalence of the Certification qualifications and that this was linked to the sovereignty crisis in the province of Quebec. Such differences would compound those that already existed, particularly those that stemmed from the fact that the College examined for the Fellowship as well as for Certification and from the College's stated policy that the Certification examination would eventually be replaced by the Fellowship examination.

Each group had good reasons to find a path to unity in respect of Certification of specialists, and it was agreed that a formal liaison committee should be established. Each would nominate three representatives, to whom would be added the Registrar of the CPMQ and the Secretary of the College. The Royal College's representatives would be drawn from the Credentials, Hospitals Approval and Examinations Committees.

The basis for future meetings between the Royal College and CPMQ on the ultimate goal of simultaneous Certification was thus firmly laid during President Kerr's presidency. It was fortuitous that he would be succeeded as President by a Quebecer, Dr. J. Turcot; at the same time, particular concerns of President Turcot on the matter of "equivalence" of Certification would influence both the meetings between the CPMQ and the Royal College's own pursuit of unity concerning specialist qualifications, Fellowship in the College and, indeed, the nature of the College itself.

The next step, therefore, was taken during Dr. Turcot's presidency, and in 1969 it was agreed that, as a pilot project, a simultaneous Certification examination in internal medicine would be planned for the fall of 1970.[17] As far as examinations were concerned, this was a logical starting point because all of the written part of the Certification examination in internal medicine would be of the objective type in 1970.

The planning for simultaneous Certification was conducted at a meeting on March 18, 1970. It was decided to include two papers in the written examination, but a simultaneous oral examination proved too difficult to incorporate owing to the College's dual standard. The plan was implemented in the fall of 1970 and the way was open to extension of simultaneous examinations in other specialties.

Of practical concern was the fee structure. Three options were put forward: for both colleges to charge the full fees; for each to charge an identical fee; and for a conjoint fee to be shared, with the CPMQ contributing to the Royal College towards the cost of the multiple-choice written examination. It was, however, difficult to devise an appropriate fee schedule when candidates were taking the same written examination that was, though, administered by two different organizations.

One other point of concern was whether the CPMQ would accept the Royal College's decision regarding the comprehensive examination to be taken at the end of two years by residents in internal medicine. This, however, was readily agreed to by the CPMQ.

In the space of five years, therefore, the College and the CPMQ had cemented a close relationship that was based on practical issues of mutual interest and on mutual respect also. The relationship was sufficiently close to withstand the tensions that arose when broader issues, such as national unity, were broached. The relationship was close enough, too, to permit the two organizations to continue their liaison in 1977 by establishing reciprocal representation in order to both review issues of common interest, such as training, evaluation and accreditation, in addition to Certification, and improved communication between them. To facilitate communication, the CPMQ accepted the Royal College's invitation of observer representation on the Advisory Board of the R.S. McLaughlin Examination and Research Centre, and the Royal College likewise accepted the CPMQ's invitation of observer representation at meetings of its Comité des études médicales.

The Association of Canadian Medical Colleges

One of the most valuable of the College's relations has been its liaison with ACMC. Like the College's relations with the CMA and CFPC, the College's link with ACMC has provided a forum for discussion of numerous issues on postgraduate medical education. If the College's relations with the CMA have been filial and those with CFPC fraternal, the College's relations with ACMC have been friendly and based on the common interests of close professional colleagues. This is not surprising, for ACMC membership then, as now, comprised the deans of the Canadian medical schools, who were, for the most part, all Fellows of the College; and, even before the College was founded, the nucleus committee that was charged from 1927 to 1929 with the responsibility of developing the College was made up of senior medical academicians, three of whom were deans.

Although ACMC had been formed in 1943, and though the College's concern over university affiliation of hospitals providing postgraduate training had been discussed by ACMC during the 1950s, Dr. J.W. Scott, attending an ACMC council meeting in 1957, was surprised to find that some of the deans knew little about the training programs of the College and that some felt that they had no responsibility in this regard. One outcome of the College's response to this lack of knowledge was a resolution of Council in October 1957 that the College ask the deans to stimulate the creation of postgraduate training programs within their affiliated hospitals and to consider including in such programs those hospitals that were not affiliated but that had adequate training facilities. Another outcome was the resolution passed by Council in January 1959, which reiterated the need to discuss the question of postgraduate training and its relationship to the universities; Council offered to send representatives to attend ACMC's 1959 meeting in order to explain the College's viewpoint and to take part in the discussions.

ACMC's annual meeting in 1959, held on November 7, was an important one. Not only did ACMC favorably receive the College's brief encouraging the medical schools to take a greater responsibility in residency training and to increase the number of university-sponsored training programs — a brief that was instrumental in the meeting's passing a resolution to these effects — but also, as 1960 dawned, the College's relationship with ACMC was placed on firm ground. The College's emphasis on the importance of a national and unified approach to university-based residency programs had made itself felt. By 1962 (when ACMC inaugurated a full-time secretariat with the appointment as Executive Secretary of Dr. J.W. MacLeod, until then a councillor and chairman of the Hospitals Approval Committee), the College and ACMC had created a fruitful relationship that was mutually rewarding. The relationship became more and more useful as the two organizations later formalized representation at each other's principal meetings.

Although the College was usually represented at ACMC's annual meetings, the College for a long time was not represented on ACMC's Executive Council. ACMC had become less of a deans' club since a full-time executive director had been appointed, and one manifestation of its involvement in medical education was the work of its research division, led by Mr. D.G. Fish. ACMC now took a greater role in medical education and it was appropriate that the College join the CMA, CFPC and the Department of National Health and Welfare in having an observer on ACMC's Executive Council. The College's Secretary, Dr. J.H. Graham, was appointed to fill this position as from 1965.

ACMC's interest in medical education had by now extended to continuing medical education. This appeared to be logical, for universities employed medical educators, had ready access to a body of knowledge, understood the teaching and learning processes and could readily organize resources on behalf of education programs at different levels. Therefore ACMC resolved, at its annual meeting in October of 1964, to recommend to its member faculties that they accept continuing medical education as one of their primary functions and that they assume a leadership role in association with other interested bodies by using teaching facilities for continuing medical education to maximum advantage. [18]

Representation of the College on ACMC's Executive Council was, therefore, most valuable. It was one of many ways in which the College could broaden its understanding of medical education and so provide an "exceptional forum" for the benefit of its Fellows.

This forum was expanded when, on August 28, 1968, representatives of the two organizations met to consolidate their relationships. The College was represented by President J. Turcot and Drs. R.B. Kerr, C.G. Drake and J.H. Graham; ACMC, by Drs. W.C. MacKenzie, E.H. Botterell, J.R. Gutelius, M. LeClair and J.W. MacLeod. The meeting agreed that ACMC should be granted observer representation on the College's Credentials, Hospitals Approval and Examinations Committees. Two years later, ACMC representation at the College's Council was invited in the form of the ACMC president and an observer. Even more importantly, the meeting agreed that a liaison committee be formed to permit the two organizations to facilitate discussions on the increasing responsibilities of medical schools in residency education.

The College and ACMC were thus enabled to discuss a wide range of topics of mutual interest. These topics included the College's policy of extending temporary Certification to specialists below the level of department head or service chief; the desirability of the straight internship following the clinical clerkship (which would shorten the period between graduation and Certification); accreditation policies; the universities' interest in developing new programs of postgraduate training; examination and evaluation methodology; the College's Final In-Training Evaluation Report mechanism; and, of course, the College's proposals of 1970 to include all certificated specialists in its membership.

The College's relations with ACMC have been peculiarly valuable. During the annual business meeting in 1960, Dr. H.K. Detweiler told his colleagues that "everything that we do is in the interests of education even though," he pointed out, "we have no classrooms or hospitals under our control." Implicit in Dr. Detweiler's observation was his awareness that the College has always achieved its objectives by the power of logical reasoning and the force of gentle persuasion. The College's close relationship with ACMC has greatly facilitated the College's use of this power and force, in part because the College and ACMC have been able to understand so immediately each other's concerns regarding the two organizations' responsibilities in specialist training.

The Canadian Society For Clinical Investigation

One of the valuable features of the College's annual meeting has been the link forged between the College and CSCI. CSCI originated in the formation, in 1951, of a "travel club for those interested in clinical investigation in Canada,"[19] but the antecedents of the club reached back to a Gynaecological Travel Club that had been formed in 1936 and to discussions between Drs.

J.S.L. Browne, A.L. Chute, J.B. Collip, R.F. Farquharson and R.B. Kerr in 1949. Then, under the leadership of Dr. Browne, 24 clinical investigators met in Montreal on September 27, 1951, on the day before the Royal College meeting. The club grew and in 1959 CSCI emerged from it. Starting in 1951, the juxtaposition of the two organizations' meetings continued unchanged except for one year when, in the interest of making a gradual change in timing of the College's meeting from January to September, the 1980 meeting was held in June — a time that was impractical for CSCI to hold its meeting.

The ties between the two organizations strengthened over the years. Two factors made these ties strong. One was that, as with the relationship between the College and ACMC, many Fellows of the College were also members of the fraternal organization of CSCI. A second factor was the continuing effort by both parties over the years to fashion a meeting that would interest both organizations. This was not easy because the investigative interests of the two organizations did not coincide, the interests of CSCI members sometimes moving more towards basic science and sometimes more towards clinical medicine. That the bond held fast is yet another example of the pursuit of unity. Equally, it marks Canada's fortune that the small size and homogeneous nature of Canada's clinicians and clinical investigators can be contained within two relatively small associations.

The efforts that the College made to create a harmonious relationship can be appreciated by taking the 1964 meeting as an example. That year no fewer than 68 papers were offered for presentation, but time permitted use of a total of only 27. Council was willing to explore the possibility of extending CSCI's program in future years to overlap with the College's annual meeting at the College's allocated meeting space. President W.C. MacKenzie was cautious and explained that the word 'explore' did not mean that the College would have to take the initiative. One reason for taking this judicious stand was that CSCI felt that the College tended to take a paternal attitude towards it, so that any proposals to maintain a closer relationship should be worked out carefully. It was also agreed that CSCI should be formally invited to attend the College's annual meeting each year.

CSCI welcomed the College's earnest offer of collaboration, for the society needed to expand its program in order to maintain the interests of its members. But the College saw that there was a risk of CSCI's moving away from the College altogether and taking with them some Fellows, which would be detrimental to the College's own program. The College had reason to be concerned about unity for, of the 270 members of CSCI, some 200 were also Fellows of the College — the cream of the crop among the younger academic group in the College. It was therefore necessary for the College to do every-thing possible to retain the interest of this group in the College rather than risk losing them to CSCI completely. The solution was to move the annual business meeting to the Friday morning in order to make it easier to hold scientific sessions on the opening day and to arrange the Royal College Lecture on the Thursday morning. This, it was thought, would demonstrate to CSCI the general willingness of the College to cooperate.

A further manifestation of the College's desire to cooperate with CSCI was the College's agreeing to provide CSCI with secretarial assistance. Though provided on a trial basis for one year as from 1964, the arrangement worked well and was continued for many years.

The growth of CSCI from a membership of 24 clinical investigators and a program of four clinical presentations and three formal papers in 1951, to a membership of over 300 and 105 presentations at the 1970 meeting reflects the growth of medical specialties in Canada in the two-decade period. The resulting problems were common to CSCI and the College, and a comment on specialization relating to CSCI could equally relate to the College. Thus, while Drs. R.A. Macbeth and G. Leboeuf wrote in relation to CSCI that "this growth and the concomitant development of 'specialty' sections within the broad framework of the Society designed to encompass the entire spectrum of clinical investigation, has spawned an inevitable and increasing dilemma that will doubtless demand the urgent attention of future councillors if CSCI is to survive,"[20] they could equally have written the same in relation to the College. The possible courses to take under these circumstances were similar for the two bodies — whether specialty groups should split off to form independent societies providing a forum for the discussion of mutual problems, or whether they should adhere to the parent organization, one that offered an "exceptional forum." Drs. Macbeth and Leboeuf, discussing this problem in the context of CSCI, reached much the same conclusions that councillors had with respect to the College — that the goal was to achieve some autonomy within the framework of the parent body relative to clinical investigation and that each specialty society's going, in succession, its own independent way would have a "disastrous" effect on the progressive achievement of excellence in Canadian clinical investigation.

The relationship between the College and CSCI was, therefore, a mutually rewarding one. Both the problems and the solutions reached in each group were similar. As far as the College was concerned, all this reflects, at least in part, the search for expediency and harmony in the broader context of the pursuit of unity.

The Canadian Association of Internes and Residents

Quite different from the College's relations with other medical organizations were its relations with CAIR. The problems with respect to the pursuit of unity by the College were different and, in dealing with a new, growing and vigorous organization, the College was required to be flexible in its approach.

The College's involvement with residents, not surprisingly, began and intensified during the restless 1960s, but the relationship had, of course, been an unwritten one since the College began examining "residents" in 1932. Most Fellows had, after all, been residents at one time or another, and many residents would sooner or later become Fellows; it was quite evident, therefore, that residents had their own contributions to make. The relationship between the College and residents, therefore, was a professional one, even though an element of distance separated the two groups.

The College's concern for residents became evident during the 1960s when the College's on-site program surveyors interviewed residents about the adequacy of the training programs; also, the College's annual scientific meetings had long been open to residents without an admission fee. As the 1960s wore on, the College was forced to take more notice of Canadian residents, and Council acknowledged the College's responsibility in January 1969. It was then resolved to consider the means whereby residents in training might be given some opportunity to participate in College affairs. Later in the year, President Turcot received a letter from the Professional Association of Internes and Residents of Ontario suggesting that discussions be held with the College, but the President pointed out that it was impossible for the College to negotiate with a provincial organization.

A national organization of residents and internes, however, was formed in October 1970, at the time of the annual meetings of ACMC and the Association of Canadian Teaching Hospitals. CAIR's purposes were twofold: first, to promote communication between CAIR and national associations whose deliberations directly affected the welfare of house staff groups; and, second, to foster communication among housestaff organs. Its founding officers were Dr. J.H. Mount (Toronto General Hospital), President; Dr. P.R. Millman (Foothills Hospital, Calgary), Vice-President; and Dr. E.G. Pavlin (Winnipeg General Hospital), Secretary-Treasurer. The first meeting of the association was held in Winnipeg in October 1971.

The College's first contact with CAIR was made in January 1971, when President R.C. Dickson invited Dr. Mount to attend the College's annual meeting. The two presidents discussed the concerns of housestaff and, in particular, the new examination process. As an outcome of this expression of concern, CAIR was invited to send representatives to the conference the College had planned on the single examination process for April 29, 1971. Accompanying Dr. Mount were Dr. Pavlin and Dr. W. Jones. The CAIR representatives "insisted on ... evaluations being made available to the resident concerned, that he must read them, and must sign them indicating he had read them and be allowed the privilege of commenting on the evaluation." On October 2, 1971, CAIR was also represented at a liaison meeting between the College, ACMC and the Association of Canadian Teaching Hospitals.

Of major concern to the residents were the College's examinations and Dr. Mount expressed this concern to Dr. Graham in the summer of 1971. Dr. Mount asked about the examinations and, in addition, about residency training and the possibility of CAIR's representation on the Examinations Committee. CAIR's questions concerned the examinations' expense; the need to pass the written examination before proceeding to the oral and clinical examinations; the delay between the written and oral examinations; any connection between the failure rate and the demand/supply ratio of specialists; failure rates; the extent of supervision of residency programs by the College; and cutbacks in residency programs. The process of answering these questions made the Executive Committee attend to what would become a new and growing relationship.

In the next two years, CAIR continued to press for representation on the College's standing committees and even on Council. CAIR had established close relationships with other organizations but, with the College, Dr. D. Wasylenki of CAIR told the Executive Committee in December 1973, CAIR seemed "stuck." This concerned CAIR, which by now had attracted 4,000 members. But progress was made and the Executive Committee recommended to Council that CAIR be invited to send representatives to the meetings of the Evaluation of Specialty Training Programs Committee and the Education Committee. Council duly approved this recommendation, and the way was now clear for a mature relationship to develop between the two professional organizations.

For its part, CAIR made its relationship with the College a constructive one. At the end of its first decade, CAIR presented a report of its study of the College's Certification process.[21] It was, in general, well received by the College and the Examinations Committee praised it as being thoughtful and comprehensive. While some of CAIR's recommendations were considered unrealistic, many were judged excellent and the Examinations Committee congratulated CAIR on providing the committee with a spur it needed to once again review the College's examination process.

The College's relationship with CAIR was thus a two-way one. It was also an example of the College's readiness to develop new relationships in order to preserve unity in the medical profession. Out of this need, which the milieu of the 1960s virtually enforced, grew a fresh outlook in the College's relationships, both within and outside the College that enabled the College to face the exciting challenges of the 1970s.

Sister Colleges

Among the College's relations with specialist colleges in other countries, those with the British colleges have been especially close — ever since 1920, when the CMA passed a resolution that referred to "a Canadian Royal College of Surgeons and Physicians in some way affiliated with those of British origin."[22] Over the years, relations between the College and its sister organizations in the United Kingdom and in the British Commonwealth, also, have remained strong and have provided close collegial ties. There have been many reasons for this closeness of collegiality, in addition to the intangible one of cultural commonality; nor are these relations based solely on formality and protocol. While it is true that the College has elected distinguished Fellows of other colleges to Honorary Fellowship, invited representatives of all sister colleges to attend its annual meetings since 1964 and exchanged gifts with many of these colleges, the College has also engaged in many educational endeavors with these organizations. Thus, for a period starting in 1963, it reached an agreement with other surgical colleges concerning reciprocity of examination at the basic science level (though this was discontinued with the introduction of the multiple-choice examinations in general surgery in 1969); on two occasions, the College has held joint meetings with other colleges — with The Royal College of Physicians of London in 1974 and with The Royal Australasian College of Physicians and The Royal Australasian College of Surgeons in 1980; and the College has taken part in several joint meetings with Commonwealth colleges on topics of mutual interest in postgraduate education, one such being held at The Royal College of Physicians and Surgeons of Glasgow in 1978.

But gifts, too, have symbolized the closeness of these collegial ties. Among these gifts, the mace and the caduceus donated in 1964 by The Royal College of Surgeons of England and The Royal College of Physicians of London, respectively, are gracious and generous ones that symbolize the close and special ties between the two English colleges and the College. The silver gilt gold mace is carried in the convocation procession and the silver caduceus is carried by the President on official occasions. A third gift was donated by The Royal College of Surgeons of Edinburgh — the presidential badge, a treasured gift from the oldest royal college in the world, its charter dating to 1505. A further symbol signifying the closeness of the College's relationship with a British college is the crest (an eagle holding a mace) of the College's coat of arms, which was intentionally designed to resemble that of the coat of arms of The Royal College of Surgeons of England.

The uniqueness of the College, comprising as it does a Division of Medicine and a Division of Surgery, has often been remarked with envy by other colleges, especially those in the United States of America. But there is another college that shares some of the College's attributes — The Royal College of Physicians and Surgeons of Glasgow. It was therefore appropriate that Sir Charles Illingworth, former president of The Royal College of Physicians and Surgeons of Glasgow, should have been the first McLaughlin-Gallie professor, visiting Canada under the terms of this professorship in 1960. The only other

Presentation of the Mace — Convocation, January 16, 1964
Lord Porritt (left) and Mr. Lawrence Abel

Conference of Presidents, Annual Meeting, Quebec, January 17, 1964

Front (L. to R.) K.B. Noad (RACP), J. Mason Brown (RCSEd.), A. Kekwick
(RCPL), G.M. Brown (RCPSC), Lord Porritt (RCS), W.W. Spink
(ACP), J.E. Dunphy (ACS)
Rear (L. to R.) W.C. MacKenzie (RCPSC), G.A. Simpson (RCOG),
K.T. MacFarlane (RCPSC), Sir Charles Illingworth (RCPSGl.),
J.H. Graham (RCPSC), E.C. Rosenow, Jr. (ACP), G.E. Judd
(ACOG), G.A. Bergeron (RCPSC), T.J. Giles (RCPSC)

Joint Conference of Surgical Colleges, Ottawa, March 29 & 30, 1973

Front (L. to R.)   J.H. Louw (CMSA), E.G. Muir (RCS), D.M. Douglas (RCSEd.),
C.G. Drake (RCPSC), A.W. Kay (RCPSGl.), F.A.J. Duff (RCSI),
J. Loewenthal (RACS), J. Ross (RCSEd.)

Mid (L. to R.)   R. Smith (RSC), R. Johnson-Gilbert (RSC), J.T. MacDougall
(RCPSC), R.B. Salter (RCPSC), G.W. Stephenson (ACS),
R.B. Wright (RCPSGl.)

Rear (L. to R.)   N. Kinnear (RCSI), G. Hurteau (RCPSC), D.R. Wilson (RCPSC),
J. Robichon (RCPSC), J.H. Graham (RCPSC), F.N. Gurd
(RCPSC)

Representatives of other Colleges, Annual Meeting, Vancouver, January 27, 1978

(L. to R.) D. Tiller (RACP), J. Goldie (RACS), R.F. Robertson (RCPEd.), J.H. Louw
(CMSA), President R.B. Salter, R. Gourdeau (CMA), J.R. Gamble (ACP),
D.W. Stinchfield (ACS)

college that is similar to these colleges in its membership of physicians and surgeons is The College of Medicine of South Africa.

Regarding the American colleges, particularly the American College of Physicians, the American College of Surgeons and the American College of Obstetricians and Gynecologists, it goes almost without saying that the College early established and then maintained close relationships with them. The College's relations with American colleges have been uncluttered by the red tape of bureaucracy, and Canadian Fellows have greatly appreciated the ever-constant southern hospitality. Many Fellows have been regents of the American College of Physicians and many value that college's continuing education expertise and courses, which have benefitted Canadian Fellows and, indirectly, Canadian patients. Of the American College of Physicians, three Canadians have served as president, and no fewer than six Canadians have become presidents of the American College of Surgeons.[23] With the American College of Surgeons, the College has reciprocated in another way: plans whereby the American Board of Surgery was created in 1937, and whereby Royal College Certification became a requirement for admission of Canadian surgeons to the American College of Surgeons, were drawn up as the result of the initiative of a founding Fellow of the Royal College, Dr. E.W. Archibald.[24]

The College's relations with medical colleges in other countries have been supplemented by other forms of relationships. The McLaughlin-Gallie Visiting Professorship and the Sims Commonwealth Travelling Professorships are two examples. All these various relationships are valuable in many respects, not the least of which is, as Platt has suggested, the preservation of unity within medicine and surgery.[25]

NOTES TO CHAPTER 5

1. L. Horlick, Executive Committee, Dec. 18, 1977, p. 4.
2. The CMA's germinal statement on approval of hospitals for residency training included the following recommendations: "With the Certification of doctors in various specialties and the probability that this listing may become more significant under any possible plan of health insurance, serious consideration should now be given to the listing of those residencies in specialties which could be recognized for the Royal College Certification.... This appraisal of residencies offered might be made either by the Canadian Medical Association... or by The Royal College of Physicians and Surgeons of Canada, which is already appraising the training received by the applicants" (CMA Committee on Approval of Hospitals for Internships, June 1946, Section 153). This section of the report was considered by the CMA's Executive Committee on Oct. 21-22, 1946, when the following resolution was approved: "That a letter be sent to The Royal College of Physicians and Surgeons of Canada, pointing out the difficulties incurred by young doctors in planning their postgraduate programme, especially with reference to Certification, and Fellowship in the College, for the reason that at the present time there is no

official designation of approved centres; and that the College be asked to inform the Executive Committee as to its future plans in this connection (A.D. Kelly, letter to J.E. Plunkett, Oct. 30, 1946).

3. A.D. Kelly, Letter to J.H. Graham, Nov. 28, 1957.
4. A.D. Kelly, Letter to J.H. Graham and W.V. Johnston, Sept. 6, 1960.
5. M.R. Stalker, Letter to J.E. Plunkett, Aug. 18, 1952. Note also that in his authoritative chapter on the College's relations with Canadian medical organizations, Dr. J.H. Graham tells that President E. Dubé asked the CFPC whether it considered that the Royal College should accredit or certify general practitioners. The answer was 'No', as the CFPC thought that "the general practitioners should do their own accreditation or Certification" (Andison and Robichon, p. 154).
6. Executive Committee, February 1953, p. 12.
7. J.E. Plunkett, Letter to G.G. Miller, Dec. 10, 1952.
8. Report of meeting of Royal College representatives with representatives of the College of General Practice of Canada, Nov. 12, 1960. RCPSC Archives.
9. P. Bolland et al., "A Proposal for Training in Emergency Medicine Leading to Conjoint Certification of Special Competence Granted by the Royal College of Physicians and Surgeons of Canada and the College of Family Physicians of Canada," April 15, 1977. See Specialty Development and Manpower Committee, May 1977, Attachment 2.
10. Draft Memorandum, "Liaison Between the College of Family Physicians of Canada and the Royal College of Physicians and Surgeons of Canada." RCPSC, December 1977.
11. J.C.C. Dawson, Letter to J.H. Graham, Aug. 24, 1966.
12. Executive Committee, August 1982, Attachment 10.
13. Executive Committee, February 1965, Attachment 1.
14. N.J. Belliveau, Letter to W.C. MacKenzie, Nov. 15, 1965. See also Executive Committee, January 1966, p. 15.
15. R. Dufresne, Letter to W.C. MacKenzie, Dec. 22, 1965.
16. Report of meeting between the College and CPMQ, June 7, 1966. In: *The Royal College of Physicians and Surgeons of Canada [RCPSC] and La Corporation professionnelle des médecins du Québec [CPMQ]: Simultaneous Certification Examinations, 1965 to 1982*, Ottawa, Royal College, mimeo, 1982. This document contains reports of meetings between the two organizations from 1965 to 1982. It is the main source of material for this discussion.
17. Liaison Committee, CPMQ, Oct. 27, 1969.
18. Executive Committee, October 1964, p. 21.
19. R.A. Macbeth, G. Leboeuf, "The Canadian Society for Clinical Investigation/La Société Canadienne pour la Recherche Clinique." *Clin Res* 1970; 18(14) (pages not numbered). This article was the source for much of this discussion.
20. Macbeth and Leboeuf, 1970.
21. D. Adamson, Report on the Certification Process of The Royal College of Physicians and Surgeons of Canada. Canadian Association of Internes and Residents, submitted on Aug. 31, 1979.
22. Lewis, p. 5.

23. Canadians have also appreciated the readiness with which Americans have elected Canadian Fellows to high office in these two American colleges. Of the American College of Physicians, Dr. C.F. Martin was president in 1928-1929; Dr. J.C. Meakins in 1934-1935; and Dr. G.F. Strong in 1955-1956. Of the American College of Surgeons, the presidency, through 1984, has been held by six Canadians: G.E. Armstrong (1920-1921); W.W. Chipman (1926-1927); W.E. Gallie (1941-1946); W.C. MacKenzie (1966-1967); N.W. Philpott (1958-1959); and C.G. Drake (1984-1985).

24. W.C. MacKenzie, "Relations with Other National Colleges." In Andison and Robichon, pp. 178-179.

25. H. Platt, "The Unity of Surgery." *Ann R Coll Surg Engl* 1972; 51:209-212.

Chapter 6

The College and National Issues

From the very beginning — even before its founding — the College was conceived of as a national organization, responsive primarily to national needs and concerned with specialty care across all of Canada. Two early statements, for example, refer to "the establishment and recognition of advanced diplomas in Medicine and Surgery *throughout the Dominion*"[italics added][1] and "the setting up of a College of Physicians and Surgeons for Canada, which shall be *entirely and distinctively Canadian* ... ." [italics added].[2] Over the years, the College's mandate did not change. When a new set of objectives was formulated in 1969, the primary role of the College was still defined in national terms; it was "to improve the health care of the people of Canada."

The College's concerns, then, have always been primarily national; as Dr. D.A. Thompson observed during the 1967 annual business meeting, "the College is a great national body with a great national duty." That is not to say that the College is unresponsive to regional needs and issues, for the membership of Council and, later, the creation of the Regional Advisory Committees confirmed the College's concern with regional matters also. It is simply that the College's responsibilities are different from those of provincial bodies or of a group of provincial organizations such as the Federation of Provincial Medical Licensing Authorities of Canada. Dr. (later, Senator) E.W. Barootes, who followed Dr. Thompson in speaking at the 1967 annual business meeting, explained that the College was indeed not a federation of provincial organizations, and he urged Fellows to keep the organization national rather than regional.

In this period of change — particularly in the 1960s when, as President R.B. Kerr observed, every aspect of medicine was undergoing development and change — the College's national role was a steadying influence. President Kerr, speaking during the annual business meeting in 1968, recognized this, stressing the College's responsibility "to continue to pursue a sound course in its function as the most important influence in the promotion and maintenance of the highest possible standards in the practice of specialties of medicine in Canada." The College's responsiveness to national needs was observed by Dr. L. Horlick, who concluded from his study of the College and the R.S. McLaughlin Examination and Research Centre in 1977 that a reason for the College's success lay in its "sensitivity . . . to the whole of the Canadian medical establishment."[3]

Between 1960 and 1980, events moved fast and many of the issues of this period affected and involved not only the Canadian medical establishment but also the Canadian people and their needs; indeed, at times, the very fabric of the nation was questioned. The College was responsive to this larger constituency and to issues such as national unity and manpower needs; and because these national issues loomed large in this two-decade period, it is instructive to consider how the College served this constituency and to examine where it stood on national issues. Examples of the College's concerns include its views on the provision of specialty health care, on specialty manpower requirements, on immigration, on bilingualism and biculturalism and on national unity.

The Provision of Specialty Health Care

Since 1929, the evolution of the College was cotemporaneous with a steady evolution in concepts of health care and health care insurance in Canada.[4] In 1929, the federal government's Standing Committee on Industrial and International Relations, in presenting a report on insurance against unemployment, sickness and disability, recommended that the Department of Pensions and National Health survey the field of public health with special reference to a national health program. The Depression underlined the need for federal funding of health care programs, and The Employment and Social Insurance Act was passed in June 1935. This Act was, however, declared unconstitutional by the Supreme Court and the Privy Council in 1937. The Royal Commission on Dominion-Provincial Relations, in its report of 1939, then recommended that responsibility for certain public health activities and for the provision of state medical services for indigent and low-income groups should rest with the provinces. Two years later, the annual meeting of the Dominion Council of Health was receptive to a health insurance plan that would cover the costs of preventive medicine and medical care, and thereafter officials of the Department of Pensions and National Health developed proposals for health insurance. These proposals embraced both an insurance program and a general public health program. Thus, when, at the war's end, the federal government called a Dominion-Provincial Conference on Reconstruction in August 1945, thinking over the previous decade had shaped ideas on health insurance for a wide variety of health care services. These ideas, in turn, yielded programs of health care insurance that developed, step by step, both federally and provincially.

Two important steps were taken in 1948 and 1957. In 1948, the National Health Grants Program assisted the provinces in ensuring the most effective use of health grants and in planning the extension of hospital accommodation and the organization of hospital and medical care insurance; it also gave grants-in-aid to existing programs such as cancer and tuberculosis control and to others such as those facilitating professional training. In 1957, hospital insurance was extended with the introduction of The Hospital Insurance and Diagnostic Services Act, which insured the in-patient and out-patient services normally provided at the standard ward level. Several provisions in this Act influenced the College's thinking. Particularly important were the provisions that made insured services "universal" and "portable" and required that provinces indicate how they would license and inspect hospitals for standards; in addition, hospitals could now afford to pay for the services of residents, whom they sought to employ more freely. Besides, it made the College more aware of the need to start considering the implications that universal health care insurance coverage would have on the education of residents, who learned much of the art and science of medicine at the bedsides of patients in "public" wards.

The move towards a comprehensive and universal health care insurance plan for Canada was irreversible, and by 1960 interest in such a plan was growing. This interest had been latent for many years, but recent events such as the election campaign in Saskatchewan (a compulsory health care insurance program was, for the first time, part of a provincial party's political platform), the generally satisfactory experience with hospital insurance and the very success of the voluntary approach to medical services insurance focussed the attention of Canadian political parties on the issues surrounding health care insurance. The CMA, aware of public interest in health services and the application of insurance methods to payment of the costs of medical services, requested the federal government to establish a royal commission to study the health services of Canada. Thus was born the first of the two royal commissions on health services that were chaired by the Honorable Justice Emmett Hall.

The College submitted a brief to both of the Hall commissions. Besides indicating what the College considered important as of 1962 and 1980, the briefs give a good idea about many aspects of the College's stand on specialist health care from 1960 to 1980 and the numbers of established specialists and trainees in Canada.

The 1962 brief reviewed the history and functions of the College, the training and examination of Canadian specialists and the supply and distribution of these specialists. The brief listed the 138 Canadian hospitals that the College approved for postgraduate training, and indicated their role in postgraduate education. The brief described a highly organized system of postgraduate medical education that made use of the scientific and clinical resources of all the Canadian medical schools and their 82 affiliated teaching hospitals, as well as the training facilities of 56 hospitals not affiliated with a university. These institutions provided 2,391 training posts in the specialties; 2,125 approved training posts were currently filled. Candidates for the Fellowship examinations numbered 129 in 1947 and 457 in 1961, and for the Certification examinations the numbers were 169 and 628, respectively; approximately 200 examiners were involved each year. As far as the College's current strength was concerned, it comprised 2,402 Fellows; 959 were medical specialists and 1,443 were surgical specialists. The brief revealed that 9,150 specialists had been certificated from 1944 to 1960 and that, as of 1962, the 7,215 specialists who were still in active practice made up 35 per cent of the estimated total number of doctors in Canada.

The brief also identified the problems underlying postgraduate medical education in the 1960s. A large problem was the cost to the medical schools and the university-affiliated hospitals. Well-organized training programs made systematic use of the basic science facilities of the medical schools, but this was costly. The universities provided many of the staff required to carry on and direct research in the teaching hospitals, and conducted medical research programs within their own departments. The facilities required for postgraduate training constituted another problem: facilities and staffing were best among the hospitals affiliated with the medical schools. A third problem was the availability of adequate numbers of patients on all teaching services. The introduction of health insurance schemes was thought likely to affect this. The College and medical educators shared the concern about the supply of patients who would be willing to cooperate with the hospitals and medical schools in their programs for clinical training. The use of paying and insured patients for teaching required new approaches and understanding by the medical profession and by the public, and the establishment of clinical teaching units in which all classes of patients might be treated. Providing facilities that would ensure a graded responsibility for patient care was another aspect of this problem.

Other problems concerned the remuneration of personnel and the shortage of personnel in certain specialties and in certain regions. As far as remuneration was concerned, some candidates for the Fellowship and Certification examinations might spend a period studying, during which they were not directly engaged in patient care or research and not eligible for financial support in the usual way. Similarly, it was thought to be the responsibility of the teaching hospital to remunerate the heads of the major clinical departments who undertook administration in addition to patient care, teaching and research. With respect to the shortage of personnel, shortages existed in anesthesia, bacteriology, dermatology, obstetrics and gynecology, ophthalmology, otolaryngology, pathology, pediatrics, physical medicine and rehabilitation, psychiatry, diagnostic radiology and therapeutic radiology. These shortages were more acute in the Atlantic provinces and, in general, in urban centres with a population of less than 25,000.

A final problem consisted of the shortage of funds, space and medical scientists to conduct the medical research program needed in Canada, which lagged behind other countries in research. Medical research was very different in 1960 from what it had been 20 years earlier, during the war. A research effort in proportion to the nation's resources was required if standards of health care were to meet the expectations of the Canadian people.

Identification of such problems led naturally to recommendations. Chief among these were the following:

- The College's authority as an independent national voluntary body that provided standards for the training and recognition of medical and surgical specialists in Canada should be preserved in any future plan of health services.
- The current minimum standards of specialty qualification as laid down by the College should be maintained.
- The facilities in hospitals across Canada for postgraduate education in the medical and surgical specialties should be gradually expanded to meet the increased needs of the people of Canada for specialist care.
- The faculties of medicine, whose budgets had been intended primarily to meet the cost of undergraduate medical education, should be assisted in meeting the costs of organizing and operating postgraduate training programs and programs of continuing medical education.
- Any new plan for health care should recognize the essential place of medical research as a basis for advance in all types of health care, and the recommendations of the recent Farquharson report concerning the establishment of additional facilities and a greater support for medical research in the faculties of medicine and the training hospitals should be accepted and expanded. (The Special Committee Appointed to Review the Extramural Support of Medical Research was chaired by Dr. R.F. Farquharson, President of the College from 1945 to 1947; it submitted its report on November 12, 1959.)

Previously, the College had refrained from making its position on matters of political importance known. The presentation of an informative and constructive brief, at a time when the Canadian health care system was beginning to undergo sweeping changes, was therefore a timely indication that the College was indeed concerned about the provision of an optimum specialist health care system.

A somewhat shorter report was the brief that the College presented to the second Hall commission on health services in Canada. The brief was prepared during the Council meeting of February 1980 by an ad hoc committee chaired by Dr. R.W. Gunton. His committee comprised the following Fellows: A.R. Cox (Dean of Medicine, Memorial University); J.H. Darragh (Executive Director, Royal College); J.B. Firstbrook (Director, Division of Training and Evaluation, Royal College); J.R. Evans (formerly President, University of Toronto); R.A.H.

Kinch (Professor of Obstetrics and Gynecology, McGill University); G.R. Langley (Professor of Medicine, Dalhousie University); and B.J. Perey (Professor of Surgery, University of Sherbrooke). The brief was presented to Mr. Justice Emmett Hall in Toronto on March 31, 1980, by Dr. R.B. Salter, who was accompanied by Drs. Firstbrook and Gunton.

As had the College's brief to the first Hall commission in 1962, the brief brought forth a number of interesting facts. Since 1964, the number of physicians graduating over an 11-year period increased from 787 to 1,567 per year, the increase being attributed to the development of four new medical schools (Memorial, Sherbrooke, McMaster and Calgary) and to an increased output of the 12 pre-existing medical schools. During the same 11 years, however, the number of physicians who immigrated to Canada almost equalled the output of Canadian medical schools. As a result, the number of physicians in Canada doubled, the overall physician:population ratio rising from 1:950 in 1964 to 1:599 in 1979. But the reverse of this situation was disturbing: during 1977, 1978 and 1979, the average net loss of physicians (half of whom were specialists) to emigration exceeded 600 — approximately the annual output of six of the 16 Canadian medical schools. Also, during this three-year period, more than one-fifth of the 4,000-odd foreign medical graduates certificated by the College were resident in the United States. And of concern to the College with respect to the emigration of physicians were unsatisfactory remuneration, governmental bureaucracy with fiscal restraints, closing of hospital beds and reduction in funding of residency training posts, particularly in Ontario and Quebec.

In short, the brief suggested that, as of 1980, something was rotten in the state of Canada's specialist health care system. The brief summarized the situation in the following terms:

> *Initial* pride and enthusiasm for the system [of Canadian health services] has been modified by the recognition that resource allocation available to, or provided by, provincial ministries of health has been insufficient to meet health care expenditures, escalated by inflation, population growth, expanding technology and the expectations of the public. Cost constraint programs presently in effect constitute implicit rationing of health care. (For example, in Ontario the recent rate of inflation has been approximately 9 per cent, whereas the annual budgetary increases have been considerably less than this — 4 per cent for some years and currently 7 per cent.) We face with reluctance the prospect of a slow but certain decline in this splendid health care program . . . . This decline will occur, from our viewpoint, as a consequence of the inability to hire the new full-time and part-time university clinical teachers who are needed to renew the physician establishment, and also as a consequence of the difficulties faced by institutions in replacing equipment, maintaining modern standards and supporting new programs in health care delivery.

The publicly financed health care system had, the brief continued, done much to alleviate the shortage of physicians that had existed in 1964 (when the first Hall commission report was published) but problems remained. One such problem was the failure of provincial administrators and public officials to consult the providers of health care adequately. The health care system would be strengthened and public accountability enhanced by developing a federal mechanism for quality assurance and for assessment of cost effectiveness.

The College offered three suggestions, in addition to altered mechanisms or amounts of funding:

- Commitment of the federal government to a program, in dimension and scope analogous to the Health Resources Development Fund of the 1960s, with the objective of capital renewal of equipment and facilities rather than manpower expansion. (This program would be considerably less costly than the original Health Resources Development Fund — possibly $100,000,000 from the federal government over a period of 10 years, to be matched by the provinces.)
- Creation of a health resources research capability supported by the federal government, with terms of reference directed towards quality control, cost-benefit analysis and determination of efficacy. A few examples of subjects requiring such study were organ transplantations, coronary artery bypass surgery and computerized tomography.
- Creation of a national institute of health, national in scope, representing both providers and the public, but at arm's length from government, to periodically assess the health services program and advise governments and public servants on their stewardships.

The concept of an institute of health was the innovative feature in the College's brief. It would be a national rather than a provincial organization, analogous in organization and external relationships to the Science Council of Canada and the Economic Council of Canada. Its terms of reference would be to identify, for study and review, issues that affected the delivery of health care; to conduct or arrange studies of qualitative health care, cost effectiveness of institutions' procedures and administrative arrangements; and to report to federal and provincial governments, the public and lay and professional organizations involved in the provision of health services.

In 1962 and in 1980, therefore, the College had taken a clear and firm stand on what it thought was required to maintain and improve specialist health care services in Canada.

Manpower Needs

In both briefs to Justice Emmett Hall, the College emphasized manpower needs. In the early 1960s, the Department of National Health and Welfare conducted a survey of the number and activities of physicians in Canada and the College set up an ad hoc committee to develop criteria of need for specialists in relation to population. The collated statistics on the supply and distribution of specialists were summarized in the College's 1962 brief. This committee's work initiated the College's interest in manpower studies, and the College later participated in the CMA's conference on physician manpower, the first and second conferences on medical manpower, the Ontario Council of Deans' study and the Task Force on the Cost of Health Services in Canada. Despite this multiplicity of studies, the Specialty Development and Manpower Committee lacked the assurance that the criteria that had been developed were valid. These criteria related to ratios of physicians to population but it seemed more reasonable to determine what specialists were actually doing. The committee, then chaired by Dr. J.M. Darte, thought it would be possible to develop an authoritative statement by taking into account, in particular, recent scientific and educational developments that might have influenced specialty practice — for example, the decline in tuberculosis and the increase in cardiovascular operations, local variations in patterns of practice of health care delivery and economic feasibility in terms of costs of health care and medical education.

In 1970 the College requested that a national study be set up on medical manpower based on the functions, distribution and utilization of specialists. Dr. R.C. Dickson and Dr. J.H. Graham indicated the College's willingness to cooperate with the Department of National Health and Welfare in such a study. For his part, Dr. Darte suggested that the College study the total manpower problem and Council resolved to take the initiative for conducting the study.

Two College activities in manpower studies were notable. The first was its representation on the National Physician Manpower Committee. With representatives from the Department of National Health and Welfare, the CMA, ACMC, CFPC, CPMQ and CAIR, the College participated in studies that were designed to establish a national inventory of physician manpower, an inventory of available training posts and a mechanism for the development of criteria of need for the various types of specialists. The last of these tasks was the responsibility of the Requirements Subcommittee, on which Dr. J.B.R. McKendry, a Fellow of the College, served as chairman. Some specialties, particularly neurosurgery and cardiovascular surgery, were recommending a reduction in their numbers, while others, especially otolaryngology, plastic surgery and orthopedic surgery, saw no increase in future requirements. In general, the trend appeared to be towards an increase in output and in some instances a continuing need to rely on immigration if the particular requirements (before 1981) were to be met. The projected 1981 requirements amounted to an annual output of 1,100 specialists, which, without immigration, would have to be derived from the 1,600 or so Canadian graduates of the cohort year of 1976.

And since half of the graduates were expected to favor family practice, Canada was not likely to be self-sufficient in terms of specialist supply in the near future.

The second College activity was a study conducted by Dr. R.W. Gunton, who became chairman of the Specialty Development and Manpower Committee in January 1972. He held that the College could not stand aside from deliberations over specialist manpower and that it should provide data from its own corps of specialists. He organized a study of manpower needs in internal medicine by sending a questionnaire to more than 300 directors of approved training programs in April 1972. The study was limited to estimating the needs for specialists in 1975 based on the numbers of candidates qualifying in 1975 and the number of specialists required in 1975. The study was restricted to internal medicine, cardiology, clinical hematology, clinical immunology, gastroenterology, neurology, respiratory disease, rheumatology, endocrinology, nephrology and dermatology.[5]

The conclusions of Dr. Gunton's study were as follows: A slight underproduction by 1975 was foreseen for internal medicine and a significant underproduction was seen for clinical immunology, respiratory disease and rheumatology. Slight overproduction was indicated for clinical hematology and significant overproduction for gastroenterology. For the other specialties, production was considered adequate. In view of these estimates, and in response to the legitimate concerns and financial constraints of governments, Dr. Gunton advised that the College and the universities should develop manpower policies consistent with the national need and ability to pay. He also thought it desirable that the College's specialty committees review and revise the projections he had detailed.

These several studies of manpower needs provided estimates only, and it proved necessary to monitor the supply of physicians each year. Most estimates yielded little more than rough approximations, and these approximations were sometimes misleading. Thus, the first Hall commission report expressed concern that Canada might not acquire an adequate number of physicians over the next three decades — yet, because of an increase in medical student enrolment and a liberal immigration policy in the 1960s and early 1970s, a physician:population ratio that was thought unattainable by 1985 was already approached in 1971.[6] The College's efforts to determine manpower needs, however, were useful, for some data were better than none. But, even as late as 1979, Dr. Gunton was still concluding that hard data were lacking.[7] In the remainder of the 1970s, therefore, the issue of manpower continued to concern the College, which monitored the supply of specialists in Canada at regular intervals.[8] The discussion of this issue by the fifth Conference of Specialties in 1980 was a further example of the College's concern with what clearly would remain a perennial problem.

Immigration of Physicians

Besides the emigration of physicians from Canada, particularly to the United States, the immigration of physicians into Canada was of interest and concern to the College. The contribution that foreign medical graduates, particularly in the two decades following the Second World War, made to specialist health care in Canada was, of course, invaluable — in the peak year of 1969, 57 per cent of new physicians were immigrants and many were specialists or wished to practise as specialists — but this influx presented problems for the College. In particular, it was often difficult to assess the previous education of foreign medical graduates, and it was disturbing that a proportion of them regularly failed to pass the College's examinations. It was therefore necessary to clarify the basic issues and the principles that might guide the College, particularly since the Training and Evaluation Committee had made headway in preparing guidelines concerning acceptable non-Canadian training programs. An opportunity to consider the approach the College should take to the broad issue of the immigration of physicians presented itself when Dr. M. LeClair, Deputy Minister of Health and Welfare Canada (and a Fellow of the College), suggested that, since the Department of Immigration was preparing a green paper on immigration, the College should prepare a brief on the immigration of physicians.

The College's statement, which was drafted by Dr. R.W. Gunton in May 1975, provided an informative background on the role that foreign medical graduates were playing in Canada. At that time it was not difficult for foreign medical graduates to practise in Canada: the College did not require a candidate for Certification to be a Canadian citizen or to hold a licence to practise. The College's responsibility was to see that a Certificant had the training, knowledge and skills appropriate to specialist practice; it was not a licensing authority and it had no statutory right to control numbers or kinds of specialist trainees. And since 75 per cent of foreign medical graduates who obtained Certification remained in Canada, the College in effect endorsed a candidate's suitability to join the specialist corps of physicians in Canada — though it exerted a more direct influence (tantamount to approval or disapproval) by assessing the credentials and later examining the competence of a candidate.

Since the end of the Second World War, Canada had come to depend increasingly on foreign medical graduates. Among specialists, only 50 per cent of specialists certificated during the quinquennium from 1968 to 1972 were graduates of Canadian schools, and approximately 30 per cent of resident and clinical fellowship positions in residency training programs were occupied by foreign medical graduates. All this, the College's statement emphasized, reflected the policy and tradition whereby Canada had been continuously enriched by "talented and vigorous new citizens." Thus, a quantitative need had developed for non-Canadian postgraduate trainees; and, even though future needs were uncertain, a continuing and relatively unrestricted flow of immigrant physicians should be permitted to fill current manpower needs.

There was, however, a reverse side to the coin. Indeed, the current policy encouraged reverse discrimination in that foreign medical graduates could become specialists in Canada by entering the system *after* their undergraduate training, while this privilege was denied highly qualified Canadians who could not enter Canadian medical schools because of the large number of applicants with superior scholastic records. Moreover, some studies from the Health Manpower Directorate indicated that the optimum physician:population ratio might be achieved in Canada without continuing immigration of physicians being required.[9] After 1970, the number of physicians graduating from Canadian medical schools continued to increase while the number of physicians immigrating to Canada steadily decreased: in 1970, whereas only 1,075 physicians had graduated from medical schools and 1,113 physicians had immigrated to Canada, in 1980 the numbers were 1,746 and 380 respectively. The guidelines that the Training and Evaluation Committee prepared on acceptable non-Canadian training in 1975, however, remained useful (see Chapter 8).

The failure rate of foreign medical graduates in the College's Certification examinations was a continuing consideration. Here the College could exert its influence where it had the authority to do so and in a manner consistent with its purposes; that is, by developing more stringent regulations regarding approval of training taken outside Canada. Any reduction in the number of foreign medical graduates entering Canadian training programs while taking the Certification examination would then result from the application of fair and equal standards to all applicants, Canadian and foreign, and not discriminative immigration regulations.

The emphasis of the College's statement on immigration of physicians was self-sufficiency in Canada but fairness to foreign medical graduates. The statement ended as follows:

> We should look forward to being able to say to Canadian citizens: there are enough Canadian medical students to satisfy our needs, there are enough postgraduate programs to satisfy their requirements if they all stay in Canada, and there are enough jobs for all if they choose to stay here. ...We will be able to accommodate some foreign medical graduates of a calibre equal to our own. There will continue to be movement across national borders.

The College was demonstrating another aspect of its continuing pursuit of unity.

The College's Policy on Bilingualism

Beginning in the mid-1960s, Quebecers in particular quite naturally felt increasingly constrained by the lack of recognition accorded to the French language. From its founding onwards, the College was a bilingual organization

— Council, for example, accepted the need for French and English versions of the Fellowship diplomas in 1930 (even though expense eventually dictated that Latin be used instead) — but it was not always easy for members of the secretariat to decide which letters and documents should be written in English or French or in both languages. It was therefore entirely appropriate that President J. Turcot, of Quebec, should suggest, in 1968, that the College would be wise to define more clearly its policies towards bilingualism in College affairs. He looked for ways that would demonstrate to all the bilingual nature and attitude of the College. Dr. J.H. Graham agreed and said that, for his part, his work would be made easier if the College possessed a definite statement of policy on bilingualism. Accordingly, the President set up an ad hoc committee to study the matter of guidelines on bilingualism for the College. Drs. J. Beaudoin and E.D. Gagnon, two Fellows from Quebec, worked with Dr. Turcot as the committee members in 1969 to prepare guidelines.

The outcome of the committee's work was a document entitled "The Use of the French Language in The Royal College of Physicians and Surgeons of Canada."[10] The document represented a résumé of what was done and a program for bilingual and bicultural development in the future rather than a set of guidelines. But it went further than this. The document was designed as an example and a model of a bilingual and bicultural attitude that Canadians, especially Fellows, might follow. Graciously, the three Fellows stated that it was "pleasant" to record that the College's attitude had been exemplary. The work of Drs. Beaudoin, Gagnon and Turcot illustrates an essential aspect of the College's pursuit of unity, and the significance of the document is partly symbolic. Thus, when the authors wrote that "all the future major developments of the College must draw their inspiration from this example," they were referring to a document that came to represent, in the daily life of the College, the essence of unity — just as does the heraldic blazon that describes the College's coat of arms. Enshrined in the document was a statement that reflected the *élan* of three Quebecers to whom unity had a special meaning and who presented to their colleagues the essence of that spirit that should guide the College in its own pursuit of unity.

This document took the following form:

The Use of the French Language in The Royal College of Physicians and Surgeons of Canada

1. Act of Incorporation

   The Act of Incorporation of the College assigned to it a bicultural and bilingual character in establishing officially its French name: "Le Collège Royal des Médecins et Chirurgiens du Canada."

2. Period of Development

   During the years which followed the founding of the College, it became clear that the participation of Fellows of the French language in the diverse activities of the College was judged indispensable.

From the beginning, the examinations for the qualification of Fellow were presented in the two languages, French and English, both at the level of the written examinations and at the oral and clinical examinations.

The representation of the French-speaking group in the Council is not numerous, because of geographic representation, but the greatest part of the time their advice and opinions gain very special attention; further, representation in the College headquarters or the Executive Committee has been maintained almost without interruption since the very beginning of the life of the College.

It is the same at the level of the various committees of the Council.

3. The Present Context

In the context of the evolution of Canadian society, the College must not follow the directives of other groups in the elaboration of a bilingual and bicultural attitude, but serve as an example and a model. It is pleasant to record that it has been thus for several years.

The use of the French language in the College can be considered and studied on an individual level and an institutional basis.

From the individual point of view, the problem has not presented itself as we have seen above. The exchanges of views between individuals can easily be carried out in one language or the other according to the circumstances.

Nevertheless, when one proceeds to the institutional level it becomes very important that the College display its bilingual character especially in its external relations with the universities, hospitals, governments and others. Thus an official document intended for a French-speaking institution must be drawn up in the French language.

The College furthermore has concerned itself for a long time with this problem and has developed gradually in the secretariat a French-speaking unit which is in a position to furnish to Fellows or to candidates of the French language a full range of reports in French.

The same spirit exists in the hospital approval surveys, in the structure of the R.S. McLaughlin Examination and Research Centre, in the organization and programs of meetings, etc. The *Annals of the Royal College* strives to develop this image or this bicultural aspect.

This does not mean, of course, that all documents coming from the College must of necessity be written in the two languages; each case must be judged according to the circumstances taking into account however the general principles enunciated above.

Certain points remain nevertheless to specify with a view to improving.

Thus it is of the greatest importance that an institution like the College which operates in the domain of teaching, research and medical life on a national scale assures an exceptional quality in its writing and documents in the two languages. To reach this in the French sector, it is necessary to have working units which operate in French as is the case in the secretariat and in the McLaughlin Centre.

All the future major developments of the College must draw their inspiration from this example. The meetings, intended for the members of the two linguistic groups are also organized in this spirit, utilizing external displays which bear witness to this bicultural character of the College such as posters, simultaneous translation, official presentations, etc.

This document is at the same time a résumé of what is done and a program for bilingual and bicultural development in the future.

The College and National Unity

In general, the College has eschewed involvement in political affairs. The College's concern with national unity therefore was unusual in that it reflected a stand on a national issue that was not directly related to specialty health care. The issue of national unity, however, as it developed in the late 1960s and much of the 1970s, concerned every Canadian citizen, and the College felt constrained to debate it.

The theme of national unity has been a recurrent one in Canadian history, waxing as movements for autonomy surfaced and waning as the strength underlying these movements weakened. Concern over national unity reached crisis proportions in 1967 (when, at the time of Expo '67, President Charles de Gaulle of France exclaimed, "Vive le Québec Libre"), in 1970 (when the Front de Libération du Québec [FLQ] separatist activities in Montreal led to the enactment of the War Measures Act) and in 1976 (when the Parti Québecois gained power in Quebec). At these times, separatism surged and reactive feelings of national unity intensified in response. Despite efforts of varying vigor to bring the "two solitudes", especially, together, true unity remained a grail to be sought and a delicate fabric yet to be woven.

In March 1977, Dr. G. Hurteau, Vice-President (Surgery), thought that it was time for the College to use its influence to sensitize Canadians in every walk of life to "the perils . . . and . . . the potential tragedy" that could surface if the nation divided.[11] He asked the President to take the initiative so that the College could play its role in the deliberations of these kinds. Dr. Hurteau suggested that the College set tangible examples of its readiness to continue demonstrating the "true spirit of Canadian life in applying to its own activities a spirit of bilingualism and biculturalism"; he recommended that the College initiate exchanges of French- and English-speaking physicians in residency programs and maintain the French sector of the McLaughlin Centre. Dr. Hurteau wished to find mechanisms that would mirror what had traditionally been the position of the College.

Dr. Hurteau's proposal was discussed by the Executive Committee in May 1977. No startling innovative recommendations emerged, but it was suggested that Dr. Hurteau and Drs L.E. McLeod and K.J.R. Wightman draft a letter that might be mailed to the Fellows. At the next meeting of the Executive Committee, it was agreed that a summary statement rather than a letter should be prepared, and the statement was presented to Council for discussion at its June 1977 meeting. The statement read as follows:

> *Your* Executive has discussed the question of Canadian unity, particularly in relation to the recent events in the Province of Quebec.
>
> The Royal College of Physicians and Surgeons of Canada since its inception has been a good example of the sort of collaboration between anglophone and francophone Canadians which has taken full advantage of the opportunity such a relationship provides.
>
> We conclude that we have entered an era of change in our country in which we must all participate if the results are to be acceptable.
>
> As a College, we should take on the responsibility to contribute to any processes which will foster national unity. Our attitude should be positive and constructive, in the hope that we can offer leadership to our members, hence to the medical profession as a whole and eventually the general public. These concerns should enter into all the deliberations of our standing committees and specialty committees. Among other things, they should give mature consideration to such matters as the development of a completely uniform process of specialty Certification across the country, admission of Certificants of the Professional Corporation of Quebec to Fellowship in the College on the same basis as our own, encouraging two-way exchanges between specialists in training, visiting professors, visiting scientists, persons on study leave and any others who contribute to the mutual understanding of the special problems existing in various sections of the country.
>
> These are examples for later detailed discussion, but we urge that the principles underlying these ideas be accepted now, and implemented without delay, by all those involved in the affairs of the College. We present this report as a means of communicating our sense of urgency of this problem to the Fellows of the College, and mobilizing their support.

Concern with national unity went beyond the desire to heal a rift between anglophones and francophones. Dr. J.R. Evans identified four major areas of concern that related to national unity in a broad context. One involved community and identity, including important matters such as language and culture, on which much of the current debate was focussed. A second comprised nationalism and international impact related to the integrity of a national unit. A third area embraced a series of economic aspects, exemplified by the concept of a customs union, which were important, but which many people understood very little. The fourth included numerous problems related to "functional federalism" — the relationships between different levels of government jurisdiction, both political and bureaucratic, and the various responsibilities of individuals at different levels in the division of powers.

Dr. Evans was particularly interested in national unity, having thought about it a great deal since November 15, 1976, when the Parti Quebecois rose to political victory in Quebec; he had had good opportunity to explore the issues for he was a member of the federal Task Force on National Unity. His concept of the goal of national unity was therefore of interest to his fellow councillors. It seemed essential to preserve the advantages of the federation in Canada and yet, at the same time, to overcome the difficulties existing in the various regions in Canada. How could the College help Canadians to reach this goal?

Three elements were proposed in this quest. The first was embodied in the first two sentences of the statement under discussion. Various mechanisms could be developed to increase the College's effectiveness in this respect. The second element was the proposal that the College could join up with other national groups having similar objectives in the hope that this would be seen not as a partisan medical approach but an assurance of goals with groups having diverse natures. The third element was more difficult to execute: the College might stimulate discussion by its own members, who would then participate in the broader debate in their own communities, not so much as members of the College as citizens with a sense of responsibility. In this way a broadened base and a heightened level of understanding might be achieved.

One danger for Quebec was recognized by Drs. J.G. Couture, R. Lefebvre and B.J. Perey, all of whom worked in Quebec. Accommodation to change, Dr. Lefebvre said, should come from anglophones rather than francophones. A low profile in Quebec would be preferable: the converted did not need statements such as just had been presented in Council, while opponents would read whatever they wished to see in various statements. Concrete proposals, rather than statements of principles, should be emphasized. Moreover, a political statement might have a negative effect, diminishing the credibility of the College in attaining these other goals and priorities. For Dr. Couture, the emphasis should rest on actions that could contribute positively towards unity within the College. And Dr. Perey reported that Quebecers felt that they were being "united to death." An attitude and a policy towards national unity was important, but more important were concrete steps taken to give effect to that policy. What the McLaughlin Centre was trying to accomplish was an example of this.

Dr. Evans then suggested courses of action for the College. One was to strengthen the national and international roles and purposes of the College in those areas that transcended regional considerations. A second was to give special attention to activities evidencing greater appreciation of and sensitivity to the realities of regional differences and needs — as could be developed, for example, through the Regional Advisory Committees. And third, Fellows themselves might, through discussion in their communities, increase their own awareness and sensitivity to regional differences and needs.

Dr. Wightman, on behalf of the ad hoc committee, then proposed, and Dr. Hurteau seconded, the following motion, which was duly carried:

Whereas, it is recognized that we are entering a period of greater uncertainty and accelerated change in Canada which will require accommodation by this College, and, whereas, the College has an important responsibility to strengthen its national and international purposes and, at the same time, demonstrate greater sensitivity to the differences and special needs of the regions,

Be it resolved that:
1. These purposes be brought to the attention of the standing committees of Council and the regional committees as important considerations in their deliberations; and that
2. Additional instruments to further these purposes be developed by the Executive Committee, in consultation with the Division of Fellowship Affairs, as a matter of priority both in timing and funding; and that
3. Regional representatives be invited to consider ways and means of implementing these purposes more effectively; and that
4. Measures be taken to ensure the widest possible dissemination of information thus generated.

In addition, it was resolved that the Regional Advisory Committees and other standing committees discuss the matter just dealt with in Council.

A further contribution to the debate was made by Dr. Perey, who discussed the issue in relation to the four areas of concern that had been identified by Dr. Evans. He placed several suggestions before the College for implementation as practical steps:

- The College should determine how to make it convenient for francophone Fellows to conduct their business in their mother tongue, so as to avoid "language stroke."
- Francophone members should be encouraged to express themselves in French at Council or other key functions.
- The growth of the francophone unit of the McLaughlin Centre should be promoted further.
- More attention should be paid to the CPMQ — for example, it could play a greater role in accrediting training programs in the province of Quebec.

- The College should subsidize access by francophones to facilities and information that are currently available in English only, especially in self-evaluation.
- Ways to make the Royal College less "royal" and more "Canadian", albeit in a symbolic fashion, might be sought; Quebecers felt that anglophone Canadians were obsessed with the monarchy of another anglophone country, and that reference to the British monarchy, if forced on them, would constitute a denial of their own cultural identity.
- The bicultural nature of the country and of the College should be further emphasized; an example of an attitude to be noted was that reflected in the fact that, in almost half a century, only two francophone Presidents had been nominated.
- The College might consider modifying its bylaws so that Quebec Certificants might be admitted to Fellowship in the College.
- The College should encourage the free flow of people across the barrier that separated the two major cultural groups; an example was the way the orthopedic examining boards had held joint meetings of the English and French members.
- That purely Canadian travelling professorships should be established, the professorship alternating between francophone and anglophone holders.
- Regional Advisory Committees might have more input into nominating members serving on College committees.

Dr. Perey's statement generated much interest. One immediate outcome was the resolution that a pilot study of simultaneous translation be conducted at the meeting of Council in January 1978.

These discussions on national unity went far to further Council's understanding of the delicate fabric that, also, was national unity. The debate reached its high point in 1978 when, on January 28, Dr. Evans delivered a Royal College Lecture on the subject of "Citizens, Societies and National Unity" and Dr. Perey delivered the Convocation Address on the subject of "The Royal College and the National Challenge."[12] Both presentations were articulate and elegant. Their addresses should be read in their entirety, but it is instructive to include here just the final paragraphs of each presentation.

> *Canada* is not a marriage of convenience. It is a marriage of inconvenience which recognizes the benefits of functioning as a collectivity rather than going our separate ways. The spirit which sustains that marriage must transcend dissatisfaction with the policies of governments of the day. National unity is not a goal in itself. It is the framework within which to achieve greater collective prosperity and an alternative to American continentalism. Economic issues and unemployment complicate the situation and are seen by some to be the primary problem. But a vicious cycle is created by the current

uncertainty and political instability of Quebec and Canada. Large corporations like General Motors can afford to risk capital but small investors cannot. And it is small investment that provides the growth in tax base and employment opportunities on which a return to prosperity depends. It is not a question of economics being more important than national unity. The two are inextricably linked, witness the importance of economic association in the concept of sovereignty association, proposed by the Parti Québecois.

The most pressing problem is Quebec. The majority of Quebecois seek accommodation of their concerns within the Canadian context. The challenge is to provide them with a sense of lasting security for their culture and identity, and full and equal participation in the responsibilities and opportunities of private and public life in Canada. As individuals they seek to be accepted and respected no more but no less than any other Canadian. Intellectual debate will not resolve the problem of attitudes. Genuine understanding is most likely to come from personal and professional association, the interaction of people, a formidable challenge but one in which national societies, business, organizations, churches, community groups and student exchanges have an important contribution to make.

The sense of collective security, respect of their culture and equality of opportunity must be communicated to French-Canadians not only by actions of the federal government but also by provincial governments in respect of their francophone minorities, by national organizations such as this College and by the attitude of the general public. And it must be conveyed as a genuine commitment, not a reluctant concession. It must be a reasoned judgement, not an emotional impulse. We can afford neither a recurrence nor a relapse. Our greatest challenge is to arouse the public, individually and collectively, to express its will positively and constructively in a sense that it is worthy of our remarkable heritage and the unmatched future potential of this country.

— Dr. J.R. Evans

Much is being done by national medical societies to promote better understanding and appreciation between our two major cultures, but much remains to be done. After surveying the list of current presidents of our 30 national medical specialty societies, and the list of former presidents of large multidisciplinary societies, I had to conclude that these organizations had only met with very modest success in bringing French-Canadians fully into their fold and in electing them to their highest office. It would be unfair for me to suggest that this state of affairs simply reflects ethnic discrimination on the part of anglophones. It must be due to a large extent to the traditionally limited enthusiasm of French-speaking Canadians for national societies in their past and present form.

If I may now leave the French-English question, I would like to suggest that there is a great deal more to the Canadian people than people of Anglo-Saxon or French origin. There are many people of other ethnic origins who are just as Canadian as everybody else and who make up about one-third of our country's population. In the medical profession alone they must constitute almost half of its manpower.

Considering only the immigrant physicians, 35 per cent of all qualified medical specialists in Canada and 36 per cent of the full-time faculty of Canadian medical schools have obtained their medical degree in another country. But I have found that their presence among the leaders of our national medical societies is marginal at best. Who is to suggest that these colleagues are not as worthy or as interested as the others? How long will they tolerate being restricted to a regional arena? In Sweden, where immigration has been very limited compared to Canada, this very situation has been described by concerned sociologists as potentially explosive if the established majority does not soon make room for the newcomers at all levels of society. How much potential for explosion is there in a country like Canada where the largest and most dominant ethnic group does not even constitute a majority? By and large, our national societies have been blessed with superb leaders and we have found comfort in the thought that we have picked the best people we knew. Perhaps it is time we started looking for the best people we should know.

This takes me back to where I started a few moments ago. If that ethnic Canadian mosaic that we claim to be so proud of continues to be nothing but a catchword to conceal the fact that we have not yet begun to develop a clear understanding among ourselves, we are headed for very difficult times ahead. But if we decide to tackle this Canadian challenge, the very diversity of our people, that threatens to be our downfall, could be turned into our greatest strength.

Let us open our eyes and wake up to the fact that in a country that is blessed with a grossly disproportionate amount of natural resources, our most valuable potential asset is still our people.

— Dr. B.J. Perey

The College's approach to the complex issue of national unity was a natural outcome of the College's evolution over the years, and even before the College was founded. As Lewis points out, the original idea of a Canadian college developed first when the British Empire was being replaced by the British Commonwealth of Nations and also when a national viewpoint was attaining ascendancy over a narrower provincial outlook.[13] Thus, the key resolution of the 1920 CMA meeting linked considerations of founding the College to the preamble that stated that "Canada has now assumed the status of nationhood within the British Empire."[14] The concept of the College as a national organization was always basic to the College's role both in the early days and in the period from 1960 to 1980 — and, in his address, Dr. Evans drew interesting parallels between the Royal College as a national organization and the Canadian political federation. The College's leaders had always thought of the College in national terms. President D.A. Thompson indeed delineated the issue accurately when he stated unequivocally that the College is a great national body with a great national duty.

NOTES TO CHAPTER 6

1. Lewis, p. 11.
2. Lewis, p. 17.
3. Executive Committee, January 1978, p. 16.
4. A useful review of the principal events in the development of health care insurance in Canada is found in the report of the 1964 Royal Commission on Health Services, Vol 1 (Ottawa, Queen's Printer). The authoritative text, however, is M. Taylor's *Health Insurance and Canadian Public Policy: The Seven Decisions That Created the Canadian Health Insurance System* (Montreal, McGill-Queen's University Press, 1978).
5. R.W. Gunton, "Manpower Needs in Internal Medicine." *Ann RCPSC* 1973; 6:136-143.
6. Canada Health Manpower Inventory, 1983. Health and Welfare Canada, Ottawa, 1983.
7. R.W. Gunton, Letter to J.H. Graham, May 17, 1979.
8. Apart from Dr. Gunton's study, which was restricted to internal medicine (see note 5), the College's records contain several sources of information on the supply of specialists in Canada in the 1970s. One is an analysis by Mr. T.J. Giles of the proportions of Canadian and non-Canadian graduates among all specialists in Canada from 1968 through 1972; this indicated that 45 per cent of the non-Canadian graduates intended to pursue their careers in Canada (see discussion in Council, June 1973). A second source is an analysis of characteristics of specialists certificated by the College from 1970 through 1979. This further study, which was completed by Mr. Giles just before the fifth Conference of Specialties met in April 1980, revealed that the College certificated 6,788 specialists during the 1970s, that these specialists constituted 37.8 per cent of active specialists in Canada as of Dec. 31, 1979, and that only one-third of Canadian graduates were entering specialty training programs. This last finding was also evident in a third study by Mr. Giles, which was based on information about residents enrolled in specialty training programs as of Dec. 31, 1978 (see *Ann RCPSC* 1979; 11:184-189). The implications of these three studies are obvious. A fourth source of information consists of the College's annual reports, which provide data concerning the numbers of successful candidates during the latter 1970s.
9. W.S. Hacon, J. Aziz, "The Supply of Physicians in Canada." *Can Med Assoc J* 1975; 112:514,517,519-520.
10. Executive Committee, January 1970, Attachments 4 and 5.

11. G. Hurteau, Letter to R.B. Salter, May 23, 1977; see Executive Committee, May 1977, Attachment 1.

12. J.R. Evans, "Citizens, Societies and National Unity," *Ann RCPSC* 1978; 11:117-123, and B. Perey, "The Royal College and the National Challenge," *Ann RCPSC* 1978; 11:150-153.

13. Lewis, p. 4.

14. Lewis, p. 5.

PART 2

THE DEVELOPMENT
OF THE
SPECIALIST

Chapter 7

Legacy of the 1950s:
The College and Postgraduate Medical
Education

The evolution of the College between 1960 and 1980 was shaped in large part by its facilitating the transition of responsibility for residency training from hospital departments to university medical faculties. This transition, which in Canada began in 1949, was part of a quiet yet profound revolution in medical education that became necessary because the education of the specialist was not organized according to a logical continuum. The responsibility for educating medical students was that of the medical schools; for interns, that of the hospitals and their administrators; and for residents, that of the individual clinical departments in hospitals. University medical schools once had the opportunity to assume responsibility for postgraduate medical education* but they did not take this responsibility; as late as 1965, for example, Coggeshall observed that in the United States most formal education after graduation was of relatively little concern to medical schools and universities.[1] This lack of concern, which was not addressed until the mid-1960s,[2] is remarkable, for the university's role is as logical and as important in medical education, both undergraduate and postgraduate, as it is in other spheres of education. After all,

> *The* university alone comprises all the fields of knowledge and disciplines related to health. The university alone can encompass the education required for all health fields. Only through the university — the locus of research — can the full benefits of scientific advance be brought to the future physician and the practitioner.[3]

Even into the 1960s, however, some North American universities were continuing to reject the responsibility for taking a full role in postgraduate medical education. It was therefore to the credit of the College that it took the initiative in changing this situation, and that it did so as early as the 1950s.

---

*The term "postgraduate medical education" is used in this book to refer to formal education in the period after graduation with the MD degree. In the United States, the term "graduate medical education" is used to denote education in this period.

The Concept of 'University Aegis' and Postgraduate Medical Education

In Canada, the College initiated its facilitatory role in 1949; its role was national in scope. In 1931, however, Dr. W.E. Gallie, the College's Vice-President (Surgery) from 1937 to 1939, had established a systematic course of training in surgery that gave residents adequate experience in the basic sciences and surgery in preparation for the College's examinations. Dr. R.I. Harris, in delivering the first Gallie Lecture before College Fellows in 1968, noted that it was the first such course in Canada and in advance of any training course in England and that the pattern was later widely adopted throughout Canada.[4] McGill University, too, organized a course in surgery, the integrated diploma course dating from 1945. Even so, the College in 1949 was still ahead of its time — in North America as a whole and not just Canada alone — in recognizing the role that university medical schools should play in postgraduate medical education and in encouraging them to fulfil this role.

The College's perspicacity in this regard can be illustrated by reference to a model — that of the collaboration between the College and certain psychiatrists that began in 1949. A prelude to the story, however, was written at the turn of the century. In 1900, in what was regarded as "departure from routine", the Faculty of Medicine of McGill University granted diplomas in public health to graduates who had taken courses in sanitation and laboratory work on hygiene and passed a special examination.[5] The editorialist who reported this event in 1900 stated that McGill University was the first medical school in North America to conduct a diploma course of this nature and suggested that what held good in public health might be applied to other lines of study. He also asked an interesting question: Why not establish "advanced courses leading to certificates or diplomas of efficiency, only to be obtained by those who really possessed special qualifications in a particular subject?"

That question concerning higher qualifications for medical graduates in Canada was asked three decades before the College was founded.

The editorialist was ahead of his time. First, he observed that "the medical degree received on graduation does not mark the end of its possessor's career as a student, but is really only the beginning of an endless course of study". He was referring to what became termed continuing medical education. This term hardly seems new, but it was adopted widely only by 1960;[6] and as recently as 1973 one writer was moved to remark that "continuing medical education is *now* recognized as a professional activity of critical importance to the quality of health care" [italics added].[7] Second, the editorialist realized that universities had a responsibility within the continuum of medical education. After indicating the importance for the physician of pursuing a career-long "endless course of study", he remarked that, as of the turn of the century, the university had provided no way of academically recognizing further progress; then he asked why Canadian medical schools had done so little to guide and encourage physicians to take postgraduate study. He asked that question in 1900; half a century would pass before it generated much interest.

Before the 1960s, then, few universities in the United States recognized that they had a responsibility in postgraduate medical education. That this situation did not obtain in Canada is attributable in part to the College's conviction, clearly demonstrated as early as 1950, that universities do indeed have a role to play and a responsibility to fulfil in the training of specialist candidates. The College's contribution, as assessed in 1962, was considerable, as was reported by one knowledgeable observer at that time:

> Very striking changes have taken place in the postgraduate training of hospital residents during the past 20 years. It has been a change from what might be called the apprenticeship system to an organized program of considerable value, and the College has played an important role in bringing about these changes.[8]

These words were written by Dr. D.S. Lewis, President of the College from 1949 to 1951. Although modesty forbade him from saying so in his history of the College up to 1960, he catalyzed the process whereby residency training of specialists did finally evolve into "an organized program of considerable value". His part in the story occurred half a century after the *Montreal Medical Journal* editorial was written.

The College's involvement with universities began in 1949. In November of that year, Dr. R.O. Jones, of Halifax, asked Council, through Dr. A.D. McLachlin, to approve psychiatric training under the auspices of Dalhousie University. This request came soon after the College had established its program of approving hospitals for training. Dr. Jones's application, which related to four hospitals in the Halifax area, was the first the College received for approval of training under university supervision.

Dr. Jones, the professor of psychiatry at Dalhousie University, was a member of the subcommittee on training of the Federal Advisory Committee on Mental Health. In the fall of 1949, he and his fellow committee members had reviewed the College's standards of hospital approval and had found that, in their words, "they do not go far enough". They accordingly suggested that the College form a committee, "fully representative of Canadian psychiatry", to consider setting up standards that would be appropriate for the assessment of mental hospitals developing methods whereby such ratings could be carried out, in a manner acceptable to the College, by those experienced in administrative psychiatry.[9]

Dr. Lewis, as President, then invited a small group of psychiatrists to consider the examination and the training requirements of the Royal College for candidates in psychiatry. The committee comprised Drs. D.E. Cameron, R.O. Jones, L. Larue, R. MacLean, D.G. McKerracher, J.C. Miller and A.B. Stokes (chairman). They expressed several concerns when they met in January 1950. First, they urged that the standard of the Certification examination should be raised at least to that of the American Board of Psychiatry and Neurology or The Royal College of Physicians of London. They noted that the College had already taken an essential step in distinguishing, for examination purposes, the disciplines of psychiatry and neurology. This important step for psychiatrists would "allow a proper range of questions extending from the physical to the social but balanced around the crucial problems of personality development". It was important also because a broadened examination would do what a Fellowship examination modified for psychiatry would, in their opinion, not do — reflect more realistically the practice of psychiatry and the principles of training based on that practice.

The committee then made an observation that altered the approach to postgraduate training in Canada: "Postgraduate training in psychiatry, as it is being developed in the training centres across Canada, is no longer a matter for a single hospital or institution in isolation. Each training centre is, in effect, made up of a number of associated establishments which together provide a whole psychiatric experience". Therefore, the committee agreed, approval for training purposes by the College should be given not to the individual hospital but to the training centre. The committee's statement contained two key recommendations. The first was the need for a unified, integrated training program, a concept that reflected Dr. Gallie's of the 1930s; the second was the need to think of approval in terms of multipartite training centres rather than individual, isolated hospitals. Both these concepts were new to the College — and to the majority of North American universities.

The committee added a third key recommendation. This stressed the role of the university:

> *In* general the training centre would be the psychiatric department of the medical faculty of a university. As such its provisions would be under scrutiny by the medical faculty and would be continuously compared with those of other medical fields. The College in granting its approval to the training centre in these circumstances would have a simpler task of assessment without the necessity of invidious arbitration on the detail of a single hospital.

The committee held that the training centres seeking approval by the College as providing an adequate postgraduate training program in psychiatry should be under "university aegis". As a corollary, it was recommended that all postgraduate students in psychiatry should be registered as such with the university — another echo of what had been implied by the Montreal editorialist half a century earlier.

The psychiatrists, who had a particular problem in training their residents because mental hospitals undertook many diverse forms of treatment and were often geographically distant from each other, had stated their position. The positions of two other groups now had to be stated — those of the universities and the College. University participation might or might not be forthcoming: while Dr. Stokes had told Dr. Lewis on March 29, 1950, that Saskatchewan's Dean Lindsay, when asked for his opinion by the College, thought that such an aegis of a postgraduate program would be undertaken by the university, he also said that in British Columbia and Manitoba "internal difficulties" in university affairs would require "skilled negotiating" to overcome. Dr. Stokes saw a useful role for the College: he told Dr. Lewis, "the effort will only be worthwhile if backed by a proper authority from the Royal College". To this last requirement Dr. Lewis responded by saying that the College was probably willing to approve of the arrangements for the approval of institutions being made on a university basis rather than on an individual basis.

Council, as Dr. Lewis had expected, did approve such arrangements, expressing its policy in three resolutions approved in the summer of 1950.

The first resolution specifically addressed the request of Dr. Jones. It was resolved that four hospitals in the Halifax area (the Nova Scotia Hospital in Dartmouth, and Camp Hill Hospital, the Children's Hospital and the Victoria General Hospital in Halifax) should be approved for one year's training in psychiatry, training in these hospitals having been integrated as part of an approved university scheme of postgraduate instruction. The second resolution referred in general to psychiatric hospitals. Council approved the resolution from Dr. A.D. McLachlin, chairman of the Hospitals Approval Committee, that psychiatric hospitals that integrated their training as part of an approved university scheme of postgraduate instruction would be approved for one year. Further, provincial mental hospitals and private mental institutions that applied to the College should be informed that applications for approval of training would be contingent on the hospitals' being grouped in a university scheme of training or some similar scheme of broad training, which would meet the approval of the Council of the College.

Psychiatry was the first specialty to recommend a university-based program of training. Council agreed with this general position, not only with respect to psychiatry but also to other specialties. The third resolution was therefore more general. Council received a resolution from the Hospitals Approval Committee that hospitals that integrated their training as part of a university scheme of postgraduate instruction would be approved for one year, provided that the training carried the approval of the chief of staff in medicine or surgery; further, it was suggested that this policy might be extended to other branches of medicine or surgery to be dealt with on an individual basis.

Council modified and approved this resolution and then defined its policy for the future in these words: "Hospitals which integrate their training as part of a university scheme of postgraduate instruction may be approved for one year, providing the training carries the approval of the head of the university department concerned." This policy was implemented immediately, for, at this same

June 1950 meeting, Council deferred action on a request from the Royal Columbian Hospital, New Westminster, B.C. for approval in anesthesia "until [the] hospital forms part of the teaching unit of an integrated university scheme of postgraduate instruction". Thereafter, an increasing number of hospitals became affiliated with universities. By 1959, for example, 93 of the 140 hospitals and institutions that were approved by the College for residency training had some form of university connection — even though not all of them participated in university-sponsored postgraduate training plans.[10] But the concept of university aegis for specialist training had been established, and one of the challenges for the College in later years was to implement policies based on this concept.

That the concept of university responsibility for postgraduate training was formulated in the 1950s is not surprising. From 1947 to 1956 advances in educational methods, especially in the United States, profoundly altered the thinking of all educators, including Fellows of the College. In 1947, the Educational Testing Service, which provided a research base to measurement in education, was established; in the 1950s influential work in medical education was reflected in the studies that led to the formulation in 1953 of a basic statement by the Association of American Medical Colleges concerning objectives of medical education,[11] in the experience that led up to the publication in 1962 of Dr. G.E. Miller's *Teaching and Learning in Medical School*[12] and in the publication in 1971 of Dr. J.P. Hubbard's *Measuring Medical Education*;[13] and in the same decade B.F. Skinner published his concepts of behavioral psychology and B.S. Bloom published his text on educational objectives.[14] All these developments influenced those College Fellows, such as Dr. D.R. Wilson, of Edmonton, who, in mid-career, became specifically interested in the developing discipline of medical education.

The 1950s, then, was a stimulating decade for medical educators. Dr. Hubbard was one of these educators. His influence on medical educators in Canada was recognized when he received the College's first Duncan Graham Award in 1973. A one-time president of the National Board of Medical Examiners, Dr. Hubbard described the educational milieu of the 1950s in three sentences that capture the essence of that formative decade:

> In the early 1950s, a change was introduced with effects more far-reaching than were appreciated at the time. Objective multiple-choice testing methods had come of age. It appeared timely to marry the science of medicine to the emerging science of educational measurement.[15]

But although the 1950s constituted so formative a period in medical education, its effects in these respects were not readily apparent for many years except to a few, and it is not surprising that the significance of the idea of university responsibility for postgraduate medical education was understood by so few medical educators when the idea was first introduced. Dr. Hubbard's words, in fact, may be said of the College's policy, implemented in 1950, concerning training in university-based programs, for in the early 1950s a change was introduced with effects that were indeed more far-reaching than were appreciated at the time.

For these several reasons, it is therefore to the credit of the College that President Lewis and his colleagues did appreciate the far-reaching significance of the concept that Drs. Jones, Cameron and Stokes and their colleagues brought to the College so early in the era of hospital approval. The faith that all these individuals — all of whom were, in one capacity or another, Fellows of the College — placed in this new concept was justified. Their faith in this concept would have gratified the spirit of Dr. S.E. Moore, who had, in 1920 on behalf of the Regina and District Medical Society, stated that "it is desirable that the best means of stimulating and promoting advanced study of, and postgraduate work in medicine and surgery, be adopted, to the end that as large a number as possible of the medical men of Canada should engage in such studies..."[16]

NOTES TO CHAPTER 7

1. L.T. Coggeshall, *Planning for Medical Progress Through Education*. Evanston, Ill., Association of American Medical Colleges, 1965, p. 11.
2. J.S. Millis (chairman), *The Graduate Education of Physicians: The Report of the Citizens Commission on Graduate Medical Education*. Chicago, American Medical Association, 1966.
3. Coggeshall, 1965, p. 41.
4. R.I. Harris, "As I Remember Him: William Edward Gallie, Surgeon, Seeker, Teacher, Friend". *Can J Surg* 1967; 10:135.
5. Anon., "Higher Medical Education". *Montreal Medical Journal* 1900; 29:470-471.
6. Anon., "History of Accreditation of Medical Education Programs". *JAMA* 1983; 250:1502-1508.
7. W.D. Mayer (chairman), *Evaluation in the Continuum of Medical Education: Report of the Committee on Goals and Priorities of the National Board of Medical Examiners*. Philadelphia, National Board of Medical Examiners, p. 10, 1973.
8. Lewis, p. 127.
9. T.E. Dancey, Letter to C.G. Stogdill, Nov. 7, 1949. This letter is one of several that constitute primary sources for this part of the chapter. RCPSC Archives.
10. Memorandum Re Graduate Training, Nov. 3, 1959. This memorandum was drafted by Dr. J.H. Graham as a brief to be presented to ACMC at a meeting with the College on Nov. 6, 1954. This meeting set the tone for regular fruitful meetings between the two organizations from then onwards.
11. Cited by G.E. Miller (ed), *Teaching and Learning in Medical School*. Harvard University Press, 1962, pp. 84-85.
12. Miller, 1962.

13. J.P. Hubbard, *Measuring Medical Education: The Tests and the Experience of the National Board of Medical Examiners*. Philadelphia, Lea and Febiger. The first edition was published in 1971; the second, in 1978.
14. B.S. Bloom et al., *Taxonomy of Educational Objectives: Cognitive Domain*. New York, David McKay Company Inc., 1956.
15. Hubbard, 1978, pp. 8-9.
16. Lewis, p. 5.

Chapter 8

The Evolution of
Training Requirements

The training and evaluation of physicians so that they may be identified as competent specialists has always been of primary concern to the College. For many years, however, training requirements were determined more by the nature and standards of the College's examinations than by carefully defined educational objectives; not until the 1970s did such objectives consistently begin to shape the nature and content of training programs. This advance came about largely as the result of the College's new approach to evaluation of specialty competence, particularly between 1970 and 1972. Thus in relation to the new concept of in-training evaluation, the College in 1972 first explicitly stated that the specialty examination process should evaluate the skills, attitudes and professional competence of candidates, in addition to their knowledge; previously, technical knowledge and technical proficiency were the principal evaluative criteria.[1] The understanding of the need for formulating educational objectives, which had grown in the 1960s, now paid dividends. The single examination process, introduced in 1972, was designed to evaluate a candidate's understanding and fulfilling educational objectives relating to skill and attitudes as much as to factual recall.

The emphasis on training and evaluation, which together make the two sides of the coin of education, was the outcome of intense study of the principles of medical education as they were understood in the 1960s. This endeavor, which was spearheaded by a handful of Fellows with a particular interest in medical education, enhanced the College's reputation in the field of specialist training and gained for the College a position of authority and respect that enabled it to convince other parties, notably the universities and the hospitals, of the logic and the validity of its various educational initiatives. It was necessary to gain such a position because, lacking direct control over the content and conduct of training programs, providing no detailed curricula or reading programs and organizing no postgraduate courses itself, the College could exert its influence only by means of moral authority and suasion. The College, as such, never trained any specialists, though of course many of its Fellows did; but what it did do, with remarkable success, was to fashion the matrix within which specialist training could be effectively developed. The College's viewpoint was simple and straightforward: "The institutions in which young men and women are to train must be capable of teaching satisfactorily and this must be the prime objective of the College in this aspect of its work."[2]

In determining the pattern of training that each specialist would take, the College, in the period from 1960 to 1980, made fundamental and often innovative contributions to postgraduate medical education. In these years, as well as stressing the need to base the content of training programs on well-defined educational objectives, the College ensured that training programs were built around core content, emphasized the importance of residents' being given progressive responsibility for patient care and, through in-training evaluation, established the principle that a resident's competence, as observed during training, should count towards evaluation during the final examination.

These several achievements took time to accomplish. Just as a series of connected steps taken in the 1960s were a necessary prelude to the development of what became an essentially new College in 1972, so logical steps taken in the 1960s and the first half of the 1970s were a necessary prelude to the development of an innovative approach to specialist training in the latter 1970s. In developing this approach, Council was guided by the activities of its three main standing committees — those dealing with accreditation of hospitals (and, later of university training programs rather than of hospitals), credentials and examinations. Each committee made its own contributions at different times in the two decades. For example, the Hospitals Approval Committee (later, the Evaluation of Specialty Training Programs Committee and, later still, the Accreditation Committee) in the mid-1960s led the way in ensuring that only hospitals and then training programs affiliated with universities would qualify for College approval. The Credentials Committee, besides having a continuing concern with assessment of credentials and eligibility of candidates for the examinations, was concerned, for much of the time, with the need to revise and update the general objectives of training programs in the different specialties. The Examinations Committee, in the mid-1960s and early 1970s, first revised and then completely changed the College's examination system, which then came to include the introduction of the innovative In-training Evaluation Report. The approach was thus a triple one, but its goal was the unitarian one of achieving a standard of specialist training in Canada that was second to none.

Emphasis on a single concern at any one time, whether this related to educational standards of hospitals, candidates' credentials or the failure rate of the College examinations, was fruitless. The problems and therefore the solutions were interrelated. In continuously striving to enhance the standard of training of specialists, it was necessary to develop better methods currently for accrediting hospitals and training institutions and assessing candidates' credentials and, particularly in the 1970s, to design an examination process that would fairly and accurately evaluate the competence of candidates. Here, the different elements of training and evaluation are considered separately, but they were, of course, interdependent and part of a concerted effort to adhere to the principle underlying the College's Act of Incorporation — "to act as an incentive to...physicians and surgeons to aspire to higher qualifications and therefore higher standards of service to the public".[3]

This chapter focusses on the approval of hospitals and training programs, the evolution of the universities' participation in specialist training, the assessment of candidates' credentials and the development of training objectives, standards and requirements.

Approval of Hospitals and Training Programs

The College's activity in accrediting the postgraduate training facilities of hospitals contributed greatly to the College's efforts to bring about excellence of specialist training. These efforts were launched in November 1944, when Council asked the Examinations Committee to consider the question of approving hospitals in which specialist candidates were taking training that would enable them to take the Fellowship examination. The guidelines that were drawn up early in 1945, though rudimentary, laid the basis for future requirements and standards. These guidelines required hospitals that sought College approval to have a public ward service large enough to provide trainees with an ample variety of clinical material, and to have on staff certificated specialists who would attend the patients in this public ward. This activity — the forerunner of the College's accreditation program — attained momentum the following year, when the CMA's Executive Committee pointed out to the College that there was "no official designation of approved centres" for residency training,[4] and in 1947, when the College's Committee on Approval of Hospitals for Advanced Graduate Training was established. Thereafter, the requirements for hospital approval were continuously refined. These endeavors reflected the College's assuming, as a 1965 statement claimed, "a moral obligation to assure trainees that approved hospitals are in fact capable of offering and maintaining standards of training and experience which will prepare them adequately for the future competent and scientific practice of their specialty as well as for the examinations of the College".[5]

A notable advance in approval of hospitals came in 1962, when the Hospitals Approval Committee appointed a subcommittee to draft a set of the regulations laying out the general policies and principles applying to the approval of hospitals as a whole and the additional requirements relating to individual specialties. This was a constructive initiative that extended the endeavor that had begun in the 1950s to integrate hospitals' training facilities into university programs.

This was a good time for the College to become also involved in surveying hospitals' and universities' training programs. The 1960s was an expansive decade,[6] and one sign of the times was the organization, within the space of a few years, of four new medical schools. Of Canada's 16 medical schools, nine had been established long before the Second World War, one (the University of Ottawa medical school, established in 1945) was a product of the 1940s and two (the medical schools of the University of British Columbia [1950] and Saskatchewan [1954]) were organized in the 1950s; but the remaining four developed in the 1960s — Sherbrooke in 1961, McMaster and Calgary in 1965 and Memorial in 1967. Therefore the College's decision in 1962 to take over the responsibility for surveying itself was timely. The decision was also logical. Dr. A.L. Chute, Chairman of the Hospitals Approval Committee, explained the background of the decision to Council in June, 1962. In the initial stages of the College's program of approving hospitals for postgraduate training, the committee and Council had to rely largely on the knowledge of local members regarding the ability of the services to provide good training. Later, the specialty committees were asked for opinions and recommendations about hospitals seeking approval in their respective specialties, and the Hospitals Approval Committee rarely acted contrary to the advice that the specialty committees gave. Still later, the College obtained on-the-spot reviews of the postgraduate training programs and facilities in approved hospitals from Canadian Council on Hospital Accreditation (CCHA) field surveyors — a step forward in providing the committee with first-hand information about the hospitals, though this method had drawbacks.

There were three drawbacks to CCHA's surveying for the College: the number of such surveys requested by the College created a burden for the CCHA surveyors; the surveys probably adversely affected the CCHA's regular accreditation surveys because priority attention was given to the training aspect of the survey in order to safeguard their approval; and the CCHA surveyors were reluctant to express any judgment about the quality of postgraduate training programs, particularly those in university teaching hospitals. These drawbacks reflected the fact that the goals of the College and the CCHA did not quite coincide. While the College greatly appreciated CCHA's generous assistance, a new approach was needed. The Hospitals Approval Committee therefore recommended to Council that the College develop its own program of surveying hospitals approved for postgraduate training.

The task would be a large one. It would be expensive and, although the College knew what to look for in conducting a survey, it would have to decide how to conduct such surveys. The committee therefore recommended to Council that an expenditure of up to $3,000 be authorized in 1963 to finance a pilot project of inspection and review of a localized group of approved hospitals. In the meantime, the subcommittee that was drafting the statement of requirements for approval of hospitals for postgraduate training was authorized to consider how the pilot study might be carried out.

The targets of the pilot study would be the hospitals that provided residency training facilities in London, Ontario. The study was conducted by Dr. R.B. Kerr, a physician, and Dr. D.R. Webster, a surgeon. They were well received in London. They appreciated "the whole-hearted cooperation" given them by the dean and the heads of services in their approved specialties. Residents also were receptive to this study, the knowledge that the College was concerned with the quality of training making a "marked and favorable impression" on them. Dr. C.G. Drake, a member of the committee, said later that he had heard no adverse comments about the survey and concluded that the survey had given a better insight into what the College was trying to do, both for those responsible for training and those being trained.

This was a pilot study and the technique of evaluation was relatively crude compared to the technique of surveying that was steadily refined thereafter. Dr. Kerr, reporting to the Hospitals Approval Committee in May 1963 did, however, list 15 items that might be used in developing accreditation techniques. These items were the following:

- A list of the medical staff with qualifications and their degree of participation in teaching programs for residents. Qualifications of the staff would include specialty status and university appointments.
- Affiliation of the hospital concerned with a university and the method of appointment of the medical staff.
- A description of facilities, particularly bed facilities and other physical arrangements.
- Organization of medical staff with respect to services.
- Arrangements concerning "staff" patients and private patients.
- The number and rank of residents in each department — both the number authorized and the number occupying the position from year to year. Numbers of applicants for the position would be of interest.
- Arrangements concerning the functions and duties of residents, rotation through services and the number of patients looked after by each resident.
- Outpatient facilities available and the nature of the work of the residents.
- The degree of responsibility and supervision provided for residents.
- Ward rounds, conferences, case presentations, pathology conferences and other group sessions.
- Programs of lectures, seminars and other educational sessions provided for basic science and other aspects of the specialty.
- Availability of library facilities.

- Clinical and other research programs of the department providing an opportunity for participation by residents.
- An opportunity for discussion with trainees, past and present, which would afford a basis for assessment of the program.
- A statement concerning remuneration and other amenities applying to each rank of resident.

Council, like the committee, was enthusiastic in its reception of the report. Dr. D.G. Cameron suggested that the fact that the survey had been carried out by such distinguished educators would encourage and facilitate heads of services in their work with trainees and, from this point of view alone, the survey might be expected to yield positive results. Dr. Chute reported that the members of the Hospitals Approval Committee had felt that further experience with this type of survey was needed before definite and final conclusions could be drawn as to the best method of carrying them out and the time and cost involved. Council then approved extension of the pilot study of hospital surveys for a further year and the appropriation of an additional $3,000 for this purpose in the 1964 capital budget.

The London on-site survey, besides establishing a precedent, signaled a second innovation. This is evident in the titles of the reports of the survey that were written by Dr. Kerr (concerning the survey of residencies in medicine and the medical specialties) and by Dr. Webster (about surgery and the surgical specialties). Each report was entitled a "Survey of Residency Programmes in Hospitals in London, Ontario", and in this title it is the word 'Programmes' that is significant. The emphasis in postgraduate medical education was changing from training centred in hospitals to training in planned programs centred in or affiliated with universities. The College was beginning to think of *coordinated* programs of training.

The College had now taken an important further step in confirming both its interests and expertise in advancing the standards of postgraduate medical education in Canada. The program would be a continuing and expanding one. Dr. W.C. MacKenzie summarized the value of the on-site program at the 1965 annual business meeting as follows:

> *This* program represents an efficient method of assuring that training taken by candidates in preparation for the Royal College examinations is taken in appointments providing a satisfactory educational experience. These teams of competent, senior medical educators, visiting and assessing the [post]graduate programs in both university-centred and non-university training centres, ensure that the programs that we are approving come up to the standards that are essential to the training of those who desire to become qualified clinical specialists in Canada.[7]

Dr. H.K. Detweiler, at the 1960 annual business meeting, had observed that everything the College did was in the interests of education, even though it had no classrooms or hospitals under its control. This further step in the interests of education, despite the College's lack of control of classrooms or hospitals, testified not only to the College's interest in education but also to its power of moral suasion. The College was ensuring that its ideas would bear fruit in those classrooms and hospitals across the country that, while not under direct College control, were nevertheless greatly influenced by the College. In fact, all parties benefitted. Hospitals and hospital departments were enabled to assess their training programs and were stimulated to improve them. The College gained expertise in a specialized field of evaluation and accreditation and it became able to systematically assess training programs across Canada.

By 1965, the College's approach to specialty training in hospitals had advanced greatly from the guidelines the College had drafted in 1945. The College was clear as to what it considered appropriate for specialist training, but it was interested especially in working out a partnership with the universities, with which hospitals providing the training facilities would be integrated. The College's approach is clear from two paragraphs in the booklet that the College published in 1965 on requirements for approval of hospitals for advanced postgraduate training:

> *While* hospitals which are not affiliated with the universities may be capable of developing complete training programs which would meet the standards for approval, the Royal College believes that the teaching hospitals closely affiliated with the medical schools are, as a rule, best equipped and staffed to conduct complete programs of graduate training in the medical and surgical specialties. University-sponsored training programs make systematic use of the basic science and research facilities of medical schools and the clinical and scientific resources of their affiliated hospitals. The place occupied by research in the medical schools and by clinical investigation units in the teaching hospitals creates an excellent scientific atmosphere in which to produce physicians and surgeons well trained in the medical sciences and in the application of their scientific knowledge to the care of patients.

> Because trainees moving from one hospital to another with only limited approval usually cannot attain graded responsibility for patient care under supervision, the Committee on Approval of Hospitals in general does not favour granting approval for limited training, such as one year, unless the training is integrated with a program providing full training in the specialty, preferably with a university plan. In such affiliations, the head of the department or service of the parent program must assume responsibility for the training in the affiliated institution. In some specialties such as cardiovascular and thoracic surgery and neurosurgery, limited independent approvals are no longer granted.[8]

The seeds of the idea for more particular approval had been sown. It was now necessary to consider withdrawing approval from hospitals that were unaffiliated with universities and whose training programs were approved for one or two years but not longer.

The deficiencies of these isolated training programs had been apparent for some time — they had been recognized, for example, in the College's 1965 document on requirements for approval of hospitals — but it was the cumulative experience of the on-site surveyors that led the College to take definitive action. The problem was a simple one. By giving approval to unaffiliated one-year training programs, the College tended to encourage the "hop, skip and jump" pattern of training by which candidates were able to technically fulfil the College's current regulations by spending a year here and another there yet did not acquire the experience, through increasing responsibility for patient care, that the College held was an implicit (though not then explicit) requirement of a good training program. The "one-year approvals" were of little educational value and did little more than satisfy, first, residents who, as foreign medical graduates, had come to Canada to wait out, for visa purposes, a two-year period before returning to the United States and, second, hospitals with service needs rather than educational interests.

On the surface, the solution to the problem was equally simple. The College was obliged to insist that hospitals providing isolated one-year training programs affiliate with a fully approved program run by a university or major teaching hospital and to withdraw approval of those one-year programs that remained unaffiliated.

Because objections were foreseen not only from the hospitals (which would lose service "bodies") but also the universities (which might be burdened financially if residency training were regarded purely as an educational function and therefore not reimbursable through the hospital insurance program), it was deemed necessary to keep ACMC informed of the College's plans. It was also deemed wise to define criteria that hospitals should satisfy to enable them to obtain College approval. Five such criteria were drawn up by Mr. T.J. Giles:

- There must be an administrative head of the program responsible for its planning, organization, direction and supervision.
- There must be a detailed outline of the content of the training program and the part to be played in it by each of the participating institutions.
- There must be provision through which the director of the program would have an effective voice in the selection and appointment of those who would be responsible for carrying out the teaching program in each of the participating institutions.
- There must be provision through which the director of the program could effectively control the initial selection and continuing reassessment of the candidates accepted into the program.
- There must be an indication from each of the participating institutions of their willingness to participate in such an integrated training

program and to accept the conditions for so doing in order to ensure the operation and maintenance of the basic principles outlined.

These criteria were approved by Council in January 1966 and the Hospitals Approval Committee discussed the issue in June 1966.

These various matters were the concern primarily of the Hospitals Approval Committee, which approved two important resolutions at its June 1966 meeting. The first was to recommend to Council that, effective as from July 1, 1969, approval of unaffiliated one-year programs would be withdrawn except under unusual circumstances. The second resolution, by which the committee reaffirmed its belief that only programs offering full training sponsored by a university or major teaching hospital should be approved, recommended to Council that the current attitude of medical schools towards this policy be ascertained by approaching ACMC. Council approved these recommendations, and the cut-off date of July 1, 1970, was agreed on with respect to one-year approvals.

Gradually, the goal of total integration of residency training programs with universities, first defined in 1949, was being reached. In the attainment of this goal, the College's insistence on a standard of postgraduate medical education that would be derived from university participation was instrumental. It was, however, not yet complete, and the further step of limiting approval to programs providing full specialty training within the university orbit had to be taken. This was a logical extension of the previous step, and the Hospitals Approval Committee recommended to Council in June 1969 that the deans of the Canadian medical schools and all approved hospitals be informed of the College's new intention. This was done and, as from July 1, 1975, integration into university-based programs became obligatory for approval of programs offering full training.

Development of the Universities' Responsibility for Specialist Training

Although the role of the universities in specialist training was first clearly established in 1950, it was not until 1975, when the College's approval of unaffiliated two-year and three-year programs was discontinued, that total responsibility on the part of the universities for residency training was completely recognized and accepted. While the College's decisions of June 1966 and June 1969 to withdraw approval of unaffiliated one-year and of two-year and three-year programs were landmarks as far as the College's policy was concerned, the entire process of transition of responsibility for residency training from hospitals to university required patient insistence by the College over a long period. As late as the 1969 annual business meeting, for example, the process was described by President J. Turcot as being one of "gradual organization"; and, as late as 1970, as many as 76 one-year approvals remained on the College's list. The process was, in fact, more gradual than in Quebec, where the CPMQ's Committee on Medical Education had already taken steps to make university affiliation mandatory for all programs as from July 1, 1970. Since the College first formulated its policy on university responsibility for postgraduate training in 1950 yet did not see it fully implemented until 1975, the process was indeed gradual, but the reasons for this seeming delay are understandable. These reasons may be understood in relation to the College's concerns on the one hand and to the concerns of the universities and hospitals on the other.

The College's customary approach in its relationships with other partners has generally been a conciliatory one. In its relationship with the universities this approach was not difficult to maintain because many Fellows, from the start, were drawn from the universities. Therefore, the College early on recognized the value of working with medical school faculties and with an organization like ACMC. Likewise, the College early on recognized the importance of training within the university environment. As early as 1937, it was recommended that one of the training requirements for Certification be a minimum of two years' postgraduate training under supervision; significantly, it was also stated that if the candidate had not taken a continuous period of postgraduate training in an approved medical school and teaching hospital, a longer period of training would be required. The College experienced no apparent difficulty in communicating its ideas on the university aegis concept to the medical schools and, once the principle of university responsibility appeared to have been established, the College regularly communicated with medical school deans. In the 1950s, the College communicated directly with medical schools on at least three separate occasions (in 1951,[9] 1955,[10] and 1957[11]), and in 1959 the College presented a brief to the deans, as represented in ACMC, on the subject of postgraduate training within the university orbit.[12]

The brief that the College presented to ACMC in 1959 was important because it explained simply and clearly the College's stand in the 1960s on the universities' responsibility for postgraduate training. Three elements of this stand are notable. First, the hospital approval program was justified on the basis that it was preferable to a system of complete freedom of choice of training in unselected institutions, which would be likely to produce inferior and superficial programs that might cause failure and disappointment in later years. Second, as the number of hospitals requesting approval for postgraduate training steadily increased, the College became more concerned that hospitals that were not associated with a formal training program would be unable to provide instruction in, for example, clinically relevant basic science and that some candidates would take some or all of their training in such hospitals. And third, the brief offered the view that it would seem logical that the College, a largely academic body seeking to establish the highest standards of postgraduate medical education and specialist qualification, should work with the medical schools, in which were concentrated the best teaching facilities. The brief concluded by saying that "since it is the view of the Royal College that the university-directed plan of training is the most desirable form of [post]graduate training, it is our hope that the medical schools will expand their work in the [post]graduate training field, accepting the assistance and collaboration of the Royal College."

The College's brief was well received, and ACMC recorded "its interest and responsibility in the field of [post]graduate training and its desire to cooperate with The Royal College of Physicians and Surgeons of Canada in these matters". ACMC also expressed the hope that hospitals would indeed be brought "into the orbit of the university in [post]graduate training".[13]

At the same time, some potential difficulties were identified by ACMC. While there was a need for a clear-cut understanding of the universities' responsibility in postgraduate education in assisting in the selection of candidates, in outlining postgraduate programs and in providing basic science courses, difficulties could arise where hospitals took full responsibility for postgraduate training. A further potential difficulty was the expense to the universities for, it was claimed, the fact that medical school staffs must usually train the residents would increase costs to the medical schools.

These reservations indicated that the principle of university responsibility was not as widely accepted as the College believed. For the universities and the hospitals a number of problems made immediate acceptance of the university responsibility for postgraduate training difficult. (In contrast, the College was not affected directly by any of these problems.) These problems may be summarized as follows:

- Before mandatory university affiliation of hospitals and training programs could be implemented, several developmental problems had to be solved. Because university affiliation impinged on the interests of several groups — the medical schools, the hospitals, the provinces and the residents, among others — time and patient negotiating were required. Relationships between universities and hospitals also varied across the country. For a considerable period there were no ready and certain answers to several basic questions: Who was responsible for the content of postgraduate programs? Who should select the candidates for training? How should the several responsibilities be divided between the university medical school and its affiliated hospitals? How should the cooperation or approval of each party be enlisted?
- Conflicts between service needs, as seen by hospitals, and educational requirements, as seen by medical faculties, also prevented ready implementation of the university aegis concept. On the one hand, a hospital administrator needed a certain complement of residents to occupy service positions; on the other, a university department head, thinking of residents as trainees, might find it

difficult to reconcile the hospital's needs for residents with the training program's requirements to teach residents. Numerous concerns occupied the department head and these often conflicted with the hospital administrator's concerns: the selection of residents; the approval of facilities for training; the appointment of teaching staff; the evaluation of residents during training; and the desirability of residents' obtaining graduated responsibility for patient care and acquiring special experience by rotating through several different hospitals.

- Hospitals' perception of university "interference" also militated against acceptance of a primary role for the university. Both individual physicians and hospitals feared possible control by universities. In some cities, some physicians whose primary interest was practice rather than teaching had access to hospital beds only by being appointed, as an expedient measure, to a part-time faculty position, and the apparent primacy of educational needs was seen as university interference with their own freedom to practise. These physicians feared losing their privileges in a process of engulfment by the requirements of the university for teaching. Similarly, hospitals that lacked the knowledge and expertise that only a university faculty possessed feared loss of autonomy and control in the anticipated need to establish and maintain a full and formal training program, and such hospitals were reluctant to enter into an agreement with the university.

- For some universities, acceptance of the responsibility for a formal training program was seen as an undesirable burden. For one that was new, such as the University of British Columbia, or one that was the only one in a large area, such as Dalhousie University, it was a large task to devise a system of affiliation with hospitals that previously had been unaffiliated. The burden appeared to have financial implications, too, and the need to fulfil added teaching and administrative responsibility, all of which increased a university's expenses, made universities hesitate before entering affiliation agreements. Nor was it certain that the hospitals, rather than the universities, would be asked to remunerate the residents.

- Not all universities shared the College's opinion that the College-approved university-based training program was necessarily the best plan. McGill University and the University of Toronto, for example, had developed their own training programs over a long period and excellent graduates emerged from these programs, some with local diplomas. The "Gallie Course" (from which the "Gallie slaves" emerged as free men) was one such example of a program that needed no help or encouragement from the College. Some universities saw no reason why they should be told how to produce well-trained graduates. Likewise, some specialty departments were unconvinced that the College's requirements for its vaunted Fellowship program were superior to their own. Psychiatrists from Montreal and Toronto, moreover, considered that the College's requirements were unrealistic; they held that the College's requirement that an entire year be spent in an internal medicine residency limited rather than broadened a psychiatrist's training. Because of the need to concentrate on the study of internal medicine, a Fellowship candidate might spend less time studying psychiatry than would a Certification candidate who had no such requirement to fulfil. This was the origin of the view, widely held among psychiatrists, that psychiatric residents should take the Certification examination, which was considered the "usual" means of achieving specialist status, rather than the Fellowship examination.

- Some educators, even in the early 1960s, were not convinced that universities should play a major role in postgraduate education, even though, in June 1957 Dr. R.M. Janes had observed that a "gradual change" was taking place in university responsibility. [14] Yet, a few months later, Dr. J.W. Scott still expressed surprise that some medical school deans knew little about the College's training program and that some felt little or no responsibility in this direction. [15] And Dr. J.W. MacLeod, Executive Director of ACMC and a former dean of medicine himself, in November 1962 felt bound to say that, in agreeing with the principle of university responsibility, he was in the vanguard of an apparently innovative movement. He would not otherwise have written to Dr. J.H. Graham, on November 15, 1962, that this movement seemed to him and some of his colleagues as "clearly 'the wave of the future' not only for the good of the training itself but also as a step towards the more rational solution of the problem of financial support of medical education". [16]

- To some extent, the College appeared to some university executives as authoritarian. Sometimes this view originated in incomplete communication by the College of its plans; on other occasions the view stemmed from inadequate knowledge in the College of local conditions. The reaction of one dean, who was in general in favor of university affiliation, is illustrative. "I resent", he told the College, "having any agency other than the Faculty of Medicine and the Senate and the Board of Governors....decide what is the function of this university, or to suggest an extension of our responsibility without approaching us on this matter". [17] He suggested that ACMC or individual medical schools be asked to give an opinion on the feasibility and desirability of affiliation before the College took action that might indicate to non-teaching hospitals that postgraduate training in these hospitals was a university responsibility. Sometimes a university might disagree with the College, and the way in which the College approached the university to broach the issue would be of paramount importance. Thus Dr. C.E. Hébert, speaking in Council in October 1957 and observing that one could not force a university to introduce a plan that it did not favor, advised that "it might be wiser to ask their advice".

None of these problems necessarily invalidated the principle of university responsibility for postgraduate medical education or negated the College's wish to improve the standards of specialty training in Canada, but these problems did emphasize for the College the importance of negotiating with care, consideration and patience with the universities. The universities were subject to many more pressures than was the College, and they understandably looked askance at further pressures. The partnership between the College and the universities was a valuable and necessary one for specialist training and specialist health care in Canada — indeed, it could even be considered unique[18] — but it was also fragile and deserving of great respect. The College's concept was a valuable one but it needed nurturing by the universities as well as the College. In this aspect of the pursuit of unity, circumspection was the order of the day for, as Dr. E.H. Botterell observed to President J. Turcot in 1968, "universities have had to learn over many generations to guard their academic independence and...Fellows of the Royal College should continue to give great heed to the preservation of the universities that spawned us".[19]

Dr. Botterell was dean of the faculty of medicine at Queen's University in Kingston. Two years before writing to President Turcot he had suggested that "active engagement in the solution of problems in the form of vigorous discussion advances understanding." He had done this in introducing the published proceedings of a conference on residency education organized and sponsored by the College and held at Queen's University on October 1 and 2, 1965.[20] The significance of this conference was profound. Virtually all those Fellows who were concerned with postgraduate medical education and specialist training met and participated not only in the formal discussions but also in the informal networks that the conference either created or strengthened anew. The conference was indeed an "exceptional forum" for discussion of current concepts and problems and a catalyst from which grew ideas that would shape the College's thinking on residency training in the next decade — the decade in which the potential of university aegis was fully realized.

As well as stimulating discussion on numerous aspects of residency education (particularly education in the university milieu), the Kingston conference yielded ideas that led, in particular, to two innovations that greatly influenced specialist training in Canada in the latter 1960s and the 1970s — the establishment of the R.S. McLaughlin Examination and Research Centre (through conversations between Drs. D.R. Wilson and R.B. Kerr) and the development of in-training evaluation (through the presence of Dr. D.D. Matson, of Boston, and of Drs. D.R. Wilson, G.R. Langley, F.N. Gurd and D.G. Cameron). The conference also enabled Fellows to gain an idea of the views of residents whose interest in specialty training became more pronounced in the 1970s.

At the Kingston conference, many stimulating papers were presented, innovative topics were discussed and emerging concepts were crystallized. The following is a summary of these papers, topics and concepts.[21]

The College's Concern With Residency Programs

In his presentation, "Interest and Concern of the Royal College in Residency Programs," President W.C. MacKenzie explained that some Fellows felt that the College should approve programs for training rather than for specific periods of training in individual hospitals. He reminded his audience that in psychiatry all postgraduate training in Canada was organized and integrated under university auspices. In neurosurgery and cardiovascular surgery, approval was granted only to a hospital or an integrated group of hospitals that provided complete training in the specialty. He raised a series of questions for later consideration:

- Who should be responsible for selecting candidates who wished to enter specialty training?
- How would educators assure continual study and assessment both of the candidate's performance and of the training program?
- Who would determine the actual content of the postgraduate training program?
- How would responsibility be divided between the university medical school and the approved teaching hospital?
- Did the College and other examining bodies, which conducted and determined the content of the examinations, have too great an influence on the postgraduate training program?
- Was the College becoming unduly pressured by hospitals for approval of residency training as a means of enabling them to attract house staff, when their interest in obtaining approval was partly determined by their need to employ junior physicians to perform a service function in the hospital, and little more than lip service was paid to the hospitals' responsibility for the training of the resident staff?
- How would the College balance training in general internal medicine and training in its subspecialties? (The same question applied to general surgery as related to the surgical specialties.)
- What effect would compulsory comprehensive medical care have on residency training?

Ideal Medical Education

Dr. J.R. Ellis, of England, suggested that there should be three stages in ideal medical education: university education to teach the grammar of medicine; general vocational training to teach the practice of medicine; and special vocational training to teach the special vocabulary of a part of medicine. The first stage would provide elasticity in the education of differing students. The last stage would provide elasticity in preparing for different branches. Until the later stages were established (under proper control with necessary facilities, with appropriate licensing, and with adequate earning and living conditions for the graduates), not much progress would be made. The undergraduate course must be radically changed if it were to provide a sound basis for a lifetime of learning and to enable each doctor to encompass the advances of the future and to apply them to the benefit of patients. Such preparation for the future could not be a reality until there was *for every single graduate* (not just those who enter specialties) a full postgraduate training to provide a preparation for the present. In Canada a great responsibility therefore fell upon the College.

Factors Influencing Residency Training Programs in Clinical Teaching Units

Drs. J.R. Evans, A.L. Chute and T.P. Morley identified four factors that influenced residency training programs: the advent of comprehensive health insurance; changing patterns of medical education and practice; subspecialization and research in clinical teaching units; and the widening gap between the supply of medical personnel and the demand for health services. The concept of the clinical teaching unit emerged as a response to two needs. The first was the need to provide the setting for specialized training of physicians in the application of existing knowledge and the acquisition of new knowledge relating to the recognition, treatment and prevention of disease. The second was the need to consider the rapid disappearance of medically indigent patients and the failure of The Hospital Insurance and Diagnostic Services Act to provide much-needed financial support for teaching and research in the clinical centres sponsoring residency programs. For proper functioning of a unit, the academic direction of the university, the cooperation of the hospital and the financial and moral support of the community were all required.

In-Training Examination and Evaluation of Programs and Trainees

Based on his work with the American Board of Neurosurgery, Dr. D.D. Matson reported the outcome of the Board's concern over the high failure rate in neurosurgical examinations. Because each candidate examined was the responsibility of an individual training program and because each took a fairly uniform minimum period of training, poor performance at examinations was attributed to one of three factors: poor examining of candidates (which seemed unlikely), deficiencies in the quality or quantity of training and retention in programs of inferior candidates. To Dr. Matson and his colleagues, it seemed essential to provide earlier in the training experience something other than a "cram" session taken just before the oral board examinations if the overall performance of candidates, and therefore their general knowledge and qualifications to practise the specialty, were to be improved. Of the various sugges-tions that were considered, the possibility of conducting a written examination at some time during the formal training rather than at the end of the training period seemed theoretically the most desirable.

In April 1963, the consensus had been reached that the written examination, given before a trainee became a chief resident, would probably provide the most useful information as to the quality of the candidate's training as well as of the training program. The in-training examination served in part as an educa-tional exercise also. If the candidate did poorly, he was so informed. Dr. Matson hoped that, in conference with the program director, the candidate would act accordingly during the training and practice period remaining before qualifying for the oral examinations.

Progressive Reassessment of Residents

In a discussion led by Dr. R.E. Rossall, interest centred around in-training and progressive reassessment of residents throughout the residency programs. Internal assessment was considered desirable, and annual examinations and machine-marked tests were two such techniques that were discussed. Some participants thought that some form of academic assessment was desirable at about three years after graduation or two of specialty training — the equivalent of the mid-training examination that was adopted by the College in 1968. Dr. J.R. Evans noted that interim evaluation would involve a departure from College tradition, but stressed that one general examination should not be the only means of testing at the end of the total period. Dr. R.C.A. Hunter, referring to internal assessment, thought it would not be difficult, for if a resident trained in a supervised and well-organized program, an enormous amount of informa-tion would be available for evaluation purposes. He observed, perspicaciously in view of the fact that in-training evaluation was not introduced officially by the College until 1972, that the best place to assess him was in his day-to-day work and not at some single arbitrary point in his career.

Objectives of Residency Programs

A discussion led by Dr. R.C. Dickson considered some basic aspects of the organization of residency programs. Fundamental to this was identification of the objectives of residency training. The Association of American Medical Colleges had defined the objectives of undergraduate medical education as the acquisition of appropriate knowledge, skills, habits, attitudes and ethical princi-ples — and these should be included among the objectives of postgraduate education. Additional objectives included the following: to prepare the medical graduate for a specific role in the practice of medicine in the community; to turn out physicians who had attained an acceptable standard of clinical compe-tence; to train academic personnel; to produce inquisitive scholars; and to provide professional service and to maintain a high standard of medical care in the hospital. A group led by Dr. J. Turcot concluded that the residency program was successful if the products were doctors in possession of a rather large body of basic and clinical knowledge, served by sound judgment and capable of taking clinical responsibilities for total medical care. Dr. J.C. Harvey, of Johns Hopkins University, emphasized an essential objective when he stated that in a residency training program there must be graded responsibilities until the most senior resident was perhaps almost acting as a consultant.

Responsibility For The Environment of Residency Programs

While the discussion groups led by Drs. Rossall and Dickson touched on coordination of programs and university integration of programs, these two aspects of residency education were regarded as desirable rather than completely accepted. The first group agreed that the problems of unsatisfactory performance of a resident came not in good four-year programs but when a trainee was taking casual years of training in different hospitals with nominal supervision only and no one was responsible for his overall training. Service requirements dominated such positions, to the neglect of educational requirements. One solution was affiliation of such one-year posts to an existing university-sponsored program — which, the speaker said, "I believe is already under discussion by the Royal College". This topic was indeed being considered, but one of the outcomes of the Kingston conference was the impetus it gave to working towards implementation of such a policy.

University responsibility for postgraduate medical education, however, evidently still constituted a "rather controversial aspect" of the subject. While Dr. A.D. McLachlin's group agreed that residency programs should, whenever possible, be organized under university aegis and that the university should be held responsible for the quality of residency training in any affiliated hospital and, consequently, should be given the responsibility of appointing a chief of service or departmental head, the group agreed that it was expressing an ideal: "Perhaps we are searching for a utopia, but we thought we should at least put down what we believe is ideal". Dr. J.C. Harvey, however, pointed out that university commitment to residency training must be real and understood not just by physicians but also by the universities. This was a problem, as Dr. Harvey explained: "University presidents apparently universally say that their biggest headache is their medical school, and now if they take on, through their departmental chairmen, the running of residency programs in many different hospitals, they may be even more disillusioned with their medical school". The affiliated hospitals had their point of view, too: personal pride on the part of the hospital and the particular direction in which a board of trustees was taking the hospital might not always be in conformity or in agreement with the training program of a university.

A further problem was identified in a discussion led by Dr. G.M. Brown. This concerned the merits of a system of approval of programs rather than of hospitals. His group was divided on this issue. Approval of programs, it was recognized, placed the responsibility on departmental heads, and this was not always viewed with equanimity by their local and sometimes ambitious colleagues. Some of the group considered that the tail of medical education was close to wagging the entire medical dog, to the disadvantage of the tail itself as well as to the inconvenience of the dog. Potential problems were numerous; it would be necessary that communication was watched and nurtured so that the community as a whole, the hospital administration, the nursing staff and the medical school were always knowledgeable of and sympathetic towards each other's needs and capabilities.

Residents' Views of Residency Training

In general, residents in 1965 were critical of the College's dominance of postgraduate medical education. Their complaints included the following:

- The increasing importance of the Fellowship in a medical career, even though the College permitted two standards of achievement.
- Whether or not the Fellowship was the operative standard for practice and hospital privileges, the belief that this was the case affected residents' training and learning experiences and their career aspirations.
- Doubt that specialty training influenced by the academic orientation of the Fellowship produced specialists suited to community practice.
- In choosing the hospital to work in, the lack of freedom on the part of the resident and the lack of direction given by the College, such that residents felt pushed from hospital to hospital "by inflexible forces" without any set course being laid down. "Everything is haphazard", it was said.
- Dissatisfaction and anxiety concerning the examinations, partly because residents felt that their training did not provide an adequate preparation for the examinations, and partly because the examination neither seemed to represent a valid test of the knowledge and ability gained in training, nor appeared to be related to what residents needed to know and practise.
- The element of chance in the examinations, such that a candidate might pass the Fellowship examination yet fail the easier Certification examination and such that a particular examiner might be so biased or purposeful that a candidate would be failed because of conflict with the examiner or because of isolated gaps in a resident's knowledge.
- Lack of alternatives to the current examination system, such as multiple-choice techniques and an ongoing system of evaluation of the candidate during the residency.

- Service responsibilities' occupying too much time, which might be better spent in studying.
- The College's manner of operating, factors other than academic excellence or clinical abilities seemingly governing admission to the examinations and contributing to the impression of the College as a "closed shop" or a "private club".

In general, this study of residents' views of residency training revealed conflict: conflict between their goals of passing the College examinations and their desire to prepare themselves for practice; conflict between a hospital's service requirements and the residents' own goals; conflict between a university program's goals and the aims of hospital administrators; and conflict between the goals of the university residency teaching programs and the goals of the College. In essence, however, "the locus of dissatisfaction lay in the examinations, not in the training itself".

This view of residents' opinions was conducted by Mr. D.G. Fish, Research Director of ACMC. Together with Mr. C.G. Clarke, of ACMC, and Mr. T.J. Giles, of the College, Mr. Fish was responsible for another corpus of information about residents. This was the census of residents in Canadian hospitals approved by the College, as of April 1965.[22] The information that the census provided was interesting because comprehensive statistics on residents in Canada had never been collated before and because it confirmed trends that were of concern to the College. The main findings of the study were as follows:

- On April 1, 1965, a total of 3,162 residents were training in the 151 institutions approved for training.
- Of these residents, 1,796 (57 per cent) were Canadian citizens, 744 (24 per cent) were foreign trainees and 593 (19 per cent) were landed immigrants.
- Of the foreign trainees (i.e., student-visa holders), the percentages from other countries or regions were as follows: India or Pakistan, 15; the Philippines, 14; Europe and USSR, 12; West Indies, 11; Central or South America, 9; Iran, 6; USA, 4; Turkey, 3; UK, Eire, Australia and New Zealand, 3; other, 21.
- A higher proportion of residency positions in Canada was filled by residents from countries other than Canada or USA than was the case in USA (42 vs. 26 per cent).
- Within Canada more teaching-hospital residency positions were filled by Canadian graduates (70 per cent) than by non-Canadian graduates.
- Canadian graduates were more likely to be in hospitals approved for full training than were non-Canadian graduates (64 vs. 48 per cent).
- More non-Canadian graduates held posts in hospitals approved for one-year's training than did Canadian graduates (28 vs. 17 per cent).

- Proportions of Canadian and non-Canadian graduates differed according to the specialties — for example, in ophthalmology, only 9 per cent of the residents were foreign graduates, versus 47 per cent were in neurosurgery.
- Canadian hospitals, therefore, played a substantial part in training foreign doctors and likewise depended substantially on foreign doctors to fill residency positions.

*   *   *

The Kingston conference was a powerful stimulus to further improvements in specialist training. The influence of the conference was great and its effects on the participants long-lasting. This conference was followed by several others on similar topics, of which those on surgical education and research (Winnipeg, November 3–4, 1967) and on residency training in internal medicine (Kingston, September 8–9, 1972) were two. At the latter conference, it was evident that the university aegis concept had taken hold at last: "....one major change that has occurred," said President C.G. Drake, "....is response of the universities of this country to the pleas of the Royal College to take more responsibility...in the organization of [post]graduate training programs, their conduct, their insistence on excellence, in a much more positive way than previously".[23]

Assessment of Training Credentials

The selection of trainees has never been a responsibility of the College; universities' training program directors and specialty training committees make the decisions regarding admission of residents. The College's responsibility and influence has been exerted at a later stage, in terms of the candidates' eligibility for admission to specialty examinations.

This aspect of the College's activities has been the responsibility of the Credentials Committee. This responsibility was not difficult to execute with graduates of Canadian medical schools, it provided some problems with graduates of American medical schools and it was sometimes difficult with graduates of English-speaking medical schools outside North America; but it was virtually impossible with graduates of other medical schools and problems arising from this last group took up most of the time of the Credentials Committee.

The work of the Credentials Committee with respect to candidates' credentials was important, for the College, in the absence of guidance from other sources, was forced to make its own decisions. The College has always been concerned about the quality of specialist care ultimately given by Fellows and Certificants, but it lacks direct control with respect to certain aspects of the training such as the quality of the training provided as opposed to the training requirements and standards that the College laid down. Also of concern, and not easy to control, was the suitability of individual residents training for a particular specialty and their innate ability as assessed by examination. These factors could be influenced to some extent, but the College's concern is illustrated in the following two paragraphs from the minutes of the May 1966 meeting of the Credentials Committee:

> *The* Credentials Committee has been disturbed that in quite a number of instances, candidates who according to reports received have shown lack of aptitude and obviously inadequate competence in training have nevertheless been permitted to continue in their training programs, or moved to other approved posts without evident difficulty. Whether such trainees have been told frankly about their shortcomings and advised regarding their future is unclear.

> The Council and Credentials Committee request chiefs of service and directors of training programs who are training physicians and surgeons in the specialties to consider most seriously the responsibility to assess performance in training. Where it is obvious that the trainee is unsatisfactory in the field he has selected, the committee feels that he should be advised that he appears unsuited to continue training for a career in that specialty and for the examinations of the Royal College or other specialty examining body. Such advice may help to direct these trainees into a more appropriate field, save time and prevent disappointment for the individual and reduce the number of inadequate candidates at the examinations.

The main problem facing the Credentials Committee in this period, then, was the assessment of credentials from graduates of "foreign medical schools" — a term usually restricted to schools in India, the Far East, the Philippines, the Middle East and Central and South America. Would-be trainees came from these countries to Canada, some finding it difficult to adapt quickly to a new environment and many lacking an adequate understanding of the basic sciences. The chief question facing the Credentials Committee was whether the College should accept for the examinations candidates who had medical degrees from medical schools about which the College could know little. Acceptability of the primary medical qualifications of foreign medical graduates was a complex matter for all licensing authorities and organizations, such as the College, that offered higher specialist qualifications. Dr. J.H. Graham summarized the nature of the problem in relation to assessment of two physicians who had been trained in China as follows:

> *We* have accepted for our examinations graduates of Chinese medical schools in the past. We have done so really without any detailed knowledge of the nature of their undergraduate medical training, and largely, perhaps, in the days before we paid much attention to the nature of the medical degree as we do now. I do not think that these two cases which I have cited should necessarily suffer in any way from possible revision of our policy, but they do illustrate some of the points with which we are faced. Probably our College can take a somewhat

more liberal attitude toward basic medical qualifications than would be the case with licensing bodies but how far that liberality should go is certainly something of a problem. We already accept a good many medical qualifications which would not be accepted by provincial licensing bodies for registration.... . There are, of course, variations from province to province in the degrees which are accepted, and one of the factors which influences such regulations is likely the supply of physicians in the province, and also, in some cases, the wording of the provincial medical act which may require that the college of physicians and surgeons be satisfied that the undergraduate teaching is comparable to what would be obtained in the home province. The assessments of training which we now handle are largely those of foreign medical graduates, if one uses that term to mean a graduate who obtained his medical degree outside of Canada. ....[and] probably 70 per cent of the applications for assessment of training are now from foreign medical graduates. Somewhat less than half of the foreign graduates come from the British Commonwealth, other than India, and the remainder, probably constituting about 40 per cent of our total assessments, come from medical schools in areas such as India, the Far East, the Middle East, the Philippines and a few from South America.[24]

This problem was not easy to solve, and the College was confronted with it, in one form or another, for many years. The problems of foreign medical graduates also concerned the Examinations Committee, because of the relatively high examination failure rate among these physicians. By the mid-1970s a high failure rate in the College's examinations was nothing new but, as Dr. B.J. Perey told Council in January 1974, the College was not attempting to identify "a specially gifted and particularly well-trained elite". (Those days had gone the way of the old Fellowship.) The concern now focused on Certification, which, Dr. Perey held, evaluated nothing but the achievement of a basic minimal standard of competence. To him, as chairman of the Examinations Committee, the 1973 failure rate of 61 per cent was unacceptable. The College controlled the approval of training programs, and "supposedly" approved only satisfactory training programs; it set the training requirements, and "supposedly" they were adequate; it decided who was allowed to take its examinations, and "supposedly" all candidates were adequately trained; and the College ran the examinations, and "supposedly" (reiterated Dr. Perey) they evaluated competence adequately. Therefore, failure should be the exception rather than the rule. Dr. Perey proposed that Council regard the average examination pass rate of 39 per cent as the mark that the College should give itself for performance in the area of training and evaluation and that the College should be congratulated on its "enormous" potential for improvement.

The high failure rate was attributable largely to the inadequate training taken by foreign graduates. In the specialties using the multiple-choice question technique, whereas the pass rate for Canadian graduates was of the order of

85 per cent, the pass rate for foreign graduates was of the order of 50 per cent. (Strictly speaking, as Dr. D.R. Wilson pointed out, the candidates who failed were below one standard deviation away from the mean.) The low pass rate among foreign medical graduates consequently blurred the perception of acceptable standards among examiners.

This problem was beyond the purview of any single College committee, and the Examinations Committee, in December 1973, recommended that a task force grapple with the problem, and particularly the delineation of more definite guidelines for acceptable non-Canadian postgraduate training programs. The committee suggested the context of these guidelines as follows: "These guidelines should be precise enough to permit entrance to the examinations only after a candidate is sufficiently prepared and has had sufficient senior responsibility in his specialty to enable him to conduct a specialty practice in a satisfactory manner and to permit him to have a reasonable chance of passing his specialty examinations". Council, in January, 1974, directed the Training and Evaluation Committee to undertake this task. Council approved a motion to set up an adequate data storage and retrieval system to provide information on all aspects of postgraduate training and performance in the examinations.

The task of drawing up guidelines on non-Canadian training was entirely appropriate for the Training and Evaluation Committee. It met on June 12, 1974, and January 17, 1975, to deal with this enormously complex problem. The Examinations Committee had suggested specific questions that the task force might answer:

- While in Canada the College approved, after detailed review, only institutions providing complete programs, were there acceptable alternatives for approving non-Canadian programs?
- Should entrance requirements for residency training be established?
- Should candidates take some of their training in North American programs?
- Should both graded, increasing responsibility and a level of senior responsibility, under supervision, be documented and certified by candidates and program directors?
- Do the guidelines for the older specialties adequately indicate the depth and breadth of experience and responsibility that is consistent with Certification?

To facilitate its work, the task force commissioned Dr. C.B. Mueller to track the records of candidates who had taken the Certification for the first time in 1972, through the examination process up to the written examinations in 1974, by which time several attempts might have been made in the written or oral examinations or both. The tracking study was done in two parts. Stage A was intended to identify the medical schools of candidates attempting the examinations in the various specialties and the results of written and oral examinations with follow-up through five sittings; Stage B, to analyze the demographic and training data of those taking the examination for the first time in the fall of 1973, and the various credentials of those passing and of those failing.

The tracking study clarified the situation concerning examination results in general and those of foreign medical graduates in particular. It clarified aspects of a confusing issue that had long concerned the Credentials Committee as well as the Examinations Committee. The highlights of Dr. Mueller's observations were the following:

1. The data base for Stage A consisted of 1175 candidates' results (502 who took medical school training in Canada; 210 in the United States of America or the United Kingdom; and 463, elsewhere).

2. For these candidates, success at the first attempt was recorded for 308 of the 502, 98 out of the 210 and 109 out of the 463. Success in the written and oral examinations at subsequent attempts was recorded for 111 out of the 502, 45 out of the 210 and 79 out of the 463. Therefore, over the whole period, overall ultimate success was achieved by 83 per cent of the graduates of Canadian medical schools, 68 per cent of those from the United States of America or United Kingdom and 41 per cent of those graduating from other countries. The overall pass rate was 64 per cent.

3. An ultimate pass rate of 83 per cent was considered acceptable and the standard that would define the required performance by foreign candidates.

4. The data base for Stage B comprised the results of 1165 candidates (471 Canadian; 185, from the United States of America or the United Kingdom; and 509, from elsewhere).

5. For graduates of Canadian medical schools, the pass rate percentage was 67; for those of the United States of America, 43; and for those of the United Kingdom 46; for Australians 82; for South Americans, 35; for Europeans, 25; for those from the Far East, 25; and for those from the Near East, 38.

6. The primary language of the candidates was English in 50.4 per cent, "Indian" (i.e., a language of Indian or the Indian subcontinent) in 12.9 per cent, Chinese in 4.5 per cent, Spanish in 1.8 per cent and "other" or "unknown" in 29.2 per cent.

7. The pass rate percentage for foreign graduates was marginally improved in a direct ratio to the length of training taken in Canada, as follows: up to 18 months, 21; up to 30 months, 34; up to 42 months, 38. In general, all foreign trainees who passed the written but failed the oral examination had taken their last training episode in an English-speaking program.

8. Within any of the three major geographic and linguistic groups (Canadian, English-speaking and foreign), candidates who passed

the written examination and failed the oral examination did not significantly differ with respect to the length of training, though their training embraced a greater number of training episodes.

The principal conclusions and recommendations to emerge from this study were the following:

- The paucity of "no show" candidates suggested that all candidates were serious about taking the examination and eventually practising in Canada.
- Abstracting of credentials data permitting computer analysis was possible and should be carried out.
- Information about the candidates' languages, which might well be important, was insufficiently documented, as was more specific and precise information regarding training level and function; these details should be included in any credentials document.
- All trainees should be required to take the last two years of training in a program in Canada or the United States.
- Previous impressions of examiners and of the Examinations Committee that a large part of the foreign medical graduate problem stemmed from deficiencies in the undergraduate curriculum were confirmed.

Dr. Mueller's study, an innovative analysis of an old problem, formed an important part of the task force's work. After analyzing the pass rate study, the task force then formulated guidelines for the assessment of credentials. The principal recommendations were the following:

- Foreign medical graduates entering Canadian programs should demonstrate a level of knowledge comparable to that of Canadian graduates by passing the MCC examination or an appropriate equivalent.
- Prospective candidates requiring recognition of foreign training a) should complete an expanded College questionnaire to document previous training, and b) must spend a minimum of one year as a senior resident in a Canadian program or in a program elsewhere characterized either by major affiliation with a United States university or by approval of medical or surgical authorities responsible for advanced specialty training and Certification in the United Kingdom, Australia or South Africa.
- Notwithstanding these two recommendations, training must meet the College's requirements and candidates must be evaluated by the Credentials Committee as being suitable to sit the examination; completion of training, therefore, was not equivalent to College approval to write the examination.
- Exceptions to these requirements might include such instances as temporary Certification with or without time limit.

This was a useful study and it greatly facilitated the work of the Credentials Committee. It was possible now to be fair to all candidates for admission or at least applying for admission to a training program, whatever their origins. Instead of relying on such outmoded general statements of suitability as "satisfactory moral and ethical standing" and "graduation from a medical school approved by the College",[25] the College could, in 1979, reasonably recommend that applicants be required to meet admission standards that were appropriate to postgraduate educational programs rather than to service programs and that all applicants should have passed the MCC examination or an equivalent screening mechanism.[26]

Training Requirements, Standards and Objectives

As of 1960, the College's requirements for training were met by the simple fulfilment that a certain amount of time be spent in hospitals that offered some teaching facilities. A resident could, however, spend all of the required years of training that were specified in the specialty training requirements without having planned the program in a coordinated manner and, especially, without having acquired experience based on increasing responsibility for direct patient care. Among the advances that were made between 1960 and 1980 was the realization of the College's potential to coordinate specialist training according to carefully defined standards and objectives rather than to simplistic requirements of time spent in hospitals A, B, C and D over X number of years. In short, the medical profession — and the public — could be assured that the specialist had "completed a program of specialty training as prescribed in the training requirements of the specialty concerned, supported by reports confirming that all such training...[was] completed to the satisfaction of the programme director concerned, including a final in-training evaluation report attesting that the candidate...[had] demonstrated sufficient professional ability to practise effectively and responsibly and act as a consultant in the stated specialty".[27] In other words, a specialist was properly qualified according to 1980 standards, the physician's skills and attitudes as well as knowledge being taken into account.

The attainment of this goal required continuous refinement of training and evaluation between 1960 and 1980. This almost alchemical refining process was catalyzed in four phases. The first followed acceptance of the principle, stated clearly by the Robertson committee in 1955, that the dual system of training should be abolished and that a series of minimum training requirements should be established for each specialty. The second phase was initiated by the 1965 Kingston conference on residency education, out of which crystallized ideas concerning specialist training that were applied in the following years. The third originated with the planning and implementation of the single examination process (including in-training evaluation) from 1970 to 1972, for this necessitated a new approach to the requirements for training, including the preparation of three new booklets for the guidance of the College's major committees and the program directors, as well as the candidates. The fourth phase was initiated by the full acceptance of university responsibility for specialist training in the early 1970s, which led the College to insure that its accreditation role in the College-universities partnership be clearly understood. The College was steered through these four phases by its three major committees, aided by the specialty committees. Here, the work of the Credentials Committee in refining candidates' requirements for training, and of the Accreditation Committee in refining guidelines for training programs, will be summarized. Taken together, all this altered the requirements, standards and objectives of specialist training programs.

Development of Uniform Requirements for the Fellowship and Certification Examinations

One of the chief conclusions reached by the Botterell committee, and transmitted in its report for discussion by Council in October 1958, was that the College should establish a single standard of first-class competence. Ultimately this would mean developing a single examination process in all specialties and in two languages, but the first step would involve working with the College's specialty committees and the national specialty societies. The specialty committees themselves had requested changes in training requirements from time to time and now Council's response to the Botterell report would give them an opportunity to shape the College's training requirements. Council, in October 1958, referred the matter to the Credentials Committee and the Examinations Committee for continued study with a request that they bring in reports for the January 1959 meeting of Council. And, as an outcome of the discussion of the duly submitted report from the Credentials Committee, Council, in January 1959, approved the key motion that the Credentials Committee be instructed to modify the training requirements in consultation with the specialty committees of the College and the national specialty societies, so that a single standard of training in each field would be required for both the Certification and Fellowship examinations.

The Credentials Committee concluded that it would not be difficult to amend and implement regulations relating training requirements to a single standard in internal medicine and general surgery but in some of the specialties difficulties might necessitate certain changes. These difficulties included the possible insistence by the Credentials Committee that candidates for examination in the specialties spend a year in general medicine or general surgery — a requirement that was not then asked of Certification candidates — and the related but logical question of determining the appropriate level for the single standard.

The significance of these difficulties and the viewpoint of the Credentials Committee, as well as the dimensions of the problem of uniformity of requirements, may be understood by referring to three paragraphs taken from the report that the Credentials Committee submitted to Council in January 1959. These three paragraphs, drafted by Dr. D.G. Cameron, were included as a preamble to the committee's report:

- The training requirements for Certification in general medicine and general surgery are now very similar to the requirements for the Fellowship. The abolition of approval for a year of supervised practice for Certification would, in fact, make the requirements identical.
- In the medical and surgical specialties there is more discrepancy between the training requirements for the Fellowship and the Certification. This is creating serious problems at the present time. It is clear that a solution to these problems must be sought which is acceptable to the College, and to the specialty groups. The establishment of a single standard of training for the Fellowship and Certification would resolve these problems effectively.
- As a practical example, the training requirements for the Fellowship in psychiatry are different from the requirements for the Certification, with the result that the vast majority of young men and women entering this specialty are seeking Certification rather than the Fellowship.

The Credentials Committee then asked the College's specialty committees and the national specialty societies for comments and recommendations on the development of a single training standard. Most of the specialties favored the move to a single standard, though psychiatry and radiology for a while insisted that there was a continuing need for both Certification and Fellowship. The psychiatrists respected the Certification examination because, paradoxically, training for it embraced a wider study of psychiatry than did the requirements for the Fellowship examination; the radiologists held that the Certification program was necessary in order to meet the country's needs for radiologists.

As the Credentials Committee had foreseen, one set of problems stemmed from the conflict between the training requirements favored by the College and those proposed by the specialty committees. How this conflict was resolved reflects credit on all parties and illustrates one facet of the College's pursuit of unity. The various attitudes on the ways in which agreement (or compromise) was reached are apparent in the College's responses to the proposals of the psychiatrists and of the otolaryngologists also.

The College had always made a year's training in either medicine or surgery mandatory for the Fellowship examination in the medical and surgical specialties, but the psychiatrists and the otolaryngologists wanted this period to be a voluntary rather than a mandatory one. Each specialty group developed requirements that reflected its particular stand for the College to consider further.

The otolaryngologists' suggested requirements were straightforward but caused concern among some members of the Credentials Committee and of Council. The Canadian Otolaryngological Society, in agreement with the College's Specialty Committee in Otolaryngology, proposed the following set of training requirements:

1. An approved general internship of at least one year.
2. Four years of postgraduate training in addition to the general internship...[which] *must* include:
   (a) Three years of approved training in otolaryngology, two years of which must be spent in an approved resident training program in otolaryngology and one year...in further approved resident training in otolaryngology or such other training in otolaryngology as may be approved by the Credentials Committee.
   (b) One year of training which may include:
      i)   One year of approved resident training in general surgery.
      ii) Six months of approved resident training in general surgery and six months in approved resident training in internal medicine.
      iii) One year in the full-time study of basic science in a department approved by the College.
      iv) One year in an approved course of study and training at a hospital or university centre in Canada or abroad.
      v)   One year as a clinical research Fellow in a department approved by the College.

These requirements represented a compromise on the part of the Canadian Otolaryngological Society, the total training period for Certification having lengthened from four years to five. At its January 1960 meeting, Council was divided on the acceptability of the proposed requirements, particularly those that meant eliminating the mandatory requirement for training in general surgery in the training of otolaryngology. But since both the Canadian Otolaryngological Society and the College's Specialty Committee in Otolaryngology — and the Credentials Committee as well — had approved these requirements, it seemed wise for Council to approve them. Moreover, as Dr. Cameron pointed out, there was nothing irrevocable in the decision to approve the requirements and the otolaryngologists would be the first to recognize whether or not the elimination of the mandatory requirement for training in general surgery was working to their disadvantage. The motion to accept the otolaryngologists' proposed requirements was carried, but only narrowly: ten councillors voted in favor, nine opposed the motion and three councillors abstained.

The otolaryngologists' viewpoint is of interest because otolaryngology was one of the specialties that suggested the discontinuation of the mandatory year's training in the parent discipline — in this case surgery. Council's acceptance of this change set a precedent, and the desire of the specialties to suggest less training time in medicine or surgery and more in the specialty concerned marked a trend that would continue. In medicine, the precedent was followed in psychiatry.

The psychiatrists' case was, however, somewhat different and their viewpoint more complex.[28] At that time, two constraints prevented them from submitting a set of single training requirements. First, the CPA believed that there was a practical and continuing need for two levels of examination. The Certification level would testify to a psychiatrist's ability to practise the specialty and would satisfy the need for psychiatrists to provide community practice and to staff clinics and mental institutions. A Fellowship level of examination would indicate a broader academic knowledge of the specialty appropriate to psychiatrists interested in teaching and academic work. Second, the CPA found the College's Fellowship examination in medicine as modified for psychiatry unsatisfactory and urged a different approach to the Fellowship, such that removal of the requirement for Fellowship candidates to spend one year in internal medicine would encourage more candidates to take that examination. (CPA also suggested that candidates for the Fellowship examination should take an additional two years of training following successful completion of the Certification examination and that the College should establish separate faculties to oversee the training and examination of candidates in each specialty.) The CPA and the College's Specialty Committee in Psychiatry were quite ready to work for the College to find a way of developing a single standard, and on March 9, 1960, a meeting between Dr. R.O. Jones, of the CPA, Dr. J.G. Dewan, chairman of the specialty committee, and Dr. F.S. Brien, of the Credentials Committee, was convened for this purpose.

At this meeting, it was suggested that agreement on a single standard could be reached, though it would require some give and take by both parties — the CPA on the one hand and the College on the other. Since the real obstacle for psychiatrists in taking the Fellowship examination was a mandatory year of residency training in internal medicine, their basis of agreement would be removal of this obligatory year of residency training in internal medicine. The College's current requirement led most would-be specialists to prefer the Certification examination to the Fellowship examination and their teachers to hold the opinion that most candidates had little or no chance of passing the Fellowship examination. If a period of training in internal medicine were optional, more psychiatrists would take the Fellowship examination. The question for the College was simply whether it could accept this change. However, the CPA's Education Committee, of which Dr. Jones was chairman, had developed a set of requirements leading to the Certification qualification that did include the options of six months of approved full-time study of a basic science and six months of approved residency training in internal medicine, pediatrics or other branches of medical practice related to psychiatry. Further, during the intensive training period of the residency in psychiatry itself, and of one year in an approved course of study and training at a hospital or university centre in Canada or abroad approved by the university concerned, it was expected that there should be contact with other medical disciplines. Overall, these requirements embraced a four-year training program in which all four years should be conducted under university supervision — one detects Dr. Jones's views here — and in which contacts between resident and teacher and resident and patients were continued. These years would be considered primarily teaching years and service consideration would be secondary during this time. The CPA proposed that, of the four training years, two should be spent in "an intensive teaching experience and organized training program of a university department of psychiatry" and the other two should include more emphasis on "learning through training and supervised clinical experience". The document had been carefully drawn up, and Dr. Jones was reluctant to reword the CPA's submission because of certain difficulties that had arisen within its own membership, and because the submission in its present form had been passed by the CPA.

Dr. Brien was impressed by the psychiatrists' presentation and advised Council to consider the setting up of the single standard along the line suggested by the psychiatrists. The discussion had compelled him to think that the change was timely, particularly when both the College and the CPA were attempting to get postgraduate training under university supervision; "if this opportunity is lost," Dr. Brien emphasized, "it may not arise again". Dr. Brien concluded his report to the Credentials Committee and Council by stating that there were sound grounds for optimism with respect to the future role of psychiatrists and psychiatry within the framework of the College.

Dr. Brien saw the need for unity in a period of change, and both his fellow members of the Credentials Committee and of Council agreed with his view. The removal of the requirement for a one-year period of training in internal medicine had become acceptable, and time would tell whether the omission of a mandatory year of training in internal medicine was a good move and would produce better psychiatrists. The Credentials Committee's recommendation on the proposed single standard of training for examination in psychiatry was approved by Council, and one more milestone in the College's pursuit of unity had been passed.

Other specialties' requirements were less controversial and, by the end of 1965, all the specialties had submitted statements on uniform requirements for the College's examinations. These statements, however, still stressed requirements of time and content rather than educational objectives. It was not until the importance of candidates' acquiring satisfactory skills and attitudes as well as knowledge was realized — which came about in part as a result of the need to design a new examination process — that formal educational objectives were stressed. The concept that a national examination process should evaluate the competence of specialist candidates necessitated national agreement on standards for all of the training programs. This, indeed, was one of the great challenges for the College in the 1970s: "provision of an unequivocal standard through the new examination process [that] constitutes a contribution to the quality of patient care in which the Fellows of the College can take pride".[29]

The Accreditation Project

This "unequivocal standard" was attained in two ways. The first was by providing clearer guidance regarding the standards desired for specialist training. This activity was stimulated by two factors: the evolution of the universities' responsibility in training and the development of the single examination process. The latter process was facilitated by the contributions of specialty examining boards and the specialty committees, which were asked to determine standards of performance that should be expected of their candidates. Each specialty's expectations were then written into the College's booklets that gave information about the regulations and the requirements of specialty training relating to the examinations. Initially, these expectations were reflected in the preamble to the regulations and requirements for training for each specialty, as published in 1972 in the booklets that related to the medical and surgical specialties (the "Blue Book" and the "Red Book", respectively). Later, with the general recognition that the new examination was designed to evaluate competence, the specialty committees assisted the Credentials Committee to go further in defining general objectives that gave more specific guidance as to the aims and designs of each specialty training program.[30]

The second way in which the "unequivocal standard" of specialist practice was attained resulted from a project undertaken by the Accreditation Committee in the latter half of the 1970s. This project was initiated in the fall of 1975, when Dr. J.B. Firstbrook was appointed Director of the Division of Training and Evaluation and when Dr. F.N. Gurd was retained as consultant to the division. The accreditation project consisted of a complete revision of the requirements and guidelines for training programs in the individual specialties.[31]

This project was undertaken by Dr. Gurd in collaboration with Dr. Firstbrook and Mr. V.H. Skinner, Director of the accreditation section of the Division of Training and Evaluation. To this project Dr. Gurd brought his experience in having recently studied specialty training in Britain and in having written a comprehensive report on it.[32] He had also just completed a nine-year term as Regent of the American College of Surgeons; Dr. Firstbrook had a broad experience of the academic aspects of specialty practice in Canada, having served as Executive Director of ACMC before joining the College secretariat. The accreditation project, therefore, was based on a sound knowledge of British and North American approaches to specialty training in addition to complete knowledge of the current Canadian approaches.

The project was accomplished in two phases. The first phase comprised the preparation of a document entitled "General Information Concerning Accreditation of Specialty Training Programs". This was designed as a reference guide for those involved in the conduct of postgraduate medical education programs in Canada and for those involved in their accreditation. Published in June 1976 and bound in a grey cover, it became known as the "Grey Book". The Grey Book dealt, first, with accreditation policies and criteria and, second, with the College's survey process.

The Grey Book served as a comprehensive summary of the state of the art of specialty training in Canada as overseen by the unique Royal College-universities partnership. It defined the objectives of the College's accreditation process and of the universities' sponsorship of specialty training clearly and concisely in a manner that had previously not been spelled out. The accreditation process, it was explained, had three main objectives: to ensure that each specialty program would meet the College's standards in terms of minimum resources; to ensure that these resources were utilized effectively and efficiently in enabling trainees to meet the College's training requirements; and to provide consultation services to the medical schools and the specialty programs. With respect to university aegis, it was stated that "the primary purpose of university sponsorship of specialty training is to make available to each trainee all resources of the university and its participating hospitals that can be mobilized to his or her advantage". The reasons for the superiority of university sponsorship — and also of the College's control — over the old system of apprenticeship in hospital were also clearly identified: "The academic and research resources of all faculties and the clinical and other facilities offered by general hospitals and special institutions are needed to provide variety and depth in educational and clinical experience. Central control is necessary to some degree to ensure optimal use of such diverse facilities".

The Grey Book detailed three elements of training programs. These were the organizational components that were considered necessary within each university (e.g., the multidisciplinary faculty committee, the program director and the specialty training committee), the clinical teaching unit (which had first been described during the Kingston conference on residency education in 1965[33]) and the requirements of academic education within each program (since "the residents in training", it was explained, "are the future guardians of quality within their chosen discipline…they must [be enabled to] preserve and strengthen the scientific base that underlines their specialty"). The Grey Book also dealt with the survey process, listing the categories of approval and describing the manner of application for approval of a program; the roles of the specialties in surveys and guidelines for surveyors were also characterized.

Underlying the publication of the Grey Book was an awareness that the College, lacking direct control over the entire arrangements of any university (and also, perhaps, understanding that some universities might soon relish and

224

claim autonomy with respect to specialty training), needed to provide a clear and authoritative statement on the state of the art of specialty training in 1976. At that time the concept of a nation-wide network of integrated programs under university control was not totally accepted; as Dr. Gurd observed, "it was a bold experiment that could still go wrong".[34] If the College's contribution to the process was to reach its full potential, it was essential that the College should point the way with intelligence, reason, logic — and tact. In this the College succeeded, for, though a few faculties and hospital staff members looked askance at the College's initiative, the majority of educators and specialists, together with the trainees themselves, appreciated the College's publishing an authoritative document. Moreover, publication of the Grey Book marked a readjustment of the balance of training and the examination in College activities. For years, the College had been obliged to focus to a great extent on examining candidates; the Grey Book testified that it was the training of a specialist that, in the last analysis, was the raison d'etre of the College.

The second phase of the accreditation project consisted of updating criteria for acceptable training programs in all the specialties. This was necessary because the existing booklet of requirements had been written in 1965, before the imperatives of integrated training and the advances in education of the 1960s had been fully understood. Ideas expressed in the Grey Book must now be adapted to the needs of each specialty in turn. This phase of the accreditation project was made possible by close collaboration with the Credentials Committee, which had begun in 1972 to press each specialty committee to define general objectives for training in its specialty. The work of the Credentials Committee in preparing general objectives formed the keystone of the training and evaluation arch. These statements made program directors and residents (and examiners, too) aware of the general expectations of the specialties as to the content of the training.

As one specialty after another settled on rational objectives, then, and only then, was it possible for the accreditation project to move on to the second phase — the formulation of well-reasoned guidelines and requirements for accreditation of training programs in each specialty. To each of the documents was coupled a specialty-specific supplement to the pre-survey used to gather data on each training program in advance of the cyclical surveys. As in the definition of general objectives for each specialty, the contributions of the specialty committees proved invaluable. Often, the specialty committees consulted the national specialty societies concerning the appropriate statements to be included. Such concentration on so wide a scale confirmed the value of the College's pursuit of unity but, more than this, it demonstrated once again the College's dependence on the expertise of the specialty committees for its credibility in postgraduate medical education.

The accreditation project was essentially complete by 1979. Medical educators across Canada generally agreed that the standards of training were higher than they had been at the beginning of the decade and far higher than they had been in 1960. As in other aspects of the College's activities, the changes that had reshaped the approach to specialist training were profound. By 1980, it appeared that the need to ensure that well-selected candidates received the finest training possible was balanced by an effective semi-quantitative as well as qualitative evaluation process. The means had changed over the years, but the end remained the same — to ensure that "a practising physician essaying to do 'special work' should have the opportunity of obtaining a distinguishing designation from The Royal College of Physicians and Surgeons of Canada whereby it may be known that he is properly qualified".

NOTES TO CHAPTER 8

1. Compare, for example, the May 1951 College booklet entitled *Regulations and Requirements of Graduate Training Relating to the Examinations for the Diploma of Fellow or Certification in a Specialty* with the June 1972 booklet entitled *General Information Concerning Requirements for Training and Examinations.*
2. RCPSC, Memorandum re Graduate Training. Drafted by J.H. Graham, Nov. 3, 1959. See Council, January 1960, Attachment 5.
3. Lewis, p. 25.
4. A.D. Kelly, Letter to J.E. Plunkett, Oct. 30, 1946.
5. RCPSC, *Requirements for Approval of Hospitals for Advanced Graduate Training.* Ottawa, 1965, p. 3.
6. I am indebted to Dr. R.W. Gunton for reminding me of this quality of the 1960s. It affected psychological, philosophical, political and physical aspects of life in the 1960s. As far as medical education was concerned, the same element of expansiveness was noted by Dr. R.B. Kerr during his presidential address to the Fellows in 1968. Dr. Kerr said that "new medical schools are being organized, existing medical schools are enlarging, curricular changes are occurring with almost incomprehensible rapidity, medical science and information is multiplying, new concepts of patient care and application of medical knowledge are developing, [and] more needs arise for specialized training" (ABM, 1968, p. 9).
7. ABM, 1965, p. 3.
8. RCPSC, *Requirements for Approval of Hospitals for Advanced Graduate Training.* Ottawa, 1965, pp. 6-7.
9. Council, June 1951, pp. 25-27.
10. Council, June 1955, pp. 28-32.
11. Council, June 1957, pp. 10-11.
12. RCPSC brief to ACMC, Nov. 7, 1959, based on the memorandum referred to in note 2.
13. ACMC, minutes of 17th annual meeting, Nov. 6-7, 1959, p. 4.
14. Council, June 1957, p. 11.
15. Council, October 1957, p. 17.
16. J.W. MacLeod, Letter to J.H. Graham, Nov. 15, 1962.
17. C.B. Stewart, Letter to R.C. Dickson, n.d. See Council January 1959, p. 31.

18. I am especially indebted to Dr. J.H. Graham for having summarized the evolution of accreditation and the universities' participation in postgraduate training. Dr. Graham concluded his summary by stating, "All of this is a remarkable accomplishment in collaboration between the Royal College and the medical schools. It is possibly unique, at least in the western world."

19. E.H. Botterell, Letter to J. Turcot, Mar. 25, 1968.

20. Proceedings of the Conference on Residency Education in the Clinical Specialties, *Can Med Assoc J* 1966; 95: 696.

21. For a full report, see Proceedings of the Conference on Residency Education in the Clinical Specialties, *Can Med Assoc J* 1966; 95:695-781.

22. C.G. Clarke, D.G. Fish and T.J. Giles, "A Census of Residents in Canadian Hospitals Approved for Training by The Royal College of Physicians and Surgeons of Canada, April 1965". *Can Med Assoc J* 1966; 94:777-784.

23. C.G. Drake, Welcoming Address to Conference on Residency Training in Internal Medicine, held at Queen's University, Kingston, Sept. 8-9, 1972. *Ann RCPSC* 1973; 6:97.

24. J.H. Graham, Letter to E.D. Gagnon, April 28, 1965. See Credentials Committee, May 1965, Attachment 1, p. iii.

25. RCPSC, *Regulations and Requirements of Graduate Training Relating to the Examinations for the Diploma of Fellow or Certification in a Specialty.* Ottawa, May 1951, p. 9.

26. RCPSC, *General Information Concerning Accreditation of Specialty Training Programs.* Ottawa, June 1979, p. 10.

27. RCPSC, *General Information and Regulations on Training Requirements and Examinations,* Ottawa, October 1981, p. 5.

28. For a full account of the psychiatrists' viewpoint, see: Council, January 1960, pp. 26 and 39; Executive, April 1960, p. 28, Attachment 9; Credentials Committee, June 1960, pp. 2-3, Attachment 2; Council, June 1960, pp. 25-26 and Attachment 2.

29. F.N. Gurd, "The Royal College: New Perspectives in Specialty Training and Evaluation." *Can Med Assoc J* 1973; 108:95-97.

30. The nature of evolution from Preambles to General Objectives may be illustrated by comparing the 1972 and 1977 versions of the requirements for training in Cardiovascular and Thoracic Surgery. The 1972 Preamble ran as follows:

    The cardiovascular and thoracic surgeon has special need of a complete knowledge of the physiology of the cardiovascular and respiratory systems. He should possess a good knowledge of diseases of the chest and cardiovascular system.

    In some centres experience in the surgery of the lungs and other structures within the thorax may be obtained on the same service with the cardiovascular surgery; in others, this experience will be gained as part of the general surgery training.

    During the course of training the candidate must acquire a knowledge of the basic sciences necessary to the understanding and practice of cardiovascular and thoracic surgery. Further training in basic science (such as anatomy, physiology, biochemistry and pathology) may be taken concurrently with the resident training or by attendance at special courses in the basic sciences.

By 1977, General Objectives had been prepared, as follows:

> Cardiovascular and thoracic surgery is concerned with diseases of the heart and great vessels, chest wall, mediastinum, lungs, pleura, esophagus, diaphragm, and arteries and veins.

> It is recognized that, after completion of their training, some surgeons will join teams in major centres with facilities for cardiac as well as esophago-pulmonary and vascular surgery. Others will settle in smaller centres where they may concentrate on vascular, esophago-pulmonary and pacemaker problems. The training requirements in this specialty are flexible enough to allow the trainee to choose, in collaboration with the director of the training program, a distributional operative experience best suited to his or her individual needs.

> All trainees are expected to have knowledge relevant to the entire spectrum of cardiac, vascular and non-cardiac thoracic surgery. However, it is recognized that some will have less experience than others in certain components of the specialty. For example, some trainees will carry out many cardiac procedures. Others might have a minimum of cardiac surgery, preferring to concentrate on non-cardiac thoracic surgery.

> During the course of training, candidates must acquire a satisfactory knowledge of the principles of surgery, including the pathophysiology of shock, nutrition and metabolism, infection, coagulation, immunity, genetics and statistics. A knowledge of the body's response to prosthetic materials is required. In addition, a detailed knowledge of congenital and acquired cardiac, vascular and thoracic disease is necessary, together with adequate exposure to patients for the necessary training in their management and actual operative experience.

> Detailed knowledge and experience is also required in the following specific areas: diagnostic procedures (including heart catheterization, angiography, ultrasonography, rigid and flexible bronchoscopy, bronchial brushing, esophagoscopy, esophageal motility and pH studies, respiratory function tests, non-invasive studies of peripheral vascular disease); cardiopulmonary bypass; ventilatory support devices; cardiac assist devices; pacemakers; chest trauma; postoperative monitoring and intensive care; intraoperative myocardial protection.

31. The material for this part of the chapter is based on information kindly provided me by Dr. F.N. Gurd. His contributions to the College (first as a councillor from 1964 to 1972, then as chairman of Examinations Committee from 1968 to 1972, then as Associate Secretary from 1972 to 1975 and finally as consultant to the Division of Training and Evaluation from 1975 to 1982) gave Dr. Gurd an unusual perception of the College's role in Canadian medicine from 1960 to 1980. This section of the present chapter is complemented by two essays by Dr. Gurd — the article referenced in note 29 and the chapter entitled "Guidelines for Training in the Specialties" published in Andison and Robichon, pp. 85-94.
32. F.N. Gurd, "Specialist Training in Britain — 1975", a report to The Royal College of Physicians and Surgeons of Canada. RCPCS, 1975.

33. "The Clinical Teaching Unit as an Effective Organization for the Education of Residents Under Changing Medical Socio-economic circumstances: I. J.R. Evans, A.L. Chute and T.P. Morley, "Objectives and Organization of the Clinical Teaching Unit: A White Paper"; II. T.P. Morley, "Contractual Relationship Between Surgeon and Patient in a Clinical Teaching Unit"; III. A.L. Chute, "Administrative and Professional Problems of a Clinical Teaching Unit Based in a Community Hospital". *Can Med Assoc J* 1966; 95:720-733.
34. F.N. Gurd, Letter to D.A.E. Shephard, June 26, 1984.

Chapter 9

Evaluation and Examination for Specialist Competence

The decade from 1963 to 1972 was remarkable for the evolution of an entirely new approach in the College to the content and conduct and the methodology of its examinations. The principal change occurred in the fall of 1972, when the Fellowship examination and the Certification examination were replaced by an entirely new single examination process. Termed the Certification examination (but in no way resembling the original Certification examination), this qualifying examination for specialists was designed so that specialist competence could be evaluated more fairly — and in any of more than 30 specialties and in either English or French. Although introduced at one stroke, it was possible to introduce the single examination process only because a number of constructive steps had been taken in the 1960s — the review of the Fellowship examination in 1963, the introduction of multiple-choice questions into the Fellowship examination in 1965, the establishment of the R.S. McLaughlin Examination and Research Centre in 1968 and the seminal discussions conducted by the Expanded Executive Committee in 1969. The flaws in the dual examination system thereby had become only too evident. The College recognized the fact that neither the Fellowship nor the Certification examination was a precise evaluative tool.

At the beginning of the 1960s, the College conducted two sets of examinations — the Fellowship and the Certification. The Fellowship examination, conducted in fewer than two dozen specialties, consisted of a written test of the essay type and an oral and clinical examination for those candidates who scored 70 per cent or more in the written examination. It was a one-shot or final-axe type of evaluation that was more a test of factual knowledge and academic aptitude than an overt assessment of clinical competence. The Fellowship examination, it was generally agreed, was designed to identify those would-be specialists who wished to engage in teaching or research (or both) as well as to practise as consulting specialists. The Certification examination was less rigorous and searching, and its purpose was to identify physicians who preferred to practise as specialists and deliver, safely and competently, specialty health care in hospitals outside the university orbit. In 1972 this dual standard was abolished in favor of a single one for all specialists. The single examination process that replaced the two former examinations was a three-phase *process* that was intended, by taking account of a resident's ability as manifested during the training period as well as during the written examination and the oral and clinical examination, to identify a physician who was competent in terms of factual knowledge and appropriate skills and attitudes. This new approach was based on a number of methodologic advances — the multiple-choice question technique, the mid-training examination and, especially, the developing concept of in-training evaluation were the most important — and thus the new qualifying examination, despite being termed Certification, was not only quite different from the College's former Certification examination but also arguably superior even to the highly respected Fellowship examination of earlier years.

Of all the changes that contributed to the transformation of the College between 1960 and 1980, those relating to the specialty examinations were among the most important. There was, moreover, a sense of purpose in the way these changes developed. Dr. G.R. Langley, writing just after the single examination process had been introduced in the fall of 1972, observed this when he commented on the "evolutionary changes" in the College's examination program in the latter 1960s and early 1970s. He pointed out that these changes were "so carefully planned on such a carefully constructed data base."[1] In this chapter these "carefully planned" evolutionary changes are described and the "carefully constructed data base" is elucidated. Because the growing understanding of evaluation was essential to this evolution, the changes in the College's examinations are discussed in the context of evaluation as it was understood in the 1960s and early 1970s.

Principles and Practice of Evaluation

None of the changes in the examination system that occurred in the latter half of the 1960s and in the early 1970s could have been implemented if the principles of evaluation had not been understood. This understanding came only gradually. The work of medical educators like Drs. J.P. Hubbard and G.E. Miller in the United States and of a handful of College Fellows in Canada, notably Drs. J.A.L. Gilbert, F.N. Gurd, B.J. Perey and D.R. Wilson, was instrumental to the application of the principles of evaluation to the assessment of clinical competence. The fundamentals of evaluation had to be learned before they could be applied; otherwise, as Miller stressed, "practices of evaluation in medical education often give the appearance of a pagan rite of worship at the altar of many ill-defined gods, practised with all the grace of an angry bull."[2]

Evaluation was much discussed in the period from 1960 to 1980, and an example of the interest evaluation generated was the Conference on Evaluation in Medical Education that was held in Edmonton in June 1969. This conference, which demonstrated a growing interest in evaluation, was held at a time when the increasing and general dissatisfaction with the College's examinations was yielding to an optimistic view that an understanding of the principles of evaluation would alleviate this dissatisfaction — and even correct the faults in the examination system. At this conference some basic principles of evaluation were enunciated. These principles are now well recognized, but the need for them to be stated at the Edmonton conference in 1969 and then for selected papers to be published in the College's *Annals* is worth noting.[3] For this reason these principles are summarized here:

- Evaluation, in general, is a process of determining what is of value, judging the attainment of these values and then reflecting on the newly collected information.
- Among the aims of evaluation in postgraduate medical education, two are paramount: first, to identify candidates who both have the potential for solving relevant questions and are suited to provide excellent patient care; and, second, to discover how well training programs are working.
- Concerning problem-solving ability — the essence of medicine — an understanding of the aims of evaluation facilitates achievement of the endeavors underlying evaluation. Three aspects of problem-solving ability are important: factual knowledge, clinical skills and personal attitudes. Dr. D.R. Wilson summarized this simply and directly when he suggested elsewhere that these three aspects could be looked at in terms of what the candidate knows, what the candidate does with this knowledge and how the candidate applies this knowledge.[4]
- No matter what form a training program assumes, the essence of training must be reflected in the preparation of students to perform certain tasks. These tasks demand not only knowledge, skills and attitudes but also the adoption of the role of the professional, whose ideal goal is to safeguard the public's well-being by delivering competent and proficient specialist health care. Therefore medical educators must indicate the level of proficiency that examination candidates are expected to attain, and this in turn requires that medical educators define educational objectives for training programs, examiners and candidates to follow.
- In seeking appropriate evaluation procedures, the correct approach is to identify those that are reliable, relevant and predictive. The steps in the evaluation process are complex, but a "deceptively simple" evaluation approach is a fourfold one: defining objectives; identifying criteria of standards by which achievement of the objectives can be judged; isolating single dimensions of competence to be measured (and designing appropriate and adequate measurement tools); and implementing further steps in the light of what has been learned up to then.[5]

- In attempting to successfully achieve the aims of evaluation in medical education, further objectives are necessary: to consider each evaluation procedure in terms of the specific purpose for which it is intended; to define as precisely as possible what is to be measured; and to recognize the strengths and limitations of the various evaluation procedures.

These principles were applied to both training and examinations, as it became realized in the 1960s that examinations should be based on the underlying concept that the training and examination of specialist candidates were part of a common goal — the production of a competent specialist physician. The purpose of training was to ensure that a candidate's experience was sufficient to permit safe embarcation on the practice of the specialty; the purpose of an examination was to assess a candidate's capacity to develop into a competent specialist. Input to evaluation therefore came from many different sources: program directors and other members of specialty departments; members of specialty committees; members of examination test committees; the staff of the R.S. McLaughlin Centre; members of the Examinations Committee; members of the Credentials and Accreditation Committees; the College secretariat, especially in the Division of Training and Evaluation; and candidates themselves. The general dissatisfaction with the College's examinations, which became strident as the 1960s passed by, thus became tempered with constructive criticism based on the sound understanding of the purposes and principles of evaluation.

But examinations have always been imperfect evaluative instruments, and it was therefore necessary for the College to be content with achieving a goal somewhere between an ideal method of objectively evaluating the competence of candidates and an expedient process aimed at determining a minimum standard of competence for identification of specialists. This challenge was a continuing one. Because competence is not easily defined, either in theory or in practice, it was not easy to examine candidates as objectively as desirable. Nor could the principal components of competence — factual knowledge, problem-solving ability and interpersonal skills and attitudes — be related clearly to standards of competence. Similarly, the degree to which reliability and validity, while essential to measurement, actually were incorporated into the final evaluation of a candidate on the particular day of the examination was uncertain. Consequently, the College's principal methods of assessment of competence — the written examination, the oral and clinical examination and in-training evaluation — remained imperfect.

The introduction of the multiple-choice question technique into the written examination in internal medicine in 1965 appeared to be an advance because the lack of reliability and validity of the essay type of examination was thereby to a large extent removed as a negative factor.[6] Yet it was necessary to retain the essay test in the examination process in the numerically smaller specialties, and even the multiple-choice question technique, it was realized, was imperfect: it did not assess all aspects of competence, and use of the technique required a great deal of education and of time and effort on the part of examining personnel. Also imperfect was the oral and clinical examination; for several reasons, logistics included, the American Board of Internal Medicine, for example, discontinued using it in 1972.[7] The traditional oral examination has been faulted on several grounds: sampling and rating errors make it unreliable; not all important areas of competence are evaluated and those that can be evaluated are not evaluated precisely because the examination is unstructured and unstandardized; candidates must behave both subserviently (to examiners) and responsibly (with respect to presented cases); the examination measures predominantly a candidate's ability to recall, rapidly and under stress, isolated and often unconnected pieces of information; and inter-rater reliability of agreement is not high.[8] But in spite of such defects, this examination technique persisted, in part because a perfect alternative was not available.[9] Even the attractive alternative of in-training evaluation had defects such as lack of standardization in all training programs across Canada and incomplete objectivity.[10]

The need to evaluate specialist candidates, however, remained, and examinations offered the most practical method of evaluating thousands of candidates yearly. One of the College's responsibilities is to be accountable to the Canadian public (and calls for the College, and other organizations, to be accountable became more strident in the 1960s and 1970s), and the identification of competence is an aspect of the College's accountability. Realizing that, as evaluative instruments, examinations remain imperfect and, at the same time, that it is accountable to the public, the College, particularly between 1960 and 1972, took a series of steps to diminish this degree of imperfection, and it is in this context that the College's work in the examinations field should itself be evaluated.

Examination Reform

The Need for Reform

In the late 1950s and early 1960s, the rising failure rate in the Fellowship examinations was a matter of great concern in the College. In 1942, the pass rate for all specialties was 60 per cent and in 1943 and 1944 it even reached 100 per cent. The pass rate fell to 54 per cent and 56 per cent in 1945 and 1946, and by 1956 it had fallen to 37 per cent. In 1960, although the overall pass rate was 38 per cent, the pass rate for neurosurgery was 13 per cent and for general surgery it was 28 per cent. In 1962, the pass rate was even lower — 30.5 per cent. Such results continued to concern the College into the 1970s; examination results from 1960 to 1971 and from 1972 to 1980 are summarized in Table 9.1. While these results, particularly in the 1960s, indicated that the College was

TABLE 9.1 Numbers of Candidates Taking, and Percentages of Candidates Passing, the Fellowship Examination and the Certification Examination in all Specialties, 1960-1971 (Part A) and the Certification Examination in all Specialties, 1972-1980 (Part B).

(Source: College Examinations Section files.)

PART A: 1960-1971

Year	Fellowship Examination		Certification Examination	
	No. of Candidates	Pass Rate (per cent)	No. of Candidates	Pass Rate (per cent)
1960	459	38.0	621	58.6
1961	457	39.2	627	64.6
1962	512	30.5	594	63.1
1963	625	43.7	621	60.1
1964	646	46.4	697	63.6
1965	725	45.8	735	64.6
1966	774	43.0	688	62.9
1967	868	39.3	785	68.1
1968	1009	42.2	935	68.0
1969	1008	45.2	1068	66.6
1970	1021	46.8	1070	67.7
1971	1120	42.4	1135	66.6

PART B: 1972-1980

Year	Single Examination Process Certification			
	Written		Oral	
	No. of Candidates	Pass Rate (per cent)	No. of Candidates	Pass Rate (per cent)
1972	1725	64.9	990	67.7
1973	1994	60.3	1079	66.6
1974	2075	59.6	1177	65.9
1975	2050	62.6	967	63.4
1976	2412	65.4	1373	65.3
1977	2197	61.9	1185	69.8
1978	2072	68.0	1212	69.3
1979	1957	69.6	1207	71.3
1980	1767	73.5	1029	73.6

Commentary on Table 9.1

Certain factors must be taken into account when Table 9.1 is studied:

1. Because the College's examination system was totally redesigned beginning in 1972, when the single examination process was introduced, the results in Parts A and B of the Table cannot be compared. The Certification examination from 1972 onwards was different from both the Certification examination of earlier years and the Fellowship examination also.

2. In Part A, the results for the Fellowship examination from 1964 to 1971 include the results of two groups of candidates — those who were successful in the fall of the year indicated and those who were successful in the supplemental examination that was held the following spring. The supplemental examination was first held in 1965.

3. In Part B, pass rates are given for the written examination and the oral examination, but it is not possible to derive overall pass rates for any one year, as was possible earlier, because candidates who passed the written examination could elect to postpone their oral examination until another year. The results for the oral examinations in any one year therefore include those of some candidates who had passed the written examination in a previous year.

4. In Part B, a trend towards higher pass rates is observable from 1978 onwards for the written examination and from 1977 onwards for the oral examination. The probable explanation is a multiple one: (a) the components of the single examination process were introduced at different times from 1970 onwards, and the influence of these several components (the mid-training comprehensive [or early written examination] in some medical specialties; the principles of surgery examination in some surgical specialties; and in-training evaluation) is likely to have been exerted only gradually; (b) the College's training requirements were revised in the mid-1970's, when the Accreditation and Credentials Committees made a concerted effort to assure a higher standard among candidates permitted to proceed to the final examinations; and (c) also in the 1970s, an increasing proportion of candidates took most or all of their specialty training in Canada, which is significant because specialty training in Canada (like medical school training in Canada) has tended to be associated with higher pass rates than specialty (and medical school) training taken in other countries.

5. Although the R.S. McLaughlin Examination and Research Centre was established in 1968, the awareness of valid and reliable examination procedures that the work of the Centre stimulated was not fully felt for several years.

upholding a certain standard, certain questions required close consideration: Was this standard realistic? Were the examinations reliable and valid? And were the candidates suitable and well trained? But reflection along these lines was discomforting, and in the early 1960s a variety of concerns caused the Examinations Committee, particularly, to take stock.

One frequent finding was that graduates of medical schools outside Canada did not generally do as well in the Fellowship examinations as graduates of Canadian medical schools. This was reported, for example, by an ad hoc committee representing the Examinations Committee and the Credentials Committee. Dr. W.G. Beattie, the Honorary Assistant Secretary, and Mr. T.J. Giles, the Executive Secretary, reviewing the files of 50 candidates who took the Fellowship examination in general surgery in 1960, reported an observation that was the first of several such observations: whereas the pass rate for candidates who had graduated from medical schools in North America, the United Kingdom or Australia averaged 40 per cent, the pass rate for candidates who had graduated elsewhere was only 11 per cent. Dr. Beattie and Mr. Giles also found that candidates who had taken all their training in fully approved, university-coordinated training programs in Canada stood the best chance of succeeding at the Fellowship examinations. This sample of 50 candidates was too small to provide statistically significant results, but later studies, such as the tracking study conducted by Dr. C.B. Mueller,[11] confirmed the validity of these two findings.

The content and conduct of the examinations also required attention. While the continued high failure rate demonstrated the discrepancy between the standard expected by the examiners and that achieved by the candidates, a second discrepancy was evident in the marking of the same questions by two examiners. This discrepancy, advised Dr. J.L. McCallum, chairman of the Fellowship examining board in medicine in 1962, might be less of a problem if examiners listed the points essential to a satisfactory answer and if they substantiated their marks by giving clear objectives for the answering of each question. Some examiners, too, were generally unhappy about the examinations: one examiner claimed that the results often hinged on "irresponsible decisions about inconsequential minutiae", and a second commented on the "wide deviation which can occur between the realm of the practical and the theoretical."

This second examiner was Dr. J.W. Rogers, chairman of the Fellowship examining board in obstetrics and gynecology in 1962. In a report that he submitted to the Examinations Committee for its meeting in December 1962, Dr. Rogers questioned the disconcertingly predominant place of pathology in the Fellowship examinations. Dr. Rogers requested Council to grant Fellowship to two candidates who, though passing the examinations as far as obstetrics and gynecology were concerned, had been failed because they had narrowly missed the 70 per cent pass mark required in pathology by margins of 0.75 per cent and 1.75 per cent, respectively. The matter that Dr. Rogers raised was not simply a protest on behalf of two candidates whom he considered "extremely capable"; it was, Dr. Rogers said, "a protest which may well concern the College as a whole and particularly the obstetricians and gynecologists as a group." It is therefore worth considering Dr. Rogers's argument further. [12]

Dr. Rogers's report brought to the fore two important issues. The first related not so much to the principles of the Fellowship examination — the purpose of which should be to assess a candidate's capacity to develop into a "first-class physician" [13] — as to the way in which those principles were executed. Was it right that the competence of a candidate in a clinical field should be assessed on the basis of detailed knowledge of a non-clinical subject (pathology) and that, in Dr. Rogers's words, the pathology examiners should fail or pass "according to their whims with no regard to other factors"? The second issue related to the unity of the College as a whole. The danger was that "splinter groups with plans for a separate College" would be only too ready to seize on "the apparently overwhelming influence [of] the result of the pathology examinations upon the successful outcome of [specialist] aspirants" as a strong point in the case for separation and autonomy. [14]

Dr. Rogers believed that "incongruities" detracted from the value of the Fellowship diploma and that they should be corrected. As far as obstetrics and gynecology was concerned, the Fellowship diploma represented the highest possible achievement available to any obstetrician and gynecologist. It was the proficiency demanded in general surgery, general medicine, basic science and pathology that distinguished the Canadian Fellowship in obstetrics and gynecology from all other higher diplomas in this specialty, and nothing should ever be done that would adversely affect the integrity and value of the Fellowship. The "overwhelming" influence pathology had had in the 1962 Fellowship examination in obstetrics and gynecology was an example of a major incongruity. Dr. Rogers urged that the College, through its examiners, be "absolutely certain that those candidates who fail our Fellowship [examination] have done so in an unequivocal manner without a possible element of doubt." The case of the two candidates on whose behalf Dr. Rogers spoke revealed that doubt that they had failed in "an unequivocal manner" indeed existed, for "no examiner", Dr. Rogers claimed, "can be accurate to fractions of a per cent, no matter what his experience has been."

Dr. Rogers's main concern was that lack of competence in the two candidates was not proven. His experience (or, rather, inexperience, since he acknowledged this in not asking the examiners to vote on the second candidate's marks) and the range of the marks assigned to the two candidates by the different examiners led him then to question the merits of the examination system. He became further concerned because, considering the marks of the 42 candidates who took the written examination in obstetrics and gynecology in 1962, he found that the pass rate was as low as 19 per cent. Dr. Rogers was led to suggest that "any examination which presents this result is a very serious cause for deep consideration, not only of the examinees but of the examination and the examiners as well, and that when such a condition exists in any academic institution, no matter at what level of education, serious consideration must be given to replacement of the examining personnel with more satisfactory individuals."[15]

Council acceded to Dr. Rogers's request and thereby acknowledged that the College's examination system was faulty. Part of the problem was that the College provided no clear guidelines regarding the level of knowledge that candidates for the Fellowship and the Certification examinations should be expected to reach. Certification was intended to indicate that a successful candidate had "a satisfactory practical knowledge of his specialty"; a Fellowship diploma attested to "equal or greater clinical proficiency and...a keener appreciation and a broader understanding of basic science and fundamental principles of medicine and/or surgery." Other than these statements, examiners received little guidance,[16] and it was not surprising that some examiners, such as the pathologist whose marks Dr. Rogers commented on, should assess Fellowship candidates at a high, academic level, whereas others, particularly clinicians, were more interested in a candidate's clinical aptitude and knowledge. Nor was it surprising that, on more than one occasion in the 1960s, a candidate passed the supposedly more difficult Fellowship examination yet failed the supposedly easier Certification examination.[17] Dr. Rogers was quite right: incongruities blurred the terms of reference relating to the Fellowship examination and it was necessary that these incongruities be corrected.

Among the profession as a whole, too, criticism of the Fellowship examination grew during the early 1960s. Criticism in the correspondence column of the *Canadian Medical Association Journal* in 1966 and 1967, for example, suggested that all was not well with the examination system. While some of the correspondents praised the Canadian approach and the College's Fellowship examination — one said that "the Fellowship examinations represent a very fair measure of a candidate's ability" although it was "the toughest examination in the English language"[18] — some correspondents were highly critical. One writer stated that "the spectre of the Royal College's Fellowship examination looms from the day of graduation from medical school; postgraduate training is thereby conditioned."[19] Another, observing that possession of the Fellowship diploma had become a prerequisite for admission to hospital staffs, concluded that the standards and future of the College needed to be reviewed, since the Fellowship diploma appeared to him to have become the "ultimate weapon in Canadian medicine."[20] A third writer admitted that, after years of scrutiny and a failed examination behind him, he had only the slightest idea of what the College's standards actually were.[21] Yet another claimed that the Fellowship examination exerted a "pernicious influence" because the intensive preparation that candidates considered necessary for the examination often meant "complete atrophy" in their desire to strike out independently in the search for new knowledge; this correspondent, a clinical neurophysiologist, contended that to make the Fellowship examination the *only* road to access to academic clinical medicine was "wrong, short-sighted and dangerous."[22]

None of these observations, taken alone, necessarily invalidated the College's examination system but, taken together, they indicated that many Fellows were dissatisfied with it. The early 1960s, therefore, was a period of unrest among those who were directly concerned with the fairness of the College's examinations. By this time, however, the College had begun to consider how the examination system might be improved. This was the task of three subcommittees of the Examinations Committee in 1963. The three subcommittees in medicine, surgery and obstetrics and gynecology were appointed in December 1962 "to critically examine the whole content and the conduct of the Fellowship examinations." The subcommittee in internal medicine, noting that the Fellowship examination had been designed in the early 1930s, concluded that it was now obsolete in several respects and that reform was "long overdue."[23] With this initial step, the College launched a process of reform of its examinations that would continue through the early 1970s.

In conducting a critique of the Fellowship examinations in medicine, surgery and obstetrics and gynecology, the Examinations Committee was faced with a complex task. The three subcommittees each met at least twice during 1963 and consulted with each other as well; they also sought comments and suggestions from senior academicians and past examiners. Early on, the subcommittees were provided with up-to-date information about failure rates for the three five-year periods ending in 1962, which revealed a significant increase in the failure rate in the three disciplines over each of the three five-year periods, 1948-1952, 1953-1957 and 1958-1962. The reasons for this steady increase could not be accurately determined, but a more detailed statistical study of the Fellowship examinations in general surgery from 1952 to 1962 revealed an increase, since 1958, in the proportion of candidates originating from foreign medical schools of from 20 per cent to 30 per cent of the total. Since the failure rate in this group exceeded the average, one factor was the location of the candidates' medical schools. Stiffer marking of the written papers was also thought to be a contributing factor. On the other hand, the failure rate in the Fellowship examination in medicine was no higher than that experienced by other comparable bodies over the same period — for example, in the United States.

The three subcommittees agreed that the current high standards of the Fellowship examination should be preserved. Their recommendations concerned various aspects of the examination. Not surprisingly, it was recommended that the place of pathology be deemphasized; what should be tested was knowledge in the basic sciences, including pathology, rather than knowledge just of pathology. The advantages of multiple-choice questions were mooted; the subcommittee in medicine wished to introduce multiple-choice questions while the other two subcommittees preferred to wait and see. The marking of written papers came under scrutiny; it was recommended that the number of examiners marking each paper be increased, in order to make the essay type paper fairer for candidates. A further recommendation concerning examiners was made: to maintain continuity from year to year in the standards and conduct of the Fellowship examination, it was recommended that a chief examiner be appointed in medicine and in surgery, to serve five years and to oversee all aspects of the examinations in medicine and surgery. Finally, it was recommended that candidates who failed the oral examination be permitted a second attempt at the oral examination the following spring, instead of having to wait a whole year and to repeat the entire examination.

The chairman of the Examinations Committee, Dr. R.V. Christie, suggested that all these recommendations, except for the introduction of the multiple-choice paper in medicine, could be implemented with a minimum of delay. He hoped that they might be implemented with the 1965 examinations. An investigation into the multiple-choice technique would be necessary, and Dr. D.R. Wilson, who was familiar with the work of the National Board of Medical Examiners and the American Board of Internal Medicine and "the obvious choice", was given the task. On Dr. Wilson would fall the responsibility of introducing the multiple-choice examination into the Fellowship examination in medicine as soon as was feasible. Meanwhile, Dr. Christie, in concluding his presentation of the comprehensively and grandiloquently entitled "Report on the Findings and Recommendations Arising Out of Studies of the Committee on Examinations on the Content and Conduct of the Fellowship Examinations in the Three Major Disciplines of Medicine, Surgery and Obstetrics and Gynecology", spoke optimistically of the reception of the report by the Fellowship.

The Christie report was presented to the 1964 annual business meeting. It was appropriate that it should be presented to the Fellows, since several had expressed concern over the increasing failure rate in the Fellowship examination at the previous meeting. The discussion yielded several good points. Dr. H.S. Morton, chairman of the Fellowship examining board in surgery in 1963, was concerned that excluding borderline candidates from the oral examination would tend to eliminate worthy candidates. Dr. I. MacKenzie agreed, and added that pathologists had unfairly borne the brunt of the criticism in the past for the high failure rate. Dr. D. Power claimed that examiners had placed too much emphasis on artificial and arbitrary assessment based on marks that could vary both among different examiners and among the same examiners on different days. It would be easier, he suggested, to categorize performance in the written papers into three groups, the candidates in the upper two broadly categorized groups proceeding to the oral examination; a similar basis of assessment of the oral examination would make possible a fairer evaluation of the overall performance of each candidate. For Dr. J.L. McCallum, the main problem was the fact that many candidates were inadequately trained. Many training programs, he thought, tended to be amorphous and unguided. A candidate might complete four years of training with little or no assessment of progress and guidance as to whether he should continue. The College appeared to be the only organization that could rectify this. For Dr. C.H. Weder, who had spoken at the previous meeting, the question of the objective of the examinations remained unanswered. "Is it to assess a safe level of competence to practise in the community or is it to be something more than this?", he asked. Dr. Weder held that it would not be possible to determine the kind of examinations necessary to achieve specific objectives until this fundamental question had been answered — a question that would not be formally debated until the Expanded Executive Committee met in 1969.

The discussion had been useful; Dr. D.G. Cameron concluded that the discussion was a "very healthy sign" of the future strength of the College. On that note, the report of the Examinations Committee was approved. The Examinations Committee and Council now had sufficient sense of the feeling of the Fellows to enable them to proceed to implement the reforms.

The Introduction of the Multiple-Choice Question Technique

Of the reforms proposed by the Examinations Committee in 1963, the introduction of the multiple-choice technique was the most innovative. This technique had been used by the National Board of Medical Examiners in the United States since 1946 and was considered more reliable in assessing factual knowledge than the essay examination. The essay examination was hardly a finely tuned instrument and it was neither sensitive nor specific. (It is question-able as to how valid an instrument an essay type of paper, consisting of just a few questions, that bore, as one did in 1965, the following 27-word title might be: *Clinically Applied Basic Science, Including Anatomy, Physiology, Bio-chemistry, Pathology, Bacteriology, Embryology, Genetics and Endocrinology with Emphasis on the Clinical Application of These Sciences to Obstetrics and Gynecology.*)

The task that confronted Dr. D.R. Wilson, of Edmonton, who took on the responsibility of developing the multiple-choice examination, was a forbidding one.[24] Dr. Wilson was one of few physicians in Canada who was interested in the technique. A few medical schools had been experimenting with the tech-nique and recognized the problems involved. While it had been shown as early as 1952 that the multiple-choice, or objective, examination evaluated a stu-dent's knowledge in its application with greater reliability and validity than did the essay type of examination,[25] preparation of a multiple-choice test required greater skill, understanding, patience, care and diligence on the part of the test-writer than was required by examiners who prepared essay questions. Most of the original work had been done in the United States, where Dr. J.P. Hubbard, of the National Board of Medical Examiners, and Dr. V. Logan, of the American Board of Internal Medicine, were leaders in the medical field. Fortuitously, Dr. A. Kekwick, senior censor of The Royal College of Physicians of London, who had recently introduced a multiple-choice screening test as Part I of that college's examination,[26] attended the College's annual meeting in 1964, and it was to him that Dr. Wilson first turned for advice. Accordingly, in May 1964, Dr. Wilson, accompanied by Dr. R.V. Christie, studied the technique in England, where it was at least five years ahead of the technique in Canada. They also met Dr. G. Smart, whose group in Newcastle had been assembling a computer-based library of multiple-choice questions for their medical students.

Dr. Wilson learned much from his English visit on basic aspects of the multiple-choice technique — how to validate questions, how to use distractors and how to use questions having a high coefficient of discrimination so that the good and poor candidates might be differentiated. The firm relationships with several educators that were established during this visit, especially with Dr. J.F. Stokes, led to stimulating exchanges of views for many years.

In the United States, Dr. Hubbard — the doyen of examination techniques at that time — and Dr. Logan were particularly invaluable sources of information. The American Board of Internal Medicine had introduced new examination techniques in the 1950s and early 1960s and was helpful to the College in introducing its own examination techniques. The Board instructed Dr. Wilson and provided the College with some 300 questions. Dr. Wilson acknowledged Dr. Logan's assistance by saying that, were it not for Dr. Logan's help and influence with the American Board, the Canadian program could not have been started so confidently. The American assistance was valuable, for the lack of experience with the multiple-choice question technique in Canada meant that few individuals in Canada had responded to Dr. Wilson's appeal for questions, while The Royal College of Physicians of London had supplied but half a score of questions.

By the beginning of 1965, the Examinations Committee agreed that a multiple-choice paper should be included in the Fellowship examination that year. This paper was to replace the discontinued paper on clinically applied pathology and bacteriology, and would cover the principles and practice of medicine and the application to medicine of the basic sciences, including pathology. Dr. Wilson collected some 400 questions from which a final set could be selected. To assist him in preparing the examination, a committee of Drs. M. Belisle, J.P. Gemmell and R.V. Christie was appointed, and Dr. Wilson was authorized to appoint a second committee to assist him locally. Progress was rapid, and in June 1965 the multiple-choice paper for the Fellowship in medicine was ready, together with the French translation done by Dr. Belisle. Dr. Wilson graciously acknowledged the value of Dr. Belisle's work by saying that "if there are any 'firsts' in the field of multiple-choice examinations, thanks to his efforts, this is the first time that a paper has been produced in two languages in the same book, hence providing candidates the opportunity to compose their answer sheet utilizing either or both languages."

A procedure for marking the paper also had to be devised. An item analysis sheet was designed with the help of the Department of Education of Alberta and constructed by a local printer, after which the mechanical marking procedure was tested twice and the score sheet analyzed for discrepancies. In order to meet objections that mechanical marking might provoke, every tenth paper was hand-marked. As well as having to devise a mechanical method of marking, Dr. Wilson and his colleagues had both to determine the cut-off score and to dovetail the marks obtained in the multiple-choice question paper with those obtained in the essay papers.

The process of scoring required consideration. First, decisions had to be made as to how to score the paper, for there were several ways in which it could be done. Dr. Wilson decided to use the procedure favored by the American Board of Internal Medicine, which allowed one mark for each correct choice and a penalty of one mark for each incorrect choice; failure to mark an answer neither gained credit nor penalized the candidate. Next, a decision had to be made concerning the cut-off score. Dr. Wilson learned from the American experience that the average proportion of candidates who passed the written portion of the examination was approximately 65 per cent; therefore it was agreed that the pass mark for the multiple-choice paper should be established at that level. And third, it was necessary to correlate the marks for the multiple-choice paper with those of the essay-question paper. Two-thirds of the candidates scored 60 points out of the possible 129, or virtually 50 per cent, and it was decided that this mark could be equated to 70 per cent, the traditional passing mark for the essay papers.

The next problem was to unravel the meaning of the marks obtained for the two types of written examinations and for the oral examinations. Would the "objective" multiple-choice examination point to some useful and interesting lessons? Dr. Wilson was able to draw the following conclusions by analyzing the marks obtained by the successful and unsuccessful candidates on the two essay papers, the multiple-choice question paper and the oral examination:

- Most apparent was the fact that the essay papers failed seriously to discriminate between candidates who did well in the entire examination and those who did not. With respect to the essay papers, the examiners' marks tended to be grouped in a narrow range on either side of the pass mark of 70 per cent. In contrast, the marks of the multiple-choice papers were more widely dispersed. This finding is illustrated in Table 9.2.
- A possible contributing factor to the lack of discrimination associated with the essay technique was the need for the essay papers to be marked by busy individuals. The marks of these examiners were

TABLE 9.2 Average marks in Written and Oral Fellowship Examination in Internal Medicine, 1965.

| Candidate | Paper | |
Group	Essay	Multiple-Choice
Failed Writtens	59.7	66.0
Passed Writtens Failed Orals	70.3	79.5
Passed Writtens Passed Orals	71.2	81.9

Source: D.R. Wilson, "Assessment of Clinical Skills From the Subjective to the Objective." *Ann RCPSC* 1975; 8:109-118. See also: D.R. Wilson, Interim Report in the Multiple-Choice Examination Pilot Project, Examinations Committee, December 1965, Attachment 14.

the best effort that a group of highly competent, but very busy, individuals could produce by marking questions whenever an opportunity presented itself. Usually this opportunity occurred at night or at weekends, or was compressed into a concentrated effort over a few days taken off exclusively for this purpose.

• More interesting and useful was the effect that the marks of the essay papers exerted on selection of candidates for the oral examinations. Because the essay marks tended to cluster close to the pass mark of 70 per cent, whereas the marks of the multiple-choice question paper were more widely dispersed, some candidates attained a pass on the written papers on account of their high score on the multiple-choice paper. Since a proportion of these candidates subsequently passed the oral examination, it may be said both that the essay technique failed an appreciable number of candidates who would otherwise have been successful and that the multiple-choice technique identified more accurately those candidates whose competence was proved at the oral examination. This held true after 1965, as Table 9.3, relating to the results of 79 candidates in 1968, shows.

After the multiple-choice question paper had been introduced in 1965, Dr. Wilson assessed its value. His main conclusion was that the multiple-choice technique was superior to the essay technique. While the essay-type examination served the limited purpose of identifying candidates who could express their clinical thinking in writing in just a few questions, it failed to bring to the oral examination some knowledgeable candidates who were identified by the more objective multiple-choice examination. The introduction of multiple-

TABLE 9.3 **Proportions of Candidates Brought Forward to the Oral Examination as a Result of Marks Obtained in the Multiple-Choice Question Paper in the Fellowship Examinations, 1968.**

Specialty Group	No. Proceeding to Oral	No. Obtaining Fellowship
General Surgery	37	19
Orthopedic Surgery	14	9
Obstetrics & Gynecology	28	8
Total	79	37

Source: D.R. Wilson, "Assessment of Clinical Skills From the Subjective to the Objective." *Ann RCPSC* 1975; 8:109-118.

choice questions was an advance, although it involved much effort and expense, and use of the technique was later extended to all the other numerically large specialties, so that some 80 per cent of candidates eventually came to be tested by this method.

Development of In-Training Examinations

Once a bank of questions had been developed — in itself no mean feat — the multiple-choice technique could be used for several different purposes. One was to compare the performance of residents at the mid-point of training with those who had completed their training. One reason for doing this was to determine the appropriate time at which to stage the written examination. Accordingly, in June 1966, through the cooperation of departments of medicine, Dr. Wilson was able to study the results of 68 residents who took the same multiple-choice question paper that specialist candidates had taken in the fall of 1965. Most of the residents had completed two core years of training, and their results compared favorably with those of the 1965 Fellowship examination candidates.

This finding led later to the introduction of in-training examinations. Interest in the concept of in-training examinations stemmed from the favorable reception that had been accorded the paper given by Dr. D.D. Matson at the Kingston conference on residency education in 1965, but more recently two orthopedic surgeons, Dr. J.C. Kennedy, chairman of the College's Specialty Committee in Orthopedic Surgery, and Dr. W.R. Harris, an examiner in orthopedic surgery, had commented on the role of an in-training examination in identifying unsuitable trainees. More positively, an in-training examination was seen as a way of convincing candidates of the need to maintain a reasonable academic level while busily involved in orthopedic training. (Dr. Kennedy equated it with the College's original primary examination, which had been discontinued in 1944.)

There were arguments for and against the introduction of an in-training examination. An advantage to it, in addition to "weeding out" undesirable trainees and stimulating trainees to keep their noses to the grindstone, was that a resident in internal medicine could take the written examination after two years of training and then concentrate on a special area of training without having to worry about the need to pass a written examination in internal medicine at the end of the total training period. A further benefit was that it would assist program directors in identifying weaknesses in their own programs. On the other hand, residents would cram harder than ever in the formative period, when they should be concentrating on exposing themselves to clinical material and clinical skills rather than to textbooks.

Council was not immediately in favor of the concept. Two principal objections were put forward. First, only one specialty (internal medicine) was being considered. The Examinations Committee's recommendation that Council approve of the concept of in-training examinations therefore needed to be looked at carefully; Dr. J. Turcot was concerned that, if the same pattern was not maintained for all specialties, it might be the beginning of the division of the College. The second objection was that the Specialty Committee in Internal Medicine had not been consulted. The matter was therefore referred back to the Examinations Committee for further study, and the concept of the in-training examination was refined also by the Executive Committee in July 1967. The Executive Committee wished to consider "the most appropriate ways and means of recognition of special branches of medicine and surgery" — a topic that went to the heart of the question as to what constituted a specialty and even what constituted Fellowship in a general sense. The question of how a specialty should be defined would become increasingly important, but it was relevant in mid-1967 because the subspecialties of allergy, cardiology, gastroenterology, clinical hematology, clinical immunology, nuclear medicine and respiratory medicine had all been seeking approval and recognition by the College. The in-training examination, therefore, not only would serve as a means of formative evaluation but also would provide a way in which a subspecialty received *de facto* recognition, for it would mean that candidates, having taken the examination, would stream in different subspecialties. Objections to the in-training examination dissipated, and the introduction of a comprehensive examination in internal medicine in 1970 for trainees who had completed two core years of training was a further advance in examination reform.

Development of the Single Examination Process

Of all the examination reforms that were introduced between 1960 and 1980, the introduction of the single examination process in 1972 was the most far-reaching. Besides providing a new approach to examination methodology, it was intimately linked to the other changes that creation of the 'new' College in 1972 necessitated. But, like many of the changes that were introduced at about this time, the single examination process evolved out of a matrix of ideas that had been forming in the latter 1950s and throughout the 1960s.

The concept of a *single* qualifying examination was introduced by Dr. G.G. Miller late in 1946 but the Executive Committee considered the proposal "impracticable." It was next expressed in the proposal of the Robertson committee in 1955 that all specialist candidates in a particular specialty should take the same *initial* set of examinations. (The results would separate the candidates into those who failed, those who would proceed to the Certification oral examination and those, thought to be potentially capable of attaining a Fellowship standard, who would advance to the Fellowship oral examination.) Council's decision three years later that Certification should eventually be phased out appeared to signal a change in policy, but it was not until the Expanded Executive Committee met in 1969 that the principle of a single qualifying examination for specialists was finally established. Until then, the several proposals that were discussed in the 1960s — Dr. N.A. Watters in 1966, for example, proposed that candidates take a single set of examinations, and that those who passed with honors should be granted Fellowship and that other successful candidates should be awarded the Certification — each accepted the dual standard as a fact of College life and thereby condoned the view that the Certificant was a "failed Fellow."

Somewhat different, though still accepting the validity of the dual standard, was the plan that Dr. F.N. Gurd, chairman of the Examinations Committee, presented to the committee in December 1968. Based on a submission prepared for the Specialty Committee in General Surgery by Dr. R.A. Macbeth, this plan proposed that all specialist candidates in surgery first demonstrate proficiency in clinical surgery and a knowledge of applied basic sciences by passing an examination for the Certificate. This qualification would be the basic form of specialist recognition by the College, but it would also permit a specialist to proceed voluntarily to the Fellowship examination, which would assess those qualities of "extraordinary scholarship" beyond first-class clinical competence. There would thus be no suggestion that the Fellowship surgeon was the better surgeon than the Certificant surgeon, for equal ability in dealing with surgical problems would have been demonstrated in the process of gaining Certification. The Fellowship would be an optional higher award in the best academic sense.

When he introduced this plan at Council in January 1969, Dr. Gurd asked Council to approve a far-reaching rider: he wanted Council to come out one way or another in favor either of the single standard (to adopt either Fellowship or Certification but not both) or of the dual standard (to retain both qualifications). He recognized that this request was not a simple one and he suggested that a special study group be set up to answer the many questions on Fellowship and Certification that faced the College at the beginning of 1969. Dr. Gurd's request was far-reaching in significance because it led to the creation in the same year of the Expanded Executive Committee, the group that ultimately proposed that all specialty candidates desiring recognition of their competence be subjected to a single examination process; it was also the group whose deliberations ultimately led to Council's defining the proposals that led to the formation of the 'new' College in 1972. By 1969 the concept of a single examination process was generally accepted, though some Fellows feared that the standard of the single examination would be lower than that of the Fellowship and that consequently the Fellowship itself would become devalued. However, the steady improvement in training programs, most of which were now affiliated with a university, and the work of the R.S. McLaughlin Examination and Research Centre offset this fear. Dr. Gurd, for example, said that the College would be provided with "a real opportunity to develop a new revamped, really good process of successful completion of training", particularly since the importance of evaluating residents throughout their training was being increasingly recognized. Dr. Gurd, therefore, had good grounds for stating that the College's proposed examination process would be a better examination than any in the past.

The Examinations Committee discussed the concept of the single examination process in December 1969 and May 1970. Towards the end of the second meeting, during which familiar problems as well as future possibilities such as a basic surgical examination had been considered, a second far-reaching proposal was made; Dr. C.B. Mueller suggested that a task force should review the College's examination structure, develop recommendations for the unification process and give some indication of appropriate timing. Council approved the plan and the following Fellows were later named as members of the task force: Drs. F.N. Gurd (chairman), J. Beaudoin, J.A.L. Gilbert, R.A.H. Kinch, G.R. Langley, C.B. Mueller and D.R. Wilson.

The work of the Task Force on the Single Examination Process enabled the College to take a quantum leap in examination methodology. No longer need the Council and a series of examiners endlessly debate the theoretical benefits of a single examination, as they had been doing throughout the 1960s, for the job of the task force — and its remarkable achievement — was to finally implement the practical procedure that would mark the transition from the dual to the single standard. This task excited Dr. Gurd; for him, the opportunity presented by this task was "without parallel" in the history of the College.[27]

The task force's charge — to review the examination structure and to make recommendations concerning the unification process — was a complex one. It was necessary to develop a master plan based on the particular requirements of the different specialties, but the task force was not starting de novo. The advances in medical education and evaluation in the 1960s and the intensive study of the interrelationship between the Fellowship and the Certification, which was most notably conducted by the Expanded Executive Committee in 1969, clarified for councillors and committee members the direction that the College should now take. In fact, an increasing number of specialties were coming to rely on a single examination (the Fellowship); the value of the multiple-choice technique was well established in the Fellowship examination in internal medicine; and the medical specialties, beginning with internal medicine, were about to introduce a mid-training comprehensive examination. Thus the task force's work consisted in part of bringing already accepted elements together in one package. Other elements, however, whose value was only just beginning to be perceived — in-training evaluation, a basic examination in the principles of surgery for surgical specialties and computer-based patient simulation tests, for example — would need to be developed and incorporated. These innovations would present a particularly worthwhile challenge. But most worthwhile was the task force's first priority: "To outline a reasonable process which...[would] identify the individual who is ready to function in his specialty — a process not too fancy or complex, not punitive or overly threatening, but clear-cut and as neat as possible."[28] The approach would be fair as well as reasonable: it had to be sufficiently capable of standardization, however, so it could be applied to all disciplines and specialties with the assurance that a fair and common standard would be set for every candidate.

The Task Force on the Single Examination Process began its studies in the fall of 1970, and these studies made it possible for the College to introduce the new single examination process only two years later. In the interim, the task force did nothing less than review all aspects of the College's examining role over the years, collate many useful ideas and rebuild the College's examination structure.[29]

The task force's first meeting was held in Montreal on September 24, 1970. The first step was to define the objectives of the examination process. It was agreed that these objectives were "to evaluate the knowledge, skills and attitudes of candidates and to certify to their professional competence in an acknowledged specialty according to standards prescribed by the College." These objectives attested to the College's readiness now to evaluate a candidate's performance against defined standards of professional competence.

The task force then considered the several components of the proposed examination process. Of the traditional components, the written examination was well established and there was general support for the objective, multiple-choice question type of examination (though it was realized that it would not be practical in all specialties); there was, however, much less support for the oral and clinical examination obtained at the end of the training period. The various defects of these traditional components were recognized. Dr. Wilson pointed out that "pencil and paper" tests that the College conducted in its written and its oral and clinical examinations occupied at the most 10 or 11 hours of a candidate's time, and that during this period examiners had to attempt to learn as much as they could about the candidate in order to make a pass or fail decision. "The examination process in its present form", Dr. Wilson stressed, "just is not designed to do this... ."[30]

The basic concept underlying the single examination process was a simple one. The ideal examination process should reflect and even monitor the training process. It would do so not at one moment in time, as examinations traditionally did, but over a period of years. It was part of a formative process, as well as being in part a summative process also. The formative aspect of the single examination process was clearly identified by Dr. Wilson in a reference to the general principles, or mid-training, examination:

> *The* great advantages of the general principles examination at the end of two years...are to identify weak candidates early and to weed them out, to identify candidates that are in trouble and need help from their program directors and, what is equally important, to identify programs that are in trouble and need help, either from the rest of the school in which the program resides, or from the College or both. ...at this particular level the objective form of evaluation is the only one that is going to give us valid information, particularly in view of the increasing numbers of candidates in all areas.
>
> This examination at the mid-point of the graduate training program could equally well serve the purpose for an in-training evaluation and might well eliminate the necessity of developing separate in-training examinations... .[31]

Dr. Wilson added that to design a single examination process without instituting or demanding evaluation over the whole four years of postgraduate training was a "sheer waste of time." Dr. Mueller put it in similar terms: "specialty competence in performance while at work should be the objective, rather than performance in a specialty examination."[32]

This was the approach that the College was taking to its examining function in 1970; it was a far cry from the approach taken 40 years earlier by the Nucleus Committee, for which examinations should be a "severe", one-shot test of the candidate's knowledge, ability and judgement rather than a multi-phase process of evaluation closely reflecting training.[33]

By the end of the first meeting, the task force had discussed the main components of the single examination process. In particular, it had unanimously endorsed the principles of in-training evaluation and mid-training examinations. In preparation for its next meeting, Dr. G.R. Langley was asked to draft a statement concerning the assessment of candidates' attitudes and performance during training. It was also agreed that the specialty committees and ACMC would be informed of the task force's preliminary conclusions.

The task force met again on November 12, 1970. The group studied a summary of the task force's "Current Status of Thoughts", prepared by Dr. Mueller. Dr. Mueller set out five elements of a tentative examination process. The first was registration of residents in a College roster, which would contain annual reports of performance. Pretesting of residents was the second element; this should be done before completion of 24 months' training, demonstrating competence in basic biological information, as indicated by passing an examination such as LMCC, FLEX, NBME Parts I, II and III or the CPMQ examination for licensure. The third proposed element of the process consisted of mid-testing, based on completion of an appropriate general principles examination for each resident in a laboratory specialty, a surgical specialty, a medical specialty or obstetrics and gynecology. In-training examinations constituted the fourth element; they would be given "intermittently" to enable a program director to define a trainee's strengths and weaknesses, performance which would not be known by the College except insofar as it was reflected in the annually submitted report of performance. The fifth element in the single examination process would be a final certifying examination, based on 18 months of progress reports by a program director, a written examination and an oral examination.

In addition to studying this summary, the task force also discussed the draft of a form that Dr. Langley, in conjunction with Drs. Wilson and Mueller, proposed be used to evaluate residents during their training. In this original version of the In-Training Evaluation Report form (ITER), evaluation was intended to assign marks in scoring attitudes and skills relating to a series of a candidate's abilities. A candidate would be judged according to his or her ability to execute certain tasks: to take an in-depth history; to carry out a physical examination; to make a clinical diagnosis; to assess critically ill patients; to resuscitate and institute supportive care for critically ill patients; to select appropriate laboratory investigations; to anticipate complications; to direct in-hospital care programs; to communicate information to the referring physician and relatives; to care for patients' emotional needs; to perform techniques necessary for a particular specialty; and to recognize personal limitations and the need to obtain additional help in solving some clinical problems. The proposed form included a question on the likelihood of the candidate's reaching "acceptable standards of competence" (a mark of 70 or greater for the overall assessment) after an additional year of training. Space was provided for the program director to include a general assessment of the candidate's performance and to make recommendations.

The progress that the task force had made by November 1970 was summarized in an interim report that Dr. Gurd prepared for the Examinations Committee's December 1970 meeting. The committee's lengthy discussions supported the task force in its work and encouraged it to aim for a target date for introduction of the new single examination process of 1972. Support and encouragement came from Council, too, in January 1971. The task force's proposals were considered innovative but sound. Dr. D.G. Cameron, for example, observed that several of the concepts in the proposals were consistent with those that seemed to have arisen spontaneously from other sources, which attested to their validity. Of the several concepts that Dr. Cameron referred to, the concept of in-training evaluation was, as Dr. Mueller had said, at the December 1970 Examinations Committee meeting "the most radical thing the task force had done." Yet it was not so much the use of the evaluation form that was new as its incorporation into an examination process. Evaluation based on behavioral objectives had been developed during the Second World War, when pilots were evaluated rather than examined with respect to critical behavior; and, in medicine, evaluation procedures had for some time been used either to protect the comprehensiveness of a resident's training or to enable a training committee to evaluate and substantiate a candidate's clinical skills as a prerequisite to the written examination.[34] The task force's concept therefore was somewhat different, the difference lying in the integration of the evaluation by a program director into the examination process. The ITER was eminently logical; as Dr. Mueller had observed in the November 1970 meeting of the task force, no other part of the overall examination process could assess "the work performance" of the trainee.

The development of in-training evaluation was assigned a high priority by President R.C. Dickson, who had told Dr. Gurd that he knew of "no very effective way" by which an examination could evaluate the candidate's attitudes and skills in collecting data and in performing necessary procedures.[35] The concept of in-training evaluation was welcomed by program directors, by examiners and, as well, by residents, who saw it as making less fearful the "final axe" that the traditional examination represented. The importance of the concept, then, was considerable, and the possibility of assigning a value of at least 30 per cent of the overall mark in the proposed examination process to the ITER was even considered.

By April 1971, Dr. Gurd was able to provide a progress report on a single examination process that elaborated on the previously developed components of the process. Progress was sufficient now to make it appropriate to communicate the details of the proposed process to specialty representatives, and a meeting of interested parties — the inaugural meeting, as it turned out, of the periodically held Conference of Specialties — was convened at College headquarters on April 29, 1971. Those attending included the chairmen of the

College's specialty committees, the presidents (or representatives) of the Canadian specialty societies and representatives of CAIR. The chairmen of the specialty committees were asked to discuss the task force's proposals with their committees and to submit their recommendations so that it would be possible to construct "a master process" that would recognize the needs of each specialty. The meeting was a successful one, in more than one respect: not only were the specialty representatives brought directly into the decision-making process with respect to evaluation and examination procedures, but also their constructive participation suggested that similar meetings on other topics would prove just as valuable.[36] The majority of specialty committees approved of the task force's proposals. Most, but not all, agreed with pre-testing and mid-testing, and the principle of in-training evaluation, in particular, received wholehearted support. The success of this conference, together with the confidence expressed by the Examinations Committee, was welcome, for it was now firmly agreed that the single examination process would definitely be introduced in the fall of 1972.

The specialty committees were kept informed and a bulletin dated August 25, 1971, was sent to them and to directors of postgraduate training programs as well. This bulletin contained a revised version of the Report on Work Performance, a prototype of the Final ITER (FITER), which was by now recognized as an original contribution that the College had made to the final evaluation of residents in specialty training programs. The form was essentially a grid on which attributes of performance could be assigned marks from one to nine. The attributes were divided into the five main categories of patient assessment, patient care, administrative ability, professional attitude and technical proficiency; guidance was given concerning the attributes of a "poor" resident and a "superior" resident. The form also requested the program director to answer the question as to whether the candidate had satisfactorily fulfilled the requirements of the training program and should thus be admitted to the written and oral examination; the resident had to sign the form to attest to having seen the program director's written evaluation.

This bulletin was warmly received, one respondent praising the College for introducing "a most imaginative and important change."[37] Other comments were constructively critical, and all helped the task force to develop a practical FITER form. There were many suggestions for improvement of the FITER form, particularly in relation to addition or clarification of certain items: the need to account for other attributes such as judgement, inquisitiveness, academic knowledge and a positive attitude to research; special strengths and weaknesses; use of a greater number of quantifying descriptors such as "outstanding", "good", "satisfactory", "doubtful" and "unsatisfactory"; and the importance of having more than one individual make the evaluation. But it was also made clear that a potential point of weakness in the FITER was the problem of achieving a uniform standard across the country.

These comments and suggestions were considered at the task force's fourth meeting, which was held on November 12, 1971, and at the Examinations Committee's meeting in December 1971. The Examinations Committee maintained its support for in-training evaluation. Dr. E. Robillard, referring to the CPMQ's experience, put the case for in-training evaluation well when he argued that at the end of the training period someone had to decide whether a person deserved to be Certificated and that the judgement must be given to the person who was the most knowledgeable. This person, of course, was the program director. It was then agreed that the three components of in-training performance, knowledge demonstrated by the written examinations and ability to apply knowledge as demonstrated by the oral examination should each provide input into the evaluation process; that a pass rate in both the in-training and written components should be a prerequisite for taking the oral examinations; and that a yet-to-be defined rating of "excellent" performance in both the in-training and written components should exempt a candidate from an oral examination and so automatically lead to the granting of Certification.

By the end of 1971, the basic work of the task force had been completed, and the finishing touches were applied by the Examinations Committee in conjunction with the specialty committees. Chairmen were appointed for each specialty committee to provide for continuity during the period of transition, and each specialty committee agreed to use an interim format for the initial examination in 1972. The examination would emphasize competence. Standards for the specialty examinations, the specialty committees agreed, should reflect the training as well as judge the worthiness to pursue the specialist career. The Examinations Committee expected nothing less than "a new conception of a well-trained specialist...by virtue of the more clear-cut objectives of the new examination process."

In both the development and the implementation of the single examination process, the role of the specialty committees was considerable. The Examinations Committee proposed, and Council approved, that the former positions of chief examiners in medicine and surgery be eliminated; specialty examining boards then achieved greater autonomy, though each was responsible to both the Examinations Committee and the respective specialty committee.

During the task force's studies, support for objective multiple-choice written examinations was sustained. When the new examination process was introduced in 1972, approximately 75 per cent of candidates taking the written examination were tested by multiple-choice questions — even though the small numbers of candidates in 20 specialties meant that the objective technique could not be used for the other 25 per cent of candidates. Nor would it be possible for the general principles examination to be made available to many candidates, though test committees were studying the feasibility of the examination in surgery and laboratory medicine.

The most interesting component remained the ITER, though the developmental work necessitated by the recommendations and observations submitted by the specialty committees prevented its being incorporated into the 1972 single examination process. In its development, the opinions of the specialty committees and program directors were taken into account. The grid format was retained but changes were made in the attributes (now termed criteria) and in the descriptors used to evaluate the attributes. The form included four categories of attributes, listed vertically in the stub of the grid. *Patient Assessment and Care* was divided into and subdivided into six criteria: history and physical examination, clinical judgement and decision-making, emergency care, comprehensive continuing care, laboratory utilization and records and reports. *Professional Attitudes* included physician-patient relationships, team relationships, ethics and sense of responsibility and self-assessment. *Technical Areas* included surgical technique, other manual skills related to the specialty, use of equipment and supervisory skills. The other attribute was an open-ended one, *Special Criteria*. The grid was completed by spaces in which marks could be assigned to criteria by reference to five descriptors listed horizontally in the boxhead of the grid: "Unacceptable" (1-2); "Poor" (3-4); "Fair" (5-6); "Good" (7-8); and "Excellent" (9-10). And, as before, a space at the bottom of the form permitted comments and the signatures of the evaluator and the resident.

The development of the single examination process was thus a cooperative effort on the part of the Examinations Committee, its task force, the specialty committees, the specialty societies and the program directors. Referred to also as a "unified examination process", the College's new examination process was another step in the pursuit of unity. It represented also a process that unified the dual roles the College and its agents played in this certifying function — the continuing monitoring and improvement of training standards and the continuing reform and refinement of examination techniques. Dr. Gurd, to whom much credit is due in the development of the single examination process, summed it up admirably when he wrote that "no separation should exist between the functions of the College which relate to training and evaluation, since they share the same objectives"[38] — the development of a well-trained, ethical and responsible specialist.

The Principles of Surgery Examination

An outcome of the work of the Task Force on the Single Examination Process was the introduction of a basic examination in the principles of surgery for general surgery and some of the surgical specialties. The idea for this examination arose when the Task Force on the Single Examination Process began to investigate the possibilities of a mid-training examination for surgical specialist candidates. The underlying principles were expressed by Dr. C.B. Mueller: "If all information in medical schools is considered basic to all physicians, there must be another level of information basic to all surgeons, regardless of specialty."[39] What, for example, should all surgeons know about infection or bone healing?

A multiple-choice question examination, available after two years of training, was used in the specialty of internal medicine as the final written examination, though candidates seeking Certification in a subspecialty like cardiology were required to take an additional subspecialty final written examination at the end of the subspecialty training period. For surgical specialties, the examination likewise would be a mid-training examination rather than a final examination, the latter being taken at the end of subspecialty training as an examination in that subspecialty. The examination was conceived as a test of a candidate's knowledge of basic biological science and of those principles of surgery that all surgeons should know, regardless of their specialty.[40] It had several further aims and advantages as an evaluative instrument: candidates would be provided with a form of self-assessment halfway through their training period; program directors could better determine where each candidate most needed help; likewise, program directors could learn where their own programs might be improved; and the final written examination could cover in some depth important elements of a particular candidate's specialty.

To develop the principles of surgery examination, Dr. C.B. Mueller chaired a committee comprising the following representatives of specialties: Dr. P. Allen (neurosurgery); Dr. R.D. Bell (otolaryngology); Dr. L. Levasseur (general and pediatric surgery); Dr. R.B. Lynn (cardiovascular and thoracic surgery); Dr. B. Mount (urology); Dr. D.C. Robertson (plastic surgery); and Dr. R.H. Yabsley (orthopedic surgery). The committee met for the first time on June 15, 1973, when it drafted an outline of the knowledge expected of each surgical trainee. Then, from 1,500 preliminary multiple-choice questions that were obtained from the McLaughlin Centre the committee eventually selected 233 basic questions that pertained to six categories of basic interdisciplinary knowledge: vital functions; body response to trauma; infections and neoplasia; bleeding, coagulation, thrombosis and surgical immunology; clinical pharmacology; and miscellaneous topics. The proposed examination was intended to be an in-training examination but it was not regarded as a prerequisite to further training. It was both a formative and a summative instrument of evaluation, and the questions were phrased as much as possible in a clinical setting.

The first examination was held in June 1974. This was a trial examination. Any surgical trainee in Canada who had completed at least 18 months of training was eligible; 462 candidates took the examination. The results impressed most of the participating specialties, but a second trial run, in which the same questions would be used, was held in May 1975. The examination now sufficiently impressed the general surgical representatives to enable them to decide that it should become mandatory for their residents; by June 1976, the representatives of the specialties of neurosurgery, plastic surgery and urology followed suit. Council approved the principles of surgery examination the same month and it became officially part of the single examination process in September 1976. It became a requirement for Certification in those specialties that had favored it (particularly general surgery, neurosurgery, plastic surgery and urology) and it was hoped that other specialties would also adopt it. However, it never became mandatory for all specialties.

Indeed, some surgical specialties never accepted the principles of surgery examination. One specialty's representatives held that it was an attempt on the part of the general surgeons to dominate the surgical specialties and that it reflected the original situation in which the specialty of general surgery regarded all other surgical specialties as subspecialties of general surgery.[41] This view, however, demonstrated something of an isolation that was self-induced. Some specialists recognized the danger that residents might share in the general trend toward isolationism of their practitioner-teachers; isolationism was a threat and the way it might be prevented was by stressing the educational value of a sound base that was built on broad general principles of surgery and medicine.[42] Building this base, of course, was what the examination was intended to achieve, and the extent to which this was not completely achieved indicated the amount of work that remained to be done in implementing the principles of surgery examination. This situation, too, revealed in a new light the concept formulated by the College's founding Fellows, of a sound educational base for all the surgical specialties. In order to build this base, they believed it necessary to hold Fellowship examinations in the parent discipline of general surgery, as opposed to examinations in the surgical specialties.

Refinement of In-Training Evaluation

During the Council meeting of June 1972, Dr. B.J. Perey explained that much remained to be done to make the new examination process a realistic and valid mechanism for measuring and certifying clinical competence. With respect to the FITER, for example, several problems made validation difficult. Standardization across Canada was one such problem. In Quebec, for example, at least six different forms were used for evaluation purposes — those used by the four medical faculties, the form preferred by the CPMQ and the one that the Royal College was developing. The deans wished to use the university form, but this was used primarily in the day-to-day evaluation of medical students and did not contain the key question as to whether the candidate had demonstrated sufficient professional ability to justify his qualifying as a specialist. There was a difference, too, between the Royal College's and the CPMQ's form, for the latter was based in part on the assessment of knowledge.

Evaluation of the FITER form itself was another problem. The Canadian Association of Professors of Medicine, after discussing in-training evaluation during the 1972 conference on residency training in internal medicine (held in Kingston on September 8 and 9), held firm views on the right way to evaluate the form. The professors thought that, for a trial period of three years, residents in internal medicine, who took a comprehensive written basic examination in medicine midway through their training, should not be prevented from attending the oral examination by virtue of a negative answer on the FITER to the question of demonstrable professional ability. Otherwise, it would not be possible to compare the value of the FITER with the value of the traditional oral and clinical examination, which a number of educators hoped might be supplanted by the FITER.[43] This position, however, conflicted with the position taken by the Examinations Committee and the Credentials Committee; it also conflicted with the principle, approved by Council in January 1973 and reaffirmed in June 1973, that an adverse FITER would deny a candidate admission for the oral and clinical examination. This issue was an important one because, properly used, the FITER permitted only those candidates who were adequately trained and considered competent to proceed to the certifying examination.

The question as to whether oral examinations might be discontinued in favor of some type of in-training evaluation also remained unanswered in the early 1970s. The question continued to generate interest throughout the decade, but no definitive answers were found. The Canadian Association of Professors of Medicine, however, was able to conclude in 1983 that they were "on the right track." They reviewed the results of a four-year study of in-training evaluation and a university system of final evaluation of professional competence and the findings of a two-year study of the College's examinations in internal medicine.[44] Although a high degree of consistency was obtained by the combination of the university final evaluations and the oral examinations, neither was satisfactory by itself in assessing professional competence. Both components were considered indispensable. The study suggested that the College could now concentrate on improving the details of both components of the final evaluation process. Reforming evaluation and examination techniques, it became clear once again, must be a continuous process.

The second half of the 1970s, therefore, witnessed a refinement of requirements and guidelines for in-training evaluation. Problems with usage of FITERs were identified, but five problems in FITERs for internal medicine were resolved by the end of the decade: residents' understanding of in-training evaluation; the opportunity for residents to see and sign FITERs; appropriate length of rotations; availability of in-training oral examinations; and yearly summative reviews. A further four problems remained at the end of the decade: direct observation of trainees' clinical skills; faculty review of trainees' clinical records; availability of tests of formal knowledge; and reviews by teachers, with each resident, at the end of each rotation.

The process of refinement was facilitated by three studies on in-training evaluation in the second half of the 1970s. One was a review by a College task force of in-training evaluation after three years of experience in the College, a responsibility that was discharged by a task force consisting of Drs. G.R. Langley (chairman), W.R. Harris and R.I. Hector and Mr. E.N. Skakun.[45] This report found, somewhat unexpectedly, that the effect of in-training evaluation was contrary to what had been anticipated when it was introduced — it had little effect on the examination component but a significant effect on training programs. The explanation was straightforward: candidates with deficiencies in their training were identified earlier than had been the case previously, and trainees were systematically and regularly evaluated. This study indicated that there was little doubt that the need to complete a detailed FITER on a trainee's clinical proficiency induced stricter entrance requirements and more careful assessment for promotion, and that indeed some programs declined to allow certain residents to proceed to the final oral examination because they had not demonstrated adequate professional competence.

With respect to the effect of ITERs on examination results, two conclusions could be drawn. The first was that there was a relation between the number, or score, on the ITER grid and the proportion of candidates passing the oral component of the Certification examination. However, all of these candidates had been assessed by their program directors as being sufficiently competent to be granted Certification. Yet some of these candidates performed poorly in their first attempt at the clinical oral examination, and the examiners were then reluctant to grant Certification. On the other hand, the second conclusion of this study was that the program directors' in-training evaluation did make it possible for the examiners to grant Certification to some candidates whose marks in the oral examination were borderline.

The task force identified faults that users had found in the FITERs. These faults included the use of numbers on the grid; the use of the terms "unacceptable", "poor", "fair", "good" and "excellent"; the characteristics evaluated; confusion as to where the failure mark lay; and an explanation as to who should submit the FITER. The task force found that the first four of these faults were corrected by a recent modification of the FITER and that the fifth fault required attention.

The task force also reached conclusions regarding the future of in-training evaluation. The task force looked for improvement in the reporting of the performance of trainees, assigning of consistent and greater weight to in-training evaluation in the making of a pass/fail decision and defining the precise purposes of the oral examination and in-training evaluation so that comparisons of the two evaluative instruments could be made and improvements in the evaluation form itself. The task force concluded that the potential of in-training evaluation was significant but largely unrealized. At the same time, the impact on the College had been considerable, for "through in-training evaluation the College is involved in almost the day-to-day operations of specialty programs, although this involvement is delegated to faculties and the jointly appointed specialty program directors."

The second useful report on in-training evaluation was a document, published by the College in June 1976, that provided accreditation requirements and guidelines relating to in-training evaluation.[46] A companion volume to the College's Grey Book (see Chapter 8), this booklet, or Orange Book, recognized that as in-training was developing — and improving — there was a need to explain the College's requirements concerning in-training evaluation and to foster consistency in evaluation and reporting across the country. This document set out clearly the College's requirements that, if understood and executed, would correct the faults that the task force had identified. It also described the components and standards of in-training evaluation. The guide explained that the College used the FITER in two ways — to determine a resident's suitability to take the final set of examinations and to aid the oral examiners in making their final assessments. The two sections that dealt with the way the College used the FITER are reproduced in order to emphasize the College's role in training, evaluation and examination in having introduced in-training evaluation:

1. *To determine eligibility to take the final examinations.*

On the front of the [ITER] form is the crucial question: "Do you consider this final-year candidate has demonstrated sufficient professional ability to practise effectively and responsibly as a Certificant in the stated specialty?"

If the answer is 'Yes', and the training requirements of the Royal College have been met, the candidate will be allowed to take the final examination.

If the answer is 'No', the candidate will not be permitted to take the final examinations. In such cases, it is important that the program director and his colleagues describe the candidate's deficiencies under "Comments" on the back of the form and provide specific guidelines to the Royal College's Committee on Credentials regarding the kind of further training needed.

2. *To aid the oral examiners in their final assessments.*

Oral examiners have only one or two hours to assess a detailed and complex mixture of knowledge, skills and attitudes in each candidate. Furthermore, they are asked to do this under conditions that are far from "real life" and often very stressful psychologically for the candidate. After the oral examinations are completed, the performance of each failed candidate is reviewed very carefully. Armed with the results of the written examinations as an indicator of knowledge and, to some extent, problem-solving ability, and armed with the final ITE report as an indicator of performance, skills and attitudes on a day-to-day basis in "real life", the examiners are in a position to make a final assessment that is more realistic than one based on the oral examination alone. The candidate who has failed in the oral examinations may be granted an overall pass on the basis of this final assessment, although the final oral mark will not be changed. The final ITE Report will *not* be used to fail a candidate who has passed the oral examinations.

The third report that clarified the value and role of in-training evaluation was the eventual outcome of a conference that was jointly sponsored by the College and the Canadian Association of Professors of Medicine. This conference, entitled "Measurement of Professional Competence for Specialty Certification in Internal Medicine", was held on May 5, 1977. The conference presented papers that were representative of the state of the art of measurement of professional competence and, in particular, a key paper that recommended implementation of a project to improve the measurement of specialty competence for Certification in internal medicine.[47] The purpose of this project was to review and evaluate the quality of in-training evaluation systems, of the final university evaluation of trainees that emerged therefrom and of the College's oral examinations for specialty Certification. In 1972, the College had requested faculties of medicine to prepare a FITER on trainees completing their training and it developed the Orange Book to provide guidelines to assist the faculties to do this. This third report on in-training evaluation summarized the position that the universities and the College had reached together, with particular reference to the faculties' familiarity with in-training evaluation and the forms that were completed. The report reviewed current systems of measurement of professional competence in internal medicine and correlated the results of multiple-choice question examinations and oral examinations with the results of in-training evaluation.[48]

This third report, prepared by a task force and writing committee for the Canadian Association of Professors of Medicine and the College, summarized the findings of a study that was conducted from 1979 to 1982. The study identified the problems that impaired the value of ITERs, recognized that these problems were largely resolved in the latter 1970s and found that, by the end of the decade, acceptable overall systems of in-training evaluation were implemented in all training programs. This comprehensive report reflected the state of the art of the measurement of professional competence for specialty Certification in just one specialty at the beginning of the 1980s. The report gives an indication of the distance and direction in which the College had travelled along the difficult path of evaluation and examination between 1960 and 1980. The main points included in the report's summary are therefore reproduced here:

- A significant improvement had occurred in in-training evaluation and in the university final evaluation of candidates training in internal medicine, and good university systems of evaluation were being used.
- The university final evaluation was comparable to that of the Royal College if the university final evaluation came from the program director in internal medicine. The Royal College and university evaluations were complementary and would continue to be inter-dependent in the measurement and assurance of national standards of professional competence.
- The multiple-choice examination dealt with clinical problems and basic information. The pass/fail cutting score changed from a relative to an absolute standard during the study.
- Study of the College's oral examination showed good agreement between individual co-examiners and between oral examiner teams. Oral examiners tended to distinguish between four grades — outstanding, above average, average and unsatisfactory.
- The predominant difficulties of the universities and the College were found to concern the difference between an unsatisfactory and an average performance. Neither the university final evaluation or the oral examination could stand alone in determining professional competence; both appeared to be indispensible.
- "We conclude we are on the right track. We should maintain the course indicated by the study. The study itself was a powerful stimulus to progressive change. In-training evaluation, used primarily to counsel trainees to reach program objectives, enhances postgraduate education. A university final evaluation, developed on the basis of an analysis of performance in an appropriate environment near the end of training, enhances the measurement of professional competence."

NOTES TO CHAPTER 9

1. G.R. Langley, "Internal Assessment of Specialty Trainees." *Ann RCPSC* 1972; 5:122-125.
2. G.E. Miller, "Evaluation in Medical Education: A New Look." *J Med Educ* 1964; 289-297.
3. The selected papers from the Edmonton conference on Evaluation in Medical Education were published in the October 1969 issue of the *Annals* (Vol 2, pp. 271-300).
4. D.R. Wilson, "Assessment of Clinical Skills from the Subjective to the Objective." *Ann RCPSC* 1975; 8:109-118.
5. See also S. Abrahamson, "Evaluation in Continuing Medical Education." *JAMA* 1968; 203:625-626.
6. See: G.M. Bull. "Examinations," *J Med Educ* 1959; 34:1154-1158; F.N. Fastier, "Consistency of Performance at Examinations," *J Med Educ* 1959; 34:761-772;

P.J. Holloway, J.C. Hardwick, J. Morris and K.B. Start, "The Validity of Essay and Viva-voce Examining Techniques," *Brit Dent J* 1967; 123:227-232; G.H. Bracht and K.D. Hopkins, "The Commonality of Essay and Objective Tests of Academic Achievement," *Educ and Psychol Measurement* 1970; 30:359-364; J.F. Calhoun, "Oral vs Written Testing in Self-Paced Individualized Instruction," *Education* 1974; 94:242-248.

7. R.G. Petersdorf and J.C. Beck, "The New Procedure for Evaluating the Clinical Competence of Candidates to be Certified by the American Board of Internal Medicine." *Ann Int Med* 1972; 76:491-496.

8. See: J.P. Guilford, *Psychometric Methods*, New York, McGraw-Hill Book Company, 1954; J.M. Mitchell, "Medical Education and Specialty Boards," *J Med Educ* 1959; 34:555-560; G.E. Miller, *Teaching and Learning in Medical School*, Cambridge, Harvard University Press, 1962; A.D. Polcorny and S.H. Frazier, "An Evaluation of Oral Examinations," *J Med Educ* 1966; 41:28-40; T. Colton and O.L. Peterson, "An Assay of Medical Students Abilities by Oral Examination," *J Med Educ* 1967; 42:1005-1014; D. Waugh and C.A. Moise, "Oral Examinations: A Videotape Study of the Reproductibility of Grades in Pathology," *Can Med Assoc J* 1969; 100:635-640; H. Levine and C.G. McGuire, "The Validity and Reliability of Oral Examinations in Assessing Cognitive Skills in Medicine," *J Educ Measurement* 1970; 7(2):63-74; P.R. Kelley, J.H. Matthews and C.F. Schumacher, "Analysis of the Oral Examination of the American Board of Anesthesiology," *J Med Educ* 1971; 46:982-988; A.M. Bold, "How to Pass Examinations: A Personal View on Good Technique in Clinical Biochemistry Examinations," *Ann Clin Biochem* 1976; 13:399-402; F.H. Goodyear and R.H. Behuke, *The Oral Examination, An Educational Evaluation*, Washington, U.S. Department of Health, Education and Welfare and National Institute of Education, 1976; C.H. McGuire, "The Oral Examination as a Measure of Professional Competence," *J Med Educ* 1976: 41:267-274; E.S. Siker, "A Measure of Competence," *Anaesthesia* 1976: 31:732-742.

9. See, for example, D. Waugh and C.A. Moise, "Oral Examinations: A Videotape Study of the Reproductibility of Grades in Pathology", *Can Med Assoc J* 1969; 100:635-640; R.A.H. Kinch, "The Position of the Royal College of Physicians and Surgeons of Canada", *J Reprod Med* 1970; 4:91-97; Examinations Committee, December 1975, p. 3; L.S. Valberg and J.B. Firstbrook, "A Project to Improve the Measurement of Professional Competence for Specialty Certification in Internal Medicine", *Ann RCPSC* 1977; 10:278-281.

10. See, for example, Examinations Committee, April 1976, p. 10-18 and also Attachment 16 (Report of the Royal College Task Force on In-Training Evaluation Reports, G.R. Langley (chairman), W.R. Harris, R.I. Hector and E.N. Skakun).

11. See Chapter 8, pp. 214 to 217, and Examinations Committee, December 1974, Attachment 12, for details of Dr. Mueller's tracking study.

12. For a full account of Dr. Rogers's argument, see Examinations Committee, December 1962, Attachment 4.

13. Examinations Committee, October 1963, Attachment 1, p. 1.

14. See also Chapter 12, pp. 351 to 360.

15. Compare with the observation by Dr. B.J. Perey made to Council in January 1974 to the effect that a low pass mark must be the pass mark the College should give itself as marking its potential for improvement.

16. Some guidance concerning the standard expected of Fellowship and Certification candidates was provided by the *Regulations and Requirements of Graduate Training Relating to the Examinations of the Royal College of Physicians and Surgeons of Canada*; the statements quoted here are from page 7 of the May 1956 edition. The lack of guidance given to examiners is illustrated by a story related by Dr. D.R. Wilson: when, as examiners for the Certification examination in medicine in 1954, he and Dr. D.G. Cameron asked of the chief examiner what standard they should attempt to establish in determining a pass mark for Certification candidates as opposed to Fellowship candidates, they were simply told, with a smile, "Oh, you two fellows know the difference between a Certified specialist and a Fellowship man." That was the only direction these two examiners received. For Dr. Wilson, this was where his dissatisfaction with the College's examination system began. (D.R. Wilson, Letter to D.A.E. Shephard, July 25, 1984.)

17. In 1964, 153 candidates sat both the Fellowship and the Certification examinations. Of these candidates, 41 passed both examinations and 60 passed the Certification examination only; one of the candidates, however, passed the Fellowship examination yet failed the Certification. In 1965, four of the 218 candidates who took both examinations passed the Fellowship examination yet failed the Certification examination. These droll occurrences were indeed strange, since the pass rates for the Fellowship were always lower than those for the (old) Certification examination.

18. I. van Praagh, *Can Med Assoc J* 1967; 96:554.

19. C.R. Scriver, *Can Med Assoc J* 1966; 95:1266.

20. C. Way, *Can Med Assoc J* 1967; 96:55.

21. L. Iffy, *Can Med Assoc J* 1967; 96:285.

22. P. Gloor, *Can Med Assoc J* 1967; 96:1071.

23. Examinations Committee, October 1963, Attachment 1, p. 1.

24. For an account of the introduction of multiple-choice questions in the College's examination system, see D.R. Wilson, Interim Report on the Multiple-Choice Examination Pilot Project, December 1965, Examinations Committee, December 1965, Attachment 14.

25. J.T. Cowles, J.P. Hubbard, "A Comparative Study of Essay and Objective Examinations for Medical Students." *J Med Educ* 1952; 27 (May, Part 2): 14-17.

26. For an English perspective, see: P.R. Fleming, W.G. Manderson, M.B. Mathews, P.H. Sanderson and J.F. Stokes, "Evolution of an Examination: M.R.C.P.(UK)." *Brit Med J* 1974; 1:99-107.

27. F.N. Gurd, Work Paper No. 1, Single Examination Process, July 24, 1970.

28. Gurd, 1970.

29. The progress made by the Task Force on the Single Examination Process from 1970 to 1972 can be studied in reports and bulletins attached to the minutes of the Examinations Committee.

30. D.R. Wilson, Letter to F.N. Gurd, Sept. 10, 1970.

31. D.R. Wilson, Letter to F.N. Gurd, Sept. 10, 1970.

32. Task Force on the Single Examination Process, Sept. 24, 1970, Attachment 3.

33. Lewis, p. 102.

34. J.C. Beck, "Internal Assessment — Another Point of View." *Ann RCPSC* 1973; 6:126-129.

35. R.C. Dickson, Letter to F.N. Gurd, Aug. 11, 1970; Task Force on the Single Examination Process, March 30, 1971, p. 1.

36. Following the first conference of specialties held on April 29, 1971, four other conferences took place — on May 11, 1976 (on continuing medical education); on May 9, 1977 (on the relationship between the College and the specialties); on Jan. 13, 1979 (on the timing of the annual meeting); and on April 26, 1980 (on specialist manpower). See Chapter 12 also.

37. W.H. Kirkaldy-Willis, Letter to J.H. Graham, Sept. 2, 1971.

38. F.N. Gurd, "Fellowship and Certification, 1972: A Unified Examinations Process." *Ann RCPSC* 1971; 4:242-252.

39. C.B. Mueller, "Basic Surgical Examination." *Can J Surg* 1977; 20:9-10.

40. J.B. Firstbrook, "The Principles of Surgery Examination: A Brief Historical Review." The Royal College of Physicians and Surgeons of Canada, June 1976.

41. F.J. Rounthwaite, Letter to P.J. Doyle, Nov. 19, 1974; Y. Morrisette, Letter to F.J. Rounthwaite, Dec. 2, 1974.

42. G.G. Laframboise, Letter to F.J. Rounthwaite, March 16, 1975.

43. See, for example, D.G. Cameron, Expanded Executive Committee, Oct. 24, 1969, pp. 5, 22 and 43.

44. G.R. Langley, J.B. Firstbrook, A. Knight et al, *University and Royal College Evaluation of Training for Professional Competence: Report of a Study in Internal Medicine.* The Royal College of Physicians and Surgeons of Canada, Jan. 12, 1983.

45. G.R. Langley (chairman), W.R. Harris, R.I. Hector and E.N. Skakun, Report of the Royal College Task Force on In-Training Evaluation Reports, April 14, 1976. See Examinations Committee, April 1976, Attachment 16.

46. *In-training Evaluation Systems in Postgraduate Medical Education: Accreditation Requirements and Guidelines.* The Royal College of Physicians and Surgeons of Canada, June 1976.

47. L.S. Valberg, J.B. Firstbrook, "A Project to Improve the Measurement of Professional Competence for Specialty Certification in Internal Medicine." *Ann RCPSC* 1977; 10:278-281.

48. G.R. Langley, J.B. Firstbrook, A. Knight et al, *University and Royal College Evaluation of Training for Professional Competence: Report of a Study in Internal Medicine.* The Royal College of Physicians and Surgeons of Canada, Jan. 12, 1983.

Chapter 10

The College and Research:
The Work of the McLaughlin Centre
and Other Aspects of Scientific
Investigation

Although the College's main concerns have been to develop requirements and standards for training and to examine and certify specialists, fostering an interest in research has likewise enhanced the College's authority in matters of postgraduate medical education. An interest in research, in the sense of scholarly or scientific investigation or inquiry, can be traced back to the pre-history of the College. In 1920, Dr. S.E. Moore, on behalf of the Regina and District Medical Society, proposed to the CMA that it was "desirable that the best means of stimulating and promoting advanced study of, and postgraduate work in, Medicine and Surgery be adopted";[1] and in 1922, the chairman of the CMA's Committee on the Formation of a Canadian College of Physicians and Surgeons included the "stimulation and promotion of postgraduate work in Canada for Canadians" as one of the objects that should be kept in mind as a college for specialists was being considered.[2]

After the College was founded in 1929, the value of research was recognized in the College's regulations governing training. A knowledge of the basic sciences, it was stipulated in 1951, was necessary to a proper understanding of any specialty, and one way a trainee could acquire this knowledge, and at the same time fulfil the College training requirements, was to spend a year as a full-time graduate student in research and teaching in a basic science department of a recognized medical school.[3] Likewise, would-be specialists planning an academic career were advised to spend a year or more in the full-time study of the basic sciences.[4] The importance of research during a specialist's training period was more explicitly stated later. In 1965, it was stipulated that, in a complete training program, the trainee should become familiar with research methods and the critical analysis of scientific data.[5] In 1975, trainees were informed that, since the maintenance of quality in medical practice requires that scholarship be based on scientific principles, the College encouraged research; and trainees, especially those intending to pursue an academic career, were advised to consider taking at least a year in clinical research related to the particular specialty.[6]

In the early years, two other activities testified to the College's concern for research. Research was first encouraged by the awarding, each year, of The Royal College of Physicians of Canada Medal to a Fellow in the Division of Medicine and The Royal College of Surgeons of Canada Medal to a Fellow in the Division of Surgery. These prizes, which were first competed for in 1946, were awarded for the best investigative work in the basic sciences related to medicine or surgery in a field of clinical research. Each medallist obtained further recognition by being invited to give a paper based on the work at the College's annual meeting. The College's annual meeting encouraged research in a second way, for the scientific program of the meeting was a recognized forum to which any Fellow could submit for possible presentation a paper based on research. As the scientific program expanded, and especially as CSCI and the growing number of specialty societies participated in the College's annual meeting, this forum attracted an increasing number of research presentations.

The value of research, therefore, was recognized early, but it was not until the Expanded Executive Committee formulated new objectives for the College in 1969 that an objective relating specifically to research was formulated. Somewhat modified, this objective was entrenched in the Letters Patent of Continuance approved by the Minister of Consumer and Corporate Affairs on November 4, 1971: the College was "to initiate, encourage, support and extend interest in research in medicine and medical education". This objective was readily achieved in the 1970s, as the College supported and fostered research in a number of specific ways.

A constructive step was the formation of the College's Research Committee in 1977. Chaired by Dr. J.C. Laidlaw, the committee was formed in order to advise Council on appropriate ways in which the College might foster medical research, not only as a source of new knowledge but also as an element in medical education. The committee's terms of reference enlarged on the committee's purpose. The committee was charged with being involved in the following specific activities: considering and emphasizing the role of research in the postgraduate training of specialists; monitoring excellence in research training posts in medical school programs and stressing the importance of research by medical school faculty in relation to the excellence of training programs; studying ways in which the College might influence governments in the funding of research; and recommending ways in which the College could further medical research of high quality, possibly through education, recognition or monetary rewards.

A second way in which the College encouraged the conduct of research was by establishing fellowships. The Merck Sharp and Dohme Travelling Fellowship and the Walter C. MacKenzie-Ethicon Travelling Fellowship both stimulated and supported scientific investigation. A further stimulus to research came in 1978, when Council approved the recommendation of the Research Committee for the establishment of the Royal College Visiting Professorships in Medical Research. Funded by the Educational Development Fund, to a value of $1,500 in each of two medical schools, two professorships were created to stimulate interest in medical research among both undergraduate and postgraduate students in medical schools.

These various developments alone would have demonstrated the College's concern with research, but two other developments between 1960 and 1980 emphasized the College's concern still further. These developments were the College's decision to admit medical scientists to Fellowship and the creation and work of the R.S. McLaughlin Examination and Research Centre. These activities did more than advance the College's evolution vis-a-vis its concern with research: they strengthened the College's credibility in matters of training and evaluation and they enhanced the College's respect and status, both in Canada and abroad. They therefore merit closer attention.

Admission of Medical Scientists to Fellowship

During the annual business meeting in 1964, President G.M. Brown referred to Council's decision to admit to Fellowship a new category of physicians — medical scientists. He explained Council's decision in these words:

> *These* are men, and there are not so far a great many of them, who play an essential role in teaching and research, and it is wrong to have them barred from Fellowship simply because they have not been fully trained as clinicians. It is also wrong for the College to be without them for that leaves us with no representation from an essential and growing part of medicine. Now Council has arranged it so that medical scientists-clinical investigators who are medical graduates of at least 10 years standing or who have reached the age of 35, and who have been engaged in medical research for at least seven years may apply for admission to the Fellowship.

Although, as Dr. Brown said, the question of admitting medical scientists was a long-standing one — the question had been raised first by Dr. A.L. Chute in Council in 1958 — it was entirely appropriate that admission of medical scientists should be inaugurated during Dr. Brown's presidency. President Brown was himself an outstanding medical scientist and, from 1965 until his untimely death in 1977, he would so discharge his responsibilities as president of the Medical Research Council that it was later said of him that "he may well have been the most important single influence on the quality of Canadian health research in the past decade".[7]

When Dr. Chute, in March 1958, had proposed that Council create a mechanism whereby medical scientists could be admitted to Fellowship in the

College, he did so aware of "the gulf" between those interested in the more strictly scientific aspects of medicine and individuals with a major clinical orientation. Admitting medical scientists to Fellowship would bridge this gap and would enrich and fertilize both medical science and clinical medicine. The College could serve as a catalyst for, as Dr. Chute saw it, one of the strengths of the College was that it was "an integrating force for all specialists". Inclusion of such an important group as the clinical scientists in the College would prevent a schism within clinical departments. Advantages would accrue to both the College and the medical scientists. The College would benefit from the influence of medical scientists, who would foster high standards of clinical investigation and educational programs for physicians; the medical scientists would gain from acquiring a closer link to their clinical colleagues (and indeed to clinical medicine) and from achieving a special credibility in the eyes of their fellow clinicians. There were, therefore, many advantages and benefits in Dr. Chute's proposal. The implementation of the proposal, however, took some five years.[8]

At its meeting in March 1958, Council agreed that a committee should be set up "to study ways and means whereby the College might provide for the future inclusion of men of science". Dr. Chute, together with Drs. F.S. Brien and G.A. Bergeron, were named members of the ad hoc committee. Through the Credentials Committee, they submitted proposals to Council in October 1958. Council approved in principle the Credentials Committee's resolution that medical scientists be admitted to the College and directed that training and examination standards be studied at the next Council meeting. Training requirements and examination regulations were drafted and, at the January 1959 meeting of Council, it was directed that this draft be considered by CSCI and the Canadian Federation of Biological Societies. Their opinion was requested as to the advisability of admitting medical scientists to the College; if this was positive, suitable regulations for admission to the Fellowship examinations could be drawn up. The College's proposals then were studied by these groups and by the medical schools.

The Credentials Committee first suggested that medical schools be consulted, and the deans were asked to consult with the heads of preclinical departments as well as with the heads of clinical departments. Among the seven medical schools that responded to the College's request for guidance, opinion was divided: Western, Montreal, Laval and Dalhousie favored the College's proposals, British Columbia and Manitoba (where only the preclinical scientists had been consulted) opposed them and Alberta reported a lack of consensus. Meanwhile, the Federation of Biological Societies (which comprised the Canadian Physiological Society, the Pharmacological Society of Canada, the Canadian Association of Anatomists and the Canadian Biochemical Society) discussed the College's proposals, but opposition within the Federation became apparent. The concern related to the training of graduate students in the basic medical sciences and to the opportunities for scientists so qualified after graduation. Because of the lack of agreement among these various groups and because of an element of opposition, which appeared to stem in part from misunderstanding of the objectives of the College's proposals, the matter was tabled indefinitely in January 1961.

The idea did not die, however, and in April 1961 the Executive Committee agreed that discussions should be resumed. It became clear that the opposition to the proposals had come not from clinically oriented individuals but from preclinical scientists, some of whom had not clearly understood what the College's proposals implied. CSCI itself had favored the proposals and had only suspended their own discussions when the College tabled further discussion. A second ad hoc committee (consisting of Drs. A.L. Chute, D.G. Cameron and J. Genest) then drafted training requirements for further study and negotiations, this time with the clinical investigators rather than the preclinical scientists. CSCI expressed its continuing interest in the College's idea — though it opposed the use of special examinations of any kind in the admission of clinical investigators to the College. CSCI thought that this might introduce the misleading concept that the College was a certifying body in clinical research.

At this time, the number of clinical investigators who were full-time faculty members in clinical departments was steadily increasing. They were able to make special contributions. Many knew more about the clinical aspects of their particular subject than did most clinicians, and more about its physiology and pharmacology than most physiologists and pharmacologists; their inclusion in teaching programs was therefore thought essential to the advancement of clinical medicine. In view of the lengthy discussions that had continued over the years, Dr. Chute now advised the Executive Committee in May 1963 that the time was finally right for Council to consider the admission of medical scientists and from two simple points of view — whether admission was in the best interests of medical education, training and research and whether admission was in the best interests of the College itself. The logical step was to devise a mechanism, other than an examination, whereby the contributions of the medical scientists could be evaluated.

Several options were open to the College. One was to consider carefully the observations already made by CSCI. Constructive comments had been made in 1960 by Dr. R.J. Slater, when he was president of CSCI. First, the number of career clinical investigators eligible for Fellowship in the College would be quite limited. This opportunity would be limited to the few individuals who were conducting clinical investigation in academic centres. Second, because the primary purpose of a clinical investigator was to master one realm of research thoroughly and although the techniques and knowledge of the basic sciences could be brought to the bedside, it was unlikely that an investigator could also be an excellent general physician and maintain that standard. And third, in view of these considerations, three criteria for admission of medical scientists to the College were debatable as a basis for discussion: the submission of a thesis on studies carried out by the investigator, with the winning of a Royal College medal as an existing standard of acceptability of such research; an oral examination in the special field of interest of the applicant as well as his background of general knowledge, the examiners being one or two scientists of repute in the scientist's field, as well as one or two Fellows of the College; and the recommendation by the chairman of the candidate's department, the candidate's personal qualifications being emphasized. To qualify and attain this level of accomplishment, a candidate in general would have received at least five years of training after graduation in medicine, and would have had to demonstrate ability to conduct independent, original research. This duration would place candidates in a position comparable to candidates for Fellowship in various aspects of clinical medicine.

These criteria were discussed by the Executive Committee in June 1963. It was suggested that physicians and surgeons who were medical scientists and medical graduates of at least ten years' duration who had devoted at least five years (later amended to seven) to medical research might become eligible for Fellowship under specific regulations. One step would be for them to take the ordinary Fellowship examination, but the fact was that many such physicians had entered research before completing the standard requirements for training. An alternative course would be for them to be evaluated on the basis of their published work; this form of "examination" would meet the requirements of Section 8 of the Act of Incorporation. Each would be assessed by a specially selected board of examiners, who would submit an opinion to the Executive Committee regarding the merits of such publications. There was a precedent for such a mechanism, since The Royal College of Physicians of London included a provision of this nature in its bylaws.

Drs. D.R. Webster and W.C. MacKenzie were then directed to nominate a group of distinguished medical scientists to be considered for election to Fellowship. As an introductory step, it was recommended that these scientists be admitted without examination. In December 1963 the Executive Committee agreed to submit the names of three medical scientists for the approval of Council — Dr. M.L. Barr, Professor and Head of the Department of Microscopic Anatomy, University of Western Ontario; Dr. J. Doupe, Professor and Head of the Department of Physiology, University of Manitoba; and Dr. S. Hartroft, Director of The Research Institute, The Hospital for Sick Children, Toronto.

This step concluded the lengthy process whereby clinical investigators were brought into the College. The program was formally introduced in 1964 and became an important part of the College's pursuit of unity among Canadian specialists. As of February 25, 1982, no fewer than 80 medical scientists had become Fellows under the provisions of the program. The criteria of admission changed little over the years, and the following statement of December 1980 indicates the nature of these criteria:

Guidelines Which Can be Utilized in the Special Form of Examination for Admission to Fellowship Under the Special Regulations Relating to Medical Scientists

1. The applicant must hold a medical qualification acceptable to the Council.
2. The applicant must have reached the age of 35 years or have possessed his/her medical degree for at least ten years.
3. The applicant must have devoted at least seven years to research.
4. The applicant should be holding at the time of submitting the application a recognized research appointment. (Most, although not all, of these have been academic appointments.)
5. The applicant must ordinarily be resident in Canada. The policy has been not to accept applications from persons outside of Canada.
6. Immigrant medical scientists should have landed immigrant status, should occupy a full-time academic post in Canada and have occupied such a post for at least three years.
7. The applicant may be an investigator in the basic sciences related to medicine or in one of the clinical branches of medicine.
8. The applicant must be a "career investigator"; those who devote a goodly part of their time to clinical practice or non-investigative work would be expected to qualify by examination in the usual way.
9. The publications of the applicant must have been accepted in journals of high standards and high standing.
10. In the case of multiple-author publications there must be some evidence that in a reasonable number of the important publications the applicant was the principal investigator with major responsibility.
11. There should be evidence in the published works that the applicant is well-trained and knowledgeable in research methods.
12. The evaluation should be of a standard which is not less than what one could compare with that of the ordinary examinations that provide an entry into Fellowship, as far as that comparison is practical.
13. There should be evidence of the contribution of some new knowledge. (This is perhaps the most difficult area to evaluate; the requirement here is reasonable and the applicant need not have achieved the level, for example, of a Gairdner Award nominee.)[9]

The medical scientist program was successful and Dr. Chute's foresight was evident when the opinions of medical scientist Fellows were analyzed in June 1982. Dr. J.B. Firstbrook, Director of Training and Evaluation, questioned the

80 medical scientists who were registered as Fellows as of February 25, 1982. He received replies from 54; virtually all the replies indicated that these scientists were pleased (and many felt honored) to be Fellows.[10] The reasons for their pleasure varied, but the comments of just one Fellow, however, do summarize the meaning of the College Fellowship for this group of physicians and surgeons. Dr. J.R. Wall, an Australian who was Associate Professor of Medicine and of Microbiology and Immunology at Queen's University, put it this way:

> *What* Fellowship into the Royal (Canadian) College as a medical scientist offers, then, is acceptance of the background, training and qualifications of a member of an associated or affiliated college who has performed mainly medical research and for whom re-examination would pose a major problem because of the disruption of the research program which would be necessary in order to pass the examination. In practical terms, Fellowship in the Royal College has, for me, meant that I can remain in Canada doing what I have been doing successfully.... . It does, however, make me feel that I have been accepted into the medical community as an equal member in that it recognizes my contribution to medical science and to the practice of medicine generally.

The medical scientist program, therefore, demonstrated the College's interest in integrating the results of scientific investigation and medicine, one of the benefits of research.

Development and Work of the R.S. McLaughlin Examination and Research Centre

A further demonstration of the College's integrating the results of investigation and medicine — and enhancing the development of the specialist — is afforded by the creation and work of the R.S. McLaughlin Examination and Research Centre. Of all the developments that shaped the transition of the College between 1960 and 1980, the contributions of the McLaughlin Centre were among the most important. Establishing the Centre was a fundamental evolutionary step. Thereafter, thinking in the College about the training, examinations and evaluation of specialist candidates was influenced by the results of the various studies conducted by the Centre; no longer would anecdotal and retrospective accounts collected by individuals determine the College's beliefs and practice. Establishing the Centre represented a further step in professionalization of the College; it catalyzed a successful fusion of theory and practice and so gave authority to the College in matters of medical education.

The Concept of the Centre

The starting point of events that led up to the formation of the McLaughlin Centre was 1963, which was also a turning point in the history of examination reform in the College. During that year, the Examinations Committee studied the content and conduct of the Fellowship examinations in medicine, surgery and obstetrics and gynecology, and two years later the College decided to introduce a multiple-choice paper into the examination for the Fellowship in medicine.

The College was embarking on a new venture. As Dr. D.R. Wilson, the Centre's founding director, said, "at this time there was no clear knowledge of the techniques involved, no one who had any experience and background in these methods, and the Royal College had no question items in its possession to begin such a new type of examination".[11] This situation was corrected to some extent by the visit of Dr. Wilson and Dr. R.V. Christie to England in May 1964, when they met Drs. A. Kekwick in London and G. Smart in Newcastle, and by the liaison that Dr. Wilson established in 1964 with Dr. V. Logan, of the American Board of Internal Medicine in Philadelphia. Dr. Logan's assistance was invaluable, for it was his providing the College with 300 test items that enabled Dr. Wilson, working with Dr. Christie, Dr. M. Belisle and Dr. J.P. Gemmell, to construct the multiple-choice paper that was introduced as planned, in 1965.

The concept of an examination centre had developed by the mid-1960s. Conversations that Dr. Wilson had in Edmonton with Dr. J.P. Hubbard, of the National Board of Medical Examiners, at the beginning of the decade constituted one stimulus. A second stimulus was provided in the latter part of 1965, when the idea of a centre was discussed informally by Dr. Wilson and Dr. R.B. Kerr while they were returning to Toronto from the Kingston conference on residency education.[12] The first formal reference to such a centre in College records was made by Dr. Wilson in a report on the initial studies of the multiple-choice examination to the Examinations Committee in December 1965. Dr. Wilson wrote as follows:

> With the increasing interest of the Medical Council of Canada in newer examination methods, it is quite obvious that this body and the Royal College should be considering one centralized facility in Canada for this purpose. Just how far the Royal College can go in the introduction of objective examinations remains to be seen, but it is now quite clear in my mind that these newer methods of examination are established beyond all doubt and are in many ways superior to our present essay methods. Although our two-year 'pilot' run is only at mid-point, I am convinced that to abandon this type of examination now would be a retrograde step from which it would take us many years to recover.

Study of the results of the first multiple-choice examination provided objective evidence of weaknesses in the College's examination system, and the evidence was strengthened by a study the following year of the marking of papers in the 1966 Fellowship examination in medicine. By 1967, it was evident that the College's examination system was seriously flawed, and Dr. Wilson

Donald R. Wilson

The First Duncan Graham Award, Edmonton, June 25, 1969
(L. to R.) President J. Turcot, Duncan Graham, J.P. Hubbard

presented the evidence for this to the Examinations Committee in May 1967. In a report entitled "Pilot Project Study in Multiple-Choice Examinations", Dr. Wilson submitted no fewer than 21 conclusions that might guide the committee in formulating policy for the future; these conclusions also were illustrative of a new interest in the research aspects of examination methodology.

The essence of these conclusions is as follows. The most obvious finding was that the introduction of multiple-choice examinations had improved the College's examination procedures.[13] Multiple-choice examinations were superior to essay examinations in measuring candidates' knowledge at all levels of achievement and they eliminated language barriers to success in some candidates. Most importantly, the discriminatory power of the multiple-choice examination was greater than that of the essay examination, which was imperfect in several respects. The essay examination, in short, was a blunt evaluation tool. Because the marking of the essay examination was neither precise nor objective, the essay examination failed to identify all knowledgeable candidates and so prevented a certain number from reaching the oral examination. Some candidates who took the examinations that included both types of questions were able to proceed to the oral examination only because of their marks on the multiple-choice question papers, and they then performed as well as candidates with a clear pass in all papers. In the previous two years, multiple-choice examinations had brought 49 more candidates to the oral examinations and, of them, 28 then succeeded in passing the Fellowship examination. The essay type of examination was flawed in other respects also: there was no correlation between the performance of candidates in either essay paper or any question in either paper with oral examination performances; only 50 per cent of examiners reached the minimum level of acceptance when pair-marking of essay questions was analyzed; and, when markers were given a particular pass mark to adhere to, they tended to mark to that standard and not necessarily to the intrinsic quality of the answer. These flaws were serious enough to suggest that essay examinations were a hazard to a significant number of candidates. Moreover, failure to utilize computer analysis meant that serious flaws in essay questions were undetected; indeed, computer analysis was now yielding much information that was not previously available. The oral examination, too, was also defective, for there was now sufficient evidence to indicate that the results of the first of the two oral examinations were being overemphasized in determining the ultimate success or failure of candidates.

A further interesting finding was that candidates who had taken two core years of training performed equally well in written examinations as did candidates with four years of training. This suggested that candidates should be permitted to sit the written portion of the examination at any time after having completed two core years of training. In brief, these findings made a strong case for radical reform of the College's examination system. They supported

Dr. Wilson's advocacy of the need for the College to develop a centre that might continue studies of the methodology of examinations and advise the College regarding the content and conduct to examinations in the 1970s. They further demonstrated the spirit of research that would come to characterize the contributions of the McLaughlin Centre in this decade.

The need for a unit to study and develop examination techniques seemed logical when multiple-choice questions were introduced in 1965 but it was compelling by 1967. The College was not the only organization that would find such a unit useful, for the MCC was pursuing inquiries concerning an examination service at that time. Dr. H.M. Stephen, Registrar of the MCC, telephoned Dr. J.P. Hubbard, of the National Board of Medical Examiners, about an "examination service" on March 29, 1967. Dr. Hubbard favored the further development of closer relationships between medical education and licensure in Canada and in the United States as desirable rather than the setting up of two separate activities, but he did comment on the matter of a Canadian testing "system". Thus Dr. Hubbard: "If Canada is seriously considering the development of a testing system for the primary purpose of developing multiple-choice examinations for medical licensure and medical education, the leadership should be in the hands of a person who has been through the medical education system itself and has real interest — and hopefully some experience — in methods and techniques of educational measurement".[14] The provincial colleges and the CFPC were likely to be interested too, so the chief question now was how to develop a centre for use by Canadians.

By mid-1967, the concept of a centre had developed into a formative plan. Dr. Wilson's interest and enthusiasm led Council in June 1967 to approve a resolution that the College should establish an operational unit. Dr. Wilson saw the centre as an operational unit for research in postgraduate medical education, the main purpose of which would be to study evaluation techniques as applicable to postgraduate students and postgraduate training programs and to introduce newer examination methods. He immediately took the initiative of discussing the project with the dean of education (Dr. H.T. Coutts) and the Vice-President of the University of Alberta (Dr. M. Wyman). By the late summer of 1967, the plans for a centre had virtually been formed in prototype, for on August 29, 1967, Dr. Wilson wrote Dr. W.C. MacKenzie that the unit then consisted of himself and Dr. S. Hunka, assisted by part-time secretaries, though no actual space was required.[15] The University of Alberta, however, was receptive to Dr. Wilson's request for space on the campus, though Vice-President Wyman would need a letter of support from Dean Coutts and Dr. W.C. MacKenzie, now dean of medicine, before the request could be granted formally.

Of much importance was the role played by Dr. F.G. Kergin in the fall of 1967. A member of Council and sharing an interest with Dr. Wilson in postgraduate medical education, Dr. Kergin was both chairman of the College's

Finance Committee and a trustee of the R. Samuel McLaughlin Foundation. Earlier in 1967, Mr. J.C. Fraser, likewise a trustee of the Foundation and close to Colonel R.S. McLaughlin, had suggested to Dr. Kergin that the latter "might give some thought to some other activity of the Foundation which would be a further service to the people of Canada by improving the excellence of medical care".[16] An examination and research centre would constitute such an activity, and Dr. Kergin consulted Dr. Wilson on the desirability of approaching the McLaughlin Foundation with this in mind. Dr. Wilson expressed his ideas at length to Dr. Kergin in a letter on August 31, 1967[17] — "the letter", Dr. Wilson noted on it later, "that started it all".[18]

Dr. Wilson's letter to Dr. Kergin was based on the theme of uniformity and evaluation. The pilot project of multiple-choice examinations in internal medicine had shown that the whole concept of evaluation by modern methods was a challenge not only for the College but also for all universities in Canada. There was no standardized basis for evaluation of students entering university; for example, in Alberta, with its three universities, patterns and standards for admission to the same faculty differed widely. The challenge to medical educators at all levels — undergraduate, licensure for practice and postgraduate — was a real one, and educators had an opportunity to make advances in the next five to ten years that were long overdue. Medical schools, licensing bodies (especially the MCC), the CFPC and the College were all interested in bringing about major changes in evaluation techniques and examination procedures. Therefore, continued Dr. Wilson, at this evolutionary stage it was important to take steps to ensure the development of a modern scientific centre that would devise uniform measuring techniques. These would apply across the country to ensure that all students had an equal chance. Such a centre would also provide the opportunity in the licensing field to set up modern uniform standards across Canada and thus to avoid a patchwork quilt of the various state requirements that existed in the United States.

Other points that Dr. Wilson made concerned the College itself. The development of an examination centre would introduce changes in examination methods that had remained essentially unchanged since the later 1930s. Change was required; Dr. Wilson emphasized that, "although our training regulations are excellent, our methods of measuring candidates' competence are somewhat shaky and archaic in the light of the data we have turned up". One new method was in-training assessment, which would benefit the College and the candidates. Existing examination methods failed to reveal hard data that could be confidently used to identify a candidate's weaknesses; the failed candidate was simply required to take another year of training (the sixth after graduation) yet received no competent advice from the College as to where his or her knowledge was deficient. This, Dr. Wilson admitted, was "a rather shocking state of affairs for a College which prides itself on its scientific excellence". Candidates were just "axed" and they learned little or nothing from their experience. This was a major reason for the College's bad public relations with candidates — particularly those bright Canadians currently in the United States who did not return to Canada or did not try the College's examinations because of the examinations' reputation of unpredictability and arbitrariness. The College, therefore, needed to take a new look and to introduce new procedures for the oral examinations. But examiners remained reluctant to assault this "sacred cow" and yet they always left the oral examinations frustrated and angered at many of the decisions that were made. Finally, Dr. Wilson told Dr. Kergin that a national examination centre would make it possible to assess training programs by evaluating impartially the graduates of such programs. This would also improve further the College's approval of training programs and do much to enhance the College's reputation in this field.

The "long rambling letter" that Dr. Wilson feared he had written was in fact a clear and informative exposition of the state of the art of evaluation in 1967. Dr. Wilson had summarized opinions that he had formed "after playing around with this rather fascinating subject for the past few years". Despite Dr. Wilson's fears, the letter was most helpful to Dr. Kergin. On September 19, 1967, Dr. Kergin wrote to Mr. J.C. Fraser concerning a project that, Dr. Kergin thought, "would very well complement the present activity of the foundation".[19] In what Dr. Kergin, like Dr. Wilson modestly claimed was "a long and rather rambling letter", yet was actually a masterful exercise in communication, Dr. Kergin made a clear and convincing case for supporting the concept of an examination and research centre.

Dr. Kergin laid down the basis of the project point by point, as he explained the situation as he saw it in 1967 to the two lay philanthropists, Mr. Fraser and Colonel McLaughlin. Dr. Kergin first explained that the College had the responsibility each year of examining about 1500 candidates for specialist qualifications in various categories, using written papers with essay-type questions and some oral examinations. "None of us who have had experience as examiners are under any delusions", Dr. Kergin admitted, "that this is a precise or accurate process". He noted that for the past two years the College had had two examiners mark the same questions and had then compared their marks. The lack of uniformity was remarkable. The College also had the same examiner return six months later to read and mark the same questions again. Once again there was little correspondence between the marks given on the two different occasions. Dr. Kergin stressed that it seemed "absolutely wrong" that physicians who had spent five or six years in postgraduate training and whose whole future in the profession rested on obtaining the higher qualification should have their future determined by "extremely inaccurate" processes. This state of affairs was the more unacceptable since, over the past 15 years, the Americans and the British had developed new examination methods based on a more sophisticated technique for the oral examination and on the use of multiple-choice questions for the written examination.

Dr. Kergin continued by explaining that multiple-choice questions could be marked with complete accuracy "as there is only one right answer to each of perhaps 180 or 200 questions." This relatively new technique tested a candidate's factual knowledge. A candidate's judgement and technical skill were assessed by newer techniques of oral examinations. The College had become interested in innovations in examination techniques and had, for example, even borrowed suitable questions for an experimental trial. "We are convinced," Dr. Kergin emphasized, "that these newer methods are now fully established, have proved their worth and must be adopted and used by the College". He explained, too, that it was not only the College that needed help: "If the College could set up an organization to develop this type of examination procedure it would render a service to the whole medical field in Canada". Since no other medical body in Canada was moving in this direction, the College should accept an important responsibility related to medical education and develop an examination centre. Deliberately, no doubt, Dr. Kergin left his final point to the end, saying that he might have managed to obscure "the important point". But his strategy was precisely to leave this last point to the end, to emphasize the way in which philanthropists, especially Colonel McLaughlin, might be of assistance. Dr. Kergin made his point as follows:

> There is a great gap here in the overall program of education of doctors in Canada. A contribution to close this gap, to improve our ability to recognize knowledge and skill, and also to do justice to these highly trained men and women by assessing them accurately would be a very great contribution indeed.

Writing this letter required considerable skill and judgement, but the task was evidently easier than the physical task that Dr. Kergin faced next, when he made the oral presentation of the proposal to Colonel McLaughlin and Mr. Fraser. Dr. Wilson described the difficulties Dr. Kergin faced at this meeting on September 27, 1967, in these words:

> Both these senior members were extremely hard of hearing and Dr. Kergin had to give the whole report by practically shouting at the top of his lungs. At its conclusion Colonel McLaughlin chided Dr. Kergin for not speaking loudly enough, but stated that although he did not understand the whole proposition, if Dr. Kergin felt that it was a good idea he would approve it. On observing Dr. Kergin nod his head in the affirmative the chairman, after a very brief consultation with Mr. Fraser, approved the project... . The sum of $50,000 was to be advanced to the College annually for five years.[20]

Thus funded, the Centre that Dr. Wilson had long envisioned was now realized. Formally approved by Council in January 1968 and named the R.S. McLaughlin Examination and Research Centre, with Dr. Wilson appointed as

Director, the College's new research unit would soon be able to begin providing service to the College and other organizations and to conduct much-needed research in the field of evaluation and examinations.

Early Work and Development

One of the first steps that Dr. Wilson, the Centre's founding director, took was to define desirable functions and objectives for the Centre. These were presented to, and approved by, the Examinations Committee in December 1967 and Council in January 1968. The objectives were the following:

- To establish a centre to explore examination methods.
- With the experience gained from the pilot project over the past three years, to establish the unit initially at the University of Alberta.
- To establish objective examinations for the College.
- To develop in-training assessment programs.
- In collaboration with the MCC and ACMC, to survey and mobilize the available qualified personnel in Canada.
- To establish test committees in the specialties, as required.
- To establish a close liaison with the CPMQ.
- To establish a working liaison between the College and organizations concerned with medical and health care examinations.
- As part of a long-term objective, to work towards the establishment of common international examinations.

An early need was the support of medical schools, and Dr. Wilson accordingly addressed ACMC in October 1967. He wished to determine the number of individuals in the various clinical and preclinical disciplines who would be willing to act on the various examinations test committees. He planned to visit each medical school in Canada and to discuss his ideas with the deans at the ACMC meeting. The deans' support was essential: now that the decision had been taken to go ahead with the Canadian centre — "a monumental task", as Dr. Wilson realized[21] — he did not want to seek further advice from American authorities like Dr. Hubbard and Dr. G.E. Miller without knowing whether a sufficient number of Canadians would be willing to work on the project. The deans were supportive, as were the Canadian academicians and specialists whose opinions Dr. Wilson sought early in 1968.

Despite the enthusiasm generated by the McLaughlin grant, it was still unclear, however, which of three courses should be pursued. The College could depend entirely on American sources for examination material; an entirely Canadian centre could be developed, though this appeared to be an unlikely possibility; or the College could create a small centre, depending initially on the good will and material resources of existing American agencies, and ultimately achieving independent status but perhaps part of a larger examination organization involving all of North America and possibly the United Kingdom as well.[22] But the uncertainty made the challenge of developing an appropriate form of centre all the more interesting though there were several problems: developing a cadre of specialists to form the test committees and to acquire and refine examination questions — in internal medicine first, then in general surgery, in obstetrics and gynecology and later in other specialties; creating a translation service so that questions could be provided in English and French; obtaining cooperation with interested organizations like the MCC, the CFPC and the CPMQ; and finding and hiring a small group of professionals with a particular expertise in evaluation and educational measurement who would staff the Centre.

In 1967, before the Centre as such had truly been established, Dr. Wilson and Dr. S. Hunka, Director of Educational Research Services at the University of Alberta, constituted the professional, part-time faculty. But at that time Dr. B. Hudson, of Monash University, Australia, was visiting Canada as a Sims Travelling Professor, and he elected subsequently to spend a sabbatical year with the Centre. His contributions were crucial then, for the Examinations Committee particularly was profoundly concerned about the high failure rates in the Fellowship examinations and the Centre was accordingly bending its chief efforts to identifying the factors involved. One of Dr. Hudson's first contributions was made in 1968, when the Centre conducted one of the initial research studies that identified it as a research centre. This was a videotaped oral examination study that was designed to demonstrate some of the flaws in the oral examination as an instrument of evaluation.

In this study, no less than "a complete replication of a normal Royal College examination in internal medicine" was filmed.[23] The film was made in a television theatre in the University of Alberta. Participating were a patient from the University Hospital; a recently qualified Fellow in internal medicine, who played the role of a resident being examined; a senior examiner; and a junior examiner. The film was shown to the examiners in Montreal who were participating in the oral examinations in 1969. Because the purpose was to highlight flaws and the variability in the marks that would be given by the 17 pairs of examiners (10 in internal medicine and seven from specialties), these 34 examiners were the objects of study that Drs. Hudson and Wilson were interested in. Among the ten pairs of examiners in internal medicine, seven "passed" the "candidate" and three "failed" him, while among the seven pairs of examiners in the specialties, only two "passed" him. The examiners' marks varied widely also. Among the internal medicine examiners, the marks given by individuals ranged from 77 to 55, and by pairs, from 76 to 56.5. Among the other examiners, the individuals' marks ranged from 75 to 50 and the pairs' marks, from 73 to 59. These findings confirmed everyone's worst fears. Dr. Wilson's comment on the experiment was the following: "This served to bring home in a factual way the wide variability known to exist in this particular phase of Royal College examinations and subsequently led to research studies being undertaken for other possible means of assessing competence of candidates performing in situations as close to real life as possible".

Dr. Hudson was one of a number of visitors to the McLaughlin Centre who, in its first decade, made valuable research contributions. During his sabbatical at the McLaughlin Centre in 1968, Dr. Hudson conducted two other research studies. Assisted by Mr. C. Hazlett, a graduate student in experimental psychology, Dr. Hudson directed basic work on computer storage and retrieval of all multiple-choice question material. He also directed the Centre's first critical studies on the shortcomings of the oral and clinical examination. He was also instrumental in developing the first working model for a computer-based examination. Studies such as these, allied to the College's earlier studies on the written examinations, formed the data base from which the Centre could develop in other directions, particularly in relation to the development of multiple-choice examinations. Until 1969, the only specialty making use of multiple-choice questions was internal medicine, but in 1969 new test committees were formed for general surgery, orthopedic surgery and obstetrics and gynecology. These specialties were followed by urology and pediatrics, in which test committees started to work on multiple-choice questions in 1970. The CPMQ also decided to use the College's multiple-choice examinations in 1970.

Satisfactory as the multiple-choice examinations were, they were not all-embracing in their evaluation of clinical competence. Comparison of the results of the written examinations and of the oral examinations showed that the multiple-choice examination technique could not be used to measure clinical competence, and the study of the oral examination technique likewise revealed that this technique was limited as an evaluative instrument. Another way of measuring clinical competence was needed, and thoughts turned to in-training assessment for this purpose. This concept had been introduced to the College during the Kingston conference on residency education in October 1965,[24] and it was a logical step now to propose that the evaluation of clinical competence should become at least partially a formal responsibility of program directors; moreover, to develop in-training assessment programs had been one of the objectives that Dr. Wilson had defined for the Centre in 1967. From this objective emerged the work that led to the development of the in-training evaluation technique, and of the in-training evaluation report (ITER) that was first used by the College in 1973.

By 1970, all of the eight objectives that Dr. Wilson had drawn up for the Centre as a Canadian, as opposed to an international, unit had been largely met. But for the Centre to develop and keep pace with fast-moving developments as more specialties sought to introduce objective examinations, a more formal organization in the Centre was necessary.

Until mid-1969, not even Dr. Wilson, the founding director, worked in a permanent capacity, though he and Dr. Hunka put in countless hours because of their interest in, and dedication to, the developing Centre. On July 1, 1969, however, Dr. Wilson resigned from the chairmanship of the department of medicine at the University of Alberta and took on half-time duties as director of the Centre. Dr. Hunka also became a part-time staff member, with responsibilities in computer science, educational psychology and psychometrics. Research studies were thereby facilitated. Research was conducted in 1969 on factors influencing pass/fail rates and on inter-judge reliability. The Centre's research studies were further facilitated when Dr. M. Grace joined the staff full-time in 1970 as a programmer.

Until this time, the McLaughlin Centre was thought of principally as a small but sophisticated unit working out of the University of Alberta, somewhat distant from the College. A key member of the staff, however, was located in Quebec City, for the need to develop the Centre as a bilingual unit was recognized early; Dr. J. Beaudoin was appointed co-director in Quebec City in February 1968. Dr. Beaudoin's responsibilities and achievements lay in translating multiple-choice questions into French, but he also enthusiastically sought to interest his colleagues at Laval University in his work and in this Centre's need for translation services. But Dr. Beaudoin was physically remote from Edmonton and, in the fall of 1969 he told President J. Turcot that, if the College wished to preserve the bilingual character of the Centre, a French section should be formally established. The Executive Committee's recommendation to Council that a French section be established was approved in January 1970. This was a desirable step, for the Centre had assumed semi-independent status as early as 1969 and, while there was no danger of disunity, a tendency towards autonomy was developing. Some degree of autonomy was not undesirable, and the very success of the Centre could not be denied. Nor was semi-independence displeasing to the director, for he had envisioned the R.S. McLaughlin Examination and Research Centre from its very beginnings as serving a larger constituency than the Royal College alone[25] — a constituency, for example, of an examination centre with national or even international aspirations and dimensions.

Yet the pattern of growth in the Centre in these early years was seen as being "rather inchoate".[26] The Centre was largely the outcome of the vision of one man who was able to create an institution through a combination of native intelligence, acute understanding of educational needs, a well-developed network linking himself to others in the evaluative and educational field and individual entrepreneurship. Dr. Wilson's dedicated leadership of a team of innovative professionals enabled the Centre to conduct original work that provided irrefutable data and gained for the Centre an unassailable intellectual position in a field that was still largely untilled in Canada. It was therefore reasonable for Dr. Wilson to take the initiative of establishing lines of communication with the College that tended to separate the Centre from the College and, to a considerable extent, from the secretariat. Dr. Wilson reported to the Executive Committee on matters related to the College and to the Examinations Committee on matters related to examinations; on local policy he reported to the University of Alberta. Because the College virtually gave Dr. Wilson carte blanche, communication tended to be "a one-way street",[27] from Dr. Wilson to the College. Because of Dr. Wilson's initiative in the Centre's early years, the College itself did not formulate any strategy.[28] The force of growth in a changing and developing field may well have led to a degree of decentralization that was unusual in the College. Despite this "inchoate" growth and various administrative anomalies, the Centre in its early years grew from a "cottage industry" with an operating cost in 1968 of a paltry $19,395 into "big business" with an operating cost in 1970 of a respectable $81,081.[29]

Growth and change continued to shape the Centre during the early years of the 1970s. The main developments in this period were the growth of the Laval unit and the creation of an advisory board. In research, part of the generous grant of $300,000 from the Gladys and Merrill Muttart Foundation made it possible to study, together with the American Board of Pediatrics and the National Board of Medical Examiners, an examination technique using computer-based patient management problems; the last was the first international effort of its kind anywhere in the world in the joint study of the feasibility of the use of computers in the evaluation of competence.[30] The Centre was flourishing — in itself a tribute to Colonel R.S. McLaughlin, whose death occurred early in 1972. The College mourned the passing of Colonel McLaughlin. His generosity, extended through the McLaughlin Foundation, had supported the McLaughlin Foundation-Edward Gallie Visiting Professorship since 1960 and had established the R.S. McLaughlin Examination and Research Centre itself in 1968 and the College was deeply appreciative of Colonel McLaughlin's philanthropic efforts.[31]

Until the end of 1971, the principal function of the Laval unit had been to translate examination questions into French. This function did not fully satisfy the unit's co-director, Dr. J. Beaudoin, who wanted the French section to create questions as well as translate them. This point of view was supported by the Executive Committee. Dr. J.T. MacDougall said that the English and the French should be working together — unity was an important consideration — and Dr. J. Turcot stated that this view reflected a Canadian problem in that the growing French unit wanted to express itself. Besides, working only on translation would not satisfy anyone who was seriously interested in medical education. The Executive Committee in January 1972 therefore recommended to Council that services of the McLaughlin Centre should function equally well in French and English, for which an increased budget was necessary. Council accepted this recommendation. Dr. B.J. Perey saw the French unit as providing a "tremendously rewarding and enriching experience" for both individuals and the medical schools who were interested in designing better evaluation procedures. Such experience was currently denied francophones, in part because some were unable to function as fully and effectively in English as in French. An increased budget would ensure that French-language medical schools could contribute more fully to this aspect of medical education.

The budget for the Laval unit was then increased from $10,000 to $35,000. More significantly, the French unit began to discuss its organized development. Both general and specific objectives were drawn up on May 12, 1972 by Drs. J. Beaudoin, J. Boulay, G. Cormier, J.G. Couture, B. Lefebvre, L. Levasseur, Y. Morin, Y. Ouellet, B.J. Perey, G.A. Sirois and J. Turcot. The general objectives were to contribute to the general objectives of the R.S. McLaughlin Examination and Research Centre in promoting the participation of a group of French-Canadians in the activities of the Centre; to promote the interests of the French-Canadian group in the methods of evaluation in medical education and to develop expertise in some aspects of personnel and facilities in this geographical area; and to ensure the bilingualism of the Centre in offering adequate translation services in both languages. The specific objectives, as defined for 1972 and 1973, were to establish the storage and retrieval system used in the Edmonton division and to store in French all the material that had been translated in the last few years; to organize two working groups, in association with the medical schools, to look at the content of the question bank for surgery (under Dr. Perey) and to review the core content of medicine and the related question bank (under Dr. Ouellet); to follow up, evaluate and analyze the in-training assessment operation that would begin in July 1972 (under Dr. G. Cormier); and to organize a secretariat and to develop on a more permanent and stable basis. These objectives reflected the interest that Canadian medical schools were taking in reorganizing their approach to evaluation and, not surprisingly, the University of Alberta and Laval University led the way in applying new techniques. The Laval unit, now more effectively integrated into the McLaughlin Centre as a whole, was in a particularly good position to stimulate the four Quebec medical schools to develop objective techniques of testing. The evolution of the Laval unit, therefore, exerted a major influence on the understanding of evaluation in Quebec.

The second area of growth in the McLaughlin Centre in this early period was the creation of an advisory board. Other organizations, especially the MCC, were interested in using the resources of the Centre. The McLaughlin Centre, however, was entirely a College operation but, because the MCC wished not only to use the resources but also to participate in its management and financing, it was necessary to develop a mechanism to enable the MCC to do this. Accordingly, an advisory board was created, five members representing the College and two, the MCC.

The MCC accepted the College's invitation to serve on the advisory board, and the board met for the first time on December 12, 1973. Dr. R.C. Dickson was elected chairman; the members of the board consisted of Drs. L. Horlick, J.T. MacDougall, G. Hurteau and B.J. Perey of the College and Drs. D.F. Cameron and A. Roy of the MCC. The ACMC and CFPC were also represented by observers. Mr. C.F. Scott, QC, who happened to be the legal advisor to both the College and the MCC, also attended the meeting.

The formation and work of the advisory board showed how medical organizations could collaborate when they wished to pursue common endeavors. The MCC's membership of the advisory board made it easy to arrange that test committees of the MCC and the College should have a common core of members; in this way money, time and manpower could be saved. The development of examination techniques and, indeed, the study of evaluation in general were also facilitated. Moreover, in a country like Canada, in which both the College and the MCC were essentially unitarian organizations, unity was thus further fostered. The MCC wished to avail itself of the McLaughlin Centre's resources because of its interest in repatriating its examinations to Canada in a manner acceptable to all parties concerned. Such cooperation as was either based on or served the cause of common national unity in this instance was of pragmatic value, day-to-day operations thus being made easier than they would have been in the absence of a commonality of interests among examining bodies — as in the United States, for example, where the pursuit of unity among similar organizations tends to be a quixotic endeavor.

In its first five years, the Centre had grown rapidly, both in developing concepts of evaluation and in applying them. The Centre's growth was apparent in several ways. Thus, by 1973, more than 6,000 examination questions were now banked with the Centre, available for use by the various specialty test committees, which themselves were developing fast, and another 2,500 questions were stored and classified at the University of Alberta; and all of these questions were translated into, and stored in, the French language.[32] A second indication of growth was the increase in professional staff. Dr. W.C. Taylor joined the Centre in 1973 as Assistant Director, and Dr. S. Kling joined the following year to assist in the development of Canadian items for the MCC. But besides the Centre's full-time staff, many other physicians were associated with the Centre; by 1975 as many as 227 Canadian physicians were giving their time and energy to the various test committees and the Centre's two main units.[33] A further indication of growth and maturity was the Centre's participation in the first joint feasibility study on the international sharing of test items, along with the United States, the United Kingdom and Australia.[34]

Research in the McLaughlin Centre also intensified in the mid-1970s. The introduction of in-training evaluation in 1973 provided an incentive to the staff of the Centre to assess this new component of the College's examination process;[35] so did the need to investigate, in terms of competence, various methods of scoring of examinations. The vexing problem of the validity of cutting scores was a perennial incentive to research. A further incentive to research in the Centre was provided by the numerous visitors to the Centre. In 1976 alone, visitors from Australia, New Zealand, Scotland and West Germany, as well as from other centres in Canada, interested themselves in the work of the McLaughlin Centre. One of these visitors was Dr. E. Nanson, from New Zealand and formerly Professor of Surgery at the University of Saskatchewan. Dr. Nanson, who spent six months in the Centre in 1975 and 1976, created patient management problems of high quality, and he assisted a doctoral student from the University of Alberta's Department of Educational Psychology, Mr. P. Harasym, use the Centre's computerized patient management problems to investigate methods of scoring of this type of problem.

The use of the computer in examination techniques was of particular interest to the McLaughlin Centre, and the generous grant of $300,000 from the Gladys and Merrill Muttart Foundation, which commenced in 1971, made it possible for the Centre to conduct several projects based on computerized techniques. One such study concerned the use of computers in the evaluation of candidates. The first international effort of its kind anywhere, this study, which was conducted in the early 1970s, was developed in collaboration with the National Board of Medical Examiners and the American Board of Pediatrics.

The research and development into computerized patient management problems (CPMPs) for inclusion in the College's Certification examination in pediatrics was one of the Centre's most important research projects. The use of computers in the instruction and examination of students had developed in the 1960s and was widely accepted by 1970. (In medicine, the Computer-Based Examination Project [CBX] of the National Board of Medical Examiners and the Model for Evaluation and Recertification through Individual Testing [the MERIT process] used by the American Board of Internal Medicine were the largest computer examination programs.) In 1972 the College entered into an agreement with the National Board of Medical Examiners and the American Board of Pediatrics to develop patient management problems in pediatrics. Patient management problems were used as part of the College's Certification examination in pediatrics in 1973 and remained part of the Certification examination in pediatrics through 1977, even though technical problems occasionally impaired their value.

The dimensions of the study of the feasibility of CPMPs were discussed by Drs. W.C. Taylor and E.N. Skakun in an informative report in December 1976.[36] Their principal conclusions were the following:

- CPMPs measure aspects of candidates' performance that are not assessed by the multiple-choice question written examination and the oral examination. CPMPs detect aspects that are separate from those detected by multiple-choice questions, oral examinations and ITERs.
- Experience from 1974 to 1976, during which CPMPs were administered to 484 candidates, showed that the technique was feasible, that candidates accepted it and that this type of examination could be administered on different days in the same city without compromising the performance of those who take the examination early as opposed to late.

- With the cost of examining 160 candidates in 1975 at $34,582.88, the cost per candidate at $216 was $34 lower than the average cost per candidate of an oral examination in pediatrics but higher than the cost of a multiple-choice examination at $62 per candidate.
- The specific variables that the CPMP technique measures include the following: data gathering and interpretation abilities reflected in the history, physical examination, laboratory tests and special procedures; the appropriateness of therapeutic, procedural and operative intervention; the sequence in which decisions are made and decision-making skills; audio as well as visual components of clinical problems; and cost effectiveness in terms of time, money expended on tests and discomfort to the patient.
- CPMPs permit unlimited branching and can trace the performance of a candidate through the clinical maze.
- The CPMP technique can instantly compute a candidate's performance in any preselected parameter without the possibility of human error caused by handling data; it also provides immediate feedback on any decision and therefore mirrors a physician-patient encounter or dialogue.
- The security of the CPMP technique is greater than that of the standard patient management problem and the multiple-choice question technique.

The CPMP project was an innovative one and demonstrated the Centre's ability to conduct research and to develop the theoretical base so that it could be applied in practice. In just this project alone, the Centre went far in fulfilling at least four of the Centre's objectives — by exploring examination methods, by establishing objective examinations for the College, by establishing a working liaison between the College and organizations concerned with such examinations and by working towards the establishment of common international examinations. The Centre was engaging in research of a high order and with important practical applications.

The Horlick Review

The McLaughlin Centre continued to grow apace in the second half of the 1970s, and in September 1976 the Executive Committee requested Council to authorize a review of the Centre. This request was prompted by several earlier statements. In April 1975, the Training and Evaluation Committee (see Chapter 4), in reviewing the College's Division of Training and Evaluation, had recommended that, "at some time in the future", a feasibility study should be conducted to determine whether the interests of the McLaughlin Centre and its major users would be better served by combining the English and the French units in Ottawa. The committee noted that as the McLaughlin Centre became more of a national resource, it must inevitably become less of a servant of the College with respect to the examination process. The Executive Committee in

September 1976 therefore advised that the administrative relationships of the College with the McLaughlin Centre should be defined and clarified, in keeping with its broad role.

Dr. Wilson supported the proposal for a review of the McLaughlin Centre. He told Dr. R.C. Dickson, chairman of the Board of Governors* of the McLaughlin Centre, that the Centre had become "quite a large operation" and suggested that the review be widened to constitute a review of all the Centre's operations, similar in scope to the on-site surveys that the College conducted of training programs in the university centres. At the same time, Dr. Wilson informed Dr. Dickson that he wished to retire from the directorship of the Centre no later than September 1, 1978.[37]

Accordingly, Council directed that a review team, including representatives from the United States and the United Kingdom as well as Canada, survey the McLaughlin Centre. The terms of reference for the survey were comprehensive. Principally, the review team would study the Centre's development and current status and report and make appropriate recommendations. It would be necessary, however, to examine the Centre's administration, budget, relationships with various organizations (including the College itself, the CPMQ, the MCC and the CFPC), English-French relationships and location (centralized or decentralized), as well as the questions of sponsorship (as by the College and possibly other organizations) and autonomy. The review team consisted of Drs. L. Horlick (chairman), G.M. Brown and G. Pigeon (from Canada), and Dr. S. Abrahamson (Director, Division of Research in Medical Education, University of Southern California School of Medicine) and Dr. J.F. Stokes (Past-President of the Association for the Study of Medical Education, United Kingdom); Mr. T.J. Giles was appointed secretary. Later, when the need for a person with expertise in business management was recognized, Dr. E.B. Shils (Professor of Management, Wharton School of Business, University of Pennsylvania) was appointed. Because illness prevented Dr. Shils from participating in the original on-site survey and in the related intensive discussion by the other team members, he was subsequently asked to consult on the complex interrelationships that existed between the Centre and other organizations and to examine and make recommendations regarding the financial and budgetary operations of the Centre. To do this, he felt obliged to conduct his own survey, covering essentially the same ground as that covered by the other members of the team. Because of this, and because Dr. Shils's report was not discussed in conjunction with that of the other members of the team, his report was appended to the main report and he was listed as consultant rather than as a member of the survey team itself.

---

*From 1974 to 1978 the Advisory Board was known as the Board of Governors.

The survey was conducted in Ottawa, Edmonton and Quebec City from March 27 to April 1, 1977. Submitted on November 17, 1977, the detailed 70-page Horlick report included 18 appendices (the last of which was Dr. Shils's own 78-page minority report) and 19 recommendations.

The recommendations engendered considerable discussion in the Executive Committee, the Council, the secretariat and the staff of the McLaughlin Centre. The following is an abridged version of these recommendations:

1. The Centre should "stand apart" from the regular line organization of the College and retain the potential of eventually becoming a free-standing independent Canadian examination Centre.
2. Since the Centre's assets were the property of the College, responsibility for the operation of the Centre should continue to rest with the College, through Council and the Executive Committee.
3. To resolve ambiguity regarding function, what was currently the Board of Governors should be renamed with the previous title of Advisory Board because this more clearly reflected its function and because it had no administrative or executive powers.
4. The Director was the Centre's chief executive officer, and he was recognized as being responsible to the College's Executive Committee.
5. The Centre's budgetary and financial controls should be centralized in Edmonton under a financial and administrative officer who would work with the College's senior financial officer and take direction from him; a subsidiary financial officer in Quebec City would work under the financial comptroller in Edmonton.
6. Membership of the Advisory Board should include representatives of external users, such as the MCC and the CPMQ, and of internal users, such as the Examinations Committee and the Fellowship Affairs Committee.
7. The chairman of the Examinations Committee should be the chairman of the Advisory Board.
8. The Centre's headquarters should remain in Edmonton, and the current decentralized structure, with units in Edmonton and Quebec City, should be maintained.
9. Affiliation agreements should be created between the Centre and its host universities, showing that the College was the responsible body and employer and paymaster of the Centre staff.
10. An advisory committee should be established for each unit, comprising members drawn from Canadian medical schools and other interested parties; the Quebec unit's advisory committee should include representatives of the francophone schools, McGill University and the University of Ottawa, and the Edmonton unit's advisory committee should include representatives from the other medical schools.

11. The bilingual nature of the Centre should be preserved and the growth and development of the Quebec unit should be fostered so that it might provide equal input into research and developmental planning and become an active partner in all new major projects.

12. A major goal should be to plan an overall strategy for research and development, which would be accomplished through an advisory committee on research and development that would report to the Centre's Advisory Board and, through it, to the College's Executive Committee and Council.

13. A director of research, at College headquarters, should be appointed to identify needed operational research and to facilitate its execution.

14. Coordination of all research and development should be the responsibility of the Centre's director.

15. Of the Centre's operating budget, five to ten per cent should be assigned to the support of research and development.

16. A permanent inter-institutional relationship between the Centre and the National Board of Medical Examiners should be negotiated.

17. Wider distribution of chairmanship of test committees through the medical schools was advisable.

18. Consideration should be given to use of the same computer language in both units.

19. The Centre's international role and offer of assistance to developing nations that are interested in testing and evaluation should be maintained.

These apparently straightforward recommendations were not devoid of controversy. The survey team had, however, identified problems and areas of conflict and unrest. The issues that generated various degrees of controversy were the following: relationships between the Centre and the College, between the Centre's two units and between the staff of the Centre and of the College secretariat; integration of the Centre and the College's total examination process; mechanisms for setting research priorities for the Centre and for meeting the College's operational research needs; financial and administrative controls within the Centre; planning by the Centre; possible relocation of the Centre to Ottawa; and contributions to the work of the McLaughlin Centre at the graduate level within the francophone medical schools. These issues received close attention during a special meeting of the Executive Committee on December 18, 1977.

This meeting of the Executive Committee was a particularly useful one. Dr. Horlick explained the views of the survey team in great detail, especially regarding differences of opinion. There was general support for the Horlick report, although the members of the secretariat expressed reservations about

some of the recommendations. The discussion also illustrated different perceptions of the Canadian medical scene.

In introducing his report, Dr. Horlick referred to the views of Dr. Shils and the
relationship between him and the other members of the survey team. Here was
the first evidence of a difference of opinion. In this instance, the difference was
too great to be accommodated within a single unanimous report. Dr. Horlick
explained this by saying that, while there were broad areas of agreement
between Dr. Shils's conclusions and those of the survey team, there were also
major and irreconcilable differences on which no acceptable middle ground
could be found. The areas of difference were related mainly to the administrative relationships of the McLaughlin Centre to the College and its clients and to
perceptions of the Canadian medical scene. Concerning the areas of disagree-
ment between the two parties, Dr. Horlick had this to say:

> We fundamentally disagree with [Dr.] Shils's recommendation that the
> McLaughlin Centre become a fourth division of the College and that it
> report to the Secretary. His proposal would essentially make the
> Centre a service division of the College and would, I think, damage its
> research potential. Also it would in one stroke abolish the stream
> of historical continuity which goes back to the foundation of the
> McLaughlin Centre. The Centre, from the beginnings, has been con-
> ceived of as more than a simple servant of the Royal College, and the
> prospect that it might one day become an independent and free-
> standing entity was never abandoned by the College. [Dr.] Shils's
> proposal would also constitute as we saw it a breach of faith with the
> Medical Council of Canada which abrogated its arrangement with the
> National Board of Medical Examiners on the understanding that it
> would have meaningful input into the McLaughlin Centre policy
> decisions. Finally, to make a move as drastic as that advocated by [Dr.]
> Shils would be to imply that somehow the McLaughlin Centre had
> failed in its mission and in its responsibilities to the Royal College, an
> implication which the survey team rejects.

> I believe the divergent views in this important matter can be explained
> in reasonable terms. Fundamentally it rests, with due respect for
> Dr. Shils and for his ability as the managerial consultant, in Dr. Shils's
> lack of knowledge of the Canadian scene and on his desire to equate
> the McLaughlin Centre with the National Board of Medical Examiners
> and the American Board of Internal Medicine, which does not hold
> water. He underestimates the importance of the historical continuity of
> relationships between the Royal College, the Medical Council of
> Canada and the Association of Canadian Medical Colleges in the
> foundation and development of the McLaughlin Centre. He under-
> estimates the paucity of Canadian resources which make it mandatory
> that there should not be competing organizations in the field of evalua-
> tion and, perhaps most seriously, he fails to understand the particular
> role of the Royal College vis-a-vis the universities, provincial health

departments, licensing authorities, federal government etc. Finally, [Dr.] Shils is a business consultant. He likes a neat and clean solution. So do we, but we realize that such solutions are obviously impossible in Canada without disrupting the delicate fabric of our complex inter-relationships.

The recommendations were then discussed in detail. Recommendation No. 1 was the important one and Dr. Horlick explained why this recommendation had been made. The major issue in the early 1970s was whether it would be better to establish an independent centre or to develop the McLaughlin Centre within the College so that it might function as a resource centre for other interested organizations. But Dr. Horlick detected a "seeming ambiguity" in the control of the McLaughlin Centre and the College's inability to decide whether it really wanted to relinquish control of the McLaughlin Centre. Added to this uncertainty was dissatisfaction on two sides. First, some individuals thought that the McLaughlin Centre staff was "not interested" in some aspects of the examination process and that the College could not influence the McLaughlin Centre in such a way that any legitimate requests for operational research could be met; second, others thought that the College had given "little if any direction" to the McLaughlin Centre and that the Centre had been obliged to make its own decisions. Lack of overall coordination of the examination process, allied to the College's ambiguity regarding control of the Centre, were, therefore, among the chief problems identified. Recommendation No. 1, which Dr. Horlick regarded as "a crucial recommendation, perhaps the most crucial recommendation in the whole report", was designed to correct some of the principal weaknesses; so were Recommendations 2, 3, 4, 6 and 7. The survey team felt that it was their responsibility to recommend an administrative structure that would allow for the solution of these problems without at the same time destroying those qualities of the Centre that had given it its excellence — the freedom of the members of the McLaughlin Centre staff to remain innovative, to maintain an acute interest in research and not to be subjected to too many day-to-day pressures for delivery of service.

In the lengthy discussion of Dr. Horlick's report, subsidiary problems were uncovered. One was "the delicate, important issue of status". The McLaughlin Centre had become a world-renowned organization and, in Dr. Horlick's view, it had brought kudos and recognition to the College; nor was it difficult for anyone to forget that the Centre, based on its own merits and on Dr. Wilson's entrepreneurial talents, had been funded in large part by the two substantial grants of $250,000 and $300,000 from the McLaughlin Foundation and the Muttart Foundation, respectively. At the same time, Dr. Horlick reported that some members of the secretariat appeared to resent the fact that members of the McLaughlin Centre staff were treated as "colleagues" by the Executive Committee and Council while they themselves were regarded as "employees or servants". Another problem stemmed from the constraints that, during the

Centre's development, had made it difficult for the College to give directions and leadership to the Centre. A third problem was the College's difficulty in attracting "top-flight academics" to its permanent staff.

Discontent among the members of the secretariat, Dr. J.B. Firstbrook explained, was not attributable to a lack of attention paid to headquarters but to a lack of communication and a lack of clear-cut responsibility. Here, Dr. Horlick observed, there was a fundamental schism that should not be passed over. This was the question of reporting structure. The survey team recommended that the director of the McLaughlin Centre should report directly to the Executive Committee. That was the structure that gave it its semi-autonomous situation. If the director were to report through Dr. Graham, he would be co-equal with the directors of the other divisions, and the McLaughlin Centre, in effect, would be a fourth division of the College; and that, Dr. Horlick pointed out, was what the survey team recommended should *not* be done. Dr. Shils, however, had clearly stated that the director of the McLaughlin Centre should report directly to Dr. Graham, the College Secretary, and that the Centre should be one of the operating divisions of the College.

The schism was the more noticeable because the senior members of the secretariat agreed with Dr. Shils. The secretariat submitted their argument to the Executive Committee in a separate memorandum. They believed that the McLaughlin Centre should be an integral part of the administrative structure of the College, that its status should be equivalent to that of the other three major administrative divisions and that its director should be responsible to the College's chief executive officer in the same way as were other division directors. While the secretariat stressed the need to control rising costs relating to the Centre's activity, which could be done only if the McLaughlin Centre were treated as an integral part of the administrative structure of the College as a whole, they disagreed with Recommendations No. 2, 4 and 5 for other reasons. They held that the operation of the Centre as an integral part of the College administrative structure would not jeopardize its potential to become a free-standing entity should the College, at any time in the future, decide on such a course. They argued that to accept that the Centre should remain apart from the regular line structure would only perpetuate and perhaps exaggerate even further the existing problems. The members of the secretariat also took the view that to provide for the Centre a function that was separate from all other segments of the College administrative structure seemed inconsistent with the basic premise stated in Recommendation No. 2, and might lead to undesirable competition within the College regarding such considerations as the setting of priorities and the allocation of financial resources. Finally, the secretariat claimed that there was a danger in emphasizing too much the possibility of the Centre's becoming independent and that this could condition those involved in directing the work of the Centre in considering that as a major objective.

In this basic difference of opinion between the secretariat and the survey team, the main question was whether the Centre should become an integral part of the administrative structure of the College or whether it should enjoy some kind of semi-autonomous existence at an "arm's length" from the College and thus preserve its potential for attaining an independent status at some time in the future. The secretariat stressed that their position had been formulated before, rather than after, Dr. Shils's somewhat similar opinion had been stated; the members had suggested, as a way of resolving these problems, the very recommendations that were now proposed. The secretariat felt that they had a considerable interest in the issues involved; they stressed that they would be assuming a major responsibility for the effective and efficient implementation of whatever ultimate decisions might be taken.

The other recommendations of the Horlick report were less controversial, both to the Executive Committee and the secretariat. Action on Recommendations 1, 2, 3, 4, 5 and 7 was deferred pending their consideration by other parties (for example, the Board of Governors of the McLaughlin Centre); Recommendations 6, 8, 9, 10, 11, 12, 14, 15, 17, 18 and 19 were approved (some in modified form); and only Recommendation 13 (to establish a director of operational research within the College) was not supported.

The Executive Committee on December 18, 1977, had provided the secretariat the opportunity of stating their views; on January 21, 1978, the Executive Committee acceded to Dr. Wilson's request to express his views. Dr. Wilson's reactions to the Horlick report were contained in a memorandum entitled "The Other Side of the Coin". He was concerned that the Executive Committee had heard the views of the secretariat but not his own, and it seemed only just that the Executive Committee should receive a balanced input on the Horlick report. In fact, Dr. Wilson was understandably upset that he had not been invited by either the Executive Committee or the secretariat to state his reactions to the report. Dr. Wilson noted the secretariat's statement that they were the ones who would assume the major responsibility for the effective and efficient implementation of whatever ultimate decisions might be taken, but he pointed out that he had no axe to grind; he had, after all, given notice of his resignation long in advance of the survey.

Dr. Wilson, like everyone else, recognized that all hung on Recommendation No.1. He emphasized that the failure to adopt this important section of the report would be not only a complete reversal of all the accumulated and approved developments of the Centre, but also "an unconscionable breach of faith" with other agencies participating in the development of the Centre, particularly the MCC. His position was the same as that of the survey team and opposed to that of the secretariat. If the Centre was to be "tucked back" into the College as another division, the whole nature of the Centre would change and the dismantling of the Centre, particularly the research component, would begin.

With respect to the other Horlick recommendations, Dr. Wilson, who had seen the Centre develop from the start, made many points, and his opinion was greatly valued. He observed that the statement in Recommendation No. 2 was only partly true, since the Centre's "assets" included the test item bank developed for MCC; the College, therefore, had a legal and moral commitment to the MCC. In relation to Recommendation No. 4 and, in particular, to the secretariat's inference that semi-independence of the Centre would perpetuate "existing problems", Dr. Wilson explained that most of the problems had arisen as a result of the "phenomenal" growth of the College and of the Centre; he was unaware of any serious problems resulting from the relationship between the Centre and the secretariat. "Tucking it back under line authority" would not solve all the "problems". Regarding Recommendation No. 5, Dr. Wilson stated that at no time had there been any desire on the part of the Centre to become a separate agency; the recommendation would in fact simplify the Centre's operation. Nor did he think that the financial situation was as gloomy as the secretariat suggested; at no time since its inception had the Centre ever knowingly exceeded its budget as approved by Council. Concerning Recommendations Nos. 6 and 7, Dr. Wilson advised that the whole examination process should be brought together under the McLaughlin Centre. His point was that the examination and research process, or in other words, the accountability for what the College did in these areas, should be an agency separate from that which sets the standards, develops the programs in collaboration with the university training centres and supervises the quality of the training programs. Finally, Dr. Wilson found that Recommendation No. 8, as stated in the Horlick report, was entirely acceptable, though the secretariat's suggestion that "a 'pro tem' condition" should be attached to the recommendation that the headquarters of the Centre remain in Edmonton was not. It would, Dr. Wilson assured the Executive Committee, meet with "universal dismay" in the Centre and prolong the uncertainty regarding the future of the Centre.

The Executive Committee emphasized that Dr. Wilson's presence at the meeting testified to the importance that the committee attached to his opinion. Now, all of the material and the different views concerning the Horlick report would be made available to the incoming Executive Committee and their minds would be "uncluttered" by previous concepts. Nor would Council take any action at its next meeting.

A further contribution to the debate on the Horlick report was made by Dr. B. Perey. He had two chief concerns. First, the Horlick report offered no practical answer to a major question: Who, at the College, was in charge of the entire examination process? No statement defined the manner in which the College intended to maintain direct control of its examinations, to ensure coordination and to ensure that the needs of the College would be met. Dr. Perey's second concern was expressed in a further question: How heavily should the hand of the Ottawa secretariat be felt in the affairs of the Centre? He expressed his concerns in a letter to Dr. Graham on January 3, 1978, and his letter was discussed during the meeting of the Executive Committee on January 21, 1978. Dr. Perey identified seven aims of the College with respect to the McLaughlin Centre and issues related to it. The College had to discharge its responsibilities of ownership of the McLaughlin Centre; to retain direct control of its examinations regarding content, standards and costs; to ensure comprehensive coordination of its own examinations; to ensure that its needs regarding examinations be met by the McLaughlin Centre or otherwise; to reflect the bicultural nature of the nation as well as its regional diversity; to consolidate the input from current and prospective customers and to be responsive to them; and to promote the growth, development and prestige of the Centre, nationally and internationally. Dr. Perey then attempted to take the best elements of the whole positions that had already been taken — those of the Horlick report itself, of Dr. Shils's minority report, of the secretariat and of Dr. Wilson. Part of the problem was the dual nature of the College: it was both owner and customer of the Centre. Was the Centre "really going to be a service centre or is it going to 'run the show'?"

Dr. Perey made three recommendations. First, a member of the College secretariat should be designated who would organize the College's entire examination process, including the part prepared by the McLaughlin Centre. This individual would coordinate the examination process and convey to the McLaughlin Centre the views and wishes of Council and its committees regarding examinations, including operational research. Second, a member of the College secretariat should be designated to take responsibility for all evaluation projects in continuing education, including the part prepared by the McLaughlin Centre. All such projects would be coordinated, and the views and wishes of Council and its committees in matters regarding continuing education, including operational research, would be conveyed to the McLaughlin Centre. And, third, a program to promote growth and development of the francophone contribution to the activities of the McLaughlin Centre should be implemented. These recommendations were complemented and accompanied by an organizational chart that Dr. Perey offered in order to stress basic concepts of communications. Dr. Perey's plan was supported by the Executive Committee. The plan would provide a means of clearly designating individuals who would recognize problems and draw them to the attention of their counterparts in the McLaughlin Centre. It would overcome a major problem that had been identified by the Horlick report and ensuing discussions — "what is lacking is a little bit of understanding", was how Dr. Perey put it. He went further: "No one dares to do too much so nothing gets done. Part of the reason for this is that nobody knows who is supposed to do what". The need now was to ensure that people began to understand who was supposed to do what. Dr. Perey's plan, it was agreed, went far to bridge the gap between the survey team's report and the secretariat's position.

Council supported the Executive Committee's position and gave its approval to the Horlick report in June 1978. The crucial Recommendation No. 1 was readily approved in principle. Of the other recommendations, all were approved except for Recommendation No. 5, which was received for information only, and Recommendation No. 13, for which the reasons for the recommendation no longer existed. Dr. Perey's plan was also approved.

The Board of Governors of the McLaughlin Centre also supported the Executive Committee's position. In particular, the Board recommended the Centre's continuation as a College enterprise, utilizing as a basis Dr. Perey's administrative plan. The director would be the chief executive officer of the Centre and report to the College's Executive Committee and Council by way of the College Secretary; he would also have responsibilities to other bodies utilizing the Centre. The only apparent difference related to Recommendation No. 7: opinion seemed opposed to the proposal that the chairman of the Examinations Committee would automatically be chairman of the Advisory Board.

By September 1978, little unfinished business remained. None of the recommendations remained controversial and many had been effected. What business was unfinished would, however, soon receive fresh attention: on September 1, 1978, Dr. S. Kling, formerly Assistant Director of the McLaughlin Centre, succeeded Dr. Wilson as Director.

With the retirement of Dr. Wilson and the succession of Dr. Kling to the directorship, the Centre's first decade came to a close. This first decade was a success story. The Centre had accomplished a great deal and its achievements were among the most remarkable of all those in the history of the College from 1960 to 1980. The Centre's accomplishments went far beyond research and medical education, for they enhanced the status of the College itself, both internationally and nationally.

NOTES TO CHAPTER 10

1. Lewis, p. 5.
2. Lewis, p. 11.
3. *Regulations and Requirements of Graduate Training Relating to the Examinations for the Diploma of Fellow or Certification in a Specialty.* The Royal College of Physicians and Surgeons of Canada, May 1951, p. 33.
4. *Regulations and Requirements of Graduate Training Relating to the Examinations for the Diploma of Fellow or Certification in a Specialty.* The Royal College of Physicians and Surgeons of Canada, May 1951, p. 33.
5. *Requirements for Approval of Hospitals for Advanced Graduate Training.* The Royal College of Physicians and Surgeons of Canada, 1965, p. 6.
6. *General Information Concerning Requirements for Training and Examinations.* The Royal College of Physicians and Surgeons of Canada, June 1975, p. 7.
7. Obituary: Malcolm Brown. *Ann RCPSC* 1977; 10:264.

8. A useful summary of the negotiations leading to the admission of medical scientists to Fellowship is provided by Dr. J.H. Graham in a "Memorandum Concerning the Admission of Medical Scientists to Fellowship in the College" (Council, June 1963, Attachment 5).

9. "Guidelines Concerning the Admission of Medical Scientists to the Fellowship". The Royal College of Physicians and Surgeons of Canada, December 1980.

10. Questionnaire Survey of Medical Scientist Fellows, June 10, 1982. Royal College Archives.

11. D.R. Wilson, Notes on the History of the R.S. McLaughlin Examination and Research Centre, The R.S. McLaughlin Examination and Research Centre, 1974, p. 1. This informal document is an invaluable source, as are Section I and Appendix I of the Report of the Survey Team on the R.S. McLaughlin Examination and Research Centre, 1977 (L. Horlick, chairman), submitted to the College on Nov. 18, 1977.

12. D.R. Wilson, "The R.S. McLaughlin Examination and Research Centre". In Andison and Robichon, Ottawa, 1979, p. 115.

13. This finding is discussed in detail in Chapter 9, pp. 245 to 247.

14. J.P. Hubbard, Letter to H.M. Stephen, Mar. 30, 1967.

15. D.R. Wilson, Memorandum to W.C. MacKenzie, Aug. 29, 1967.

16. F.G. Kergin, Letter to J.C. Fraser, Sept. 19, 1967.

17. D.R. Wilson, Letter to F.G. Kergin, Aug. 31, 1967.

18. Dr. Wilson's letter was a long one; indeed, with tongue in cheek, he suggested to Dr. Kergin in his letter of Aug. 31, 1967, that "if the length of this letter bears any relation to our ultimate success with the McLaughlin Foundation we should be good for at least half a million over the next five years".

19. F.G. Kergin, Letter to J.C. Fraser, Sept. 19, 1967.

20. D.R. Wilson, in Andison and Robichon, Ottawa, 1979, p. 115.

21. D.R. Wilson, Letter to R.B. Kerr, Oct. 1, 1967.

22. D.R. Wilson, Letter to C.B. Stewart, Dec. 28, 1967.

23. For further details, see D.R. Wilson's Notes on The History of the R.S. McLaughlin Examination and Research Centre, The R.S. McLaughlin Examination and Research Centre, 1974, p. 11-13, and "Assessment of Clinical Skills from the Subjective to the Objective", *Ann RCPSC* 1975; 8:109-118 (particularly p. 114, with reference also to erratum notice referring to Table 3 as corrected by an erratum notice on p. ii preceding p. 161 in volume 8 [July 1975 issue]).

24. See Chapter 8, pp. 206 to 207.

25. Report of the Survey Team on The R.S. McLaughlin Examination and Research Centre, 1977 (L. Horlick, Chairman), submitted to the College on Nov. 18, 1977 (hereinafter the Horlick Report), p. 30.

26. Horlick Report, p. 20.

27. Horlick Report, p. 31.

28. Horlick Report, p. 20.

29. Horlick Report, pp. 20-21; see also Minority Report by E.B. Shils, p. 12, Table 2.

30. D.R. Wilson, in Andison and Robichon, Ottawa, 1979, p. 118.

31. Three months after Colonel McLaughlin died, the trustees of the Foundation found themselves unable to recommend a further grant — a source of disappoint-

ment that was relieved somewhat by the generosity of the grant of $300,000 awarded by the Gladys and Merrill Muttart Foundation, which was announced on Dec. 6, 1971.

32. D.R. Wilson, in Andison and Robichon, 1979, p. 119.

33. D.R. Wilson, in Andison and Robichon, 1979, p. 120.

34. D.R. Wilson, in Andison and Robichon, 1979, p. 119.

35. See, for example, two papers by E.N. Skakun, D.R. Wilson, W.C. Taylor and G.R. Langley: "A Preliminary Examination of the In-Training Evaluation Report", *J Med Educ* 1975; 50:817-819; and "The In-Training Evaluation Report — Stability of Structure and Relationship to Other Certifying Examinations", *Ann RCPSC* 1976; 9:315-317.

36. W.C. Taylor and E.N. Skakun, The Computerized Patient Management Problem — A Report to the Committee on Examinations of The Royal College of Physicians and Surgeons of Canada, reproduced as Attachment 4, Examinations Committee, December 1976. Two pertinent publications from the McLaughlin Centre are: W.C. Taylor et al, "The Use of Computerized Patient Management Problems in a Certifying Examination", *Med Educ* 1976; 10:179-182, and E.N. Skakun et al, "Computerized Patient Management Problems as Part of the Pediatric Certifying Examination", *J Computer-based Instr* 1978; 4(4):79-83.

37. D.R. Wilson, Letter to R.C. Dickson, Aug. 17, 1976.

PART 3

THE MAINTENANCE OF COMPETENCE

Chapter 11

The College and Continuing Medical Education

During the College's first decade and a half of existence, a specialist could remain informed about advances in a particular specialty, and even in medicine as a whole, by simply reading a few textbooks and journals and attending the College's annual meeting. In the next 15 years, however, medicine became increasingly specialized and compartmentalized, and the remarkable advances that came with the introduction of antibiotics and steroids, for example, radically changed the face of medical practice. Change of such magnitude profoundly altered the ability of physicians to keep themselves informed, for the traditional techniques of continuing education were ill-adapted to deal with the mushrooming explosion of information. The amount of information that specialists were required to digest in order to keep abreast of advances in their specialty — to say nothing of advances in medicine as a whole — now increased by quantum leaps.

For a long time, however, little was done in an organized manner to overcome this problem. But in 1950 the University of Toronto developed a program in continuing medical education (CME) for specialists, and in 1951 Dalhousie University developed one for general practitioners. The concept of CME was taking hold.

Beginning in the 1960s, the enormous problem of simply keeping informed was compounded by the consequences of another phenomenon — the public's growing interest in and insistence on the delivery of quality medical care. By the mid-1970s, the obsolescence of knowledge and the additions to the body of knowledge then existing necessitated, as a current report claimed, "professional reorganization".[1]

Between 1960 and 1980, therefore, CME became increasingly important to physicians in enabling them not only to keep informed but also to demonstrate high standards of practice. One of the primary concerns of the medical profession became the maintenance of competence — "the presence in a given individual of aptitudes, knowledge and experience necessary to assume professional responsibility in a satisfactory way."[2] Both individual physicians and educational organizations within the medical profession responded to the challenges that faced them. In the United States, for example, the number of

CME courses offered by accredited institutions and organizations rose by a factor of five between 1971 and 1977, as did the enrolment of physicians in CME courses in the same period.[3] But the problem was a universal one, and the College responded appropriately to the challenges that confronted the medical profession in Canada.

Since no occupation in which professionalism exists as a form of control is static and unchanging,[4] the College had to take a flexible and dynamic approach to CME and the maintenance of competence. This the College did. Indeed, the College was compelled to do so, for the new and larger membership that came with the transformation of the College in 1972 required the College to assume a leadership role in CME. The outcome of the College's leadership was the quiet evolution of a responsible role in encouraging and facilitating the maintenance of competence among Canadian specialists — and a remarkable though untrumpeted aspect of the history of the College between 1960 and 1980.

In this chapter, three aspects of the impact of the concerns surrounding CME and the maintenance of competence in the College in this period are discussed. First, the principal issues are identified. Second, the evolution of the College's role is reviewed. And, third, the development of the College's role with respect to two of its CME instruments — the annual meeting and the *Annals* — is summarized.

Issues in CME and the Maintenance of Competence

In 1974, Dr. R.B. Salter identified continuing education and continuing assessment as being "pressing" issues for the College to consider.[5] These issues were pressing in 1974 for two reasons: in part because awareness of the importance of CME and maintenance of competence coincided with the awareness in the College of its own responsibility concerning the needs of the large number of specialists who were now members of the College, and in part because, currently, the understanding of the core principles of CME and the maintenance of competence was relatively primitive. Indeed, as late as 1981 it was observed, on good authority, that CME was even then in its "infancy phase".[6]

Although hard data on CME were largely lacking in this period, the literature on CME burgeoned in the 1970s, and by the end of the decade appropriate and pertinent questions were being asked. Listing some of these questions makes it possible to identify some of the important issues on the maintenance of competence that the College had to consider from 1960 to 1980.

What is Competence and the Maintenance of Competence?

These questions were asked frequently in the latter 1960s and early 1970s. To some extent they were as theoretically complex as the question as to how many angels can dance on the head of a pin, and many of the discussions on these questions were academic and of interest only to medical educators rather than immediately useful to a variety of clinical specialists.[7] It is, however, necessary to define competence and its maintenance, and simple definitions are here preferable to complex ones. Regarding competence, one definition in the College literature holds that it is "the ability to perform according to such standards in a way that will provide the expected results"; and regarding the maintenance of competence, a second definition states that competence is maintained by "study, comparison of results with peers, observation and self-critique".[8]

What is CME?

Definitions of CME similarly abound in the literature. A simple definition of CME appeared in one article in the *Annals*: "continuing medical education...may be defined as those activities undertaken by practising physicians to maintain and upgrade their professional competence and clinical performance."[9]

How Effective is CME?

Although it is likely, on *a priori* grounds, that CME does maintain competence, a paucity of objective data makes it difficult to be certain of the efficacy of CME. Several problems prevent one from being certain of the value of CME. First, until the late 1970s, few studies had been conducted specifically to answer this question. Dr. O.E. Laxdal and his colleagues in Saskatoon, for example, noted that prior to 1973 the published literature revealed "scant evidence" that physician knowledge, physician performance or patient health was improved by traditional CME courses or programs.[10] A second problem was the quality of the studies on CME, a problem that Dr. J.C. Sibley and his colleagues from McMaster University addressed. They applied basic methodologic standards to those evaluations of the effectiveness of continuing education that had been published up to the mid-1970s. They concluded that none satisfied key criteria for validity and generalizability.[11] These authors remained skeptical; although, by means of objective tests, they found that physicians learned from continuing-education packages, they observed little effect of this learning on the overall quality of patient care.

Because CME is so young a discipline, and because it is difficult to avoid methodologic problems in the assessment of CME, the lack of positive results of CME is not surprising. Rigorous research and objective evaluation were, for the most part, lacking before 1980. As the 1970s drew to a close, however, the quality of the literature improved. The thoughtful study of CME by Dr. Laxdal and his colleagues, for example, did reveal an improvement in the performance of physicians following their exposure to a CME program, and the admirably skeptical study by Dr. Sibley and his colleagues did indicate that one subset of conditions was associated with important and significant improvements in the quality of care. These two studies are examples of work by College Fellows that have elucidated aspects of CME that must be emphasized in future studies. As well as the need for rigorous research and evaluation, these aspects concern identification of needs assessment, consideration of different learning styles and learning preferences, CME content and techniques and, above all, motivation of individual physicians.

Which Is the Best CME Method?

Although reading of journals and textbooks appears to be the most practical way of keeping up to date, a wide range of CME methods is available to specialists. There are many such methods in addition to reading: formal or information consultation; rounds of one sort or another; lectures and demonstrations; postgraduate courses, refresher courses and conventions; medical society and specialty society meetings; audio cassettes and video cassettes; clinical traineeships; self-assessment and self-instructional learning packages; computerized modules; record review for medical audit; and pharmaceutical handouts.[12] Since adults learn in different ways and since specialists in different specialties have different priorities as far as CME methods are concerned, it is unlikely that, apart from reading, any one CME method is greatly superior to another.

Other problems complicate the issue. The CME literature, for example, has concentrated on the effects of CME on clinical knowledge and its application. There is little information on the effects of CME on skills, the elements of which are soon forgotten unless practised or brought into consciousness frequently, and on attitudes, which are likely to be modified by CME. Nor is there much information on the effects of CME on patient care, as mediated through physicians' skills and attitudes.

It is probable that each individual learns in one way more effectively than in others. Each individual's level of knowledge and skills and each individual's attitudes are, indeed, individual factors that must be taken into account when CME programs are being considered (or evaluated). Yet individual factors may be misleading, particularly when an individual physician assesses his or her own learning needs. Nor is research helpful here, either, for there is no clear answer to the question as to how the best way of learning for a given physician can be determined.

Until clear answers are available, the advice of Dr. V.R. Neufeld may be the most useful: "Perhaps the best guidance for the individual practitioner is to concentrate on those methods of learning that result in changes of strategies for patient care and that, at the same time, are feasible."[13]

Should CME Be Mandatory or Voluntary?

In the early 1970s, much attention was given to relicensure and recertification of specialists. The essence of the problem was simple. When licensure was originally introduced, few physicians took postgraduate training and all physicians who were licensed to practise were thought to be capable of performing the current range of services. The sole restriction was a physician's own estimate of his ability. As medical knowledge increased, neither changes in licensure regulations nor requirements for postgraduate education paralleled the advances in medical practice. Even the availability of postgraduate education opportunities did not solve the basic problem of ensuring that a physician keep up to date; as Dr. R.C. Dickson observed, "the availability of educational activities and their use are not synonymous, and the fact that the doctor has attended a meeting or course does not guarantee that most of his time is not spent on the golf course."[14] How, then, could postgraduate learning be enforced? With the cost of health care being borne by the public's tax dollars, questions about maintenance of competence were being asked in the public domain as well as in the College. The College, as a responsible national body, had to show that it was taking reasonable steps to ensure the accountability of all specialists in Canada. Was recertification by the College as the national specialty certifying body the answer?

Whether recertification is the best way of ensuring that a physician maintains an acceptable level of competence is not certain, even though this has been brought into effect by some of the American specialty boards. The case for recertification seems logical; in Canada the case was argued well by Dr. B.J. Perey.[15] Recertification would serve as a motivating force that would encourage specialists to take CME seriously and would indicate that the College recognizes the importance of accountability. However, a reliable and practical technique was lacking, and the drawback to recertification is that, to a varying degree, it seems threatening and potentially punitive. As Dr. Dickson pointed out, although the punitive approach to continuing education has been tried repeatedly since the Code of Hammurabi was introduced about 2500 B.C., no evidence has ever shown that this approach leads to improvement in the delivery of health care.

The College, therefore, has encouraged the educational approach. But this approach, too, has limitations, for its success is largely dependent on each physician's own motivation to maintain competence. The conditions for success were summarized by President K.J.R. Wightman: "In general terms, the need for continuing education will be met if the practitioner can be persuaded that he wants it, that he needs it, what it is he needs, what to do to get it and how to make sure that he got it."[16]

Although the question as to whether CME should be mandatory or voluntary is still unanswered, the need for the College to develop a logical and useful role in CME remained paramount. The final answer to this vexing question would depend on the College's contribution to CME.

The Evolution of the College's Role in CME

Between 1960 and 1980, the College's role in CME changed greatly, both qualitatively and quantitatively. In 1960, the College's role was limited to organizing a short annual meeting and arranging the recently introduced regional meetings. By 1980, the College's role had greatly expanded, as the following inventory indicates: The entire program of the meeting lasted five days and its scientific portion was designed to satisfy the needs of such varied groups as CSCI and 27 specialty societies as well as the College itself; the College supported the expenses of guest speakers at meetings of some of the specialty societies across Canada; fellowships available to College members included the Detweiler Travelling Fellowships, the Merck Sharp and Dohme Travelling Fellowship, the W.C. MacKenzie-Ethicon Travelling Fellowship and the Royal Canadian Legion Fellowships in Geriatric Medicine; clinical train-eeships were also available to Fellows through the Regional Advisory Committees; short courses for specialists in many Canadian cities were supported by the College; the content of the *Annals* and the *Canadian Journal of Surgery* was clearly attuned to CME needs; a film library was available; a self-assessment program was under development with one of the specialty societies and others were under consideration; a directory of self-assessment programs enabled Fellows to identify those programs in North America that might be available to them; and bibliographies of methods of self-assessment, medical audit and peer review acquainted Fellows with sources of information about these innovative approaches to CME. (Other vistas would open up in the 1980s and, while that is to some degree another story, these exciting vistas — those afforded by teleconferencing, videotext and computer-assisted instruction, for example — would open up as a continuum of ideas that were conceived in the 1960s and 1970s unfolded to reveal how the College's role in CME has been a continuing one.)

What factors contributed to the expansion of the College's role in CME between 1960 and 1980? Apart from the general recognition of the importance of CME and the maintenance of competence, the factors in the College were primarily the interest in these aspects taken by individual Fellows and their endeavors in certain of the College's committees to develop an effective CME program for Fellows.

The evolution of the College's role in this modern period began in 1959. Two of Council's decisions had far-reaching implications. The first was announced by President J.W. Scott during the annual business meeting in January 1959. President Scott told the Fellows that Council recognized that it should assume increasing responsibility in postgraduate medical education in Canada apart from the program of the annual meeting. The College, President Scott said, would, as from October 1959 in Halifax, organize regional meetings. The provision of regional meetings, which would continue through 1978, was important not only because Fellows could be provided with an alternative to the annual meeting (which not more than 10 per cent of the Fellows ever attended) but also because Certificants were invited — the beginning of one path to unity that was fully opened when Certificants were invited to apply for admission to Fellowship in the College in 1972.

Council's second decision with a bearing on CME was reported to the Fellows a year later, at the annual business meeting on January 21, 1960. Dr. H.K. Detweiler told the Fellows that Council, in June 1959, had decided to launch an endowment fund that would support educational purposes. The fund would be known as the Educational Endowment Fund, the interest accruing to it being used to fund such CME activities as bursaries and short-term postgraduate Fellowships for young Fellows. Dr. Detweiler was appointed chairman of the fund committee. The choice of Dr. Detweiler was a wise one. An academician — a gold medallist of the University of Toronto, a graduate of the same university with an MD degree *cum laude* and Chief Physician at Toronto Western Hospital — Dr. Detweiler recognized the educational needs of Fellows, particularly those from non-academic centres. A young Fellow promised a university teaching post might be awarded a McLaughlin Fellowship but no similar opportunity was open to Fellows outside of university centres. The purpose of the Educational Endowment Fund was to rectify that; among the proposed objectives were to increase the educational activities of the College outside of university centres, to fund short-term training grants for specialized studies or refresher courses and to endow lectureships, perhaps at regional meetings. Dr. Detweiler set $500,000 as his goal and he immediately began to solicit contributions for the fund. Dr. Detweiler was a remarkable chairman of this fund, for he not only executed his duties as chairman with great vigor and enthusiasm but also became the College's biggest single benefactor as an individual, both to the fund and to the College as a whole.[17]

The Educational Endowment Fund (not to be confused with the Educational Development Fund that was created in 1972 to make use of the admission-to-Fellowship fees that the pre-1972 Certificants forwarded to the College) soon made its mark on CME activities. By 1968, when the Educational Endowment Fund was worth $324,660, the following activities had been conducted with the support of the fund: 19 Royal College lectureships at the annual meetings; 30 guest lectureships at the regional meetings; 22 Royal College Travel Fellowships for Fellows; the publication and supply of reprints of the proceedings of the 1965 conference on residency education; and the holding of the 1967 conference on surgical education and research. 1968 was a significant year in another respect, for the first volume of the *Annals* was published in 1968.

Honorary Fellows Admitted at Convocation, January 21, 1966

(L. to R.) Sir Charles Illingworth, President Walter MacKenzie, Lord Brock,
Sir Peter Medawar

Honorary Fellows Admitted at Convocation, January 22, 1976

(L. to R.) Monseigneur Roger Maltais, Lord Smith, President K.J.R. Wightman,
Sir Ferguson Anderson, Sir Ludwig Guttman

Herbert Knudsen Detweiler

By the end of the 1960s, therefore, the College had made remarkable headway in fulfilling the responsibility of CME that President Scott had envisioned in 1959. A firm base for CME activities was laid during the 1960s. Further headway was made in the 1970s through the efforts of four committees in particular — the Education Committee; its successor, the Continuing Education Committee; that committee's successor, the Fellowship Affairs Committee; and the Maintenance of Competence Committee. These committees expanded the College's role in CME by studying Fellows' needs, particularly in the 'new' College with its increased membership, identifying appropriate activities and facilitating the provision of programs. Collaboration with the national specialty societies and with regional CME authorities also characterized the College's role in the 1970s.

The initial step in the 1970s was the formation of the Education Committee in 1970. The committee was charged with considering how activities that were supported by the Educational Endowment Fund might be more effectively administered and coordinated. It was suggested that a committee on educational policy would make recommendations to Council on the educational activities and fiscal responsibilities that might be discharged by the Educational Endowment Fund. This new committee would have overall responsibility, especially in CME, so that the College might develop a coordinated educational program.

The Education Committee held its initial meeting on November 20, 1970. Terms of reference were discussed. The College's principal CME activities consisted of the scientific programs at the annual meeting and the regional meetings and of the program developed by each McLaughlin-Gallie Visiting Professor. These activities could be expanded and improved, the committee's chairman (Dr. D.G. Cameron) suggested, by adding other activities — postgraduate courses, short on-site training courses tailored to individuals' needs, instruction utilizing audio visual resources and greater use of the *Annals* to publicize available CME opportunities, for example — and by conducting pilot studies of innovative educational techniques. Any CME program should fit logically into whatever pattern of self-assessment might be developed for specialists, and the College should cooperate and liaise with other organizations having an interest in CME in order to clarify individual roles in CME and to use resources effectively. CME programs should incorporate methods of determining the needs of different individuals and of different regions, together with methods of evaluation of the benefits derived by participants in such programs.

With respect to the College's role in CME, the committee would be able to guide and coordinate the activities of several of the College's existing committees — notably those on the scientific meeting, publications, films and arrangements for the McLaughlin-Gallie Visiting Professorship as well as the Educational Endowment Fund Committee.

This coordinating role was soon applied to CME at the regional level. At the committee's next meeting, held in May 1971, attention was focused on the development of a program of continuing education for Fellows. It was proposed that a mechanism be set up at a regional level to facilitate the planning and implementation of refresher courses — a logical extension of the College's regional meetings. A program of this nature was needed, for there was a dearth of CME opportunities for specialists in Canada, and the committee agreed that the College bore a responsibility towards its members in this area. The basis of a regional structure for CME was laid with the formation of regional committees in continuing education, which were established in 1971. Each of these committees would consist of the councillors for the region, two Fellows at large, representatives of the provincial licensing authority or authorities and the university director or directors of CME in the region. The committees formulated ideas for CME, with emphasis on what could be provided by refresher courses and regional meetings. Their existence confirmed the feasibility and value of a decentralized structure.

A further step was taken in 1972, when the Continuing Education Committee was formed. Chaired by Dr. H.O. Murphy, this committee was at first a subcommittee of the Education Committee, charged with giving "operational direction" to the implementation of the program of regional meetings and refresher courses. Considerable authority, however, was soon delegated to this committee, for two reasons. First, with the formation of the Training and Evaluation Committee in January 1972 to coordinate the activities of the three principal committees that dealt with pre-Fellowship affairs (Credentials, Evaluation of Specialty Training Programs and Examinations), the need for the additional coordination of post-Fellowship educational activities was then recognized. It was therefore resolved that the Education Committee, then chaired by Dr. R.B. Salter, should primarily emphasize CME, "though not to the total exclusion of concern for medical education in its broader context." The terms of reference for the Continuing Education Committee were three: to coordinate, guide and direct the regional meetings and postgraduate courses that Council approved; to provide broader coordination of regional and national elements in the College's CME program and of those of the medical schools and specialty societies; and to give major attention to assessing the continuing education needs of the College membership, to evaluating and testing better methods of fulfilling the identified needs and to finding ways of measuring the end result of continuing education programs in terms of improved patient care. These well-defined and goal-directed terms of reference laid the basis for the College's CME activities in the remainder of the 1970s.

The second reason for the Continuing Education Committee's authority lay in the fact that the College's membership doubled in 1972 with the admission of the pre-1972 Certificants to Fellowship. (The monies accruing to the College thereby greatly strengthened the College's financial resources that were now available to support CME and these were placed in the Educational Development Fund for this purpose.) The needs of all these Fellows, especially in CME, had to be considered. The Education Committee, for example, identified six areas for future development: continuing educational objectives of the annual and regional meetings that might be emphasized by means of programs specially designed to meet the needs of the practising clinicians; direct involvement of the College in the publication of scientific journals in medicine and surgery; development of medical knowledge self-assessment programs; study and promotion of patient care evaluation methods; promotion of an educational approach for reexamination and recertification; and use of audiovisual instructional techniques in CME. Clearly, such needs could best be attended to by a committee that focused specifically on CME; so the Executive Committee decided, in 1974, that the Continuing Education Committee should be enlarged and reconstituted, at the expense of the Education Committee, which was disbanded.

In expanding the role of the Continuing Education Committee, the College wished to emphasize further its role and responsibilities regarding the increased membership's needs in CME. More importantly, Council wished to stress the College's concern with what was the responsibility of each physician — the maintenance of competence. Now to be answered was the question as to the efficacy of the College's CME activities, and answering this question pointed ways in which the College might move in the future. As of 1974, the College was engaged primarily in four CME activities, but with only varying success. Dr. R.B. Salter found that, while the annual meeting was "increasingly successful", the regional meetings had been "poorly attended" during the previous year in particular, the postgraduate courses were only "moderately successful" and the Annals were apparently "not widely used".[18]

The climate of great interest in CME, which was tinged with skepticism and tempered by a perceived need to avoid dogma, greatly advanced and clarified the College's thinking on the maintenance of competence from 1974 to 1976; indeed a new role for the College was envisioned in this period.[19] In 1974, a memorandum on a possible expanded role for the College in continuing education and continuing assessment was discussed by the Continuing Education Committee at its meeting in September; a second memorandum detailing ways in which the College should move, including liaison with the national specialty societies, was discussed by the committee in December; motions on self-assessment and medical audit and peer review were also approved at the committee's December meeting; and at the same meeting the committee further considered the thoughtful position paper on CME that President K.J.R. Wightman had prepared for the Joint Conference Committee on Education. In addition, the important motion to consider establishing, in each of the five geographic regions, an advisory committee (the Regional Advisory Committee

[RAC] in each region), originated in the Continuing Education Committee's meeting of September 1974.

The more significant of these ideas were developed further in 1975. In January, Council approved resolutions from the Continuing Education Committee that the College accept responsibility for aiding specialists in "maintaining competence in their practices"; that self-assessment, medical audit and peer review likewise be responsibilities of the College; that the College develop Royal College-sponsored lectureships at specialty society meetings; and that postgraduate courses also be supported by the College. Where possible, the College would work with the national specialty societies in these endeavors.

Council approved further resolutions bearing on CME in January 1976. The responsibility was recognized of assisting the Fellows to keep abreast of information that would enable them to maintain high standards of practice, and two courses of action were advocated. The first was to negotiate purchase of medical and surgical knowledge self-assessment programs from The American College of Physicians and The American College of Surgeons, respectively; the second, to convene a conference of the national specialty societies to discuss, with the College, self-assessment evaluation in CME. These various policy decisions in Council set the pattern of latter 1970s for the College's role in CME and the maintenance of competence.

A further development was the replacement, in January 1976, of the Continuing Education Committee by the Fellowship Affairs Committee. At first chaired by Dr. E.R. Yendt and later by Dr. W.B. Spaulding, this committee took over the responsibility for carrying out functions relating to continuing education, publications, awards and fellowships — in short, those functions of concern to established Fellows.

An idea of the College's approach to CME in the mid-1970s is obtained by studying the report of the Horizons Committee.[20] Although this report was not completed until 1977, many of the issues it addressed, including CME, were being discussed both in the committee and by other Fellows in 1974 and 1975. CME was the focus of a position paper prepared for the Horizons Committee by Dr. L.K. McNeill, and the final version of this paper, submitted in August 1976, took into account current opinions on CME. Some of the points that were made in the report of the Horizons Committee concerning CME were the following:

- Although CME had been emphasized in the previous few years, available CME programs were too few and their content was inadequate. The needs of Canadian specialists were not being met.
- Canadian specialists looked to the College for leadership and participation in the CME process, but they also believed that the College should collaborate, rather than compete, with medical schools and specialty societies in providing CME programs.

319

- A useful role for the College, which had demonstrated its competence in evaluation of training, would be to design, prepare and conduct self-assessment programs. The information thus derived could determine the most appropriate content for CME programs. Knowing that such programs had been designed to correct deficiencies of individual specialists would encourage these specialists to engage in CME activities. These activities could include home-study and reading courses as well as workshops and seminars.

- An extension of this role would be to investigate the application of innovative CME techniques. Prototype programs in peer review and medical audit and patient care appraisal could be developed for the evaluation of specialty practice.

- The College would be expected to evaluate all CME programs sponsored by the College and therefore to develop expertise in testing participants before and after they had engaged in any CME activity.

- The College's role in CME in the latter 1970s and beyond was summarized in the following recommendation: "...it will be appropriate for the College to accept the major responsibility for the identification of specialty physicians and surgeons in need of continuing medical education and also for stimulating and ensuring the participation of specialists so identified in suitable remedial continuing medical education programs."

By the middle of the 1970s, the College's approach to CME had advanced greatly in comparison with its somewhat primitive approach in 1960. The College in 1960 had no stated policy on CME and its participation in CME was virtually limited to the scientific program of the annual meeting and the newly introduced regional meetings. By 1977, the situation was quite different. Two of the College's stated objectives specifically concerned CME and the maintenance of a high standard of practice. A variety of activities facilitated achievement of these objectives, both at the national level and at the regional level. Short courses were sponsored and supported by the College in university centres and the larger cities; lectureships at the national specialty society meetings were similarly supported by the College; appropriate material was published in the *Annals* and the *Canadian Journal of Surgery*; various travel fellowships and clinical traineeships were available; and the McLaughlin-Gallie Visiting Professorships remained valuable. Other activities were being discussed with a view to their support by the College, particularly self-assessment programs, medical audit and peer review. Although minimum guidelines for CME had not as yet been defined, the College was ready to provide guidance to Fellows, realizing that they regularly required a certain amount of updated information to enable them always to improve care of their patients — the ultimate test of clinical competence.

In the remaining years of the 1970s, the College was able to consolidate these advances and to relate them to specialist competence by forming a new committee, the Maintenance of Competence Committee, in 1977. The activities of this committee, which is a subcommittee of the Fellowship Affairs Committee, enabled the College to carry some of Council's resolutions of 1975 and 1976 into effect. The Maintenance of Competence Committee, which was first chaired by Dr. W.B. Spaulding, did much to stimulate investigation into CME, to focus attention on feasible CME methods and to apply these methods to the College's CME program.

From 1977 to 1980, the Maintenance of Competence Committee endeavored primarily to identify CME activities that would be of value to Fellows, particularly in the context of the interest of the national specialty societies. Publishing the "Update" series in internal medicine in the *Annals* was one such activity. The College continued to sponsor a variety of CME events across Canada (more than 50 such events were organized in 1979 alone). A third popular activity comprised clinical traineeships, of which, in 1979, more than 100 were awarded by the RACs. The College also took an interest, on the Fellows' behalf, in self-assessment programs such as MKSAP V from the American College of Physicians; for example, the College obtained permission to prepare, with the assistance of Dr. J. Boulay, of the McLaughlin Centre's Laval unit, a French-language version of the multiple-choice question items of MKSAP V. Useful, too, were two other projects that were investigated at this time. One was the preparation of bibliographies on CME methods, medical audit and peer review. The other project was a joint one on the development of a self-assessment program with the Canadian Anaesthetists' Society. The society had already developed two self-assessment programs on its own, and it now agreed to share the cost of developing a third program together. Recognizing that other specialty societies would wish to develop self-assessment programs, the College regarded this joint project as a model for cooperation with other specialty societies in the future. The College also made a directory of self-assessment programs available to Fellows.

The closing years of the 1970s were, therefore, most productive as far as the College's role in CME and the maintenance of competence were concerned, and the College's role in CME as of 1980 was the subject of two resolutions to Council that were drafted during the Executive Committee's retreat in August 1980. It was resolved "that the College do everything feasible to encourage and support continuing competence and performance of high quality by Fellows of the College." It was also resolved "that the College offer incentives and help to the Fellows in assessing their competence in order to assist them in planning their continuing medical education."

The Annual Meeting and the *Annals*

The scientific program of the annual meeting is the College's oldest CME instrument, the first program having been held in 1933. Much newer is the *Annals*, which started publication in 1968. Because of their relevance to the College's role in CME, the evolution of these two instruments in the 1960s and 1970s is briefly reviewed.

The Scientific Program of the Annual Meeting

Between 1933 and 1959, the scientific program was an important but small part of the College's annual meeting. The entire annual meeting lasted only one day until 1946, when half a day was added. At first, a single topic was the focus of the meeting, and the scientific program was divided into one section for medicine and another for surgery. The main changes in these years were the addition of a new section of the program devoted to obstetrics and gynecology in 1950 and the gradual replacement of the formal presentations of the early years by a larger number of shorter papers, many on research topics.

Between 1960 and 1980, the scientific program continued to grow both in duration and in the number and type of presentations. The evolution of the scientific program reflects not only certain changes in the College but also the advances in medicine in this period. Described during the meeting of the Annual Meeting Committee in 1966 as "the showcase for the achievements of Canadian medicine", the annual scientific program was more than an important CME instrument, for increasingly an underlying objective of the meeting was to provide a forum in which the College, specialty groups and CSCI could meet together and learn from each other. More than that, the annual meeting served a purpose in the College's pursuit of unity. An objective of the meeting, it was also observed in the November 1966 meeting of the Annual Meeting Committee, was "the demonstration of the unity of the various specialties".

The principal changes that occurred in the scientific program of the annual meeting between 1960 and 1980 can most readily be summarized by comparing the chief elements of the meeting in 1960 with that of the meeting in 1979. (The 1980 meeting is not used as the end point because, for this year only, the CSCI did not meet in conjunction with the College and it was held in June rather than in January of that year.) This comparison is set forth in Table 11.1. The scientific program in 1979 was both bigger and more varied than the program in 1960; it lasted five days and included a debate, free communications, poster sessions, symposia, panel discussions and lectures. Impressive though the increase in the total number of sessions was from 1960 to 1979, even more impressive in the 1979 program was the abundance of specialty-interest and multidisciplinary interest sessions. Indeed, the most single notable difference between the meeting in 1960 and the meeting in 1979 relates to the

TABLE 11.1 The Annual Meeting: 1960 and 1979 Compared.

Item	1960	1979
Duration (days)	2.5	5
Hospital Sessions	6	0
Scientific Sessions		
Royal College	18	52
Royal College/CSCI	0	5
CSCI	0	2
Specialty Society	0	28
Lectures		
Royal College	2	3
CSCI	0	1
Specialty Society	0	8
Residents' Presentations	0	2
Specialty Groups Participating	7	27

way the overall meeting, of which the scientific program was a part, was designed to satisfy the interests of the specialties. The 1960 meeting was centred around just the Division of Medicine, the Division of Surgery and the Section of Obstetrics and Gynecology; the only indication of specialty interest was a joint session for orthopedic surgery and neurosurgery and another for thoracic and cardiovascular surgery. In 1979, not only was the scientific program planned so as to satisfy the interest of 27 specialty groups but also the annual meeting was planned so that the annual meetings of 17 national specialty societies and of CSCI were held during the week of the College's meeting. The suggestion, considered at the Executive Committee meeting in December 1978, that the College should be renamed "The Royal College of Specialties of Medicine",[21] while unrealistic in one sense, was reflective of the creature that the College had become.

Between 1960 and 1980, then, there was a gradual progression from the old format to the new. This progression can be traced by dating major changes in the program from year to year. These changes are summarized as follows:

1960 Extension of duration of meeting to three days.

1961 First use of the term 'scientific papers' to designate sessions.

Symposia introduced, substituting for previous hospital sessions.

Fellows invited to annual meeting of CSCI held the day before start of College meeting.

1963 Coat of arms represented on front cover of program.

First use of color television during meeting.

Last evidence of separation into The Royal College of Physicians of Canada and The Royal College of Surgeons of Canada in relation to the Medallist in Medicine and the Medallist in Surgery.

1965 CSCI meeting now one and one-half days in duration, with second morning coinciding with start of College meeting.

1966 Last occasion on which there was a lecture in Medicine, a lecture in Surgery and a lecture in Obstetrics and Gynecology.

Inauguration of the Gallie Lecture.

1967 First meeting in which each of the three main lectures was designated 'Royal College Lecture'.

1968 Change to a new format for the program book from the distinctive program that had become a tradition in the College (abstracts included, and plastic spiral spine); related to publication of the new *Annals* and provision of bibliographical reference of abstracts.

CSCI now two days in duration, but held on the two days preceding the College's meeting.

1969 Meeting now lasted three full days.

First meeting in which joint CSCI/Royal College symposia held (on afternoon before first day of College meeting).

1970 New cover format for program book.

Last meeting in which medicine, surgery and obstetrics and gynecology sessions were individually identified by a specific program content.

1971 First meeting with some sessions given jointly by College and specialty societies.

1972 First year in which annual scientific meetings of specialty societies (gastroenterology, pediatric surgery, hematology and neuropathology) held in conjunction with College meeting.

1973 First specialty society lecture — for example, R.D. McKenna in Gastroenterology.

1974 New cover for program book and inside format similar to current program with new type, etc.

First meeting of the College "and affiliated societies"; meeting now of four days' duration.

First "Royal College Scientific Session".

1979 Forty-eighth annual meeting, the logo "50/1929-1979" recognizing the College's half-century as a professional organization.

The attendance reached a peak of 2,104 in 1977, when the meeting was held in Toronto. In view of the fact that the Fellows represented more than 30 specialties and came from all over Canada to attend what in essence had become a multidisciplinary conference, the College's annual scientific meeting was by now a successful event in the calendar of all Fellows.

The problems that the College faced in developing its annual meeting were those of the unique, multidisciplinary organization that it had become. These problems are different from those of other specialists' colleges, particularly those in the United States. The observations of Dr. Edward C. Rosenow, Jr., then Executive Vice-President Emeritus of the American College of Physicians, are interesting in this respect. Dr. Rosenow was asked to report on the 1978 annual meeting and had these observations, among others, to make:

> Your College has a different problem than ours, but we're moving in your direction. You have already accomplished what we're only moving towards. You really have a congress of over 30 specialty societies meeting at the same time under the umbrella of the College. This is to my mind a very significant accomplishment. The dilemma is the visibility of the College. I don't see this as big a problem as many of you do. Almost everybody I talked with seemed to be happy to be meeting with the several societies... . Several of the people that I talked with said that they came to this meeting to hear original papers in their specialty, to see friends and attend the main lectures. For more general meetings, both surgical and medical specialists apparently like to go south to meetings of the American College of Surgeons or Physicians or other large specialty societies.[22]

The Annals

The *Annals*, like the annual meeting, has served not only as a CME instrument but also as a bond between Canadian specialists. In fact, the *Annals* originated in some Fellows' recognizing that, while complete integration of the Certificants was not possible in the mid-1960s, it was still desirable to find ways of bringing them into a closer relationship with the College. Dr. G.M. Brown, then chairman of the Publications Committee, was one of these Fellows. At the same time, some Fellows were interested in the College's publishing a journal, and a committee to review the position of the College in relation to publications was established in 1963. Under the active leadership of Dr. Brown, the committee studied the prospects for a new medical journal in Canada. Among the factors to consider, one was the obvious connection between a College journal and the proposal of the Committee on Policy in 1964 that the Certificants be brought into a closer relationship with the College. The hope was that a College journal would serve not only as a scientific journal but also as a vehicle providing news and information about the College and so link specialists, both the Fellows and the Certificants, closer together.

The journal was, however, seen primarily as an interdisciplinary journal, to emphasize the clinical sciences in particular. Two unanswered questions concerned the effect a new journal would have on existing Canadian journals and the attraction it would have for Canadians who customarily submitted material to American journals. The first question mainly related to the *Canadian Medical Association Journal* and the *Canadian Journal of Surgery*, but the increasing volume of scientific work conducted by Canadians made it less likely that those journals would suffer. With respect to the second question, Dr. Brown was prepared to leave it to Canadian authors themselves to decide whether they would publish in Canada. This was a reasonable stand, since a proportion of Canadians would always wish to publish some of their work in a Canadian journal; moreover, there was no Canadian journal devoted primarily to medical science. He personally believed that medicine in Canada was rapidly approaching the stage at which it should be able to stand on its own.

By January 1966, the Publications Committee was ready to present specific recommendations. It was thought that, as soon as it was possible to do so, the College should embark on the publication of a scientific journal. Preferably this journal should be published monthly from the beginning, unless the editor felt that initially it should be only a bimonthly publication. It was considered that the journal should have the breadth of appeal of such journals as the *New England Journal of Medicine* and the *Lancet*. As far as the content was concerned, although the journal should emphasize internal medicine, it was thought that it should be regarded as being a journal for all specialties of medicine and surgery and, as well, that it should be recognized as the official organ of the College, reflecting the two cultural groups within the College in more than the sense of the use of the two languages.

Now that it appeared probable that the College would proceed, Council approved these recommendations in January 1966. President R.B. Kerr agreed with Dr. Brown that the CMA should be informed of the College's intentions for, when the concept of a College journal had first been put forward, the College had agreed that the CMA would be kept informed. A meeting with the CMA was held on May 17, 1966. Dr. G. Dickinson, editor of the *Canadian Medical Association Journal*, expressed "grave reservations" about the availability of high-quality scientific material and feared that the new journal, especially a multispecialty one, might force the *Canadian Medical Association Journal* to publish bimonthly or even monthly, and the *Canadian Journal of Surgery* to cease publication. Dr. F.G. Kergin, editor of the *Canadian Journal of Surgery*, was also pessimistic, since that journal was having difficulty in obtaining suitable material. But Dr. Brown remained optimistic in view of the increasing amount of good scientific literature that would be available within the next few years. Canada would soon have 15 medical schools and, as of 1966, the Medical Research Council would be supporting 1,400 medical research investigators; accordingly, the amount of publishable material would certainly increase. Dr. Brown admitted, without apology, that his approach was nationalistic, and he cautioned that if the College did not start a journal another group would.

Despite Dr. Brown's optimism (which, as it turned out, was well founded), the situation was sufficiently uncertain to warrant further study. Dr. S.S.B. Gilder, former editor of the *Canadian Medical Association Journal*, was invited to conduct a feasibility study.

Dr. Gilder visited Canada in February 1967. He followed three lines of inquiry by checking the amount of material in the clinical sciences published by Canadians outside Canada each year, by interviewing individuals, including heads of departments across Canada and by comparing the situation in Canada with that elsewhere.[23] With respect to the proposal that a journal oriented to medical science be published, Dr. Gilder detected considerable opposition, which was summed up by saying that "here and there a few voices were raised in favor of another Canadian journal, but by and large opinion was against it." He therefore found himself unable to recommend that the College start a general-purpose journal, at any rate for the moment.

Dr. Gilder did, however, favor the College's publishing a house journal. He commented on the success of the *Annals of the Royal College of Surgeons of England*, which included among its aims the publication of material that would keep its Fellows and Members informed about recent advances in surgery and various surgical subjects as well as the affairs of the college. Dr. Gilder had detected a "deplorable gap" in communication between the College and its Fellows and Certificants, and for this reason as much as any other, he urged the College to publish an organ that would be more attractive than a mere newsletter, perhaps following the pattern of the *Annals of the Royal College of Surgeons of England*.

In view of the heady nature of the 1960s, it is perhaps surprising that opinion was unfavorable to the idea of a Canadian journal of medical science, and another decade would elapse before such a journal would be published.[24] Dr. Gilder's report was a realistic one and the Publications Committee accepted it in April 1967. The committee agreed with Dr. Gilder concerning the lack of communication between the College and the Fellows. Because thousands of Certificants would now probably wish to affiliate themselves with the College, the need for effective communication would become urgent. Mr. T.J. Giles commented on this in a memorandum dated April 6, 1967. The first paragraph of this memorandum read as follows:

> *The* negative outcome of the feasibility study relating to the publication of a College scientific journal lends renewed urgency to the consideration of an alternative means of obtaining improved communication with the Fellows. The lack of adequate communication

with the Fellowship at large has been recognized by Council in recent years as one of the chief reasons for the lack of understanding and appreciation of what the College is attempting to do and has led to a number of areas of criticism and unrest among the Fellows as evidenced by the pressure from certain areas to introduce constitutional reforms and in letters to the editor of the *Canadian Medical Association Journal* concerning the standards and place of the Fellowship examinations and qualification. In addition, with the Fellowship now numbering approximately 4,000 and with the distinct possibility of an additional 2,000 or more Certificants electing to take up the new relationship with the College, continuation of the present procedure of communication regarding specific matters, such as announcements of annual and regional meetings, by mimeographed form letters, is becoming impractical and inefficient from the point of view of the limited duplicating facilities of the College and is regarded as an antiquated and amateurish method of operating for an organization of the size and prestige of the Royal College.[25]

Council also recognized the need to improve communication with its Fellows and now with the Certificants. In June 1967, Council directed that publication of *The Annals of The Royal College of Physicians and Surgeons of Canada* be embarked upon at the earliest possible date.

A few loose ends remained. One step was to confirm the nature of the publication; the name, "The Annals of The Royal College of Physicians and Surgeons — Les Annales du Collège Royal des Médecins et Chirurgiens du Canada", was duly approved. The second step was to nominate an editor and an editorial board; Dr. J. Robichon, Honorary Assistant Secretary, and the members of the Publications Committee were accordingly nominated. A third step was to affirm that the primary function of the *Annals* should be that of "a medium of communication with Fellows and Certificants regarding College activities"; this was done also. A fourth step concerned the date of publication of the first issue; this was slated for January 1968. Later, Mr. Giles was named managing editor. All was now set for the new venture, and the first issue of the *Annals* reached Fellows at the beginning of 1968. The first issue consisted almost entirely of College news, as Table 11.2 reveals. During the 1968 annual business meeting, however, President R.B. Kerr told the Fellows that he thought this new development would "contribute greatly to the work of the College and also to medicine in Canada", and over the next decade the *Annals* indeed evolved in the direction that President Kerr had predicted. The *Annals* came to serve successfully both as a scientific journal with relevance to the CME needs of its readers and as a house organ for providing College news. To illustrate this evolution and to compare the content of the first issue of the first volume of the *Annals*, the titles of the contents of the last issue of the *Annals* for 1979 are also listed in Table 11.2.

TABLE 11.2 The Annals: Contents of Vol. 1, No. 1 (1968) and Vol. 12, No. 4 (1979) Compared.

Vol. 1, No. 1 (1968)	Vol. 12, No. 4 (1979)
A New Venture — Une nouvelle entreprise	New Chief Executive Officer
To Improve Communications/Pour accroître nos relations	Editorial: The *Annals* — The Next Decade
Editorially Speaking/Commentaire éditorial	Understanding Backward and Looking Forward: The View From Genetics
McLaughlin Foundation Grant Awarded for Research Centre	Meetings/Assemblées
The New Examinations in Laboratory Medicine	Symposium on Hypertension
The Educational Endowment Fund	Tonin-Angiotensin II Systems in Hypertension
La caisse des oeuvres d'enseignement	The Role of Sodium in Hypertension
Surgical Education: University Role Stressed in Graduate Programs	Hypertension in Children
1968 Regional Meetings	The Influence of Sodium Intake on Incidence of Hypertension in Newfoundland
1968 Annual Meeting	
College Medallists	
Abstracts/Sommaires 1968	Symposium on Entry into Life-Sustaining Systems
The College and Its Functions	Introduction
	Accès aux systèmes de support vital au Canada — Situation actuelle
	Entry into Life-Sustaining Systems — Resources Allocation
	Decision-Making Respecting Entry into Existing Life-Sustaining Systems and the Initiation of Life-Sustaining Systems
	Discussion
	Guidelines for the Appropriate Use of Medical Laboratory Services in Canada
	The Certification Procedure — How the System Works
	From the Division of Training and Evaluation/De la division de la formation et de l'évaluation
	From the Division of Fellowship Affairs/ Le Collège cherche un nouveau directeur des affaires des associés
	Continuing Education Opportunities

NOTES TO CHAPTER 11

1. Anon, "CME Task Force Presents Report on Continuing Medical Education." *Can Med Assoc J* 1975; 112:1119-1127.
2. R. Gourdeau, "The Royal College and Recertification." *Ann RCPSC* 1982; 15:467-468.
3. Anon, "Continuing Education of Physicians: Conclusions and Recommendations." Association of American Medical Colleges Ad Hoc Committee on Continuing Medical Education, September 1979.
4. T. Johnson, *Professions and Power*. London, The Macmillan Company, 1972, p. 59.
5. R.B. Salter, Letter to K.J.R. Wightman, Jan. 30, 1974. Attached to Minutes of Continuing Education Committee, April 1974.
6. J.S. Lloyd, Maintenance of Competence Committee, November 1981, p. 14.
7. See, for example, Proceedings of Conference on The Measurement of Physician Competence: The Current State of the Art — Where Do We Go From Here? (D.R. Wilson and E.N. Skakun, eds.), Banff, Alberta, Aug. 25-26, 1978; and Proceedings of the Conference on Definitions of Competence in Specialties of Medicine, American Board of Medical Specialties, Chicago, Sept. 19, 1979.
8. R. Gourdeau, Maintenance of Competence Committee, November 1981, p. 5.
9. D.A. Davies, T. Delmore, A.M. Bryans et al, "Continuing Medical Education in Ontario." *Ann RCPSC* 1983; 16:136-142.
10. O.E. Laxdal, P.A. Jennett, T.W. Wilson and G.M. Salisbury, "Improving Physician Performance by Continuing Medical Education." *Can Med Assoc J* 1978; 118:1051-1058.
11. J.C. Sibley, D.L. Sackett, V. Neufeld et al, "A Randomized Trial of Continuing Medical Education." *New Eng J Med* 1982; 306:511-515.
12. These methods are discussed in several articles in the College's *Annals*. See, for example, V.R. Neufeld, "An Overview for Clinicians", 1983; 16:223-227; I.E. Purkis and L. Curry, "Learning Preferences of Specialists", 1983; 16:408-414; and D.A. Davies, T. Delmore, A.M. Bryans et al, "Continuing Medical Education in Ontario", 1983; 16:136-142.
13. V.R. Neufeld, "An Overview for Clinicians." *Ann RCPSC* 1983; 16:223-227.
14. R.C. Dickson, "Limited Licensure." *Can Med Assoc J* 1973; 109:842-843.
15. B.J. Perey, "The Future of Specialty Recertification in Canada: A Proposal." *Ann RCPSC* 1975; 8:1-2.
16. K.J.R. Wightman, Position Paper on Continuing Education, June 23, 1974; Presented to the Joint Conference Committee on Education, See Continuing Education Committee, December 1974, Attachment 5.
17. During his lifetime, Dr. Detweiler donated more than $20,000 to the Educational Endowment Fund; after his death, a further $600,000 was bequeathed to the Fund (ABM, September 1981, pp. 6-7). He was the College's greatest benefactor, a Fellow whom the College was fortunate to count among its own.
18. R.B. Salter, Letter to K.J.R. Wightman. See Continuing Education Committee, April 1974, Attachment.

19. Continuing Education Committee, September 1974, pp. 7-8. See also: R.B. Salter, Draft Statement on The Expanded Role of the Royal College in Continuing Education and Continuing Assessment, Continuing Education Committee, September 1974, Attachment 1; R.A. Davis, Statement on Continuing Education and the Royal College of Physicians and Surgeons of Canada, Continuing Education Committee, December 1974, Attachment 7; and K.J.R. Wightman, Position Paper on Continuing Education, June 23, 1974, Education Committee, December 1974, Attachment 5.

20. Report of the Committee on Horizons, pp. 98-116 especially.

21. Executive, Canadian Association of Pathologists, Memorandum to Council of the Royal College, Nov. 8, 1978. See Executive Committee, December 1978, Attachment 2.

22. E.C. Rosenow, Jr., Report to the Annual Meeting Program Committee, Annual Meeting Committee, April 1978, Appendix II.

23. S.S.B. Gilder, "The Publications Policy of the Royal College of Physicians and Surgeons of Canada." The Royal College of Physicians and Surgeons of Canada, Feb. 27, 1967. See also Executive Committee, April 7, 1967, Attachment 5.

24. The journal *Clinical and Investigative Medicine* was founded in 1977, with Drs. W.O. Spitzer, D.A.E. Shephard and S.O. Freedman as the moving spirits behind this publication. Little difficulty was encountered in obtaining material for this journal, most of it originating in Canada. Its emphasis lies in the field of medical science.

25. Executive Committee, April 1967, Attachment 6.

PART 4

RELATIONS
WITH THE
SPECIALTIES

Chapter 12

The College and Specialty Development

S ince 1929, when the College was founded, there have always been close relations between the College and the specialties embraced by the Division of Medicine and the Division of Surgery. The College's original Object recognized the desire of some physicians to devote themselves to "special work", and a large part of the College's activity has stemmed from the need to identify and distinguish those physicians who could prove themselves, through training and examinations, competent in the practice of "special work".[1] As medicine grew more complex, the College and the specialties developed together, but their relations also became complex — and sometimes problematic, as the College held one viewpoint and some of the specialties another. Thus, the College did not favor the fragmentation of medicine into numerous specialties; it did not want, as Dr. R.V. Christie put it to Council in January, 1965, "the central core of general surgery and internal medicine to be 'nibbled away' until there is nothing left." The newer specialties wanted recognition on their own as free-standing specialties and some wanted their own colleges, pointing to the situation in other countries and believing that their needs and desires would be better fulfilled by branching out on their own than by remaining under the roof of an all-embracing single college. The issue that recurred between 1960 and 1980 was a perennial one for the College — that of association versus autonomy. Is it better for specialty groups to associate with a larger, multidisciplinary whole or is it better for them to each become autonomous?

That the vast majority of specialties did in fact remain associated with the College is one of the remarkable phenomena of these two decades, for, in this respect, the College is virtually unique among specialists' colleges. It is remarkable that the College, as a single, national organization, has continued to execute the three principal functions of determining requirements and standards of training, designing and conducting examinations and certifying would-be specialists as being competent as well as providing opportunities for continuing medical education for established specialists — in all the specialties

335

recognized by the College and for both English- and French-speaking physicians. Stresses and strains there have certainly been, but the College has been not unsuccessful in discharging its several responsibilities in a multidisciplinary context. Moreover, the College has discharged these responsibilities in specialist health care with ever-present respect for the bicultural and bilingual nature of Canada. These achievements have not gone unnoticed, and other colleges respect and admire, and even envy, the College for its attainment of unity.

The reasons for the College's success in this aspect of its pursuit of unity cannot readily be pinpointed. It may, however, be useful to discuss the several aspects of the College's relations with the specialists by bearing in mind the importance of commonality of interest, communication, cooperation and collegiality. There were three principal concerns from 1960 to 1980: the increase in the number of specialties and the need for the College to recognize them and to find ways to mark competence among specialists in the new specialties and subspecialties; the desire on the part of some specialty groups for autonomy rather than association; and the importance of enhancing the College's relationships with the increasing number of specialty groups.

Recognition of the Specialties by the College

A phenomenon that characterized the development of medicine in the early 1960s was its fragmentation into more and more specialties. For the College a major concern was the burgeoning of specialties and the question of how to recognize medical and surgical specialties that were clamoring for recognition as independent specialties or subspecialties.

From 1930 to 1947, the number of specialties that the College recognized as *bona fide* specialties with their own examinations by Council approval grew steadily from two to 21. These are listed in Table 12.1.

By 1950, the College was conducting Fellowship examinations in 19 specialties and Certification examinations in 21. By then, the demand for specialty recognition that would have seemed insatiable to the founders of the College had been satisfied, and the number of specialties recognized remained at 21 until 1961, when the specialty of cardiovascular and thoracic surgery was recognized. Until 1961, there had been a 15-year period without recognition of new specialties, but then, in the mid-1960s, "the flood gates opened again."[2] The College was now faced with one of the problems of the expansive decade of the 1960s, that of the enormous and rapid growth of both knowledge and technology. The main need was to contain and satisfy the demands of specialty recognition without dangerously fragmenting and splintering the body medical to the extent that unity would be lost — forever. The rapid development of the specialties between 1960 and 1980 may be considered in two phases — the 1960s and the 1970s.

TABLE 12.1 Dates of Recognition of Specialties and First Examinations by The Royal College of Physicians and Surgeons of Canada, 1929-1947. (Comparative information concerning incorporation of specialty board in USA is included from data kindly provided by the American Board of Medical Specialties, 1983.)

Specialty	Council Approval	Fellowship	Certification	USA
Internal Medicine	1929	1931	1946	1936
Surgery	1929	1931	1946	1937
Dermatology	1937	1947	1946	1932
Ophthalmology	1937	1947	1946	1917
Otolaryngology	1937	1947	1946	1924
Pediatrics	1937	1947	1946	1933
Diagnostic Radiology	1937	1949	1946	1934
Therapeutic Radiology	1937	1949	1946	1934
Urology	1937	1947	1946	1935
Neurology	1941	1947	1946	1934
Obstetrics & Gynecology	1941	1947	1946	1930
Orthopedic Surgery	1941	1947	1946	1934
Psychiatry	1941	1947	1946	1934
Anesthesia	1942	1951	1946	1938
Physical Medicine and Rehabilitation	1944	1957	1946	1947
Medical Microbiology	1945	1962	1946	1949[a]
Neurosurgery	1945	1947	1946	1936
General Pathology	1945	1956	1946	1939
Plastic Surgery	1946	1952	1947	1948
Thoracic Surgery	1946	—	1950	1948
Public Health	1947	—	1950	1948

[a] Certificate of Special Competence in Medical Microbiology, from American Board of Pathology, incorporated in 1936.

Recognition of Specialties in the 1960s

In the first phase, the opening of the "flood gates" was recognized in June 1963, when the Specialty Committee in Pathology reviewed the training requirements and examinations for that specialty. The committee members agreed that there was a need in Canada for four different types of pathologists — generalists, morbid anatomists, clinical pathologists and academic pathologists. They concluded that it was time to broaden the training requirements for Fellowship and Certification in pathology and to modify the examinations to take into account the various training possibilities for the candidates. The College, it was suggested, should broaden the content of the Certification examination in order to grant a certificate in pathology with emphasis, for example, on anatomical pathology or clinical pathology. At the same time it should continue to grant a single Fellowship in medicine modified for pathology (to take account of general pathology as well as more specialized areas such as anatomical pathology, neuropathology, pediatric pathology, clinical chemistry, bacteriology, virology and hematology).

The situation became more complex in September 1963, as the president of the Canadian Association of Medical Biochemists, Dr. A.H. Neufeld, told Dr. J.H. Graham that the association wanted the College to establish a Fellowship examination modified for biochemistry. This issue was considered by the Credentials Committee in September 1963. The committee agreed that the recommendations of the Specialty Committee in Pathology should be referred to the Examinations Committee for study of modifications in the examinations in pathology, including consideration of whether further subdivision of the specialty might be necessary. But the Examinations Committee, at its December 1963 meeting, held that the time was not right. Dr. E.F. Ross thought that the recommendations of the Specialty Committee in Pathology were not entirely in line with studies by a committee of the Canadian Association of Pathologists, and Dr. R.V. Christie suggested that a decision on changes in the Fellowship examination should be deferred pending the results of the Examination Committee's review, then underway, of the Fellowship examination.

The various aspects of the issue were next formally discussed during the Credentials Committee's meeting in May 1964. Dr. G.A. Bergeron, Vice-President (Medicine) and co-chairman of the Credentials Committee, explained that the Specialty Committee in Pathology had made its suggestions on the training requirements and examinations relating to Certification in anatomical pathology and clinical pathology in order to elicit Council's reaction. The Credentials Committee supported the view of the specialty Committee in Pathology; there was general agreement that the pathologists' proposals were in accord with the position that clinical pathology now occupied in scientific medicine, and in line with the practice of the American Board of Pathology in granting a diploma in clinical pathology. The Credentials Committee recommended to Council that the specialty of pathology should be divided into the separate specialties of anatomical pathology and clinical pathology at both the Fellowship and the Certification level.

The Credentials Committee also considered the proposal, submitted by Dr. Neufeld, that biochemistry be recognized as a specialty through the development of a Fellowship examination in medicine modified for biochemistry. This matter was even more complex because the medical biochemists' proposal was opposed by a group of clinical chemists from Toronto.

The medical biochemists' case was expressed in a submission to the College signed by Dr. Neufeld and Dr. K.R. MacKenzie, the secretary-treasurer of the Canadian Association of Medical Biochemists; both were qualified in biochemistry as well as in medicine. Three paragraphs from the letter accompanying their submission, dated November 11, 1963, convey a sense of their argument:

> *Advances* in medical biochemistry and the physiological implications have developed rapidly in the 20th century, and the rapidity and magnitude of these developments have resulted in the growth of a highly specialized branch of laboratory medicine, namely medical biochemistry. By demonstrating the significance of biochemical alterations and of the constantly increasing number of recognized abnormal biochemical states, medical biochemistry has correspondingly increased its value to clinical medicine and surgery as well as to the laboratory. This specialty now represents the application of present scientific knowledge regarding aberrations of chemical, endocrine, and enzymatic functions, abnormalities of organic and inorganic metabolism, nutrition, etc. in all branches of medicine as well as in pre- and post-operative treatment.
>
> This brief commentary on the development of the present status of the specialty is presented to emphasize the need to be recognized in Canada, not only for the sake of recognition but, more important, that this will lead to improved medical practice.
>
> It is not the intent of this submission to propose an administrative separation of the medical biochemists from the other laboratory specialists, but rather to allow for the allocation of the immediate responsibility of the direction of medical biochemistry to those having the necessary qualifications in medicine and biochemistry.[3]

Some clinical chemists, learning of the medical biochemists' proposal, wrote to the College on January 19, 1964, to ask that no precipitate action be taken without a full assessment of its possible implications on the practice of clinical chemistry. They were concerned especially about the possible "repercussions" of the introduction of a Fellowship in biochemistry restricted to medically qualified persons in the practice of clinical chemistry. The clinical chemists represented biochemistry departments in several leading Toronto hospitals. Three paragraphs from their letter summarize their argument:

> The clinical chemists in Canada are represented by the Canadian Society for Clinical Chemistry [CSCC]. ...This society numbers both PhD's and MD's in its membership and includes the directors of nearly all the major hospital clinical chemistry laboratories in Canada, as well as university professors engaged in the teaching of clinical chemistry. Recently the CSCC has initiated a "Certification program" by means of which certain clinical chemists who meet stringent requirements of education and experience may become "certified" after oral and/or written examination. It is possible for either PhD's or MD's to qualify.

> This "program" is similar in intent to a fellowship program though we recognize that it has a long way to go to attain the professional recognition of a Royal College Fellowship. The introduction of a Fellowship in Biochemistry, though it would be available only to MD's, would produce a double standard of professional attainment. If the PhD biochemist cannot hope to attain the same professional stature as the MD in this paramedical field it will become impossible to induce the best talent in biochemistry to enter clinical chemistry.

> It should be pointed out that most of the large hospital clinical chemistry laboratories are under the supervision of PhD biochemists. It is doubtful that, if the supply of PhD biochemists entering clinical chemistry should be cut off, the medical profession would be able to provide MD's with suitable graduate training to meet the demand.[4]

The Credentials Committee was swayed more by the arguments of Drs. Neufeld and MacKenzie than those of the clinical chemists. Dr. W.A. Cochrane concluded that the decision must be based on what was good for the College and that the opposition of a group from one local area should not influence their decision. Dr. W.M. Goldberg wondered why the national society had not prepared an official communication on a matter that was of national significance. President W.C. MacKenzie, concerned that the College was placed in the middle of a family quarrel, thought it wise to defer action until more was known. Dr. E.D. Gagnon wondered whether the Credentials Committee could play a useful role in bringing all of the interested parties together to try to obtain agreement as to a proper course of action. The committee then agreed in principle to the recognition of biochemistry as a specialty, and its recommendations were submitted to Council for consideration in June 1964.

The June 1964 meeting of Council was both important and interesting. It was important because it established the Fragmentation Committee (later, the Specialty Development and Manpower Committee), a committee that was struck to deal with the problem of evaluating claims for recognition of "an apparently endless succession of new specialties."[5] It was interesting in that it illustrated aspects of decision-making in Council.

Council initially considered the recommendation of the Credentials Committee that medical biochemistry be recognized as a specialty, the means for this being establishment of a Fellowship in medicine modified for biochemistry. Dr. Gagnon, senior chairman of the Credentials Committee, reiterated that the committee might bring the various interested groups together to try to obtain unanimity as to a proper course of action. Dr. J.P. Gemmell, who found the whole situation "very confused", advocated tabling the matter until there had been time for members of Council to sort out in their minds a proper course to follow. Dr. G.M. Brown said that Council should know more about the direction in which the College was going before coming to any definite decision. For Dr. D.F. Moore, the confusion was further clouded by the fact that medical biochemists were a varied lot. Some medical biochemists were medically qualified and some were not, and there was, besides, a variety of sub-specialties, including hematology, microbiology and pathological chemistry. Dr. Moore, himself a pathologist, stated that the College obviously could not make any recommendations concerning those who did not possess a medical degree.

The need now was to bring interested and knowledgeable people together within the College in order to pool ideas. Dr. D.R. Wilson saw the problem in broad terms; the problem was not limited to biochemistry since other basic disciplines such as pharmacology and genetics were also becoming increasingly involved in clinical and paraclinical settings. This problem, he noted, was separate from that of further fragmentation of the clinical specialties — among which cardiology was one, notice of the Canadian Cardiovascular Society's wish to have a Fellowship in medicine modified for cardiology having been given in February 1964.

Rather than table the motion, Council voted on the issue and unanimously defeated the motion to approve the recommendation of the Credentials Committee in approving the establishment of a Fellowship in medical biochemistry. The Credentials Committee suffered a second reversal in this meeting of Council, for its recommendation of May 1964 that the specialty of pathology be divided into anatomical pathology and clinical pathology was also defeated. Council then struck a special committee, comprising senior officers of the College, to study the matter further. The committee, which in effect would be a task force, became known as the Fragmentation Committee. Its task would be to look into the implications of the splintering of medicine into specialties and to recommend a policy for Council to consider on specialty development.

The problem before Council amounted, in part, to the need to reach a decision on which two standing committees had taken different positions. The Credentials Committee's discussion of the recommendation of the Specialty Committee in Pathology had led the Credentials Committee to recommend acceptance of the principle of separate branches of the specialty of pathology at both the Fellowship and Certification levels. In contrast, as Dr. Christie explained, the Examinations Committee had reached a different position: a single qualification should be maintained, at both the Fellowship and Certification levels, with multiple questions on the examinations from which candidates might choose according to the specialty in which they had trained. The Examinations Committee had raised an important issue — that of fragmentation, the implications of which were now becoming clear.

Councillors responded in different ways. During the meeting of the Examinations Committee in June 1964, Dr. C.C. Ferguson had suggested that some basic denominator should be preserved — for example, the Fellowship in medicine, general surgery or pathology — and, if necessary, that the College should recognize training in more specialized areas. Dr. Christie told his colleagues in Council that the existence of the two types of pathologists (anatomical pathologists and clinical pathologists) was a fact of life requiring a different training and a different outlook. In summarizing the Examinations Committee's discussion, Dr. Christie stressed that this was a case of fragmentation that was not confined to anatomical pathology and clinical pathology, as evidenced by the submissions already before Council from the clinical chemists and the neuropathologists also. It was necessary to consider the matter from the policy point of view as to how far the College wished to go in permitting or disallowing or preventing further fragmentation of the specialties.

This was the crucial question: to what extent would the College, an essentially unitarian body, go in accepting the fact of fragmentation?

The Credentials Committee's motion regarding the division of pathology into the specialties of anatomical pathology and clinical pathology having been defeated, it was moved that the matter should be referred back to the pathology committee for consideration of the general principle of fragmentation in the light of Council's discussion. Dr. G.M. Brown, however, pointed out that the problem of fragmentation cut across more than just pathology and that it therefore should not be considered only by the Specialty Committee in Pathology. The motion was then amended so that the matter would be considered by a committee consisting of the chairmen of the Examinations Committee, the Credentials Committee and the Specialty Committee in Pathology and three others to be named by the chair — the Fragmentation Committee.

The formation of the Fragmentation Committee was an important step in resolving an issue that would have to be addressed periodically in the 1960s and 1970s. Once the Fragmentation Committee met, a decision about the future development of specialties was soon made. At the committee's first meeting, held on December 10, 1964, the conclusions reached were the following:

- The training and examinations relating to pathology were unsatisfactory. Separate Fellowships should be established in anatomical pathology and neuropathology.
- A qualification in general pathology should be retained, but at both the Certification and Fellowship levels rather than at the Certification level.
- Specialist qualifications in hematology and medical biochemistry were needed, but it was unclear whether the qualifications should be the responsibility of the examining board in laboratory medicine or whether they should be regarded as separate specialties under the Fellowship in medicine. The opinions of the biochemists were required and those of the specialty committees in pathology and internal medicine would also be evaluated.
- Because further subspecialization in medicine was inevitable, recognition of such specialties should be granted at the appropriate time in order to encourage their development. Specialties in line for recognition included cardiology, respiratory disease, allergy, gastroenterology and endocrinology. But the advice of the Specialty Committee in Internal Medicine would first be necessary.

Meanwhile, there was an urgent need to make a decision concerning appropriate changes regarding pathology. Dissatisfaction with the examinations, particularly in relation to clinical pathology, had led two pathologists to resign from the Fellowship examining board. President W.C. MacKenzie suggested that the Executive Committee might recommend to Council acceptance of changes on which the specialty committee and the Fragmentation Committee could agree. For the moment, therefore, Fellowship examinations might be established in pathology modified for anatomical pathology, for neuropathology and for medical biochemistry (and in medicine modified for cardiology). Council approved recognition of these specialties in January 1965, as the floodgates leading to recognition of still more specialties swung open.

The debate from 1963 to 1965 on specialty development clarified the criteria of recognition in this first phase of specialty growth and provided reference criteria for the second phase, which came in the mid 1970s. A paragraph from the minutes of the discussion of the report of the Fragmentation Committee to Council in January 1965 summarizes the views of that time:

> Dr. Christie commented that pressure is being brought to bear on the College by cardiologists, allergists and pathologists to divide the Fellowship into further specialties, as has been done in most other Colleges. The pathologists in particular were anxious for a change and go so far as to say that the present regulations of the College are preventing the proper training of pathologists. This was the problem which was put to the Fragmentation Committee and it was not an easy problem because there were two opposite points of view, both of which are valid. On the one hand, specialization is part of medical

progress and if we do not recognize it and encourage it and help to organize it, the Royal College will be left behind. On the other hand, we must not allow the central core of general surgery and internal medicine to be "nibbled away" until there is nothing left. It was a reasonable compromise between these points of view which the committee had to consider.

It was compromise that the College, too, would have to consider as an increasing number of specialties requested recognition. The decision-making process was both difficult and deliberate, as Dr. R.W. Gunton indicated:

These decisions were taken only after a most exhaustive examination of the proposals among the various committees of Council. They were undoubtedly influenced by the generally expansive mood of the sixties, by corresponding actions taken in the United States and by the genuine conviction that these new separate disciplines offered scientific advances and improved health care; moreover, they recognized career decisions already taken by the trainees.[6]

To summarize the sequential recognition of specialties in the 1960s, Table 12.2 lists the specialties and the year in which each was recognized.

TABLE 12.2 **Dates of Recognition of Specialties and First Examinations by The Royal College of Physicians and Surgeons of Canada, 1961-1970. (Comparative information concerning specialty recognition in USA is included, from data of American Board of Medical Specialties, 1983.)**

Specialty	Council Approval	Fellowship[a]	USA[b]
Cardiovascular and Thoracic Surgery	1961	1962	1949: Certification by American Board of Thoracic Surgery
Medical Science	1964	1964	—
Cardiology	1965	1970	1941: CSC from Internal Medicine Board
Anatomical Pathology	1965	1968	1959: CSC in Forensic Path. from Path. Bd.
Neuropathology	1965	1968	1947: CSC from Path. Bd.

Specialty	Council Approval	Fellowship[a]	USA[b]
Medical Biochemistry	1965	1968	1950: CSC in Chemical Path. from Path. Bd.
Hematological Pathology	1966	1968	—
Hematology	1966	1971	1952: CSC from Path. Bd.
Gastroenterology	1968	1971	1941: CSC from Internal Medicine Board
Respiratory Medicine	1968	1972	1941: CSC from Internal Medicine Board
Clinical Immunology	1968	1971	1971: Board of Allergy and Immunology estab.
Rheumatology	1970	1972	1972: CSC from Internal Medicine Board

[a] Except in medical science, Certification was obtained through success in the Fellowship Examination.

[b] It is not possible to give a precise equivalent for recognition of specialties in USA in view of minor differences in the names of specialties and the degree of autonomy of specialties there. As of 1972, there were 21 independent specialty boards in USA, Internal Medicine and Pathology granting Certificates of Special Competence (CSCs) in specialties that were established free-standing ones in Canada. CSCs, therefore, have been taken as the principal equivalent, although in this College CSCs were not granted until 1975. (Source: American Board of Medical Specialties, 1983.)

In this first phase of specialty recognition, contributions by two other senior Fellows foreshadowed developments in the second phase. When the Executive Committee considered how to recognize "special branches" of medicine and surgery in July 1967, Dr. F.G. Kergin suggested the following as criteria to be used in defining a specialty: a sufficient volume of problems or patients having these problems to require in a major hospital at least two or three qualified persons devoting their time to them; special knowledge or techniques of diagnosis and treatment; organization of hospitals for the handling of a particular specialty; a recognized literature in the field; and probably a specialty society. These criteria antedated those that were formulated in 1974 in a formal statement on guidelines for the College.

The Executive Committee's wide-ranging discussion on subspecialty recognition and allied problems in this era was also facilitated by study of a memorandum on subspecialty recognition that Dr. J.H. Graham prepared in 1967.[7] This memorandum, besides reflecting the thinking on specialty development as of 1967 and facilitating the development of recognition of guidelines later, presented four options regarding the recognition of additional specialties and the conduct of examinations in them. These four options were the following:

- To establish each new specialty as a separate and independent entity with its own training regulations and its own examination regulations. This course had been adopted in approving the 26 specialties to date, with an effort being made to retain some consistency in the patterns of training and the patterns of examining.
- To establish a common basic training program in internal medicine (or general surgery), with a common preliminary examination after an agreed-upon period of residency training (of perhaps two years), followed by a differentiated training program in each specialty and a differentiated final examination in that specialty. This was the general nature of the proposal of the Examinations Committee.
- To require the completion of training that would make a candidate eligible for the Fellowship examination in internal medicine (or general surgery) with training in the specialty being included in that program, the candidate then being required to pass a general Fellowship examination and, after a period of training, to take an additional examination in the chosen specialty. This was the proposal of the Specialty Committee in Internal Medicine; it was similar to the pattern of the American Board of Internal Medicine and three other American specialty boards. The committee proposed that the second qualification should be Fellowship, and there was the additional alternative of this being a certificate.
- Some other technique.

Preparation of this memorandum was stimulated by current discussions on recognition of subspecialties of internal medicine (allergy, gastroenterology, clinical immunology, nuclear medicine and respiratory medicine). Guided by this memorandum, the views of the Specialty Development and Manpower Committee, the report of the Specialty Committee in Internal Medicine and the conclusions of the Examinations Committee, the Executive Committee then approved five important resolutions:

- That a Fellowship in Internal Medicine be not a mandatory prerequisite to obtaining a Fellowship qualification in the subspecialties of internal medicine.
- That it be recommended to Council that recognition in a subspecialty of internal medicine be at the Fellowship level only.
- That the principle be accepted that the training requirements for the new subspecialties of internal medicine must include two years of satisfactory training in general internal medicine beyond the internship year, and further, where the general medical service was divided into subspecialty services, not more than six months might be spent in any one of the subspecialties.
- That the content of the two core years of training in the subspecialties of internal medicine be determined in each case by the Credentials Committee in consultation with the specialty committee for that subspecialty.
- That it be recommended to Council that, in the new subspecialties of internal medicine, a comprehensive objective type of examination in the broad field of general internal medicine be permitted at the time of the candidate's choosing following the satisfactory completion of the required two years of resident training in general internal medicine beyond internship.

While these resolutions related more to training and examination than to means of specialty recognition, they do reflect the growing complexity of recognition of specialties in the 1960s.

Recognition of Specialties in the 1970s

The second phase in the College's recognition of new specialties was initiated in 1973, when nuclear medicine was recognized. In this phase the College formulated guidelines for recognition of new specialties and introduced the Certificate of Special Competence to mark recognition of a subspecialty subordinate to Certification in a primary specialty.

The equivalent of the Fragmentation Committee (and its successor, the Specialty Development Committee) in the 1970s was the Specialty Development and Manpower Committee. Formation of this committee was authorized in February 1970. It was chaired by Dr. J.M.M. Darte until 1972, when Dr. R.W. Gunton took over and chaired it for the remainder of the decade.

Concern about the growing number of specialties in the 1970s was first expressed at the Council meeting of January 1974, when Dr. R.W. Gunton raised the question of recognition of pediatric surgery, medical oncology, community medicine, pediatric neurology, emergency medical care, geriatrics and infectious diseases. Dr. J.C. Beck was sufficiently disturbed to state that, until the College faced this issue squarely and developed recommendations, a moratorium should be declared on the recognition of any new specialty — a course that had recently been taken by the American Board of Medical Specialties in order to reassess the situation in the United States. Dr. J.R. Evans, while not wanting to claim that specialization was bad or that it should be held back, favored a framework that would prevent the development of undesirable consequences of fragmentation or temporary dead-end specialties. He suggested that an additional type of recognition, such as Certificate of Special Competence or Training, or a Certificate of Secondary Certification, might obviate the need to recognize new primary specialties — there were, after all, already 32 recognized specialties in Canada (community medicine had just been added to the list). Recognizing the need for further study, Council established a moratorium on the development of new specialty certificates until it had had an opportunity to develop a policy for the recognition of new specialties. The President was empowered to appoint a committee for this purpose. To this committee were appointed Dr. R.W. Gunton, as chairman, and Drs. J.C. Beck, J.R. Evans and J.R. Gutelius as members.

The committee first identified the problems. It then discussed considerations that had earlier guided the Specialty Development and Manpower Committee when it recommended recognition of nuclear medicine. These considerations, or criteria, however, were not easy to interpret; nor was it easy to assign weight to each, or to substitute other criteria by interested groups. Thus, with nuclear medicine, it was not easy to decide that there was *a separate body of knowledge or separate skills identifiable with the specialty*; laboratory medicine specialties, radiology and internal medicine could be regarded as having equal claim to the new specialty with respect to knowledge and techniques. With geriatrics, *to improve specialized health care* was undoubtedly an objective favoring recognition. A certificate in infectious diseases was sought because it would encourage recruitment of a *body of highly trained individuals with special knowledge in the field*. A certificate in medical oncology would attest to the value of *combining the knowledge and special skills of two or three earlier recognized specialties into a new specialty devoted to one disease*. And with community medicine, the proposed changes in public health and preventive medicine were influenced by the desire to *make the specialty more attractive, and bring it into line with modern medicine, current social structure or changing patterns of health care delivery*.

These purposes and objectives — and others such as the *availability of a corps of specialists able to support training programs and the examination process* and the creation of a specialty *without adversely affecting other specialties or the delivery of specialized health care* — were legitimate, but certain other problems remained. The main problem was to decide when any of a number of considerations were convincing enough to warrant granting of recognition. Could the College sustain five or more additional specialties without bringing about further fragmentation and "administrative strangulation" and so weakening the College and impeding the preservation of unity? Another problem was raised by the suggestion that geriatrics, pediatric surgery and pediatric neurology be recognized: should subdivisions of specialties be related to age groups?

The committee then considered current assumptions:

- Educational forces that had promoted fragmentation — increasingly specialized knowledge and skill being the chief ones — would persist. The College would remain the major force guiding postgraduate education and the certification of specialists, whether or not provincial colleges tied Certification to licensure (and perhaps limited licensure) and whether or not the College introduced recertification.
- Licensure changes might aggravate fragmentation since it would involve levels of remuneration of physicians and so promote the guild phenomenon.
- The College could identify core educational content and skills common to many specialties that were or would be seeking recognition.
- Overlaps of educational and jurisdictional areas would leave the College to define policy that would establish legitimacy of qualification in several fields by individuals certified in only one.
- Governments and other agencies would increasingly demand certification of competence in determining qualification of specialists for remuneration of services, regardless of the mechanism of remuneration.

It was entirely possible, however, to look at the future positively. The committee made four proposals in this light:

The College, now a stronger organization than ever, should not arbitrarily halt the recognition of new specialties out of concern for weakness resulting from division, but should rather continue to evaluate each proposal for a new specialty carefully.

To facilitate this, officially accepted criteria for recognition of new specialties should be developed.

An integrated rather than a compartmentalized approach should be taken, consisting of the granting of a Certificate of Special Competence over and above the previous acquisition of a specialist's Certificate in one of the general or primary specialties.

The general or primary specialties and their interrelationships with those subspecialties recognized by Certificates of Special Competence should be defined.

These were the main recommendations, and Council approved them when it accepted the report of the Specialty Development and Manpower Committee in January 1975. The committee's suggested guidelines for the recognition of a new specialty, as revised in September 1974 and approved by Council in June 1975, became policy in the following form:

Guidelines for the Recognition of a New Specialty

- ...the Royal College will consider the recognition of a new specialty or grant a Certificate of Special Competence when a substantial deficiency in patient care of Canadians has been identified and it is clear and apparent that the creation of this new specialty will help to rectify this deficiency.
- There should be a body of knowledge separately and specifically identifiable with the new specialty.
- There should be separate and specific skills or expertise associated with the practice of the specialty. This guideline can be applied readily to the procedural skills of many specialties.
- The specialty should have encouraged or attracted enough de facto recognition that there exist individuals already possessing the knowledge and skills to practise it.
- The number of such individuals identifiable at the time of application for the new specialty or anticipated to be identifiable, employable and needed in the country, should be large enough to provide a corps of these professionals able to sustain training programs, annual scientific meetings and the examination process.
- Recognition of a specialty should have as one of its important objectives advancement of the science and practice of medicine in that discipline, including such matters as development of appropriate training programs, evaluation procedures and the attraction of research funds.
- The creation of the specialty should lead to improved specialized health care in Canada.
- Creation of the new specialty should be reviewed in the light of its effect on the other specialties, the College as a whole and the delivery of specialized health care in the country.
- Recognition of the specialty in other jurisdictions, particularly the USA and UK, would be a positive factor in the decision.
- Existence of national specialist societies and journals devoted to the discipline would be a positive factor in the decision.
- A specialty may be recognized if it is overwhelmingly in the public's interest, even though some of the more specific criteria are not met.
- There should be a clearly recognized need for specialists in the new discipline outside the teaching centres as well as within them.

Formulation of these guidelines permitted Council to reconsider recognition of the next group of specialties. Many of these were granted recognition in the form of a Certificate of Special Competence. The moratorium was in effect lifted when Council, in January 1975, approved the recognition of pediatric general surgery as a specialty by means of a Certificate of Special Competence. This innovation could be regarded in two different ways — either as a manifestation of the desirability of recognizing and so facilitating subspecialty practice, or as one more example of the trend by which the role of the generalist was steadily being narrowed.

Recognition of other specialties followed. For completeness, and to complement Tables 12.1 and 12.2, specialties that were recognized between 1970 and 1980 are listed in Table 12.3.

By 1980, the College had recognized 39 specialties. In 50 years, the number of specialties recognized by the College had grown from two to almost twenty times that number.

TABLE 12.3 Recognition of Specialties by The Royal College of Physicians and Surgeons of Canada, 1971-1980[a].

Specialty	Year of Council Approval
Nuclear Medicine[b]	1973
Community Medicine[b]	1974
Pediatric General Surgery	1975
Geriatric Medicine	1977
Nephrology	1977
Thoracic Surgery	1977
Perinatal Medicine[c]	1978
Emergency Medicine[b]	1980
Infectious Diseases	1980
Vascular Surgery	1980

[a] Occasionally, recognition would be granted by Council but not implemented. This occurred with medical genetics. Recognition was granted in 1979 but, owing to differences with the Canadian College of Medical Genetics, the Royal College never implemented recognition. The medical geneticists wanted recognition by primary Certification, not by a CSC. Here the College's pursuit of unity failed, as it did too, perhaps, with emergency medicine (see Chapter 5, pp. 129 to 132). With child psychiatry recognition was granted in January 1969 but Council rescinded its own decision in January 1972; the factor of age differentiation within a specialty was not considered an adequate reason for granting recognition.

[b] Granted recognition as a free-standing specialty; the others listed here were granted recognition by means of a CSC.

[c] On the basis of primary Certification in obstetrics and gynecology. Neonatology, on the basis of primary Certification in pediatrics, was recognized by means of a CSC in 1982.

Association Versus Autonomy

Recognition of new specialties by the College was the first half of the association-autonomy equation; the second half consisted of the expression of some specialty groups' desires, stated with varying intensity, to separate from the College and become autonomous.

The spectre of fragmentation and separation always haunted the College. At its very first meeting in 1929, Council required all its conciliatory facility to counter the move to create two colleges instead of one; and even as long after as 1960, one Fellow could still foresee the division of the College into a college of physicians and a college of surgeons.[8] Over the years, various specialty groups felt the need for autonomy and independence. The degree of independence varied. Some groups, like the psychiatrists, sought greater freedom in terms of training requirements (see Chapter 8). Others, like the obstetricians and gynecologists and the laboratory medicine specialists, sought a measure of autonomy — a type of sovereignty-association — within the structure of the College. Dissent among obstetricians and gynecologists was first evident in the late 1940s when negotiations between the College and the newly formed SOGC led to changes in the training requirements and examinations and to creation of a third section of the annual meeting's scientific program devoted to obstetrics and gynecology.[9] Dissent that again led to changes in the examination procedure occurred in 1958 and then reached a head in 1960. The concerns of laboratory medicine specialists were expressed in the early 1970s. These two instances of dissent constitute a model that is worth examining in order to understand one aspect of a threat to unity.

Dissent Among the Obstetricians and Gynecologists

A letter dated December 20, 1960, expressed a dissenting view that forced the College to react. Dr. G.B. Maughan, chairman of the Fellowship examining board in Obstetrics and Gynecology, felt that the recent oral examinations for the College Fellowship raised "once again" the question of the conduct of the examinations;[10] he was referring in particular to a letter that he had written earlier, on December 13, 1958,[11] and to dissatisfaction and unrest concerning "our Fellowship" in the College. In his 1958 letter, Dr. Maughan himself urged that obstetricians and gynecologists should have the final word as to which obstetrical and gynecological candidates passed the examination. In 1958, it had been medical and surgical examiners who had had the final word, and in

1960 it was a pathology examiner who "adamantly" refused to raise his mark.[12] Control by the obstetricians and gynecologists over their own candidates was Dr. Maughan's principal request, but he was also concerned that further dissatisfaction and unrest among some obstetricians and gynecologists caused by irritating examination practices would fuel the threat to unity. Three paragraphs from his 1958 letter explain the problem and its possible consequences:

> *There* is a growing movement afoot in this country among obstetricians and gynecologists to establish their own college and conduct affairs separately from those of The Royal College of Physicians and Surgeons of Canada as was done in England some thirty years ago. I believe this would be a mistake at this time, because with a small number of Fellows, not only in our discipline, but in medicine and surgery in this country, there is strength in unity. I believe we need this strength in these years of great change in medical and surgical practice.
>
> It is inconceivable to me that a general surgeon has any proper place on the examining board in gynecology, or a physician any proper place on the examining board in obstetrics, any more than an obstetrician and gynecologist should have a place on the examining board of medicine and surgery. Obstetrics and gynecology is not an offshoot of either medicine or surgery, but historically preceded both of the other major disciplines. Practically, in modern times, we are prepared to stand on our own feet as the third main branch of the Royal College.
>
> ...I would request your Examinations Committee and Council give very earnest consideration to my remarks above. I am convinced that the proper step by the College at this time will forestall action by the prematurely hot-headed individuals in our discipline, and allow us to continue in a unified Fellowship group. Failure of serious consideration or a misstep by the College now will add fuel to the fires of separation and this I would not like to witness.

This letter was considered by the Examinations Committee in January 1959, together with the committee's resolution recommending the creation of an independent board of examiners for obstetrics and gynecology as submitted to Council. But Council, because of the policy recently adopted of a single standard of training requirements and ultimately of examinations, tabled the resolution until further information could be obtained about the Fellowship examinations modified for the specialties and until the problem could be more fully investigated. By the end of 1960, however, such further information did not seem to be available, and Dr. Maughan, now believing it to be time that the results of these studies were promulgated, duly wrote his second letter.

Dr. Maughan's 1960 letter was more direct and his demands more stringent. He wanted no less than the following changes: the establishment of a third division of the College to make it henceforth "The Royal College of Physicians, Surgeons and Obstetricians and Gynaecologists"; full representation of obstetricians and gynecologists on Council; complete control of the examinations in obstetrics and gynecology in the hands of an examining board or committee of obstetricians and gynecologists; the omission of the physician from the examiners in obstetrics and the deletion of a surgeon from the examiners in gynecology; and the inclusion of a gynecological pathologist as one of the two pathologist-examiners. He ended by saying "this country is not large enough for the divisive actions which characterized the Royal Colleges in England some 30 or 40 years ago, and the American Colleges more recently." Dr. Maughan urged Council to likewise keep an eye on history.

Dr. Maughan's letter was effective. The Examinations Committee reaffirmed its previous stand that a separate Fellowship examining board be established. Council, however, rather than accepting Dr. Maughan's recommendations, directed in January 1961 that the College's Specialty Committee in Obstetrics and Gynecology be consulted and a questionnaire was sent to the 215 Fellows in obstetrics and gynecology. Over 50 per cent of the 156 respondents supported Dr. Maughan's position in general, although some 65 per cent opposing the removal of a physician and a surgeon from the examining board. The Examinations Committee adopted a further resolution based on the belief that in most other countries obstetrics and gynecology was not regarded as a subspecialty of medicine or surgery and the view that the granting of autonomous status in regard to the conduct of the examinations in obstetrics and gynecology would not constitute a precedent for the granting of similar autonomy in the conduct of the examinations in other specialties. The committee resolved that a separate examining board in obstetrics and gynecology be created; it would not come under either medicine or surgery, and a chairman from the discipline would report directly to the Examinations Committee and the College. It did not, however, go so far as to suggest removing a physician or a surgeon from the examining board or replacing the general pathologist by a gynecological pathologist. This resolution was then considered by Council in June 1961.

During the debate in Council, Dr. K.T. MacFarlane, an obstetrician, reported that about 75 per cent of persons he had canvassed felt that there should be a separate division, and even a separate Fellowship diploma, for obstetricians and gynecologists. He felt that these recommendations might "weld rather than separate." Dr. G. Hooper agreed that if concessions were not made discontent would result. Dr. P.E. Ireland was not concerned about precedents — which are necessary to establish if progress is to be made. The thinking in Council had changed and a firm decision could now be made. The motion that the resolution approving a separate examining board for obstetrics and gynecology be adopted was carried unanimously, aside from one abstention.

Ten years later, obstetricians and gynecologists expressed further concerns. In a letter dated February 13, 1970, the president of the SOGC drew the College's attention to certain of the Society's concerns. Dr. F.L. Johnson wrote to Dr. J.H. Graham on the problem of organization in obstetrics and gynecology and in the broad field of reproductive biology. He, too, urged the College to seek unity:

> In some countries, a multiplicity of organizations has developed, representing the field of reproduction, and there is concern that this may develop in Canada and it is a wish of many individuals that all these organizations could work under one umbrella.
>
> At the present time there is no one group who could speak on behalf of the area of reproduction in Canada. It is the belief of many individuals that better progress could be made if all of the efforts relating to this field could be channelled through one organization.
>
> I...believe [that] a study committee should be formed to explore this entire area. I would suggest that the Royal College appoint three members to this committee and the Society of Obstetricians and Gynaecologists of Canada appoint three members to this committee.[13]

In response to this request, the Executive Committee appointed Drs. F.J. Tweedie, G. Hurteau and R.P. Beck to represent the College. The first meeting of the study group was held on May 15, 1970, when Dr. Tweedie was named chairman of the subsequent meeting. The discussion covered topics beyond the relationship between the College and SOGC, and Dr. Tweedie suggested that the discussions could be useful if they concentrated on matters affecting the two organizations. Such discussions, Dr. Tweedie suggested, must be useful to the College as an example of efforts at cooperation with a national specialty society. This would not be too difficult as Dr. Tweedie was chairman of the study group and the members representing SOGC (Drs. M. Caouette, P. Harding and T.M. Roulston), being specialists, were also Fellows of the College; as so often happened, Fellows were likely to share common concerns with members of the second group in discussions of this nature.

The study group met again in November 1970 and January 1971 and produced their final report in May 1971. The group defined six problems, all of which had relevance in general to the College and, in principle, to other specialties:

- The need to develop guidelines leading to a representative and official specialty position on matters of current public interest (e.g., oral contraception, therapeutic abortion and sex education) and to develop mechanisms to designate a spokesman for the specialty on such matters when appropriate.

- The need for more coordination of scientific programs between specialty groups, and particularly the SOGC and the obstetrics-gynecology section of the Royal College.
- The need for stimulation and the development of research in obstetrics and gynecology.
- The need for active recruitment of quality candidates to the specialty.
- The need for a program to develop obstetrical-gynecological direction and leadership in the broad field of reproductive biology in its relationship to the future of specialty and subspecialty development.
- The need for improved liaison and communications between specialty groups generally.

The report then identified changing trends and new developments in obstetrics and gynecology, and the responses of various organizations to them. Although these trends and developments concerned chiefly obstetricians and gynecologists, the group's concerns were of general interest, and they illustrate how medicine was evolving. Thus, the specialty was seen as rapidly emerging from its traditional stance of a highly clinical discipline based largely on mechanical obstetrics and surgical gynecology, to one with many active fringe interests, with expanding scientific potential and awakening social responsibility. The specialty's new horizons extended to intrauterine genetics, endocrinology of the fetal placental unit, the intensive care monitoring of high-risk labor and perinatal medicine, as well as oral contraception, therapeutic abortion and sex counselling and education. In addition, the advent of Medicare, and, with it, the interest and participation of government in many aspects of medicine, had shaped thinking in the medical profession further.

The study group's members admitted that, as a specialty, they had responded to these trends only slowly and sporadically and even ineffectively. Because the specialty had lagged behind other disciplines in research and its applications, full partnership in research would be lost by default. There was a chronic problem in recruiting good quality candidates to the specialty, even though medical students found obstetrics and gynecology "exciting and dramatic". Other problems included dissatisfaction with the content of scientific programs; the expanding power of government in various areas of medicine and, through "budgetary necessity", the effects of this on specialist manpower and on the consultant's role; and criticism within and outside the profession regarding lack of cohesion within the specialty in reactions to medical social issues. The specialty needed to actively respond to such matters and to recognize its opportunities in the challenges around it.

As an interim mechanism, the study group recommended formation of a Coordinating Advisory Council, comprising representatives from SOGC, the Canadian Society for the Study of Infertility, the Obstetrics-Gynecology

Research Group, the Obstetrics-Gynecology Professors Group and the College. This council would work towards the desired objectives by providing a focal point for discussion and liaison with representative groups.

With respect to the relationship between SOGC and the College, three points were made by the study group. First, the traditional role of the College in training and assessment was affirmed. Second, in continuing education, the roles of the College and the specialty society should be complementary; the multidisciplinary philosophy and organ-system orientation of the College was appropriate and should be developed further. And third, for scientific programs, the SOGC-Royal College Program Committee liaison should be formalized by making the chairman of each program committee an official of the other, and a special liaison for scientific programs in obstetrics and gynecology should be formed (under the Coordinating Advisory Council), with representation from SOGC, the Infertility Society, the research group and the College. Conjoint meetings with specialty groups and the College would be useful, too.

The study group's report was approved by Council in January 1972. The College had responded positively to the request of a large and important specialty group for the College to play the role that, compared to the situation in other colleges, was unique. The uniqueness of this role was often the subject of comment; as Dr. R.C. Dickson, among many who made similar observations, told Council in September 1972, "our College is envied for its gathering of specialties under one roof." Such a role was not to be neglected, for it contributed in no small measure to the College's success in the pursuit of unity. For the College, it was a role of partnership rather than power; for a specialty group, the College hoped, satisfaction would be derived from association with the College rather than autonomy.

In these years, the College, for unity's sake, made its own efforts to increase the representation in College affairs by Fellows in the specialty of obstetrics and gynecology. Dr. MacFarlane was appointed Honorary Treasurer in 1957; and the appointment to this office later of Drs. F.J. Tweedie and R.A.H. Kinch meant that an obstetrician and gynecologist was always a member of the Executive Committee from 1960 to 1980. In addition, Dr. G. Hurteau was elected to Council in 1974 and served as Vice-President (Surgery) from 1976 to 1978, and Dr. W.B. Paul likewise was elected to Council in 1978 and served as Vice-President (Surgery) from 1980 to 1982. Other obstetricians and gynecologists represented on Council were Dr. F.E. Bryans from 1962 to 1970, Dr. N.K. MacLennan from 1967 to 1972 and Dr. W.R.C. Tupper in 1972, the latter two being Certificant representatives under the Certificant affiliation plan.

Dissent Among the Laboratory Medicine Specialists

A second example of dissent among specialty groups is provided by the desire of laboratory medicine specialists for a measure of autonomy. Communications between them and the College in 1971 and 1972 provide another facet of the model of unity versus disunity and of association versus autonomy vis-a-vis the College and specialty groups.

The concerns of the laboratory medicine specialists were raised in a letter written by Dr. D. Magner, president of the Canadian Association of Pathologists, on October 14, 1971.[14] Dr. Magner proposed that a separate division in the College be formed to represent the particular interests of specialists in laboratory medicine. He stated that some laboratory physicians, more than any other specialists in the Division of Medicine, argued that they were not adequately represented by clinicians on Council, even those with an interest in the laboratory specialties. Many laboratory physicians found this arrangement unsatisfactory, and Dr. Magner advocated creation of an additional division in the College to serve the needs of laboratory medicine. He pointed to the situation in the United Kingdom, where pathologists had gained autonomy in The Royal College of Pathologists. In Canada, the College attempted to represent specialists but the laboratory medicine specialists, whose role was becoming increasingly important, wanted representation at a high level. The changes that had occurred in medicine seemed to demand it and, in this time of change in medicine, among those specialties most affected by the currents of change were those embraced by laboratory medicine. Dr. Magner thought that, particularly at this time, it was important for laboratory medicine to have continuing representation at the highest decision-making level of the College.

Dr. Magner was supported by Drs. J.M.S. Dixon and D.M. Robertson.[15] Dr. Dixon, president of the Canadian Association of Medical Microbiologists, wrote the College on December 7, 1971, to state that his association supported Dr. Magner. Dr. Dixon's opinion was similar to that of Dr. Magner: laboratory medicine comprised a large and ever-increasing variety of specialties and had evolved to the stage at which laboratory physicians must govern their affairs to a much greater extent than before. In Australia, as well as the United Kingdom, pathologists had formed a separate College. Dr. D.M. Robertson, chairman of the Canadian Association of Neuropathologists, wrote to Dr. J.H. Graham on December 8, 1971 to state that his association supported this stand.

The pathologists' request was discussed by the Executive Committee in January 1972. President R.C. Dickson, though not in favor of creation of a separate division in the College (the Act of Incorporation referred to medical and surgical divisions only), considered the matter important enough to warrant a committee being set up. The Executive Committee recommended, and Council then approved, that a joint study group comprising representatives of the College and the Canadian Association of Pathologists be set up. The SOGC-Royal College study group served as a model.

The first step in establishing a working liaison was to hold a meeting between representatives of the College and of laboratory medicine specialists. The College was represented by the President, Dr. J.H. Graham, and the chairmen of the College Specialty Committees in Pathology, Microbiology and Medical Biochemistry; the laboratory medicine group, by Drs. D. Magner, W.E.M. Corbett, W.L. Dunn, J.M.S. Dixon and J.C. Nixon.

The points made by the two sides may be compared by listing them in parallel:

Laboratory Medicine View	*Royal College View*
Discipline distinct from medicine and surgery.	College strength derived from its multidisciplinary character.
Discipline represented by six of 21 medical specialties currently recognized by College.	Continuous representation for all specialties on Council not feasible.
Discipline crosses the boundaries and serves as a coordinating influence for both medicine and surgery.	Specialty interests represented by specialty committees, and by the Examinations, Credentials and Accreditation Committees.
Interests so distinct as to preclude adequate representation by physicians or surgeons.	Granting division status to a small group (700 or 5 per cent of total) impossible without establishing precedent for other groups of equal or greater numbers.

The meeting decided to form a working party comprising Drs. D. Magner, A.C. Ritchie, J.H. Graham and F.N. Gurd. They would attempt to define ways in which the role of laboratory medicine could be enhanced in College activities under the present constitution.

The working party, which met on June 28, 1972, developed four proposals. These called for creating specialty committees in hematological pathology and anatomical pathology; changing the name of the Specialty Committee in Pathology to the Specialty Committee in General Pathology; establishing a Specialty Committee in Laboratory Medicine, comprising the chairmen of the specialty committees in the individual laboratory specialties; and adding up to five more seats to Council, not subject to the biennial electoral process, to broaden specialty representation "in the most appropriate fashion".

The last proposal took account of the fact that the size of Council had recently been reduced with the discontinuation of representation by the five Certificants. It was sufficiently interesting to lead the Executive Committee to recommend, at its September 1972 meeting, that a study be conducted to determine how specialty representation at Council might be improved. Council considered this recommendation in January 1973.

Council's reaction to the recommendation hinged on a preposition. Dr. R.B. Salter thought that the proposal touched on the whole concept of what Council really was. A Council member did not represent his geographic area, his language or his specialty, for Council was a group of individuals who sat together attempting to work out medical and surgical problems for the whole nation. Therefore, increased specialty representation *to* Council rather than *at* Council was what should be sought.

Dr. L. Horlick opposed the recommendation because it conflicted with the trend of recent years towards greater grassroots representation on Council. If specialty representation was to be improved, inviting representation to Council would be one answer. But, as Dr. Gurd pointed out, the main question was how laboratory medicine specialists could more effectively and physically be represented on Council. It was then resolved that specialty representation to Council be studied with a view to its improvement. Once again, it was necessary to find ways of enhancing the College's relationship with a specialty group.

Enhancing the College's Relations with the Specialties

The College's relations with the specialties have been fostered in two ways — cooperation directly with the national specialty groups and liaison through the College's specialty committees. The value of the College's relations with the specialties has long been recognized, but it received increasing attention in the 1970s.[16]

Cooperation with the National Specialty Societies and Associations*

The College's relationship with national specialty groups does not constitute true affiliation, for which there is no constitutional provision in the College. Rather, the relationship is based on a commonality of interests. Conversely, some of the specialty groups' interests are of no direct interest to the College and vice-versa. Even so, there are many areas of interest that lead to cooperation between the College and the various specialty groups. Because the specialty groups themselves form a matrix of such varied professional interests, the College benefits enormously from its relations with the specialty groups. To

---

*Here, the term 'specialty group' is used. The term 'national specialty society' is not precisely defined, and some groups use the term 'Association' rather than 'Society'. Moreover, while the term could be applied to groups representing specialties in which the College offers a specialty qualification, the College's relations cover several groups in which it does not (e.g., Canadian Critical Care Society, Canadian Society of Clinical Pharmacology and the Canadian Society for Surgery of the Hand [now Manus]).

some degree, the benefits are mutual, because for each individual specialty group the College, too, forms a matrix of varied professional interests that provide an opportunity for cross-fertilization of ideas.

The principal areas of cooperation are the following:

- The specialty groups are consulted on impending changes in training and evaluation policies. They were consulted in 1959 and 1960 on uniform training requirements for the Fellowship and Certification examinations and in 1971 on the single examination process. Two groups offered financial assistance for the development of multiple-choice question examinations in the specialties and some have prepared detailed educational objectives for residency training.
- Particularly in the 1970s, the College encouraged the specialty groups to integrate their annual meetings with the College's. By 1980, 18 specialty groups were meeting with the College in this manner, and 14 others were cooperating with the College in the development of the program for the College's annual scientific meeting.
- The College's Awards Committee and Fellowship Affairs Committee cooperate with some specialty groups in providing "speaker grants" to support Royal College-sponsored lectures at their meetings and in "event grants" for such meetings.
- The Canadian Anaesthetists' Society's work in developing a self-assessment program has been of interest to the College's Fellowship Affairs Committee, which has cooperated with the anesthetists in this respect.
- From 1971 to 1980 the College held five conferences to which were invited the presidents of the specialty groups as well as the chairmen of the College's specialty committees. Each Conference of Specialties dealt with a topic of general interest, but the conference in 1977 dealt specifically with the College's relationship with the specialties.
- The College regularly invites the specialty groups to submit the names of specialists to serve on the College's specialty committees.
- The specialty committees are encouraged to maintain liaison with the national specialty groups, including reporting to both the respective specialty group and the College.

Of these areas of cooperation, the Conference of Specialties has proved of great value in enhancing the College's relationship with the specialties, while liaison through the specialty committees has had its own unique value. Liaison provides two-way communication, and the specialties at times took the initiative in establishing communication. Often, indeed, officers of specialty groups presented their concerns directly to officers of the College, and joint study committees likewise proved useful channels of communication. A common complaint from specialty representatives was that their representation was not necessarily extended to the highest decision-making level (i.e., Council); and it may be that, in the future, alternative channels of communication may have to be devised. One such channel would be to establish a bicameral legislative system, consisting of a board of directors (similar to the present Council) and a Council of Specialty Representatives, which would have a consultative and advisory role and serve as a two-way link with the specialty groups.[17]

The Conferences of Specialties enhanced communication and cooperation between the College and the specialties by addressing specific issues of mutual interest. The 1971 conference, convened to discuss the College's plans for the single examination process, established a precedent, and a standing committee made up of specialty representatives was formed in 1972 as a result. By 1975, there was sufficient business for the Continuing Education Committee to justify formal consultation with the specialty groups, and in 1976 the Conference of Specialties was convened to discuss issues of common interest with specific reference to self-assessment evaluation and continuing medical education. This second conference established a tradition, for further conferences were held in 1977 (on the relationship of the College with the national specialty societies), in 1979 (on the timing of the annual meetings held by the College and the specialty societies) and in 1980 (on specialist manpower). These conferences proved valuable. The College provided leadership and a forum, while specialty representatives (specialty committee chairmen and the presidents or other representatives of the national specialty societies) presented the views and arguments of all the specialties in this common forum. The conferences were based on a commonality of interests, the need for communication and cooperation and the element of collegiality that joined together physicians who were, at the same time, both Fellows of the College and practising specialists.

At the third conference, which was convened to discuss the relationship between the College and the specialties, President R.B. Salter presented a position paper entitled "The Relationship Between the Specialties and the Royal College."[18] Drafted by the President in consultation with Vice-Presidents G. Hurteau and L.E. McLeod, this statement served as a working document for the 1977 conference. The President observed that virtually every decision made by the College had implications not only for the 16,000 Fellows but also for the specialty committees, the national specialty societies, the directors of the specialty training programs and the national associations of chairmen of academic departments. Despite existing mechanisms of written communication with these various groups and subgroups, communication had emanated mostly *from* the College and two-way communication required greater activity on the part of specialty groups. Specialties had, from time to time, suggested altering the composition of Council or all its many committees in order to have every specialty represented, but this was a logistical impossibility. A more useful approach was to augment and enlarge the Conference of Specialties. The previous two conferences, Dr. Salter emphasized, had produced "gratifying results" and improved the important relationships between the College and its specialty groups.

President Salter proposed a six-point plan for consideration by Council and by the specialties:

- National specialty societies should be further encouraged to nominate lists of proposed members of the specialty committees.
- A formal mechanism should be created to enable the specialty committee chairmen to report regularly to their members on College affairs and to the College on relevant specialty affairs.
- The Conference of Specialties should meet once every two years to discuss specific pre-Fellowship and post-Fellowship items of business.
- The membership of the committee should include the College's Executive Committee, the chairmen of the major College committees, the chairmen of the College specialty committees, and the presidents or secretaries (or both) of the national specialty societies.
- Mechanisms for communication between the program directors and chairmen of academic departments and the College should be developed.
- These recommendations should constitute the principal item for discussion at the 1977 Conference of Specialties.

The President's position paper was fully endorsed by the 1977 conference. Most of the comments suggested the need for clarification of a few points or for extension of the direction taken by Dr. Salter's paper. Specialty representation on Council was not an issue; rather, the absence of general criticism of the organization of Council indicated that, given some improvement in communication, the current structure was acceptable to the specialties. The complex fabric of the College's relationships with the specialties was being strengthened. The advantages of the College's being the single collective body representing all specialists was re-emphasized. The only other obvious alternative to this Council structure was a large encompassing confederation of societies. The overall result of the 1977 conference was to develop a more clearly defined and understood mechanism linking the College, the specialty societies and the medical schools. In summarizing the 1977 conference, Dr. L.E. McLeod posed six questions for further consideration, assuming that both the College and the societies would wish them to be answered in the affirmative. The questions were the following:

Would the societies accept the administrative inconvenience of preparing nomination lists for the specialty committees?

Would the national specialty societies provide the chairmen of the College specialty committees with "a clear voice and hearing" at key levels of the societies, each national society even accepting the College specialty committee chairman as the chairman of the society's education committee?

Would the national societies transmit information concerning education and research throughout their membership?

Would the College choose its specialty committees from the national society's nomination lists and look upon chairmanship as a form of joint appointment (each retaining its right of veto) and clarify issues when differences arose?

Would the College expedite management problems submitted?

Would the College ensure better communication with the program directors and reflect the concerns of the standing committees, the specialty committees and, hence, the national societies?

The fourth Conference of Specialties was held on January 13, 1979, principally to discuss the timing of the College's annual meeting in relation to the annual meetings of other organizations. Pressure for a change in timing from January had been growing for several years, the chief pressure point being the inclemency of the Canadian winter. Fellows, through their Regional Advisory Committees, had argued for change, and their argument carried more weight now that the College was giving attention to post-Fellowship affairs — as was indicated, for example, by the establishment of the Fellowship Affairs Committee and the formal addition of a Division of Membership Services (later, the Division of Fellowship Affairs) to the existing Division of Training and Evaluation and the Division of Administration and Finance. It was not easy to find a time of year for the meeting that would be acceptable to the many groups that held their annual meetings in conjunction with that of the College. The decision that had been already taken to hold the 1980 meeting in June was influenced in part by the wishes of the Canadian Association of General Surgeons (CAGS), but this decision meant that many members of CSCI would not be able to attend the College meeting in June, when numerous medical meetings always took place. Beyond 1980, however, the College would take no decisions, and the 1979 conference was convened to take up the matter from there.

A round-robin discussion at the 1979 conference yielded the following arguments for and against meetings at particular times of the year. June being a popular month for meetings in Canada, no fewer than 15 societies representing College-recognized specialty groups had traditionally held their annual meetings in that month; with the decision of the newly formed CAGS to meet in June, the total was 16. Of these 16, only two specialties (anesthesia and pathology) were interested in holding their meetings in conjunction with the College's should the College continue to hold its annual meeting in June. The reasons for this lack of interest included a fear that the character and identity of specialty meetings would be lost or altered, removal of the advantage for small societies in being able to rotate their meetings through a wider range of Canadian centres and the possibility that the social aspects of individual societies' meetings would be lost or diminished. An example of this position was provided by the neurosurgeons and neurologists; while they valued the opportunity to attend the College's meeting, June was an important time for them because the Canadian Neurosurgical Society, the Canadian Neurological Society, the Child Neurology Association, the Canadian Association of Neurological Nurses and the Canadian Society for Neuroscience all met together in the Canadian Congress of Neurological Sciences, which was clearly a unique forum and not to be missed. Thirteen specialty groups (six College-recognized specialties and seven other specialty groups) customarily met in conjunction with the College, and, of them, at least eight felt an equal or even greater affinity to CSCI. In addition, two of the societies that met yearly in June but had actively participated in the College's January meetings would find it "extremely unfortunate" if the College and the CSCI meetings were divorced from one another. This situation might be avoided if a joint College-CSCI meeting was found possible in the middle of September or early October. A meeting date in early September or early October would avoid CSCI-related conflicts, and other groups would probably participate at this time, even if it were on a reduced scale. Finally, even a date in September or October was not perfect, for some people were still on vacation, others were concerned about their children's school year or their own academic year and others observed the Jewish religious holidays. The final decision, however, would be the College's. While consensus at the conference was one of sympathetic understanding of the problem and difficulties by all concerned, it was agreed that the College must make a decision on the basis of its own interests, needs and objectives. The specialty groups would then attempt to adapt to any change to the extent that they might find it possible or desirable.

A fifth conference was held on April 26, 1980. This concerned specialist physician manpower. Its format was more structured than the previous conferences, the program consisting of specific presentations in the morning, to which the specialty groups responded in the afternoon. The topics included the following: the College's role and record in physician manpower matters (R.W. Gunton); the Manpower Requirements Committee report (J.B.R. McKendry); stock flow and projection of physicians by specialty (W.A. Mennie); characteristics of specialists certificated by the College from 1970 to 1979 (T.J. Giles); the CMA's plans for a national physician data bank (D.L. Wilson); and the CFPC's dilemma, "Who are the Practising Doctors?" (D.I. Rice).

These conferences of the specialties proved most useful, even though their real value and benefits were at times questioned. In general, however, the College's relations with the specialties always reflected the College's concern about working through consent rather than control. The conferences testified to the College's attempts to foster its complex relationships and its efforts to pursue unity. The importance for the College of its liaison with the specialties was clearly summarized in the report of the Committee on Horizons: "Doubtless the most crucial category of organizations with which the College has close relationships, from the standpoint of the continued good health of the Royal College, are the national specialty societies."[19]

Liaison Through the Specialty Committees

The College's specialty committees have served as a link between the College and the specialties since 1937. Originally, the committees were associated with the Committee on Specialists and were designed to facilitate the introduction of the Certification program. They later became associated with the Credentials Committee when, after 1949, the Committee on Specialists merged with the Credentials Committee. It was not until 1956 that the advisory specialty committees were disengaged from the Credentials Committee to play a broader role that was advisory in relation to many College activities and policies. Because, since the presidential term of 1964-1966, the chairmen of the specialty committees have been appointed by the College's Executive Committee, the specialty committees provide the direct link between the College and each specialty. The wise appointment of a chairman means that both the College and the particular specialty benefit: the College, by being apprised of a specialty's opinions, needs and wishes; the specialty, by being provided with a clear channel of communication that facilitates appropriate and prompt discussion, cooperation and action. The specialty groups are invited by the College to submit nominations for membership in the specialty committees, which makes for checks and balances in the total membership of a specialty committee. Ideally, the chairmen and the committee members enjoy the confidence of both the College and the respective national specialty group.

The specialty committees are primarily advisory, though the recommendations that they make carry much respect and weight. The committee may be consulted by any standing committee or by Council. The evolution of their consultative roles and functions has thus been dependent on the evolution of the structure of the College; the list of these functions that is set forth in Table 12.4 therefore reflects many of the important developments in the College from 1960 to 1980.

The roles and functions listed in Table 12.4 evolved slowly and in conformity with the evolving activities of the various College committees. With respect to the manner in which the advisory specialty committees operated, relatively few

TABLE 12.4 Consultative Roles and Functions of the Specialty Committees with Respect to Standing Committees.

Consulting Standing Committee(s)	Subject of Role/Function of Specialty Committee
Executive	Advice regarding important issues involving specialty. Names of individuals for Royal College lectureships, Honorary Fellowships, special ad hoc committees.
Accreditation	Basic accreditation requirements in specialty. Applications for accreditation of Canadian residency programs. On-site accreditation survey reports and follow-up progress reports. Choice of surveyors to serve on residency program accreditation visits.
Credentials	Statements of training objectives in specialty. Minimum requirements of training for eligibility for examinations. Credentials of candidates with unusual training.
Examinations	Recommendations of nominees for examining boards and multiple-choice question test committee. Review of content, conduct and standards of examinations.
Specialties and Manpower	Existing and projected physician needs. Impact of recognition of new specialties or subspecialties.
Annual Meeting Program	Specialty participation in scientific program and arrangements for annual meeting.
Publications and Communications	Electoral policy and content of publications.
Biomedical Ethics	Bioethical issues and relationship to specialty training and practice.
Maintenance of Competence	Suitable forms of CME, including self-assessment programs, peer review, medical audit and patient care appraisal.
Regional Advisory	CME programs and activities at regional level.

changes were made between 1960 and 1980. Such changes in operation that were made are the following:

- Terms of reference were first drafted in January 1964.
- Regular scheduling of meetings, as opposed to occasional holding of meetings, was instituted in 1964.
- The policy that a committee chairman shall not serve for more than three consecutive two-year terms was established in January 1968.
- Terms of reference, as approved in January 1964, were reviewed and confirmed in February 1970 and since.
- The Canadian Association of Professors of Medicine was invited to propose names for membership in the Specialty Committee in Internal Medicine as from January 1977 — the only instance of an association of departmental heads recommending membership of a specialty committee.
- The position of Director of Specialties to improve liaison with and to provide service for the specialty committees and groups was created in January 1980. Dr. J.H. Graham was appointed to this post after he retired from the post of Secretary at the end of 1979.

NOTES TO CHAPTER 12

1. Two definitions of the term 'specialist' are useful in this connection. The first was proposed by Dr. F.S. Patch, who had a great interest in the College's Certification program. He wrote that a specialist is "one who devotes himself to a particular branch of a profession, science, or art; one who has a special knowledge of some particular subject" ("Certification of Specialists", *Can Med Assoc J* 1947; 51:261-264). The second is that given by Dr. E.S. Ryerson, whose editorial in the *Canadian Medical Association Journal* (1933; 29:72-73), entitled "The Qualification of Specialists in Canada", was most influential. In a report of the CMA's Committee on Specialists for Oct. 23, 1934, he wrote as follows: "A practitioner of medicine entitled to call himself a 'specialist' is one (a) who has fulfilled certain minimum educational requirements in the special field of practice which he is desirous of practising, along with the attainment of a superior knowledge in the fundamental subjects (anatomy, physiology, biochemistry, pathology, etc.) which underlie diagnosis and treatment in this special branch of practice; and (b) who has successfully passed a 'specialist' examination conducted for the purpose of determining whether or not he is adequately qualified to practise in this special field of practice."
2. R.W. Gunton, "The Development of the Specialties." In Andison and Robichon, pp. 71-76.
3. A.H. Neufeld, K.R. MacKenzie, Letter to J.H. Graham, Nov. 11, 1963.
4. J.A. Dauphinee, et al, Letter to J.H. Graham, Jan. 19, 1964.
5. R.W. Gunton, p. 75.
6. R.W. Gunton, p. 75.
7. Executive Committee, July 1967.
8. J.C. Beck, Letter to J.H. Graham, Oct. 2, 1960.

9. Lewis, pp. 71-72. See also Council, June 1950, pp. 12-14, for an account of a meeting between the SOGC and the Council of the College. The SOGC had requested that obstetrics and gynecology be placed "on an equal footing" with medicine and surgery in the College, but this was not permitted by the Act of Incorporation. "It was apparent throughout the meeting", the minutes record, "that each group understood the problems and difficulties of the other, and a very pleasing spirit of amicability and compromise pervaded the entire discussion." The minutes of Council reported that the Credentials Committee discussed nine requests and suggestions by the SOGC. While not all of these requests were granted, the fact that they were discussed and granted in part is illustrative of the College's willingness to go as far as commonality of interests and collegiality would permit.

10. G.B. Maughan, Letter to J.H. Graham, Dec. 20, 1960.

11. G.B. Maughan, Letter to J.H. Graham, Dec. 13, 1958.

12. A similar criticism of marks given by pathologists was made in 1962 (see Chapter 9).

13. F.L. Johnson, Letter to J.H. Graham, Feb. 13, 1970.

14. D. Magner, Letter to J.H. Graham, Oct. 14, 1971.

15. J.M.S. Dixon, Letter to J.H. Graham, Dec. 7, 1971; D.M. Robertson, Letter to J.H. Graham, Dec. 8, 1971.

16. For a detailed account of this topic, see the memorandum by J.H. Graham, "The Royal College and the Specialty Societies", reproduced in Executive Committee, December 1981, Attachment 17.

17. Report of the Committee on Horizons of the Royal College of Physicians and Surgeons of Canada to the Council of the Royal College, 1977 (R.A. Macbeth, chairman), pp. 185-190.

18. R.B. Salter, "The Relationship Between the Specialties and the Royal College", Executive Committee, January 1977, Attachment 1.

19. Report of the Committee on Horizons, 1977, p. 152.

PART 5

THE DELICATE FABRIC

Donald A. Thompson

Chapter 13

The Quintessence of Fellowship: Biographical Sketches of the Presidents, 1960-1980

In the period covered by this history, the College was led by 11 Presidents. That each of them became President because of outstanding personal and professional attributes almost goes without saying, and the biographical sketches of the Presidents drawn in this chapter serve mainly to highlight these attributes, but these sketches serve other purposes besides. First, through the medium of the presidency something of the essence of Fellowship in The Royal College of Physicians and Surgeons of Canada becomes manifest, albeit clothed in the individual style of a particular Fellow. In the collective portrait of the Presidents is distilled a flavor of this essence. Second, each President was a Fellow and a specialist long before being elected to the presidency, and each participated in various of the College's activities. These biographical sketches therefore reveal something of these activities and the College's concerns from 1960 to 1980. And third, each of the Presidents dealt with problems, issues and challenges that were peculiar to specialist practice in Canada. Hence these sketches are portraits of the "delicate fabric" out of which specialist practice in Canada has been woven and of the matrix from which The Royal College of Physicians and Surgeons of Canada has evolved as an individual and singular specialists' college in Canada. The Canadian College has developed in response to Canadian circumstances and needs; and, while the history of the College is more than a collection of biographies of its great men, these biographical sketches do illustrate how a few of its Fellows shaped the College's response to Canadian circumstances and needs between 1960 and 1980.

Donald Arthur Thompson, 1960-1962

Born on November 2, 1908, in Stellarton, Nova Scotia. Graduated MD, CM from Dalhousie University in 1933. Became a Certificant of the College in 1944 and a Fellow in 1949. Died in Halifax on January 5, 1980, aged 71 years.

G. Malcolm Brown

Dr. Donald Thompson brought sound common sense, a practical approach and leadership to his work as a general surgeon in Bathurst, New Brunswick. Trained at The Montreal General Hospital in general surgery from 1933 to 1937, he did much to raise the standard of surgery in his county. Dr. Thompson was granted a Certificate in the initial phase of the Certification program, but he did not rest on his laurels; he proceeded to study for the Fellowship examination while in full-time practice and was successful in his effort to obtain the Fellowship in general surgery by examination in 1949.

Elected to the Council of the College in 1953, he brought to Council the perspective of one who practised in a non-academic setting. While a councillor, he chaired the Hospitals Approval Committee in the early years of the hospitals approval program, bringing to the committee his experience as a CMA representative on the Canadian Commission on Hospital Accreditation.

It was entirely appropriate that a surgeon who was well versed in the problems of rural practice should become President when the College had just taken a decision to abolish the dual standard of specialist examinations and practice. In his valedictory address to the Fellows at the 1962 annual business meeting, he offered an observation that was precisely pertinent to the issues of the day. "The years ahead," Dr. Thompson ventured, "should bring all groups in the College closer together — an amalgamation of academic interests fused with high principles of service." The President's observation was a perceptive recognition of one aspect of the College's pursuit of unity.

George Malcolm Brown, 1962-1964

Born on July 16, 1916, in Campbellford, Ontario. Graduated MD, CM from Queen's University in 1938. Became a Fellow of the College in 1946 *ad eundem gradum.* Died in Toronto on May 19, 1977, aged 60 years.

The promise of a notable career was evident early in Dr. Malcolm Brown's life. He obtained his MD degree at the age of 21 and, as a Rhodes Scholar, his D.Phil. from Oxford University at the age of 23. After service with the Armed Forces during the Second World War, Dr. Brown returned to Queen's University and in due course was appointed Professor of Medicine. Noted for his clinical competence and teaching ability, Dr. Brown will be remembered longest for his influence on Canadian medical research. He became president of the Medical Research Council of Canada in 1965, and of his contributions between then and his death it was said of him that he might well have been the most important single influence on the quality of Canadian health research from the mid-1960s to the mid-1970s. He was an Officer of the Order of Canada.

Dr. Brown's stature as a leader in medicine was evident in many ways outside research. In organized medicine, he became president of the CPSO in 1956 and, unusually, was president for two years instead of one. Of the CPSO and

Walter C. MacKenzie

the Royal College, he was the youngest President ever elected. His ability to lead derived in part from laserlike precision of intellect and crystal clarity of expression. In the Royal College, before becoming President, Dr. Brown's presidential potential became apparent when he served as the member of the Executive Committee chosen at large from the Council from 1955 to 1957, when he chaired the Credentials Committee and when he was a member of the Hospitals Approval Committee. After his term as President, chairmanship of the Publications Committee led him to steer the *Annals* to publication of its first issue in 1968. He was also a valued member of the Expanded Executive Committee in 1969 and of the team that surveyed the McLaughlin Centre in 1977.

Despite his academic preeminence, Dr. Malcolm Brown remained at heart a practising physician whose primary concern was the care and cure of the sick. He insisted that medicine means the total care of the patient, and he demanded that a physician work only at the full range of his capability. The nearly good, Dr. Brown held, could never reasonably be substituted for the best; and less than the nearly good was intolerable.

Dr. Brown's unrivaled qualities of intellect, integrity and leadership contributed in no small measure to the respect that the College was beginning to earn in the 1960s, both nationally and internationally.

Walter Campbell MacKenzie, 1964-1966

Born on August 17, 1909, in Glace Bay, Nova Scotia. Graduated MD, CM from Dalhousie University in 1933. Became a Fellow of the College in 1948. Died in Edmonton on December 15, 1978, aged 69 years.

Dr. Walter Mackenzie took his surgical training at The Royal Victoria Hospital in Montreal and at the Mayo Clinic. At the Mayo Clinic, his surgical ability was recognized when he became one of only a few who served as surgical assistant during the training period. His personal charm and magnetism enabled him to develop lasting friendships and respect among American surgeons; later in life, he became one of only six Fellows of the College to be elected to the presidency of the American College of Surgeons and, with Dr. C.G. Drake, one of only two Fellows to be elected to the presidency of the American and the Canadian Colleges. Dr. MacKenzie also achieved the unusual distinction of being elected to the presidency of no fewer than one-half of the professional organizations to which he belonged — the American College of Surgeons, ACMC, the International Federation of Surgical Colleges and the James IV Association of Surgeons being among the most notable. His international renown was further evident in his election to the Moynihan Lectureship of The Royal College of Surgeons of England, the Sir Arthur Sims Travelling Professorship and the Digby Lectureship of the University of Hong Kong. He was an Honorary Fellow of The Royal College of Surgeons of Edinburgh and the same honor was bestowed on him in Glasgow and England and Ireland.

Robert B. Kerr

In Canada, after service in the Royal Canadian Navy during the Second World War, he likewise achieved renown. He was appointed Professor and Chairman of the Department of Surgery at the University of Alberta in 1949 and Dean of the Faculty of Medicine in 1959. Honors such as the Centennial Medal (1967), officership in the Order of Canada (1970), the College's Duncan Graham Award (1971) and the CMA's F.N.G. Starr Award (1974) confirmed the respect in which he was held in Canada.

In the College, Dr. MacKenzie was chairman of the Ethics Committee, Vice-Chairman of the Educational Endowment Fund Committee and Vice-President (Surgery) from 1962 to 1964, before becoming President. The period of his presidency was notable for the first steps that were taken to bring the Certificants into a closer relationship with the College; the Committee on Policy, which he chaired, made recommendations that led to the affiliation of the Certificants in 1967. Afterwards, he lent his counsel to the Expanded Executive Committee in 1969, and to the Fellowship Affairs Committee, as the first chairman of the Awards Committee from 1976 to 1979.

Dr. Walter MacKenzie was a gregarious man who was attracted to others and who likewise attracted others, both in Canada and around the world. His personal qualities, allied to his surgical knowledge and skill, stood the College in great stead and further enhanced the College's growing stature in his native country and abroad.

Robert Bews Kerr, 1966-1968

Born on August 20, 1908, in Hamilton, Ontario. Graduated MD from the University of Toronto in 1933. Became a Fellow of the College *ad eundem gradum* in 1945.

Dr. Robert Kerr's interest in internal medicine was awakened before he completed his medical studies, and it was heightened by working with Professor Charles Best on protamine zinc insulin in 1935 and with Sir Harold Himsworth on diabetes mellitus in London immediately before the Second World War. Wartime service rounded his education and brought him some unusual experiences: he looked after more than 400 patients with diphtheria and some 650 concentration camp victims. Both his pleasing personality and his devotion to duty inspired all he came into contact with, and when he returned to Toronto after the war he was the complete physician. He became head of the Department of Therapeutics at the University of Toronto, where Professor Duncan Graham set the example of academic practice and teaching that so many followed. Dr. Graham's approach to teaching was a valuable model and, when Dr. Kerr moved to the University of British Columbia in 1950 to become the first head of the new department of medicine there, something of the Duncan Graham school went with Dr. Kerr. At the University of British Columbia, Dr. Kerr established himself as a fine clinician and teacher, and his

Jacques Turcot

talents were recognized in 1959 by his appointment as the Sir Arthur Sims Commonwealth Travelling Professor.

Dr. Robert Kerr's contributions to the College, besides the presidency, included membership in and chairmanship of the Bylaws Committee. He was also a member and chairman of the Hospitals Approval Committee, in which capacity he was, with Dr. D.R. Webster, the first to conduct a Royal College survey of training programs. His presidency was notable for the inception of the arrangement whereby Certificants were able to affiliate with the College, and the knowledge and understanding he gained thereby served him well when he participated in the discussions conducted by the Expanded Executive Committee in 1969. Dr. Kerr's presidency was also notable for the publication of the first volume of the *Annals*.

Outside the College, Dr. Kerr's other contributions to Canadian medicine included his work with the MCC and his historical writings. Dr. Kerr was president of the MCC in 1968, a time of great progress in evaluation and examination methodology, both in the MCC and in the College. His interest in history led him to write a much admired history of the MCC, which was published in 1979. Dr. Robert Kerr continues to interest himself in history and in the College, and is engaged in writing the biographies of two of the College's Past-Presidents, Drs. Duncan Graham and Ray Farquharson.

Jacques Turcot, 1968-1970

Born on October 26, 1914, in Quebec City. Graduated MD from Laval University in 1940. Became a Fellow of the College in 1943. Died in Quebec City on April 9, 1977, aged 63 years.

Dr. Jacques Turcot came from a Quebec family whose members all distinguished themselves in the professions. He trained as a general surgeon and spent his professional career in Quebec City. A charming and athletic man, he was a fine teacher and an able administrator and in due course became Professor and Head of the Department of Surgery at Laval University.

Dr. Turcot made many contributions to the College. He was an examiner in general surgery from 1947 to 1955 and a councillor from 1962 to 1972 — a decade in which profound changes reshaped the College. He was a member of many committees, including the Bylaws, Credentials, Finance and Publications Committees and chairman of the Ethics Committee from 1966 to 1968. He was Vice-President (Surgery) from 1964 to 1966. As President, he led Council, and especially the Expanded Executive Committee, in 1969, into defining new objectives for the College and in launching the process of examination reform that culminated in the introduction of the single examination process in 1972.

Dr. Jacques Turcot was an ardent and respected Quebecer who recognized the value of the College to his colleagues in Quebec. His perspective as a French-Canadian was an important one in the College in a period in which

Robert C. Dickson

national unity was challenged and even threatened. His viewpoint was a factor in the decision to term the new examination 'Certification' and in the drafting of guidelines for bilingualism in the College. At the same time, as President of the College, he recognized the national role that the College had in Canada — "the role of the sole able national institution to keep high identical standards from the Atlantic to the Pacific," as he put it. He did much to ensure that the College did this "always with the respect of the bicultural and bilingual character of our country." His services to his country were fittingly honored when the Order of Canada was bestowed on him.

Robert Clark Dickson, 1970-1972

Born on September 24, 1908, in St. Mary's, Ontario. Graduated MD from the University of Toronto in 1934. Became a Fellow of the College in 1945. Died in Vancouver on February 18, 1984, aged 75 years.

Dr. Robert Clark Dickson's scholastic ability was evident long before he graduated; he was elected to membership in the Alpha Omega Alpha Medical Society in 1932. He graduated with honors, and the Cody Silver Medal, and immediately took five years' training in internal medicine at The Toronto General Hospital. As were Presidents R.B. Kerr and K.J.R. Wightman, President Dickson was greatly influenced by Professor Duncan Graham, who headed the Department of Medicine and was, during Dr. Dickson's residency, President of the College. After serving in the Royal Canadian Army Medical Corps during the Second World War, Dr. Dickson returned to the University of Toronto. Here, his ability to teach won him lasting respect. After a period as Physician-in-Chief at The Wellesley Hospital, he was appointed Professor and Head of the Department of Medicine at Dalhousie University in 1956. Over the next 18 years, Dr. Dickson's outstanding ability as a teacher was confirmed as his residents obtained superior results in the Fellowship examinations; the presentation to him of the Duncan Graham Award in 1974 marked his excellence as a medical educator. But he was a fine clinician, too, with a primary interest in gastroenterology. His stature is remembered in the Robert Clark Dickson Lectureship at Dalhousie University and in the Robert Clark Dickson Centre for Ambulatory Care and Oncology Research in the Victoria General Hospital in Halifax.

Before he became President, Dr. Robert Clark Dickson made numerous contributions to the College. As chairman of the Bylaws Committee from 1960 to 1962, he oversaw a review of the College's Bylaws. He then co-chaired the Credentials Committee, during the period when the College was attempting to bring uniformity to its training standards and requirements for the Fellowship and Certification examinations. He was also a member of the Ethics Committee. From 1964 to 1966, Dr. Dickson was the member of the Executive Committee chosen at large from the Council.

Charles G. Drake

When Dr. Dickson became President, both his knowledge of the College and his dedication to it were profound. To his concept of the College and of the presidency, he brought also his experience as a Governor and then a Regent of the American College of Physicians. Such a broad perspective was invaluable. It was Dr. Dickson's responsibility to lead the College in replacing the dual standard of specialty qualification with a single standard. In short, Dr. Dickson presided over the emergence of the 'new' College. He discharged this heavy responsibility with wise statemanship, particularly as he explained Council's proposals to the Fellows, endeavoring to reach a consensus at the same time by learning the views of the Fellows themselves. He discharged this responsibility with dogged tenacity of purpose also, for he visited no fewer than 21 cities in the Fall of 1970 — even though he was in constant pain from osteoarthritis. That Council's proposals for change were approved and implemented was in large measure the result of Dr. Robert Dickson's unselfish dedication to the College, and thereby to Canadian medicine. His appointment to the Order of Canada was a singularly well-deserved honor.

In his capacity as chairman of the Board of Governors of the R.S. McLaughlin Examination and Research Centre Dr. Robert Dickson continued to serve the College after he completed his presidential term.

Charles George Drake, 1972-1974

Born on July 21, 1920, in Windsor, Ontario. Graduated MD from the University of Western Ontario in 1944. Became a Fellow of the College in 1951.

Dr. Charles Drake has achieved international as well as national fame, both in clinical medicine and in organized medicine. In the clinical field, his singular achievements in neurosurgery (especially the surgery of cerebrovascular aneurysms) have led to his being recognized world-wide. Dr. Drake trained at the University of Western Ontario (in physiology, neurophysiology and surgery), Yale University (as J.H. Brown Fellow in neurophysiology) and the University of Toronto (in neurosurgery and neuropathology); he also studied in England (in London at the National Hospital, Queen's Square, and in Oxford) and in Sweden (in Stockholm). In organized medicine, he is one of only two Royal College Presidents to have become President of the Royal College as well as the American College of Surgeons. He has been prominent also in the Canadian Neurosurgical Society, the Canadian Association of Clinical Surgeons, the American Academy of Neurological Surgeons, and the Harvey Cushing Society, and he has served as editor of publications for the World Federation of Neurological Societies and he has been a member of the editorial board of the *Journal of Neurosurgery*. He is an Officer of the Order of Canada.

Dr. Charles George Drake, therefore, brought to the College a broad perspective on the training and practice of specialists and on the roles of specialists' colleges. After serving for four years as an examiner for neurosur-

K.J.R. Wightman

gery, he was elected to Council in 1962. As a councillor, he made contributions in two particular areas — the chairmanship of the Hospitals Approval Committee from 1966 to 1972 and membership in the Expanded Executive Committee in 1969. As chairman of the Hospitals Approval Committee, he played an important role in initiating the College's program of on-site surveys of approved postgraduate programs; as a member of the Expanded Executive, he participated in the discussions that led to the formulation of new objectives for the College and their approval in 1972. Dr. Drake was Vice-President (Surgery) from 1968 to 1970. As President, he continued the work of his predecessors by ensuring that the 'new' College would represent the interests of all specialists in Canada.

Much of Dr. Drake's time and energy during the first half of his Presidency was spent in an intensive effort to achieve unity among the Fellows, some of whom opposed the admission of pre-1972 Certificants to Fellowship without their having passed the Fellowship examination. Matters came to a head at the 1973 annual business meeting, held in Edmonton. It was largely Dr. Drake's statesmanship as President in 1972 and as chairman of the 1973 meeting that prevented the interests of elitism from jeopardizing the integrity of the 'new' College.

Keith John Roy Wightman, 1974-1976

Born on May 12, 1914, in Sandwich, Ontario. Graduated MD from the University of Toronto in 1937. Became a Fellow of the College in 1942. Died on March 10, 1978, in Toronto, aged 63 years.

Dr. "Kager" Wightman trained as an internist at the University of Toronto, where he came under the influence of Professor Duncan Graham; he also took some of his training in the United Kingdom. His special interests in clinical medicine were hematology and oncology. His academic career was spent in Toronto, where he was Professor of Therapeutics and then Professor and Chairman of the Department of Medicine at the University of Toronto. In the latter part of his career, his interest in education was reflected in his directorship of the Division of Postgraduate Medical Education in the university. He was Medical Director of The Ontario Cancer Treatment and Research Foundation, and he worked closely with the Canadian Hepatic Foundation and the Canadian Society for Chemotherapy. He was always a fine clinician; his sharp intelligence combined with modesty and sincerity of manner and clarity of expression won him wide respect; and his sometimes serious mien combined with friendliness and an undercurrent of humor gained him trust from patients and physicians alike. (Dr. Wightman had a neat turn of phrase: he admitted to playing the violin "for my own amazement" and having to learn by trial and error, and it always seemed to him that "my first trial is bound to be an error.")

Robert B. Salter

Dr. Wightman was elected to Council in 1964. He was co-chairman of the medical division of the Credentials Committee from 1964 to 1970 and chairman from 1970 to 1972. Before becoming President he was chairman of the Publications Committee and a member of the Education Committee, the Educational Endowment Fund Committee and the Specialty Development Committee. He was also the member of the Executive Committee chosen at large from the Council from 1968 to 1970 and a member of the Expanded Executive in 1969.

As President, Dr. Wightman was concerned particularly with the organization and structure of the College, with the College's regional organization and with the need to develop the College's educational expertise to the needs of the Fellows. For him, the presidency meant establishing himself as an asset for the College rather than being a figurehead. He stressed the importance of communication — "I don't think it's a matter of trying to take credit for things that are accomplished," he said, "but really one of trying to produce more effective communication." One of the innovations during his presidency was the creation of the Regional Advisory Committees, which have enhanced communication between Council and the Fellows.

Robert Bruce Salter, 1976-1978

Born on December 15, 1924, in Stratford, Ontario. Graduated MD from the University of Toronto in 1947. Became a Fellow of the College in 1955.

Dr. Robert Salter's interest in medicine was awakened during childhood, when he was inspired by the example of the family physician's care of his brother. Likewise, his interest in teaching grew after he coached his sick brother so that he would not fall behind in his school work. He trained in general and orthopedic surgery by enrolling in the Gallie Course in Toronto and spent a year in England as a McLaughlin Travelling Fellow. He returned to Toronto to join the staff of The Hospital for Sick Children, where he became Surgeon-in-Chief in 1966. The surgical problems of children were of deep interest to him; the dedication to his patients is summarized in the remark about him that "he wants to put dancing shoes on them all." His authority as a pediatric orthopedic surgeon came from his research into Legg-Calvé-Perthes disease and from the operation of innominate osteotomy that he designed for children with congenital hip disease; and his renown was enhanced by his publishing a standard textbook on disorders and injuries of the musculoskeletal system. Numerous awards and professorships testify to his international stature — a Gairdner International Award in 1969, the Sir Arthur Sims Commonwealth Travelling Professorship in 1973, the Nicolas Andry Award in 1974 and the Charles Mickle Award in 1975. He is an Officer of the Order of Canada.

Dr. Salter, after being elected to Council in 1968, became a member of the Hospitals Approval Committee, the Educational Endowment Fund Committee

389

Douglas G. Cameron

and the Education Committee. He was chairman of the Grants and Awards Committee and of the Continuing Education Committee. He was Vice-President (Surgery) from 1970 to 1972.

Some of Dr. Salter's deepest concerns were reflected in the innovations made during his presidency. His interest in moral and ethical issues led him to establish the Biomedical Ethics Committee in January 1977; he was chairman of the committee from 1978 to 1980 and a member of it from 1980 to 1982. His interest in research convinced him that the College should create a vehicle in order to monitor research activities, and the Research Committee was established in January 1977 also; he was a member of this committee from 1978 to 1980. A third committee that was formed during his presidency was the Maintenance of Competence Committee; struck in June 1976, this committee reflected Dr. Salter's interest in continuing medical education and the contributions he had already made to the theoretical base of the College's approach to this activity. President Salter also helped forge a closer relationship between the College and the national specialty societies, and his position paper on this subject clarified aspects of this relationship.

One of Dr. Robert Bruce Salter's avocations is the study of heraldry. He was president of the Canadian Heraldry Society for one term and he has advised the College on heraldic matters. His chapter on the College's armorial bearings in the College's fiftieth anniversary volume is both informative of this aspect of the College's life and reflective of his own contribution to the College as a Canadian professional organization.

Douglas George Cameron, 1978-1980

Born on March 11, 1917, in Folkestone, England. Graduated MD, CM from McGill University in 1940. Became a Fellow of the College in 1951.

Dr. Douglas Cameron, after graduating from McGill University and winning the Wood Gold Medal and the Francis Stewart Memorial Prize, interned at The Montreal General Hospital. Although he was named the Rhodes Scholar for Saskatchewan in 1940, Dr. Cameron immediately joined the Royal Canadian Army Medical Corps and served as a medical officer throughout the Second World War. He was awarded the Military Cross while serving as a Regimental Medical Officer with the Royal Canadian Regiment.

With the cessation of hostilities, Dr. Cameron was able to take up his Rhodes Scholarship at Oxford University. He studied with Professor L.J. Witts and commenced a long series of important original contributions to medicine by reporting the relationship of macrocytic anemia to gastrointestinal structure and function. He returned to Canada as a Senior Medical Research Fellow of the National Research Council of Canada and became one of a small number of clinical investigators who greatly influenced clinical research in Canada. In 1957 he became physician-in-chief at The Montreal General Hospital and

Bernard J. Perey

chairman of the Canadian Clinical Travel Club, the forerunner of CSCI. In the same year he became Professor of Medicine at McGill University, and from 1964 to 1969 and from 1974 to 1981 he was chairman of the Department of Medicine at McGill University. His spirit of scholarly scientific enquiry influenced all he worked with and ultimately, through them, faculties of medicine across the country. His influence spread far and wide, for he led McGill University in plans to improve medical care in both the Canadian Arctic (the Baffin Zone Project) and Kenya (the McGill University-Canadian International Development Agency Kenya Medical Development Project). He is an Officer of the Order of Canada.

Dr. Douglas Cameron's interest in the College grew as he became a close associate of Dr. E.S. Mills, who was Vice-President (Medicine) from 1953 to 1955. Dr. Cameron's service to the College was distinguished, both in itself and in its length. He served not only as President for longer than any other (for two and one-half years) but also as a councillor for longer than any other (for 14 years). His knowledge of the College was therefore profound. He was a member of the Credentials Committee, the Hospitals Approval Committee and the Educational Endowment Fund Committee and he was chairman of the Annual Awards Committee, the Scientific Meetings Arrangements Committee and the Education Committee. He was Vice-President (Medicine) from 1970 to 1972. Clarity of vision and expression were prominent among Dr. Cameron's personal attributes, and these attributes were of great value to the College during the meetings of the Expanded Executive, of which he was a member in 1969.

Like his predecessors in office, Dr. Cameron realized that the College's pursuit of unity was essential to the incorporation of so many specialties in the College; he realized that the "creative tensions" that arose from such an association could either cause division or create harmony. "Certainly for the foreseeable future," he wrote in 1979, "the advantages of a strong, united College far outweigh any benefits fragmentation might seem to offer."

Bernard Jean François Perey, 1980-1982

Born in Paris, France, on April 28, 1930. Graduated MD from McGill University in 1956. Became a Fellow of the College in 1962.

Dr. Bernard Perey trained in general surgery in Montreal and Boston. His training completed, he was appointed to the Department of Surgery at The Royal Victoria Hospital, Montreal. A dynamic personality together with clarity of viewpoint and skills in organization led him to facilitate organization of la Fédération des médecins spécialistes du Québec and of the Association of Surgeons of the Province of Quebec. Deeply interested in all aspects of medical education, he became the founding professor and chairman of the Department of Surgery in the stimulating environment of the University of Sherbrooke. In

1983, he became Professor and Chairman of the Department of Surgery at Dalhousie University. He has been president of the Canadian Association of Gastroenterology and of the Canadian Association of General Surgeons.

Dr. Perey's contributions to the College began in 1967, when he became an examiner in general surgery. In 1968, he was appointed a member of the Educational Endowment Fund Committee and of the Supply and Distribution of Specialists Committee; and in 1970 he was appointed to the Examinations Committee. He became more widely known in 1970, when a speech he gave in proposing a motion concerning "the structure of the Nominating Committee, the election of Council and the structure of Council itself" marked him as a Fellow with great potential vis-a-vis the future of the College. He joined Council in January 1972 and was immediately appointed chairman of the Examinations Committee. This office provided him with a forum in which he exerted a profound influence on the thinking of many important issues, quite apart from those of education, evaluation and examination. He was Vice-President (Surgery) from 1974 to 1976.

As President, Dr. Bernard Perey stressed the importance of management skills and the planning process. He emphasized the need for each incoming Executive Committee to address outstanding issues afresh, and the retreat that he organized for the Executive Committee in August 1980 was an indication of a new businesslike approach of the College.

Chapter 14

The College and Medicine in Canada: A Conclusion

I

Whatever the shortcomings of the College, the fact of its survival... presupposes some good qualities, which must include tenacity of purpose and adaptability. The massive social, political, economic, and scientific changes that have occurred...have inevitably altered the structure of the College, modified the views of the fellows...and affected its place within the medical world and the larger world outside. The College has for the most part obtained and held the loyalty of the great majority of its fellows.... If the College's affairs have sometimes seemed to be largely in the hands of the President and officers, it is because these men have spent much more time and trouble on College business than the generality of the fellows... .[1]

These words were written not about The Royal College of Physicians and Surgeons of Canada but about The Royal College of Physicians of London, yet they are relevant to the much younger Canadian College, which celebrated its 50th anniversary in 1979. They also serve as a text for a concluding discussion on the evolution of the Canadian College. Both shortcomings and good qualities have characterized the Canadian College, and the latter have indeed included tenacity of purpose and adaptability. Between 1960 and 1980, social, political, economic and scientific changes were indeed massive, and these changes in turn induced changes in the structure of the College, in the views of its Fellows and in the place of the College within the medical profession and within Canadian society. As the College changed and grew — and change and growth were acute in these two decades — the majority of its Fellows remained loyal to the College, whose officers did indeed spend much time and trouble on College business.

The broad similarity in the effects of change and growth of The Royal College of Physicians and Surgeons of Canada to that of The Royal College of

Physicians of London is, perhaps, not surprising. Both are colleges whose members have been concerned with developing and maintaining competence in the service of their patients; both have endeavored to ensure that their members deliver high-quality specialist health care; and both colleges have fulfilled their several responsibilities within the framework of professionalization. Professionalization, whereby the production of knowledge and skills shapes, and becomes integrated into, the precepts and practices of a profession,[2] is attuned to and indeed is determined by change. Professionalization is a dynamic process, and unless a professional organization adapts to the primacy of change that organization will not survive. The Canadian College has survived because, like the London College, it has recognized the imperative of change, and the remarkable events that characterized the College's transformation between 1960 and 1980 can be explained within the context of professionalization and the College's reaction to the imperative of change.

In these several ways the College has had an immense impact on health care in Canada.

One of the ways in which the College has made an impact, therefore, has been the manner in which it has served as an instrument of professionalization of the specialist cadre in Canada; it has served, in Dr. A.L. Chute's words, as "an integrating force for all specialists".[3] This integrating force has been exerted and developed through a network of formal and informal networks operated by or in association with the College. At the level of a formal network, the College has exerted an impact by being one of those organizations whose functions are "to replenish the profession's supply of talent and to expand its fund of knowledge".[4] The College has molded the structure and organization of specialist practice in Canada. At the level of informal networks, the College has fostered professionalization on the basis of more personal affinities through the existence of Council, its committees and its task forces, the annual meeting and various committees. Fellows have shared membership in specialty groups (and thus have developed group identity), knowledge and techniques, a sense of obligation to patients, and sometimes family, religious or ethnic background.

The impact of the College in relation to professionalization and the activities within informal networks is illustrated well by the statements of two councillors.[5] The statements of these two Fellows not only shed light on the workings of Council and its committees but also illustrate another facet of the impact of the College — on the Fellows themselves. Dr. W.M. Goldberg, a councillor from 1964 to 1972 and chairman of the Hospitals Approval Committee for part of this period, was intrigued by the almost alchemical power that Council exerted:

> *From* a very personal point of view, the amazing thing that I experienced in my years on the College's Council was to see the dedication of the individuals concerned and their willingness to get together, to

compromise and to come out with an approach that was best for the group as a whole, even if they did not agree with some of the details. Certainly, in my experience and being involved with the universities and hospitals and medical societies, to name a few, I had never seen better group leadership at work. I don't know what the spark was that gave this group such a common purpose because they certainly were from diverse backgrounds, however, they seemed to come together under the leadership at the time which posed, I think, the appropriate questions to which they were able to find solutions. Individually, many members of Council did not appear to be liberals, free thinkers, or even the type of persons that wanted a change, and yet when the proper questions were posed and the problems presented, they were able to be extremely radical, willing to take risks to change things, and to bring the whole membership along with their thinking. It may well be that one of the important ingredients of the whole system was that personal economics were never involved, personal pride did not seem to play a big part in the picture but somehow they were able to divorce themselves from their own personal medical environment and apply a more liberal approach in group discussions. I think a great deal of this was accomplished by the leadership of the secretariat of the College, the various Presidents and the chairmen of the subcommittees, all of whom seemed to have mutual respect and could demonstrate informed leadership.

For his part, Dr. B.J. Perey offered a somewhat different view of the College's impact, mediated through Council and its committees. His view expresses the role of informal networks in professionalization, which were quite evident in College committees:

...at any one time, 800 or more faculty members who are Fellows work on the many (more than 130) standing committees, examining boards, test committees and task forces of the College. Their work is done in an environment that is largely detached from the pressures, contingencies and politics of medical schools and teaching hospitals. Consequently, committee members can express themselves with greater freedom and can often create nationally what may be impossible on home ground. Committee members often relate that it is sometimes easier to introduce a change in the whole country, through the College, than it is to do the same thing locally through the medical school structure. The committee system of the College became recognized as a training ground in medical education, as well as a major "grapevine" and official channel of communication between faculties and between specialties. Through the R.S. McLaughlin Centre, the College has tapped most of the Canadian technological expertise in the science of medical education and has provided a milieu for these experts to exchange views, to work together and to promote research and education. The College also became a source of academic 'promotion', each faculty member across the country proudly recording in his/her curriculum vitae any appointment and chairmanship in the committee and examining board network. Department chairmen, deans and prominent faculty members used the College committee systems to promote their most promising protégés as well as to identify and recruit new faculty members. Another strong area of partnership with the medical schools has been the process of accreditation of the specialty training programs. Many changes which have been introduced by the accreditation process in the schools have been good (administrative structure, in-training evaluation, distribution of resources, guidelines etc.) and have frequently helped undergraduate medical education as well. Deans have routinely used accreditation visits to obtain better support from the direction of their university and to force change on some of their faculty members. Program directors have also used accreditation to obtain needed resources from their deans or other departments.

These councillors' observations also illustrate another aspect of professionalization, which, according to a second definition, is the "process by which a heterogeneous collection of individuals is gradually recognized, by both themselves and other members of society, to constitute a relatively homogeneous and distinct occupational group".[6] The basic elements of this process of professionalization are similar in the London and Canadian Colleges, but the two have existed in different environments and under different circumstances; in Canada for example, the interrelationship of the two principal divisions of the College, the multidisciplinary nature of the College, its bilingual nature and its geographical representation of Fellows on Council must be noted. Therefore the particular impact of each College in its own country has been different, being determined by such factors as the objectives of training of specialists, national needs for specialists and the development of the specialties. In what ways, then, has the impact of The Royal College of Physicians and Surgeons of Canada been felt specifically in Canada?

II

The College was founded as a response to the situation that existed in Canada in the 1920s. It was the perception among a few Canadians of that time that Canada needed broadly trained specialist-consultants. This perception led to the formation of the College and its Fellowship program in which medical and surgical specialists would share a common purpose of achieving a high standard of specialist health care for Canadians. This perception and the College's unitarian nature have always underlaid the impact of the College. The various activities of the College have, remarkably, all been conducted in and by a single college, for the benefit of all specialists in Canada — and of all patients these specialists look after. In this manner the College has had an impact on the training and evaluation of specialist candidates, the continuing medical education of established specialists, the practice of medical and surgical specialists, the development of the specialties, the interrelationship of medical organizations and government bodies — and on the Fellows themselves and the Canadian medical profession as a whole.

It was likewise the response of a few individual Fellows to the Canadian situation, first in the 1930s and then in postwar Canada, that created the College's original Certification program. It was the response of a few Fellows to the awareness of the Canadian need for some well-trained, journeyman specialists, particularly in non-academic areas, that led to the concept of a second specialist qualification. The decision to introduce this Certification program had several consequences, among which the creation of the dual standard, though the most obvious one, was neither the most important nor the most problematic. Less well remembered, yet far more significant, was the fact that the Certification program preserved unity among Canadian specialists in the 1940s and so preserved the unitarian nature of the College — and it is unity that has always been one of the keys to the College's impact. The simple fact is that, if in the mid-1930s, the College had not initiated planning for the Certification program, it is likely that radiologists, especially, together with anesthetists, ophthalmologists and otolaryngologists, and other specialists later, would have formed their own colleges or boards or faculties. The College of 1960, of 1972 or of 1980 would then have been a radically different organization, having a totally different impact.

But the impact has not been unidirectional. Many groups have had an impact on the College; indeed, the College has sometimes acted only in response to initiative or crisis elsewhere.[7] Although the College has always exerted a large influence on residents in training (residents' views were well summarized by Fish during the 1965 Kingston conference[8]), residents themselves have influenced the College, as the critiques of the College's Certification process that CAIR prepared and its reception by the Examinations Committee clearly indicated.[9] Similarly, the College-universities impact has been bidirectional; in the latter 1960s and early 1970s the College's convincing the universities that they should undertake the responsibility for residency training is regarded as a success on the part of the College, but it was in fact university psychiatrists who made the original proposal to the College. (Once approached, however, the College moved swiftly to develop the concept of university aegis for specialty training.)

III

The major area in which the College has had an impact has been that of the training and evaluation of specialist candidates. On these activities the College's impact has been immeasurable, but its magnitude can be better understood in relation to advances in training in hospitals and university programs and in evaluation and examination methodology.

The College's single-minded efforts to steadily improve the standard of residency education in a growing number of specialties changed the approach to specialty training in a relatively short period. The standards and requirements it formulated for specialty training were most influential. But perhaps the College's principal contribution was its insistence that the responsibility for training residents lay with the universities rather than hospitals. Before the Second World War, and also in the few years following it, formal postgraduate training in a university environment was offered principally in only two cities, Montreal and Toronto. Elsewhere, some universities encouraged the development of postgraduate programs, especially after the war, when returning veterans could not be accommodated in the few existing university training programs, but some universities offered no programs at all. For the most part, training was taken in hospitals and, to a large extent, most residents learned their craft where they could, usually in an unplanned manner. But beginning in 1950, and intensifying in the 1960s and 1970s, the College's conviction that residents should be trained in integrated university programs totally changed the character and consequences of specialty training. The College's impact here has been enormous. Dr. B.J. Perey, among many others, has singled out the relationship between the College and the medical schools as "the outstanding success story of the 1970s".

The relationship between the College and the medical schools benefitted both parties. As far as the College was concerned, the universities were the logical centres for training and it was easier to deal with a small number of universities (with which many academic Fellows were associated) than with a large number of hospitals (many of which were service-oriented rather than education-oriented). In general, the universities welcomed the College's initiative, even if the responsibility for training residents seemed to carry with it financial burden — though this was offset to a large extent by payments from the Federal Health Resources Fund. Creation of a postgraduate faculty was a natural development in view of the concept of a continuum of education in medicine, and two other College programs — the temporary Certification program and the medical scientists program — facilitated this development. The medical faculties welcomed the challenge to their training potential that the College's requirement brought with it, just as they appreciated the College's surveys of their postgraduate programs.

The impact of the College was not, however, always viewed favorably by universities. One potential problem concerned the integrity and autonomy of university departments. The College wished to vest the authority for postgraduate training in the universities, through the divisions of postgraduate education. While some training programs were university-based, in many places they were set up independently by strong clinical departments in hospitals. The College's requirement for central coordination and documentation of training therefore did not always meet with university approval, for departmental autonomy sometimes seemed threatened. On such occasions, the College's pursuit of unity intensified.

The net result of the College's initiative was, however, a gain for all concerned, and the impact spread far and wide, as Dr. W.M. Goldberg has indicated:

> I think this was a very bold step which took a lot of courage to implement and resulted in the training programs in Canada being, I think, of a uniform good quality and really raised the standard throughout the country. I think what is most important is [that] it brought people together even within universities to organize their programs and forced them to work together, something that many of them had never done before, and I think this must have had a great deal of spin-off in improving even the health care delivery within the communities where this occurred. I think this was important even in the major centres such as Montreal and Toronto...where they have a lot of the hospitals acting in isolation, thinking they were providing superb training, but I think when they got together and had a more unified program it even resulted in better candidates and most importantly brought people together with a common purpose. I am sure that this must have had an effect...and it certainly resulted in the small centres such as Winnipeg, Saskatchewan, Western Ontario and the new program such as McMaster developing greater in-depth programs than they had in the past, prior to that time.

With respect to the College's concern with specialty training requirements and guidelines for specialty training programs, the impact of the College, then, has been far-reaching. Hospitals and university departments were stimulated to improve their programs, program directors and staff to upgrade their teaching and would-be specialists to look for the best overall programs in which to take their training.

Residents also looked for programs that would prepare them well for the College's examinations. Here again, the impact of the College was considerable. This is particularly true of the College's efforts, starting in 1972 with the single examination process, deliberately to relate training to the examinations, and vice versa. In the College's early years, the examining function, supported by the accrediting function, was regarded as the most important function; it was believed that anyone who passed the stiff Fellowship examination was obviously competent to practise. As people began to realize that even the sacrosanct Fellowship examination system was fallible, perceptions and practices changed; as the importance of well-planned training programs based on sound educational principles became recognized, so the emphasis shifted to the role of training, especially allied with in-training evaluation, in the identification of clinically competent specialists. The need for the triad of training, evaluation and examination became understood, and in this respect the College's influence was profound. Before 1960, the College was mainly concerned with the examination process and assuring itself and the country of the quality of the trainees through the examination of specialist candidates. As the 1960s developed, the College began to realize that it was more than just an examining body and that it should take a lead in seeing that first-class training would be provided in Canada. Training was seen to be as important as examining. This was one of the most important developments in the 1960s and 1970s, and the College was probably the first examining board anywhere to organize and oversee in such detail a revision of the training requirements leading to the certifying examination.

The impact of the College was also being felt outside Canada, as other countries came to realize that the Canadian Fellowship identified clinical competence rather than, as in the United Kingdom, for example, readiness for higher training. This achievement was emphasized by Dr. J.T MacDougall, who wrote that, during the latter 1960s and early 1970s, "the College evolved from a strictly examination and accreditation body to an important — indeed *the* important — educational force in specialty medicine and surgery in Canada, and became an example to other similar bodies in the world".

The College's work on evaluation and examination methodology made a profound impact in the latter 1960s and early 1970s. The efforts of the Examinations Committee to reform the examination process, which started in 1963 and reached a high point in 1972, were productive, and to these efforts were added the endeavors of the R.S. McLaughlin Examination and Research Centre. The work of the McLaughlin Centre was particularly fruitful; indeed, the high regard for the College outside Canada was based largely on its research and development, through the McLaughlin Centre, in applying theoretical aspects of educational psychology and evaluation to the training and assessment of competence of specialists. Thus Dr. B. Hudson, of Melbourne, Australia, and an Honorary Fellow who led the computer-based examination project during his year at the McLaughlin Centre, wrote that "it was a year that enabled me to introduce a number of the philosophies of training and examining of the Canadian Royal College to our own Royal Australasian College of Physicians...in Australia and New Zealand". And from England, writing of the College's high reputation in the international field and of the McLaughlin Centre as one of the College's important assets, Dr. J.F. Stokes had this to say of the impact produced through the McLaughlin Centre:

From the international standpoint, the impact of [Dr.] Don Wilson's work and the importance of the McLaughlin [Examination and] Research...[Centre] should not be underestimated. Even though the international bank of multiple-choice questions held in Edmonton may not be used as fully as had been hoped, the fact that the resource is there is an encouragement to developing countries setting up their own examinations (Saudi Arabia is the latest example). This project...took shape after a series of meetings at the CIBA Foundation, London, to see how far examination test material could be shared between English-speaking countries. [Dr.] Don [Wilson] played a leading part here, especially as we had developed nothing comparable to the McLaughlin Centre in Britain.

In these respects the impact of the College on medical education in general and on evelution technology in particular has been profound, and the existence of the Centre has given the College a leading edge in this field. The work of the McLaughlin Centre enabled the College to develop and introduce multiple-choice questions into its examinations and to support the work of the necessary test committees; and the Centre's expertise facilitated the development of the College's innovative in-training evaluation program. Nor was the impact of the McLaughlin Centre felt only in College circles, for the MCC, which participated as a user in the McLaughlin Centre's work, benefitted also through the multiple-choice question examinations that the Centre prepared for the MCC.

The base that the College developed in specialty training and evaluation has given it considerable expertise and authority. This expertise and authority likewise has meant that the impact of the College was felt by other organizations that shared a common interest in training and evaluation. Of these organizations, the CPMQ, ACMC and the CFPC have worked closely with the College from time to time and have benefitted from the College's knowledge and expertise; and the College itself has benefitted from the knowledge and expertise developed by these organizations also.

IV

The College has made an impact not only on the training, evaluation and Certification of specialist candidates, but also in its encouraging some established specialists to maintain a high level of competence in their practice and others to conduct research. Since its early days, the College emphasized the value of continuing medical education (through, for example, the scientific program at the annual meeting) and of research (as in the awarding of the College's medals in the Division of Medicine and the Division of Surgery), but it was not until the period from 1960 to 1980 that the College went to extraordinary lengths to emphasize their importance. The basis for both these activities was laid in the 1960s, when the numerous awards and Fellowships supported by the Educational Endowment Fund and the publication of the College's *Annals* facilitated Fellows' efforts in continuing medical education and the creation of the McLaughlin Centre stimulated a greater interest in scientific enquiry among Fellows. But it was not until the 1970s that these efforts bore fruit. In continuing medical education, not only did opportunities for Fellows flourish but also the College gave a positive commitment to assisting Fellows maintain their level of competence by making programs such as self-assessment available and by tuning the *Annals* and the *Canadian Journal of Surgery* to the needs of continuing medical education. In research, the College's establishing its Research Committee and its Visiting Professorships in Medical Research have emphasized the contribution of scientific investigation to specialist training and practice.

These endeavors reflected a new concern of the College. The College doubled in size in 1972, after the 'new' College emerged following the admission of thousands of pre-1972 Certificants into Fellowship. The needs of an enlarged membership became important. For now some 11,000 College Fellows were delivering specialist health care, and the College felt increasingly accountable for the standard of specialist health care in Canada.

V

The College has made a further impact in relation to the recognition and development of specialties in Canada. This impact has been felt in three ways. The impact was first felt when, in the early 1960s and again in the early 1970s, the College requested the specialty committees and the national specialty societies to revise the training standards and requirements. (The impact was not unidirectional, for the College benefitted greatly from the opinions of the specialty groups.) The College's influence was strengthened, too, by the College's actively fostering its relationship with the specialty groups in other ways. This relationship, too, benefitted both parties. The specialties gained from the opportunity to share in the College's multidisciplinary acitivities, whether this was provided by the College's annual meeting or by the periodic meetings of the conferences of specialties; the College benefitted from the contributions that the many specialties made to advances in training and evaluation and from the participation by specialty representatives in Council and committee activities.

An impact was also felt when new specialties sought recognition. Twice in the period from 1960 to 1980, the danger of fragmentation of medicine due to the development of new specialties was considered serious enough to warrant study in a committee, and on each occasion good came out of the crisis. One result was the formulation of useful criteria for recognition of new specialties and ultimately the acceptance of the principle that the development of new specialties should not be hindered, provided the criteria for specialty recognition were fulfilled.

In one sense, however, the impact of the College has been controversial. In pursuing unity with vigor and determination, the College appreciated, as Dr. J.R. Evans noted, "the breadth of viewpoint of specialty representatives that permitted them to seek out their narrower objectives within the framework of one Canadian College rather than balkanizing into separate specialty regional and linguistic organizations". In this respect, most of the specialty groups have welcomed the impact that the College has had in providing them with "an exceptional forum". [10] But for some specialty groups the impact of the College has been negative; the unitarian structure and nature of the College has been too confining. A tendency to separate has so far been contained, but this tendency is likely to make itself felt as more and more specialties develop. The question has often been asked as to how long the College, in the name of unity, can contain this tendency.

VI

Whatever the impact of the College in these several ways, all of it would have been to no avail if the College's various activities had not shaped specialist health care in Canada. If, at the same time, patients had not benefitted, directly or indirectly, The Royal College of Physicians and Surgeons of Canada would have failed to achieve its objectives.

The College's endeavors concerning the training, evaluation and Certification of specialists, the maintenance of competence among established specialists and the recognition of medical and surgical specialties are, on *a priori* grounds, likely to have improved health care in Canada, but this effect is difficult to define and even more difficult to quantify. One way of solving this problem is to consider a discrete and relatively well-defined model. This model is the role of the College in medicine in Newfoundland. [11]

Newfoundland became a province of Canada in 1949, when the College had been in existence for only 20 years. The College immediately admitted three surgeons in the province to Fellowship and granted Certification without examination to several physicians and surgeons, most of whom were heads of hospital departments. These gestures were symbolic, but the presence of the College was felt from the start of Newfoundland's provincehood.

Prior to Newfoundland's entry into Confederation, specialist health care had been concentrated mostly in the 100-year-old General Hospital in St. John's. This hospital was accredited by the American College of Surgeons and then the Joint Commission on Accreditation of Hospitals. A year of training was recognized by the General Medical Council of the United Kingdom and most of the interns were Newfoundlanders who had graduated from Dalhousie University or from British or Irish medical schools. Medical licensure was facilitated by means of a reciprocal agreement between the Newfoundland Medical Board and the General Medical Council. Surgery was strong at the General Hospital and, though surgeons like to suggest that membership in the department of medicine was determined by a lack of surgical skill, medicine and pediatrics also attracted physicians of high calibre.

The College contributed to the development of specialist health care by assisting the province build on this base in four ways. First, the College granted Fellowship and awarded the Certification qualification to selected specialists between 1949 and 1959. Second, the College included significant activities in Newfoundland in all its programs, ranging from sponsoring visits of distinguished specialists and encouraging and hosting regional meetings (for example, the 1959 meeting in Halifax and the 1962 meeting in St. John's) to nominating Newfoundland candidates for College committees and awards. (Drs. I.E. Rusted and J.M.M. Darte were early Newfoundland councillors.) Third, as from 1967, the College granted temporary Certification to specialists coming from outside Canada to facilitate the development of specialist departments, particularly as Memorial University was emerging as the major academic force in Newfoundland. And, fourth, the College manifested a clear sensitivity to existing needs in Newfoundland, such as the approval of training posts, and to the future potential of the rich clinical material that could be made available to residents, particularly at the beginning and at the end of their training. Of these, the most important was the fourth.

Instrumental in initiating a planned teaching program in Newfoundland, particularly at the General Hospital, were Dr. L. Miller (Director of Medical Services in the Provincial Department of Health, and later the first Deputy Minister of Health) and Dr. I.E. Rusted. The first Newfoundlander to complete successfully the College's formal requirements for the Fellowship in internal medicine, Dr. Rusted was concerned about the lack of an organized teaching program in Newfoundland and therefore looked forward to the development of a teaching program for interns at the General Hospital, so that the General Hospital might finally become a recognized teaching hospital:

> This would be a great step in the direction of solving the intern problem which occurs year after year [Dr. Rusted wrote] to plague the Department [of Health] and which has so often led to the importation of interns from other countries. I recall from conversations with the dean of medicine at Dalhousie University that the main objection to allowing interns to go to Newfoundland was that there was no organized instruction, even though they got excellent practical experience.[12]

The College's impact was strengthened in the early 1950s, when recognition was granted for one year of training in pathology at the General Hospital.

Recognition of training posts in other specialties followed. In psychiatry a regional plan for postgraduate training was introduced into Newfoundland in 1952 by Dr. R.O. Jones, Professor of Psychiatry at Dalhousie University (who, with Dr. A.B. Stokes and others, had convinced the College of the need to involve universities in residency training as early as 1950) and Dr. C. Pottle, Superintendent of the Hospital for Mental and Nervous Diseases. In medicine and surgery, one-year approvals for single trainees were recognized for the General Hospital in 1955 and for two trainees in 1958. These were gradual beginnings, which were followed over the next decade and a half by approval of other major specialties and subspecialties. By 1967, Newfoundlanders could proudly say that the entire teaching program had been expanded to constitute the integrated program of postgraduate and continuing education at Memorial University, and all major hospitals in St. John's were now formally affiliated with the program.

In these developments, which were fundamental to delivery of specialist health care to Newfoundlanders, the College played a distinct role. The importance of this role is best summarized by quoting Dr. Rusted, whose membership on Council from 1964 to 1972 (and his serving as Vice-President [Medicine] from 1968 to 1970) was another way in which the College's impact was felt in Newfoundland:

> ...*Newfoundland* would probably not now have a medical school or a health sciences centre — with the virtual revolution in health care standards that has resulted from its presence — if it had not had a well-organized postgraduate medical education program which, by the mid-1960s, had already attracted many excellent individuals who, after one or two years at the General Hospital in St. John's, went on to other centres in a manner that was usually carefully planned in advance. Of the first 50 residents in internal medicine, for example, all but one (who withdrew for health reasons) went on to pass the Royal College examinations. Several of these are now heads of departments or divisions in our own or other schools of medicine and most of them are faculty members on either full-time or part-time basis. On a more personal bias, I am certain that I could not have made my own contribution to medical education in Newfoundland, (and perhaps elsewhere) if it had not been for the opportunities, experience, stimulation and help of colleagues provided by or through the Royal College — first by the standards established by individuals, which helped me throughout much of my own postgraduate education; secondly, by their standards for hospitals and, after the late 1960s for university-integrated programs. My own experience has, I know, been shared by many others to varying degrees and, in Newfoundland, this has been demonstrated by developments not only in internal medicine but in most other specialties.

In 1929, just before the College was founded, Dr. M. MacLaren, Member of Parliament for Saint John, New Brunswick, explained the purpose of the bill that would introduce and eventually lead to Royal Assent to the College's Act of Incorporation. "It was", Dr. MacLaren observed, "to act as an incentive to medical men, both physicians and surgeons, to aspire to higher qualifications and therefore higher standards of service to the public."[13] This observation succinctly expressed the primary objective of The Royal College of Physicians and Surgeons of Canada at its founding, and this primary objective did not change over the years, either in Canada as a whole or in its provinces. In Newfoundland, as in the other provinces of Canada, the College has indeed assisted its members in achieving and maintaining ever higher standards of service to the public, and it is in this manner that the College's impact has mainly been felt.

VII

In its first half-century, the College evolved to assume a prominent and unique position in Canadian medicine. Its impact has been profound. It is appropriate to conclude with a perspective of the 1980s:

> The College has a unique position. It is not parochial, that is involving the day-to-day function of one's division or department or even local hospital or university. It is national, inter-provincial, federal and bilingual. It is not involved with those necessary but sometimes contentious issues of the business of practice, medical politics and economics. Its ethos is at a higher plane — scholarship, fellowship, collegiality and dedication to the highest level of skill and training in the practice of medicine.[14]

This is the conclusion that Dr. R.W. Gunton drew in 1984. The implication is clear. The College has remained true to its motto, *Mente Perspicua, Manuque Apta* — With a Keen Mind and Skilful Hand.

NOTES TO CHAPTER 14

1. A.M. Cooke, *A History of The Royal College of Physicians of London*, vol. 3. Oxford, Oxford University Press, 1972, p. 1126.
2. M.S. Larson, *The Rise of Professionalism: A Sociological Analysis*, Berkeley, University of California Press, 1977, p. 50.
3. A.L. Chute, Executive Committee, May 1963, Attachment 2, p. 2.
4. See E. Greenwood, "Attributes of a Profession", *Social Work* 1957; 2(3):44-55, reprinted in H.M. Vollmer and D.L. Mills (eds.), *Professionalism*, Englewood Cliffs, Prentice-Hall Inc., 1966, pp. 10-19; and E. Gross, *Work and Society*, New York, Thomas Y. Crowell Company. 1958, p. 77.
5. Unless otherwise made clear, the individuals whose statements are quoted herein made known their views in letters to the author.

6. S.E.D. Shortt, "Medical Professionalization: Pitfalls and Promise in Historiography". hstc Bulletin, 1981; 5(3,Sept.), *Journal for the History of Canadian Science, Technology and Medicine, no. 19.*

7. Report of the Committee on Horizons of The Royal College of Physicians and Surgeons of Canada, December 1977, p. 2; and B. Perey, "The Role of the Council", Executive Committee retreat, Aug. 22, 1980, Attachment 11.

8. D.G. Fish, "The Resident's View of Residency Training in Canada". *Can Med Assoc J* 1966; 95:711-716.

9. Canadian Association of Internes and Residents, Report on the Certification Process of The Royal College of Physicians and Surgeons of Canada, mimeo, 1979. A more recent and more readily available statement is that of G.D. Adamson and H. Rowe, "Certification of Specialists: Survey of Candidates and Review of the Literature", *Can Med Assoc J* 1984; 130:586-590.

10. G.A. Bergeron, Executive Committee, February 1965, Attachment 1, p. 2.

11. I am greatly indebted to Dr. Ian E. Rusted, Vice-President, Health Sciences and Professional Schools, Memorial University of Newfoundland, for making material available to me.

12. I.E. Rusted, Letter to L. Miller, June 2, 1949.

13. Lewis, p. 25.

14. R.W. Gunton, Letter to D.A.E. Shephard, April 11, 1984.

APPENDICES

Compiled by

James H. Graham, CM, MD,CM, FRCPC
Associate Honorary Archivist

These appendices have been prepared from information and data contained in the College's official documents, records, minutes, *Annals RCPSC*, and files including copies of correspondence involving a number of persons. The information can be verified in those sources. A separate listing of credits through notes and references has not been prepared for the appendices.

APPENDICES

1 – Chronology 1959-1980
2 – Documents of Historical Interest 1958-1981
3 – Act of Incorporation and Letters Patent of Continuance
4 – Elected Officers 1960-1986
5 – Members of Council 1960-1988
6 – Additional Offices 1958-1986

    6.1 Honorary Archivists and Librarians 1958-1985

    6.2 Editors of the *Annals RCPSC* 1967-1985

    6.3 Executive Committee members "chosen at large" 1949-1986

7 – Executive Officers 1960-1985
8 – Headquarters Management, Personnel 1960-1985
9 – Headquarters Staff with long service 1960-1985
10 – R.S. McLaughlin Examination and Research Centre — Officers and long service staff 1968-1985
11 – Honorary Fellowships 1960-1984
12 – Lecturers 1960-1984
13 – Medallists 1960-1985
14 – Gallie Lecturers 1966-1984
15 – McLaughlin Foundation Edward Gallie Visiting Professors 1960-1984
16 – Sims Commonwealth Travelling Professors from Canada
17 – The Duncan Graham Award — Recipients 1969-1985
18 – The Robert M. Janes Memorial 1970-1984
19 – The K.G. McKenzie Memorial Awards 1968-1985
20 – Brief Historical Notes

    20. 1 The Mace

    20. 2 The Caduceus

    20. 3 The Presidential Badge of Office

    20. 4 The Past-President's Badge

    20. 5 The Presidential Chair

    20. 6 The College Gavels

    20. 7 The College Seals — Past and Present

    20. 8 The Portrait of Jonathan Campbell Meakins

    20. 9 The Silver Cigar Boxes

    20.10 The 50th Anniversary Silver Plate

    20.11 The College Tie

APPENDIX 1

CHRONOLOGY 1959-1980

1959

Commitee on Trauma established, the predecessor of the Committee on Emergency Medical Care: Council, January pp. 7-9.

ACMC – decision to approach regarding integrated postgraduate training programs: Council, January p. 33.

Uniform training requirements for Fellowship and Certification examinations – decision to adopt: Council, January p. 57.

Department of National Revenue ruling declaring the College a charitable organization for purposes of receiving tax exempt donations, February 27: Executive, April p. 7.

College Building – laying of cornerstone by the Rt. Hon. Vincent Massey, Governor General (Canada), June 1.

Auditors for the College – Frazer and Otton appointed: Council, June p. 22.

College Building – Canadian Nurses Association agreed to lease the second floor: Council, June p. 23.

Educational Endowment Fund – founding and appointment of committee: Council, June pp. 23-30.

First Regional Scientific Meeting, Halifax, October 30-31.

ACMC – presentation of a brief on postgraduate medical education to ACMC, Winnipeg, November 6.

College Building – gift of $50,000 from Johnson and Johnson for panelling and furnishing the Council Room, August 10.

College Building – occupation by the staff, November.

Mace – offer of a gift from the Royal College of Surgeons of England accepted: Executive, November p. 34.

1960

Uniform training requirements for Fellowship and Certification examinations – first six specialties approved: Council, January pp. 22-30.

The McLaughlin Foundation Edward Gallie Visiting Professorship in the Royal College of Physicians and Surgeons of Canada founded: Council, January p. 64.

Annual Meeting – first three-day scientific program, Montreal, January 21-23.

Future of the Certification program – meeting of representatives of the CMA and the Royal College to discuss, Toronto, April 21.

Permanent secretariat on medical education – meeting of representatives of the CMA, ACMC and the Royal College to discuss its establishment, Toronto, April 21.

College Building – first meeting of Council in the new Headquarters, June 8-9.

ACMC – Royal College support for the establishment of a permanent secretariat: Council, June pp. 14-15.

McLaughlin-Gallie Visiting Professorship – Professor Charles F.W. Illingworth, Regius Professor of Surgery at the University of Glasgow, appointed first Visiting Professor: Council, June pp. 19-21.

Annual Meeting – first decision to provide simultaneous translation: Council, June p. 16.

1961

College Building – acceptance of an offer from the MCC to donate $15,000 to finish and furnish the Roddick Memorial Room: Council, January pp. 7-8.

Archives and Library Committee established: Council, January p. 8.

Cardiovascular and Thoracic Surgery – specialty qualification approved: Council, January pp. 25-26.

Dichotomy of fees and Itinerant Surgery – Council statements: January pp. 49-53.

Certification program – summary of the position of Council: Council, January p. 70.

College Building – official opening by the Rt. Hon. John G. Diefenbaker, January 19.

1962

History of The Royal College of Physicians and Surgeons of Canada, 1920-1960, by Dr. D.S. Lewis published by McGill University Press, February.

Royal Commission on Health Services (first "Hall Commission") – brief prepared by the Executive Committee and the Council presented to the Ottawa hearings of the commission, March 21 by a group headed by President G.M. Brown.

Conference of Presidents of Colleges of Physicians in the Commonwealth and associated Republics – first participation by this College (President G.M. Brown), Edinburgh, October 3-5.

College Grace – English version prepared by Dr. D.S. Lewis and the Reverend Dr. G.A. Brown and French Version by Dr. G.A. Bergeron: Council, June p. 11.

Minister of National Health – Committee to advise on drug regulations, Drs. F.S. Brien (Chairman), R. Dufresne and E.A. Sellers appointed: Executive, June p. 26.

College Building – Roddick Memorial Room, official opening, September 10.

Coat of arms granted by the College of Arms, London, England, November 20.

1963

Surveys (on-site) of postgraduate training facilities – approval of their inauguration: Council, January p. 11.

Fellowship examinations in Medicine, Surgery, and Obstetrics and Gynecology – approval of a study of their "conduct and content": Council, January pp. 11-12.

Merck Sharp and Dohme Travelling Fellowship approved: Council, January pp. 12-14.

Obstetrics and Gynecology – separate certificates in the two branches discontinued effective 1967: Council, January p. 26.

Annual Awards (Medals) in Medicine and in Surgery – major modification of the governing regulations: Council, January pp. 42-46 and Att. 9.

First on-site survey of postgraduate training facilities, by Dr. R.B. Kerr and Dr. D.R. Webster, in London, Ontario, March 19-23.

Joint Conference of Surgical Colleges – first representation from this College (Dr. W.C. MacKenzie), Royal College of Surgeons in Ireland, Dublin, May 3, 1963: report, Executive, June Att. 8.

Regional Scientific Meetings – decision to increase to two per year commencing in 1966: Council, June p. 15.

Traffic Injury Research Foundation – agreement to sponsor its formation: Council, June p. 16.

Annual Meeting – initial decision to invite representation from Colleges in the United Kingdom, Ireland, South Africa and Australia: Council, June p. 21.

First Royal College (subsequently Detweiler) Travel Fellowships awarded to Drs. I. Holubitsky, Y. Perigny and R. Wilson: Council, June p. 24.

First Merck Sharp and Dohme Travelling Fellowship awarded to Dr. D.L. Schatz: Council, June p. 25.

Portrait of William Harvey – copy of the Jannsen painting presented by Dr. D.H. Paterson FRCPC, October 10: Executive, October Att. 1.

1964

Medical Scientists – approval of mechanism for their admission to Fellowship: Council, January pp. 3-4.

Gallie Lecture – acceptance of funds from the Gallie Club and Foundation to endow a lecture in surgery for each annual meeting: Council, January pp. 7-8.

College Building – decision to develop the Hooper Room to honor Dr. G. Hooper, Chairman of the Building Committee 1955-1970: Council, January p. 10.

Accreditation of postgraduate training facilities – first comprehensive statement of requirements: Council, January p. 11.

Council Elections – adoption of the secret ballot under the bylaw: Council, January p. 31.

Fellowship examinations – approval of amendments to the content and conduct including introduction of the supplemental (springtime) oral examinations and a multiple-choice written examination in internal medicine: Council, January pp. 14-15.

Mace – gift from the Royal College of Surgeons of England presented by Mr. Lawrence Abel at the Convocation, January.

Caduceus – gift from the Royal College of Physicians of London presented by Dr. A. Kekwick at the Convocation, January.

Committee on Films established: Executive, February p. 3.

Fragmentation Committee, predecessor of the Specialty Development Committee, established: Executive, October p. 8.

1965

Certificated specialists – affiliation with the College, approval in principle: Council, January pp. 8-11.

Pathological Anatomy – specialty qualification approved: Council, January pp. 13-14.

Neuropathology – specialty qualification approved: Council, January pp. 13-14.

Cardiology – specialty qualification approved: Council, January p. 15.

K.G. McKenzie Memorial Award – agreement that it be established, supported by endowment funds provided through the Canadian Neurosurgical Society: Council, January p. 51.

College Tie – design approved: Council, January p. 53.

First supplemental oral examinations for Fellowship, March 15.

Election to the Office of President – approval of enacting a bylaw amendment to provide that in addition to active Council members persons who have served two full terms on Council will be eligible for nomination: Council, June pp. 9-10.

Medical Biochemistry – specialty qualification approved: Council, June pp. 15-16.

College Building – official opening of the Hooper Room, June 11.

Presidential Badge of Office, a gift from the Royal College of Surgeons of Edinburgh, received formally in Edinburgh, June, by President W.C. Mac-Kenzie.

Affiliation of certificated specialists with the College – referendum to the Fellows on the proposal, September 1.

First Royal College multiple-choice written examination (in internal medicine), September.

Conference on Resident Education in the Clinical Specialties, organized and sponsored by the Royal College, held at Queen's University, Kingston, Ontario, October 1-2.

1966

First Gallie Lecture delivered at the annual meeting by Dr. R.I. Harris, January 20.

Notice of motions (seven) to amend the bylaws given at the annual business meeting by a group of Fellows from Saskatchewan: minutes of the annual business meeting, January 20. pp. 20-22.
Motions defeated at the annual business meeting, January 19, 1967 pp. 11-21.

Specialist Certificate – extensive revision of the format: Council, June p. 7.

Hematology – specialty qualification approved: Council, June pp. 24-26.

Hematological Pathology – specialty qualification approved: Council, June pp. 24-26.

Bacteriology – name of the specialty qualification changed to microbiology (and subsequently to medical microbiology): Council, June p. 27.

"One-year approvals" – decision to discontinue as of July 1, 1970, approval of a hospital for one year of training in a specialty unless the residency were affiliated with a fully approved program of a university or major teaching hospital: Council, June pp. 39-40.

University-sponsored postgraduate training programs in the recognized medical and surgical specialties – reaffirmation of support: Council, June p. 41.

Affiliation of certificated specialists with the College – enactment of the appropriate amendments to the bylaw: Council, June pp. 56-59.

Regional scientific meetings – first year for two meetings, Sudbury, November 11-12, and Saskatoon, November 24-25.

CFPC – meeting with representatives, Toronto, November 10.

1967

Temporary Certification without examination – approval of its availability to physicians and surgeons brought to Canada for full-time academic appointments: Council, January pp. 8-9.

Fellowship examination in medicine – name modified to Fellowship examination in internal medicine: Council, January p. 55.

Affiliation of certificated specialists with the College – confirmation of new bylaws: annual business meeting, January 19 pp. 9-10.

Presidential chair for the Council Room, gift of the Royal College of Obstetricians and Gynaecologists: Executive, April p. 23.

Council elections – approval of the policy of circulating a curriculum vitae for each nominee: Council, June p. 13.

Examination and Research Centre – resolution to establish: Council, June p. 20.

"The Annals of the Royal College of Physicians and Surgeons of Canada" established: Council, June pp. 43-46.

Examination and Research Centre – offer on September 27 of financial support from The R. Samuel McLaughlin Foundation: Executive, October pp. 3-5 and Att. 2.

College administration – systems analysis by TRW Systems of California, November.

1968

Subspecialties of internal medicine – adoption of general principles regarding their recognition: Council, January pp. 9-20 and Att. 1.

Internal Medicine – written examination after two years of resident training approved in principle: Council, January p. 18.

Gastroenterology – specialty qualification approved: Council, January p. 20.

Pulmonary Disease (later "respiratory medicine") – specialty qualification approved: Council, January p. 20.

R.S. McLaughlin Examination and Research Centre established: Council, January pp. 21-23.

Federation of Provincial Medical Licensing Authorities of Canada – agreement to participate in this new body: Council, January p. 25.
Federation founded February 7, and associate membership for this College approved by Executive, September 1969 pp. 12-13.

Automation – decision to introduce into College administration: Council, January pp. 34-35.

Annual Meeting – approval of seeking a cooperative approach with specialty societies and the CSCI: Council, January p. 57.

Clinical Immunology – specialty qualification approved: Council, June pp. 25-26.

Straight internships – first approval as equivalent to residency training: Council, June pp. 32-35.

Single examination for Fellowship and Certification – Examinations Committee asked to explore: Council, June pp. 48-51.

Robert M. Janes Memorial Lecture in Surgery – offer of funding from the Janes Surgical Society accepted: Council, June p. 19.

Conference on Surgical Education and Research sponsored by the Royal College, the Medical Research Council and the University of Manitoba, Winnipeg, November 3-4.

1969

Dual standard examination system – resolution to study it and the relationship of certificated specialist to the College (the origin of the "Expanded Executive"): Council, January pp. 29-35.

College Seal – authorization of a new version: Council, January p. 45.

Child Psychiatry – specialty qualification approved: Council, January p. 51. Rescinded: Council, January 1972 p. 8.

Residents – resolution favoring their participation in College affairs: Council, January pp. 54-55.

Accreditation to be granted only to programs providing full training: Council, January pp. 58-59.

Expanded Executive Committee – first meeting to study the dual examination system and the relation of certificated specialists to the College, April 26. Subsequent meetings June 4, October 24 and December 13.

Expanded Executive – approval of initial proposals for a single standard of examination and the mechanism of admission to Fellowship: Council, June pp. 13-34.

Straight internships – policy on their acceptability broadened with agreement that the duration of training might thereby be reduced by one year: Council, June pp. 44-47.

Royal College Travel Fellowships become the Detweiler Travel Fellowships: Council, June p. 101.

Letter to Fellows and Affiliated Certificated Specialists on the future status of the Fellowship and Certification qualifications, December 8: Executive, November Att. 6.

1970

McLaughlin Examination and Research Centre – francophone division established: Council, January pp. 13-14.

Single standard examination – further proposals from the Expanded Executive Committee approved: Council, January pp. 19-64.

Nephrology – specialty qualification approved: Council, January p. 86.

Rheumatology – specialty qualification approved: Council, January pp. 86-87.

Perey-Trias motion requesting a review of the bylaws governing the Nominating Committee and the structure and election of the Council, made by Drs. B. Perey and A. Trias adopted by the annual business meeting, January 23 (minutes p. 26).

Specialty Development and Manpower Committee created through merging the Committee on Supply and Distribution of Specialists with the Specialty Development Committee: Executive, February p. 3.

Committee on Education established: Council, June pp. 13-15.

Task Force on the Single Examination Process established: Council, June pp. 66-67.

Criteria for accrediting postgraduate training programs – modification of policy ("Mustard Report"): Council, June p. 70.

President R.C. Dickson's tour of 21 cities across Canada to present the proposals of the Council for a single standard of examination and entry of certificated specialists into the College, September-November.

First comprehensive examination in internal medicine for trainees who had completed two years of resident training, September.

Plebiscite among the Fellows on the Council proposals for the new single examination process and mechanisms of admission to Fellowship, November.

Mace – Executive member chosen-at-large from the Council to be the Mace Bearer: Executive, November p. 7.

1971

ACMC – first attendance of their president and executive director at the Royal College Council meeting, January.

New mechanisms of admission to Fellowship – alternative proposals developed: Council, January pp. 19-20.

Committee on Approval of Hospitals – change in name to Committee on Evaluation of Specialty Training Programs: Council, January p. 30.

Single standard of examination and mechanisms of admission to Fellowship, approval of Council proposals: annual business meeting of Fellows, Ottawa January 22, minutes pp. 2-23.

First Conference of Specialties, Ottawa, Thursday, April 29, to discuss proposals for the new single examination process.

Letters Patent of Continuance – decision to apply to the Minister of Consumer and Corporate Affairs: Council, May pp. 37-38.

New Bylaw No. 1 – approval of the first draft: Council, May pp. 38-39.

Certificated specialists – approval of a liberal mechanism for their admission into Fellowship: Council, May pp. 46-64.

Past-President's Badge – gift of the die from Dr. R.C. Dickson: Council, May p. 80.

Regional Committees on Continuing Education established: Council, May p. 100.

Code of Ethics and Guide to the Ethical Behavior of Physicians prepared by the CMA endorsed: Council, May p. 109.

Letters Patent of Continuance – approval of the formal application to change the constitutional status of the College: Council, October pp. 2-4.

New Bylaw No. 1 – approval of the draft bylaw to implement changes to be effected under the authority of the Letters Patent regarding admission to Fellowship and the new single examination process: Council, October pp. 5-11.

Letters Patent of Continuance approved by the Minister of Consumer and Corporate Affairs, November 4.

Referendum to the Fellows on the proposed mechanism of admission of Certificants into Fellowship, November.

Grant of $300,000 from the Gladys and Merrill Muttart Foundation for research in the development of computer-based simulated patient management problems, December 6.

1972

Training and Evaluation Committee established: Council, January p. 14.

New Bylaw No. 1 approved by the annual business meeting of Fellows, Toronto January 28.

Committee on Emergency Medical Care established to succeed the Committee on Trauma: Executive, February p. 5.

Letter to the Fellows from President C.G. Drake reporting the decisions of the 1972 annual business meeting, March 27: Executive, April Att. 1.

Certificated specialists – invitation from President C.G. Drake May 5, to apply for Fellowship under the provisions of Bylaw No. 1.

Concerned Fellows of Victoria – first letter and questionnaire to the Fellows regarding Bylaw No. 1, May.

Laboratory Medicine – meeting of representatives with College officers to discuss the status of this field in the College, Ottawa, June 7.

Emergency Medicine – acceptance of the concept of this field as a specialty: Council, June pp. 45-46.

Concerned Fellows of Victoria – second letter to the Fellows, August 10, reporting on the May questionnaire.

Conference on Residency Training in Internal Medicine, Queen's University, Kingston, Ontario, September 8-9 conducted in co-operation with the Canadian Association of Professors of Medicine.

Council – extraordinary meeting September 23, to consider a submission from the Concerned Fellows of Victoria.

Educational Development Fund created: Council, September pp. 14-15.

Concerned Fellows of Victoria – first letter to the Fellows from President C.G. Drake explaining the views of the Council, October 20, Executive, December 2 Att. 2.

Concerned Fellows of Victoria – letter from President C.G. Drake November 3, to those Fellows who had sent to the College "Appendix A" from the Victoria document of August 10: Executive, December 2 Att. 3.

Laboratory Medicine – establishment of Specialty Committees in Hematological Pathology, Anatomical Pathology and Laboratory Medicine: Executive, December 2 pp. 9-10.

Concerned Fellows of Victoria – third letter to the Fellows, November 30: Executive, December 28 Att. 1.

Concerned Fellows of Victoria – letter to all Fellows from President C.G. Drake expressing further Council views on the Victoria proposals, December 13: Executive, December 28 Att. 2.

Concerned Fellows of Victoria – meeting with College officers, Ottawa, December 27-28.

1973

Concerned Fellows of Victoria – fourth letter to the Fellows, January 5: Council, January Att. 1.

Concerned Fellows of Victoria – defeat of motions to amend Bylaw No. 1, annual business meeting, Edmonton, January 26.

Joint Conference of Surgical Colleges held at the College headquarters, March 29-30.

The Royal Society of Medicine – acceptance of the availability of affiliate membership for Fellows of the Canadian College: Council, June p. 11.

Canadian Journal of Surgery – agreement to co-sponsor with the CMA: Council, June p. 20.

McLaughlin Examination and Research Centre – establishment of the Advisory Board: Council, June p. 33.

Nuclear Medicine – specialty qualification approved: Council, June p. 52.

Committee on Horizons appointed: Executive, September p. 9.

In-training Evaluation Report – first use in the College examinations, autumn.

Advisory Board, McLaughlin Centre – inaugural meeting December 12.

1974

CAIR – approval of representation on the Committee on Evaluation of Specialty Training Programs: Council, January pp. 11-12.

Community Medicine – specialty qualification approved (with phasing out of Certification in Public Health): Council, January pp. 35-40.

Moratorium (temporary) on approval of new specialty qualifications: Council, January p. 40.

International Federation of Surgical Colleges – meeting in Montreal January 22-23 in association with our annual meeting.

Conference on the Quality of Care and Medical Education, Ottawa, April 25-26: Co-sponsored by the Royal College, CFPC and ACMC.

Joint scientific meeting with the Royal College of Physicians of London, May 8-9, London, England.

McLaughlin Centre – responsibility to produce examinations for the MCC: Executive, April 16 p. 7, Att. 4.

Principles of Surgery examination first held June 1.

Resident participation in surveys of postgraduate training programs approved: Council, June p. 20.

Internal Medicine – requirement for three "core" years of resident training: Council, June pp. 24-25.

New specialties – report of the ad hoc committee on related policy: Council, June pp. 48-52 and Att. 1.

Royal College Speakers at specialty society meetings – first approval (for the Canadian Association of Radiologists): Council, June pp. 38-39.

First computer-based patient management problem examination in pediatrics, autumn.

MCC – first official representation from this College at their annual meeting, Ottawa, September 9-10.

1975

Specialty Committee in Radiology replaced by Specialty Committee in Therapeutic Radiology and Specialty Committee in Diagnostic Radiology: Council, January p. 8.

Regional Advisory Committees replace Regional Committees on Continuing Education: Council, January p. 9.

Pediatric General Surgery – approval of a Certificate of Special Competence (first such qualification): Council, January p. 65.

Anesthesia – Retreat at Queen's University, Kingston, sponsored by the College to study undergraduate and postgraduate education and the role of research in anesthesia, February 27-28.

CSCI – first meeting of officers with the College Executive Committee, April 2.

Certificates of Special Competence in the subspecialties of internal medicine – decision to explore: Council, June p. 49.

1976

Division of Fellowship Affairs founded: Council, January p. 4.

Fellowship Affairs Committee replaces the Committee on Continuing Education: Council, January p. 11.

Therapeutic radiology – name of the specialty changed to radiation oncology: Council, January p. 17.

Examinations Committee – approval of representation from CAIR and la Fédération des médecins résidents et internes du Québec: Council, January p. 30.

Second Conference of Specialties, Ottawa, May 11 on CME.

Committee on Evaluation of Specialty Training Programs – approval of representation from la Fédération des médecins résidents et internes du Québec: Council, June p. 13.

Committee on Evaluation of Specialty Training Programs – change of name to Committee on Accreditation of Specialty Training Programs: Council, June p. 27.

Thoracic surgery – approval of a Certificate of Special Competence based on prior Certification in general surgery: Council, June pp. 32-34.

Communications Committee replaces the Committee on Publications: Council, June pp. 39-40.

Maintenance of Competence Committee founded: Council, June pp. 39-40.

CFPC – liaison representation of senior officers at Board of Directors and Council meetings inaugurated October 2 and January 23, 1977.

1977

Biomedical Ethics Committee established: Council, January pp. 15-16.

Research Committee established: Council, January pp. 16-18.

Geriatric medicine – approval of a Certificate of Special Competence based on prior Certification in internal medicine: Council, January pp. 26-27.

Medallists, past and current, breakfast at annual meeting, initiated Toronto, January.

McLaughlin Examination and Research Centre – survey (chairman, Dr. L. Horlick) week of March 28.

Conference on In-training Evaluation and Certification in Internal Medicine, Ottawa, May 5, jointly sponsored with the Canadian Association of Professors of Medicine.

Third Conference of Specialties, Ottawa, May 9 on the relationships between the Royal College and the specialties.

Respiratory disease – change in the name of the specialty qualification to respiratory medicine: Council, June p. 12.

Nephrology – establishment of a Certificate of Special Competence based on prior Certification in internal medicine or pediatrics: Council, June pp. 49-50.

McLaughlin Examination and Research Centre – grant of $100,000 for research from The R. Samuel McLaughlin Foundation: Executive, October p. 4.

Last computerized patient management problem examination in Pediatrics, September.

McLaughlin Examination and Research Centre – survey report submitted November.

Committee on Horizons – report submitted, December.

G. Malcolm Brown Memorial Lectureship accepted for annual meeting scientific program on rotation with CSCI and the Canadian Federation of Biological Societies: Executive, December 19 p. 3.

1978

Simultaneous translation – first use at Council meetings, January.

Annual Meeting – decision to move the time to June in 1980: Council, January pp. 14-15.

American Board of Medical Specialties – inauguration of official exchange of representation through senior officers at meetings, March (Chicago) and June (Ottawa).

Perinatal Medicine – approval of a Certificate of Special Competence based on prior Certification in obstetrics and gynecology: Council, June pp. 44-45.

Royal College Visiting Professorships in Medical Research established: Executive, December pp. 12-13.

1979

Fourth Conference of Specialties, Ottawa, January 13, on the timing of annual meetings.

Annual meeting celebrating the 50th anniversary of the College, Montreal, February 6-9.

Annual meeting – decision to move the time to mid-September commencing in 1981: Council, February p. 12.

Walter C. MacKenzie – Ethicon Surgical Travelling Fellowship established: Council, February p. 44.
First awards in 1980 to Dr. S. Dubé of Montreal and Dr. R.J.D. Honey of Toronto.

Oral examinations – decision to schedule at the conclusion (June) of the final year of training in specialties with early written examinations: Council, February pp. 18 and 30.

Subspecialties of internal medicine and pediatrics – decision to recognize through Certificates of Special Competence: Council, June pp. 20-21. To be effective 1985: Council, June 1980 p. 31.

Medical genetics – approval of a Certificate of Special Competence based on prior Certification in an appropriate specialty: Council, June p. 21. Rescinded: Council, September 1983 p. 48.

1980

President-Elect – enactment of an amendment to Bylaw No. 1 to provide for this office: Council, February pp. 14-20.

Scientific meeting with The Royal Australasian College of Physicians and the Royal Australasian College of Surgeons, Auckland, New Zealand, February 19 and Sydney, Australia, February 24-29.

Fifth Conference of Specialties, Ottawa, April 26 on physician manpower.

Infectious diseases – approval of a Certificate of Special Competence based on prior Certification in internal medicine or pediatrics: Council, June pp. 33-35.

Vascular surgery – approval of a Certificate of Special Competence based on prior Certification in general surgery: Council, June pp. 35-36.

Emergency medicine – primary specialty qualification approved: Council, June pp. 36-40.

First Executive Committee Planning Retreat, Mont Ste-Marie, Quebec, August 22-24. Policy proposals: Executive, March 1981, Att. 13.

R.M. Janes Visiting Professorship in Surgery, to replace the Janes Surgical Lectureship, established by the Janes Surgical Society and the Awards Committee, October 16.

APPENDIX 2

DOCUMENTS OF HISTORICAL INTEREST, 1958-1981

1958

Report of the Nucleus Committee Concerning the Relationship of the Certificated Specialists to The Royal College of Physicians and Surgeons of Canada and the Future of the Certification Examination Program in Canada (Botterell Report), June 27, 1958: College Archives and Examinations Committee, January 1959, Att. 1.

1959

Charitable status for receiving gifts; letter of confirmation February 27, from The Honorable George C. Nowlan, Minister of National Revenue: College files and Executive, April p. 7.

Brief to ACMC on the role of the University in postgraduate medical education. November 6: Council, January 1960, Att. 5.

1960

Certification program – historical memorandum: Executive, April Att. 10.

Certification program – letter to Fellows October 25, summarizing studies 1955-1960 and inviting comment: letter and replies in College files.

1961

Council statement on dichotomy of fees and the principles of financial relations in the professional care of the patient: Council, January pp. 49-52.

Council statement on itinerant surgery: Council, January p. 53.
Amended by Council, January 1965 and January 1966.

Brief to the Royal Commission on Government Organization (Glassco Commission): Council, June pp. 8-9.
Full brief in College files.

1962

History of The Royal College of Physicians and Surgeons of Canada, 1920-1960, by Dr. D.S. Lewis, published by McGill University Press, February.

Brief to the Royal Commission on Health Services (Hall Commission), March 21, College archives.

College Grace – approved text: Council, June pp. 11-12.

Grant of arms from the College of Arms, London, England, November 20.

ACMC – establishment of secretariat and its relationship with the Royal College, letter from Dr. C.B. Stewart: Executive, November, Att. 1.

1964

Requirements for approval of hospitals for advanced graduate training, approved by Council, January and published 1965. College records.

Brief to the Canadian Universities Foundation on the financing of the costs of higher education, October: Executive, October Att. 11.

1965

Council statement on the practice or oral surgery: Council, June pp. 8-9. Amended by Council, June 1966 and January 1967.

Letter and referendum to the Fellows on the affiliation of certificated specialists with the College, September 1: College archives.
Report on referendum, Executive, January 1966 Att. 1.

1966

Brief on examinations in laboratory medicine prepared jointly by the Canadian Association of Pathologists and the Canadian Association of Medical Bacteriologists, January 6: College files and Committee on Specialty Development, April Att. 1.

Proceedings of the Conference on Residency Education, October 1965: *Can Med Assoc J*, 1966; 95:695-781, October 1 and 8 (a reprint).

Affiliation of certificated specialists – letter to all Fellows Oct. 14, reviewing the plan and proposed new bylaw provisions: Executive, September Att. 6.

1967

Report of the Specialty Committee in Internal Medicine on the establishment of qualifications in the subspecialties of internal medicine: Executive, January Att. 8.

The Publications Policy of The Royal College of Physicians and Surgeons of Canada, report by Dr. Stanley S.B. Gilder, February: Executive, April Att. 5.

Letter from President Robert B. Kerr to all certificated specialists inviting them to affiliate with the College under new provisions in the bylaw, April 17: Executive, April 1967 Att. 7.

1968

Information Data Processing System (for the Royal College), final report by TRW Systems of California, January College records.

Annals of The Royal College of Physicians and Surgeons of Canada, Volume 1, No. 1, published January.

Brief to the Commission on the Relations between Universities and Governments, December: Executive, October Att. 15.

1969

Brief to the Special Committee of the Senate on Scientific Policy, March 26: Executive, March Att. 3.

1970

The use of the French language in The Royal College of Physicians and Surgeons of Canada – report of an ad hoc committee: Executive, January Atts. 4&5.

Brief to the House of Commons Standing Committee on Finance, Trade and Economic Affairs: Executive, April Att. 1.

College organization and staffing – memoranda by T.J. Giles, Executive, April Atts. 5&6, and by Dr. R.C. Dickson, Executive, June Att. 3.

"Council Proposes Single Qualification and New Approach to Fellowship", by Dr. R.C. Dickson, *Ann RCPSC*, 1970; 3:171-80.

Plebiscite concerning Fellowship and Certification examinations and qualifications, November: Executive, November Att. 3.

1971

Plebiscite of November 1970 – report by T.J. Giles, *Ann RCPSC*, 1971; 4:3-4.

Task Force recommendations, preliminary, on a new single examination process: Council, January Att. 2, and final, Examinations Committee, April Att. 9.

Health Hazards of Cigarette Smoking – statement on: Executive, March Att. 5.

Nominating Committee, Council elections and structure (a memorandum): Executive, April Att. 1.

Letter to the Fellows Sept. 13, describing proposed changes in the Constitution of the College and in the electoral procedures for Council: College files.

Referendum with accompanying letter on the method of admitting certificated specialists into Fellowship in the College, November 8: College files.

1972

Obstetrics and gynecology – report of the Joint Study Committee (College and SOGC): Executive, January Att. 7.

Emergency medical care in Canada – letter Jan. 17, from five Fellows regarding the role of the College in its improvement: Executive, January Att. 10.

Letter of March 27, to the Fellows from President C.G. Drake regarding approval of Bylaw No. 1 at the annual business meeting of January 28: Executive, April Att. 1.

Letter of May 5, from President C.G. Drake to certificated specialists inviting them to apply for admission into Fellowship under Bylaw No. 1: Executive, April Att. 2 and in College files.

"Green book" – first edition of general information concerning requirements for training and examinations approved: Council, June; revised 1975, 1977, 1980 and 1981: College records.

Concerned Fellows of Victoria – first letter and questionnaire to the Fellows regarding new Bylaw No. 1, May: College files.

Concerned Fellows of Victoria – second letter to the Fellows reporting on the May questionnaire, August 10: Executive, September Att. 2.

Fellowship Diploma – new (1972) version: Executive, September pp. 11-13.

Concerned Fellows of Victoria – first letter to the Fellows from President C.G. Drake, Oct. 20, explaining the position of the Council: Executive, December 2 Att. 2.

Concerned Fellows of Victoria – letter from President C.G. Drake, Nov. 3, to those Fellows who had sent to the College "Appendix A" from the Victoria document of Aug. 10: Executive, December 2 Att. 3.

Concerned Fellows of Victoria – third letter to the Fellows, November 30: Executive, December 28 Att. 1.

Concerned Fellows of Victoria – further letter to all Fellows from President C.G. Drake, December 13, expressing additional Council views: Executive, December 28 Att. 2.

Limited medical licensure – statement of views of Dr. R.C. Dickson: Executive, December 28 Att. 11.

1973

Concerned Fellows of Victoria – letter to President and Council, January 5: Executive, January Att. 1.

Concerned Fellows of Victoria – fourth letter to the Fellows, January 5: Council, January Att. 1.

Chairmen of examining boards – definition of their role: Council, January p. 25.

Specialist physician and surgeon manpower – a survey by Dr. R.W. Gunton, reported to Council, January: College files.

Preregistration internship education and training – statement (1973) of the Council: Council, June Att. 1.

Admission of certificated specialists into Fellowship – second letter from President C.G. Drake to certificated specialists reminding them of the opportunity available under Bylaw No. 1 to apply for Fellowship, September 24: College files.

Preregistration internship education and training – extended statement of College views, a brief to the Noakes Committee, prepared by Drs. R.W. Gunton and E.R. Yendt, December: College files.

1974

Standing committees – review of status as of 1973: Executive, January Att. 1.

Clinical immunology – brief from the Canadian Society of Allergy and Clinical Immunology, October 25, 1973: Executive, January Att. 2.

New specialties – report of the ad hoc committee on their recognition: Council, June Att. 1.
(An important document that set down guidelines for recognition of a specialty and introduced the concept of the certificate of special competence.)

1975

Guidelines for acceptable non-Canadian training programs – reports of the Committee on Training and Evaluation: Council, June 1974 Att. 2 and Council, January Att. 5.

Preregistration internship education and training – reports of the Committee on Medical Education and Licensure of the Federation of Provincial Medical Licensing Authorities of Canada (Noakes Committee): Council, January Att. 1.

The expanded role of the Royal College in continuing education and continuing assessment – a draft statement from the Committee on Continuing Education, written by Dr. R.B. Salter, chairman, with three related major resolutions: Council, January Att. 6.

Performance of candidates at the College examinations – a "tracking" study (1972-74) by Dr. C.B. Mueller for the Training and Evaluation Committee, reported 1975: College files, and conclusions, Executive, June Att. 1.

The function of the Division of Training and Evaluation – report by the Training and Evaluation Committee, Dr. L. Horlick, chairman, February: Executive, April 26 Att. 1.

Statement on Immigration of Physicians by Dr. R.W. Gunton, presented May 16 to the Special Joint Committee of Parliament on Immigration Policy: Executive, April 26 Att. 1a, and *Ann RCPSC*, 1975; 8:279-82.

Specialist Training in Britain, 1975 – a report to The Royal College of Physicians and Surgeons of Canada, by Dr. F.N. Gurd: College files.

1976

The Administrative Organization of the College Secretariat, memorandum by T.J. Giles: Executive, January Att. 12.

Report of the Requirements Committee of the National Physician Manpower Committee, 1975-76 (multiple volumes). College records.

"Grey book" – general information concerning accreditation of specialty training programs, first edition approved: Council, June p. 25 and College records.

Certificate of Special Competence – approved format of the document: Executive, December pp. 24-25.

1977

The Relationships Between the Specialties and the Royal College – a position paper prepared by Drs. R.B. Salter, L.E. McLeod and G. Hurteau: Executive, January Att. 1.

"Yellow book" – requirements and guidelines for accreditation of specialty training programs, a revision of the standards in the individual specialties: Council, January pp. 47-49 and College records.

Report of the Survey Team on the R.S. McLaughlin Examination and Research Centre, submitted November 18, by Dr. Louis Horlick, chairman, also the related report of a survey of administration by Edward B. Shils Ph.D., consultant: College records.

Report of the Committee on Horizons of The Royal College of Physicians and Surgeons of Canada to the Council of the Royal College, submitted by the chairman, Dr. R.A. Macbeth, December: College records.

1979

The Royal College of Physicians and Surgeons of Canada – 50th Anniversary, 1979, a book published in February; editors, Drs. A.W. Andison and J.G. Robichon.

First catalogue of Library and Archival holdings 1978, by Dr. H.R. Robertson and Ruth Clark.

Report on the Certification Process of The Royal College of Physicians and Surgeons of Canada — prepared by CAIR 1979: Examinations Committee, December 1979.

1980

Commentary on the CAIR report by the Royal College Examinations Committee: Examinations Committee, April Att. 8.

Brief to the Health Services Review 1979 (second Hall Commission): Council, February pp. 53-54, and Executive, April Att. 1.

Medical Council of Canada – text of agreement with the College for the McLaughlin Centre to produce the whole MCC Qualifying examination: Executive, June Att. 16.

McLaughlin Examination and Research Centre – summary of development and functions, a memorandum by Dr. S. Kling: Executive, August Att. 29.

Specialty committees – appointment and structure, a review and analysis: Executive, December Att. 1.

1981

Statement of the status of interns and residents by Dr. B.J. Perey: Council, March Att. 4, and *Ann RCPSC*, 1981; 14:88-91.

Annual report for 1980 (published April 1981), the first College Annual Report in this mode.

APPENDIX 3

ACT OF INCORPORATION
AND
LETTERS PATENT OF CONTINUANCE

An Act to Incorporate The Royal College of Physicians and Surgeons of Canada*

WHEREAS The Canadian Medical Association, a corporation constituted by chapter sixty-two of the statutes of 1909, has by its petition prayed in effect that it may be enacted as hereinafter set forth; and whereas His Majesty King George V, has been graciously pleased to grant permission to the College to use the title "Royal"; and whereas it is expedient to grant the prayer of the said petition: Therefore His Majesty, by and with the advice and consent of the Senate and House of Commons of Canada, enacts as follows:—

1. In this Act unless the context otherwise requires —
    (a) "The College" means the corporation constituted under the provisions of this Act;
    (b) "The Council" means the Council of the said College;
    (c) "Fellows" means members of the College;
    (d) "Charter Fellows" means members of the College who become such upon the coming into force of this Act, together with those persons selected and admitted as Fellows within two years thereafter.

2. Those persons holding, at the date of the coming into force of this Act, appointments as professors in medicine, surgery, gynaecology or obstetrics in a Canadian university together with the persons from time to time selected and admitted as, or otherwise being, Fellows of the College pursuant to this Act, upon their consent so to act, are hereby constituted a corporation under the name of "The Royal College of Physicians and Surgeons of Canada", and when the French language is used to designate that corporation the equivalent name shall be "Le Collège Royal des Médecins et Chirurgiens du Canada."

*19-20 George V. Chapter 97, Assented to 14th June, 1929.

As amended   George VI, 1939. Chapter 63, Assented to 3rd June, 1939.
              George VI, 1945. Chapter 54. Assented to 18th December, 1945.

and with further constitutional amendments through Letters Patent of Continuance issued by the Minister of Consumer and Corporate Affairs on November 4, 1971.

3. The General Secretary of The Canadian Medical Association shall call together, at Ottawa, within six months of the passing of this Act all those entitled to become Fellows of the College, as set out in section two of this Act. All those present at such meeting shall constitute a provisional Council. It shall be their duty at this meeting to elect a Council with such officers and officials as they may deem necessary. The elected Council, officers and officials shall hold office in accordance with the provisions of this Act and with the by-laws, rules and regulations of the College.

4. The Council shall hold office for a period of four years, and until their successors are elected and hold their first meeting.

5. The Council may, at any time after the coming into force of this Act, and without examination, select and admit as Fellows, physicians and surgeons of distinction who are graduates of at least twenty years' standing of a medical school or university, who are domiciled in Canada, and who, in the opinion of the Council, have given evidence of high ability in one or more branches of medicine.

6. The Council may, without examination, select and admit as Fellows, physicians and surgeons domiciled in Canada and holding a diploma or fellowship issued or granted after examination by a recognized medical or surgical organization constituted by the laws of the United Kingdom of Great Britain and Northern Ireland, the Irish Free State, any of the British Dominions, the Republic of France, or of such other countries as the Council may direct, if in the opinion of the Council such diploma or fellowship is of equal status to the fellowship of the College, and the candidate shall have submitted evidence of at least five years supervised study and/or practice subsequent to graduation from a medical school or university, and of continuous activity in medicine or surgery up to the date of application for fellowship in the College.

7. The Council may, without examination, select and admit as Honorary Fellows such distinguished physicians, surgeons or other persons resident within or without Canada as the Council may deem fit.

8. (1) Except as hereinbefore mentioned no person shall become or be admitted as a Fellow of the College until he shall have complied with such by-laws and regulations as the Council shall from time to time consider expedient, and unless he shall have passed such special examinations, in either the English or the French language, by the examiners of the College as the Council shall from time to time prescribe and direct for candidates for fellowship, but every fit and proper person, qualified as hereinafter set forth and having complied with such rules and regulations and passed such special examination, as hereinbefore set out, shall be entitled to be admitted as a Fellow of the College.

(2) A candidate wishing to be examined in either the English or the French language for fellowship in the College shall be a graduate of not less than five years' standing of a medical school or university approved by the Council.

(3) The Council may by by-law provide for the organization of the College into medical and surgical divisions, and for admission into fellowship in the College in one or other of such divisions, in which event a Fellow of the Surgical Division may be known and designated as a Fellow of the Royal College of Surgeons of Canada, or in the French language as "Associé du Collège Royal des Chirurgiens du Canada", and a Fellow of the Medical Division may be known and designated as a Fellow of the Royal College of Physicians of Canada, or in the French language as "Associé du Collège Royal des Médecins du Canada".

9. (1) The admittance of every Fellow or Honorary Fellow of the said College shall be by diploma under the seal of the said College in such form as the Council shall from time to time think fit, provided that one or more general diplomas may be granted or issued covering the admittance to the College of such Charter Fellows.

(2) The Council shall cause the name of every Fellow or Honorary Fellow for the time being of the College to be entered, according to the priority of admittance or otherwise as the Council may direct, in a book or register to be kept for that purpose at the headquarters of the College or such other place as the Council shall direct, and such book or register, subject to such reasonable and proper regulations as the Council for the time being may direct shall be open to the inspection of any Fellow of the College.

10. (1) The business and affairs of the College shall be administered by a Committee of the Fellows to be known as "The Council" of the College.

(2) The Council shall have power to provide for and hold special examinations for physicians and surgeons in Canada and make such by-laws, rules and regulations concerning the nature of the said examinations and qualifications of candidates as the Council may consider expedient from time to time.

(3) The Council shall have power to grant special certificates to persons who shall have shown such degree of proficiency in such examination as the Council may consider entitles them to such special certificates; Provided that the granting of such special certificates shall in no way qualify such persons to be Fellows of the College.

(4) The Council shall have power to grant certificates to graduates in specialties without further examination if such graduates have certificates or diplomas in specialties issued from a recognized Canadian university.

11. The Council may make such by-laws, rules and regulations not inconsistent with the provisions of this Act as it may deem necessary or advisable for the government and management of its business and affairs and specially with respect to the qualifications, classification, admission and expulsion of Fellows, and provide for examinations and the granting of certificates pursuant to Section 10 hereof, the fees and dues which it may deem advisable to impose, and the number, constitution, powers, duties and mode of election of the Council or any sub-committees thereof, and of the officers of the College, and may from time to time alter or repeal all or any of such by-laws or rules as it may see fit.

12. The College may receive, acquire, accept and hold real and personal property by gift, purchase, legacy, lease or otherwise, for the purpose of the College, and may sell, lease, invest of otherwise dispose thereof in such manner as it may deem advisable for such purposes; provided, however, that the annual value of the real estate held by the College shall not exceed the sum of fifty thousand dollars.

13. No Fellow of the College shall merely by reason of such fellowship be or become personally liable for any of its debts or obligations.

Letters Patent of Continuance

WHEREAS, in and by section 159 of Part II of the Canada Corporations Act, it is in effect enacted that any corporation without share capital incorporated by Special Act of the Parliament of Canada for the purpose of carrying on, without pecuniary gain to its members, objects, to which the legislative authority of the Parliament extends, of a national, patriotic, religious, philanthropic, charitable, scientific, artistic, social, professional or sporting character, or the like objects, may apply for letters patent continuing it as a corporation under Part II of the Canada Corporations Act;

AND WHEREAS it has been established that THE ROYAL COLLEGE OF PHYSICIANS AND SURGEONS OF CANADA — LE COLLEGE ROYAL DES MEDECINS ET CHIRURGIENS DU CANADA (hereinafter referred to as "the Corporation") was incorporated by an Act of the Parliament of Canada, being Chapter 97 of the Statutes of Canada, 1929 as amended by Chapter 63 of the Statutes of Canada, 1939 and Chapter 54 of the Statutes of Canada 1945, upon the prayer of The Canadian Medical Association, His Late Majesty King George V having been graciously pleased to grant permission to the Corporation to use the title "Royal";

AND WHEREAS the Corporation has applied for letters patent continuing it as if it had been incorporated under Part II of the Canada

Corporations Act as a body corporate and politic without share capital under the name of THE ROYAL COLLEGE OF PHYSICIANS AND SURGEONS OF CANADA — LE COLLEGE ROYAL DES MEDECINS ET CHIRURGIENS DU CANADA.

NOW KNOW YE that the Minister of Consumer and Corporate Affairs, by virtue of the power vested in him by section 159 of the Canada Corporations Act, does, by these letters patent, continue the Corporation as if it had been incorporated under Part II of the said Act, subject to the following provisions:—

The objects of the Corporation are:

(a) To further the excellence of professional training and the standards of practice in the various medical and surgical specialties in Canada;

(b) To contribute to the improvement of health care of Canadians through the provision of designations for specially trained physicians and surgeons, whereby it may be known that they are properly qualified;

(c) To maintain a high standard of professional ethics, conduct and practice among medical and surgical specialists;

(d) To encourage, assist and promote continuing medical education;

(e) To initiate, encourage, support and extend interest in research in medicine and medical education

(f) To encourage, assist and promote the study of quantitative and qualitative aspects of specialized health care in Canada;

(g) To encourage, assist and have continuing concern with health matters.

Such objects are to continue to be carried out in more than one province of Canada.

The head office of the Corporation shall be situated at the City of Ottawa, in the Province of Ontario, or such other place in Canada as the Corporation may by by-law determine from time to time.

The Corporation is to be carried on without pecuniary gain to its members and any profits or other accretions to the Corporation are to be used in promoting its objects.

The powers of the Corporation shall be extended by the insertion of the following clauses:

(a) Anyone who has a medical qualification acceptable to the Corporation and who possesses the qualifications established by or pursuant to the by-laws of the Corporation, and no other, may be admitted to membership by the Corporation, and the members shall continue to be known as Fellows; provided that the Corporation may continue, without examination, to select and admit as Honorary Fellows distinguished physicians, surgeons and other persons resident within or without Canada as the Corporation may deem fit. The Corporation may prescribe the qualifications for Fellowship notwithstanding any provision, restriction or qualification in the Act incorporating the Corporation, as amended. The Corporation may prescribe the qualifications for certificates to be granted to persons who have shown such proficiency as the Corporation may consider entitles them to such certificates. Notwithstanding Section 10 of the Act incorporating the Corporation, as amended, the Corporation may provide for the admission to Fellowship of holders of any certificate heretofore or hereafter granted.

(b) The business and affairs of the Corporation shall be managed by a board of directors who shall be known as The Council, the members of which shall be elected or appointed as the Corporation may prescribe by by-law and which shall have the powers set out in the by-laws of the Corporation.

(c) The Corporation may make such by-laws and provide for rules and regulations thereunder, not contrary to law, as it may deem necessary or advisable for the government and management of its business and affairs and, without restricting the generality of the foregoing, with respect to the qualifications, classifications, privileges, rights, admission and expulsion of Fellows, the granting of certificates, the fees and dues which it may deem advisable to impose subject to the approval of the members in respect of fees and dues imposed upon the members, and the number, constitution, powers and duties and mode of election of The Council, committees, sub-committees, and of its officers, and may from time to time alter or repeal all or any such by-laws as it may see fit.

(d) In addition to the general powers accorded to it by law, the Corporation shall have power:

(1) to purchase, take, lease, exchange, hire or otherwise acquire by gift, legacy, devise or otherwise and to own and hold any estate, property or rights, real or personal, movable or immovable, or any title or interest therein; to sell, exchange, alienate, manage, develop and to mortgage or hypothecate and to lease or otherwise deal therewith as it may deem advisable for the purposes of the Corporation;

(2) to establish and support or aid in the establishment and support of associations, institutions, funds, trusts and projects calculated to advance the science or practice of medicine in Canada.

(e) The present officers and The Council of the Corporation shall continue to be the officers and The Council of the Corporation upon issue of these letters patent until replaced by others in accordance with the by-laws of the Corporation.

(f) The present by-laws of the Corporation shall be the by-laws of the Corporation upon issue of the letters patent and shall continue in effect until changed at an annual meeting of the members of the Corporation held in accordance with the present by-laws of the Corporation when such by-laws may be revoked, amended or adopted, as the case may be, by the majority of those present at such annual meeting.

GIVEN under the seal of office of the Minister of Consumer and Corporate Affairs at Ottawa this fourth day of November, one thousand nine hundred and seventy-one.

APPENDIX 4

ELECTED OFFICERS, 1960-1986

Presidents

Donald Arthur Thompson	1960-62
George Malcolm Brown	1962-64
Walter Campbell MacKenzie	1964-66
Robert Bews Kerr	1966-68
Jacques Turcot	1968-70
Robert Clark Dickson	1970-72
Charles George Drake	1972-74
Keith John Roy Wightman	1974-76
Robert Bruce Salter	1976-78
Douglas George Cameron	1978-80
Bernard Jean François Perey	1980-82
Lionel Everett McLeod	1982-84
Jean Georges Couture	1984-86

Vice-Presidents
Division of Medicine

Lennox Gordon Bell	1960-62
Georges-Albert Bergeron	1962-64
Ronald Victor Christie	1964-66
Donald Robert Wilson	1966-68
Ian Edwin Lawman Hollands Rusted	1968-70
Douglas George Cameron	1970-72
Jean-Luc Beaudoin	1972-74
Louis Horlick	1974-76
Lionel Everett McLeod	1976-78
Hamish William McIntosh	1978-80
George Ross Langley	1980-82
Pierre-Paul Demers	1982-84
Campbell Joseph Coady	1984-86

Division of Surgery

Charles Edouard Hébert	1960-62
Walter Campbell MacKenzie	1962-64
Jacques Turcot	1964-66

Edouard Donat Gagnon	1966-68
Charles George Drake	1968-70
Robert Bruce Salter	1970-72
John Taylor MacDougall	1972-74
Bernard Jean François Perey	1974-76
Charles Arthur David Gilles Hurteau	1976-78
Jean Georges Couture	1978-80
William Morris Paul	1980-82
John Hamilton Duff	1982-84
Donald Richards Wilson	1984-86

APPENDIX 5

MEMBERS OF THE COUNCIL, 1960-1988

Division of Medicine

Henry Joseph Macaulay Barnett	1980-84
Jean-Luc Beaudoin	1968-76
Johannes Christian Beck	1972-76
Lennox Gordon Bell	1953-62
Georges-Albert Bergeron	1955-64
Agnes Joyce Bishop	1982-86
George Malcolm Brown	1953-57, 1960-66
John Herbert Burgess	1981-88
Douglas George Cameron	1957-64, 1968-72, 1978-81
Victor Chernick	1974-82
Ronald Victor Christie	1960-68
Andrew Lawrence Chute	1955-64
Campbell Joseph Coady	1980-88
Robert Francis Patrick Cronin	1977-81
John Marie Marcel Darte	1970-71
Pierre-Paul Demers	1976-84
John George Dewan	1955-64
Robert Clark Dickson	1957-66, 1970-74
Henry Begg Dinsdale	1984-88
Guy Drouin	1967-72
Ronald Douglas Drysdale	1970-78
John Robert Evans	1972-80
Robert Gordon Fraser	1976
Thomas William Fyles	1970-74
John Patmore Gemmell	1962-70
Jacques Genest	1964-72
James Alan Longmore Gilbert	1968-72
William Morton Goldberg	1964-72
Richard Ballon Goldbloom	1971-74
Jean Grandbois	1964-68
Ramsay Willis Gunton	1972-80
Ian Ritchie Hart	1984-88
James Earle Hickey	1982-86
James Harvey Bruce Hilton	1964-72
Charles Herbert Hollenberg	1980-88
Louis Horlick	1970-78

Clarence Stuart Houston	1984-86
Robin Cyril Adair Hunter	1970-72
Sydney Israels	1968-72
Robert Bews Kerr	1960-70
George Ross Langley	1978-86
André Lanthier	1972-74
René Lefebvre	1974-80
William Brien MacDonald	1978-84
John Wendell MacLeod	1953-62
John Reginald Martin	1974-78
Douglas Fraser McAlpine	1970-72
Hamish William McIntosh	1972-80
John Douglas McLean	1979-82
Lionel Everett McLeod	1972-80, 1981-85
Donald Freeman Moore	1962-70
Yves Morin	1980-88
Harold Ormond Murphy	1970-72
Gérard Eugène Plante	1984-88
Ian Edwin Lawman Hollands Rusted	1962-70
James Robert Sparling	1978-79
William Bray Spaulding	1980-84
Brian Jessup Sproule	1980-88
Lea Chapman Steeves	1957-62, 1966-70
Douglas Oliver William Waugh	1970
Keith John Roy Wightman	1964-72, 1974-78
Donald Robert Wilson	1960-68
Edmund Reinhold Yendt	1972-80

Division of Surgery

Laurent Gabriel Archambault	1970-73
Gordon Wallace Bethune	1970-78
Frederick Edward Bryans	1962-70
Leslie Raymond Chasmar	1970-74
Ralph Marenus Christensen	1978-82
Cecil Edwin Corrigan	1953-62
Albert Douglas Courtemanche	1982-86
Clayton Heber Crosby	1957-66
Jean Georges Couture	1976-87
Pieter Josef Erasmus Cruse	1984-88
Luc Deschênes	1984-88
Charles George Drake	1962-70, 1972-76
John Hamilton Duff	1978-86
Frederick Wardell DuVal	1978-86

445

Colin Campbell Ferguson	1962-70
Murray Macdonell Fraser	1982-86
Paul Joseph Fugère	1972
Edouard Donat Gagnon	1962-70
Claude Gaudreau	1970-74
Robert Humphrys Gourlay	1970-78
Fraser Newman Gurd	1964-72
Charles Edouard Hébert	1953-62
George Hooper	1949-55, 1957-62
Charles Arthur David Gilles Hurteau	1970-78
Percy Egerton Ireland	1955-64
Frederick Gordon Kergin	1962-70
Robert Clarence Laird	1964-67
William Hall Lakey	1976-84
Carroll Alfred Laurin	1980-88
Louis Levasseur	1972-76
James Forest Lind	1976-80
Robert Alexander Leslie Macbeth	1972-76
John Taylor MacDougall	1970-78
Walter Campbell MacKenzie	1960-68
Neil Kenneth MacLennan	1967-72
Stephen Clair MacLeod	1982-86
Michel Mathieu	1982-86
Robert Malcolm McFarlane	1970-78
James Overgard Metcalfe	1968-72
Walter Douglas Miller	1962-70
David Alton Murphy	1978-86
Eric Mustard Nanson	1966-70
Edgar Paul Nonamaker	1966-70
Jean-Maurice Parent	1974-82
Frank Porter Patterson	1953-62
William Morris Paul	1978-86
Bernard Jean François Perey	1972-83
Edwin Fraser Ross	1957-66
William Oswald Rothwell	1967-70
Louis-Philippe Roy	1955-61
Robert Bruce Salter	1968-80
Gordon Waddell Thomas	1974-82
Donald Arthur Thompson	1953-64
William Roderick Carl Tupper	1972
Jacques Turcot	1961-72
Donald Robertson Webster	1955-64

Carman Holden Weder 1974-82
Wilfred Keith Welsh 1953-62
Donald Richards Wilson 1980-88

APPENDIX 6

ADDITIONAL OFFICES, 1958-1985

6.1 Honorary Archivists and Librarians

D. Sclater Lewis	1958-69
Edouard Desjardins	1970-74
H. Rocke Robertson	1974-

6.2 Editors of the "Annals"

Jacques Robichon	1967-79
James H. Darragh	1980-81
Robert Gourdeau	1982-

6.3 Executive Committee Members Chosen at large from the Council 1949-1986

The Executive Committee of the Council was established by the Council by resolution on November 2, 1945 and held its first meeting on January 19, 1946. Its membership of seven was prescribed as being the President, the two Immediate Past-Presidents, the two Vice-Presidents, the Honorary Treasurer, and the Honorary Secretary. In June 1949 the Council modified this structure by deleting the senior Past-President (who in reality was not a member of the Council) and replacing him with "one other member of the Council chosen at large". This change was formally recognized through bylaw amendments in 1950 when the Executive Committee first became a standing committee under the bylaw.

From 1949 to 1966 the member chosen at large was elected by the Council (on one occasion by the Executive itself), at times being suggested by the Nominating Committee. From 1966 to 1976 the member was appointed by the President with advice from Executive colleagues, but in 1978 the Council resumed election of this Executive member, a procedure now mandatory under a bylaw amendment of 1980.

Dr. A.D. McLachlin was elected in November 1949 as the first Executive member chosen at large from the Council and served two terms (1949-51 and 1951-53) in that role, the only person ever to do so. Thereafter the custom evolved of selecting the member chosen at large from the Division of the College other than that of the President, a mechanism intended to help medical-surgical balance in the Committee. That custom persisted until 1982 when Dr. W.B. Spaulding, a physician, became the member chosen at large during the presidency of Dr. L.E. McLeod, also a physician.

The members of Council chosen at large for membership on the Executive Committee have made major contributions to the work of the Council and the Executive Committee and are listed below. Since these persons were not recorded in Volume I of the history (Lewis), all appointees since 1949 are included here.

Angus D. McLachlin	1949-51
Angus D. McLachlin	1951-53
H. Rocke Robertson	1953-55
G. Malcolm Brown	1955-57
Percy E. Ireland	1957-60
A. Lawrence Chute	1960-62
Donald R. Webster	1962-64
Robert C. Dickson	1964-66
Frederick G. Kergin	1966-68
K.J.R. Wightman	1968-70
John T. MacDougall	1970-72
Louis Horlick	1972-74
Gordon W. Bethune	1974-76
Ronald D. Drysdale	1976-78
Gordon W. Thomas	1978-80
William B. MacDonald	1980-82
William B. Spaulding	1982-84
David A. Murphy	1984-86

APPENDIX 7

EXECUTIVE OFFICERS, 1960-1985

Honorary Treasurers

Kenneth Turville MacFarlane	1957-66
Frederick John Tweedie	1966-72
Robert Arthur Hugh Kinch	1972-82
Frederic Wardell DuVal	1982-84*

Honorary Secretary and Secretary

James Hutcheson Graham	1953-79**

Executive Director

James Hilton Darragh	1980-

Honorary Assistant Secretaries

William Gordon Beattie	1955-68
Jacques Robichon	1968-80**

Associate Secretary

Fraser Newman Gurd	1972-75**

*Office discontinued 1984
**Office discontinued 1980

APPENDIX 8

HEADQUARTERS MANAGEMENT, PERSONNEL 1960-1985

Executive Secretary*

Theodore J. Giles	1958-79

Office of Training and Evaluation

Directors
Fraser N. Gurd, MD, CM	1972-75
John B. Firstbrook, MD	1975-82
J. Lester McCallum, MD, CM	1982-85
Robert F. Maudsley, MD	1985-

Section Heads
Credentials
Barbara L. Wilson	1964-67
Dorothy Gates	1967-72
Jean Burrow	1972-75
Sheila Waugh	1975-

Accreditation
Victor H. Skinner	1968-83
Josephine M. Cassie	1983-

Examinations
Françoise Lemieux Moreau	1962-80
Louise Papineau	1980-

Office of Fellowship Affairs

Directors
James H. Darragh, MD, CM	1977-79
Robert Gourdeau, MD, CM	1980-

Associate Director
Robert A. Davis	1974-85

Director, Section of Communications
Theodore J. Giles	1980-84

Division of Specialties
Director, James H. Graham, MD, CM	1980-81**

Division of Administration and Finance**

Director – Peter L. Muir, CA	1976-82
Office Manager – Freda Roy	1979-

Administrative Assistant to the Executive Director and
Assistant Registrar – Jean Dunn   1981-

Financial Manager – F. Glen McStravick, CA   1982-

*Office discontinued, 1980. Pauline L. Crocker had been Executive Secretary, 1946-58 and Associate Executive Secretary 1958-64.

**Merged with the Office of the Executive Director and its sections, 1982.

APPENDIX 9

HEADQUARTERS STAFF, LONG SERVICE*, 1960-1985

Grace Allen	1954-59, 1971-74
Elinor Axton	1952-63
Emma Bayley	1947-66
Nicole Breton	1977-
Shirley Brown	1974-76, 1977-
Jean Burrow**	1964-84
Irène Chartrand	1959-64
Monique Coté	1969-74
Darquise Courval	1979-
Carmelle Couvrette	1973-
Dorothy Gates**	1960-72
Joseph P. Hamelin	1960-73
Laura Hamelin	1955-75
Denise Johnston	1966-81
Hélène L'Abbée	1967-74
Denise LaCharity	1975-
Pierrette Landry	1975-83
Richard Landry	1972-
Rita McClymont	1959-62, 1964-
Isabel Mitchell	1955-64
Françoise Lemieux Moreau**	1948-80
Peter L. Muir**	1972-82
Margaret Mulvihill	1962-
Andrée Newberry	1973-78
Marcia Palef	1974-
Louise Papineau**	1965-
Georgette Patenaude	1963-70, 1972-73
Diane Pilon	1966-79
Rosemary Poggione	1965-74
Toni Layton Robertson	1964-79
Wilma Tinnish	1979-
Heather Trencher	1964-73
Marjorie Troy	1969-78
Elsie Young	1963-79

*Persons who served five or more years
**See also Management listing, Appendix 8

APPENDIX 10

R.S. McLAUGHLIN EXAMINATION AND RESEARCH CENTRE
OFFICERS AND LONG SERVICE STAFF 1968-1985

Directors

Donald R. Wilson, MD, CM	1968-78
Samuel Kling, MD	1978-85

Co-Directors

Jean-Luc Beaudoin, MD	1968-75
Jacques Turcot, MD	1975-77

Assistant Directors

William C. Taylor, MB, Ch B	1973-
Samuel Kling, MD	1974-78
Jean-Marie Loiselle, MD	1978-
Olav Rostrup, MD	1978-84
Ernest Skakun, M Ed	1979-

Long Service Staff

Beatrice Ross	1968-
NaDeane Werner	1968-
Ronald Von Kuster	1970-
Danielle St-Maur	1970-
Huguette Simian	1970-
Donna Kuhn	1973-83
Ernest Skakun	1974-
Dan Vervynck	1976-
Rosemarie Henley	1976-
Colin Park, PhD	1979-

Chairmen of the Advisory Board

Robert C. Dickson, MD	1973-76
D.F. Cameron, MD	1976-79
Frederic W. DuVal, MD	1979-

APPENDIX 11

HONORARY FELLOWSHIPS 1960-1984

1961

Colonel R. Samuel McLaughlin, Oshawa, Ontario
Sir Walter Mercer, Edinburgh, Scotland
Major-General Georges P. Vanier, Montreal

1964

The Rt. Hon. Lord Porritt, London, England
Professor Leslie J. Witts, Oxford, England

1965

Dr. William B. Castle, Brookline, Massachusetts
Dr. Lester R. Dragstedt, Gainesville, Florida
Dr. Chester M. Jones, Boston, Massachusetts

1966

The Rt. Hon. Lord Brock, London, England
Sir Charles Illingworth, Glasgow, Scotland
Sir Peter Medawar, London, England

1967

Sir John Bruce, Edinburgh, Scotland
Sir Charles Dodds, London, England
Dr. R. Gordon Douglas, Providence, Rhode Island
Dr. J. Englebert Dunphy, San Francisco, California
Dr. Frank L. Horsfall, Jr., New York, New York
Professeur Jean Patel, Paris, France
Sir John Peel, West Tytherley, England

1968

The Rt. Hon. Roland Michener, Toronto

1969

Sir Hedley Atkins, London, England
Sir Benjamin Rank, Melbourne, Australia
The Rt. Hon. Lord Rosenheim, London, England

1970

Sir Lance Townsend, Melbourne, Australia
Sir Reginald Watson-Jones, London, England
Madame Pauline Vanier, Montreal, and Oise, France

1971

Sir Edward Rowan Boland, Ashford, England
Dr Roger Gaudry, Montreal
Sir John McMichael, London, England
Dr. Francis D. Moore, Boston, Massachusetts

1972

Sir Andrew Kay, Glasgow, Scotland
Dame Sheila Sherlock, London, England
Louis Albert Cardinal Vachon, Quebec

1973

Dr. Benjamin Castleman, Boston, Massachusetts
Professor Norman M. Dott, Edinburgh, Scotland
Professeur Jean Hamburger, Paris, France
Dr. Charles Huggins, Chicago, Illinois
Sir Norman Jeffcoate, Liverpool, England

1974

Dr. D. Harold Copp, Vancouver, British Columbia
Dr Armand Frappier, Montreal
Dr. J.D. Mills, Braeside, Ontario
Dr. Jonathan E. Rhoads, Philadelphia, Pennsylvania
Professor Witold Rudowski, Warsaw, Poland

1975

The Rt. Hon. Jules Leger, Ottawa
Dr. Frank B. Walsh, Baltimore, Maryland

1976

Sir Ferguson Anderson, Glasgow, Scotland
Sir Ludwig Guttman, Aylesbury, England
Monseigneur Roger Maltais, Sherbrooke, Quebec
The Rt. Hon. Lord Smith, London, England

1977

Professor Eric G.L. Bywaters, London, England
Sir John Dacie, London, England
Sir Edward Hughes, Melbourne, Australia
The Honorable Pauline McGibbon, Toronto

1978

Sir Cyril Clarke, Liverpool, England
Professor Jan Hendrik Louw, Cape Town, South Africa
Professor Guan Bee Ong, Hong Kong
Dr. William E. Swinton, Toronto
Dr. Cecil J. Watson, Minneapolis, Minnesota

1979

Professeur Jean Bernard, Paris, France
Sir Arnold Burgen, London, England
Professeur Lucien Léger, Paris, France
Dr. H. Edward MacMahon, Cambridge, Massachusetts
Dr. Orvar Swenson, Rockport, Maine
Dr. Claude E. Welch, Boston, Massachusetts

1980

The Rt. Hon. Edward R. Schreyer, Ottawa

1981

Dr. Bruce Chown, Winnipeg, Manitoba and Victoria,
British Columbia
Professor Bryan Hudson, Melbourne, Australia

1982

Dr. Joseph B. MacInnis, Toronto
Sir Alan Parks, London, England

1983

Dr. James V. Maloney, Jr., Los Angeles, California

1984

Professeur Gilles Edelmann, Paris, France
Sir John Walton, Newcastle-upon-Tyne, England

APPENDIX 12

THE LECTURERS
OF
THE ROYAL COLLEGE OF PHYSICIANS AND SURGEONS
OF CANADA
1960-1984

These Lectures were inaugurated at the annual meeting of 1940. There was a Lecture in Medicine and a Lecture in Surgery until 1966 and an obstetrical and gynecological lecture 1963-1966 inclusive. In 1967 the lectures were re-named as the Royal College Lectures and are still so designated. They have always been appointments of distinction and prestige in the scientific program of the annual meeting.

(See also Lewis, p. 70-1, and p. 221.)

1960 – Montreal, January 21-23

H. Rocke Robertson
Montreal

Venous Thrombosis

K.J.R. Wightman
Toronto

The Era of Rational Therapeutics

1961 – Ottawa, January 19-21

Jacques Genest
Montreal

Angiotensin, Aldosterone and
Hypertension in Humans

Walter C. MacKenzie
Edmonton

Surgery of the Pancreas

1962 – Toronto, January 18-20

John Eager Howard
Baltimore, Maryland

The Urinary Stone

Robert M. Zollinger
Columbus, Ohio

Hormones Effecting Gastric
Secretion

1963 – Edmonton, January 17-19

E. Harry Botterell
Kingston, Ontario

The Cerebral Circulation and
Cerebral Vascular Surgery

Ray F. Farquharson Toronto	Anorexia Nervosa: The Course of Patients Seen Over Twenty Years Ago
E. Stewart Taylor* Denver, Colorado	Acute Renal Insufficiency in Obstetrics and Gynaecology

1964 – Quebec, January 16-18

Wilfred G. Bigelow Toronto	Some Physiological and Philosophical Observations Concerning the Peripheral Vascular System
Duncan E. Reid* Boston, Massachusetts	Diabetes in Pregnancy
Leslie J. Witts Oxford, England	Anaemia After Operations on the Stomach

1965 – Toronto, January 21-23

William B. Castle Boston, Massachusetts	Polycythemias
Joseph E. Murray Boston, Massachusetts	Organ Transplants: A Type of Reconstructive Surgery
Sir John Peel London, England	Diabetes and the Gynaecologist

1966 – Montreal, January 20-22

Allan C. Barnes Baltimore, Maryland	The Postmenopause
Albert Jutras Montreal	Facteurs physio-pathologiques dans la detection du carcinome intramuqueux de l'estomac
Sir Peter Medawar London, England	The Current Position of Research on Transplantation

1967 – Ottawa, January 19-21

Douglas G. Cameron Montreal	Anaemia Associated with Disorders of the Small Intestine
Sir Alexander Haddow London, England	Progress and Prospects in Cancer Research

Jean Patel
Paris, France

Le côté chirurgical de la question des adenomes Langerhansiens

1968 – Toronto, January 18-20

Claude Bertrand
Montreal

The Evolution of Surgery –
A Neurosurgeon's Viewpoint

Alan C. Burton
London, Ontario

A Virtue of Ignorance: A Biophysicist
Asks Simple Questions About
Medical Science and Medicine

Victor A. McKusick
Baltimore, Maryland

Genetics and the Practice of Medicine

1969 – Vancouver, January 23-25

Carlton Auger
Quebec

General Considerations on Benign
Tumours

John C. Beck
Montreal

Graduate Medical Education – Crisis
and Challenge

Thomas E. Starzl
Denver, Colorado

Topics in Organ Transplantation

1970 – Montreal, January 22-24

G. Malcolm Brown
Ottawa

Medical Research – Servant or Master

Robert A. Good
Minneapolis, Minnesota

Relationships Between Immunity, the
Lymphoid System and Malignancy

Lucien Léger
Paris, France

Pathophysiologie de l'hypertension
portel

1971 – Ottawa, January 21-23

Gustave Gingras
Montreal

Rehabilitation Medicine, 1970

James Jandl
Boston, Massachusetts

Spleen Function and Splenomegalic
Disorders

Paul Sanazaro
Washington, District of Columbia

Assessment of the Quality of the
Delivery of Health Care

461

1972 – Toronto, January 26-29

Norman C. Delarue
Toronto

Clinical Studies in the Realm of
Tumor Biology

Robert O. Jones
Halifax

Psychiatry, Medicine and the 1970's

Sheila Sherlock
London, England

The Natural History of Viral Hepatitis

1973 – Edmonton, January 24-27

John C. Laidlaw
Toronto

Hypertension

H. William Scott, Jr.
Nashville, Tennessee

The Use of Intestinal Bypass
Procedure in the Control of
Atherosclerosis

William H. Sweet
Boston, Massachusetts

Pain

1974 – Montreal, January 23-26

Jean-Louis Amiel
Paris, France

La place de l'immunologie et de la
chimiothérapie dans la stratégie et le
traitement du cancer

Henry J.M. Barnett
London, Ontario

Transient Cerebral Ischemia:
Pathogenesis, Prognosis, and
Management

Donald B. Effler
Cleveland, Ohio

The Place of Surgery in the
Management of Coronary Artery
Disease

1975 – Winnipeg, January 22-25

Charles H. Hollenberg
Toronto

The Fat Cell and the Fat Patient

M. Vera Peters
Toronto

Cutting the "Gordian Knot" in Breast
Cancer

Donald R. Wilson
Edmonton

Assessment of Clinical Skills – From
the Subjective to the Objective

1976 – Quebec, January 21-24

Pierre Grondin
Montreal

Pre-operative Left Ventricular
Function versus Survival After
Coronary Artery Surgery

Robert L. Noble
Vancouver

A New Approach to the Hormonal
Cause and Control of Experimental
Carcinomas, Including Those of the
Breast

William B. Spaulding
Hamilton

Implications of the Core Content
Concept in Medical Education

1977 – Toronto, January 26-29

Hector F. De Luca
Madison, Wisconsin

The Vitamin D Endocrine System in
Health and Disease

Jacques Genest
Montreal

Bioethics and the Leadership of the
Medical Profession

Lloyd D. MacLean
Montreal

Shock and Sepsis in 1977

1978 – Vancouver, January 25-28

John R. Evans
Toronto

Citizens, Societies and National Unity

Balfour M. Mount
Montreal

Palliative Care of the Terminally Ill

Louis Siminovitch**
Toronto

Genetics and Cancer

1979 – Montreal, February 6-9

Jean Bernard
Paris, France

Hématologie géographique

John H. Dirks
Vancouver

Kidney Electrolyte Transport:
Implications for the Clinician

Samuel O. Freedman
Montreal

The Immunological Monitoring of
Human Tumors

1980 – Ottawa, June 4-6

Jules Hardy
Montreal

Microsurgery of Pituitary Disorders

Jean Loygue
Paris, France

Les polyposes digestives

J. Fraser Mustard
Hamilton

The Role of Platelets and Thrombosis
in the Development of Atherosclerosis
and its Complications – A Canadian
Research Story

1981 – Toronto, September 15-17

Richard L. Cruess**
Montreal

Musculoskeletal Effects of
Corticosteroids

Richard B. Goldbloom
Halifax

"Take a Number" (The Modern
Teaching Hospital as an Instructional
Model)

Bryan Hudson
Melbourne, Australia

Virility and Fertility: Some Aspects of
Endocrine Function in the Male

1982 – Quebec, September 13-16

Joseph B. MacInnis
Toronto

The Arctic: A Drama of Cold and
Courage

Sir Alan Parks
London, England

Stoma Prevention

1983 – Calgary, September 19-22

Joseph B. Martin
Boston, Massachusetts

The Brain as an Endocrine Gland

David L. Sackett
Hamilton

On the Need for Skepticism in
Medicine

1984 – Montreal, September 10-13

Jacques Genest**

Clouds Threatening Medical
Research

William B. Weil, Jr.
East Lansing, Michigan

Patient Autonomy and Ethical
Problems in Medicine

*E.E. Poole Lecture
**G. Malcolm Brown Memorial Lecture

APPENDIX 13

THE ANNUAL MEDALLISTS
OF
THE ROYAL COLLEGE OF PHYSICIANS AND SURGEONS
OF CANADA
1960-1985

The Annual Medals were inaugurated in 1949 with the objective of encouraging research, basic or clinical, by younger physicians and surgeons. One medal is awarded annually in the Division of Medicine and one in the Division of Surgery. The two scientific papers that have received the medallist awards in the most recent competition are presented by the authors in the program of the College's subsequent Annual Meeting and the prizes are presented formally at that time.

(See also Lewis, p. 137-8, and p. 222.)

Division of Medicine

1960	J. Cyril Sinott	The Control of Pulmonary Ventilation in Physiological Hyperpnea
1961	John O. Parker	Quantitative Radiocardiography
1962	Charles R. Scriver	Familial Hyperprolinemia, Occurring Independently, in a Pedigree Containing Hereditary Nephritis and Deafness and Other Familial Diseases
1963	Carl A. Goresky	The Nature of Transcapillary Exchange in the Liver
1964	Peter T. Macklem	Bronchial Dynamics in Health and Obstructive Airway Disease
1965	David Osoba	Evidence for a Thymus Hormone
1966	Phil Gold	Studies in the Antigenic Analysis of Human Cancers

1967	Douglas R. Wilson	Micropuncture Studies of the Pathogenesis and Prophylaxis of Hemoglobinuric Acute Renal Failure
1968	W. Robert Bruce	Normal and Malignant Stem Cells and Chemotherapy
1969	Norman K. Hollenberg	Acute Oliguric Renal Failure in Man: Evidence for Preferential Renal Cortical Ischemia
1970	Morton A. Kapusta and Jack Mendelson	The Inhibition of Adjuvant Disease in Rats by the Interferon Inducing Agent Pyran Copolymer
1971	David M.P. Thomson	Diagnosis of Human Digestive System Cancer by Radioimmunoassay of Carcinoembryonic Antigen
1972	Murray M. Fisher	Bile Acids, Sex and the Liver
1973	Hiroko Watanabe	Regulation of ACTH Secretion by Glucocorticoids
1974	Mitchell L. Halperin	Pathogenesis of Type I (Distal) Renal Tubular Acidosis: Re-evaluation of Diagnostic Criteria
1975	Hulbert K.B. Silver	The Clinical Significance of Alpha 1 Fetoprotein
1976	Clayton Reynolds	Abnormalities of Endogenous Glucagon and Insulin in Unstable Diabetes
1977	Alan B.R. Thomson	Experimental Demonstration of the Effect of the Unstirred Water Layer on the Membrane Transport Process for D-Glucose in Rabbit Jejunum
1978	Roger A.L. Sutton	The Excretion of Calcium by the Kidney: Micropuncture Studies

1979	Morris A. Blajchman	Shortening of the Bleeding Time in Thrombocytopenic Rabbits by Hydrocortisone
1980	Emil Skamene	Genetic Control of Natural Resistance to Infection
1981	Hans-Michael Dosch	Detection, Characterization and Treatment of Immunoregulatory Abnormalities Associated with Antibody Deficiency
1982	Ranjit K. Chandra	Numerical and Functional Deficiency in T Helper Cells in Protein-Calorie Malnutrition
1983	Bernard Zinman	Definition of Open Loop Insulin Infusion Waveforms for Postprandial Exercise in Type I Diabetes
1984	Leo P. Renaud	In-vivo and In-vitro Characterization of the alpha-Noradrenergic Receptors on Vasopressin-secreting Neurosecretory Neurons in the Hypothalmic Supraoptic Nucleus
1985	Philip F. Halloran	The Regulation of the Expression of the Major Histocompatibility Complex Products in the Kidney

Division of Surgery

1960	Robert B. Salter	An Experimental Investigation of the Effects of Continuous Compression on Living Articular Cartilege
1961	John S. Speakman	The Structure of the Trabecular Meshwork and Corneal Endothelium in Relation to the Problem of Resistance to Outflow in Open-Angle Glaucoma

1962   No Award

1963   Joseph Schatzker   An Experimental Investigation of the
                                      Normal Blood Supply to the
                                      Proximal End of the Femur of a
                                      Newborn Pig

1964   William J. O'Callaghan   Factors Influencing Axonal
                                      Regeneration in the Mammalian
                                      Spinal Cord

1965   Gustavo Bounous   Cellular Nucleotides in Hemorrhagic
                                      Shock

1966   Robert J.W. Blanchard   Esophageal Motility in Children after
                                      Successful Operation for Esophageal
                                      Atresia and Tracheoesophageal
                                      Fistula

1967   Raymond O. Heimbecker   Surgery for Massive Myocardial
                                      Infarction

1968   George K. Wlodek   Gastric Mucosal Competence and its
                                      Relation to the Pathogenesis of Peptic
                                      Ulcer Disease

1969   Ronald J. Baird   The Reasons for Patency and
                                      Anastomosis Formation of the
                                      Internal Mammary Artery Implant

1970   T.H. Brian Haig   Cellular and Subcellular Mechanisms
                                      in Acute Pancreatitis

1971   Charles J. Wright   Septic Shock: A Problem of Hemo-
                                      dynamics or of Primary Cellular
                                      Damage

1972   T. Derek V. Cooke   Immunoglobulin Synthesis and the
                                      Significance of Persisting Antigen in
                                      a Chronic Experimental Antigen-In-
                                      duced Arthritis

1973	Ronald M. Becker	The Effect of Platelet Inhibition on Platelet Phenomena during Cardiopulmonary Bypass in Pigs
1974	Dennis W. Jirsch	Experimental Allograft Tolerance and Transplantation of the Mouse Heart
1975	Steven M. Strasberg	Bile Flow Studies in the Primate
1976	Richard J. Finley	The Metabolic Basis of Severe Sepsis in Man
1977	Barry N. French	The Value of Computerized Tomography (CT) in the Management of 1000 Consecutive Head Injuries
1978	Thomas R.J. Todd	Pulmonary Capillary Permeability During Hemorrhagic Shock
1979	John R. Little	Superficial Temporal Artery to Middle Cerebral Artery Anastomosis for Occlusive Disease of the Internal Carotid Artery: Evaluation of the Cerebral Microcirculation and Regional Blood Flow
1980	Leonard Makowka	Immune Modulation and Control of Neoplasia by a New Synthetic Polymer
1981	Julia K. Terzis	Patterns of Cutaneous Innervation and Reinnervation Following Nerve Transection
1982	Leonard Makowka	Studies into the Reversal of Experimentally Induced Fulminant Hepatic Failure
1983	Marcus J. Burnstein	Evidence for a Potent Nucleating Factor in the Gallbladder Bile of Patients with Cholesterol Gallstones

1984   Rollin K. Daniel   An Absorbable Anastomotic Device
                                    for Vascular Surgery

1985   Nicolas V. Christou   Predicting Septic Related Mortality of
                                    the Individual Surgical Patient Based
                                    on Admission Host Defence
                                    Measurements

APPENDIX 14

THE GALLIE LECTURERS, 1966-84

The Gallie Lecture was instituted in 1966 as a part of the scientific program of the Division of Surgery in the annual meeting of the College. It honors the late Dr. William Edward Gallie, former professor of surgery and dean of the faculty of medicine at the University of Toronto.

The financial support for the lectureship is provided by funds placed in 1965 in the College's Educational Endowment Fund by the Gallie Club and its Foundation. The Gallie Club is composed of former students of Professor Gallie. There was an additional grant in 1976 from the R. Samuel McLaughlin Foundation.

1966	Robert I. Harris Toronto	As I Remember Him: William Edward Gallie – Surgeon, Seeker, Teacher, Friend
1967	J. Englebert Dunphy San Fransicso, California	The Healing of Wounds
1968	Norman C. Tanner London, England	The Management of the Oesophageal Complications of Hiatal Hernia
1969	William V. McDermott, Jr. Boston, Massachusetts	Medical and Surgical Management of Hepatic Encephalopathy
1970	Angus D. McLachlin London, Ontario	Venous Thrombosis and Pulmonary Embolism
1971	Francis D. Moore Boston, Massachusetts	The Quality of Care
1972	Andrew W. Kay Glasgow, Scotland	Duodenal Ulcer – A Quest for a Policy of Selective Surgery
1973	Frederick G. Kergin Toronto	William Edward Gallie: An Appreciation
1974	G. Tom Shires Dallas, Texas	Some Aspects of Emergency Medical Care

1975	E. Harry Botterell Kingston	A Model for the Future Care of Acute Spinal Cord Injuries
1976	Frederick P. Dewar Toronto	The Gallie Course: A Retrospective Study of its 40 years
1977	E. Bruce Tovee Toronto	The Malpractice Situation in Canada – Past, Present and Future
1978	Charles G. Drake London, Ontario	On the Surgical Treatment of Intra-cranial Aneurysms
1979	Donald R. Wilson Toronto	Vascular Surgery – Then, Now and Whither
1980	Norman C. Delarue Toronto	Lung Cancer in Historical Perspective – Implications for Prevention and Individualized Management
1981	Hiram C. Polk, Jr. Louisville, Kentucky	Infection in the Surgical Patient: Current Practice and Future Prospects
1982	Clyde F. Barker Philadelphia, Pennsylvania	Studies of Immune Mechanisms and Transplantation in Pathogenesis and Treatment of Diabetes
1983	James V. Maloney, Jr. Los Angeles, California	Health Care: The North American Experiment
1984	Gilles Edelmann Paris, France	Maladie de Crohn colo-rectale: aspects chirurgicaux

APPENDIX 15

THE McLAUGHLIN FOUNDATION EDWARD GALLIE VISITING PROFESSORS
1960-1984

This annual visiting professorship in The Royal College of Physicians and Surgeons of Canada was established in 1960. It commemorates the late Dr. W.E. Gallie of Toronto, a close friend of Colonel R.S. McLaughlin. The Visiting Professor may be selected from any country and from any branch of medicine, and spends two to four weeks visiting medical schools in Canada to participate in teaching undergraduates, graduates and the profession at large.

1960	Sir Charles Illingworth, Glasgow, Scotland
1961	Sir George Pickering, Oxford, England
1962	Raoul Kourilsky, Paris, France
1963	Sir Lance Townsend, Melbourne, Australia
1964	Johannes Mortens, Copenhagen, Denmark
1965	Joseph Pierre Hoet, Louvain, Belgium
1966	A.L. d'Abreu, Birmingham, England
1967	Sir Richard Bayliss, London, England
1968	William P. Longmire, Jr., Los Angeles, California
1969	Marcel Legrain, Suresnes, France
1970	Sir Andrew Kay, Glasgow, Scotland
1971	Henry G. Miller, Newcastle-upon-Tyne, England
1972	Gilles Edelmann, Paris, France
1973	Edward B.D. Neuhauser, Boston, Massachusetts
1974	A.P.M. Forrest, Edinburgh, Scotland
1975	Vacant
1976	J. Gordon Robson, London, England
1977	Etienne-Emile Baulieu, Paris, France
1978	Claude E. Welch, Boston, Massachusetts
1979	Christopher C. Booth, Harrow, Middlesex, England
1980	Jean Loygue, Paris, France
1981	Bryan Hudson, Melbourne, Australia
1982	David C. Sabiston, Durham, North Carolina
1983	Gene Usdin, New Orleans, Louisiana
1984	Sir Peter Tizard, Oxford, England

APPENDIX 16

SIMS COMMONWEALTH TRAVELLING PROFESSORS FROM CANADA

The Sir Arthur Sims Commonwealth Travelling Professorships were endowed with the Royal College of Surgeons of England in 1946 by Sir Arthur Sims, a New Zealand industrialist with international business interests. The first professorship was held in 1948, and the first to visit Canada was Sir Reginald Watson-Jones in 1950. The objectives include promotion of liaison between scientific workers in the British Commonwealth and those in the United Kingdom, and to contribute to Commonwealth unity.

The professor may be selected from the United Kingdom or a country of the British Commonwealth. The appointment is made by the Council of the Royal College of Surgeons of England on the recommendation of an Advisory Board on which the President of the Canadian College (or his representative) has had a seat since 1952 and to which he can submit nominations. One or two professors are named each year; over a period of three to six months they visit parts of the Commonwealth to lecture and teach.

The Sims Professorship is a prestigious appointment, and the following Canadians, all Fellows of this College, have received this honor:

1955	Robert I. Harris, Toronto
1958	Robert M. Janes, Toronto
1959	Robert B. Kerr, Vancouver
1962	Walter C. MacKenzie, Edmonton
1966	A. Lawrence Chute, Toronto
1967	Angus D. McLachlin, London, Ontario
1970	Jacques Genest, Montreal
1973	Robert B. Salter, Toronto
1976	Arnold Naimark, Winnipeg
1978	Charles G. Drake, London, Ontario
1980	Charles H. Hollenberg, Toronto
1983	Jules Hardy, Montreal
1986	Richard B. Goldbloom, Halifax

APPENDIX 17

THE DUNCAN GRAHAM AWARD – RECIPIENTS 1969-1985

This award was introduced in 1969 in honor of the late Dr. Duncan Graham, long-time Professor of Medicine at the University of Toronto. It is conferred, ordinarily each year at the annual convocation of the College, on a distinguished teacher of medicine. It is supported financially by donations to the Royal College's Educational Endowment Fund from students and friends of Dr. Graham.

1969	John P. Hubbard, Philadelphia, Pennsylvania
1970	No award
1971	Walter C. MacKenzie, Edmonton
1972	Douglas E. Cannell, Toronto
1973	No award
1974	Robert C. Dickson, Halifax
1975	William Boyd, Toronto
1976	Eugène Robillard, Montreal
1977	John F. McCreary, Vancouver
1978	Lea C. Steeves, Halifax
1979	J.S.L. Browne, Montreal
1980	J. Wendell MacLeod, Ottawa
1981	Donald R. Wilson, Edmonton
1982	Angus D. McLachlin, London, Ontario
1983	Ronald V. Christie, Vancouver
1984	Martin M. Hoffman, Vancouver
1985	Fraser N. Gurd, Ottawa

APPENDIX 18

THE ROBERT M. JANES MEMORIAL

In 1968 the Janes Surgical Society agreed with this College to establish a fund within the College's Educational Endowment Fund for the purpose of honoring the late Robert M. Janes, professor of surgery at the University of Toronto and President of the College 1955-57. The memorial took the form initially of The Robert Janes Memorial Lecture delivered at a Royal College regional meeting. With the phasing out of regional meetings between 1975 and 1978 it became necessary to change the form of the memorial, and in 1981 agreement was reached to introduce a Janes Surgical Visiting Professorship. The latter was inaugurated in 1982, the professor visiting one or more medical schools in Canada over two to three weeks.

Janes Memorial Lecturers

1970	Robert Milnes-Walker, Emeritus Professor of Surgery, University of Bristol, England "Robert Janes and His Ideals" Winnipeg, Manitoba, November 7
1971	Josep Trueta, Barcelona, Spain "The Decay of the Human Frame" Sherbrooke, Quebec, September 24
1972	George Crile, Cleveland, Ohio "Newer Concepts in the Management of Carcinoma of the Breast" Hamilton, Ontario, October 27
1975	Oliver H. Beahrs, Rochester, Minnesota "Some Surgical Aspects of the Management of Inflammatory Bowel Disease" Victoria, British Columbia, October 2
	J. McAlpine, Paisley, Scotland "Variations in the Presentation of Disease in the Elderly" Victoria, British Columbia, October 2

1978   Douglas Wilmore, San Antonio, Texas
"Overview of the Status and Problems of Nutrition in the Critically Ill Patient"
London, Ontario, October 5

Janes Surgical Visiting Professors

1982   N. Tait McPhedran, Calgary

1983   John A. Palmer, Toronto

1984   Vacant

APPENDIX 19

THE K.G. McKENZIE MEMORIAL AWARDS

In 1965 the College agreed with the Canadian Neurosurgical Society to accept funds donated into the College's Educational Endowment Fund by neurosurgeons and other friends of the pioneer Canadian neurosurgeon Dr. Kenneth G. McKenzie of Toronto. The object of this special fund was to support educational awards that would serve as a memorial to Professor McKenzie.

The first K.G. McKenzie award was made early in 1968 to Dr. S.J. Peerless, then a neurosurgical resident at the University of Toronto, to assist with expenses associated with his attendance in October 1967 at the Congress of Neurological Surgeons in San Francisco, where he delivered a paper on von Hippel-Lindau's disease. As the fund and its revenues increased, two types of awards were created and offered on a regular annual basis from 1973. The first such award (No.1), open only to neurosurgical residents, is for the best scientific paper presented to the annual meeting of the Canadian Neurosurgical Society; the winner receives a citation, cash award and travel expenses. The second award (No. 2), open also to neurosurgical residents in Canada or those who have very recently completed training, supports a specific neurosurgical educational project including the related travel.

The recipients of the K.G. McKenzie memorial awards, selected by a committee of the Canadian Neurosurgical Society, have been as follows:

1968	S.J. Peerless, Toronto
1973	Kenneth C. Petruk, Edmonton (Award No. 1)
1974	Barry N. French, Toronto (Award No.1)
	Michael L. Schwartz, Toronto (Award No. 2)
1975	Paul Steinbok, Vancouver (Award No. 1)
1976	Paul Steinbok, Vancouver (Award No. 1)
	Eugene F. Kuchner, Montreal (Award No. 2)
1977	Paul J. Muller, London, Ontario (Award No. 1)
	Neal F. Kassell, Toronto (Award No. 2)
	John D. Wells, Montreal (Award No. 2)
1978	Richard C. Branan, Montreal (Award No. 1)
1979	Fred Gentili, Toronto (Award No. 1)
1980	E.J. Dolan, Toronto (Award No. 1)
1981	Richard C. Chan, Vancouver (Award No. 1)

1982	Frederic A. Lenz, Toronto (Award No. 1)
1983	Quentin J. Durward, London, Ontario (Award No. 1)
1984	A. Allan Dixon, Halifax (Award No. 1)
	G.R. Cosgrove, Montreal (Award No. 2)
	R.W. Griebel, Saskatoon (Award No. 2)
1985	F.A. Lenz, Toronto (Award No. 1)

APPENDIX 20

THE MACE

The Great Mace was donated to the College in 1964 by the active and past members of the Council and the Court of Examiners of The Royal College of Surgeons of England. The idea of the gift was conceived by Mr. A. Lawrence Abel, FRCS, of London who was largely responsible for carrying the project to a successful conclusion. Mr. Abel presented the Mace to the College at the convocation in Quebec City on January 16, 1964.

The best description of the Mace is contained in the handsome illuminated address that accompanied it:

> "The head of the Mace is surmounted with a crowned eagle, the crest of the Canadian College which is reminiscent of that of the English College, standing on an orb, holding in its dexter claw a miniature mace with a maple leaf as its finial.

> "The eagle is supported on four beaded arches of a monarchial crown, the coronet of which consists of four maple leaves alternating with four fleurs de lys. On a shaped band below the coronet is embossed the motto of the Canadian College 'Mente perspicua manuque apta'.

> "The main body of the head of the mace is mounted with four shields, each embossed with a caduceus topped by an imperial crown entwined with a serpent, the armorial bearings of the Canadian College, the serpent being the ancient symbol of the healing art which is common to the arms of both colleges.

> "The staff is plain, with two bosses, the lower of which bears an inscription recording the donors. The 'Heel' which represents the last survival of the old fighting weapon, is decorated on the upper surface with alternating maple leaves and fleurs de lys; on the lower part the caduceus and serpent emblem is repeated.

> "The Mace is made of silver and has a heavy gold deposit: its weight is 135 troy ounces and its length 3 ft. 8 ins."

The Mace is symbolic of the corporate power of the College. In the colleges of the United Kingdom the Mace is seen at most official and formal occasions but in this College its use is now confined to the annual convocation where it is carried by the member of the Executive Committee chosen-at-large from the Council. The Mace is permanently on display in a specially constructed glass cabinet in the foyer of the College building in Ottawa.

The offer of the gift of the Mace stimulated the Council to seek properly designed and registered armorial bearings so that these might be incorporated into the design of the Mace. The coat of arms was granted by the College of Arms in London late in 1962. For more detail about this see "The Armorial

Bearings" by Robert B. Salter, pages 35-46 in the 50th Anniversary commemorative volume. On page 45 of that article there is a picture of the Mace and reference to it will enhance appreciation of the description quoted above.

20.2   THE CADUCEUS

The Caduceus is a gift to the College from The Royal College of Physicians of London. The official presentation was made by Professor Alan Kekwick, Vice-President of the London College, at the annual convocation in Quebec City, January 16, 1964.

The Caduceus is a silver rod 26 inches in length and 17 ounces in weight. At its head it bears the arms of The Royal College of Physicians of London and four serpents. This Caduceus is an exact replica of the one designed and presented about the year 1556 to The Royal College of Physicians of London by Dr. John Caius, its President.

The Caduceus is the personal symbol of office of the College President and is carried only by him. The Royal College of Physicians of London have quoted Dr. Caius as writing "The silver rod indicates that the President should rule with gentleness and clemency, unlike those of olden time, who ruled with a rod of iron. The serpents, the symbols of prudence, teach the necessity of ruling prudently, while the arms of the College, placed on the summit, indicate that gentleness and prudence are the means by which the College is sustained."

In the Canadian College the President carries the Caduceus at the convocation and at certain formal social functions. It is not used at other times. There is an excellent picture of it in the 50th Anniversary commemorative volume, page 44. It is on display, together with the Mace, in the lobby of the College building in Ottawa.

20.3   THE PRESIDENTIAL BADGE OF OFFICE

The presidential badge is a gift received from The Royal College of Surgeons of Edinburgh. Mr. James J. Mason Brown, President of that College and a pediatric surgeon, attended the annual meeting in Quebec City in January 1964. Shortly after his return to Edinburgh the President received the offer of the badge and there is no doubt that Mr. Mason Brown played a leading part in initiating this handsome and generous gift. Unfortunately he died in June 1964 and thus was regrettably absent at the formal presentation of the medallion by President George I. Scott to the President, Dr. Walter C. MacKenzie, in Edinburgh on June 30, 1965.

The badge was made by the Edinburgh firm Hamilton and Inches. It is in actuality a full reproduction in 18 carat gold of the armorial bearings of the

College suspended from an arch bearing the word "President". All colours of the shield, the crest, the motto and the mantling are truly reproduced in enamel on the gold. The badge is 3¼ inches in length and 2 inches in width. It is worn at the neck suspended from a scarlet and purple ribbon, the colours being those of the Divisions of the College.

The President wears the badge at official occasions such as convocation, lectures and the annual meeting, at formal social functions, and when representing the College at official ceremonies and formal social events elsewhere.

It is of interest that Dr. John W. Scott, President of the College 1957-1960, raised the question at an Executive Committee meeting in November 1959 "whether the Council should consider a chain of office for future Presidents." No action was taken on this suggestion at the time, but his idea became a reality in 1965.

20.4   THE PAST-PRESIDENT'S BADGE

Dr. Robert C. Dickson, President of the College 1970-72, initiated the custom of a past-presidential badge. In April 1971 he told the Executive Committee of his view that there should be such a medallion that could be a replica of the President's badge but reduced in size. Dr. Dickson offered to present to the college the die for the production of such an emblem. His proposals and the offer of the gift were accepted with gratitude by the Executive Committee and subsequently by the Council in June 1971.

The badge is a miniature of the President's badge, its dimensions being approximately two thirds of the latter. It is therefore also a reproduction of the full coat of arms of the College done in appropriately coloured enamel on silver gilt. There is an arch over the badge bearing the words "Past-President", with the whole suspended from a bar on which is engraved the name of the possessor. The reverse side of the bar has a clasp for fastening to the clothing although customarily the badge is worn at the neck suspended from a purple and scarlet ribbon. All the badges have been manufactured by the Canadian silversmiths, Henry Birks & Son.

Past-presidential badges were presented to all living Past-Presidents early in 1972. The majority received them at a ceremony at the convocation at the annual meeting in Toronto. Recipients that year were Duncan Graham (presidential term 1933-35), Wilder G. Penfield (1939-41), D. Sclater Lewis (1949-51), John W. Scott (1957-60), Donald A. Thompson (1960-62), G. Malcolm Brown (1962-64), Walter C. MacKenzie (1964-66), Robert B. Kerr (1966-68) and Jacques Turcot (1968-70). Since 1972 each President has received the badge on retirement from office in a ceremony performed at convocation.

20.5 THE PRESIDENTIAL CHAIR

The presidential chair in the Council Room of the College building in Ottawa is a gift from The Royal College of Obstetricians and Gynaecologists. The President of the latter College, Sir John Peel, attended the annual meeting in Ottawa in January 1967 to represent his College and to receive Honorary Fellowship in this College. During that visit he toured the headquarters building, and shortly after his return to London he wrote to the President, Dr. Robert B. Kerr, proposing the gift of a presidential chair or "something which would be more useful or acceptable". The Executive Committee with the support of Dr. George Hooper, Chairman of the House Committee, accepted with gratitude the offer of the chair.

It was agreed that the chair should be made in Canada so that it could conform with the chairs already in place in the Council room. The design was prepared by Mr. Harold E. Devitt of Montreal, an interior decorator who was responsible for the finishing and furnishing of the Council room, lounge, Secretary's office, Roddick Room (Library) and the foyer. The design was approved by the officers of the Royal College of Obstetricians and Gynaecologists and the chair was manufactured by Mr. Devitt's firm, "The Iron Cat Limited".

The armchair is 40 inches in height and 26 inches in breadth. It is constructed of mahogany with an upholstered cushioned seat and back, the latter being shallowly winged. It was completed and placed in the Council room in August 1967 and has been in regular use for meetings since that time. The Royal College of Obstetricians and Gynaecologists expressed the wish that the chair "will represent the good relations existing between our two Colleges for many years to come."

20.6 THE COLLEGE GAVELS

The College over the years has been the recipient of a number of gavels of considerable interest. We have also presented some gavels to other organizations.

The gavel currently utilized at Council meetings in Ottawa was carved by Past-President R.C. Dickson and presented at the Council meeting held at the 50th Anniversary annual meeting in Montreal, February 3, 1979. The wood is Nova Scotia oak; the gavel is 11¼ inches in length; Dr. Dickson carved the College coat of arms on one side of the head and the original seal of the College on the other side. The block is a 4-inch square, 2 inches in height. On one side of it the dates 1929 and 1979 are cut and two other sides bear engraved plates recording, one in English and one in French, the origin of this gift. Dr. Dickson also made a wooden box for the gavel and the block; it is lined in purple and scarlet cloth, the College colors.

In 1976, the year of the bicentennial of the United States of America, Dr. Dickson carved three gavels of Canadian maple; one was given to each of the American College of Physicians, the American College of Surgeons and the American College of Obstetricians and Gynecologists at the time of their annual meeting.

This College has received as gifts four other gavels. In March 1950 Sir Reginald Watson Jones, while in Canada as Sims Commonwealth Travelling Professor, presented a gavel on behalf of The Royal College of Surgeons of England. Of simple lines, it was carved by Sir Henry Souttar, former Vice-President of The Royal College of Surgeons, and has a small accompanying block. The wood is "teak rescued from the ruins of the Hunterian Museum", bombed during the Second World War.

In October 1953 Dr. Daniel C. Elkin of Atlanta, Georgia, Lecturer in Surgery at the annual meeting that year, gave to the College a wooden gavel "made from a newel post of the stairs leading to the office of Dr. Crawford W. Long", the latter in 1842 being a pioneer in the use of anesthesia in surgery.

Professor Charles Illingworth during his visit to Canada in the autumn of 1960 as the first McLaughlin Foundation Edward Gallie Visiting Professor presented at the request of Mr. Arthur Jacobs, President of the then Royal Faculty of Physicians and Surgeons of Glasgow, a wooden gavel with stand on which was a cradle for securing the gavel when not in actual use.

The College of Medicine of South Africa, through its President, Professor Francis Daubenton, gave to this College at the 50th Anniversary meeting in February 1979 a handsome gavel made of stinkwood, a South African hardwood valued for the production of such articles.

20.7   THE COLLEGE SEALS – PAST AND PRESENT

From its earliest days the College has had an official seal that is impressed upon important documents. Its most frequent use is on the Fellowship diplomas. The original seal was circular in shape; centrally there was a maple tree with prominent leaves "on which, slung couche, a Gothic shield of arms", the latter in its three segments showing respectively a chamomile flower (physicians), a scalpel and forceps (surgeons) and the staff and serpent of Aesculapius. The College motto "Mente perspicua manuque apta" was inscribed at the foot of the maple tree. At the top of the circle there was a royal crown and at the base the date "1929", the founding year of the College. Around the perimeter of the circle there were the identifying words in Latin "Sigill Collegii Regii Medicorum et Chirurgorum Canadensis". This seal became widely known through its regular use as an emblem engraved or printed on College stationery and publications. A wooden replica, hand carved at St-Jean Port Joli, Quebec, was affixed for many years over the front door of the College building and is now in the archives. The origins and heraldic aspects of this seal are well described in Dr. D.S. Lewis's history of the College (pages 41-43) and in the 50th Anniversary commemorative volume, Chapter 3, "The Armorial Bearings" by Dr. R.B. Salter.

In 1962 the College received its registered new armorial bearings from the College of Arms in London, England. The shield of this coat of arms differs almost completely from that in the original seal. Nevertheless Council at that time agreed in the case of the seal to continue to use the original one rather than change its central design by introducing all or part of the new coat of arms. By 1968 however it was felt that it would be more appropriate and consistent if the College were to use in its insignia only one shield which should be the new one in the armorial bearings. Bylaw amendments to effect this change in the seal were approved in 1969 and 1970.

When the constitutional status of the College changed in 1971 it again became necessary to modify the seal. Under the Canada Corporations Act it was required to discontinue the use of Latin on the seal for purposes of identifying the organization. The Council elected to replace the previous Latin inscription with the name in both official languages. The word seal (Sigill) was deleted, and the full name of the College is now displayed in the left semicircle of the seal in French and on the right side in English.

The maple tree with its handsome leaves was removed from the central part of the seal which is now occupied by the full coat of arms of the College. Features of the original seal of 1930 that remain in the new one are the royal crown at the top and the date 1929 at the bottom. They now separate neatly the French and English versions of the name. In addition there is the rod and serpent and the motto can still be seen (in Latin) in the coat of arms although for most this would require use of a hand lens.

20.8 THE PORTRAIT OF JONATHAN CAMPBELL MEAKINS

Jonathan Campbell Meakins was the first President of The Royal College of Physicians and Surgeons of Canada. His term of office was 1929-31, and at that time he was professor of medicine at McGill University and physician-in-chief of The Royal Victoria Hospital in Montreal. He was an internationally renowned physician, researcher, teacher, author and administrator.

A portrait of Professor Meakins was painted in 1934 by the eminent Montreal portrait artist Alphonse Jongers. It is said to be the only one in existence. Shortly after Professor Meakins's death in October 1959 this portrait was offered to the College by Dr. J.F. Meakins and Miss Diana Meakins, son and daughter of Professor Meakins. This offer was accepted with gratitude by Council and the portrait was presented during the Council meeting of June 9, 1960, at a ceremony in which the principal participants were President D.A. Thompson and Dr. J.F. Meakins.

The portrait of Professor Meakins hangs centrally on the wall facing the foyer of the College building and above the main staircase. It is therefore clearly on view to visitors to College Headquarters. It depicts Professor Meakins seated in an armchair wearing red academic gown with blue trim and academic hood.

When the portrait was donated the College also received Professor Meakins's Royal College presidential gown and cap and 10 of his diplomas for the Archives.

20.9   **THE SILVER CIGAR BOXES**

In 1959 Dr. R.B. Kerr of Vancouver visited South Africa during his tour as Sims Commonwealth Travelling Professor. The Council of the College agreed that Dr. Kerr should carry with him a gift of silverware to the College of Physicians, Surgeons and Gynaecologists of South Africa (now the College of Medicine) which had been founded in 1955. The Honorary Treasurer, Dr. Kenneth T. MacFarlane, was assigned the responsibility of selecting a suitable gift. In consultation with the Montreal silversmith Petersen a sterling silver cigar box with distinctive Canadian decor was produced. It was presented by Dr. Kerr to the South African College on May 8, 1959.

The silversmith retained the original design solely for the College. The box is somewhat more than 9 inches in length and 5 inches in width, its depth being 2¼ inches. On the superior aspect of the lid there is fashioned a tree branch with 11 handsome maple leaves and two beautifully sculpted Canadian beavers. Engraving relevant to the gift is inscribed ordinarily on the anterior aspect of the box.

This particular gift, intended chiefly for other colleges and medical organizations, proved popular and nine more of them were presented between 1960 and 1968. These went to The Royal College of Obstetricians and Gynaecologists in 1960 (on the official opening of their new building), The Royal Australasian College of Physicians in 1963 (on their 25th anniversary), The Royal College of Physicians of London in 1964 (on the official opening of their new building), The Royal College of Surgeons of Edinburgh in 1965, the Australian Regional Council of The Royal College of Obstetricians and Gynaecologists in 1966, The Royal College of Surgeons of England in 1967 (at the Lister Centenary Conference), The Royal College of Physicians of Ireland in 1967 (at their tercentenary) and the Royal Australasian College of Surgeons in 1968.

Dr. MacFarlane while Honorary Treasurer donated a box to the College in 1961. The Council gave one to Dr. D.S. Lewis on the occasion of his retirement as Honorary Archivist and Librarian in 1970. Dr. Lewis was the only person to receive this gift from the College. It was the last of the stock of this unique piece of silverware; none has been given since that time.

20.10   **THE 50th ANNIVERSARY SILVER PLATE**

The Royal College of Physicians and Surgeons of Canada had its 50th Anniversary in 1979. Considerable attention had been paid to the planning of projects to recognize this milestone in a suitable fashion. In the spring of 1978 the College was approached by the Franklin Mint of Franklin Center, Pennsylvania, to determine interest in the production of a commemorative silver plate. The Mint had carried out a similar project for a number of Canadian universities. The plate would be of solid sterling silver and produced in a limited edition with each plate numbered and registered in the purchaser's name. It would be offered only once and for a limited period solely to Fellows of the College. In addition to producing the plates the Franklin Mint, with the help of its Canadian branch at Rexdale, Ontario, would handle the preliminary mailings and the ultimate distribution. A portion ($30.00) of the purchase price of $235.00 would be remitted to the College.

The Fellowship Affairs Committee believed that the proposal of the Franklin Mint was particularly appropriate as a 50th Anniversary project, and Council agreed that the committee could proceed. The offer of purchase of the plate was mailed to all Fellows in the early autumn of 1978. Experience suggested that the number of plates ordered would be modest (probably less than 200) but 1,354 Fellows subscribed to the offer within the time limit, a response far exceeding what had been anticipated. The resulting considerable sum of money accruing to the College ($40,620) was placed in the Educational Endowment Fund to be used for educational projects.

The sterling silver plate is eight inches in diameter and is engraved centrally with the full coat of arms of the College. Also engraved on the plate are the full name of the College in English and in French and the dates 1929 and 1979. One of the plates is displayed permanently in a case in the corridor outside the Council Room in the College Headquarters where it can be seen by visitors.

20.11   **THE COLLEGE TIE**

The announcement that the College had been granted new armorial bearings stimulated Ian Van Praagh, FRCSC, to write to the College Secretary on August 14, 1963, to propose consideration of the production of a College tie. Dr. R.M. Janes had raised the question of a College tie at an Executive meeting in April 1961 but no firm action had followed. This time the Executive Committee's reaction was immediately favorable and the proposal had the subsequent approval of Council. After consultations with several firms and review of multiple designs the College contracted in June 1965 with Rathbone & Company of Toronto to produce the first order of 500 ties. These became available in November 1965 for sale at the annual meeting in Montreal in January 1966.

The original tie was made of silk. The fabric was midnight blue with a pattern that reproduced at intervals of 1½ inches the shield of the College's coat of arms with the right (dexter) half of the shield purple (physicians) and the left half scarlet (surgeons), and the centrally placed coronet and rod of Aesculapius in gold thread. The width of the tie at the broadest point was 2½ inches.

At irregular intervals of time it has been necessary to place further orders for up to 1000 ties. With changing sartorial styles the width of the tie has varied tending now to be considerably wider than the original and the silk fabric has been replaced by synthetics. The basic design and colors have remained aside from one significant change. On the dark blue background the purple half of the shield was poorly perceptible. This distressed Dr. R.B. Salter, longtime Council member and President 1976-1978. Dr. Salter is an heraldic expert, and in December 1975 the Executive Committee approved his suggestion that ties produced thereafter should have the shields clearly outlined by gold thread. This has improved the visibility of the purple part of the shield in the tie. It is the model currently available.

But were some child of yours alive that time,
You should live twice, in it and in my rhyme.

— Shakespeare, Sonnet XVII

ABOUT THE AUTHOR

David Shephard, a Fellow of the College and a Regina, Saskatchewan anesthetist, has attempted, with varying degrees of success, to combine in his career interests in anesthesia, editing, writing and medical history. A graduate of St. Thomas's Hospital Medical School and the University of London, Dr. Shephard trained in anesthesia at the Peter Bent Brigham Hospital, Boston, the Montreal Neurological Hospital and Institute and the Montreal Children's Hospital. He practised as an anesthetist in Halifax, Nova Scotia, from 1966 to 1972, during which time he was Editor of the *Nova Scotia Medical Bulletin*. He then joined the staff of the Department of Biomedical Communications at the Mayo Clinic as a Consultant in Publications and spent three years there editing manuscripts for publication. He returned to Canada in 1974 and for a period served as Scientific Editor of the *Canadian Medical Association Journal*. In 1977, he returned to Montreal to teach medical communication at the Kellogg Centre for Advanced Studies in Primary Care and, with Drs. W.O. Spitzer and S.O. Freedman, founded *Clinical and Investigative Medicine*. He resumed clinical practice in 1979, first at The Montreal General Hospital, then at Sydney Hospital and St. Rita's Hospital, Sydney, Nova Scotia, and then at Pasqua Hospital, Regina. From 1982 to 1984 he was Directing Editor, Medical Education CIBA-GEIGY Corporation. Since 1984, he has been Associate Professor of Anesthesia in the Department of Anesthesia in the University of Saskatchewan, at Regina.

Dr. Shephard's interest in the history of medicine, particularly in Canada, has grown steadily over the years. A strong interest in biography is reflected in publications on Harvey Cushing, Alexander Graham Bell, Thomas Alva Edison and Norman Bethune. A member of the Canadian Society for the History of Medicine, David Shephard hopes that his history of the College will help to make Canadian physicians more aware of the uniqueness of medical history in Canada — as well as of the uniqueness of the College's own history.

INDEX

Individuals' names and subjects are combined in a single Index. The names of individuals are set in bold face; those of books and journals, in italics. A number followed immediately by a lower-case letter (f, n or t) refers to a page on which an indexed item is mentioned in the text in a figure, a note at the end of a chapter or a table. Not indexed are items in the following categories: the Appendices, because of the profusion of names therein and because there is a list of Appendices and their content; illustrations; and the majority of references to Council or its Executive, because of a similar profusion of references to these committees. Abbreviations are used, mainly of organizations' names; these abbreviations are explained on page xii.

Abrahamson, S., 293

Accreditation
of training programs, 110
discussed by College and ACMC,
147
early history, 193
items in basic techniques of, 195-196

Accreditation Committee, 99, 105, 109,
144, 192, 196, 234, 237, 317
assuring qualification of training
programs for College approval, 192
decision that College should conduct
own program of surveying training
in hospitals, 194
discussion of criteria for College
approval of hospital training
programs, 194, 195
drafting of regulation for hospital
training programs, 193
formation of, 193
relations of specialty committees to,
367t
representation of CAIR on, 151
representation of CPMQ on, 143
representation of public on, 117
revision of requirements and
guidelines for training, 223-226
university aegis as requirement for
training hospital approval, 187

Accreditation of Training
requirements for, 225

Accreditation of Training Programs
objectives of, 224

Accreditation Project
in revision of training standards and
requirements, 223-226

Act of Incorporation
amendment as prerequisite for
Certification program (1939), 17
to empower granting of specialist
Certificates, 14, 25
avoidance of need for amendment
through Letters Patent of
Continuance, 97
compatibility with admission of
medical scientists to Fellowship,
274

desirability of leaving undisturbed, 39
exemplifying community sanction of
specialty practice, 3
incompatibility of with voting by
Certificants on Council, 97
incompatibility with holding of
specialist examination earlier than
five years' post-graduation, 97
incompatibility with of Fellowship
examination's being held four years
after graduation, 42, 52, 57
in relation to formulation of objectives
1969, 32
integration of Letters Patent with, 79
limiting College to hold special
examinations and to grant specialist
certificates, 140
limiting Fellowship to successful
Fellowship examinees, 77
need for change, 145
need to avoid conflict with in
terminology of specialist
qualification, 89
not permitting Certificants to vote at
Council, 84
Parliamentary Bill presenting, 3, 11,
408
prescribing that Charter Fellows be
university professors, 12
presentation to Governor General
through petition from CMA, 126
principle underlying, 193
problems of opening to admit
Certificants to Fellowship, 52, 78
purpose of bill introducing, 408
relationship to Letters Patent of
Continuance, 78
requiring only medical and surgical
divisions in College, 358
requirement that interval of five years
be held since graduation before
Fellowship examination be held,
39, 44, 47, 57, 78
restricting College membership to
Fellows, 39, 60, 77
revision reflecting changes in
College's constitutional powers, 95
Saskatoon Fellows' proposals
incompatible with, 82

Advisory Board for McLaughlin
Examination and Research Centre,
100
see also McLaughlin Centre

Africa
specialist trainees from, 210
see also Foreign Medical Graduates

Alberta, 109
reliance on Certification for
recognition of specialists, 22, 136

Allen, P., 258

Allergy
desire of specialty for College
recognition, 248, 343
see also Immunology, Clinical

American Board of Internal Medicine,
296, 346
assistance to College in supplying
multiple-choice examination
questions, 244
discontinuance of oral and clinical
examination, 235
experience with multiple-choice
question examinations, 242, 244
marking procedure for multiple-
choice question examinations
College's use of, 245
use of the model for evaluation and
recertification through individual
testing (MERIT process)

American Board of Medical Specialties
moratorium on recognition of new
specialties, 348
College's relationship with, 126

American Board of Neurosurgery
studies on in-training examination,
206

American Board of Pathology
practice of granting diploma in clinical
pathology, 338

American Board of Pediatrics
computerized technique for

evaluation of candidates
joint study by with McLaughlin
Centre and National Board of
Medical Examiners, 291
computer-based patient management
problems
McLaughlin Centre's development
of with, 288, 291

American Board of Psychiatry and
Neurology, 186

American Board of Surgery
creation in 1937, 155
plans for drawn up by College
Fellow, 155

American College of Obstetricians and
Gynecologists
relationship with College, 155

American College of Physicians
Canadian Fellows as presidents of,
155, 157n, 385
nature of Fellowship in compared to
College's, 42
purchase from of medical knowledge
self-assessment program, 319, 321
relationship with College, 155

American College of Surgeons
Canadian Fellows as presidents of,
155, 157n, 377
nature of Fellowship as compared to
College's, 42
purchase from of surgical knowledge
self-assessment program, 319
relationship with College, 155
role in accreditation
exemplified in Newfoundland, 405

Anesthesia
as specialty recognized by
Certification, 18
manpower shortage of, 162
recognition of as a specialty, 337t

Anesthetists
autonomy avoided by Certification
program, 399
desire for autonomy, 16

Annals of the Royal College of Physicians and Surgeons of Canada, The, 109, 114, 233
  as medium of communication
    between College and Fellows and Certificants, 325
  bilingualism in, 171
  CME content of, 97
  development of, 325-330, 377
  facilitating CME, 312, 316, 404
  function, 328
  in publicizing CME opportunities, 316
  publication of article on Council's proposals (1970), 59
  publication of CME-related material, 320
  publication of first volume, 1968, 313, 328, 381
  "Update" series as CME content, 321
  use of, 318

Annals of the Royal College of Surgeons of England
  as model for College's *Annals*, 327

Annual Meetings
  see College

Annual Meetings Committee
  scientific program as "showcase" and demonstrating unity, 322

Annual Meeting Scientific Program
  activities coordinated by Education Committee, 316

Approval of Hospitals
  see Hospitals, approval of

Archibald, E.W., 155

Archives and Library Committee, 96

Armstrong, G.E., 157n

Aronoff, A., 84

Association of American Medical Colleges
  definition of objectives of undergraduate and postgraduate medical education by, 188, 207

Association of Canadian Medical Colleges, 296, 377
  and National Physician Manpower Committee
    participation with College on, 166
  College's relationship with, 5, 25, 145-147, 148, 200
  College's discussions with concerning postgraduate medical education, 145, 200-201
  in discussions on single examination process, 253
  in selection of McLaughlin-Gallie Visiting Professor, 96
  liaison meeting with College, Association of Canadian Teaching Hospitals and CAIR, 150
  McLaughlin Centre's need for medical school support, 284
  mutual benefits of College's relationship with, 403
  observer representation on McLaughlin Centre advisory board, 289
  problems with university aegis concept discussed, 201
  representation on Continuing Education Committee, 98
  university participation in training programs
    ascertaining of medical schools' attitude towards, 199
    need for College to inform regarding, 145-146, 198
  value for College of working with, 88, 146

Association of Canadian Teaching Hospitals
  liaison meeting of College, ACMC and CAIR, 150

Association of Canadian University Departments of Anaesthesia
  College's discussion with on education liaison, 126

Atlantic Provinces, 109

Audiovisual Instruction
  potential for CME activity, 318

Australia
    participation in joint feasibility study
        of international sharing of test
        items, 290
    specialist trainees from, 210, 215
        see also Foreign Medical Graduates

Automation of headquarters operations,
    103t, 109

Autonomy
    of specialties, 149
        versus association with College,
        149, 335, 352-360

Awards Committee, 96, 109
    cooperation of with specialty societies
        regarding speaker and event
        grants, 361

Bacteriology
    manpower shortage in, 162

Baird, D.A., 71, 72

Baird, J.D.B., 26

Barootes, E.S., 82, 159

Barr, M.L., 274

Barton, W.B., 26

Bazin, A.T., 11, 16

Bean, I.W., 127

Beattie, W.G., 238

Beaudoin, J., 28, 66, 170, 250, 288,
    289

Beck, J.C., 347, 348

Beck, R.P., 355

Beddoe, A., 85

Belisle, M., 244, 277

Bell, R.D., 258

Belliveau, N.J., 141

Bergeron, G.A., 25, 272, 338

Berman, M., 89

Best, C., 379

Bethune, G., 117

Bicameral legislative system proposed,
    362

Bilingualism
    College policy, 169-172, 383

Bilingualism and biculturalism, 173,
    176, 336

Biochemistry, Medical
    recognition as a specialty, 338-343,
    345t

Bioethics Committee, 106

Biomedical Ethics Committee, 3, 106
    relations of specialty committees to,
    367t

Bloom, B.S., 188

"Blue Book, The"
    reflecting regulations and
        requirements for training in medical
        specialties, 223

Botterell Committee and Report
    on Certification program, 23, 25,
    26-28
    recommendation for single standard
        of clinical competence, 218

Botterell, E.H., 13, 23, 24, 25, 27, 85,
    88, 147, 204

Boulay, J., 289, 321

Bourgeois, E.G., 17

Brien, F.S., 221, 222, 272

British Columbia, 109, 187
  orthopedic surgeons' emigration
    because of lack of recognition of
    Certification, 37
  reliance on Certification for
    recognition of specialists, 22

British Columbia, University of, Medical
  School
  establishment of, 194
  university participation in training
    programs
    problems with, 202

British Commonwealth of Nations
  development of
    in original concept of College, 178
  foreign medical graduates from, 213

British Medical Association
  as association rather than examining
    body, 16

Brown, G.M., 24, 40, 41, 42, 44, 46,
  50, 51, 52, 53, 75n, 97, 128, 209,
  271, 293, 325, 326, 327, 341, 342,
  375, 377

Browne, J.S.L., 148

Bryans, F.E., 84, 357

Bucher, R., 2

Budget
  see College, Budget

Burns, C.W., 22, 23

Burrow, J., 113

Bylaws
  original
    approval of (1930), 11
    numbering of, 77
    revision reflecting changes in
      College's constitutional powers, 95
  No. 1 (1972), 69, 92, 93, 95
    development of, 77-79
  No. 2 (1976)
    flexibility in committee

appointments censuring of
  specialists, 93
No. 3 (1978)
  regularization of FRCPC and
    FRCSC; introduction of Chief
    Executive Officer as synonym for
    Secretary, 93-94
No. 4 (1980)
  creation of office of President-Elect;
    change in designation of Chief
    Executive Officer from Secretary
    to Executive Director;
    clarification of Council
    membership, 94

Bylaws Committee
  proposal that it study Nominating
    Committee and Council, 92

Bylaw Amendments
  1964: greater protection in proper use
    of ballot papers, 80
  1966: greater flexibility in election of
    President, 83
  1967: affiliation of Certificants with
    College, 84
  1969: representation of Certificants
    on Council; use of coat of arms in
    shield, 84-85
  1970: ratification of wording of coat
    of arms description; revision of
    wording on Fellowship diploma;
    deletion of reference to President
    as chairman of annual meeting
    arrangements committee;
    rescinding of need for affiliative
    Certificants to give notice by 1970;
    voting for Council in all geographic
    areas, 86-87

Caduceus
  donated by the Royal College of
    Physicians of London, 152

Calgary, University of, Medical School
  establishment of, 194
    as factor in increase in number of
      medical graduates in Canada,
      164

Cameron, D.E., 185, 189

Cameron, D.F., 289

Cameron, D.G., 50, 51, 56, 58, 66, 70, 75n, 98, 141, 196, 204, 219, 220, 243, 254, 273, 316, 391, 393

Camp Hill Hospital, Halifax, NS, 187

Canada Corporations Act (Part II), The
  permitting continuance of College's constitution, 78-79
  enabling College's conversion to a corporation, 78, 97

Canada Medical Act
  not empowering Medical Council of Canada to certify specialists, 16

Canadian Anaesthetists' Society
  interest in meeting with College in June, 365
  knowledge self-assessment program joint development with College, 321
  self-assessment program, 321, 361
  interest to Maintenance of Competence Committee, 321

Canadian Association of Anatomists, 272

Canadian Association of Clinical Surgeons
  view that Certification in urology would be unwise, 17

Canadian Association of General Surgeons
  desire for College's annual meeting to be held in June, 364

Canadian Association of Internes and Residents
  and National Physician Manpower Committee
    participation with College on, 166
  and single examination process
    participation of in development of, 255
  College's relationship with, 5, 125, 149-151, 255

critique of Certification process and impact of College, 399
formation and purpose, 150
participation in first Conference of Specialties, 255
requests for representation on College committees, 151

Canadian Association of Medical Biochemists
  request for Fellowship in medicine modified for biochemistry, 338

Canadian Association of Medical Microbiologists
  support for autonomy among laboratory medicine specialists, 358

Canadian Association of Neurological Nurses
  see Canadian Congress of Neurological Sciences

Canadian Association of Pathologists
  membership in joint study group with College, 358
  views on pathology subspecialty development, 338

Canadian Association of Professors of Medicine
  and invitation to propose names for membership in Specialty Committee in Internal Medicine, 368
  College's relationship with, 126
  in-training evaluation study of, 260
  in-training evaluation report form opinion on assessment of, 260
  measurement of professional competence for Certification in internal medicine, 263
  cosponsorship of conference on with College, 263

Canadian Association of Radiologists
  desire for recognition of specialty, 16

Canadian Biochemical Society, 272

Canadian Cardiovascular Society
request for Fellowship in medicine
modified for cardiology, 341

Canadian Clinical Travel Club, 393

Canadian College of Medical Genetics
difference with College regarding
genetics as free-standing specialty,
352t

Canadian Congress of Neurological
Sciences
annual meeting in June as potential
conflict with College's, 365

Canadian Commission on Hospital
Accreditation, 375
priority of its annual meeting in June,
365

Canadian Council on Hospital
Accreditation
College's relationship with, 125
surveying of hospital training
programs for College, 194

Canadian Critical Care Society
College's relationship with, 360

Canadian Federation of Biological
Societies
admission of medical scientists to
Fellowships
consideration of draft training
requirements and examination
regulations for, 272

Canadian Film Institute, 97

Canadian Journal of Surgery
CME content of, 312, 320
College's co-sponsoring with CMA of,
97, 127
cosponsoring of with CMA, 127
effect on of proposed publication of
Annals, 326
facilitating CME, 404

Canadian Medical Association

and National Physician Manpower
Committee
participation with College on, 166
Certification program, 15-17, 126
discussed with College, 4, 15-17
code of ethics, 127
collaboration with College in
formulating Code of Ethics, 127
College's relationship with, 5, 125-127
Committee on the formation of a
Canadian College of Physicians
and Surgeons, 269
Committee on Specialists, 15
co-sponsoring with College in
developing Canadian Journal of
Surgery, 97, 127
need to inform regarding proposed
publication of Annals, 326
observation by Executive Committee
on lack of approved training
centres, 193
observer representation on ACMC
Executive Council, 146
physician manpower conference on,
166
presentation of Act of Incorporation
through petition to Governor
General, 126
representation on Continuing
Education Committee, 98
request that federal government
establish Royal Commission on
health services, 160
resolution (1920) leading to formation
of College, 151-152, 178, 189, 269
section of radiology, 16

Canadian Medical Association Journal
correspondents' criticism of
Fellowship examination, 240-241
effect on of proposed publication of
Annals, 326
Fellowship examination discussed in,
240-241, 328

Canadian Neurological Society
see Canadian Congress of
Neurological Sciences

Canadian Neurosurgical Society

see Canadian Congress of
Neurological Sciences

Canadian Oncology Society
College's relationship with, 360

Canadian Otolaryngological Society
training requirements in
otolorayngology, proposal to
College regarding, 220

Canadian Physiological Society, 272

Canadian Psychiatric Association
College's relationship with, 5
Education Committee, 5
proposed training requirements
leading to Certification, 221-222
Fellowship examination thought to be
in need of revision, 221
opposition to child psychiatry as
specialty, 352t
training requirements in psychiatry
discussions with College on,
221-222
two levels of examination thought
necessary, 220

Canadian Society for Clinical Chemistry
concern regarding Fellowship in
medical biochemistry, 339-340

Canadian Society for Clinical
Investigation, 147-149, 393
admission of medical scientists to
Fellowship
consideration of draft training
requirements and examination
regulations for, 272
favoring of, 273
observations concerning, 273-274
opposition to special examinations
relating to, 273
annual meeting
coinciding with College's, 148-149,
324, 365
held preceding College's, 148, 323
joint symposia with College
inaugurated, 324
College's relationship with, 5, 125,
147-149, 322

concern over medical research
funding, 106
participation in College's annual
meeting, 270, 312, 322-324, 364
affinity of some specialty societies to,
365

Canadian Society for Neuroscience
see Canadian Congress of
Neurological Sciences

Canadian Society for Surgery of the
Hand
see Manus

Canadian Society for the Study of
Infertility
membership in Coordinating Advisory
Council, 356, 357

Canadian Society of Clinical
Pharmacology
College's relationship with, 360

Canadian Society of Endocrinology and
Metabolism
College's relationship with, 360

Caouette, M., 355

Cardiology
desire of specialty for College
recognition, 243, 248
Fellowship in medicine modified for
request for as example of
fragmentation of specialties, 341
need for final written examinations at
end of training, 258
recognition as a specialty, 341, 343,
344t
specialists required
estimation of number of, 167

Cardiovascular and Thoracic Surgery
Fellowship examination favored as
single standard of competence, 39
lack of approval of non-university
affiliated training programs, 197
limited independent approval of
training programs no longer
granted, 197, 204

recognition as specialty, 336, 344t
session for in annual meeting, 323
specialists required
    recommendation concerning
        reduction in, 166

Central America
    specialist trainees from, 210
    see also Foreign Medical Graduates

Certificant
    distinction between Fellow and
        difficulty of making, 37, 39

Certificants
    admission of to Fellowship, 49, 52,
        53, 54, 59, 66, 67, 79
    basis for laid by Expanded
        Executive Committee, 41-54, 98
    affiliation with College, 32, 57, 84,
        114, 328, 381
    closer relationship with College
        proposed, 23, 25, 27, 28, 32, 57,
        84, 114, 325
    College's relationship to, 6, 63, 84,
        97
    College's responsibility towards a
        priority, 38
    comprising a variety of specialists, 65,
        74
    elected to Council, 57, 84
    extension of representation on
        Council, 84
    formal designation as such, 57
    granted Certification by "grandfather"
        clause, 1942-1947, 18
    granted representation on Council,
        57, 84
    invited to attend regional meetings,
        313
    not permitted to become Fellows by
        reason of Act of Incorporation, 78
    participation in College's scientific
        meetings, 57
    pre-1972
        admission to Fellowship of, 1, 48,
            53, 54, 57, 59, 66, 67, 79
        as majority of specialists, 2, 26, 28
        College's obligation to, 38, 73
        College's relationship with, 6
        privileges granted by College,
            1967, 57, 84

Quebec certificate holders and
    admission to College Fellowship,
        173
resolution concerning, 157
status of (e.g. "Failed Fellows"), 2,
    24, 74, 249
relationship with College, 6
referendum on, 97
closer with 1967 bylaw
    amendment, 84, 97
relationship with Council, 57, 84, 97
support for retention of Certification,
    38

Certificate(s) of Special Competence
    as form of recognition of new
        specialties, 348, 349, 351
    discussion of value of with Canadian
        Association of Professors of
        Medicine, 126
    in USA, 345t
    introduction of, 349
    problems of multiplicity of, 131
    suggested as means of obviating need
        for recognizing new primary
        specialties, 348, 349

Certification
    and measurement of specialist
        competence, 41
    arguments favoring use as term for
        single examination process, 47, 57,
        60
    as basic specialty qualification, 37-39,
        48, 59, 250
    national importance of, 44
    use by CPSO, 137
    as "constraint of history", 39
    as prerequisite for Fellowship in
        College, 2
    as requirement for admission to
        American College of Surgeons, 155
    as standard in provinces for
        recognition of specialists, 22, 139
    as stimulus to approval of residency
        training positions, 155n
    as term for basic specialty
        qualification, 37-40, 47, 48, 50
    as term for single examination
        process, 47, 48, 60, 383
    as stated by Council (1970), 59
    granting without examination, 405,
        406

as problem for College, 137
in internal medicine
  measurement of professional
    competence for, conference on,
    263
in psychiatry
  preferred by psychiatrists to
    Fellowship, 221
need for in addition to Fellowship
  expressed by psychiatrists and
  radiologists, 219
need to keep College and CPMQ
  Certification of equivalent standard,
  144
origin of concept of, 15
paradoxically more important than
  the Fellowship, 41, 42
retention as College's competence
  qualification
  arguments for, 24, 25
uniform process of across country
  urged, 173

Certification Examination
and foreign medical graduates
  relative simplicity of admission to,
  168, 169
as basic examination for specialist
  competence, 2, 44, 46, 213
as less academic alternative to
  Fellowship examination, 14
as prerequisite for admission to
  Fellowship, 2
CAIR study of, 151, 399
decision to abolish in neurology,
  neurosurgery, orthopedic surgery
  and thoracic surgery, 25, 37
different reasons for specialists taking,
  65, 74
essential difference between
  Fellowship examination and, 22,
  37
lack of valid definition for, 37
evaluation of only minimal standard
  of competence by, 213
failure in but success by same
  candidate in Fellowship
  examination, 37
failure to reflect ideal of high standard
  of specialist practice, 19
first held fall 1946, 18

lack of precision as evaluative tool,
  231
nature and purpose, 36, 232
need for defined objectives, 45
objectives previously not well defined,
  44
of province of Quebec, 38, 57, 141
oral
  quality of, 263
pass rates, 24, 213, 236t
planning for
  negated by Council's 1959
  decision, 32, 97
post-1971
  replacing previous Fellowship and
  Certification examinations, 2,
  231, 232
  success in as prerequisite for
  admission to Fellowship, 2
  superiority of as examination, 2,
  232
pre-1972 Certification examination
  replaced by new Certification
  single examination process, 231
proposals to abolish, 22, 23, 24, 26,
  27, 28
purpose of, 231, 240
resolution favoring abolition of (1958),
  23, 32, 97, 249
standard of
  lack of guidance for examiners,
  240
standard proposed, 15
uniform requirements for with
  Fellowship examination, 218-223
see also Examination(s)

"Certification Mentality", 39

Certification administered in Quebec
  see Quebec

Certification of Family Physicians
  collaboration by College with CFPC
  on, 129
  pilot projects on, 129

Certification of Specialists, 4

Certification Program, 15-28
  arguments in favor of, 18, 41

as peripheral concern of College, 5, 18
CMA's role in initiating, 126
concern expressed over, 22-27
deficiencies in, 23
faults of, 21, 23
greater importance than Fellowship, 41, 42, 45
impact of, 18-19, 399
inaugurated by amendment of Act of Incorporation 1939, 14
introduction of, 1942, 5, 18, 366
need to amend Act of Incorporation, 17
origins, 15-18
preserving unity among specialists, 5, 399
proposal to discontinue, 27

Certification, Simultaneous, 140-145
and College's relationship with CPMQ, 140-145
conducted jointly by College and CPMQ, 57
in internal medicine
introduction of, 144
of College and CPMQ
fees for, 145
origin and development of, 141-145

Certification, Temporary
and College's relationship with CPSO, 136-139
as problem for College, 138
extension of program
discussed by College and ACMC, 147
facilitating development of specialty departments in Newfoundland, 406
facilitating growth of postgraduate faculties, 400
impact of, 138, 139
modifications to, 138, 139
origin and development of, 136-139

Change
Council's proposals for, see Council
radical need for, 87, 88, 89, 174
1960s as era of, 32, 34, 159, 358, 395

Charter Fellows
nature of
representing different specialties, 16

Chevalier, P., 64

Child Neurology Association
see Canadian Congress of Neurological Sciences

China
specialist trainees from, 212
see also Foreign Medical Graduates

Chipman, W.W., 157n

Christie, R.V., 141, 142, 242, 244, 277, 335, 338, 342, 343

Chute, A.L., 24, 26, 28, 148, 194, 196, 206, 271, 272, 273, 275, 396

CIBA Foundation, 402

Clarke, C.G., 210

Clinical Clerkship
experience provided
similarity to junior internship, 143
influence of on interval between graduation and Certification, 48
discussed by College and ACMC, 147
provision of by medical schools, 47

Clinical Teaching Unit
as element of training program, 206, 224

Clinical Traineeships
as form of CME, 310, 312, 320, 321

Coat of Arms
as symbol of nature of College and its pursuit of unity, 85, 170
crest
intentional similarity to crest of The Royal College of Surgeons of England, 152
use in College seal authorized by bylaw amendment, 85

Cochrane, W.A., 340

Cockings, E.C., 80, 83, 84, 85, 87

Cockshott, W.P., 138

Code of Ethics
see Ethics

Coggeshall, L.T., 183

College
accountability to public of, 404
administrative structure
changes in, 106-123
affiliation with Certificants (pre-1972),
32
and ACMC, 5, 145-147, 148, 200,
403
and an examination centre
need for College to develop, 277,
280
and CAIR, 5, 149-151
and Canadian Association of
Professors of Medicine
cosponsorship of conference on
measurement of professional
competence for Certification in
internal medicine, 263-264
and Certificants
close relationship proposed, 325
lack of communication with, 327,
328
relationship with, 6, 97
closer with 1967 bylaw
amendment, 84, 97
referendum on, 97
and Certification, 5, 15-18
policy on abolition of, 23, 32, 38,
39
and CFPC, 5, 125, 403
basis for liaison with, 133
and change, 1, 2, 31, 87, 88, 89,
101, 395
and CMA
relationship with, 5, 125-127
and CME
evolving role in, 312-321, 403, 404
increased interest in, 308, 312
objectives related to, 34, 320
regional committees in, 98, 104,
316, 317

resolutions on, 321
and Coordinating Advisory Council,
356
membership in, 356-357
and CPA, 5, 221-222
and CPMQ, 5, 140-145, 403
comité des études médicales
liaison committee with College,
144
observer representation on, 145
and CPSO, 5, 136-140
and evaluation and examination
methodology, 281
and Fellows
lack of communication with, 327,
328
responsibility for needs of, 32, 308,
316, 318
and health care, 34
and immigration of physicians,
168-169
and in-training evaluation, 253-257,
261-262
study of with Canadian Association
of Professors of Medicine, 126,
263
and laboratory medicine
membership in joint study group
with Canadian Association of
Pathologists, 359
and laboratory medicine specialists
additional division in College urged
by some, 358
desire for autonomy among some,
358-359
and maintenance of competence,
318-321
and manpower needs, 165-167
and specialty development, 335-368
and MCC
common membership of
examination test committees,
290
McLaughlin Centre's development
of Canadian examination
questions for, 403
relationship with, 5, 125, 134
and McLaughlin Centre
aims identified by Dr. B.J. Perey,
301
membership of Advisory Board of,
289

need for study of administrative
   relations with, 293
and medical scientists, 270-276
   guidelines for admission to
   Fellowship of, 275
and national issues, 159-179
and national unity, 172-179
and postgraduate medical education,
   183-189
and professional incompetence
   discussions with CPSO on,
   139-140
and psychiatrists, 184-187
and regional issues, 159, 175
and research, 269-302
   encouraged by annual meetings,
      270
   encouraged by Royal College
      medals, 270, 403
   fostered by admission of medical
      scientists, 271-276
   fostered by establishment of
      fellowship, 270-271
   fostered by Research Committee,
      270
   fostered by Visiting Professorships
      in Medical Research, 270, 404
   objectives relating to, 34, 269, 270
   recognition of value of, 269, 270,
      403
and residency programs
   concern with, 205
and residents, 150
and SOGC
   joint study committee, 355-357
      deliberations of, 357
   relationship with, 5, 357, 369n
and specialist competence
   cosponsoring with Canadian
      Association of Professors of
      Medicine of conference on
      measurement of in internal
      medicine, 263
and specialist manpower, 365
and specialty committees
   dependence on, 225
and specialty health care in
   Newfoundland, 405-408
and specialty societies, 360-366
   relations, 391
      discussed at Third Conference of
         Specialties, 361

and specialty training
   partnership with universities in, 32,
      197, 204
and temporary Certification, 136-139
and The Royal Australasian College
   of Physicians
   influence of College's training and
      evaluation methods on, 402
   joint meeting with, 1980, 152
and The Royal Australasian College
   of Surgeons
   joint meeting with, 1980, 152
and The Royal College of Physicians
   of London
   joint meeting with, 1974, 152
and the specialties
   relations enhanced, 360-368
and training requirements in
   otolaryngology, 220
   discussions with Canadian
      Otolaryngological Society and
      Specialty Committee on
      Otolaryngology on, 220
and training requirements in
   psychiatry, 221-222
   discussion with CPA and Specialty
      Committee in Psychiatry with,
      221-222
and unity, 6
   proposal for two colleges instead of
      one, 4
   proposal to establish Division of
      Obstetrics and Gynecology, 354
and universities, 200
   impact on, 400-401
annual and regional meetings
   scientific programs
      as CME activities, 316
annual meetings, 320, 322-325
   desirability of joint annual meeting
      with CSCI, 148, 149
   potential for CME activity, 312,
      320, 322, 403
   scientific program, 148-149, 150,
      316, 322-325
   timing discussed at Third
      Conference of Specialties, 364
   1930, 11
   1960, 196
   1964, 80, 148, 242
   1966, 80, 84
   1967, 81, 82, 84

1969, 85, 159, 199
1970, 86, 87, 91, 92, 109
1971, 63, 64, 92
1972, 69, 73, 79
1979, 322
as an educational force, 402
as an elite vs. a democratic body, 2,
  14, 36, 40, 53, 58, 68, 72, 90, 91,
  210
as national organization, 81-83, 85,
  159, 178, 179, 383
as unified body, 4, 66, 91
  call for, 91
as "an integrating force for all
  specialists", 272
"authority" of, 140, 147, 163, 191,
  197, 225, 269, 276, 403
bilingualism
  policy on, 169-172
  statement on, 170-172
brief to ACMC (1959), 200-201
brief to 1964 and 1982 Hall
  Commissions, 161-165
budget
  growth of, 107, 108f
calls for change in, 80-81, 85, 87-92
Certificants (pre-1972)
  admission to Fellowship of, 31, 49,
  52
  referendum concerning, 66-69
challenges confronting, 88-92
  need to address, 100, 101
change
  reaction to, 101, 395
claim of slowness to change, 87, 88,
  89
coat of arms
  represented on annual meeting
    program cover, 324
  blazon of, 86
  granted by College of Arms, 85
constitutional and governing structure
  deficiencies in, 109
  proposal for improvement of, 109
convocation address
  B.J. Perey: "Citizens, Societies and
    National Unity", 176, 177-178
Council
  problems of representation of
    Fellows, 81-83
criticisms of, 80-83, 85, 87-92

"culture" of, 1, 3-4
democratization, 88, 89
  claim of its resistance to, 88-92
Division of Medicine
  annual meeting originally centred
    around Division of Surgery and,
    4
Division of Surgery
  annual meeting originally centred
    around Division of Medicine
    and, 4
evaluation
  lack of modern ideas on, 90
Executive Director, 107
  change of title from Secretary, 94
  introduction of term for Chief
    Executive Officer, 94
financial assets, 74
founding, 11, 335, 398
function
  as conceived by charter Fellows,
    398
  identification of specialist
    competence, 41, 42
  no longer breeding an elite, 40, 41,
    42
  opportunities for CME, 335
  provision of national standard of
    competence, 90
  training, examining and certifying,
    257, 335
granting Fellowship, Certification
  without examination
  as problem, 137
impact of
  by means of CME, 399
  effected through College's unitarian
    nature, 398
  on medical profession, 399
  on other countries, 402
  on other organizations, 403
  on specialist practice, 396, 399
  on specialists, 396
  on specialty development, 404-405
  on specialty health care, 398, 404,
    405-408
  on universities, 399
  through maintenance of
    competence, 403
  through training and evaluating,
    399, 401, 402

importance of accepting all
certificated specialists, 90
influence on residents, 209-210, 401
leadership in specialty practice
desirability of undertaking role in,
101
Lectures
see Royal College Lectures
lectureship at regional meetings, 312,
320
letters to Fellows
Oct. 14, 1966, 81
Dec. 8, 1969, 55
Nov. 8, 1971, 66
Oct., 20, 1972, 73
Nov. 3, 1972, 73
Dec. 13, 1972, 73
liaison meeting with ACMC,
Association of Canadian Teaching
Hospitals and CAIR, 150
maintaining highest standards in
specialty practice
role in, 159
membership, 36-71, 107
acute growth in 1972, 31, 73, 113,
114, 317, 404
all, 36, 53, 54, 65
change with admission of pre-1972
Certificants, 31
desirability of single class of
specialists, 53, 88
growth of, 107f
importance of including all
specialists, 36, 53, 54, 60, 65,
88, 90
limited to Fellows by Act of
Incorporation, 39
need for inclusivity rather than
exclusivity, 48, 52, 58, 59, 65
motto (Mente Perspicua Manuque
Apta), 85, 408
multidisciplinary nature of, 103t, 336
view contrasted with that of
laboratory medicine specialists,
359
nature and purpose, 33, 42
change with change in
membership, 31
objectives
broader, in Canadian medicine, 45,
73

early statements on, 12, 13, 159,
192, 269, 408
formal statement on, 33-34, 59,
398
lack of definition before 1969, 33
need to broaden objectives, 60
need to formulate new objectives,
31, 58, 159, 381
formulation of, 32-34
original single object, 11, 32, 33,
40, 226, 335
organization
proposal for changes in, 109, 110
original concept of, 178
partnership with universities
value and uniqueness of, 204
power
urged to share rather than
monopolize, 88
pre-1972 Certificants
relationship to, 62
privileges granted pre-1972
Certificants 1967, 57
publication of journals
potential for CME activity, 318
purpose, 32
reaction to crisis, 399
regional meetings
defects in, 104
guest lectures funded by
Educational Endowment Fund,
313
inauguration of in Halifax, 313
poor attendance, 318
potential for CME activity, 313
1959 (Halifax), 406
1962 (St. John's), 406
relations with Certificants, 6
relations with other medical
organizations, 5, 102t, 125-155
relations with other medical colleges,
126, 151-155
representation in geographic areas,
80, 81, 82, 84, 87
responsibility towards Certificants as a
priority, 38
revolution in medical education
lack of advanced understanding of,
90
Roddick Memorial Room
and College's relationship with
MCC, 134

role in Canadian medicine, 159
greater than identifying
competence, 33, 52, 60
role in postgraduate education,
1949-1959, 184-189
seal
replacement by official coat of
arms, 85
secretariat
administrative organization of,
106-110, 113-114, 116-123
recommendation concerning,
109-110, 116-120
administrative structure
changes in 1980, 106-108, 113,
116, 117, 118t, 119t, 120, 121
associate secretary, 113
abolition of post of, 120
chief executive officer and
Executive Director
appointment of Dr. J.H. Darragh
as, 122
communications office created, 122
directorship of specialties
created and Dr. J.H. Graham
appointed to, 122
divisional structure of Training and
Evaluation, Administration
and Finance and Membership
Affairs
formalization of, 120
Division of Administration and
Finance, 107, 113, 120, 364
Division of Fellowship Affairs, 107
creation, 364
demonstrating College's attention
to post-Fellowship affairs, 364
J.H. Darragh appointed Director
of, 122
Division of Membership Affairs,
113, 120
Division of Training and Evaluation,
107, 113, 114, 364
Credentials Section, 113
problems concerning, 116, 119t
Evaluation of Training Programs
Section, 113, 118t, 119t, 120
problems concerning, 116
Examinations Section, 113
problems concerning, 116, 118t
problems identified and

recommendations made by
Horlick report (1975), 116-117,
118t, 119t, 120
reviewed by Training and
Evaluation Committee,
114-115, 118t, 119t
role in evaluation, 234
Dr. J.H. Graham's secretaryship
appreciation of, 121-122
growth of, 113
Honorary Assistant Secretary
retention of post of, 120
organization and staffing of, 109
proposal for changes in, 109
post of assistant secretary created,
113
remuneration of senior personnel
need for Finance Committee to
consider, 120
resignation of Dr. J.H. Graham
from secretaryship, 120-121
Secretary
designation as Chief Executive
Officer, 93, 120
change of title to Executive
Director, 94
Chief Executive Officer as synonym
for, 93
Section of Obstetrics and Gynecology
annual meeting centred around
Division of Medicine, Division of
Surgery and, 322
slowness to change, 88, 89, 90
specialty designations provided, 11,
13, 19, 34
the 'new' College, 50, 60, 249
affirmation of, 63-74
basis for laid by Expanded
Executive Committee, 32-54, 98
concept of, 32, 50, 52, 110, 249
constitutional basis for, 79
creation of, 249, 250
emergence of, 31, 69, 113, 192,
385, 404
requiring formulation of new
objectives, 33
evolution of
Council's proposals for (1970),
59
integrity of, 387
meaning of, 57, 69, 74

nature and role of, 72

tie, 86

training requirements in psychiatry
  discussion with CPA on, 221-222

transformation into, 1, 31, 114

travel fellowships
  supported by Educational
    Endowment Fund, 313

university participation in training
  programs, 184-189, 199-211
  brief to ACMC regarding, 200-201
  communications with medical
    schools regarding, 200

unitarian nature, 290, 342, 398, 399,
  405

use of French language, 169-172

College of Arms
  granting College its coat of arms, 85

College of Family Physicians of Canada,
  5, 99
  and National Physician Manpower
    Committee
    participation with College on, 166
  change of name from College of
    General Practice of Canada
    permitted under Canada
    Corporations Act (Part II), 78
  College's liaison with, 129, 132, 133
    basis for, 133
  College's relationship with, 5, 125,
    127-134, 293
  cooperation sought by McLaughlin
    Centre, 285
  emergency medicine conjoint
    committee with College, 129-132
  interest in an examination centre, 280
  interest in changes in evaluation and
    examination techniques, 281
  mutual benefits of College's
    relationship with, 132, 133
  observer representation on
    ACMC Executive Council, 146
    College committees
    McLaughlin Centre Advisory
      Board, 289
  "Who are the practising doctors?"
    (paper by Dr. D.I. Rice), 365

College of General Practice of Canada
  see College of Family Physicians of
    Canada

College of Medicine of South Africa
  division of general practice in, 128
  similarity in membership to College,
    128, 155

College of Physicians and Surgeons of
  Ontario
  and professional incompetence
    discussions with College on,
      139-140
  College's relationship with, 5, 136-140
  Dr. G.M. Brown president of, 375
  recognition of foreign specialty
    qualifications
    Education and Registration
      Committee's reluctance
      concerning, 137
  role in development of temporary
    Certification program, 136-139

College of Physicians and Surgeons of
  Saskatchewan
  enquiry of College re term 'specialist',
    1934, 15

Collip, J.B., 148

Committee(s)
  CAIR's request for representation on,
    151
  manifesting professionalization, 396
  on arrangements for scientific
    meetings, 98, 109, 316, 322
    representation on Continuing
      Education Committee of, 98
  on Certificant Relationships, 95, 97
  on Horizons, 100-104, 122, 319
    creation, 100
    emphasis on importance to College
      of good relations with
      specialties, 366
    regarding College's future, 100-104
  on Policy, 95, 97, 325
  on Specialists
    as antecedent of specialty
      committees, 17, 366
    plans for Certification, 16, 17, 366
  on Trauma, 98, 109
  regional, in continuing education, 98,
    316, 317
    defects, 104
    nature and activities of, 317

representation on Continuing
Education Committee, 98
see also Committees listed under
individual names (e.g.,
Examinations Committee)

Committees, Structure of
changes, 95-106

Communications Committee, 97

Community Medicine
recognition as a specialty, 347, 348,
351t

Competence
certificate of,
need for, 37
definition of, 309
measurement of
by specialty qualifying examination,
46
of specialists, 1
assessment by one examination or
two, 43
College's future in providing
national standard of, 90
question as to whether Fellowship or
Certification examination should be
retained as test of, 37-41, 45
single standard of
recommended, 43, 45, 53, 218
specialist, 2, 37, 41, 42, 43, 44, 45,
46, 47, 51, 52, 60, 61, 231-264
as aspect of College's
accountability to public, 235
College and, 404
components, 234
dangers of lack of, 12
evaluation and examination of, 37,
231-264
identification by basic examination,
41
measurement of,
internal medicine conference,
263
related to Certification, 263
need for certificate, 37
need for standard of, 45
need to recognize, 41
single examination process
emphasis on, 256

value of in-training evaluation in
measuring, 263
see also Evaluation, Examination
Methodology, In-Training
Evaluation
specialty,
single basic examination reflecting
motion relating to, 44, 46, 47
see also Dual Standard

Competence, Certificate of Special
see Certificate(s) of Special
Competence

Competence, Maintenance of, 311
College's impact on, 308
definition of, 307, 309
increased interest of College in, 308,
318
issues in, 308-312
see also Maintenance of Competence
Committee

Comprehensive examination
see In-Training Examination

Computer-Assisted Instruction, 312

"Concerned Fellows of Victoria, The",
71-73

Conference(s)
on evaluation in medical education
(1969), 232
on Measurement of Professional
Competence for Specialty
Certification in Internal Medicine
(1977), 263
on residency education in the clinical
specialties, 140, 204-211, 217, 224,
247, 277, 286, 399
proceedings publication cost
supported by Educational
Endowment Fund, 313
on residency training in internal
medicine, 211, 260
on surgical education and research,
211
costs supported by Educational
Endowment Fund, 313

Conference(s) of Specialties, 98, 361-366
  demonstrating College's relations with specialty societies, 361-362
  fifth (1980), on specialist manpower, 167, 362, 365
  first (1971), on single examination process, 254, 361, 362
  fourth (1979), on timing of annual meeting, 362, 364-365
  origin of, 254, 362
  second (1976), on self-assessment and CME, 319, 362
  third (1977), on College's relations with specialty societies, 362-364

Continuing Education Committee, 98, 318
  and CME, 316
  and regional structure for College, 104
  discussions on self-assessment, medical audit and peer review, 318-319
  expansion of role, 318
  formation of, 98, 317
  inauguration of first Conference of Specialties, 362
  replacement by Fellowship Affairs Committee, 105, 319
  terms of reference of, 317

Continuing Medical Education
  ACMC's interest in, 146
  activities facilitating attainment of, 320
  areas identified by Education Committee for development, 316
  audiovisual instruction in, 316
  College and, 307-330
  College's impact on, 319
  College's principal activities, 316
  College's role in, 34, 45
  conditions for success, 311
  content and techniques of, 310
  definition of, 309
  early use of term, 184
  effectiveness of, 309-310
  facilitated by clinical traineeships, 312, 320, 321
  facilitated by College-supported lectures at specialty society meetings, 312, 320

  facilitated by College-supported short courses, 312, 316, 320
  facilitated by travel fellowships, 312, 313, 320
  Horizons Committee report recommendations on, 101t, 319-320
  identification of needs assessment in, 310, 316
  increase in courses offered and in enrolment, 308
  issues in, 308
  learning styles and preferences in, 310
  methods, 310
    bibliographies of, 321
  motivation of individuals in, 310
  nature of programs, 312, 313, 316, 318, 320
  recertification and, 311
  regional committee structure for, 98, 104, 316, 317
  value of recognized, 403-404

Convocation
  presence of president of CMA at, 126

Convocation Address
  B.J. Perey
    "The Royal College and the National Challenge", 176

Coordinating Advisory Council, 356, 357

Corbett, W.E.M., 359

Core Content
  central importance of in specialist training, 192

Cormier, G., 289

Corporation Professionnelle des Médecins du Québec, la
  and National Physician Manpower Committee
  participation with College on, 166
  Certificants of
    admission to Royal College Fellowship urged, 173
  Certification of, 38

Comité des études médicales
College's observer representation
on, 145
action to make university affiliation
of training programs mandatory,
200
cooperation sought by McLaughlin
Centre, 285
evaluation of residents by
form used for, 259
difference from College's, 259
experience with in-training evaluation,
256
greater role in program accreditation
urged, 175
relationship with College, 5, 140-145,
293
mutual benefits of, 141
revolution in medical education
advanced understanding of, 90
role in development of simultaneous
Certification with College, 140-145
temporary certificates granted by, 136
university involvement in
postgraduate training, 143, 200
use of College's multiple-choice
question examinations, 286, 294

Council
as sole obligatory College committee,
95
basic aims, 1970-1972, 63
call for change in, 80-81, 91-92
changes in structure deferred, 92
discussion of Expanded Executive
Committee's deliberations, 49-50
influence on councillors
demonstrating professionalization,
396-398
manner of working, 68
need to be more representative,
80-82
principal aims of, 1970-1972, 60
program of communication regarding,
75n
proposals for change (1970), 55-64,
86, 97, 98, 147
relating to the 'new' College
including alternative versions,
62-63
in original form, 59
relationship with Certificants, 84, 97

Coutts, H.T., 280

Couture, J.G., 174, 289

Cox, A.R., 163

Credentialling
of specialist candidates, 114

Credentials Committee, 95, 99, 105,
109, 142, 144, 192, 215, 234, 237,
238, 317
and admission of medical scientists to
Fellowship, 272
and revision of training requirements,
225
assessment of examination eligibility,
211-217
assessment of foreign medical
graduates' credentials, 211-217
definition of objectives for specialty
training, 225
definition of objectives for training
programs, 192
development of uniform (single)
standard of training for Fellowship
and Certification examinations,
218-223
discussions on recognition of
pathology subspecialties, 338-342
discussions on training requirements
in otolaryngology, 220
discussions on training requirements
in psychiatry, 221-222
early association with Committee on
Specialists, 366
position of on value of in-training
evaluation report
and conflict with Canadian
Association of Professors of
Medicine, 260
problems facing, 211-214
proposed function of evaluating
Fellowship candidates, 41, 48, 53,
57
observer representation of CPMQ on,
143
relations of specialty committees to,
367t
resolution that medical scientists be
admitted to Fellowship, 272
study of Botterell Committee report,
23, 28

view on use of FITER, 260
work of, 217-217, 225
   facilitated by tracking study, 217

Credentials, Training
assessment
   see Training Credentials

Crocker, P., 106

Cross-Country Tour (1970)
undertaken by President R.C.
Dickson, 59, 60, 65

Cut-Off Score
   see Examination Methodology,
      multiple-choice question technique

Dalhousie University Medical School
CME program for general
   practitioners developed, 307
internships for Dalhousie graduates in
   Newfoundland, 406
proposed admission of medical
   scientists to Fellowship
   response to, 272
psychiatric training under auspices of
   request for, 185
university participation in training
   programs
   problems with, 202

Darragh, J.H., 107, 122, 123, 138, 163

Darte, J.M.M., 166, 347, 406

Davis, R.A., 113

Dawson, J.C.C., 136, 139

de Gaulle, C., 172

"Delicate Fabric, the"
as aspect of national unity, 125
concerning complex interrelationships
   in Canadian health care scene, 297
in relation to specialist practice in
   Canada, 373
reflecting College's relations with
   other organizations, 125

Denton, R.L., 25

Department of Consumer and
Corporate Affairs
Council advised to apply to for
   Letters Patent of Continuance, 78

Department of Immigration
green paper on immigration, 168

Department of Health, Newfoundland,
406

Department of National Health and
Welfare
and National Physician Manpower
   Committee
   participation with College on, 166
observer representation on ACMC
   Executive Council, 140
study of medical manpower
   College's willingness to participate
      in, 166
survey of number and activities of
   physicians, 165

Department of Pensions and National
Health
interest in national health program,
   160
proposals for health insurance, 160

Departments of Health,
College's relations with, 125

Depression, The
need for funding of health care, 160

Dermatology
manpower shortage in, 162
recognition as a specialty, 337t
specialists
   estimation of number of, 167

Dermatology/Syphilology
as specialty for early Fellowship
   examination, 14
as specialty recognized by
   Certification, 18

Deschenes, L., 100

Desjardins, E., 96

Detweiler, H.K., 147, 196

Detweiler Travelling Fellowships
in context of CME, 312

Dewan, J.G., 221

Dickinson, G., 326

Dickson, R.C., 21, 52, 59, 60, 62, 64,
66, 68, 69, 70, 75n, 79, 83, 92, 110,
150, 166, 207, 208, 254, 289, 293,
311, 357, 358, 383, 385

Dixon, J.M.S., 358, 359

Dominion Council of Health
interest in health insurance, 160

Dominion-Provincial Conference on
Reconstruction
in relation to health insurance, 160

Doupe, J., 274

Drake, C.G., 32, 33, 36, 40, 43, 45,
46, 48, 52, 54, 71, 72, 73, 74, 75n,
100, 117, 147, 157n, 195, 211, 377,
385, 387

Drouin, G., 97

Drucker, W.R., 138

Dual Standard
abolition of, 231, 375, 385
condemned by Fellows, 55, 89
defects of, 21, 26, 60, 63, 231
move to resolve initiated in 1953, 22
of examinations, 24, 231, 249
continuation of, 89
deficiencies of, 24
inappropriateness, 88, 90
request for Council to retain or
reject, 250
of Fellows, 36
of membership, 36, 53
of specialists, 1, 63
importance of abolishing, 65

of specialist competence, 1, 21, 36,
42, 89
dissatisfaction with, 19-21
germ of idea, 29n
identified by Dr. R.I. Harris, 21
no longer needed, 46, 47, 59, 60
origin and early moves to resolve,
19-29
problems caused by, 21, 31
question of retention, 24, 25, 42
preventing simultaneous oral
Certification examination with
CPMQ, 144
request for Council to accept or
reject, 250
solution to, 31
of specialist status, 1, 21, 89
of training, 89, 217

Dubé, E., 22, 128

Dufresne, R., 141

Duncan Graham Award
first award (1973), Dr. J.P. Hubbard,
188
second award (1974), Dr. R.C.
Dickson, 383

Dunn, W.L., 359

Economic Council of Canada, 165

Education Committee, 317
ad hoc antecedent of, 95-96
CAIR representation on, 151
CME responsibilities, 316, 318
terms of reference, 98, 316

Educational Development Fund, 74,
108f, 313, 318
CME activities supported by, 313,
316
providing support for Royal College
Visiting Professorship in
Medical Research, 271

Educational Endowment Fund
facilitating CME, 313, 316
purpose, 313
representation on Education and

Continuing Education
Committees, 98, 316
support of CME activities, 404

Educational Objectives
understanding of need for, 191, 192,
207-208, 217, 222-223, 225, 233,
234

Educational Standards Committee, 14

Educational Testing Service, 188

Education Committee, 96, 98, 110
and CME, 98
coordination of activities of
Educational Endowment Fund
Committee, 316
coordination of activities of Films
Committee, 316
coordination of activities of
Publications Committee, 316
coordination of activities of Scientific
Program for Annual Meeting
Committee, 316
coordination of arrangements for
McLaughlin-Gallie Visiting
Professorship, 316
disbanded, 318
formed to administer Educational
Endowment Fund activities, 98
identification of Fellows' CME needs,
318
reorganized as Continuing Education
Committee, 98, 318
representation of CAIR on, 151
terms of reference, 98, 316

Education, Medical
advances in 1950s and 1960s, 2, 46,
47, 225, 250
expansiveness of in 1960s, 136, 226n
objectives, 207-208
principles of
understanding of in 1960s, 191
stages of, 205

Education, Medical, Postgraduate
College's innovative contributions to,
192
College's role 1949-1959, 183-189

hospitals' role in, 161
issues discussed with ACMC, 145
problems underlying in 1960s, 162
residency education in the clinical
specialties
conference on (Kingston, 1965),
140, 204-211
standards of
advanced through College's survey
of training programs, 196
see also College, Universities

Eire
specialist trainees from, 210
see also Foreign Medical Graduates

Electoral Reform
ballot for Council election not voided
by voting for incomplete candidate
list, 77
1970 amendment introducing, 87
motions from Saskatchewan Fellows
proposing, 1966, 80-83, 85
provided by 1970 bylaw amendment,
77

Ellis, J.R., 205

Emergency Medical Care Committee,
98
and joint meetings with CFPC, 99,
130-132
recommendations of for primary
specialist qualification in emergency
medicine, 132

Emergency Medicine
as specialty
problems for College recognition of
on basis of CFPC training
program, 131, 132
conjoint interest with College of
Family Physicians of Canada in,
129-132
development of as specialty, 98
formation of special interest
committee in, 98, 130
joint training committee with CFPC
in, 131-132
recognition as a specialty, 99, 132,
347, 351t

collaboration with CFPC, 99,
129-132
College-CFPC proposal for joint
recognition of, 131
joint College-CFPC plans for
aborted, 98
recognition of
through demands for College-
granted primary specialist
qualification in, 131-132

Emigration
of physicians, 164

Employment and Social Insurance Act
(1935), The
declared unconstitutional, 160

Endocrinology
recognition as specialty, 343
specialists required
estimation of number of, 167

Essay Question Examination Technique
see Examination Methodology

Ethics
high standard of as College
responsibility, 34

Ethics Committee, 3, 109

Ethics, Code of
Collaboration with CMA in
developing, 127

Europe
specialist trainees from, 215
see also Foreign Medical Graduates

Evaluation
aims of, 233, 234
College's lack of modern ideas on, 90
definition of, 233
improvements in, 53
lack of uniformity of in Canada, 281
methodology
discussed by College and ACMC,
147
need for centre to devise uniform
measuring techniques, 281

need for changes in evaluation and
examination techniques, 281
of examination candidates, 232-235
by computerized techniques, 288,
291-292
of residents, 90
changes needed, 282
College's impact on, 402-403
College's new approach, 191
Final In-Training Evaluation Report,
255, 259-264
discussed by College and
ACMC, 147
discussions of value of with
Canadian Association of
Professors of Medicine, 126
through in-training examination
of specialist candidates, 4
principles of, 232-235
sources of, 234, 256
steps in, 233
see also In-Training Evaluation, In-
Training Evaluation Reports

Evaluation of Specialty Training
Programs Committee
see Accreditation Committee

Evans, J.R., 163, 173, 174, 175, 176,
177, 179, 206, 348, 405

Examination Centre, An
benefits of, 283
general interest in, 277
need and rationale for, 280
need for College to develop, 277
need for to devise uniform measuring
techniques, 281
need for to study and develop
examination techniques, 280
see also McLaughlin Examination and
Research Centre, The R.S.

Examination Methodology
banking of examination questions
at McLaughlin centre, 290
at University of Alberta, 290
comprehenisve examination
see below at in-training
examination
computerized patient management
problems

inclusion of in Certification
  examination in pediatrics, 291
McLaughlin Centre's international
  development of in evaluation
  of competence, 288
  study of feasibility of, 291
computers in examination techniques,
  286
computer-based examinations, 286,
  288, 291, 292
  first working model for developed
    by McLaughlin Centre, 286
Computer-based Examination Project
  (CBX)
  developed by National Board of
    Medical Examiners, 291
cutting scores
  incentive of to research in
    McLaughlin Centre, 290
deficiencies in examination methods,
  231
discussed by College and ACMC,
  147, 253
essay question technique, 99
  deficiencies of, 143, 234, 243, 252,
    279
  disadvantage of, 234, 245-246
  lack of discriminatory ability, 245
factors determining pass/fail rates,
  213, 238, 241
  McLaughlin Centre's studies on,
    287
improvement in, 53
inter-judge reliability
  McLaughlin Centre's studies on,
    287
in-training (comprehensive, mid-
  training) examination
  advantages and disadvantages of,
    206, 248
  as component of single
    examination process, 252, 253,
    258, 260
  as formative aspect of single
    examination process, 248, 252,
    253, 257
  development of, 247-248, 257-259
  introduction of, 247-248, 258-259
  rationale for, 279
  see also below at principles of
    surgery examination

Model for Evaluation and
  Recertification through Individual
  Testing (MERIT process)
  used by American Board of
    Internal Medicine, 291
multiple-choice questions
  computerized storage and retrieval
    of, 286
multiple-choice question technique,
  37, 99, 209, 283
  advantages and disadvantages,
    234-235, 243, 245-246
  as component of single
    examination process, 232
  conclusions based on analysis of
    introduction of, 245-247
  cutting score
    determination of, 245
  development, 286
  development of test committees,
    286
  discriminatory superiority over
    essay question technique, 279
  extent of use of, 143
  imperfections in, 235, 286
  improvement of College's
    examination procedures resulting
    from introduction of, 53, 188
  introduction of into College's
    examination system, 231, 234,
    242, 243-247, 277, 403
  limitation in measurement of
    clinical competence, 235, 286
  need for College to use, 283
  preparation of, 244-245
  scoring procedure, 245
  study of international sharing of test
    items
    McLaughlin Centre's participation
      in, 290
  superiority of over essay question
    technique, 243, 246, 277, 279
  test committees for, 99, 234, 286,
    403
    College and MCC common
      membership of, 100
  value established, 251
multiple-choice question technique
  and orals
  results of correlated with results of
    in-training evaluation, 263

need to introduce changes in, 282
new approach to, 231
oral and clinical examination
  deficiencies demonstrated, 235,
    252, 279, 286
  flaws in as evaluation instrument
    demonstrated by videotaped
    simulated examination, 285
patient management problems
  in investigation of examination
    scoring, 291
principles of surgery examination
  advantages of, 6, 258
  aims of, 258
  as component of single
    examination process, 251, 254,
    256, 259
  basic concept of, 258
  development and introduction of,
    257-258
  rejected by some specialists, 259
scoring of examinations
  incentive of to research in
    McLaughlin Centre, 290
single examination process, 2, 37, 47,
  59, 98, 99
  antecedents, 24, 25-27, 249
  basic concept of, 232, 249, 251
  components of, 251, 253
  development of, 218, 223,
    249-257
  discussed by Expanded Executive
    Committee, 47
  for all specialists, 31, 44, 47,
    249-257
  introduction of, 2, 4, 98, 114, 232,
    249, 254, 381
  motion on, 44, 46, 47
  objectives of, 191, 232
  replacing previous Fellowship and
    Certification examinations, 2,
    231, 232
  specialist competence emphasized,
    31, 44, 46, 256
  specialty societies consulted, 361
  superiority of to College's previous
    Fellowship examination, 60, 232
  task force on
    see Task Force on the Single
      Examination Process
  study and development of

examination techniques
  need for unit for, 277, 280, 281

Examination(s)
  after two years of training, 279
  anomaly of candidates' taking same
    training for either Fellowship or
    Certification or both, 37
  basic qualifying
    to be available after four years of
      training, 44, 48
    to be taken by all specialists, 31,
      44
  comprehensive
    see Examination Methodology, In-
      Training Examination,
      Mid-Training Examination
  defects in, 209, 234, 277
  discussed by CPMQ and College,
    142-143
  dual standard of, 231, 232
  Fellowship examination
    pass/fail rates, 13, 231, 236t
    reasons for failure in, 206, 213
  marking impaired by lack of
    uniformity, 282
  multiple-choice question type as
    assessment of competence, 37
  need for both Fellowship and
    Certification
    expressed by psychiatrists and
      radiologists, 219
  need for reform of, 27, 32, 92, 279,
    281
  of College
    dissatisfaction with, 210, 233, 234,
      238, 240, 241, 251
  oral
    for Certification
      quality of, 263
  perennial problems with, 32
  primary, for Fellowship, 13, 248
  purpose of, 234, 251
  reform of, 14, 235-264, 279
  relationship to training, 191, 225, 401
  uniform requirements for Fellowship
    and Certification, 218-223
  whether both Fellowship and
    Certification should be held, 36
  see also Certification Examination,
    Fellowship Examination

Examinations Committee, 95, 99, 105, 109, 142, 144, 192, 234, 238, 277, 279, 284, 294
agreement to introduce multiple-choice question examination, 242-244
and comments on CAIR's report on Certification, 399
and revision of College's examination system, 241, 242, 402
and revision of College's training requirements, 218
CAIR representation on, 151
concern over examination pass rate of foreign medical graduates, 213, 215, 238, 241
CPMQ representation on, 143
discussions on recognition of pathology subspecialties, 338, 342
guidance on future policy, 279
in drawing up early training requirements, 193
in-training examinations recommended by, 248
position of value of in-training evaluation report and conflict with Canadian Association of Professors of Medicine, 260
recommendations for study of acceptable training by non-Canadian residents, 214
relations of specialty committees to, 367t
recommendation of separate examining board in obstetrics and gynecology, 353, 354
reform of examination process, 192, 241-264
role in development and implementation of single examination process, 192, 250-257
study of Botterell report, 23, 28
study of content and conduct of Fellowship examination, 241-242
view on use of FITER, 260
views on specialty recognition, 338, 342, 346, 353
whether competence should be assessed by one or by two examinations, 43

Examining Boards
and single examination process
contribution to development of, 223

"Exceptional Forum, an"
College's impact on specialty groups through providing, 405
Kingston conference on residency education as example of, 204
provided for College by ACMC Executive Council, 147
reflecting College's relations with other organizations, 140

Executive Committee
relations with specialty committees, 366, 367t
retreat, 394

Executive Director
see College, Executive Director

Expanded Executive Committee
basis laid by for the 'new' College, 32-54, 98
creation of, 32, 98, 250
development of new criteria for admission to Fellowship, 36-54, 97
discussions of, 32-34, 36-54, 231, 249, 250
formulation of new College objectives by, 32-34, 98, 270
membership of, 75n
studies of benefitting postgraduate medical education, 88
task of, 32, 42

"Failed Fellows"
as a view about Certificants, 2, 24, 74, 249

Far East
specialist trainees from, 213, 215
see also Foreign Medical Graduates

Farquharson Report
see Reports

Farquharson, R.F., 24, 148, 163, 381

Federal Advisory Committee on Mental Health, 185

Federal Health Resources Fund
offsetting costs of residency training programs, 400

Federation of Biological Societies
proposed admission of medical scientists to Fellowship
opposition to, 272

Federation of Provincial Medical Licensing Authorities of Canada, 159
College's relationship with, 134

Fellows
distinction between Certificants and
difficulty of making, 37, 39

Fellowship (in College)
admission of Certificants to, 41-54, 79
as stated by Council (1970), 59
basis for laid by Expanded Executive Committee, 41-54
discussed by College and ACMC, 147
incompatibility with Act of Incorporation, 78
motion proposing, 51, 54
admission of medical scientists to, 270-276
admission of pre-1972 Certificants to, 31, 404
fees, 74, 108f, 313, 317
admission of Quebec-Certificate holders, 173, 176
admission to
Certification as prerequisite for, 48, 59
Certification (post-1971) as prerequisite for
as stated by Council (1970), 59
criteria for, 36, 44, 48
development of criteria for, 36-71
discussion of criteria for, 43, 48, 50-54
admission to of pre-1972 Certificants, 31, 49, 52
referendum concerning, 66-69

admission to without examination, 82
ad eundem gradum permitted under Act of Incorporation, 77, 82
as an elite, 2, 14, 43, 58
as 'hallmark of academic man', 13
as stipulated in Act of Incorporation, 77
distinctive nature of, 239
fear of its becoming devalued, 17, 45, 52, 55, 68, 71, 250
granting without examination, 405, 406
as problem for College, 137
Honorary, 77, 103t, 153
importance of to Quebec, 57, 64
inability to define, 50, 52
meaning and nature of, 14, 31, 50, 57, 276
agreement by Expanded Executive Committee on, 37
change in, 1, 2
newer concept, 36, 50, 57, 73, 74
need to be more representative, 80-82
origins, 11-15
post-1971
criteria for admission, 36
to embrace wider membership, 36
purpose of, 50
quintessence of, 373
reflecting professional and Collegial values, 41, 45
retention as College's competence qualification
arguments for, 39-40, 45

Fellowship Affairs Committee, 96, 105, 113, 294
and CME, 316
cooperation with specialty groups regarding speaker and event grants, 361
demonstrating College's attention to post-Fellowship affairs, 364
interest in self-assessment program of Canadian Anaesthetists' Society, 361
replacement of Continuing Education Committee by, 319
terms of reference, 105, 319

Fellowship Diploma
    indication of passing a rigorous test,
        13, 240

Fellowship Examination
    case for retention as single standard
        of competence, 39-40, 46, 231
    content and conduct of, 238
    criticisms of, 209, 238, 239, 240,
        241, 352
    discontinuation of, 2
    emphasis on general medicine and
        surgery, 13
    essential difference between
        Certification examination and, 22,
        37
    lack of valid definition for, 37
    flaws in, 209, 231, 239, 240, 241,
        402
    foreign medical graduates and, 238,
        241
    in early years
        nature of, 13-14
    in medicine, surgery and obstetrics
        and gynecology
        content and conduct of, 238
        reviewed by Examinations
            Committee subcommittees,
            241-242
        recommendations for reform of
            content and conduct of, 241-242
    in obstetrics and gynecology
        separate board approved by
            Council, 355
        separate board recommended by
            Examinations Committee, 354
    lacking precision as evaluative tool,
        231
    modification to permit examination in
        specialties, 14
    nature and purpose, 41, 50, 73, 231,
        238, 240
    objectives previously not well defined,
        44
    pass/fail rates, 13, 14, 24, 90, 235,
        236t, 238, 241
    primary examination, 13, 248
    reflecting ideal of high standard of
        specialty practice, 13, 19, 239
    replaced by post-1971 Certification
        examination, 231

    review of, 231
    uniform requirements for with
        Certification examination, 31
    standard of
        lack of guidance on for examiners,
            240
    success in yet failure in Certification
        examination, 37, 209, 240
    see also Examination(s)

Fellowship, Honorary
    election to of Fellows of sister
        colleges, 152
    permitted under Act of Incorporation,
        77

Ferguson, C.C., 90, 342

Films Committee, 97, 109
    activities coordinated by Education
        Committee, 316

Film Library
    College's, 97
        in context of CME, 312

Final In-Training Evaluation Report
    see In-Training Evaluation

Finance Committee, 120

Firstbrook, J.B., 114, 117, 120, 163,
    164, 223, 275, 298

Fish, D.G., 146, 210, 399

Fitzgerald, J.G., 15

Foreign Medical Graduates
    acceptable specialist training, 168,
        169
        guidelines for, 168, 214
    acceptable training of, 169
        study by Training and Evaluation
            Committee, 169, 214-217
    assessment of credentials, 168,
        211-217
    Canada's dependence on, 166, 167,
        169
    certificated
        proportion resident in USA, 164

contribution to specialist health care,
168
credentials
assessment of, 212-217
examination pass rates, 168, 169,
214-215, 238, 241
Examinations Committee's concern
over, 238
tracking study, 214-216, 238
requirements for practice in Canada
simplicity of, 168
types of residency programs filled by,
210-211
see also Immigration, of physicians

Fragmentation Committee, 95, 96, 340,
341
conception and formation of, 340,
341, 342
conclusions on specialty recognition,
343

Fragmentation of Specialties
see Specialties, Fragmentation of

Fraser, F.M., 128

Fraser, J.C., 281, 282, 283

French Language
use of by College, 170-172, 175

Front de Libération de Québec
separatist activities in Quebec, 172

Fyles, T.W., 66, 70, 71

Gagnon, E.D., 32, 33, 38, 41, 42, 45,
46, 52, 75n, 82, 85, 136, 141, 142,
143, 144, 170, 340, 341

Gagnon, H., 141

Gallie Course, 389
as example of established
independent university-based
training program, 184, 186, 202

Gallie Lecture
first, 184, 324
inauguration, 324

Gallie, W.E., 15, 17, 157n, 184

Gass, C.L., 128

Gastroenterology
desire of specialty for College
recognition, 248
recognition as a specialty, 343
specialists required
estimation of number of, 167

Gaudreau, C., 66

Gemmell, J.P., 244, 277, 341

General Hospital, St. John's, NFLD,
405, 406, 407

General Motors
affording risk capital, 177

General Practice, CMA Section of
chief objective of, 128

General Surgery
as educational base for all surgical
specialties, 259
as "mother discipline" for surgical
specialties, 104t
as specialty recognized by
Certification, 18
formation of test committee for
multiple-choice question
examination, 286
participation in principles of surgery
examination, 258-259
recognition as specialty, 337t

Genest, J., 106, 273

Genetics, Medical
College recognition but not
implementation as specialty, 351t

Geriatric Medicine
recognition as a specialty, 347, 349,
351t

Gilbert, J.A.L., 232, 250

Gilder, S.S.B., 327

Giles, T.J., 59, 75n, 106, 109, 113, 114, 117, 120, 122, 179n, 198, 210, 238, 293, 327, 328, 365

Gingras, G., 143

Gingras, R., 143

Goldberg, W.M., 56, 396, 340, 401

Goldbloom, V., 141, 142

Government, Federal
College's relations with, 125

Grace, M., 287

Graham, D., 15, 16, 17, 18, 379, 381, 383, 387

Graham, J.H., 33, 40, 49, 55, 75n, 106, 107, 117, 120, 121, 122, 133, 136, 137, 139, 141, 143, 146, 147, 166, 170, 203, 212, 298, 301, 338, 346, 355, 359, 368

Great Britain
specialty training in
memorandum on, 223

"Grey Book, The"
as summary of specialty training overseen by College-universities partnership, 224, 225
summarizing accreditation policies and survey process, 224, 262

Gunton, R.W., 3, 100, 130, 163, 164, 167, 168, 344, 347, 348, 365, 408

Gurd, F.N., 25, 26, 37, 38, 39, 41, 45, 46, 48, 75n, 90, 113, 114, 116, 204, 223, 225, 232, 249, 250, 359, 360

Gutelius, J.R., 88, 89, 147, 348

Gynaecological Travel Club
as forerunner of CSCI, 147

Hall Commission(s) on health services
brief to from ad hoc committee on

specialist manpower, 1960, 96, 161-163, 167
brief on health services, 1980, 163-165

Hall, Justice Emmett, 161, 164, 165

Hammurabi, Code of
negative effect of approach of in continuing education, 311

Harasym, P., 291

Harding, P., 355

Harris, R.I., 21, 22, 184

Harris, W.R., 247, 261

Hartroft, S., 274

Harvard University, 122

Harvey, J.C., 208

Hazlett, C., 286

Health Care, Specialty
College's impact on, 398, 404, 405-408
College's objective relating to, 34
defects in, 164-165
provision of in Canada reviewed, 160-165

Health Insurance
as factor influencing residency training programs, 206
as stimulus to approval of residency training positions, 155n
evolution of concepts of, 160-161
interest of Dominion Council of Health in, 160
proposals for developed by Department of Pensions and National Health, 160
report by Standing Committee on Industrial and International Relations, 160

Health Manpower Directorate
physician/population ratio
estimate of optimum by, 169

Health Resources Development Fund
program similar to required in 1980,
165

Heal, F.C., 26

Hébert, C.E., 203

Hector, R.I., 261

Hematological Pathology
see Pathology, Hematological

Hematology, Clinical
desire of specialty for College
recognition, 248
recognition as a specialty, 343
specialists required
estimation of number of, 167

Himsworth, H., 379

Holland, C.W., 23

Honorary Fellowship
see Fellowship

Hooper, G., 354

Horizons Committee
see Committee on Horizons

Horlick Report (1975)
concerning Division of Training and
Evaluation, 116-120
as candid self-appraisal of College,
116
problems identified and
recommendations made, 116,
117, 118t, 119t, 120
origin in work of Training and
Evaluation Committee, 113, 114
regarding relationship of College and
McLaughlin Centre, 117

Horlick Report (1977)
see McLaughlin Examination and
Research Centre, The R.S.

Horlick, L.R., 58, 66, 114, 120, 121,
125, 159, 289, 293, 295, 296, 297,
298, 360

Hospitals
isolated training programs in
withdrawal of College approval,
198, 199
training programs in, 32
criteria for College approval, 187,
198

Hospitals Approval Committee
see Accreditation Committee

Hospitals, Approval of
by College and CPMQ
differences relating to, 142
CMA statement on, 126-127, 155n
development of, 193-199

Hospital Approval
by College and CPMQ, 142
inauguration, 127
requirements necessitating integration
with universities, 187

Hospital Insurance and Diagnostic
Services Act (1957), The
failure to provide support for teaching
and research, 206
influence on College's awareness of
implications of health care
insurance, 160

Hould, F., 143, 144

Hubbard, J.P., 188, 189, 232, 244,
280, 284

Hudson, B., 285, 286, 402

Hunka, S., 280, 285, 286, 287

Hunter, R.C.A., 207

Hurteau, G.D., 114, 172, 173, 175,
289, 355, 357, 362

Illingworth, C., 152

Immigration
   of physicians, 164, 168-169
   College's reliance on, 166-169
      effect on physician/population ratio,
         164

Immunology, Clinical
   recognition as a specialty, 345t
   desire of specialty for College
      recognition, 248
   specialists required
      estimation of number of, 167

Incompetence, Professional
   discussed by College and CPSO,
      139-140

India
   specialist trainees from, 210-213
   see also Foreign Medical Graduates

Infectious Diseases
   recognition as a specialty, 347, 351t

"Integrating Force for All Specialists,
   an"
   College as, 272
   College as instrument of
      professionalization, 396

Internal Medicine
   as specialty for Certification, 18
   formation of specialty test committee
      for multiple-choice question
      examination, 286
   mid-training examination in, 258
   recognition as a specialty, 337t
   specialists required
      estimation of number of, 167

International Federation of Surgical
   Colleges, 377

International Sharing of Test Items, 290

Internships
   CMA's role in identifying and
      approving, 126
   report on by CMA Committee on
      Approval of Hospitals for
      internships, 126-127

Internship, Junior
   abolition of, 143

Internship, Straight
   desirability of, 47
      discussed by College and ACMC,
         147

In-Training Evaluation, 36, 90, 209, 217
   accreditation requirements and
      guidelines for, 262
   assessed by Canadian Association of
      Professors of Medicine, 261
   assessed by McLaughlin Centre, 290
   as component of single examination
      process, 116, 192, 253-257
   as new examination method, 191,
      192, 257, 281
   as "radical" innovation, 254, 255
   components and standards of, 262
   defects, 235, 255
   development, 207, 253-257,
      259-264
      facilitated by McLaughlin Centre,
         286, 403
   discussed with ACMC, 147
   experience of CPMQ, 256
   final in-training evaluation report
      (FITER), 255, 259-264
      assessments, 260
      problems, 259, 260, 261
      prototype of, 255
      use, 262
   in measurement of specialist
      competence, 192
   in-training evaluation report (ITER)
      attributes assessed by, 253, 255,
         257
      form, 253, 254
      original version of, 253
   problems with and value
      studied by College and Canadian
         Association of Professors of
         Medicine, 126, 263
   refinement of, 259-264
   results of, 261
      correlation with results of multiple-
         choice question and oral
         techniques, 263
   reviewed by College task force,
      261-262

systems for assessed, 263-264
through FITER
  difficulty in validating, 260
  faults in, 255, 261
  future of, 261, 262, 264
  effect on examination results, 261
  problems with, 259, 260, 263
unique assessment capability of, 254

In-Training Evaluation Report (ITER)
  see In-Training Evaluation

In-Training Examination
  see Examination Methodology

Iran
  specialist trainees from, 210
    see also Foreign Medical Graduates

Ireland, P.E., 26, 27, 354

Izaak Walton Killam Hospital, Halifax, NS, 187

James IV Association of Surgeons, 377

Janes, R.M., 28, 203

Johnson, F.L., 355

Johnston, W.V., 128

Joint Commission on Accreditation of Hospitals
  role in accreditation
    exemplified in Newfoundland, 405

Joint Conference Committee on Education
  position paper by Dr. K.J.R. Wightman on, 318

Joint Training Committee
  with CFPC, 130, 131

Jones, R.O., 185, 187, 189, 221, 222, 407

Jones, W., 150

Jones, W.A., 16, 23

Kekwick, A., 244, 277

Kelly, A.D., 127, 128

Kennedy, J.C., 247, 248

Kergin, F.G., 50, 56, 64, 143, 280, 281, 282, 326, 345

Kerr, R.B., 23, 39, 43, 49, 75n, 80, 85, 97, 141, 143, 144, 147, 148, 195, 196, 204, 206, 207, 379, 381, 383

Kilgour, J.M., 26

Kinch, R.A.H., 164, 250, 357

Kling, S., 290, 302

Kucherepa, J.W., 139

Laboratory Medicine Specialists
  autonomy-oriented view of discipline
    view contrasted with that of College, 359
  desire for autonomy among, 352, 358-360
  request for representation higher in College, 358
  working party with College, 359-360
    proposals for change regarding pathology specialty committees, 359-360
  study group with College, 358-359
  see also Pathologists

Lachaine, G.A., 141

Laidlaw, J.C., 270

Lancet, The
  as content model for the Annals, 326

Langley, G.R., 164, 204, 232, 250, 253, 261

Larue, L., 185

LaSalle, G., 143

Latour, P., 143

Laval University
leadership in application of new
evaluation techniques, 289

Laval University Medical School
proposed admission of medical
scientists to Fellowship
response to, 272

Laxdal, O.E., 309

Leboeuf, G., 149

LeClair, M., 147, 168

Lefebvre, B., 289

Lefebvre, R., 174

Lemieux, F.
see Moreau, F.

Lemieux, J.R., 128

Lemieux, R., 26

Letters Patent of Continuance
as means to avoid amendment of Act
of Incorporation, 78, 97
development of
1971, 77-79
exemplifying community sanction of
specialist practice, 3
granted, 77, 79
inclusion of objective regarding
research in, 270
objectives stated in seeking support
from Fellows, 73
relationship of Bylaw No. 1 to
1971, 78

Levasseur, L., 258, 289

Lewis, D.S., 96, 178, 185, 187, 189

Licensing Authorities
see Federation of Provincial Medical
Licensing Authorities of Canada

Licentiateship of Medical Council of
Canada
as basic form of medical licence, 134

Lindsay, W.S., 187

Logan, V., 244, 277

London (Ontario)
on-side survey of hospital training
programs in, 195-196
precedent set by, 196
training programs in hospitals in
College's pilot study of, 195-196

Lynn, R.B., 258

Lyon, E.K., 128

Macbeth, R.A., 100, 149, 249

MacDonald, R.I., 139

MacDougall, J.T., 288, 289, 402

Mace
donated by The Royal College of
Surgeons of England, 152

MacFarlane, K.T., 354, 357

MacKenzie, I., 242

MacKenzie, K.R., 242, 339, 340

MacKenzie, W.C., 33, 36, 37, 38, 39,
43, 46, 47, 48, 75n, 85, 97, 104,
136, 137, 139, 141, 147, 148, 157n,
205, 274, 280, 340, 343, 377, 379

MacLaren, M., 408

MacLean, R., 185

MacLennan, N.K., 39, 97, 357

MacLeod, J.W., 13, 23, 146, 147, 203

Magner, D., 358, 359

Maintenance of Competence
see Competence, maintenance of

Maintenance of Competence
Committee, 105
and CME, 105, 316, 321

relations of specialty committees to, 367t
work of, 105

Manitoba, 109, 187

Manpower
ad hoc committee on, 166
conferences on, 166
national physician data bank, 166
needs, 165-167
shortages in specialties, 166, 167

Manpower, Specialist
College's role and record in study of, 166-167, 179n
Manpower Requirements Committee report, 365
needs, 165-167
shortages, 162
specialist supply
projections of, 166, 167

Manus
College's relationship with, 360

Marian, J.J., 83

Martin, C.F., 157n

Mathieu, J., 143

Matson, D.D., 204, 206, 207, 247

Maughan, G.B., 352, 353, 354

McCallum, J.L., 238, 243

McCoy, E.C., 128

McGill University
diploma course in surgery, 184
diploma in public health, 184
multiple-choice question technique used by, 143
representation on McLaughlin Centre advisory committee, 294
university participation in training programs
problems with, 202

McKendry, J.B.R., 166, 365

McKenna Lecture in Gastroenterology, The R.D.
as first specialty society lecture during College's annual meeting, 324

McKerracher, D.G., 185

McLachlin, A.D., 185, 187, 208

McLaughlin Examination and Research Centre, The R.S., 110, 114, 116, 117, 160, 237
advisory board, 100, 289
development of, 289-290
MCC membership in, 100, 134, 289, 290
observer representation by ACMC on, 289
observer-representation by CPMQ on, 145
observer-representation of CFPC on, 133, 289
and College's examination section
desirability of closer relationship with, 116
and medical education, 397
and research, 3, 280, 287, 290-292
and the College
aims of College in relation to identified by Dr. B.J. Perey, 301
need for study of administrative relations with, 293
approval by Council of, 283
banking of examination questions with, 290
bilingualism in, 171, 288, 295
computerized patient management problems, 291-292
concept of, 204, 276-284
demonstrating flaws in College's examinations, 40, 90, 285
demonstrating sensitivity to Canadian medical establishments, 160
development and work of, 231, 276-302
Dr. D.R. Wilson appointed director, 283
Dr. D.R. Wilson's notice of resignation as Director, 293
Dr. J. Beaudoin appointed co-director, 287

Dr. S. Kling succeeds Dr. D.R. Wilson as Director, 302
evaluation procedures, 234
  improvements designed
    value of Laval bureau to francophones, 288
grant to from McLaughlin Foundation, 283
growth of francophone unit urged, 287
impact,
  international, 402
  on training and evaluation of specialist candidates, 402
  in understanding and application of evaluation, 3
Laval bureau, 173, 175
  achievement of, 288, 289, 321
  creation as French unit, 287
  development of, 287-289
  objectives, 289
multiple-choice question test committees, 286, 290
  Examinations Committee's involvement with, 99
need for support of medical schools, 284
objectives and functions of, 284, 286
oral examination
  videotape study, 285
relation to College and vice-versa considered in Horlick Report (1975), 120
review by Horlick Committee, 120, 160, 292-302
  discussion of by Dr. B.J. Perey, 300-301
  members of, 293
  reaction of College secretariat to, 297, 298, 299
  reaction of Dr. D.R. Wilson to, 299
  reaction to by McLaughlin Centre advisory board, 302
  recommendations of, 294-295
  recommendations of discussed by Executive Committee, 295-301
  terms of reference of, 293
role in context of national unity, 174, 175
stimulation of scientific enquiry among Fellows of, 404

studies indicating improvements in training and examination, 46
studies of computerized patient management problems in pediatrics, 291-292
supplying questions for principles of surgery examination, 258
uncertainty regarding financial support for, 110
use of by MCC for production of examinations, 134
work of contributing to impact of College on training and evaluation, 250

McLaughlin Fellowship
  awarded to Fellows in university orbit rather than outside, 313

McLaughlin Foundation, The R. Samuel
  grant to McLaughlin Centre, 283, 284, 297
  in selection of McLaughlin-Gallie Visiting Professor, 96
  interest in improvement of medical care, 281
  support of McLaughlin Foundation-Gallie Visiting Professorships and McLaughlin Centre, 281, 288

McLaughlin, Col. R.S., 281, 282, 283, 288

McLaughlin-Gallie Visiting Professorship
  as CME activity, 316, 320
  committee on arrangements for, 316
  reflecting College's relationship with sister colleges, 155
  Sir Charles Illingworth as holder of first, 152

McLaughlin-Gallie Visiting Professorship Committee
  arrangements for, 96

McLeod, L.E., 114, 173, 362, 363

McMaster University Medical School
  establishment of, 164, 194
    as factor in increase in number of medical graduates in Canada, 164

impact of College on training
programs, 401

McNally, W.J., 23, 25

McNeill, L.K., 100, 319

Meakins, J.C., 157n

Measuring Medical Education
(Hubbard), 188

Medical Audit
approval of motion by Continuing
Education Committee, 319
as method for CME, 312, 320
bibliographies of methods, 312, 321
concern of Maintenance of
Competence Committee, 105
resolution on, 318
responsibility for
of Fellowship Affairs and
Maintenance of Competence
Committees, 105
see also Continuing Medical
Education

Medical Biochemistry
recognition as specialty, 338, 339,
340, 341, 343, 345t

Medical Council of Canada, 296, 299,
300, 381
as client of McLaughlin Centre for
production of examinations, 134,
289, 290, 294, 403
Canadian examination questions
developed by McLaughlin Centre,
134, 289, 290
College's relationship with, 5, 125,
134, 293
donation to College to furnish
Roddick Memorial Room, 96, 134
interest in an examination centre,
277, 280
interest in changes in evaluation and
examination procedures, 281
McLaughlin Centre
membership on advisory board of,
100, 134, 289, 290
not empowered to certify specialists,
16

Medical Education
see Education, Medical, and
Education, Medical, Postgraduate

Medical Knowledge Self-Assessment
Programs, 321
Canadian Anaesthetists' Society
program, 321
College's interest in MKSAP V from
American College of Physicians
and program from American
College of Surgeons
as CME activity, 321
College's translation of MKSAP V
purchased from American College
of Physicians, 321

Medical Oncology
recognition as specialty, 347

Medical Profession
College's impact on, 399

Medical Research Council of Canada
Dr. G.M. Brown's presidency of, 271,
375
increasing volume of work of medical
research
resulting prospects for College
journal, 326
funding for medical research, 106

Medical Schools
admission of medical scientists to
Fellowship
reaction concerning, 272
and responsibility regarding residency
training, 146
need to extend, 146
and specialist training in Quebec
responsibility of, 143
and university participation in training
programs, 143, 144, 146, 147
College's communications with
regarding, 200
in Quebec, 143
College's relations with, 125, 200,
400
deans of, 145, 200
and membership of ACMC, 145
desire that specialist competence
examination be taken four years

after graduation, 44, 47, 57
establishment of, 164, 194, 326
interest in changes in evaluation and
  examination techniques, 201, 225,
  253
provision of clinical clerkship year for
  medical students, 47
see also Universities

Medical Science
  recognition as a specialty, 344t

Medical Scientists
  admission to Fellowship, 270-276
    facilitating growth of postgraduate
      faculties, 400
    guidelines for, 275
    satisfaction expressed by medical
      scientists, 276
  contributions to clinical medicine of,
    273

Medical/Surgical Self-Assessment
  Programs
  directory, 321

Medicine
  see Internal Medicine

Membership
  see College, Membership

Memorial University
  as academic force in Newfoundland,
    406

Memorial University Medical School
  establishment of, 164, 194, 407
    as factor in increase in number of
      medical graduates in Canada,
      164

Mennie, W.A., 365

Merck Sharp and Dohme Travelling
  Fellowship
  as stimulus to and support of
    research, 270
  in context of CME, 312

Microbiology, Medical
  recognition as a specialty, 337t

Middle East
  specialist trainees from, 213
    see also Foreign Medical Graduates

Mid-Training Examination
  see Examination Methodology

Miller, G.E., 188, 232, 284

Miller, G.G., 128, 249

Miller, J.C., 185

Miller, L., 406

Millman, P.R., 150

Mills, E.S., 128, 393

Minister of Consumer and Corporate
  Affairs
  approving Letters Patent of
    Continuance, 270
  authority to grant continuance of
    College's constitution under
    Canada Corporations Act, 79

Mitchell, I., 107

Montreal General Hospital, The, 39

Montreal Medical Journal, 185

Moore, D.F., 50, 83, 341

Moore, S.E., 188, 269

Moreau, F. (née **Lemieux**), 107, 113,
  114

Morin, Y., 289

Morley, T.P., 206

Morris, L.E., 138

Morton, H.S., 242

Mount, B., 258

Mount, J.H., 150

Mueller, C.B., 138, 214, 215, 238, 250, 252, 253, 254, 257

Muir, P.L., 113

Multiple-Choice Question Technique
see Examination Methodology

Murphy, H.O., 317

Mustard, R.A., 24

Mutrie, R.R., 26

Muttart Foundation, The Gladys and Merrill
grant to McLaughlin Centre, 288, 291, 297

Nanson, E., 290, 291

National Board of Medical Examiners
computer-based patient management problems
McLaughlin Centre's development of with, 288
computerized technique for evaluation of candidates, 286, 291
joint study by with McLaughlin Centre and American Board of Pediatrics, 288, 291
development of computer-based examination project (CBX), 291
relationship with McLaughlin Centre, 295
use of multiple-choice question examination technique, 243
work on multiple-choice question examination technique, 242

National Health Grants Program
facilitation of provinces' health care programs, 160-161

National Institute of Health
creation recommended by College, 165

National Physician Manpower Committee
College representation on, 166

requirements subcommittee of, 166
definition of criteria for need for specialists, 166

Near East
specialist trainees from, 215
see also Foreign Medical Graduates

Neonatology
recognition as a specialty, 351t

Nephrology
recognition as a specialty, 351t

Neufeld, A.H., 338, 339, 340

Neufeld, V.R., 310

Neurology
decision to abolish Certification examination in, 25
estimation of number of, 167
Fellowship as sole qualification in, 39
recognition as a specialty, 337t

Neurology/Psychiatry
as specialty for early Fellowship examination, 14
as specialty recognized by Certification, 18

Neuropathology
recognition as specialty, 342, 343, 344t

Neurosurgery
as specialty for early Fellowship examination, 14
as specialty recognized by Certification, 18
decision to abolish Certification examination in, 25
Fellowship as sole qualification in, 39
lack of approval of non-university affiliated training programs, 197
recognition as a specialty, 337t
recommendation concerning reduction in, 166
session for in annual meeting, 323

New England Journal of Medicine, The
as content model for the *Annals*, 326

New Zealand
  specialist trainees from, 210
  see also Foreign Medical Graduates

Newfoundland
  development of specialist health care
    College's role in, 405-408

Nineteen-Sixties, the
  advances in education and
    evaluation, 2, 46, 47, 225
  an expansive decade, 194, 336, 344
  as period of change, 32, 34, 89, 159,
    226
  changes in Canadian society, 88
  examinations appropriate to, 36
  spirit of, 89
  temper of, 80
  "widening restlessness" of, 80, 85

Nixon, J.D., 359

Noble, W.H., 139

Nominating Committee, 81, 91, 93, 110

Nova Scotia Hospital, Dartmouth, NS,
  187

Nuclear Medicine
  desire of specialty for College
    recognition, 248
  recognition as a specialty, 347, 348

Nucleus Committee
  concept of function of examination,
    252

Objectives of College
  see College, objectives

Obstetricians and gynecologists
  desire for autonomy and
    independence, 5, 239, 352-357
  elected to office in College, 357

Obstetrics and Gynecology
  as specialty for early Fellowship
    examination, 14
  desire for autonomy within specialty,
    239, 351, 352-357

formation of specialty test committee
    for multiple-choice question
    examination, 285, 286
  manpower shortage in, 162
  participation as section in annual
    meeting, 323
  recognition as a specialty, 337t

Obstetrics-Gynecology Professors
  Group
  membership in Coordinating Advisory
    Council, 357

Obstetrics-Gynecology Research Group
  membership in Coordinating Advisory
    Council, 357

Oncology, Medical
  see Medical Oncology

Ontario, 109
  problems consequent on physician
    emigration, 164
  reliance on Certification for
    recognition of specialists, 22

Ontario Council of Deans
  physician manpower
    study of, 166

Ontario Health Insurance Plan
  as stimulus to introduction of
    temporary Certification, 136

Ontario Subcommittee
  on need for Certification in some
    specialties, 23, 24-25

Ophthalmologists
  autonomy prevented by Certification
    program, 399
  desire for autonomy, 16

Ophthalmology
  manpower shortage in, 162
  recognition as a specialty, 337t

Oral and Clinical Examination
  Technique
  see Examination Methodology

"Orange Book, The"
providing College's requirements standards and components of in-training evaluation, 262, 263

Orthopedic Surgery
as specialty for early Fellowship examination, 14
decision to abolish Certification in, 25, 37
formation of specialty test committee for multiple-choice question examination, 286
Fellowship as sole qualification in, 39
recognition as a specialty, 337t
session for in annual meeting, 323
specialists required
lack of likely increase in number of, 166

Otolaryngologists
autonomy prevented by Certification program, 399
desire for autonomy, 16
proposed training requirements of, 220

Otolaryngology
manpower shortage in, 162
recognition as a specialty, 337t
specialists required
lack of likely increase in number of, 166

Ottawa, University of, Medical School
establishment of, 194

Ouellet, Y., 289

Pakistan
specialist trainees from, 210
see also Foreign Medical Graduates

Parkhouse, J., 138

Parti Québecois
economic association and sovereignty association linked, 177
rise to power, 172, 174

Patch, F.S., 18, 19

Pathologists
desire for autonomy and independence, 5, 358-360
interest in holding specialty society meeting with College in June, 365
see also Laboratory Medicine Specialists

Pathology
as specialty recognized by Certification, 18
manpower shortage in, 162
place of in Fellowship examination, 238, 239, 241, 353
recognition of subspecialties of, 338-344

Pathology, Anatomical
recognition as specialty, 342, 343, 344t
evolution of, 338, 342, 343

Pathology, General
recognition as a specialty, 337t, 343

Pathology, Hematological
recognition as a specialty, 345t

Patient Care
progressive responsibility for in specialist training, 192

Patient Care Evaluation Methods
potential for CME activity, 318

Patient Management Problems, Computerized
see Examination Methodology

Patterson, F.P., 23

Paul, W.B., 357

Pavlin, E.G., 150

Pediatric General Surgery
recognition as a specialty, 347, 349, 351, 351t
recognition by Certificate of Special Competence, 351

Pediatric Neurology, 347

Pediatrics
as specialty for early Fellowship
examination, 14
as specialty recognized by
Certification, 18
formation of specialty test committee
for multiple-choice question
examination, 286
manpower shortage in, 162
recognition as a specialty, 337t
use by specialty of computerized
patient management problems in
Certification examination, 288, 291
use by specialty of computers in
evaluation of candidates
joint study by McLaughlin Centre,
National Board of Medical
Examiners and American Board
of Pediatrics, 288, 291

Peer Review
approval of motion by Continuing
Education Committee, 319
as method for CME, 312, 320
bibliographies of methods, 312, 321
concern of Maintenance of
Competence Committee, 105
resolution on, 318
responsibility for
of Fellowship Affairs and
Maintenance of Competence
Committees, 105
see also Continuing Medical
Education

Perey, B.J., 86, 87, 88, 89, 90, 91, 92,
100, 109, 110, 114, 120, 164, 174,
175, 176, 213, 232, 259, 288, 289,
300, 301, 302, 311, 393, 394, 400

Perey-Trias motion, 86, 92, 394

Perinatal Medicine
recognition as a specialty, 351t

Pharmacological Society of Canada,
272

Philippines
specialist trainees from, 210, 213
see also Foreign Medical Graduates

Philpott, N.W., 22, 157n

Physical Medicine and Rehabilitation
as specialty recognized by
Certification, 18
manpower shortage in, 162
recognition as a specialty, 337t

Physician-to-population ratio, 164

Pigeon, G., 293

Plastic Surgery
recognition as a specialty, 337t
specialists required
lack of likely increase in number of,
166
training program at The Montreal
General Hospital, 39

Platt, H., 155

Plebiscite
on Council's proposals for change
(1970), 59, 61-62, 63, 65

Plunkett, J.E., 128

Pottle, C., 407

Power, D., 242

President, The
election of, 83

Presidency, The
medium and roles of, 373, 389

President-Elect
office created, 94

Presidential Badge
donated to College by The Royal
College of Surgeons of Edinburgh,
152

Primrose, A., 15

Principles of Surgery Examination
see Examination Methodology

Problem-solving
elements of, 233

Professional Association of Internes and
Residents of Ontario
request by for discussions with
College, 150

Professionalism
see Professionalization

Professionalization, 2-4, 7n
as a form of control, 308
College as an instrument of among
specialists, 3, 396, 397, 398
determined by change, 396
facilitating pursuit of unity, 2
of College
enhanced by establishment of
McLaughlin Centre, 276

Professorships
McLaughlin-Gallie visiting
committee on arrangements for, 96
Royal College visiting in medical
research, 271

Program Directors
as components of training programs,
224, 234, 251, 254, 256

Provinces
relations with College, 125, 139, 140
responsibility of for public health
programs, 160
see also Federation of Provincial
Medical Licensing Authorities of
Canada, Provincial Medical
Colleges

Provincial Licensing Authorities
interest in changes in evaluation and
examination techniques, 281
see also Federation of Provincial
Medical Licensing Authorities of
Canada

Provincial Medical Colleges
College's relation with, 125, 134,
136-145
see also CPMQ, CPSO

Psychiatrists
desire for autonomy and
independence, 3, 352

expression of need for both
Certification and Fellowship, 186,
203, 219
proposal of regarding university
responsibility for training, 186, 399
proposed training requirements,
221-223

Psychiatry
development of training under
university auspices, 185-187
manpower shortage in, 162
recognition as a specialty, 337t
training in
under auspices of Dalhousie
University, 187
training requirements for, 186-187,
221-223

Psychiatry, Child
lack of recognition as specialty, 351t

Publications Committee, 97
activities coordinated by Education
Committee, 316
and prospects for a College journal,
325, 326
representation on Continuing
Education Committee of, 318

Public
representation on College
committees, 117

Public Health
recognition as a specialty, 337t

Quebec, 109
Certification in, 38, 57
importance of Fellowship to, 57, 64
problems consequent on physician
emigration, 164
Parti Québecois victory in, 174
province's Certification as reason for
College's need to retain
Certification, 38, 57
see also Certification, Corporation
Professionnelle des Médecins du
Québec

Quebec Medical Act, 142

Quebec Medical Association
Education Committee,
conclusion regarding simultaneous
Certification, 141

Québecois,
need for acceptance and respect, 177

Queen's University,
conference on residency education
held at, 204-211, 211
development of residency program in
family medicine, 129

Radiologists
autonomy prevented by Certification
program, 399
concern over lack of training and
examination organization, 4
desire to form own college, 5
expression of need for both
Certification and Fellowship, 219
resolution to establish Canadian
College of Radiology, 16
see also Canadian Association of
Radiologists

Radiology
as specialty recognized by
Certification, 18
Canadian College of
movement to establish, 16
CMA Section of, 16
manpower shortage in, 162
need for Certification, 219

Radiology, Diagnostic
manpower shortage in, 162
recognition as a specialty, 162, 337t

Radiology, Therapeutic
manpower shortage in, 162
recognition as a specialty, 162, 337t

Railton, S.V., 26

Recertification
in relation to CME, 311
potential for CME activity, 311
responsibility for
of Fellowship Affairs and

Maintenance of Competence
Committees, 105
see also Continuing Medical
Education

"*Red Book, The*"
reflecting regulations and
requirements for training in surgical
specialties, 223

Redford, J.W.R., 138

Referendum
on College's relationship with
Certificants, 97

Referendum, on Admission of Pre-1972
Certificants to Fellowship
by College (1971), 66-69
by concerned Fellows of Victoria
(1972), 71-72

Regina and District Medical Society
resolution expressing desirability of
advanced postgraduate work in
medicine and surgery, 189, 269

"Regina Bronchos, the"
(D. Johnstone, D. Low, S.E. Moore),
12

Regional Advisory Committees,
104-105, 113
benefits of, 104
clinical traineeships funded by, 312,
321
confirming College's concern with
regional matters, 159
conveying Fellows' desire for change
in time of annual meeting, 362
funding clinical traineeships, 312
motion proposing establishment of,
318
role in fostering national unity, 175,
176
specialty committees' relations with,
3, 1ℓ

Reports
Botterell
recommendation for single

standard of clinical competence, 26-27

Farquharson, on research, 163

Horizons Committee (1977), on future of College, 100, 101, 101t, 102t, 103t, 104t

Horlick (1975), on College Secretariat, 116, 117, 118t, 119t

Horlick (1977), on McLaughlin Centre, 294-295

Robertson (1955), on Certification program, 23-24

Research
at McLaughlin Centre, 3, 280, 287, 290-292
College objective relating to, 34, 269, 270
College's emphasis on, 163, 165
College's interest in, 269, 270
fostered by College's annual meeting, 270
fostered by establishing Fellowships, 270
fostered by establishing Visiting Professorships in Medical Research, 270
importance in faculties of medicine, 106
influence of College on allocation of funds for, 106
posts allied to specialty training programs
monitoring of quality of, 106
quality of
enhancement by College, 106
role in specialist postgraduate education, 106
Royal College medals as standard of medical research, 270, 274
shortages in funds, space and personnel, 162
through admission of medical scientists to Fellowship, 270-276
value of recognized by College, 269, 270, 403-404

Research Committee
emphasizing contribution of scientific investigation to specialist training and practice, 404

formation of fostering medical research, 270
terms of reference of, 106, 270

Residency Programs
CMA statement on, 155n
College's concern with, 126, 205
importance of university aegis, 208
see also Training Programs

Residency Training
and responsibility for by universities need to extend, 146
conferences on, 204-211, 211
coordinated educational opportunities in, 32
see also Training, and Training, Specialist

Residents
census of, 210
College and, 150, 195, 399
views on training programs, 209-210

Respiratory Medicine
desire of specialty for College recognition, 248
recognition as a specialty, 343, 345t
specialists required
estimates of number of, 167

Rheumatology
recognition as a specialty, 345t
specialists required
estimation of number of, 167

Rice, D.I., 129, 131, 133, 365

Richards, R.N., 87

Ritchie, A.C., 359

Robertson Committee and report
on need for Certification, 22-24, 42
proposal of same initial training and examination for all candidates in a specialty, 24, 217, 249

Robertson, D.C., 258

Robertson, D.M., 358

Robertson, H.R., 22, 23, 26, 96

Robichon, J., 75n, 328

Robillard, E., 256

Roddick Memorial Room,
furnished through donation by
Medical Council of Canada, 96,
134

Roddick, T., 96

Rogers, J.W., 238, 239, 240

Rosenow, E.C., Jr., 325

Ross, E.F., 338

Rossall, R.E., 207, 208

Rothwell, W.O., 48, 49, 54, 75n, 97

Roulston, T.M., 355

Roy, A., 141, 143

Roy, L.P., 25

Royal Australasian College of Physicians
influence of College's concepts of
training and evaluation on, 402
joint meeting with College 1980, 152

Royal Australasian College of Surgeons
joint meeting with College 1980, 152

Royal Canadian Legion Fellowship in
Geriatric Medicine
in context of CME, 312

Royal College Lectures
first designation as such, 324
funded by Educational Endowment
Fund, 313
J.R. Evans,
"Citizens, Societies and National
Unity", 176

J. Genest,
"Bioethics and the Leadership of
the Medical Profession", 106

Royal College Medals, 270, 403

Royal College of Pathologists, The
reflecting pathologists' autonomy in
United Kingdom, 358

Royal College of Physicians and
Surgeons of Glasgow, The, 377
and postgraduate education, 152
meeting of Commonwealth
colleges as held at, 152
similarity in membership to College,
152

Royal College of Physicians of London,
The
as examining body, 16
assistance in supplying multiple-
choice examination questions, 244
donation of caduceus to College, 152
joint meeting with College 1974, 152
provision concerning publications as
requirement for membership
in relation to admission of medical
scientists to Canadian College,
274
similarities of circumstance with those
of College, 395
standard of specialty qualifying
examination, 186

Royal College of Surgeons of
Edinburgh, The, 377
donation of presidential badge to
College, 152

Royal College of Surgeons of England,
The, 377
as examining body, 16
donation of mace to College, 152
relationship to College through coat
of arms, 86

Royal College of Surgeons of Ireland,
The, 377

Royal College Visiting Professorships in Medical Research
  as stimulus to and support of research, 271

Royal Columbian Hospital, New Westminster, BC, 188

Royal Commission on Dominion-Provincial Relations
  recommendation on provincial responsibility for public health activities, 160

Royal Commission on Health Services (1964)
  see Hall Commission(s)

Royal Commission on Health Services (1982)
  see Hall Commission(s)

Rusted, I.E., 33, 45, 75n, 84, 406

Ryerson, E.S., 15, 16

Salter, R.B., 33, 45, 46, 47, 52, 53, 58, 65, 66, 75n, 85, 98, 106, 120, 121, 164, 308, 317, 318, 360, 362, 363, 389, 391

Saskatchewan, 109
  election campaign in, 1960, 161
  see also Regina and District Medical Society, "Regina Bronchos"

Saskatchewan College of Physicians and Surgeons, 15

Saskatchewan, University of, Medical School
  establishment of, 194

Saskatoon Fellows' proposals for bylaw amendments, 80-83

Saucier, J., 23, 25

Saudi Arabia, 402

Schlesinger, A., 80, 85

Science Council of Canada, 165

Scott, C.F., 33, 42, 70, 75n, 78, 79, 97, 139, 289

Scott, J.W., 128, 145, 203, 312, 316

Scriver, W. de M., 25

Secretary
  see College, Secretary

Self-Assessment of Medical and Surgical Knowledge, 318
  as form of CME, 312, 320, 321
  concern of Maintenance of Competence Committee, 105
  medical
    approval of motion by Continuing Education Committee, 319
    program for
      purchase from American College of Physicians, 319
      translation of, 321
  methods
    bibliographies of, 312, 321
  programs
    as form of CME, 404
    directory of, 312, 321
    of Fellowship Affairs and Maintenance of Competence Committees, 105
  surgical
    program for,
      purchase from American College of Surgeons, 319
  see also Continuing Medical Education

Separatism, 172

Shils, E.B., 121, 293, 294, 296, 297, 298, 299, 301

Sibley, J.C., 309, 310

Simpson, C.A., 71

Sims Commonwealth Travelling Professorship, 285, 377, 381, 389
  reflecting College's relationship with sister colleges, 155

Single Examination Process
    see Examination(s), Examination
        Methodology

Single Standard
    of clinical competence
        recommended, 27, 39, 43, 47, 59,
            61, 63, 218
    of examinations
        request for Council to adopt or
            not, 250
    of specialty competence,
        as practical and desirable
            attainment, 4
    of training, 218

Sirois, G.A., 289

Skakun, E.N., 261, 291

Skinner, B.F., 188

Skinner, V.H., 113, 116, 223

Slater, R.J., 273

Smart, G., 244, 277

Society of Obstetricians and
    Gynaecologists of Canada
    concerns regarding specialty, 355
    discussion on sectional session in
        annual meeting, 352
    discussion on training and
        examination requirements, 351
    membership in Coordinating Advisory
        Council, 356, 357
    relationship with College, 5, 351,
        355-357, 369n

Society, Canadian
    changes in 1960s, 88
    issues identified by Horizons
        Committee, 102t

South America
    specialist trainees from, 210, 213, 215
        see also Foreign Medical Graduates

Sovereignty-association (Quebec), 177

Spaulding, W.B., 319, 321

Specialist
    concept of, 256
    definition and use of term, 15, 368n
    dual standard, 1
    enquiry by Saskatchewan College on
        use of term, 1934, 15

Specialist Manpower Committee
    ad hoc committee, 96, 166

Specialists
    censuring of, 93
    need for, 162, 165-167
    need for Certification and recognition
        of, 15, 18
    numbers certificated, 162
    qualified
        need to identify, 11, 12, 40, 45
    remuneration, 162
    standard for qualification
        need for, 15, 17
    the qualification of (editorial, 1933),
        15
        see also Committees

Specialization
    controversies regarding, 343-344
    development of, 12

Specialties
    development and recognition of,
        336-351
        College's impact on, 404, 405
    development of
        reflected in College recognition,
            337t, 344t, 345t, 351t
    Director of
        enhancing liaison between College
            and specialties, 368
    growth and fragmentation of
        as general issue for College, 149,
            336, 340, 341, 348, 352
    recognition of, 336-351
        by College, 336-351
        by CSCs, 347
        conclusions of Fragmentation
            Committee, 343
        criteria for, 345-346
        guidelines for, 347, 350
        moratorium on, 347, 348
        options for consideration in, 346

resolutions of Executive Committee
on, 347
views and proposals of ad hoc
committee on, 349

Specialty Boards (U.S.)
existence favoring use of term
Certification for single examination
process, 57
possibility of Canadian specialty
groups' joining, 52
recertification enforced, 311
similarity to of one part of College's
role, 52
subspecialty recognition by, 346

Specialty Committees, 98, 123, 361,
366
and single examination process
and hospital approval, 132
contribution to development of,
223, 253, 255, 256, 257
contributions of to evaluation, 234
coordination of, 123
College's invitation to specialties to
nominate members, 366
in development of single training
standard for both Fellowship and
Certification examinations, 218,
219, 256, 257
in emergency medicine, 132
in general surgery
proposal of same initial
examination for all candidates in
general surgery, 249
in internal medicine
in relation to concept of in-training
examination, 248
in relation to subspecialty
development, 343, 346
in medical biochemistry
chairman of as member of College-
laboratory medicine liaison
group, 359
in microbiology
chairman of as member of College-
laboratory medicine liaison
group, 359
in neurosurgery, 39
in obstetrics and gynecology
consultation regarding autonomy,
354

in orthopedic surgery, 39
in otolaryngology
training requirements
proposal to College regarding,
220

in pathology
discussions on recognition of
specialty and subspecialties,
338-344
chairman of as member of College-
laboratory medicine liaison
group, 359
review of training requirements for
Fellowship and Certification
examinations based on
subdivision of specialty, 338
in psychiatry
opposition to child psychiatry as
specialty, 352t
training requirements,
discussions with College on,
221-222
linking College and specialties,
366-368
membership of, 366, 368
participation by in first Conference of
Specialists, 255
operational changes in, 368
relating to training objectives, 225
roles of, 366, 367t, 404
terms of reference for, 368

Specialty Development
College and, 335-368
College's impact on, 399, 404-405

Specialty Development and Manpower
Committee, 96, 109, 123, 347, 348
and recognition of emergency
medicine, 130
concern over lack of validity of
criteria for manpower studies, 166
considerations of in recognition of
nuclear medicine as specialty, 348
formation of, 96
relations of specialty committees to,
367t
report on guidelines for new specialty
development, 349-350
successor to Fragmentation
Committee, 340

views on specialty recognition, 346

Specialty Development Committee, 96, 347

Specialty Practice
impact of College on, 396, 399
minimum standard for, 15

Specialty Qualification
basic
need for a realistic one in Canada, 44

Specialty Societies, 98
affinity to CSCI, 365
annual meetings
held at same time as College's, 312, 361
College's collaboration with in CME activities, 312, 318, 319, 361
College's cooperation with, 255, 360-366, 391
impact of College on, 404
in development of single training standard for both Fellowship and Certification examinations, 218, 219, 404
nomination of members for specialty committees, 361
participation in conferences of specialties, 113, 255, 361
participation in College's annual meeting, 270, 312, 322, 324
Royal College lectureships at meetings of, 319, 361

Specialty Society Meetings
and CME
College-supported lectureships facilitating, 312, 319, 320

Specialty Training
in Great Britain, 114

Specialty Training Committees
as components of training programs, 224

Specialty Training Programs, Evaluation of
see Accreditation Committee

Stalker, M.R., 128

Standing Committee on Industrial and International Relations
report on unemployment, sickness and disability insurance, 160

Steeves, L.C., 26, 50

Stephen, H.M., 280

Stokes, A.B., 185, 187, 189, 407

Stokes, J.F., 293, 403

Strauss, A., 2

Strong, G.F., 157n

Supply and Distribution of Specialists Committee, 96

Surgery, General
see General Surgery

Survey Process
components of, 194, 224
initial study, 195-196
value, 196

Tallon, J.A., 64

Task Force on National Unity, 174

Task Force on the Cost of Health Services in Canada
physician manpower, study of, 166

Task Force on the Single Examination Process, 96
achievement of, 251
formation of, 250
goals of, 250, 251
membership of, 250
see also Examination(s), Examination Methodology

Taylor, W.C., 290, 291

Teaching and Learning in Medical School (Miller), 188

Teleconferencing, 312

Temkin, O., 80

Temporary Certification
facilitating development of specialist departments in Newfoundland, 406
facilitating growth of postgraduate faculties, 136-139
see also Certification, temporary

Test Committees
see Examination Methodology, multiple-choice question technique

Thomas, G.W., 94

Thompson, D.A., 26, 28, 82, 128, 159, 179, 373, 375

Thoracic Surgery
decision to abolish Certification in, 25, 37
recognition as a specialty, 337t, 351t
see also Cardiovascular and Thoracic Surgery

Training
acceptable standards
guidelines concerning non-Canadian specialist candidates, 216
anomaly of candidates' taking same training but either Fellowship or Certification or both, 37
College's impact on, 349
coordinated, according to defined standards and objectives, 217
dual standard of, 24, 25
essence of reflected in task performance, 233
flaws in, 402
importance recognized, 402
of foreign medical graduates guidelines for acceptable, 216
purpose, 234
relationship to examinations, 401
requirements for specialties

of interest to College and CPMQ, 142
requirements, standards and objectives, 217-226, 400
specialty
programs
accreditation of
uncertainty regarding financial support for, 110
uniform requirements for Fellowship and Certification examinations, 31, 114, 218-223, 361

Training Credentials, assessment, 211-217

Training and Evaluation Committee, 99, 105, 317
formation of, 99, 113
guidelines on acceptable non-Canadian training, 99, 168, 169, 214-217
ITER assessment, 99
review of Division of Training and Evaluation, 99, 114-117, 118t, 119t
see also Horlick Review (1975)
role of, 99
study of McLaughlin Centre suggested, 116, 292

Training Programs
approval of and criteria for acceptability, 126, 193-199, 225
College's impact on, 401
components, 224
deficiencies, esp. isolated one-year programs, 198
development of new
universities' interest in discussed by College and ACMC, 147
full integration of under university auspices, 199, 225
improvements, 53
in clinical training units
factors influencing, 206, 224
need for multipartite training centres, 186
need for national agreement on standards, 223
need for unified integrated approach, 186

objectives, 207
surveys of, 195-196
university responsibility for, 183-189, 199-211

Training Requirements
educational objectives increasingly important, 191
evaluation of, 191-226
for Certification and Fellowship examinations, 126
need for uniformity, 31
revision of, 223-226, 402
uniform
for Fellowship and Certification examinations, 217
specialty societies consulted on, 361

Training, Specialist
British approach to, 223
College's impact on, 400-403
coordinated according to standards and objectives, 223, 224
North American approach to, 223
purpose of, 233
regulations and requirements concerning, 223
requirements for
evolution of, 191-226
summary of state of art in College-universities partnership, 224
universities' responsibility for development of, 191-211
university responsibility for problems for hospitals and universities with, 201-204

Trauma, Committee on,
see Committees

Travelling Fellowships
providing CME, 312, 313, 320

Travelling Fellowships in Continuing Medical Education
as stimulus to and support of research, 313

Trias, A., 86, 92, 109

Trudeau, Prime Minister P.E., 106

Tupper, W.R.C., 357

Turcot, J., 23, 32, 33, 38, 42, 43, 44, 48, 53, 54, 55, 58, 65, 66, 75n, 82, 88, 89, 140, 141, 144, 147, 150, 170, 199, 204, 208, 248, 287, 288, 289, 381, 383

Turkey
specialist trainees from, 210
see also Foreign Medical Graduates

Turnbull, A.R., 139

Tweedie, F.J., 68, 75n, 143, 355, 357

United Kingdom
participation with McLaughlin Centre in feasibility study of international sharing of test items, 290
specialist trainees from, 210, 215
see also Foreign Medical Graduates

United States
credentialling of specialist candidates approach to, 114
participation with McLaughlin Centre in feasibility study of international sharing of test items, 290
specialist trainees from, 215

Unity
advantages of united College, 393
among specialists
preserved through Certification program, 399
through admission of pre-1972 Certificants, 63
as Canadian quest, 4
call for College to act as unified body, 88
College's attainment of envied by other colleges, 6
College's opportunity to be unifying factor in medical profession, 92
College's unitarian operation, 4, 118, 398, 399
compromise in interest of, 131
desire for a unified College, 66, 72

essence of in College
illustrated by coat of arms, 85, 86
illustrated by guidelines on use of
French, 170
importance for College, 4-5
important consideration in
formulation of
College's role, 4-5
in relation to Saskatchewan Fellows'
motion, 1966, 83
national, 64, 172, 383
College and, 172-179
resolution on, 175
threat to from abolition of
Certification, 38
need for in period of change, 222
of College, 387
preservation of by College's
democratic evolution, 91
pursuit of, 1-6
among specialists, 6, 144
facilitated by admission of
medical scientists to
Fellowship, 274
demonstrated by College's policy
statement on bilingualism, 170
demonstrated in statement on
physician immigration, 169
demonstrated by College's fusion
of academic interests with
principles of service, 375
derived from College's relations
with specialties, 336
enhanced by cooperation between
English and French McLaughlin
units, 288
enhanced by membership of
McLaughlin Centre advisory
board, 290
facilitated by inclusion of all
specialties in College, 405
failure of in relation to recognition
of medical genetics as specialty,
352t
in College's relationship with
CFPC, 127, 128, 130
in College's relationship with CMA,
127
in College's relationship with CSCI,
148, 149

in context of College's relationship
with CPMQ, 64, 140, 144
in relation to agreement reached
by College and specialty
committees and societies on
training requirements, 219
in relation to Certification of
specialists by College and
CPMQ, 144, 225
in relation to collaboration with
CFPC on emergency medicine,
130
in relation to College's partnership
with universities, 204
influencing College's decision
regarding temporary
Certification, 137
reflected in coat of arms, 85, 86
reflected in College's discussions
with CPA on training
requirements, 222
served by democracy in College,
83
shown in response to "Concerned
Fellows of Victoria" stand, 71
spirit guiding College in, 170
stimulated by College's desire for
university responsibility for
training, 401
through admission of medical
scientists to Fellowship, 272
through annual meeting, 322
through College's joint membership
with MCC on test committees,
290
through College's nurturing
relations with specialty groups,
366
through College's relationship with
CSCI, 148
through development of single
examination process, 257
through inclusion of all specialties
in College, 6, 88, 313
through invitation of Certificants to
regional meetings, 313
through preservation of College's
relations with other organizations,
125
through professionalization, 2, 3,
396

through publication of *Annals*, 325
views on in critical period, 88
threat to,
    from provinces' need to compete
      for specialists, 37
    from desire for autonomy among
      obstetricians and gynecologists,
      239, 353, 355
    from "forces of disunity", 127
    from fragmentation of specialties,
      342
    from possible failure to maintain
      same examination pattern in all
      specialties, 248
    from separation within College, 4,
      336, 349, 352
through specialists grouped in "one
    house", 6, 88, 89, 114, 336, 357
within a national context as ideal for
    College, 42
underlying College's impact, 399

Universities
and interest in new training programs
    discussed by College and ACMC,
    146
and specialty training
    partnership with College in, 197,
    224
CME authorities
    College's collaboration with, 316
College's relations with, 197, 400
departmental autonomy
    threat to of College's proposals
      regarding university responsibility
      for specialist training, 401
impact on College, 399, 400
partnership in specialist training with
    College and hospitals, 32, 197
partnership with College
    value and uniqueness of, 204
relationship with College on in-
    training evaluation, 263
responsibility for specialist training,
    183-189, 199-211, 218, 223, 400
    reasons for delay in complete
      acceptance of, 200-204
responsibility of for specialist training
    in Quebec, 200
role in postgraduate education,
    183-189

see also individual universities,
    Medical Schools

University Aegis of Specialty Training,
    184-188, 199-204, 222, 224, 225,
    400

University of Alberta
and an examination centre
    support for space for, 280
Department of Education
    assistance in designing examination
      item analysis, 245
leadership in application of new
    evaluation techniques, 289
local policy concerning McLaughlin
    Centre, 287-288
storage and retrieval of McLaughlin
    Centre examination questions, 290
support in development of
    McLaughlin Centre, 280, 284

University of Alberta Medical School
proposed admission of medical
    scientists to Fellowship
    response to, 272

University of British Columbia Medical
    School
established, 194
proposed admission of medical
    scientists to Fellowship
    response to, 272
university responsibility for training
    programs, 202

University of Calgary
and pilot project for Certification of
    family physicians, 129
established, 164, 194

University of Hong Kong
Digby Lectureship, 377

University of Manitoba Medical School
impact of College on training
    programs, 401
proposed admission of medical
    scientists to Fellowship
    response to, 272

University of Montreal Medical School
proposed admission of medical
scientists to Fellowship
response to, 272

University of Ottawa Medical School
established, 194
representation on McLaughlin Centre
advisory committee, 294

University of Saskatchewan Medical
School
established, 194
impact of College on training
programs, 401

University of Sherbrooke
established, 164, 194
in-training evaluation at, 90

University of Toronto
CME program for specialists
developed, 307
course in surgery for residents
organized by Dr. W.E. Gallie, 184
university participation in training
programs
problems with, 202

University of Western Ontario Medical
School
impact of College on training
programs, 401
pilot project for Certification of family
physicians, 129
proposed admission of medical
scientists to Fellowship
response to, 272

Urology
as specialty for early Fellowship
examination, 14
as specialty recognized by
Certification, 18
formation of specialty test committee
for multiple-choice question
examination, 286
granting Certification unwise, 17
recognition as a specialty, 337t

Valin, R.E., 17

Vascular Surgery
recognition as a specialty, 351t

Victoria General Hospital, Halifax, NS,
187

Videotext in CME, 312

Visiting Professorships in Medical
Research
emphasizing contribution of scientific
investigation to specialist and
practice, 404

Wall, J.R., 276

Walter C. MacKenzie-Ethicon Travelling
Fellowship
as stimulus to and support of
research, 270
in context of CME, 312

War Measures Act (1970)
enactment of, 172

Wasylenki, D., 151

Watters, N.A., 249

Webster, D.R., 195, 196, 274, 381

Webster, J.W.R., 139

Weder, C.H., 243

Wightman, K.J.R., 33, 39, 44, 45, 48,
50, 53, 56, 66, 75n, 104, 113, 139,
173, 175, 311, 318, 383, 387, 389

Wilson, D.L., 24, 139, 365

Wilson, D.R., 26, 43, 45, 46, 49, 75n,
121, 143, 188, 204, 214, 232, 233,
242, 243, 244, 245, 246, 247, 250,
252, 253, 277, 279, 280, 281, 282,
283, 284, 285, 286, 287, 293, 299,
300, 301, 302, 341

Witts, L., 391

Wodehouse, G.E., 24, 26

Wyatt, E.R.S., 139

Wyman, M., 280

Yabsley, R.H., 258

Yendt, E.R., 319

Young, G.S., 18, 25